MAN'S PRIDE,

GOD'S HUMILITY

I dedicate this book to the Magnificent Seven
whose assistance in reading the text and
suggesting many improvements was invaluable:
Chris B, Robert and Renée K-D, Elizabeth L,
John M, John W, and Tim Y.
I am hugely grateful for their kindness,
as a result of which the book has ended up
much better than it would have been otherwise.

MAN'S PRIDE,

GOD'S HUMILITY

"A God without wrath brought men without sin into a kingdom without judgement through the ministrations of a Christ without a cross".
Richard Niebuhr, commenting on the preaching at some churches in his day

A catalogue record for this book is available from the British Library.

First published Winter 2021

ISBN 978-1-8382577-2-9

Designed by Tim Underwood   timund@hotmail.com
Printed by Sarsen Press   22 Hyde Street, Winchester, SO23 7DR

CONTENTS

Author's Preface 1

How to read this book 4

Introduction 5

Part 1 – Yahweh is King

I   1:1-9 The political and religious Background 9
      Meditation The great Love Story

II   1:10-20 Religious Hypocrisy and the Need to admit it 12
      Meditation When Religion becomes nauseating

III   1:21-31 The decadent City and God's Reaction to it 15
      Meditation The Message that stings will restore or destroy

IV   2:1-9 The City of God and the City of Man 17
      Meditation What People want may not be good for them

V   2:10-18 What God has in Store for human Pride 20
      Meditation When Pride will become unfashionable

VI   2:19-22 The terrifying Presence of Yahweh 23
      Meditation The great and terrible Day of the Lord

VII 3:1-15 How God judges us in the Here and Now 25
      Meditation People get the Leaders they deserve

VIII 3:16-4:1 Our absorbing Trivialities and their Destiny 28
      Meditation The Emptiness of earthly Glory

IX   4:2-6 After the Cleansing, a new Glory 31
      Meditation God's People are refined and contracted

X   5:1-7 The Parable of the unfruitful Vineyard 33
      Meditation God's Parable is explained

XI   5:8-23 The six (or perhaps seven) Woes 36
      Meditation The seven Woes of the Messiah

XII 5:24-30 The Avengers of Yahweh 40
      Meditation God is in control of History

XIII   6:1-8 The Call of the Prophet Isaiah...42
          Meditation The Holiness of the God who is Three

XIV   6:9-13 An exceptionally difficult Call...46
          Meditation The perennial Difficulty of God's Call

XV   7:1-9 Isaiah urges King Ahaz to trust in God 48
          Meditation Trust and obey; there is no other Way

XVI   7:10-25 The Sign of Emmanuel...51
          Meditation Are all People helped by Signs?

XVII   8:1-15 Trusting God when everything goes wrong...................55
          Meditation The Signs of true Godliness

XVIII   8:16-22 Isaiah instructs his Disciples......................................58
          Meditation The godly Remnant

XIX   9:1-7 The Dawning of the Messiah 61
          Meditation The Child that would be born

XX   9:8-10:4 The Sins that God will judge 63
          Meditation Justice will be meted out in full

XXI   10:5-19 The Assyrian Scourge will also be judged...................67
          Meditation The Proud deceive themselves

XXII   10:20-34 The Repentance of the Remnant 69
          Meditation In Whom do we place our Trust?

XXIII   11:1-5 The Humility of the Messiah 73
          Meditation The Sevenfold Spirit of God

XXIV   11:6-16 Life under the Messiah...76
          Meditation A Chapter full of Hope

XXV   12:1-6 The Song of the Saved 80
          Meditation A Song of Wonder and Joy

Part 2 – Lord of the Nations

XXVI   13:1-16 Babylon's Day of Reckoning..83
          Meditation From Babel to Babylon

XXVII   13:17-22 The Overthrow of Babylon 85
          Meditation The Doom of godless Civilisation

XXVIII   14:1-11 The Proud will be brought low...................................88
          Meditation The Bully who made it to the very Top

XXIX   14:12-23 The Day Star falls from Heaven.................................90
          Meditation The diabolical Son of the Dawn

XXX   14:24-32 The Fate of Assyrians and Philistines 93
          Meditation The Reiteration of basic Lessons

XXXI   15:1-9 Moab will be defeated and must flee...........................95
          Meditation God weeps as he smites

XXXII   16:1-14 Moab's Hope, Pride and Fall......98
     Meditation The timeless Nature of God's Word

XXXIII   17:1-14 Damascus and the Northern Tribes 101
     Meditation The Folly of heathen Cuttings

XXXIV   18:1-7 The Destiny of Ethiopia 105
     Meditation No to political Scheming

XXXV   19:1-15 The Folly of Egypt......107
     Meditation Why rely on the Unreliable?

XXXVI   19:16-25 The Repentance of Egypt...... 110
     Meditation Prophecies and their Fulfilments

XXXVII   20:1-6 The Crisis of Ashdod......112
     Meditation The naked Prophet as a Sign

XXXVIII   21:1-10 Babylon, the Wilderness of the Sea 115
     Meditation Babylon – the Reality not the Symbol

XXXIX   21:11-17 Dumah and Arabia 118
     Meditation Questions and their Answers

XL   22:1-14 The Valley of Vision 120
     Meditation The unforgivable Sin of Jerusalem

XLI   22:15-25 Two senior Officials are found wanting...... 124
     Meditation No Privileges without Responsibilities

XLII   23:1-18 Tiresome Tyre, destroyed and restored 127
     Meditation Yahweh, the Lord of the Nations

Part 3 – Yahweh's Plans

XLIII   24:1-13 The World in Chaos 131
     Meditation The Fall and Rise of Planet Earth

XLIV   24:14-23 Godly Praise lightens the Gloom...... 134
     Meditation The Subject no one may talk about

XLV   25:1-12 The great Deliverance 137
     Meditation What the next Life will lack

XLVI   26:1-13 The City of God will endure 140
     Meditation A profound Psalm born of Experience

XLVII   26:14-21 Waiting for the Resurrection 143
     Meditation An extraordinary new Insight

XLVIII   27:1-13 The Root, the Shoot and then the Fruit 145
     Meditation An Apocalypse written ahead of its Time

XLIX   28:1-13 So simple! Anyone could understand it......148
     Meditation Keep it simple and clear

L   28:14-29 Foundation Stone or stumbling Block?......151
     Meditation God's strange and alien Work

LI   29:1-8 A miraculous Reprieve for Jerusalem 154
      Meditation God is committed to his People

LII   29:9-24 The Darkness deepens and is dispelled 156
      Meditation The Challenge of Isaiah's Words

LIII   30:1-17 Our Reliance should be on God............................160
      Meditation Activism or quiet Waiting?

LIV   30:18-33 Future Blessings and purifying Fire 163
      Meditation Grace upon Grace from God's Fullness

LV   31:1-9 On Whom do we depend?............................ 167
      Meditation What an extraordinary God!

LVI   32:1-8 The honourable King and his Subjects...................169
      Meditation The Messiah

LVII   32:9-20 True Peace does not come easily........................172
      Meditation Waiting for the Holy Spirit

LVIII   33:1-16 From Impenitence to Terror 175
      Meditation The consuming Holiness of God

LIX   33:17-24 The Land of the Forgiven............................ 178
      Meditation Twelve Blessings of the New Jerusalem

LX   34:1-17 The universal Judgement............................180
      Meditation The last Thing that People talk about

LXI   35:1-10 The flowering Wilderness 184
      Meditation The Wonder of returning Home

Part 4 – In God we Trust

LXII   36:1-12 The Tactics of Intimidation 188
      Meditation The Half Truths that are hurtful

LXIII   36:13-22 The Meekness of the Bullied............................191
      Meditation A terribly clever Man

LXIV   37:1-13 Man proposes but God disposes............................ 193
      Meditation The Word of Man and the Word of God

LXV   37:14-20 The Prayer of King Hezekiah............................196
      Meditation How can the Prayerless pray?

LXVI   37:21-32 The Promises of the living God............................198
      Meditation A fine Prayer gets a wonderful Answer

LXVII   37:33-38 God fulfils his Promises 201
      Meditation How did God do it? Did People repent?

LXVIII   38:1-8 The Illness of King Hezekiah............................ 204
      Meditation Why God changes his Mind

LXIX   38:9-22 King Hezekiah prays for Healing............................ 206
      Meditation Death had not yet been swallowed up

LXX   39:1-8   The Pride of King Hezekiah 208
       Meditation   Extraordinary Prophet, but flawed King

Part 5 – A New Beginning

LXXI   40:1-11   A Herald of good Tidings......................213
       Meditation   Something amazing was going to happen

LXXII   40:12-20   Yahweh of Israel, incomparable God 216
       Meditation   The intractable Problem and its Solution

LXXIII   40:21-31   The Disposer who can also empower us 219
       Meditation   Waiting – so easy and yet so hard

LXXIV   41:1-7   God Challenges the Nations 222
       Meditation   Specific Prophecies versus vague Auguries

LXXV   41:8-20   Reassurance for God's Servants 224
       Meditation   Two wonderful Promises

LXXVI   41:21-29   The Futility of Idols 227
       Meditation   The God who controls Events

LXXVII   42:1-9   The first Servant Song................................230
       Meditation   New Things I now declare

LXXVIII   42:10-17   Praise to the Lord Almighty 234
       Meditation   When parallel Lines meet

LXXIX   42:18-25   When the Blind lead the Blind.....................236
       Meditation   The right Question to ask

LXXX   43:1-13   Grace for God's disobedient People 239
       Meditation   When Grace meets Disobedience

LXXXI   43:14-28   Provident God, indifferent Israel 242
       Meditation   The God who takes the Initiative

LXXXII   44:1-8   God will richly bless his People 246
       Meditation   A Promise for our Times

LXXXIII   44:9-28   The Ridiculous and the Sublime.....................248
       Meditation   When the Godly become scornful

LXXXIV   45:1-13   God and the pagan Cyrus 251
       Meditation   Called and successful – but responsive?

LXXXV   45:14-25   The Nations come to God 254
       Meditation   The God who hides himself

LXXXVI   46:1-13   The helpless Gods of Babylon 257
       Meditation   The Carriers and the Carried

LXXXVII   47:1-15   The inevitable Doom of Babylon.................. 260
       Meditation   Babylon – great but evil

LXXXVIII   48:1-22   God's Love for the Unlovely.....................263
       Meditation   When God captures your Imagination

LXXXIX   49:1-13 The second Servant Song..............................267
      Meditation Aspects of Servanthood

LXXXX   49:14-50:3 God comforts Zion and her People..............270
      Meditation Has God given up on his People?

LXXXXI   50:4-11 The third Servant Song..............................273
      Meditation The Teachability of the Servant

LXXXXII   51:1-16 A Hope that rekindles Faith..............................276
      Meditation Hope will ward off Discouragement

LXXXXIII   51:17-52:12 Rescue is on the Way..............................279
      Meditation Yahweh, Judge and also Redeemer

LXXXXIV   52:13-15 The great Surprise..............................282
      Meditation The great Reversal

LXXXXV   53:1-3 The great Suffering..............................284
      Meditation The great Rejoicing

LXXXXVI   53:4-6 The great Substitution..............................288
      Meditation The great Replacement

LXXXXVII   53:7-9 The great Silence..............................291
      Meditation The great Restraint

LXXXXVIII   53:10-12 The great Spoils..............................294
      Meditation The great Reward

LXXXXIX   54:1-17 Yahweh and his People reconciled..............................298
      Meditation What a great Salvation!

C   55:1-13 Invitation to Live..............................302
      Meditation A fruitful Conversation

Part 6 – The Future in Store

CI   56:1-8 Yes to Outcasts, No to corrupt Leaders..............................307
      Meditation God's Ways are not our Ways

CII   56:9- 57:13 Old Evils are to be avoided..............................310
      Meditation The severe Warnings of God

CIII   57:14-21 The God of Grace speaks..............................313
      Meditation The dwelling Places of Almighty God

CIV   58:1-14 Worship - hypocritical or true?..............................316
      Meditation Yahweh and his Servant agree

CV   59:1-15a God will deal with Injustice..............................319
      Meditation Sin spoils, Sin spreads, Sin separates

CVI   59:15b-21 The solitary Saviour..............................323
      Meditation Both Word and Spirit

CVII   60:1-16 The Triumph of the Faith..............................325
      Meditation Treasures for the Glory of God

CVIII 60:17-22 God is the Glory of his People 328
         Meditation What will the next Life be like?

CIX 61:1-11 What God's Servant will be like 331
         Meditation The Saviour and the Saved

CX 62:1-12 The Joy and Beauty of Zion 334
         Meditation The Guardians of God's City

CXI 63:1-6 The solitary Avenger 337
         Meditation A necessary but lonely Mission

CXII 63:7-19 Thanksgiving and Penitence 339
         Meditation Answers to difficult Questions

CXIII 64:1-12 Prayer for renewed Mercy 343
         Meditation The Prophet intercedes for Israel

CXIV 65:1-16 Owned by God or disowned? 345
         Meditation God's Answer to the Prayer

CXV 65:17-25 New Heavens and new Earth 349
         Meditation How can you describe the next Life?

CXVI 66:1-14 Trembling at God's Word 352
         Meditation The Birth of religious Hatred

CXVII 66:15-24 The Reign and Judgement of God 355
         Meditation The End

Appendices

Appendix 1 A most intriguing Text – Isaiah 45:7 359

Appendix 2 For Isaiah: the End and the Beginning 361

Appendix 3 For us: the Arrival of the Messiah 362

Appendix 4 The last Word is for Yahweh 365

For Further Reading 369

Acknowledgements 370

AUTHOR'S PREFACE

For many readers of the Bible, the book of the Prophet Isaiah is the highlight of the Old Testament. It sparkles with beautiful poetic passages in which the prophet conveys Yahweh's steadfast love for his people, as well as his disapproval of their behaviour, in words that are in turn plaintive, haunting and engaging.

One of the most inspiring scenes in the film *Chariots of Fire* (1981) takes us into the English Church in Paris in 1924, for a Sunday service just before the start of the Olympic Games. The lesson appointed for this service is Isaiah 40:28-31. It is read out by the runner who would win the gold medal in the 400 metres. He is Eric Liddell, a Christian who would later become a missionary in China. As he reads of God's power to restore those who are faint and weary, we see footage of Olympic athletes collapsing with fatigue. "Even youths will faint and be weary, and the young will fall exhausted. But *those who wait for Yahweh* shall renew their strength, they shall mount up with wings like eagles, they shall run and not be weary, they shall walk and not faint" (40:30-31). The idea here is that as we *wait for Yahweh* we shall be restored. This insight has brought hope to millions of Isaiah's readers during the past two and a half millennia.

In fact the concept of "waiting for Yahweh" lies at the heart of Christian hope, and yet it is hardly ever mentioned in sermons or Bible studies today. Together with faith and love, hope is one of the three Christian graces (1 Cor 13:13). Unlike faith and love, hope is much ignored and little understood. And yet hope is essential for us. It is the human quality that helps us to keep going. It has been said that there are two ways of destroying a person: one is to give him no hope, the other is to give him a false hope. In Isaiah's day the heathen nations had no hope. Hope was the exclusive prerogative of the Jewish people. Their hope lay in Yahweh, the Holy One of Israel, who was their covenant God and whom they knew by name. But there was an ongoing danger that the followers of Yahweh might adopt a false hope.

This is a recurring theme in the book of Isaiah. With his keen spiritual insight, the prophet poured scorn on any Israelite who thought it would be good to seek help from either Assyria (8:5-8) or Egypt (30:1-5), the two strongest nations of that time. Instead, Yahweh's people had been brought up to trust in *him*. They were to rest the full weight of their faith on Yahweh. They were to rely on the rock from which they had been hewn (26:4, 51:1).

Life has its ups and downs. There are times when selfish human pride seems to dominate the affairs of our world, and this may cause our hope to fade. But in spite of such unhappy realisations and other disappointments, God remains the same. On account of our pride we may prove to be unreliable and flawed, but God is always dependable because *he is humble*. It is in the book of Isaiah that we learn that although God dwells in the high and holy place, he also condescends to live along-side those who are contrite and humble in spirit. He loves to revive the spirit of the humble, and to revive the heart of the contrite (57:15).

In spite of having been written centuries before the birth of Jesus the Messiah, the book of Isaiah is full of prophecies about the Messiah's birth, childhood, ministry, death, resurrection and exaltation. Because of this, it has always been a great favourite of Christians. It is quoted sixty-six times in the New Testament. Only the book of Psalms is quoted more often, a total of seventy-nine times. But apart from the direct quotations, there are many clear allusions to the text of Isaiah in the New Testament. One example is the fifteen verses in Isaiah 52:13-53:12, thirteen of which are quoted or referred to.

The evangelist John was convinced that the book of Isaiah bore witness to Jesus Christ. Near the halfway point of his gospel (Jn 12:38-41), he quotes Isaiah twice in succession. First, 53:1, "Lord, who has believed our message, and to whom has the arm of the Lord been revealed?" Then, 6:9-10, "He has blinded their eyes and hardened their heart, so that they might not look with their eyes, and understand with their heart and turn – and I would heal them". John proceeds to join together these two passages from Isaiah by stating that "Isaiah said this because he saw [the Lord's] glory and spoke about him". Isaiah did indeed see the glory of the Lord in his vision of Yahweh in 6:1.

Two chapters of the book of Isaiah stand out as prophetic mandates. In chapters 6 and 40 the prophet in question is assigned special tasks to carry out. In chapter 6 he is commissioned to proclaim God's judgement, and in chapter 40 he is instructed to declare God's comfort. *Judgement* is the dominant note of chapters 1-35, and *comfort* of chapters 40-66. In between these two largely poetic halves, there is a shorter section consisting mainly of historical prose in chapters 36-39, which brings the first half of the book to an appropriate end. God's people must be forewarned about God's judgement, but this judgement will sometimes be followed by God's restorative work, whereby he gives them a new start.

Any follower of Jesus the Messiah will inevitably be encouraged and envisioned by studying Isaiah. Many are the parallels between Isaiah and the New Testament gospels. It is good to realise that it is the same God who is the central figure in both the Old Testament and the New. In each part of the Bible God is described as being holy and loving. In the book of Isaiah, he is both the Holy One of Israel and also the self-giving servant who would love us and give himself for us.

The book of Isaiah is divided into 66 chapters, but in my book I divide its text into 117 sections, which I have numbered in Roman numerals. As a result these sections are relatively short, each about three or four pages long. If you were to read this book at a rate of one section per day, it would take you around fifteen minutes each time, and after four months you would have studied every verse. I hope that you would then have discovered new panoramic views of the Messiah, Jesus Christ, and that your love for him would be much deeper than it was. You would also have considered in some depth many of the principal themes raised by the text of John. I have amplified these in what I have called *Meditations* at the end of each section.

Just as John's Gospel is arguably the most enriching book in the New Testament, so Isaiah is the gold mine of the Old. I have discovered immense and priceless riches as a result of studying it. I ardently long that, as you study its 66 chapters, you too may discover the immeasurable goodness and love of Yahweh and of his suffering servant. To read your way through Isaiah's prophecy is a captivating adventure. May it also bring you many and unexpected benefits.

HOW TO READ THIS BOOK

The purpose of this book is to help the reader to understand the meaning of the text of the Old Testament book of Isaiah. Christians believe that Isaiah is a book inspired by God himself, and it is therefore best read in a prayerful and reflective frame of mind. You may or may not find the following approach helpful:

Begin with a short, simple prayer. Ask God to help you to learn about Jesus the Messiah from your reading of what Isaiah wrote centuries before his birth. Ask God's Son, Jesus the Messiah, to make himself real to you as you read the inspired words which Isaiah wrote about him.

Then read thoughtfully the section of Isaiah which you have reached. If possible, use a good Bible translation such as the New Revised Standard Version, the New International Version or the English Standard Version. In this book, all the quotations from the Bible are taken from the New Revised Standard Version, and the commentary is on the English text of this particular translation. The only change I have made in the quotations is to use the divine name Yahweh instead of the usual modern alternative the LORD. The name Yahweh was the covenant name for the living God, and for God's people it would have been full of meaning, reminding them of the rich blessing of their personal relationship with him.

As you read the Biblical text, be aware that you are reading a book that millions of people down the ages have regarded as the word of God. If anything strikes you, make a mental note of it (or better a written one). If something doesn't seem to make sense, think about it.

Then read the verse-by-verse commentary. Go through each verse of Isaiah once again, comparing your thoughts with those in this commentary. Hopefully the comments here will clear up some of the difficulties you may have.

Then read the meditation at the end of the section.

Finally, try to think of one thought or idea that you would like to remember during the day to come. Maybe at some convenient moment later on, think about it.

These are just suggestions. The main thing is to read the book of Isaiah and try to understand its text. If this book helps you to do this, it will have succeeded in its main purpose.

INTRODUCTION

The Historical Context
We do not know much about the life of the Prophet Isaiah, but there are some clues which are suggestive. He was overawed by the personality of King Uzziah (6:1). We know that he spoke to King Ahaz and sought to influence him (7:3-17). He was also a close adviser of King Hezekiah (37:1-7, 14-35). From this we may deduce that Isaiah was of noble birth and had contacts in court circles. He refers to his wife as *the prophetess* in 8:3, and this suggests that she in turn exercised a prophetic ministry. Isaiah gave long and strange prophetic names to at least two of his sons, who seemingly included themselves among their father's followers. The close disciples of the prophet all belonged to an informal "school of Isaiah", into which we are allowed one tantalising glimpse (8:16-18).

Isaiah lived in the southern half of the divided kingdom of Israel, which is often referred to as the southern Kingdom of Judah. His ministry stretched from 740 B.C. until at least the year 700, by which time the siege of Jerusalem, mentioned in chapters 36-37, had been lifted. A Jewish tradition has it that he was martyred by the evil King Manasseh. If this is true, Isaiah may have lived on until after the year 686, when Manasseh finally succeeded Hezekiah. That would be 54 years after God had called him to be a prophet. By then Isaiah would have been well into his seventies.

During this period of time the kings of the southern Kingdom of Judah (which included the capital, Jerusalem) were Uzziah, Jotham, Ahaz, Hezekiah and Manasseh. In the Old Testament history books (Kings and Chronicles), the kings are classified as being either generally good, or else a mixture of good and evil, or in some cases thoroughly evil. Hezekiah was one of the few good kings although, as we shall see, even he was far from perfect. Uzziah and Jotham were a mixture of both good and evil. Ahaz and Manasseh were two very evil kings, although Manasseh had an unexpected change of heart during a period of exile and imprisonment (2 Chron 33:10-13).

Isaiah was called to be a prophet of Yahweh in the year 740 B.C. He describes his call vividly in chapter 6. In a vision he saw Yahweh, *the* King of all kings, high and exalted, and the whole earth was full of his glory. After this vision, Isaiah would always speak boldly to the kings of Judah. He was fearless when Judah came under attack, even when the aggressors were the mighty Assyrians. Assyria was the great superpower of the time, and its emperor the most powerful man on earth. Isaiah, however, knew that Yahweh was King of kings, and because Isaiah feared Yahweh, he did not fear the high and mighty of this world.

During Isaiah's time, Assyria was ruled by a succession of predatory super-emperors. Their names were Tiglath-Pileser III (745-727), Shalmaneser V (727-722), Sargon II (722-705) and Sennacherib (705-681). Their aim was to extend the rule exercised by the Assyrian empire. On several occasions the southern Kingdom of Judah would suffer from invasions by the Assyrian army, or by joint attacks from armies of other nations that were allied against Assyria.

The people of God were vulnerable to armed attack, and the ongoing threat of invasion by neighbouring nations intimidated them. In the light of this, the main choice they had to make was whether to trust in Yahweh, who had promised to protect his people if they remained faithful to him, or to rely on desperate alliances with heathen nations. In 734 B.C. Syria and the northern Kingdom of Israel invaded the southern Kingdom of Judah, and Isaiah courageously confronted King Ahaz of Judah concerning this choice. Sadly, Ahaz had decided not to rely on Yahweh, but instead to stake everything on an alliance with Assyria. This decision would convert the southern Kingdom of Judah into a vassal state of Assyria. Judah would have to pay an extortionate annual tribute, and in the long term their subjection would have other serious consequences.

Ahaz was succeeded as King of Judah by Hezekiah. Hezekiah was eager to trust Yahweh and was therefore described in Jewish histories as one of the few good kings. Nevertheless, Isaiah had his job cut out to keep him from joining in anti-Assyrian alliances. In the end, led by some courtiers who wanted Judah and Jerusalem to ally with Egypt, Hezekiah revolted against Assyria, and this brought the full might of the superpower down on Judah. Such an unequal struggle was destined to bring to an end the southern Kingdom and its capital Jerusalem in 701 B.C., but an extraordinary divine intervention took place. A summary in prose of what happened is preserved for us in chapters 36-37 of Isaiah. Abbreviated versions also appear in 2 Kings, chapters 18-20, and 2 Chronicles, chapter 32.

The final parts of the book of Isaiah (chapters 40-66) refer to later events, and there are indications that they were written partly around 550 B.C., during the period of exile in Babylon, and partly after the return of the Jews from exile in 539 B.C., which was decreed by the Persian Emperor Cyrus.

The Authorship of the Book of Isaiah

The question of the authorship of the book has been a matter of controversy during the past two centuries. There are two principal approaches, and problems have arisen because the proponents of each approach have armed themselves with impressive arsenals of convincing but contradictory arguments. Many fine commentaries have been written by supporters of one or other position.

First of all, there are those who adopt the single authorship theory. Until modern times the book of Isaiah had always been regarded as a unity, authored and edited by the 8th century prophet who bore the book's name. Some scholars continue to take this view. Among the recent commentators who steadfastly hold to the unity of Isaiah are E. J. Young (*The Book of Isaiah*, 1965-1972) and Alec Motyer (*The Prophecy of Isaiah*, 1993). Also favouring a single author, but more generously and open-mindedly, are Derek Kidner (*The New Bible Commentary*, 1953) and Barry Webb (*The Message of Isaiah*, 1996).

There are also commentators who prefer the multiple authorship theory. In the 19th and 20th centuries many scholars pointed out some clear differences in style between the first 39 chapters of Isaiah and the last 27. Chapters 1-39 were attributed in the main to the prophet Isaiah and were considered to have been written during the years 740-700. Chapters 40-66 were thought to have been written much later. Eventually a consensus was reached, whereby most of the material in chapters 40-55 was dated to around 550 B.C. or shortly after, and was regarded as the work of an unknown prophet who lived among the exiled Jews in Babylonia. Most of the material in chapters 56-66 was considered to be post-exilic, from around 530-520 B.C. It may have been the work of the editor who then took the various prophecies from the 8th to the 6th centuries that we find in the book of Isaiah, and ordered them into the form in which they have come down to us today. Two 19th century British commentators who propounded this theory and wrote excellent commentaries were George Adam Smith (two volumes, *The Expositor's Bible*, 1888-1890), and John Skinner (two volumes, *The Cambridge Bible for Schools and Colleges*, 1896-1898).

The present author has read through the book of Isaiah over fifty times, and is convinced that chapters 40-66 concern issues that faced God's people some 150 years after Isaiah wrote. It is of course possible that God could have revealed to Isaiah the mood of the Jewish exiles before and after their restoration to Jerusalem over a century in advance. After all, everything is possible to God. However, it seems more in keeping with the mysterious ways in which God reveals his purposes to his people that he should have entrusted the revelation which formed chapters 40-66 to later prophets just prior to the end of the exile (chapters 40-55) and soon after the return to Jerusalem (chapters 56-66). The principle that should be applied here is that prophets always spoke primarily about the circumstances of their own time. There are few exceptions to this rule.

There is evidence in the early part of the text that the Prophet Isaiah set up a school of prophecy for his close followers (8:16-18). He asked his disciples to share with him the responsibility for preserving the oracles that Yahweh had revealed to him (v 16). He knew that they constituted a testimony of immense value, which needed to be bound up and stored away. The scrolls on which they were written would have been placed in jars, which were then sealed and looked after by the members of this school of prophecy. Over the years, Isaiah and maybe some other members of this school would have added further oracles to the collection. When Isaiah himself died, his disciples would have dedicated themselves to preserving the precious scrolls, and further prophets may in turn have continued the tradition and contributed further material to it.

Around 550-540 B.C., towards the end of the exile, a remarkable prophet seems to have joined the ranks of Isaiah's school. It was he who wrote chapters 40-55. It is not unlikely that he too was called Isaiah: this would have made it perfectly natural for his writings to be incorporated into the growing "scroll of Isaiah".

Finally, a third notable prophet seems to have arisen after the return from exile. His work did not possess the towering grandeur of the oracles of the two Isaiahs, but he was, like them, a superb poet, who may also have had a gift for editing. It was he who wrote much of chapters 56-66, after which he may have proceeded to edit the entire *corpus*. He imposed his majestic style on some of the earlier material, thereby bringing a sense of unity to the whole book.

This explanation of the authorship of Isaiah explains both its stylistic unity and the noticeably different feel of the later chapters when compared to the earlier ones. It has been pointed out by some readers that its first 39 chapters have an Old Testament feel to them, while the last 27 (chapters 40-66) are full of the hope and expectation that characterise the New Testament. Here is an odd coincidence which amuses mathematically-minded readers. The Bible is really a library containing 66 books: the first 39 make up the Old Testament, and the remaining 27 make up the New. The book of Isaiah has 66 chapters that echo the books of the Bible: the first 39 have an ancient aura about them, while the remaining 27 are fresh with new hope. The book of Isaiah is like the Bible in miniature.

PART 1

I

1:1-9 The political and religious Background

The first five chapters have no indication of a possible dating. They consist of separate oracles concerning the people of Israel, Judah and Jerusalem. They are now no longer linked to the historical events that gave rise to them, but are pieced together in a topical arrangement. Some of them describe the initial circumstances of Isaiah's ministry in the years 740-735 B.C.

1. The name Isaiah appropriately means "Yahweh is salvation", for the vision of this prophet is all about God's great rescue plan for mankind. We know a little bit about Isaiah's family and upbringing. During his ministry he was closely connected to the royal court, and he may have belonged to a noble family. His prophetic ministry began during the year that King Uzziah died (740 B.C., see 6:1). It continued during the reigns of three other Kings of Judah: Jotham, Ahaz and Hezekiah, until at least the year 700 B.C., after the lifting of the siege of Jerusalem in 701 B.C. mentioned in chapters 36 and 37. If, as Jewish tradition has it, Isaiah was martyred by being sawn in half by the evil King Manasseh, he would have lived on until after 686 B.C., which was when Manasseh fully succeeded Hezekiah. That would be 54 years after God called him to be a prophet, so he may have lived well into his seventies. Notice how Isaiah *saw* what God was purposing for the Jewish people of his day. This is a *visionary* book, *revealed* by God to the prophet. The vision reaches out to every nation on earth. It concerns not only Isaiah's times but also the future, until the end of time itself.

2. The first prophetic oracle in the book is a lament by God. Notice the claim that this message is a revelation from God: "Yahweh has spoken". According to this oracle, God had taken great care and lavished his love on the Israelites. They were his children, and he had brought them up, educating and protecting them. But instead of reciprocating the love of their Creator and Father, they (of all people) had rebelled against him. It is a paradox that he, who is Lord and God of all, had to experience "How much sharper than a serpent's tooth it is to have a thankless child" (Shakespeare, *King Lear*, Act 1, Scene 4). This was a very serious matter, for the welfare of the entire world depended on the conduct of the people of God: their destiny was to be a light to lighten the nations (42:6, 49:6). Because of this, the heavens and the earth are summoned to the heavenly courtroom, to listen to the charges that Yahweh will bring against his children.

3. Even animals know and respond to their owners and masters, but Israel does not know God. The people simply do not understand what is most important, that their most basic purpose and need is to know God and love him forever. They have missed the point of their lives.

4. Yahweh sadly reproves his chosen people. They have burdened themselves with the heavy load of their iniquity. In spite of being God's offspring, they persist in evil ways and corrupt dealings. Because they have forsaken Yahweh, they are utterly estranged from him. They have despised *the Holy One of Israel*. This title for God occurs twelve times in the first 39 chapters of Isaiah, and thirteen times in chapters 40-66. Elsewhere it only occurs twice in scripture (in 2 Ki 19:22, where Isaiah is being quoted, and in Ps 71:22). It is therefore almost peculiar to Isaiah and his followers, and was probably coined by him to express the majestic purity of God which he experienced so vividly in his visionary call to be a prophet. The title *the Holy One of Israel* echoes the angelic cry, "Holy! Holy! Holy!" in 6:3, and combines it with the tenderness of God's self-giving to the people of Israel. It sums up the two principal attributes of God's nature, his holiness and his love. Jesus similarly addressed God as "Holy Father" (Jn 17:11).

5. Yahweh continues his lament, marvelling at his people's wish for further punishment by persisting in rebellion against him. Fortunately for them, Yahweh is a humble God. He is slow to anger. As we shall see, his patience will eventually run out, but in the meantime he is gentle and persevering with his rebellious people. They have been, and still are, extremely difficult. Their whole head is sick, which tells of their closed minds. Their whole heart is faint, which explains their utter lack of resolve to turn their lives around.

6. Here is a national calamity: from head to toe, no soundness can be found in Yahweh's people. Morally and spiritually they are covered in bruises, sores and self-inflicted wounds. They have not come to God for the right treatment, because they have not recognised the seriousness of their condition.

7. Isaiah foresees that their land will be invaded by foreign conquerors, as indeed would happen in 701 when Sennacherib, King of Assyria, captured 46 Israelite towns, overthrew many villages and took more than 200,000 prisoners.

8. Jerusalem is here called *daughter Zion*, a name used 47 times in the book of Isaiah. The city would be left standing, like a labourer's booth in a vineyard after the vintage, or a farmer's shelter in a cucumber field. On more than one occasion Jerusalem would be besieged for several months. In much of the book of Isaiah the people of God and their beloved city constitute the background of the narrative. In the introductory five chapters of his book, the prophet paints a poignant picture of them. Loved by Yahweh, they nevertheless ignored him.

9. The sparing of a few survivors marks the first appearance in the book of Isaiah of the important theological concept of a *godly remnant*. This idea will become

clearer in due course. We shall see that although the remnant would become smaller, it would also become godlier. In the end it would culminate in the work and sacrifice of the one truly just person, the Messiah, referred to in this book as *the Branch*, *Emmanuel*, and *the Servant of Yahweh*. His arrival on earth was recognised by a tiny group of godly people. Without the remnant, the people of Yahweh would have become like Sodom and Gomorrah (Gen 19:12-26).

Meditation: The great Love Story

The story of the Bible concerns a wonderful Father God and his rebellious children. A recurring lament appears several times in the Old Testament: God "reared children and brought them up" but they repeatedly "rebelled against [him]" (v 2). Their behaviour was worse than that of the beasts. Oxen know their owners and donkeys know their masters' cribs, but most of Israel, the people of Yahweh, did not know or understand the God who made them (v 3).

They had been given the most wonderful heritage in the world. They knew the law of God. From past experience, they knew that a great blessing would be theirs if they followed and obeyed it, but they did not do so. Instead they chose to be a sinful nation, offspring who did what was evil. They forsook Yahweh and despised none other than *the Holy One of Israel*. As a result they became utterly estranged (v 4). From head to foot they were morally and mortally sick (v 5-6). Their land would in due course be ravaged and in ruins; only their capital city would be spared for them (v 7-8).

It is interesting that John's Gospel has a similar sad lament in its prologue. The Son of God, who was the promised Messiah of God's people, *was* in the world. Indeed, the world had come into being *through him* – and yet the world *did not know him*. He came to his own land of Israel, and even there his own people did not accept him (Jn 1:10-11). As a general rule, the love of God towards his people would be unrequited. This was a tragedy.

Fortunately, a very positive note follows. Ultimately the story told in the Bible is not a tragedy but a romance. Although most people would despise and forsake the Messiah, there were *some* who did welcome and receive him. They believed in his name, which means that they trusted him as their saviour and obeyed him as their Lord. As a result, they were born from above and became God's adopted children (Jn 1:12-13). There was in the Messiah's day a faithful and growing remnant, and this remains the case today.

Isaiah likewise follows an initial divine lament with the divine assurance that there was and would continue to be a godly remnant. "If the Lord of hosts had not left [them] a few survivors, [they] would have been like Sodom, and become like Gomorrah" (v 9). But this would not be the case. God had a few godly followers who survived the mass rebellion and remained faithful. They were his *remnant*. In every period God's people have been afflicted with attacks from outside the church and temptations to compromise within it. However, the work of God has continued throughout the ages, and there have always been a few who faithfully follow him and live, by grace, according to his standards.

II

1:10-20 Religious Hypocrisy and the Need to admit it

10. The tone of the rebuke is devastating. To be addressed by Yahweh as *Sodom and Gomorrah* (see also v 9) amounted to being accused of infamous and ungodly misconduct. There is an implicit threat that Jerusalem, the home of God's people, would become a disaster area like Pompeii or Hiroshima. Even so, there was still some hope, because Yahweh is humble and patient. If this had not been so, the Israelites would not have been exhorted to hear his word or attend to his teaching. The later rejection by Israel of the Messiah of the Jews would be a much more serious sin than anything spoken about here (Mt 11:20-24).

11 Like other prophets, such as Jeremiah (7:5-11), Hosea (6:6), Amos (5:21-24) and Micah (6:6-8), Isaiah protests that elaborate religious performances are of no value unless they are accompanied by social justice and a lowly spirit of worship. Here he makes clear that Yahweh utterly rejects meaningless sacrifices, however numerous and impressive they may be. God has no pleasure in burnt offerings and the blood of beasts *per se*.

12. The reason for Yahweh's displeasure at this endless parade of offerings lies in the disobedient lives of those who were offering them. God had not authorised these sacrifices so as to assuage unrepentant and guilty consciences, but rather in order to enable people to worship him wholeheartedly. To offer worship while persistently disobeying him was to trample the courts of his Temple.

13. Where there is no change of heart, offerings are futile and incense used in worship is an abomination. Yahweh is displeased with the goings-on during new moons, Sabbaths and callings of convocation. He cannot endure these solemn assemblies when the participants are guilty of iniquity. The sins of priests are worse than the sins of the ungodly. Religious piety and irreligious perfidy do not belong together, and the presence of the second renders the first unacceptable.

14. Yahweh hated the solemn assemblies that took place during new moons and other appointed festivals of the Israelites. Those who participated in them did not have humble and contrite hearts, and the gatherings were therefore a burden for God just as much as they were for those who were involved in them. Yahweh himself was weary of bearing them.

15. The conclusion of all this is that Yahweh would turn his eyes away when the people stretched out their hands towards him. However many fine prayers they offered, he would neither listen nor respond. The reason now becomes apparent:

their hands were full of blood. They had failed to look after those who were poor and weak. They had oppressed the meek, driving them to despair and to an early death. They had signally failed to share in God's care for the underprivileged.

16. A string of imperatives follow. They were the requirement of Yahweh for his people, and constituted the only way forward for them. They were to wash and make themselves clean. In what way? By removing *the evil of their doings* from before his eyes, in other words, by ceasing to do evil. They were to turn themselves around. They were to be sorry enough to stop doing what was evil.

17. Instead, they were to learn to do what is good. They were to seek social justice. They were to rescue the oppressed, defend the orphans and plead for the widows. Instead of trampling all over the vulnerable, they were to care for them and do what they could to improve their lot. This is what Yahweh desires, because Yahweh is humble and meek, and he cares for the downtrodden.

18. Yahweh makes his offer in the divine law-court. It is sheer grace, for it is undeserved and wonderful. He asks his people to reason with him! They would argue things out together. God *reasons* with people: revelation is not magical, but *rational* and *moral*. Religion is a dialogue between *intelligent beings*. Their sins were scarlet like blood, yet their hearts could become as white as snow. What was crimson could become whiter than bleached wool. There is nothing whiter than snow: a clean white cloth looks grey when held up against a background of freshly fallen snow. Scarlet and crimson were loud colours and stayed fast, but Yahweh is able to alter what is unchangeable and to erase what is indelible. God's offer of free grace is a remarkable concept and is unique to the Judeo-Christian religion. The idea that God forgives and cleanses us free of charge is life-changing. It will be put across even more clearly later in the book of Isaiah (e.g. 55:1-2, 6-7).

19. If God's people were willing to change, he would help them to do so, but their willingness and obedience was essential. By turning from what was wrong, they would once again enjoy the good things that life had to offer them.

20. It was, however, possible for God's people to refuse his offer. They had the freedom to do so, but what a terrible freedom it was. Rebellion against God would result in destruction. The mouth of Yahweh had affirmed this from the start (see Deut 30:15-20). There are, and have always been, two possible responses to God's offer of grace.

Meditation: When Religion becomes nauseating

There comes a time when organised religion becomes unacceptable to God, and this even applies to the Jewish and Christian religions. One of the most disturbing human qualities ascribed to God in the Bible is that there are some things that make him *vomit*. Two generations after Jesus Christ's ascension, church life had become so tepid in the church at Laodicea that Christ spoke to them through John the Seer, saying, "I know your works; you are neither cold nor hot. I wish that you were either cold or hot. So, because you are lukewarm, and neither cold nor hot, I am about to *spew* you out of my mouth" (Rev 3:15-16). The bland and meaningless services that took place in the church at Laodicea made God vomit. Their services were nauseating to him because the Laodicean churchgoers lived a double life, adopting the right forms on Sundays but otherwise trusting in their prosperity and not in him. He would spew them out of his mouth, unless . . .

It was the same in the years after 740 B.C., when Isaiah wrote chapter 1 of his prophecy. The religious services which Yahweh himself had ordained at the Temple were turning his stomach. He cared nothing for the many sacrifices offered by his people (v 11), even though he himself had instituted the sacrificial system in order to educate them and prepare them for the coming of "the Lamb of God who takes away the sin of the world" (Jn 1:29). The regular services had become an offence to the one for whose benefit they were enacted (v 12). Sacrificial offerings were futile; the sweet odour of incense was abominable; special convocations and solemn assemblies were iniquitous; the regular appointed festivals were odious (v 13-14). When his people prayed to him, Yahweh would hide his eyes and refuse to listen (v 15).

Why? Because the hands of his people were "full of blood". Their sins were "like scarlet" and "red like crimson" (v 15, 18). Because of their sinful indifference, the disadvantaged were dying. Instead of multiplying their religious services, they were required by God to cleanse themselves from their uncaring attitude (v 15). They were also to "cease to do evil, [and] learn to do good; seek justice, rescue the oppressed, defend the orphan, [and] plead for the widow" (v 16-17). Their root problem was their neglect of social justice; from now on they were to care for those who were poor and disadvantaged.

If they repented and followed the path laid out by Yahweh, then by the sheer grace of God they would be cleansed and forgiven, and would once again enjoy life in the land that God had given them (v 19). But if they refused and rebelled, they would be settled on a way that would lead to their destruction (v 20).

A similar offer of grace was made by the risen Jesus Christ to the Christians at Laodicea. God would spew them out of his mouth, unless . . . what? Christ said to them, "I reprove and discipline those whom I love. Be earnest, therefore, and *repent*" (Rev 3:19). The Christians at Laodicea needed to turn their lives around. They were to turn away from their complacent trust in their prosperity (Rev 3:17) and ask the risen Christ to come into the house of their lives (Rev 3:20). Christ promised that he would then come in and share their lives. He would transform them. He would forget about their rebellious complacency and revolutionise their lives. This too was sheer undeserved grace, but grace is precisely what God lavishes upon his people. To those who repent, he gives rich blessings that are totally undeserved. It is, of course, striking that Christ is here calling those 'from within' to repent from their indifference, as opposed to non-believers! This is an unpopular but very important insight. The fact is that much the greater part of the book of Isaiah is addressed to God's people rather than to the heathen nations.

III

1:21-31 The decadent City and God's Reaction to it

21. The divine lament for Jerusalem begins with the word *How*, as in David's famous lament for Saul and Jonathan, "How the mighty have fallen!" (2 Sam 1:19). Here it is the *glory* of the City of God that has fallen and vanished. This is not so much a reference to the glory of empire and wealth, but to moral glory. The faithful city has been unfaithful like a prostitute. Gone is her glorious justice; the home of righteousness is now the dwelling-place of murderers. Similar pairings of justice and righteousness come sixteen times in the book of Isaiah.

22. It is as if the silver treasures of Jerusalem have been taken away by foreign kings and replaced instead with metallic tarnish and rust. Likewise her wine is now adulterated. Instead of holiness there is impurity.

23. The social injustices are exposed: princes are companions of thieves; ordinary people lust for bribes and gifts; no one cares what happens to the vulnerable. In the Bible, what happens to orphans and widows is of the first importance.

24. Because of this God responds. His response is terrifying, for he declares that he is the Sovereign, Yahweh of the armies, and the Mighty One of Israel. He will pour out his wrath on his enemies. Time and time again, the "Mighty one of Israel" had saved the people of Israel from foreign enemies. Now it was his enemies within Israel who would be recipients of his wrath. The wrath of God is his settled and righteous anger, directed against those who prefer the darkness of evil to his good and perfect way. God avenges himself on his foes. "Vengeance is mine; I will repay, says the Lord" (Deut 32:35, Rom 12:19). Revenge is God's prerogative and his alone, ours is to forgive rather than to seek redress. When God avenges himself, his retribution will be just. Every wrong that has been committed on earth will in the end be put right.

25. God will begin the work of refining humanity with his own people, for "the time has come for judgement to begin with the household of God" (1 Pet 4:17). This is merciful judgement, for although Yahweh is turning his hand against his own, his purpose is to smelt away their metallic tarnish and remove their alloy, leaving only unadulterated silver. The process will be painful but the end will be marvellous to see – God's people will once again be pure metal, precious and radiant with God's glory.

26. After the refining will come the restoration. The judges will be just and the coun-sellors wise, as in the glorious early years of King David. Then Jerusalem will be

known as the city of righteousness and faithfulness. Once again its people will be able to rely on one another, because once again there will be a city-wide priority on behalf of the needy and the downtrodden.

27. The renewed Zion, which is another name for the city of God, will be spared because of its social justice. Likewise, among its people, those who repented will be spared because of their righteousness. Here we have justice and righteousness paired once again. Together, they satisfy the requirements of God's holiness.

28. The fires of judgement are merciful to some, refining and redeeming them. Sadly they do not have a positive effect on everyone. There are those who will not repent, but instead will stubbornly persist in their selfish rebellion against Yahweh. For them the fires will bring destruction. They will be consumed.

29. The trees and gardens mentioned here were the pride and shame of idolatrous Israelites. The sacred oaks and the well-kept gardens were connected with the high places, where the Amorites used to worship idols. When the Israelites took over the Promised Land, they did not destroy these high places. Many of God's people actually worshipped the idols there. But what absorbed and delighted them would become a source of shame for them, and what they had previously favoured would in the end bring them great embarrassment. The pride of man is dark and fading, but the humility of God is lasting and full of light.

30. The unrepentant Israelites would be like an oak struck by drought, its leaves brown and withering. They would resemble a blighted garden, dry as sand.

31. Those who had gloried in their strength would be as dry and brittle as tinder, and their exploits like a smouldering spark. These people would burst into flame and burn down to ashes, and nobody would be able to extinguish the blaze. The human work that they were very proud of and once considered glorious would be the spark that set off the deadly conflagration.

Meditation: The Message that stings will restore or destroy

It was (and still is) difficult to be a prophet of the Holy and Mighty One of Israel. Isaiah knew that his message would have a polarising effect (6:9-13). The same sun that softens wax also hardens clay. Yet it was vital that someone should preach the need for repentance.

The people of Jerusalem had become degenerate; they behaved towards God as if they were whores. Instead of seeking justice, they became murderers (v 21). There was no purity in them: they had turned to dross, and at best they were like adulterated wine (v 22). Instead of encouraging one another, they manipulated and used each other. They thrived on bribery and corruption, and shut their eyes and ears to the cries of the needy (v 23).

They desperately needed to be restored, but nothing other than repentance and refining would lead to restoration. Even then, there was the awful prospect of Yahweh dispensing his just retribution (v 24-26). Into the sinful city Isaiah was sent as Yahweh's spokesman. His words promised righteousness to those who turned from their evil ways, but he also prophesied that any rebels would be destroyed, and that those who forsook Yahweh would be consumed (v 27-28).

What had previously seemed a source of beauty, security or strength would be the undoing of those who had chosen a godless path. The people and the objects that they had trusted in would in the end bring them shame. They would be burnt away, and those who had been so misguided as to trust in them would themselves likewise be destroyed in the apocalyptic fires (v 29-31).

It was a very sharp and divisive message. That this would not go down very well in our 21ˢᵗ century is obvious. We shall see that it did not go down well in Jerusalem in Isaiah's day. Less obvious is the realisation that this message *never* goes down well. It is a message that is always necessary, but seldom gladly received, except in times of religious awakening such as England experienced in the Methodist and Welsh revivals. In the fullness of time, the One towards whom Isaiah's prophecies pointed forward came into this world. When he first set out on his itinerant preaching ministry, this was the very message that he preached: "The Kingdom of God has come near; *repent* and *believe* in the good news" (Mk 1:15). The bad news must precede the proclamation of the good news. In order to become aware of our great need for a saviour, we must first acknowledge the great sins from which we need to be saved, and realise how offensive they are to God. Thanks be to him for the few faithful Isaiahs of our own day.

IV

2:1-9 The City of God and the City of Man

Early in the fifth century St Augustine of Hippo wrote a book entitled *De civitate Dei contra paganos*, usually shortened in English to 'The City of God'. In it he compared and contrasted the ideal city of God with the earthly city of man, and in passing considered and developed several important aspects of theology. The idea for the title of his book was not Augustine's own; it was Isaiah's. In this section the prophet looks forward to the glorious future which awaits Jerusalem, the city of God (v 2-4) and contrasts it with the city he lived in, which was just a city of men (v 5-9).

1. There is something unusual about this verse. One would expect, "The word that Isaiah son of Amoz *heard* concerning Judah and Jerusalem" but, as in 1:1, we read that Isaiah *saw* this prophetic word. Perhaps it came to him in the form of a vision, and he was given the ability to interpret it.

2. Verses 2-4 are very similar to Micah 4:1-3. Although Micah was younger than Isaiah, their lives overlapped and they may have known each other. The language is more typical of Isaiah's writings, so the citation is probably on Micah's part. The oracle looks ahead to "days to come", to the future glory of Jerusalem, built on the mountain of the Temple, which was Yahweh's house. The glory of the

city would be established and it would be outstanding among the nations, for Yahweh would dwell among his people.

3. People from foreign lands would be drawn to the city of God, eager to visit its Temple. They wanted to encounter Yahweh, and in his city they would find him. Their wish was to learn his ways so that they could walk humbly with him. They longed for his clear truth and kindly rule. They would know that Jerusalem was the place to learn about him, where they would encounter Yahweh's message.

4. The outcome of this would be peace and harmony between the nations. Yahweh would himself arbitrate between them, and enable them to be reconciled. As a result, wars would cease, and weapons devised for killing people would be turned into agricultural implements. Yahweh is "the God of peace" (Heb 13:20), and when people begin to follow him they find a new inward longing for peace with those from whom they were previously estranged. An example of something akin to this taking place in our own time is given in *The Secret of Nabelan Kabelan* by Jacques Teeuwen. A recently converted tribe, in Dutch New Guinea, burnt all their weapons of war and went, unarmed, to evangelise a neighbouring village with whom they had fought many battles.

5. The prophecy prompts an appeal for immediate action. It is in one sense a vision of an ideal future, but it is imperative to begin to build that future *now*. The sight of people obeying the one true God will act as a magnet for those who do not know this God. Therefore Isaiah plaintively pleads, "Oh house of Jacob, come, let us walk in the light of Yahweh". We find echoes of these words, "let us walk in the light", in John's gospel and in his first epistle (Jn 12:35, 1 Jn 1:7).

6. The present reality was far from the ideal future envisaged in the vision. The descendants of Jacob were abandoning the paths of godliness. Their city, which was supposed to be the city of God, was in fact the city of fallen man. Instead of trusting in Yahweh, they had pursued diviners and soothsayers who claimed to predict the future, and had thereby got entangled in a dark web of superstition. They had opted for foreign alliances when they should have trusted in the One who had rescued them from servitude. This pursuit of false religion or false security occurs time and time again in the Old Testament.

7. They had forgotten their God and put their trust in wealth. They had acquired everything except God. With their riches they had purchased armaments. They thought they had obtained security apart from God, and this made them proud.

8. In their arrogance they turned to their own idols. With their own hands they had crafted them, and they then worshipped what they themselves had made. As they bowed down before these idols of their own creation, they degraded their dignity as human beings made in God's image (Gen 1:26-27). Isaiah was struck by the fact that the Hebrew noun for *idols* is identical to the Hebrew adjective for *worthless*, and he would make much play of this in his prophecy.

9. One of Isaiah's great themes is the contrast between the pride of man and the humility of God. The prophet foresaw the inevitable end of the story: "And so people are humbled and everyone is brought low". So Isaiah interjects, "Do not forgive them!" Forgiveness is almost impossible for proud people who persist in their refusal to walk in the light of the Lord, and who are determined never to repent. But there are some exceptions, such as King Manasseh (2 Chron 33:10-13) and Saul of Tarsus (Acts 9:1-19), which serve to highlight the grace of God.

Meditation: What people want may not be good for them

What do people look for in life, above anything else? We build our cities and equip ourselves with three things that we believe will be just what we need. We want *reassurance concerning the future*, so we import diviners and soothsayers (v 5-6). In 21st century France the number of people earning a living in occult practices is now greater than the number of doctors, and it is ten times greater than the number of mission-minded pastors and priests.

We want *financial security*, so we hoard treasures and collect expensive luxuries, including means of transport (v 7). In the Western world most people belong to the middle class. Their standard of living is so high that it would have been unattainable to at least 95% of people in ancient times and in the time of the Messiah. And yet we in the Western world want more. We always want a little bit more than what we already have.

We want *fulfilment through worship*, so we seek it in idols, which may be either man-made images or actual celebrities (v 8). In 21st century Europe practically every person spends more time adoring his or her idols than they do worshipping the living God – and this includes deeply committed Christians, who look to politicians or sportsmen rather than to Jesus Christ as their role models. All of this leads to humiliation (v 9). Those who *exalt themselves* through their idols will be humbled (Lk 14:11, 18:14).

God has a much better plan for the citizens of this world. Those who dwell in the city of man tend to become isolated from one another. They become alienated because of their preoccupations, their over-work and their selfish ambitions. In the city of God, on the other hand, the citizens aspire to *live outstandingly*, so that their excellence may be noted and copied by others (v 2-3a). The lifestyle in the city of God is God-centred rather than man-centred, and it promotes godliness (v 3b), social justice and peace (v 4).

The writer of Proverbs summed it up well: "Righteousness exalts a nation, but sin is a reproach to any people" (Prov 14:34). When any country's legislation makes sinful behaviour legal, and also actively encourages selfish enrichment and hedonistic behaviour, that country is in decline and its fall is not far away.

How can we know what is the right course to take? God has given us a guide-book, the Bible. There are principles in it that will apply to our present situation, whatever it is, whichever century we are living in. If we wish to know what is the right and good course to adopt, we would do well to read the Bible regularly and adopt its standards. It is sometimes pointed out that in Victorian times there were many Bible-believing Christians. The next generation largely lost its faith, but it kept some morality by attempting to live by Biblical standards. The third generation abandoned both. We are reaping the consequences today.

V

2:10-18 What God has in Store for human Pride

10. The arrogance of those who have transformed the city of God into the city of man prompts Isaiah to reflect on the judgement that lies ahead for them. This passage is one of the highlights of his book. In a poem of extraordinary power he outlines the fate that awaits the proud and arrogant. The day will come when they will seek to hide themselves behind rocks and in caves, in a vain attempt to run away from the wrath of Yahweh and from his incinerating, white-hot glory. There are two ominous refrains in the poem. The first is "Enter . . . and hide . . . from the terror of Yahweh and from the glory of his majesty" (v 10, 19, 21). God in person will rise and terrify the earth. This is the final consequence of delighting in the superficial glory of celebrities, of choosing to rely on one's achievements, and of bowing down to idols.

11. The second ominous refrain of this poem (v 11, 17) is that "Haughty eyes shall be brought low" (see Prov 6:16-19, 21:4), "and the pride of everyone shall be humbled". On the great and final day, only one person will capture everyone's attention. Only one being will be lit up by the spotlights of glory. The radiance of the entire universe will light up his majesty. He alone "will be exalted on that day". This is so important that Isaiah repeats it in v 17.

This being is God, but what is his name? Isaiah often calls him *Yahweh*, which was the familiar name by which he revealed himself in a personal way to his people. They knew him as Yahweh; he was their God (Ex 6:7, Jer 32:38). In our day, God makes himself known to us by the familiar name of *Jesus Christ*. He is the same God, even though he is a person distinct from Yahweh. This is because there are three different persons within the plural Godhead, which consists of God the Father, God the Son and God the Holy Spirit.

Isaiah wrote about all three. Yahweh equates to none other than God the Father. The Messiah, about whom Isaiah has much to teach us, beginning in chapter 4, is God the Son, whom we know as Jesus Christ. The one and only Son of God, who is close to God the Father's heart, is the one who makes God the Father known to us (Jn 1:18). When Isaiah wrote about him, he had not yet been "made flesh" (Jn 1:14). Yet the prophet associates him so closely with God that he sometimes gives him the name *Emmanuel*, which means "God is with us". Isaiah also has some great truths to declare about God the Holy Spirit, beginning in chapter 11.

12. Yahweh of hosts, meaning God, the commander of all the armies of heaven, "has a day". He has appointed a final day of reckoning. Only he knows when it will be (Mk 13:32). Because he is aware of this fact, Isaiah's preaching is far-sighted and purposeful. As a result it is deeply satisfying, even when his message is negative and unpalatable. Today's church tends to disdain its privilege of feeding the people of God with nutritious spiritual food, because its message lacks this ultimate dimension. Very seldom is the solemn truth of the final day mentioned from the pulpit nowadays. Christian people are simply unaware that there will be a final reckoning, when perfect justice will be seen to be done. Nevertheless Isaiah presses home the point that Yahweh of the armies has a day, and this day is described as being "against" various groups of people and their proud attitudes. God will be seen to be against all those who are proud and lofty, and also against all those who are lifted up and high. To be high and mighty could well be thought of as being an advantage now, but it will be a terrible liability on that day. Why? Because God hates human pride. He will not bless those who are proud, but instead he will actively oppose them (2 Sam 22:28, 1 Pet 5:5).

13. Yahweh of the armies is also against people who stand out among their peers and receive glory from them. These celebrities have become epic heroes, like the proverbial cedars of Lebanon, lofty and lifted up, and like the lesser-known oaks of Bashan, long-lived and mightily dominant trees.

14. Other proud people are like high mountains or lofty hills. They are marked out by a seemingly impregnable solidity. In this world they seem impervious to attack. It is impossible to undermine a mountain. But this invincibility of theirs will be blown away by a single exhalation from the God of armies. Inevitably all will fall – Alexander the Great, Napoleon, Hitler, and their equivalents today.

15. There are also those who are like a high tower or a fortified wall. They in turn will not be safe from being utterly humbled on the great day of the Lord of hosts. Now they may look down on other people from a great height, treating them as insignificant ants. This is not pleasing to the God and Father of the One who went around doing acts of kindness on behalf of the needy and marginalised.

16. Even the insignia of escapist security, the mighty ships of transport, war or hedonistic living, will be brought low. They will be sunk. The arrogance of the affluent (Lk 12:13-21) will face up to the divine judgement on that day.

17. On that great day all the material things will be stripped away and we shall see the one who creates and upholds all things. Then the attention will not be on the bright lights, nor on the superficial glamour of this world's celebrities. It will not even be on the great achievements of mankind. "The haughtiness of people shall be humbled, and the pride of everyone shall be brought low; and Yahweh alone shall be exalted on that day".

18. It is not only human pride that will bite the dust. So will man-made religion. Idols are usually man-made things which have become objects of worship. They can also be fallen humans who have attained celebrity status and are being worshipped. All idols will utterly pass away. Yahweh alone is worthy of our worship, for all glory rightly belongs to him and to him only. It is he who will be exalted and adored on that day.

Meditation: When Pride will become unfashionable

"Pride goes before destruction, and a haughty spirit before a fall". So wrote the writer of Proverbs (Prov 16:18). This was shortened to become the well-known English saying, "Pride comes before a fall". Until three-quarters of the way through the twentieth century, the large majority of people were taught (and they believed it) that pride was both an unpleasant trait in someone else, and a fault to be fought against in oneself. In the Middle Ages pride was considered to be the deadliest sin. The words "pride" and "sin" had this in common: they were both spelt with an "I" in the middle. This reflects the basic problem in our human nature: I in the middle of everything. Me first. What I want is what matters. Life is all about me.

During the 1970s there was a radical shift in people's attitudes. It is now old-fashioned to think of pride in pejorative terms. We are all encouraged to "take pride" in our work and our achievements. Nowadays it is fine to say, "I am proud of what I have done". Today we think of ourselves as being not only *good* (which is unrealistic enough – see Mk 10:18), but also *better than others*. So much is this so, that everyone has to be excellent or outstanding at school and in their job, which is impossible! And yet, a certain unease remains. People in the public eye may be adulated by some, but they are also vilified by others. Standards vary according to convenience and expediency. Today's hero may become tomorrow's villain, and vice-versa. Perhaps the pendulum will swing back, and qualities like humility, modesty and unassuming quietness will come back into fashion.

It is often the case, even in this life, that the haughty eyes of people are brought low, and their pride is humbled (v 11), even though the day when "the Lord alone will be exalted" is still in the future. We are promised that if we humble ourselves under the mighty hand of God, *he* will exalt us "in due time" (1 Pet 5:6), and this will not necessarily be only in the life to come. It may also happen in the here and now. Jesus himself said on various occasions that, "All who *exalt* themselves will be humbled, and all who *humble* themselves will be exalted". God is the great reverser of fortunes: he delights to lift up the lowly and to bring down the haughty.

Isaiah pioneered this insight by declaring in majestic verse that this humbling of the proud is something that will characterise the final day. On that day, when God will judge the secrets of men through Jesus Christ (Rom 2:16), the haughtiness of people *will be humbled*, and the pride of everyone *will be brought low* (v 17). Yahweh alone will be exalted on that day.

VI

2:19-22 The terrifying Presence of Yahweh

19. The Old Testament is consistent in declaring that fallen man is incapable of enduring the sight of God in his perfection and holiness. Yahweh said to Moses, "You cannot see my face; for no one shall see me and live" (Ex 33:20). He went on to advise Moses to go into a cleft in the rock in order to survive (Ex 33:21-23); this is a clear parallel with the verse we are studying. The vision of the great day of Yahweh begins with a scene of madness and panic. People are trying to escape from the divine presence by entering caves in the rocks or holes in the ground. They are utterly unable to think in their terror. They want to hide "from the terror of Yahweh and from the glory of his majesty", for Yahweh has risen in order to terrify the earth. This verse repeats verse 10 and is in turn repeated in verse 21, with minor variations in the hiding places that these terrified people will enter into in order to hide "from the terror of Yahweh and from the glory of his majesty". Who are these people? They are the *proud* of the earth (v 17). There is no terror like that of proud people who know that they are about to be brought low. They realise that they will lose all their power, position and privilege. They will be humbled. It would have been better if they had humbled themselves.

20. The phrase "that day" is often used by Isaiah. He points us ahead to the great day, the day of Yahweh, and not simply to a time in the near future. For us, "that day" has already dawned with the coming of the Messiah, but it will not reach high noon until the Messiah returns to wind up this present age and inaugurate the new one. In the vision we see the proud throwing away the idolatrous images they have made. They are throwing all their idols of silver and gold to the moles of the ground and the bats of the caves. They had made them in order to worship them, and on the day of Yahweh these idols will be tangible evidence that they have rebelled against *him*. They have ignored and disobeyed *him*. They have acted as if *he* did not exist. They had an innate desire to worship something, but they did not wish to worship God – and so they have worshipped their *idols*. Some may even have worshipped *themselves*. But none of them devoted themselves to the one who alone was the rightful object of their adoration.

21. Why do they cast off their idols? Partly out of a guilty conscience, to destroy the evidence of their idolatrous worship. But they also need to dispossess themselves of unnecessary possessions in order to be able "to enter the caverns of the rocks and the clefts in the crags", so as to flee "from the terror of the Lord, and from the glory of his majesty, when he rises to terrify the earth".

22. What is the lesson that Isaiah wants his readers to learn from this awesome vision of God in his majesty? Could it be this: that only *God* should occupy the supreme place in our thoughts? When it comes to resting the full weight of our trust on someone else, we are to "turn away from mortals, who have only breath in their nostrils, for of what account are they?" Other people's hold on life is as slender as ours, and if it is eternal life that we are after, only God's Son Jesus Christ can be depended upon for true guidance as to how to attain it. Only he can give us eternal life, and he wishes to give it to us as a free gift – even though it cost him the very high price of his lifeblood (Jn 10:28, 3:16).

Meditation: The great and terrible Day of the Lord

The book of Isaiah is a huge source of ideas and inspiration for the writers of the New Testament. Jesus Christ quoted from it on several occasions, as we shall see, and there are quotations from it in several of the books of the New Testament. The vision given to us in verses 10 and 19-21 of Isaiah 2 is repeated in the terrifying glimpse of the Day of Judgement in Revelation 6:12-17:

When he opened the sixth seal, I looked, and there came a great earthquake; the sun became black as sackcloth, the full moon became like blood, and the stars of the sky fell to the earth as the fig tree drops its winter fruit when shaken by a gale. The sky vanished like a scroll rolling itself up, and every mountain and island was removed from its place.

Then the kings of the earth and the magnates and the generals and the rich and the powerful, and everyone, slave and free, hid in the caves and among the rocks of the mountains, calling to the mountains and rocks, "Fall on us and hide us from the face of the One seated on the throne and from the wrath of the Lamb; for the great day of their wrath has come, and who is able to stand?"

John the Seer, who wrote the book of Revelation, highlights the fact that it is those who have risen highest in this life who will suffer the greatest fall on that day. He mentions kings, magnates, generals, the rich and the powerful. On that day, they will all be terror-struck at the prospect of seeing the perfectly humble and pure faces of God the Father and of his suffering servant Jesus Christ.

Lest we who are small and powerless should think the vision cannot apply to us, John continues by saying that *everyone* who is proud and haughty, whether slave or free, will join the mighty as they try to hide away in caves and among the rocks of the mountains. *Anyone* who was proud, *anyone* who was lifted up and high, will try to run away from the One who, being himself humble and meek, wishes to exalt those who are humble and meek.

At the end of this meditation we may reflect on the sayings of Mary, the mother of our Lord Jesus Christ. Her words are few but well worth studying. In the *Magnificat* she praises God for reversing the fortunes of people. "God my Saviour . . . has looked with favour on the *lowliness* of his *servant*. The Mighty One has done great things for *me*, and holy is his name. His mercy is for those who *fear* him from generation to generation. He has scattered the *proud* in the thoughts of their hearts. He has brought down the *powerful* from their thrones, and lifted up the *lowly*. He has filled the *hungry* with good things, and sent the *rich* away empty" (Lk 1:46-55). In the light of this we should heed the advice, which is of universal application, that she gave to some servants at a party: "Do whatever [Jesus] tells you" (Jn 2:5). We should therefore renounce our pride, which will only lead to a fall. Instead we may delight in our great God, being content to lead a lowly and humble life.

VII

3:1-15 How God judges us in the Here and Now

In this section and the next, the background is no longer a future day of judgement as in Isaiah chapter 2, but rather the political scene in Jerusalem and Judah in the years 740-730 B.C. In chapter 2 we read about the overwhelming apocalyptic catastrophe that would engulf all ungodly people; here we witness the process of gradual disintegration of society. The invisible ties that bind people together in community would gradually be eroded. The unruly desires and intentions of selfish men and women would be given free rein, and they would prey on one another. This would lead to a state of anarchy in which all the people would do what seemed right in their own eyes.

1. God's judgement on those who have no time for him is not always postponed until the great Day of Judgement. Not infrequently, it begins here and it begins now. The Sovereign One, Yahweh the God of armies, overrules the dispositions of the mighty so as to bring scarcity to the disobedient city. Food would be rationed, and sources of clean water would run dry. Moreover the staff of the leaders would be taken away. Rule would be replaced, first by misrule and then by unruliness. The people would feel abandoned and unsupported.

2. The scarcity would extend beyond food and drink, and would include reliable leadership. Fewer people would be upright soldiers or police or lawyers, for the budgets of the armed forces and the metropolitan police would be cut, and lawyers would over-charge their clients so as to fill their own pockets. Those who were able to discern future trends would also become scarce: prophets and diviners would be ignored, as would wise elderly leaders. It is not unlikely that the latter might be used as scapegoats for the tribulations.

3. Local leaders would likewise make themselves scarce. No-one who could offer encouragement would be around. The type of charlatan who would normally have provided advice concerning the future, such as the "skilful magician" or "expert enchanter", would now be conspicuous by his absence.

4. The young would be ambitious for power, and even the extremely young and capricious would rise to occupy the empty positions of leadership.

5. In the resulting anarchy, people would be oppressed by their peers and by their neighbours. The restraints of discipline and order would be removed, and there

would be unseemly and unpleasant rudeness. Rebellious teenagers would be insolent to the elderly, and the uneducated would abuse the cultured and urbane.

6. The result would be anarchy and irreversible ruin. During elections people would be disaffected with those in authority, and would try and set up young family members as rulers. They would provide them with a cloak of office, but who would they rule over? All that would be left of civilization would be a "heap of ruins" and a collection of desperate people.

7. Even the youths chosen for high office would turn it down, preferring the freedom that accompanies lawlessness. Their excuse would be that they had no cure to offer those who were hurting, and no gift or aptitude for the sort of compassionate healing that everyone would need and desperately seek.

8. Both city and surrounding countryside would fall prey to decadence and decay. It would be their own fault, for they were guilty before God. "Their speech and their deeds are against Yahweh, defying his glorious presence".

9. The very expressions of their faces, their youthful lusts and arrogant bravado, would provide evidence of their rebelliousness. Isaiah likens their free-thinking immorality to the notorious people of Sodom (Gen 13:13, 19:4-11 and 24-26), who were condemned not only for their sexual depravity but also because they were haughty, and "had pride, excess of food and prosperous ease, but did not aid the poor and needy" (Ezek 16:49-50). The pride of the people of Jerusalem and their indifference to social needs would be an affront to Yahweh. These people would have defied his glorious presence and "brought evil on themselves".

10. Not everyone would be godless. Some would fear God, and as a result would be innocent of this proud rebelliousness. They would be the fortunate ones who would become the favoured objects of a beatitude: Blessed are those who are innocent, "for they shall eat the fruit of their labours".

11. Not so the guilty. They would be unfortunate, and would be placed under a curse: "Woe to the guilty, for what their hands have done shall be done to them". Divine retribution will be just. It will be terrible for those who brought about this state of affairs. To affront the glory of Yahweh is to deny it. There is ultimately no other source of true glory apart from him, and without his glory people will be left with nothing that is worth believing in. Once the godless have taken over, there will be nothing but an empty sea of despair, and people will find themselves adrift in it, able to float for a while but in the end doomed to drown.

12. God's people would be oppressed by immature and irresponsible leaders. The verse suggests that they would also suffer from some of their women leaders. God will look on in tender pity and say, "O my people, your leaders mislead you, and confuse the course of your paths". The old established signposts for godly living would have been discarded, and nothing would remain but confusion concerning the nature of goodness.

13. We now find ourselves in a divine courtroom. "Yahweh rises to argue his case". It is time for him to judge his people, those who supposedly follow him. He is just in all his ways, and we shall have to give an account of our lives.

14. He is particularly concerned with the religious elders and the royal princes. As we shall learn in chapter 5, they have "devoured the vineyard". They left no gleanings for the poor (Lev 19:9). Instead they plundered their meagre chattels. It is unacceptable for the spoils of the poor to be in the houses of the mighty.

15. What do they mean by crushing Yahweh's people in this cruel and inhuman way? How can the followers of the God who enjoins love (Deut 6:4-5, Lev 19:18) grind the faces of the poor? The God of the armies has spoken, and there can be no excuse. No answer is forthcoming.

Meditation: People get the Leaders they deserve

There have been various times in history when a nation has found itself in ever-increasing decline. At the same time its leaders have become increasingly corrupt and self-seeking. This is not a coincidence. A decadent people will wish to be governed by decadent leaders. When the prevailing lifestyle is hedonistic, the aspirants to leadership are likely to be of the same stamp. Their selfish lifestyle, normally a handicap for high office, will become a good credential under these circumstances. Most people like to create their leaders in their own image.

Here and elsewhere, the Bible suggests that when a civilization is in an advanced state of corruption, its leaders will also be corrupt. A vicious circle will be the result, where what is rotten will enhance the prevailing corruption. Things will inevitably get worse. There will not even be the hope that "things must get worse before they get better", for the spiral of decline can only accelerate. Without God, there can be no answer to the ever more distressing problems of society.

Where is God when the prevailing mood is godless? The answer is that he is still very much at work in the lives of individual people. In some cases he is preserving and purifying a "holy remnant". In other cases, perhaps the great majority, he is afflicting people with a kind of judicial blindness, so that it becomes more and more difficult for them to appreciate the seriousness of their situation.

No-one expressed this more starkly than the Apostle Paul in the second half of the first chapter of his great Epistle to the Romans. "For the wrath of God is revealed from heaven against all ungodliness and wickedness of those who by their wickedness suppress the truth" (Rom 1:18). Among the numerous unpopular passages of the Bible, none is hated more than this one, from Romans 1:18-32.

God himself is not to blame, says Paul. What can be known about him is plain to all people, for God has shown them his eternal power and divine nature through his wonderful creation. So those who reject God are without excuse (Rom 1:19-20). In spite of the instinctive grasp that such people have of God's power and goodness, they neither honour God nor thank him for his undeserved kindness. Instead their thinking becomes futile. Their minds become incapable of thinking rightly about God (Rom 1:21). They claim to be wise, but the more they do this, the more foolish they become. They exchange the glory of the immortal God for images of their fellow humans or of other living beings (Rom 1:22-23).

Therefore God gives up on them. It is because they dishonestly *suppress the truth*. They choose to exchange the truth about God for a lie, and as a result they worship and serve an *idol* instead of *the living God*. Their idol may be a fellow human being, created by God, or worse, an object of their own creation. They adore the creature rather the Creator, who is blessed forever! (Rom 1:25). *That* is why God gives up on them. *That* is why God gives them up to impurity and sexual depravity (Rom 1:24, 26-27). *That* is why God gives them up to a debased mind and abandons them to the practice of evil actions and attitudes (Rom 1:28-32).

God brings on those who dishonestly dismiss him an inability to think aright. Because they are *wilfully blind* to God, he strikes them with *judicial blindness* so that they become *incapable* of helping themselves. Where then can help be found for them in their hope-less plight? Isaiah's answer will be: in the godly remnant. The remnant, however, would have to diminish in size. But even when it became tiny and consisted of only a few godly and humble believers, they would not be competent to save the lost. In the end, Yahweh himself would have to intervene. The decisive moment would arrive when the holy remnant was represented by one person, and one person only: the suffering Servant of Yahweh.

VIII

3:16-4:1 Our absorbing Trivialities and their Destiny

Isaiah launches into a scornful exposure of the frivolity and extravagance of the wives and daughters of the leaders of Jerusalem. Like their husbands who practised extortion on the poor and vulnerable, these pampered women would be brought to account before Yahweh. Their subsequent degradation would be a total contrast to their carefree and showy display of luxury. Isaiah is about to bring their trivial pursuits ruthlessly to light, but first he minutely describes and exposes their showy display of pride.

16. They are *haughty*: we can see them as they walk with *outstretched necks*, and *glance wantonly* with their eyes. They *mince around*, walking with affected nicety and *tinkling* the bells on their feet. Yahweh has already pronounced judgement (3:13-15). Here he brings to light the besetting sin, and in the next verse he will put the sentence into effect.

17. Yahweh will act for this reason: it is because this ostentatious showmanship is costly, and its ultimate cost is that godly people are crushed and the poor are ground into the dust. So God will afflict the heads of these carefree women with leprous scabs. He will "lay bare their secret parts". Scarred and disgraced, they will be brought very low.

18. In verses 18-23 Isaiah proceeds to list 21 little items of finery which would have occupied the minds of the women who wore them. This catalogue of high fashion begins with anklets and headbands to adorn opposite ends of the female body, and crescents from Arabia to be worn as ornaments.

19. It continues with pendants and bracelets that add lustre to their ears and wrists, and scarves that bring colour to their necks.

20. There are also headdresses to wear at the royal racecourse, and armlets and sashes to enhance their designer clothing. There are perfume boxes to provide a pleasing aura, and amulets to charm away an evil spirit. Amulets were and still are associated with superstitions and false beliefs about God.

21. There are signet rings with which to sign cheques at the Jerusalem branch of Harrods, and nose rings which were the trendy and daring jewellery of the day.

22. There are festal robes, mantles and cloaks for every social occasion and for showing off in the streets. There are handbags, perhaps imported from Italy. How these self-important ladies liked to collect handbags!

23. There were ultra-fine erotic see-through garments of gauze for summer parties, and linen garments for winter ones. There were exotic turbans and veils to give a lady a mysterious air. All this finery would suddenly be destroyed, and with it the world of these wealthy women of the court.

24. Not only would the Lord "take away the finery" (v18). He would also replace it with less desirable alternatives. Instead of perfume there would be a stench, and instead of a sash around one's waist, a rope. Instead of well-set hair there would be baldness. Instead of a rich robe, there would be a binding of itchy and abrasive sackcloth. Instead of beauty, there would be shame. Unnecessary luxury would be replaced by destitution, exile and slavery.

25. In their turn, the men of Jerusalem would fall by the sword, and the warriors would perish in battle. All the details of this prophecy would indeed be fulfilled some 150 years later. After a long siege, the Babylonians under Nebuchadnezzar would overrun and destroy the city in the year 586 B. C.

26. The gates of Jerusalem would themselves lament and mourn. Ravaged, the people would sit on the ground in silence. It would prove the darkest of days for the Old Testament people of God. Their superficial triviality would suddenly be turned into utter tragedy.

4:1. Isaiah's description of Jerusalem on the terrible day of Yahweh's judgement is shocking. He brings it to an end with a gruesome and terribly pathetic scene. On that day, seven women would plead with one man, declaring that they would fend for themselves as regards food and clothing. What they longed for was that the man would consent to their being called by his name, in order that the reproach and disgrace of being unmarried might be taken away from them.

Meditation: The Emptiness of earthly Glory

We can hardly complain that this passage is sexist. Isaiah's message is that if the ladies are corrupt then the state is moribund. Nor can we seek to pretend that the trivialities mentioned in verses 18-23 are the luxurious whims of a bygone age. We ourselves, in our sophisticated Western civilization of the 21st century, also love to adorn ourselves with designer clothes and items of jewellery. A visit to Ascot on the day of the Gold Cup will reveal the same excessive self-indulgence that afflicted the wealthy women of Jerusalem in Isaiah's day. It is not only the inequality and the social injustice of such ostentation that Isaiah has been scorning, but also the mindless pettiness of it all. The superficial lifestyle of high society flyers is pitiful, with its solemn absurdity and vanity. To seek earnestly for worldly glory instead of the glory that comes from God is to prefer superficial glitter to lasting treasure.

Earthly glory is empty. It will be put to shame before the glory of God. The glory of God is about to be revealed to us in chapter 4 of Isaiah. By comparison, the glory of this world is like a mist that will be burnt away by the sunshine of the divine glory. It is like a palace made of snow that inevitably melts and washes away when exposed to the reality of God's sun.

The underlying reason for this is very important. Earthly glory is vain because it is created by pride, and is also the cause of it. The pride of man is a fading and insubstantial thing. Like the love of money, it is the root of all evil (1 Tim 6:10). God hates pride and arrogance (Prov 8:13). A person's pride will duly bring humiliation (Prov 29:23). In our passage, Isaiah is promising that the pride of God's people will bring them low (3:16-17). 135 years later the prophet Jeremiah prophesied in identical terms: "Hear and give ear; do not be *haughty*, for the Lord has spoken. Give glory to Yahweh your God before he brings darkness, and before your feet stumble on the mountains at twilight; while you look for light, he turns it into gloom and makes it deep darkness. But if you will not listen, my soul will weep in secret for your *pride*; my eyes will weep bitterly and run down with tears, because Yahweh's flock has been taken captive" (Jer 13:15-17).

It would take around 150 years before Isaiah's prophecy was fulfilled. God is patient and slow to anger. It would take around fifteen years before Jeremiah's prophecy came true. God remained patient after putting up with the rebellious pride of the people of Jerusalem for over a century. But even God's patience will not persist for ever. There are limits to how far he will allow people to reject and ignore his warnings. In the end, Jerusalem fell in the year 586 B. C., and terrible was its distress when it was besieged for eighteen months and then razed to the ground. You and I may indulge in superficial escapist vanities for a while. This will not bring us satisfaction, and in the end God's radiant glory will burn up the tinder of our worldly glory. It is to the wonderful glory of God that we now turn.

IX

4:2-6 After the Cleansing, a new Glory

The judgement, the humbling and the purification of God's people will be a painful process, as we have seen. After its completion, Isaiah is given a vision of the glorious age that will follow for the survivors of the Day of Yahweh. The land will be wonderfully fertile, men and women will be holy and humble, and the world will be enveloped within God's protecting umbrella.

2. "On that day the branch of Yahweh shall be beautiful and glorious". The branch of Yahweh is the shoot of new growth that will emerge from the stump of Israel after the dead wood has been chopped away from the tree. Who exactly is Isaiah referring to? At first sight the verse might seem to be speaking of the remnant of God's people, the godly citizens of Jerusalem and Judah, the true church within the visible church, after God has intervened to purify them. Many readers conclude that Isaiah is referring to the people of God who, after their failure and the consequent divine judgement, would be cleansed and holy. We are to think of them as if they had been re-born. Only a few survivors would remain, but God will have taken away their worldly glory. From these roots a new crop will spring up. So the godly remnant is in view in this passage, but most commentators believe that this verse is talking about one person only, he who is "the Branch of Yahweh" and "the fruit of the land". As God's remnant became godlier, it would contract. In the end, a small number of godly people would be represented by one person, the Messiah. It is he, "the Branch of Yahweh" and "the fruit of the land", who would be "the pride and glory of the survivors of Israel". Here a true and worthy pride is in view. We are right if we take pride in God and in his glorious Branch (as in Jer 9:23-24).

3. The people of God's city will be a renewed community. They will be holy and "recorded for life", inscribed in God's book as his holy people, those who have been rescued from judgement.

4. This would not happen without God's personal intervention, which would be extremely painful. God would have to wash away the inward "filth" of the daughters of Zion and cleanse the bloodstains of social violence in Jerusalem "from its midst". He would do this "by a spirit of judgement and a spirit of burning". Human glory cannot evolve into divine glory. It has to be taken away and be replaced by something that is quite different. God alone can do this. It is a process that will inevitably involve much pain, not only for us but also for God.

5. Then, after the fiery cleansing, God's manifested *Shekinah* glory would return to accompany his people, as in the old days of the Exodus. Throughout God's city Yahweh would be worshipped by his renewed community. Above it, a cloud would rest by day and the shining of a flaming fire would hover by night. Above

this glory there would be a canopy of protection to ensure the ongoing blessing and holiness of God's people. This is a reference to God's very presence: it would encompass and take care of his holy ones.

6. This canopy would serve as a giant tent, providing shade from the heat of the sun during the day, and shelter from the elements in stormy and rainy days. All the needs of God's people would be met. God's presence would abide with them.

Meditation: God's people are refined and contracted

After God's day of judgment and refining, and as a result of it, says Isaiah, a new growth would arise which would replace what had been destroyed. As a result of the cleansing, there would be holiness and righteous living.

In the book of Isaiah we shall see how the godly remnant was to become smaller and smaller. This contraction would reach its climax at a time when it would be a tiny group of people represented by one perfect person, the Messiah. An early indication of this is the statement that "A shoot shall come out from the stump of Jesse, and a Branch shall grow out of his roots" (Isa 11:1). But the first mention of a godly remnant consisting of the Messiah alone comes in Isaiah 4:2.

Isaiah was the first prophet who spoke of the Messiah as being like a shoot or a Branch. He introduces this idea in v 2 of our passage. He goes on to describe the Branch as "the fruit of the land". It would be "the pride and glory of the survivors of Israel". Initially we might wonder whether the branch he speaks of is a *plural* godly remnant of survivors, but then he focuses on a *singular* fruit, the coming Messiah, who would be the glory of the plural survivors. The singular *fruit* is one and the same as the *Branch*.

This description of the Messiah being like a Branch was later echoed by other Old Testament prophets. Jeremiah took Isaiah's metaphor of the branch and wrote that "The days are surely coming, says Yahweh, when I will raise up for David a righteous Branch, and he shall reign as king and deal wisely, and shall execute justice and righteousness in the land. In his days Judah will be saved and Israel will live in safety. And this is the name by which he will be called: Yahweh is our righteousness" (Jer 23:5-6). Jeremiah repeated this in similar words a little later: "The days are surely coming, says Yahweh, when I will fulfil the promise I made to the house of Israel and the house of Judah. In those days and at that time I will cause a righteous Branch to spring up for David; and he shall execute justice and righteousness in the land. In those days Judah will be saved and Jerusalem will live in safety. And this is the name by which it will be called: 'Yahweh is our righteousness'" (Jer 33:14-16).

Like Isaiah and Jeremiah, the prophet Zechariah also used this metaphor. "I am going to bring my servant the Branch . . . and I will remove the guilt of this land in a single day" (Zech 3:8-9). "Thus says Yahweh of the armies: Here is a man whose name is Branch: for he shall branch out in his place, and he shall build the temple of Yahweh" (Zech 6:12).

From this we can see that in Isaiah 4:2 we have the first of several Old Testament occurrences of the idea that the coming Messiah would be the Branch that would grow out of a dead stump, the people of Israel. Out of death would come life; out of a stump, a live Branch; out of scorched ground, a shoot. "For he grew up before him like a young plant, and like a root out of dry ground" (53:2). Out of very unpromising material, God can and does bring life and glory. It is a beautiful idea. It had lodged itself in Isaiah's mind and captured his imagination. Through his prophetic writings, it may capture ours as well.

X

5:1-7 The Parable of the unfruitful Vineyard

In this section we have a remarkable parable, composed by Isaiah. It is easily the best parable in the Old Testament, a worthy forerunner of the parables of Jesus Christ. The prophet has already used the metaphor of the vineyard in 3:14, with Yahweh's accusation against the elders and princes of his people: "It is you who have devoured the vineyard". But now he expands the metaphor into a beautiful allegory that has all the hallmarks of a parable.

1. Isaiah begins by begging our leave to sing a love song concerning his beloved. The fact that it is a plaintive love song catches our imagination. We ask, who is Isaiah's beloved? It is Yahweh. This is astonishing. The song is Isaiah's, but the words of lamentation are words spoken by God. He is mourning the utter failure of his vineyard, into which he had poured such love and care. Like a walled garden, it would afford sustenance and protection for the people he loved. The vineyard was ideally placed, on top of a hill and with very fertile soil.

2. Yahweh dug this vineyard, and cleared it of stones. The soil was now very good: there was no hard ground, for it had all been dug up and turned. There were no rocky areas, for all the stones had been collected and placed elsewhere. No doubt any visible weeds had also been taken away and burnt. Yahweh then proceeded to plant it with choice vines, specially selected and prepared by himself. He built a watchtower in the midst of it, so that the watchmen could look out for potential thieves (Mt 21:33). He even hewed out a wine vat in the middle of the vineyard, where the grape-juice would ferment. Yahweh expected his vineyard to yield grapes, and the grapes to become the finest of wines, admired and respected throughout the world. But all that came from his vineyard was wild grapes, sour and completely lacking in sweetness, unsuitable even as edible fruit.

3. Isaiah's listeners would have listened with displeasure at this turn of events. As the citizens of Jerusalem and the people of Judah, they were then consulted by the prophet concerning what they thought. It was up to them to answer the big question. Their reply was awaited. Was it Yahweh's fault or the vineyard's?

4. After lavishing such attention and love on it, what more could Yahweh possibly have done than what he did? Why then, when he had every right to expect good

fruit, did it yield wild grapes? At this stage, the listeners would have been indignant. They would have cried out, "This is an appalling disgrace! The people who ruined this vineyard should be brought to account! What more could they have asked for? Why, all that could have been done to help them was done!"

5. It is not yet time for the punchline, and Isaiah continues with Yahweh's song of lamentation. God could not simply ignore what had happened. He would take action. This is what Yahweh would do to his vineyard: he would remove its protecting hedge, and the wild beasts would devour it. He would break down its wall, and vagrants would trample it down. "Good!" said the disgusted listeners.

6. Yahweh would go further, ensuring that the vineyard would became a waste. No-one would prune the vines, nor would anyone hoe the ground. It would become overgrown and choked with briers and thorns. Yahweh would then direct the elements, and bring into being a great drought that would leave the vineyard as dry as sawdust. This retributive action might have made the listeners feel nervous. Just *what exactly* was this vineyard?

7. Isaiah presses his message home in the final verse of the song. "The vineyard of Yahweh, the God of armies, is *the house of Israel*, and *the people of Judah* are his pleasant planting". This is the moment when the listeners suddenly realise that they have been listening to their own trial, condemnation and sentencing. The second half of this verse is brilliantly concise and terse. It consists of a double play on words which is difficult to translate. "Did Yahweh find right? No, it gave him a fright! Did he discover good? No, there was a lot of blood!" Instead of the mellow taste of wine, Yahweh drank bitterness. Instead of looking at fine claret, he saw scarlet blood.

Meditation: God's Parable is explained

The vineyard of Yahweh is the house of Israel and the people of Judah (v 7). Yahweh had spared no trouble in preparing an ideal home for them. He had found and reserved a "very fertile hill" (v 1) for them to live in. Prior to their moving there, he had educated them through hardship, teaching them to rely on him for protection and fruitfulness. It had not been easy to take them out of Egypt and give them this land. First Yahweh had to raise up an outstanding leader, and then he had to work one miracle after another.

Nor was it an easy task to prepare the land of promise for their arrival. It had to be cleared: its digging and the removal of its stones (v 2a) meant the elimination of many of its corrupt Canaanite inhabitants – and it was not going to be easy to square up that bit of ethnic cleansing with the much-vaunted love of God for all the people of the world (Jn 3:16). The land had to be cleared in order to be planted with "choice vines" (v 2b). These choice vines referred to the people of Yahweh, whom he had chosen and prepared in order that they might be a light to lighten the other nations (2:2-3).

Then Yahweh built a watchtower in the midst of his people (v 2c). This must be a reference to the leaders of the Israelites, once they had settled in the land he had promised them. These leaders were to watch over the people, providing protection from their enemies. The best of them was their second king, David, but although he was outstanding among the kings of Israel, even he was flawed. As for their other leaders, the princes were "rebels and companions of thieves" (1:23), and just judges, true prophets and wise elders were becoming fewer (3:1-2).

Finally, Yahweh hewed out a wine vat in his vineyard (v 2d). This could refer to the way he provided his people with priests and prophets who would teach them the *Torah* and communicate his living word to them. These divine instructions and principles would enable them to rise above the other nations and become a model for them to follow (2:2). Sadly, there were only a few good prophets and many bad ones. The bad ones were popular because they proclaimed comforting news, but invariably they misled the people. The good ones were hated by rulers and people alike, and not infrequently were put to death by them.

Having done all this, Yahweh expected his vineyard to yield grapes (v 2e). They had every privilege and opportunity to live lives that were pleasing to him. How he would have rejoiced to see them take their turn at teaching the other nations how to avail themselves of the life that was truly life. What a wonderful plan he had devised, whereby the light of goodness would spread until all the nations pursued the path of peace (2:4). But instead of producing a rich and refreshing vintage, his vineyard "yielded wild grapes" (v 2f).

Yahweh protested! Not because this was not good enough, but because it was appalling. His own people would judge who was to blame. Was it Yahweh or was it themselves (v 3)? What more could he have done for them than what he had already done (v 4a)? When every circumstance was propitious for a rich yield of good grapes, why did his vineyard yield wild grapes (v 4b)?

After his lament, Yahweh would take action against his vineyard. He is slow to anger, but when he is persistently provoked, his anger is greatly to be feared. He would take away the defences of the vineyard (v 5) and it would be invaded by weeds and thorn-bushes. He would remove the clouds with their clear water, allowing the baking sun to scorch the land (v 6). The very fertile hill would become a wilderness, and then a desert. He was not going to deal like this with a heathen nation – that would have been understandable to Isaiah's hearers. He would do this to his own people whom he loved and set apart to be his servants.

Why? Because quite rightly he expected justice, but instead he saw bloodshed. Because quite rightly he wished to see righteousness, but instead he heard a cry!

He would do this because his love for the Israelites was unrequited. He had reared children and brought them up, but they had rebelled against him (1:2). Even domesticated animals could love and serve their masters, but Israel did not know how to do this. Sadly, the people of God did not know and did not want to know (1:3).

In his brief but helpful commentary, Derek Kidner wrote that this parable brings home, as nothing else could, the unreasonableness and the indefensible nature of sin. We find ourselves searching for some external cause of the vine's failure, and there is none. Only humans could be so capricious.

XI

5:8-23 The six (or perhaps seven) Woes

Because the leaders of God's people had rebelled against him and become like "wild grapes" (v 2, v 4), God cursed them. Verses 8, 11, 18, 20, 21 and 22 begin with the word usually translated "Woe to", but which the New Revised Standard Version renders as a sigh of dismissive resignation, "Ah!" In Yahweh's all-seeing eyes, the high and mighty in Jerusalem were depraved. Greed and sensuality had eroded public virtue. Many of the religious leaders had only the form of religion left; there was no reality in their profession or in their belief. Power had corrupted the mighty, wealth had corrupted the rich. This passage is a penetrating exposure of this corruption and of the undesirable suffering that followed from it.

8. The first woe was aimed at rich landowners who seized property belonging to the poor by means of extortion (v 8-10). They acquired the dwellings and fields of the poor, cruelly evicting the former owners. Eventually no one could afford to live there, and these wealthy landlords ended up in splendid isolation. The aim of monopolies and multinationals has always been to squeeze out the smaller businesses. The result is great loss: of community, and often of quality as well.

9. Yahweh of the armies had promised ruin for such unfeeling people. Their own homes would be desolate. Large mansions they might be, and long the driveways that led to them, but what use were they if they were accursed and empty?

10. The bath or ephah was about six gallons, and the homer was equivalent to ten ephahs. The verse is saying that vintages and harvests would be disastrous. An acre of vine bushes would only produce five bottles of wine; similarly the yield of grain would be about a tenth of what was sown.

11. The second woe was uttered against rich people whose lives were dissipated by drink (v 11-14a). They drank spirits in the morning and wine at night.

12. They gave themselves to feasting. Their feasts were accompanied by chamber music and much wine. They indulged themselves and evaded their responsibility to "regard the deeds of Yahweh" and to "see the work of his hands".

13. They were indulging in sheer escapism, but they would be unable to escape the consequences of their actions. They would suffer exile, hunger and thirst, and yet they would not know what had hit them, or why.

14a. Derek Kidner points out the ironic consequence in his commentary. Because of their social injustice, these rich hedonists would not only lose the purpose for which they lived, but also find that they were themselves the objects of an appetite that was even more insatiable than their own. In the Old Testament Sheol is the shady underworld, the abode of the dead. It would "[enlarge] its appetite and [open] its mouth beyond measure". Those who had pickled their livers through alcoholic addiction would "go down" into the wide-open Mouth of Hell.

14b. The Biblical text may have been corrupted at this point. Some commentators think that this may originally have been the start of another woe (the third of seven in all), directed against both the nobility and the multitude of Jerusalem. The multitude followed the bad example of their richer fellow citizens and envied their intoxicating lifestyle (v 14b-17).

15. Those who had previously been proud would now be bowed down; without exception they would be brought low; their haughty eyes, once accustomed to coveting, would now look down in deep humiliation and shame.

16. How different it is with Yahweh: he is humble and lowly, but he would be exalted by his justice. Yahweh, the one true God, is holy. His holiness would be plain to all people because of his righteous deeds of judgement.

17. The self-indulgent city would suffer destruction. The day would come when lambs would graze there, and fatlings and kids would find food among the ruins.

18. At this stage the woes start coming more rapidly. The third (or fourth?) was pronounced against sceptical mockers who despised true religious teaching (v 18-19). They arrogantly defied God, and were progressively dragging down the bondage of iniquity and sin upon themselves, first with strong cords and later with unbreakable cart ropes.

19. These freethinkers spoke blasphemously yet fearlessly. They challenged Yahweh to make good the words spoken by the prophet, and to do so at once. The fact that Yahweh is not to be rushed in his mysterious work of judgement would grant them a stay of execution, but they were not the sort of people that would make use of it and reverse their attitude.

20. The fourth (or fifth?) woe was then spoken against those whose hearts were so hardened that they called evil good and good evil. The Messiah would speak strongly against similar people in his own day, those who attributed his acts of healing and deliverance (which were evidently *good* works) to the devil (Mk 3:22-30). They said that darkness was light and that light was darkness; for them bitterness was sweet and sweetness was bitter. Such people were guilty of unforgivable sin.

21. The fifth (or sixth?) woe was uttered against conceited politicians who considered themselves to be wise and shrewd. Astute they may well have been, but they were liable to find their cleverness rebounding against them.

22. The sixth (or seventh?) woe was aimed at judges who perverted justice because they were inebriated (v 22-23). They were fearless drinkers, heroes of the bottle, who played with fire as they mixed their drinks.

23. In their drunkenness they presided over serious miscarriages of justice. In exchange for a bribe they acquitted the guilty, and they also deprived innocent people of their rights.

Meditation: The seven Woes of the Messiah

One of the great misconceptions of modern times is that there exists a vast ocean of difference between the God of the Old Testament and the God of the New. In particular, some critics of the Old Testament voice their belief that in it God is a God of judgement and wrath, whereas in the New Testament he is a God of love and forgiveness. According to them, our passage in Isaiah 5:8-23 would fit into this pattern. In it Yahweh, the God revealed in the Old Testament, curses his disobedient people. You would never get curses like that in the New Testament, say these people. Jesus the Messiah was quite different. He always spoke words of life, and never words of judgement. He never pronounced woes, but only beatitudes. Such a view is completely wrong.

The fact is that there are various woes pronounced by God in the New Testament, including several spoken by his Son Jesus Christ. In Luke's version of the beatitudes, each of the four beatitudes is balanced by a corresponding woe (Lk 6:20-26). Furthermore – horror of horrors – in the 23rd chapter of Matthew's Gospel we actually hear Jesus Christ as he pronounces seven woes against some of the religious teachers of his day, the scribes and the Pharisees. There are several correspondences between the Old and the New Testaments, and if there were originally seven woes in Isaiah 5:8-23, perhaps this would explain why on this occasion Jesus was prompted to utter seven himself.

Jesus uttered **his first woe** because the teaching of the scribes and Pharisees was more liable to keep people out of the kingdom of heaven than to encourage them to enter into it (Mt 23:13). The scribal or Pharisaic way panders ultimately to man's pride, and is therefore out of step with God's humility.

Jesus spoke **his second woe** because the scribes and Pharisees went to a great deal of trouble in order to make a single convert, and their convert would then become "twice as much a child of hell" as themselves (Mt 23:15). To seek for converts is, in itself, a neutral thing. What makes it good or bad is whether the way of life that people are being converted to is good or bad. The scribal or Pharisaic way would make their converts into children of hell even more "double" (i.e. devious or hypocritical) than those who had converted them.

Jesus then pronounced **his third woe** because of the extremely unhelpful nonsense that the religious leaders of his time taught on the subject of swearing and making oaths (Mt 23:16-22). The relative validity of certain oaths was, in spite of its extreme casuistry, a characteristic concern of the legalism of the scribes and Pharisees, and one that illustrated their utterly distorted system of values.

His **fourth woe** was spoken because the scribes and Pharisees tithed their herbs religiously, but were not interested in justice, mercy and faithfulness. They were therefore like blind guides who strained out a gnat but swallowed a camel (Mt 23:23-24). Their sense of proportion had completely gone out of the window!

Jesus directed **his fifth woe** at them because they presented a squeaky-clean exterior but inside, in their heart of hearts, they were full of greed and self-indulgence (Mt 23:25-26). They kidded themselves that their external correctness was matched by internal purity. This was the root cause of their hypocrisy.

Jesus pronounced **his sixth woe** on these scribes and Pharisees because they were like whitewashed tombs – alive with beauty and tidiness on the outside, thanks to marble-and-lime plaster, but inside full of dead bones and rotting flesh (Mt 23:27-28). They concentrated on minor and easily performable acts of piety, and never even made a start on the great principles of the life that is truly life.

Jesus uttered **his seventh and final woe** on them because they built monuments for those very prophets and righteous men of old who had been put to death by their ancestors (Mt 23:29-36). This was nothing but hypocrisy on their part. They themselves hated true prophecy and humble goodness, and would therefore "crucify" (v 34) some of those sent to them by God, *including his own Son.*

So if cursing people for their rebellion and disobedience is something to be avoided, then the New Testament is as difficult to swallow as the Old, for Jesus Christ was as prone to speak woes as Yahweh. One could almost say that the woes are even sharper in the New Testament. With the arrival of the one who was Messiah and Son of God, the revelation of what God is like was now complete. There was now no excuse for anyone who ignored God's love and disobeyed him. Indeed, Jesus's condemnations were even more penetrating than Yahweh's.

In six of his seven curses, Jesus began with the words, "Woe to you, scribes and Pharisees", and went on immediately to call them *hypocrites.* By this he was castigating not only their insincerity but also their complete failure to see that their teaching and practice were bound to be displeasing to God. Their entire religious system was so ill-conceived that it constituted a complete perversion of God's revealed will. This is something that should cause the Christian shepherds of our day to think twice before they thrust their clever but unnecessarily radical innovations on their docile but vulnerable sheep, thereby depriving them of the godly and scripturally-based traditions that have served them so well for centuries.

XII

5:24-30 The Avengers of Yahweh

24. The people of God (probably, in this case, the ten northern tribes) proudly and persistently disobeyed Yahweh their God. The consequence had to be divine judgement. This was as inevitable as when stubble and dry grass are consumed by flames. The Israelites' roots were corrupt and their young people possessed all the solidity and reliability of dust. Why? What had they done? They had rejected the teaching of Yahweh, and despised the words of the Holy One of Israel.

25. Therefore, "the anger of Yahweh was kindled against his people". Such references to God's anger or wrath are sometimes misunderstood by today's Bible readers, who think of anger as an essentially human and sinful quality. These references need to be understood, not in connection with human qualities like vindictiveness and malice, but in the light of God's consistent righteousness and holiness. R. V. G. Tasker writes that "Just as human love is deficient if the element of anger is entirely lacking, so too is anger an essential element of divine love. God's love is inseparably connected to his holiness and his justice. When confronted with sin and evil, he *must* therefore manifest anger".

On this occasion he would stretch out his hand to strike the people of Israel with a deadly earthquake. Dead bodies would be left decomposing in the streets inside walled towns. A refrain sounds a note of doom. It also appears in quick succession on four other occasions (9:12, 17, 21 and 10:4) in the earlier part of the same poem. It tells us that worse is to come:

> "For all this his anger has not turned away,
> and his hand is stretched out still".

It is likely that verses 24-30 have been dislocated, and that they used to be found immediately after 9:8-10:4, which is a poem telling of the judgement of Yahweh on the ten northern tribes of Israel. The final two stanzas (in the passage we are studying) shift the focus of God's judgement from the ten northern tribes to the two in the south, Judah and Benjamin. At some stage they found their present position, at the end of five chapters on God's judgement on Judah and Jerusalem.

26. What could be worse than an earthquake? The terrifying instrument of punishment is at Yahweh's beck and call. It is an army. He will signal for its coming, and whistle for it to appear like an obedient hound. Its arrival might take a little while, but it was assuredly on the way.

27. God's avengers would be like an army of super-powered automata. They would not get tired or trip up; they would not require any sleep; their uniforms would be impeccable, with their buckles always gleaming.

28. Their weaponry would be invincible. Sharpened arrows, supple bows, newly shod horses, chariots faster than the wind. Who are these people? They are the soldiers of the Assyrian army. Anyone can see what they would have looked like when they were on the march by visiting the British Museum in London. They are carved on stone reliefs from Nineveh. The avengers of Yahweh are indeed impeccably and immaculately attired, and the wheels of their chariots turn like whirlwinds as they head purposefully to do God's work.

29. Their roar and their deadly strike would be like those of young lions. Loudly and fiercely they would seize and carry away their prey. Rescue was impossible.

30. On that terrible day of God's retribution, these young lions would roar like infuriated waves of the sea during a tempest. They were approaching fast, a dark and sinister army, leaving distress in their wake. The clouds were gathering; light was rapidly fading. Yahweh's wrath was aroused and his punishment for sin was now inevitable. No hope was left for the disobedient rebels; only darkness.

Meditation: God is in control of History

This terrifying army, precise in its movements and ferocious in its strikes, machine-like and yet resembling a beast, is that of the superpower Assyria. Even though the Assyrians did not know Yahweh, their army, which was the mightiest one on earth, was nevertheless at Yahweh's disposal. Yahweh could *raise a signal* and *whistle* for it. It would do whatever Yahweh desired, for Yahweh was the God of the armies, the Lord of hosts, the organiser of all the details of history.

As is the case everywhere else in the Bible, the Old Testament prophets present us with a God who is in control of all events. Yahweh works out his purposes over the ages, and no-one can stop him. The Jewish nation was at the height of its glory during the two long reigns of King David and his son King Solomon. When Solomon died (around 930 B.C.) and his son Rehoboam inherited the crown, the nation divided in two. The ten northern tribes seceded from Judah and Benjamin and formed what became known as the northern kingdom of Israel, sometimes simply referred to as *Israel*. The tribe of Benjamin was progressively absorbed into Judah, and so the southern kingdom was usually known as *Judah*. Sometimes it was identified with its capital Jerusalem.

During its 208 year history, the northern kingdom, Israel, was plagued by one bad king after another, and in spite of the prophets sent to its people by Yahweh, they became immersed in a great moral and social darkness. A terrible judgement struck them in the year 722 B.C., when the Assyrian army overran them and they were all exiled. That marked the end of Israel.

Things were better in the south, in Judah. After David and Solomon, Judah's kings were a mixed group. Two of them were described as very good (Hezekiah and Josiah), a few others (including Uzziah and his son Jotham) were presented as godly but flawed, usually by pride, and the remainder were either bad or very bad, worshipping idols and gods other than Yahweh. Ahaz and Manasseh, two of the kings that overlapped with Isaiah's ministry, were exceptionally bad.

Judah survived an invasion from Syria and Israel from 734 to 732 B.C., and thanks to a miracle they were spared destruction after a very dangerous and destructive invasion from the Assyrians in 701 B.C. Their miraculous deliverance by Yahweh was a high point in their history, but their trajectory was largely downhill afterwards. The Babylonians invaded them in 597 B.C., and returned a decade later with terminally destructive intent in 587-6 B.C. They besieged and in due course captured Jerusalem. Then they destroyed the city and its Temple, and deported nearly all of the remaining Jews.

In all these ups and downs, Yahweh was working out his purposes for both Israel and Judah. He repeatedly sent warnings to his people of the coming judgement incurred by their idolatry and social injustice. Occasionally he would rescue them from destruction, always in answer to their repentant attitude and pleas for his intervention. In the end, however, the opportunities for wholeheartedly turning back to Yahweh ran out, both for Israel in the north in 722 B.C. and for Judah in the south in 586 B.C.

We may conclude from this that, no matter how grim things may become in our own time, no matter how secularised and anti-Christian current trends may be, God is nevertheless sovereign and in control. He is working out his own purposes (11:9), thereby overruling the sinister designs of those who hate and ignore him. And however bad the turn of events may appear to be, we may still "rejoice in Yahweh" and "exult in the God of [our] salvation" (Hab 3:17-18).

XIII

6:1-8 The Call of the Prophet Isaiah

According to John Skinner, "This chapter stands unrivalled in the Old Testament both for the grandeur of its conception and the majestic simplicity of its style". It gives us a rich portrait of Isaiah. He was a man with a great vision of God (v1), a profound awareness of his own flaws and unworthiness (v5), a vivid experience of the grace and forgiveness of God (v7), and a desire to serve God (v8), even though this would prove to be difficult and heart-breaking (v9-13).

The call of Isaiah to be Yahweh's spokesman to his generation took place in the year that King Uzziah died, which was 740 B.C. The vision Isaiah saw focused on the majestic holiness of God, and on his radiant glory which filled the Temple. Isaiah was cut to the quick by the presence of the holy One, by whose side he was not only insignificant but also foul-mouthed and filthy.

1. The long reign of King Uzziah (also known as Azariah) lasted from 792 until 740 B.C. He was a godly man and a powerful king, "but when he had become strong he grew proud, to his destruction". He attempted to usurp the role of the priests and burn incense on the altar of incense in the Temple. When he was rebuked by eighty courageous priests, he raged at them and was immediately struck down

with leprosy. He lived in disgraceful isolation until his death (2 Chr 26:16-21). It was on an amazing day during the year in which the king of Judah died of leprosy that, during a visit to the Temple, Isaiah "saw the Lord sitting on a throne, high and lofty; and the hem of his robe filled the Temple". Isaiah saw the true King, the Lord high and lofty. Yahweh was so magnificent a King that the hem of his royal robe completely filled the great Temple of Jerusalem. These same paired adjectives, "high and lofty" are applied to Yahweh again in 57:15. In 52:13 they are used to describe the Messiah, the suffering Servant of Yahweh.

2. Seraphs were fiery angels, sometimes serpent-like, but here human in form. Of their six wings only two were used for flight. With the others they covered their faces (to protect their eyes from the dazzling perfection of the Lord), and their feet (to hide their imperfections from him out of fear and respect, for he was very near). As an ancient Jewish commentary on this passage puts it, "With two wings they covered their faces so that they might not *see*; with two they covered their bodies so that they might not *be seen*". With wings unfurled, they would have looked like flames. Isaiah would soon be touched with a burning coal by one of them (v6-7).

3. The seraphs called out to one another, saying, "Holy, holy, holy is Yahweh of the armies; the whole earth is full of his glory". With these words they announced the nature, the name and the power of God, and then described the scope and splendour of his dominion. His *glory* means the radiance of his nature, which shines forth not only before his chosen people but also throughout the whole earth. People were created in order to receive him and be filled with his glory.

4. At the sound of the seraph's words, the foundations of the Temple shook and smoke filled the vast building. At first the hem of the Lord's robe filled the Temple (v1), then his glory filled the earth (v3), and then the smoke that hid him filled the Temple so that Isaiah could not see his glory (v4).

5. Later on, during his ministry, Isaiah was to pronounce various woes on God's people. The first woe that he ever spoke, however, was against himself. Isaiah's sin (unclean lips) does not seem to us to be very serious, and his vision (seeing the King of kings, Yahweh of the armies) not particularly dangerous. The two of them were, however, incompatible. Isaiah knew that he was lost. His *eyes* had seen, but his *lips* were impure. Whatever message he might later receive from God would inevitably be delivered by one sinner to others. He knew it ought to be delivered by a *forgiven* sinner. But in order for forgiveness to be granted to him, the lips that had once spoken unclean profanities would need to be cleansed (Zeph 3:9). This would prove to be a painful experience.

6. A seraph used a pair of tongs to carry a red-hot coal from the altar to Isaiah. Alec Motyer makes some pertinent points: "The perpetual fire on the altar (Lev 6:12-13) went beyond symbolising divine wrath, for the altar was the place where the

holy God accepted and was satisfied by a blood sacrifice (Lev 17:11). [The altar held] together the atonement, propitiation and satisfaction required by God, and the forgiveness, cleansing and reconciliation needed by his people. This was achieved through a substitutionary sacrifice and brought to Isaiah, encapsulated in the single symbol of the live coal".

7. The seraph touched the prophet's lips with the live coal, bringing with it searing pain and cleansing. The coal had come from the place of sacrifice. Its purpose was to atone for Isaiah's confessed sins of speech. Gone forever was his guilt; these sins of his were instantly blotted out. After the pain of the burn, he was filled with the assurance that he was forgiven. It is interesting that Yahweh is said to have touched Jeremiah's mouth when calling him to be a prophet (Jer 1:9). It is a serious matter to speak about God. When we do so, we should ask ourselves what other types of speech come from our mouths.

8. Having reconciled Isaiah to himself, the Lord now spoke to him. Whom was he to send as his spokesman? Who would go for him, or rather for them, for there is a plurality in the Godhead? Moses would have asked the Lord to send someone else; Jeremiah would have shied away in diffidence. But Isaiah said, "Here am I; send me!" This remarkably bold declaration of willingness and eagerness to be the mouthpiece of Almighty God is sufficient to define the wonder and the grace of the forgiveness that Isaiah experienced that day, and which would sustain him during the very difficult years of ministry that lay ahead for him.

Meditation: The Holiness of the God who is Three

In the Old Testament God's name is qualified by the adjective *holy* more often than all the other adjectives applied to him put together. The Hebrew word for *holy* is connected to the ideas of "brightness" and "being set apart". His brightness means that he is incomparable (40:25), distinct from mortal people (Hos 11:9), exalted and unapproachable (57:15a, 1 Tim 6:16). He is set apart from other beings by his unique moral majesty. In the Bible, the fear of God is not so much the consciousness of weak humanity in the presence of divine power, but rather the consciousness of sin in the presence of perfect moral purity. Holy fear is one of the themes of Mark's Gospel. People marvelled at the Messiah's authority, his healing powers, his nature miracles and finally at the amazing news of the empty tomb and the resurrection.

In Isaiah's vision in the Temple, he heard the seraphs describing to each other their vivid awareness of what God was like. The reason why Isaiah would later refer to God as the holy One of Israel at various stages in his book is because the seraphs kept emphasising the word "holy" to describe him: "Holy, holy, holy is Yahweh of the armies; the whole earth is full of his glory" (v3). By this they were suggesting that there is a plurality in the godhead. Although God is one being, he is also three persons. This explains why the seraphs described him as "Holy, holy, holy". It also explains why later, in v 8, God

asks, "Who will go for *us*?" Furthermore, the difficult saying of verse 10, which as far as Isaiah was concerned was a command from God who is the Father, is clearly described in John 12:39-41 as referring to God the Son, and in Acts 28:25-27 it is quoted as having been spoken by God the Holy Spirit.

There is a similar foreshadowing of the great New Testament truth of the Trinity in the first chapter of the Bible, Genesis 1. God the Father appears in verse 1, God the Spirit in verse 2, and God the Son as the creative Word in verses 3, 6, 9, 14, 20, 24, 26. There are other Old Testament passages that Christians find suggestive of the plurality in the Godhead. Among them are Genesis 11:5-7 and 18:1-33, Job 28:23-27, Psalm 33:6 and Proverbs 8:22-31.

God is one being but three persons, which means that we may get to know him in three different ways. We may know the Father as our loving creator (Jn 3:16), the Son as our self-giving saviour (Titus 2:13-14) and the Holy Spirit as the one who comes alongside us to help and strengthen us (Jn 14:16-17). The early church realised that the truth of the Trinity was implicit in the New Testament, and that it followed on from the deity of Jesus Christ. In the early creeds the church declared its belief that God is one being, and yet that from eternity he is three persons: Father, Son and Holy Spirit. He is the God who is three-in-one. The three persons of the Godhead are not three Gods, nor are they three modes of God, but rather they are co-equally and co-eternally God. The Trinity is the Tri-Unity. There is no contradiction between the Trinity seen clearly in the New Testament and the uncompromising monotheism of the Old that points to Yahweh as the loving unseen Creator, the caring Word or Messenger, and the Breath or Spirit that imparts life and brings gifts to people.

The great contribution of Isaiah chapter 6 to the Old Testament thinking about God is its insistence that the Trinity is a *holy* Trinity: "Holy, holy, holy is Yahweh of the armies; the whole earth is full of his glory" (v3). God is absolutely holy (Lev 19:2). In the New Testament, God the Father is called holy (Mt 6:9, Jn 17:11), God the Son is described as holy (Mk 1:24, Lk 1:35, Jn 6:69, Acts 2:27), and God the Spirit is often named the Holy Spirit (e.g. Jn 14:26). The vision of Isaiah has inspired some great hymns, most notably Bishop Reginald Heber's *Holy, holy, holy! Lord God Almighty!* and John Michael Talbot's modern hymn *I, the Lord of sea and sky*. It should be a constant reminder to us all that we are answerable to God for everything we say, especially if we read, intercede or preach in a church service.

When people meet God for the first time, what they often find most striking is his holiness: his utter purity, his absolute majesty and his complete righteousness. God is absolutely good and clean and humble. He is beautifully and wonderfully holy. He is light and in him is no darkness at all (1 Jn 1:5). When people first come up against God in his holiness their first reaction is not to run *to* him but *from* him (2:19). They find themselves saying, like Isaiah, "Woe is me! I am lost . . . for my eyes have seen the King, Yahweh of hosts!"

XIV

6:9-13 An exceptionally difficult Call

9. God accepts Isaiah's voluntary enlisting in his company of prophets. He does not at this stage inform Isaiah about the content of his message, but instead tells him what the effects of the message will be: it will harden the hearts of his hearers and lead to the devastation of their land. Isaiah's mission would consist of urging the people to continue to listen without really grasping what the message was, and to continue to search for truth without really understanding the lessons that God would have them learn. This was not because the prophet would obscure his message with incomprehensible concepts or excessively complex arguments. Nor would his words be unreasonable or lacking in lucidity. On the contrary, a single reading of his prophecy will suffice to show that he taught profound truths with a simple clarity that any teacher would envy.

10. The extraordinary command of v 9, which at first reading seems to be something that God could not possibly have said, turns into a repeated decree of hardening. Isaiah is to stupefy, deafen and blind the people by urging them, at God's request, to see, listen and think about the truth. In theory, this would enable them to repent and be healed. The trouble, in most cases, was that their hearts were set and their minds were already made up. Their inability to respond would be part of God's judgement upon them. They had wilfully opted for arrogance and disobedience, so they must reap the bitter fruits. Our world is one in which actions have consequences. They had settled on the course they wished to follow, and it was a bad course. Now they were destined to find out exactly where it led. This remarkable teaching would be echoed over 750 years later by the Messiah in his explanation as to why he spoke in parables. Straight teaching may bring a few people to repentance, but it will usually harden many hearts as well. Soft teaching will achieve nothing except a general spiritual torpor.

11. Isaiah asks the Lord how long he was to continue this fruitless ministry of prophecy. The answer was, until the consequences of the people's idolatry and rebellion were fully worked out. This means: until their cities were devastated and deserted, their houses were uninhabited, and their land was utterly desolate.

12. It also means: until Yahweh had caused the Jewish people to be exiled, and until there was an enormous emptiness in the land of Israel.

13. A small fraction of the cities and settlements would survive the devastation. They would then be ravaged by further conflagrations. The land of promise would be like an enormous tree that is felled, and only the stump remains. Here, at the outset of his ministry, Isaiah is already told the end result of it. There would be a catastrophic destruction of the existing order. Its cause would be, quite simply, that the people of God had heard the word of Yahweh, the Holy One of Israel,

and had despised and rejected it. The last line of the verse is the one ray of light in this gloomy commission: within that old, dead-looking stump there would be life. "The holy seed is its stump". This provides the starting point for Isaiah's message about the godly remnant. Just as a terebinth or oak, when felled, retains life in its roots and its stump, and is therefore able to spring up again into a great tree, so the devastated people of Israel and Judah would contain the indestructible germ of the future kingdom of God. The vision of the Holy One of Israel that transformed Isaiah's life therefore ends with hope. As well as *offspring who do evil* (1:4), there would be a *holy seed* that would survive.

Meditation: The perennial Difficulty of God's Call

In this very difficult passage, Isaiah is told to precipitate the hardening of the hearts of his hearers by telling them the truth. Although his ministry was destined to meet with very little success, it was nevertheless extremely important. God's people had come to the point where further exposure to the only message that could save them was likely to result in their final and absolute rejection of that message. When they did reject it, they would be rejecting Yahweh himself. It follows that Isaiah's preaching and teaching would, in the providence of God, be the means by which his hearers would bring upon themselves God's righteous condemnation and judgement for their persistent sinful rebellion.

Isaiah's dilemma was that there was only one way of coaxing the sinful people with whom he lived, and whom he knew, towards salvation. This was to present them with the very truths whose continued rejection would condemn them utterly. With the erosion of Christian values, those who speak for God today will likewise find that the good news of Jesus Christ is not a neutral message that leaves people unchanged: it always either softens or hardens their hearts towards Christ.

Alec Motyer has written that all faithful preachers find that there are times when their hearers are so resistant to the truth, that the only course left is to tell them the truth yet again, even more clearly than before. By doing this, however, they expose those who are listening to the risk that they will reject the truth yet again, and by doing so, increasingly harden their hearts. Indeed, perhaps this may prove to be the final straw for them. It may be the moment when their hearts will become irreversibly hardened. We cannot tell in advance when such a moment might arrive, and the moment will probably pass by unnoticed by us. But God knows when that moment arrives, for it is he who appoints it. He does this in perfect justice, presiding over human psychological processes that he has created.

It was at a difficult moment in history that Isaiah was called to preach a clear message of repentance, promising forgiveness and restoration to those who turned from evil and followed Yahweh wholeheartedly. He preached it with unparalleled clarity and amazing attractiveness. A very small minority listened and became his followers, the "godly remnant". The large majority could not countenance what he said, and reached the point of no return in their disobedient lives.

In the preface to his translation into German of the book of Isaiah, Martin Luther wrote as follows: "You should not think of Isaiah except as one who was despised by his fellow Jews, and considered a fool and a madman. For it was the habit of the people to mock the prophets and treat them as insane. The same treatment has been meted out to every preacher and servant of God down the ages. This still happens now, and it will continue to happen until time ends".

The fact that each of the four gospels quotes Isaiah 6:9-10 in the context of Jesus Christ's teaching should serve to remind us that the world hated and rejected his words (Mt 13:14-15, Mk 4:12, Lk 8:10, Jn 12:39-41). The fact that this part of Isaiah is also quoted in Acts 28:25-27 is a warning that the world will usually hate and reject Christians when they pass on the good news. If the people of God rejected the message when it was so beautifully put across by the prophet Isaiah, and if they even rejected it when it came to them in the matchless words of Jesus the Messiah, it will hardly be a surprise if they reject it when we in turn put it across with whatever little skill we may have at our command.

XV

7:1-9 Isaiah urges King Ahaz to trust in God

Chapters 7-12 mention a child called Immanuel (7:14). He would be special and would reign over God's people (9:1-7, 11:1-10). This was a message of comfort for the people at a time when the existence of Judah was under threat (7:1-2). There was a real danger that they would be exiled to distant parts of the world (11:11). The prophecies of these chapters arise from contemporary events, but they would also apply to a "latter time" (9:1) and affect the whole world (11:9-10, 12:4-5). Isaiah was a member of the court and a statesman, and he sought to persuade the King of Judah to follow a policy of trust in Yahweh. After failing in this venture and temporarily retiring from public life, the prophet proceeded to found a school of disciples (8:16).

Chapter 7 dates from 734 B.C. The northern kingdom of Israel had allied itself with Syria (which was then known as Aram), and they were seeking to unite all the neighbouring states in order to protect themselves against Assyria, the great superpower of that time. The southern kingdom of Judah and Jerusalem refused to co-operate, and as a result Israel and Syria invaded them in force. They wished to replace Ahaz, the King of Judah, with their own man, the son of Tabeel (v6). Then they might together be able to resist the might of the Assyrians.

1. Ahaz was the son of King Jotham, who was in turn the son of King Uzziah (mentioned in 6:1). In 735 B.C. Ahaz became King of the southern kingdom of Judah. Early in his reign King Rezin of Syria and King Pekah of Israel invaded Judah, intent on capturing Jerusalem and getting rid of Ahaz. They got as far the gates of Jerusalem and laid siege to the city, but could not breach its walls.

2. When the people of Jerusalem heard that Israel had allied with Syria, they were overcome with fear. King Ahaz was as fearful as the next man.

3. At this juncture, Yahweh spoke to Isaiah, whose son was prophetically named *A-remnant-shall-turn*, and was therefore "a sign and portent" not only of judgement but also of salvation (8:18). Isaiah and his son were to go and confront Ahaz at the end of the conduit of the upper pool on the highway to the Fuller's Field. This same place would witness a more ominous confrontation 33 years later (36:2). King Ahaz was anxiously attending in person to the water supply of Jerusalem, ensuring that the reservoirs and cisterns inside the city were filled. He was also ensuring that no sources of water would be available to the enemy armies, for in the various historic sieges of Jerusalem the besiegers had always suffered more from lack of water than the defending citizens. The construction of an adequate conduit was later completed by King Hezekiah around 702 B.C. It is interesting to traverse this tunnel today: there is a kink in the middle caused by the fact that it was being constructed from its two ends, and the engineers of King Ahaz did not quite get their directions synchronised.

4. Isaiah was sent to tell Ahaz to keep calm and not to be afraid. The enterprise that Syria and Israel had embarked on was just the final flicker of two dying torches. It would be unseemly for the King of Judah to become faint-hearted because "two smouldering stumps of firebrands", Rezin and Pekah, were angry with him. They would soon be snuffed out: Syria would be crushed by the Assyrians in 732 B.C., and Israel would suffer grievous losses at Assyrian hands in 734 B.C. before being finally destroyed by them in 722 B.C. This was the first of many calls from Isaiah to stand firm and keep trusting in Yahweh instead of seeking for compromises or political alliances (v 9b, 8:12-13, 28:16 and 30:15). Similar calls to faith had sounded previously to God's people in Old Testament times (Gen 15:6, 2 Chr 20:20-21, Hab 2:4). Never before, however, had it been so important that the national leader and his people should trust fully in Yahweh and his promises. Faith means trust in God and in God's good purposes. It is not the prerogative of prophets alone. God's will is that his people, be they prophets, nobility, or labourers, should *all* look to him in humble trust.

5. Rezin and Pekah had to join forces to plot together against Ahaz, for each was too weak on his own. Both countries had suffered from internal strife. Indeed, Pekah had usurped the throne of Israel, so Isaiah could not even bring himself to call him by his name. Instead he referred to him as "the son of Remaliah".

6. Rezin and Pekah had invaded Judah and got near to Jerusalem. They wished to conquer the city and install the son of Tabeel as King. Nothing is known for certain about either Tabeel or his son.

7. The Lord God, however, had decided that Judah would not be subjugated at this time. Why? Because God himself was looking after his people, and his purposes

for them would most certainly be fulfilled. Isaiah spoke of Yahweh's majestic greatness, hoping that this would make faith appear a realistic policy for Ahaz to adopt. It would also leave him without any excuse for his unbelief. Isaiah was convinced that Syria and Israel were in a different class from Judah. They were not looked after by God but by mere men, and very poor men at that! When Isaiah referred to them, it was only in order to dismiss them.

8, 9a. The head or chief city of Syria was Damascus, and the ruler of Damascus was the feeble Rezin. Likewise (v 9a), the head or chief city of Ephraim was Samaria, and the ruler of Samaria was the usurper king, Pekah. Isaiah did not bother to add the obvious third line: "The head of Judah is Jerusalem, and the head of Jerusalem is *Yahweh, Lord of armies*". Israel, here called *Ephraim* after her most populous tribe, would herself be shattered. She would lose her northern lands later that same year, 734 B.C. She would then cease to be a nation in 722 B.C. when her capital, Samaria, was overrun by the Assyrians. Finally, she would lose her racial identity when her people were exiled and her land was variously re-populated, so that the northern tribes would in effect "no longer [be] a people" by the end of the reign of King Esarhaddon in 669 B.C. That would be 65 years later, as Isaiah had prophesied.

9b. Ahaz was to stand firm in faith, otherwise he would not be able to stand at all. This last injunction is a play on words. It could be translated, "If you hold God in doubt, you'll be out!", or alternatively, "Are you perhaps unsure? Then you'll certainly be insecure!"

Meditation: Trust and obey; there is no other Way

King Ahaz of Judah was determined to ignore God's warnings. His father Jotham had been a godly king (2 Chron 27:2, 6), who was still alive when Ahaz took over the reins of power from him in 735 B.C. It is likely that Jotham had been in weak health; he was certainly unable to control his son. Ahaz must have thought that he would make a better king than his father. Unlike Jotham, he worshipped other gods apart from Yahweh, and his idolatry and syncretism would prompt him to offer his sons as a burnt offering to the pagan god Molech. He cruelly forced some of the royal princes to "pass through fire". As a result, Ahaz earned the condemnation of the chronicler of the Kings of Judah (2 Chron 28:1-4).

In 734 B.C. the combined armies of Syria and Israel crossed over into Judah. When Ahaz and the people of Judah heard of this invasion, their hearts "shook as the trees of the forest shake before the wind" (v 2). Not long after this, Ahaz received two appalling bits of news. On the one hand, King Rezin of Syria had captured a great number of his people and taken them to Damascus. On the other, King Pekah of Israel had killed 120,000 of his valiant soldiers in one day (2 Chr 28:5-8). More bad news would come later: the Edomites and the Philistines would send their armies to Judah, carrying away captives and taking several towns and their neighbouring villages (2 Chr 28:17-18). Ahaz would have been terrified out of his wits, and also thoroughly demoralised.

Prompted by Yahweh, Isaiah went to see Ahaz, taking his son with him. The name of his son was Shear-Jashub, which means *A-remnant-shall-turn*. This name by itself constituted a sign for Ahaz, as we shall see in the next section. In addition, Isaiah told Ahaz that the Kings of Israel and Syria were "two smouldering stumps of firebrands" (v 4). By virtue of his long and unusual name, *A-remnant-shall-turn* would have been an acted proclamation of God's purposes, a visual aid to help Ahaz realise what Judah's future would be.

King Ahaz was under pressure from his advisers to act astutely and ally Judah with the superpower of Assyria against the northern powers Israel and Syria. Isaiah's message for him was equally pertinent, because Israel and Syria were weakened by internal battles and internecine fighting. Before long they would count for nothing on the international stage. Isaiah's special insight was that this whole matter was not a question of politics but of faith. If he could persuade Ahaz not to enter into any compromising alliances, there was a chance that the King and the people of Judah would trust Yahweh to keep his promises to David and protect his people. Yahweh was strong enough to deal with foreign threats. Would Ahaz trust in him or would he seek a solution dictated by human wisdom?

The choice weighed on him. It was a seminal moment in his life. The same decision has faced many people down the ages. Do you trust God and obey him, or do you go the way of the world? It is a decision with eternal consequences. Decisions such as these are so important that they go beyond being a mere matter of life and death. The hymn writer John Henry Sammis expressed it in words that are memorable for their simplicity: "Trust and obey / For there's no other way / To be happy in Jesus – / But to trust and obey".

XVI

7:10-25 The Sign of Emmanuel

10. Isaiah had some further things to say to King Ahaz. The first was a direct challenge to his will. If he were given a sign, would he be willing to trust Yahweh? Signs play an important part in the Old Testament (in Isaiah, see 37:30 and 38:7, 22). Perhaps the most familiar case of someone seeking for a sign is Gideon, who asked for three in quick succession (Judg 6:17-22 and 36-40) and was granted all of them. The signs helped him to be certain in his faith in Yahweh; asking for them was an expression of commitment to Yahweh.

11. Isaiah asked King Ahaz to choose a sign of Yahweh *his* God. It was up to him to choose what the sign would be. He was free to choose any kind of proof of God's trustworthiness, be it as deep as the grave or as high as heaven.

12. Ahaz evaded the offer. He ostensibly declined to ask Yahweh for a sign on the grounds that this would "put Yahweh to the test". This was just pious talk. As John Skinner observes, "To put Yahweh to the proof is indeed a mark of unbelief (Deut 6:16), but to refuse a proof which Yahweh himself offers is an insult to the divine majesty which exhausts the patience of the Almighty". Ahaz had in fact already made up his mind; no amount of proof would induce him to change it. He was intent on forming an alliance between Judah and the mighty superpower of Assyria. His way of outwitting his political enemies was to make friends with the mightiest of them (2 Ki 16:7-9). Little did he realise what a mixed blessing his friendship with the Assyrians would prove to be (v 17-25). By seeking to escape from his enemies through putting his trust in an even bigger enemy, he was in effect jumping out of the frying pan into the fire.

13. This time referring to Yahweh as *my* God, Isaiah laments the King's unhelpful attitude, which was wearying both for the prophet and for Yahweh himself.

14. Because of this, the Lord would himself give Ahaz a sign, but it would be a veiled sign, and Ahaz would not understand it. A young woman (the word can also mean a virgin) would bear a son. His name would be Immanuel, which means *God-is-with-us*. Who was he? For the moment Isaiah does not make this clear, but he would soon provide further clues (9:1-7, 11:1-10). King Ahaz was intent on asking a superpower for help. Through Isaiah, Yahweh was pointing Ahaz to a very weak and insignificant person, to a tiny new-born infant.

15. The curds and honey could be a positive sign of plentiful rich food or, indeed, a negative one of massive depopulation (v 22).

16. A positive aspect would be that the two nations of Syria and Israel would be wiped out before the little baby reached the age of conscious choice.

17. There would also be a negative aspect. The King of Assyria was a bully, and having him as one's protector and friend would bring very difficult days. In 701 B.C. the land of Judah would be devastated by his troops, and Jerusalem would only be saved by a spectacular and miraculous intervention by Yahweh.

8. Yahweh was sovereign. In due course he would just whistle for the fly (the Egyptians) and for the bee (the Assyrians, as in 5:26). The two strongest armies of that age were but swarms of insects that would fly anywhere at his signal.

19. Swarms of looting soldiers would come to Judah and install themselves in steep ravines, in the clefts of the rocks, beside all the thorn bushes and on all the pastures. They would be Yahweh's scourge on the land of Judah.

20. Ahaz thought that he had hired a razor, but this razor from beyond the Euphrates River (another reference to the Assyrian army) would prove to be the razor of the Lord. Yahweh would shave the head and the hair of the legs, and also the beard. The rebellious people of both Israel and Judah would be like unwanted hair that the Lord would simply shave off.

21. Few people would remain; sheep and cattle would outnumber the people.
22. The survivors would be well fed; they could eat curds and honey.
23. The vineyards would become fields of briers and thorns. Valuable land would become worthless. The Promised Land would revert to jungle and wilderness.
24. To visit it, one would have to be armed with bow and arrows, because of the wild beasts that would take over the wilderness.
25. On the hills that were previously cultivated people would no longer be found, because of the briers and thorns. There would only be wild cattle and sheep. The wild state would be a proof of the decline of God's people.

Meditation: Are all People helped by Signs?

Isaiah was opposed to any foreign alliances. To become the partner of a country whose people worshipped other gods would constitute disloyalty to Yahweh and mistrust of the One who was the Lord of Armies. Isaiah saw the international crisis as a test of the religious inclination of the people of Judah. It was an opportunity for them to trust fearlessly in the promise of Yahweh. Only God could guide them safely through the difficulties of the immediate future and bring them to the joy and freedom that lay ahead. That was why Isaiah longed for Ahaz to adopt his own attitude of calm reliance on Yahweh, instead of seeking an alliance with Assyria. And the method Isaiah made use of in order to encourage Ahaz was to present him with divine signs.

The trouble was that Ahaz stubbornly ignored every sign that purported to come from Yahweh. It is quite likely that Ahaz already knew Isaiah when the latter received his call to be a prophet (6:1), and if so, Ahaz would have seen the burns and swellings on his lips. That was perhaps the first sign for Ahaz, a sign that he too needed to repent of sins of speech, but Ahaz nonchalantly ignored this, as he also ignored Isaiah's early prophecies. Because of this proud indifference, Yahweh proceeded to send the armies of Syria and Israel to Judah. When Ahaz and his court heard the terrible news of how the campaign was going, they shook and trembled like trees in a storm. Isaiah then gave Ahaz a second sign.

The prophet came to see him, bringing along his son who was called *A-remnant-shall-turn*, in order to press home the growing urgency for Ahaz to execute an about-turn by repenting of his ungodliness. *A-remnant-shall-turn* was a name suggesting both promise and disaster. The promise was that Yahweh would not cause his people to perish utterly, but would rescue and keep for himself a small remnant who would turn or repent. The disaster was that the remnant would only be a small one. Isaiah also promised Ahaz that King Rezin and King Pekah would be snuffed out. This was no empty promise; it duly happened.

Sensing an indifference in Ahaz's reaction, Isaiah also urged him to choose for himself a further sign that Yahweh would offer him. Ahaz immediately declined, saying, "I will not put Yahweh to the test". This confirmed Isaiah's worst fears. Ahaz was afraid that the proof that might be provided by the occurrence of the sign would force him to repent and trust in Yahweh. This was the one thing he was absolutely resolved not to do. Isaiah realised that his pleas were only hardening the king's heart, just as Yahweh had predicted (6:9-13).

At this stage Isaiah offered Ahaz a sign of his own, the sign of Immanuel. The name Immanuel means *God-is-with-us*. The message to Ahaz was that Yahweh would still be with Jerusalem and a reduced part of Judah, protecting them from their enemies. The king, however, was steadfast in his refusal to read the signs that Yahweh was sending. This would have unfortunate consequences. Ahaz was intent on having his own way and consummating an alliance with the King of Assyria. Because of this, Judah would later have to endure an Assyrian invasion that would be far more devastating than the ravages being caused by the armies of Syria and Israel.

What exactly was the sign of Immanuel? "The young woman is with child and shall bear a son, and shall name him Immanuel". The sign must have had an immediate context and application, even if its ultimate fulfilment lay far in the future, with the coming of the Messiah. What was the immediate context?

One very plausible theory is that there may have been a royal birth in the year 734 B.C. Like many other Kings of Judah, Ahaz probably had more than one wife as well as several concubines. One of the latter, a young woman, may have given birth, and named her son *God-is-with-us*. In ancient times concubines were the only women who gave names to their sons; wives would look to husbands to do this. If this was the case, Isaiah cited this birth as a divine sign for Ahaz. In effect he was saying to Ahaz, "Why don't you take your new son's name *God-is-with-us* seriously and believe it?"

A less plausible theory, suggested by certain commentators, is that the young woman is a symbolic woman representing Jerusalem, and her new-born son a symbolic child representing the faithful remnant that would emerge from her labour pains. The child's name, *God-is-with-us*, would then suggest to Ahaz that Yahweh would be with the faithful remnant that would gather round Isaiah (8:16), and not with sceptical Ahaz and his worldly courtiers.

The preservation of the remnant in Isaiah's day was part of God's ongoing plan which would culminate in the coming of the Messiah. Indeed, the Messiah was the sharp point of the arrowhead of the godly remnant. He was the one towards which the members of the godly remnant were pointing by their holy and obedient lives. All of God's promises would come to their fulfilment in him.

Whoever the original child may have been, the fulfilment of the sign of Immanuel would arrive some 730 years later. In Matthew's Gospel we read that Jesus Christ was the ultimate Immanuel (Mt 1:22-23). The final fulfilment of the sign given to Ahaz is quite simply the birth of the Messiah. The ideal King of the future would be born to his people during their hour of adversity. He would share their tribulations all his life, and yet his delight would be in the fear of Yahweh (11:3). His presence would be a sign that *God-is-with-us*. Later, when the God-appointed hour arrived, justice would be denied him. He would be despised and rejected by his people. He would himself bear their infirmities, their diseases and their sins (53:4-6). After that, the government would be placed upon his shoulder, and the perfect kingdom of God would be established.

XVII

8:1-15 Trusting God when everything goes wrong

1. Yahweh told Isaiah to take a large writing tablet, possibly a slate, and inscribe on it in ordinary handwriting, "Belonging to Maher-shalal-hash-baz". This was to be another child with an unusual name: *Quick-pickings-Easy-prey*. His name was once again a sign for King Ahaz. It would tell him that Syria and Israel would soon be overwhelmed by Assyria and cease to be a threat, confirming Isaiah's earlier prophecy (7:7-9, 16). It would also imply that Assyria's next victim would be the kingdom of Judah itself (7:17-25).

2. Yahweh also told Isaiah to have the writing attested by two reliable witnesses, a priest called Uriah and a man called Zechariah. This careful attestation would confirm that the naming of the child had taken place before the fulfilment of the prophecy, and therefore that the name was an authentic message from God.

3. Then Isaiah went to his wife, whom he refers to as the prophetess, and she conceived and bore him a son. Following Yahweh's instruction, he was named *Quick-pickings-Easy-prey* – yet another child with a strange but significant name.

4. Before this son of Isaiah learnt how to speak, the King of Assyria would carry away the wealth of Damascus in Syria, and the spoils of Samaria in Israel, as Isaiah had predicted in 7:16.

5. "The waters of Shiloah" flowed gently into Jerusalem on an open aqueduct, reaching the Pool of Siloam (Jn 9:7) and ensuring a water supply if the city was ever besieged. Isaiah may have had these waters in his mind ever since his meeting with Ahaz at the conduit of the upper pool of water (7:3). They are a picture of God's gentle ways with people. At this stage Yahweh spoke again to Isaiah, mentioning these tranquil waters.

6. Ahaz and the rulers of Judah had turned away from Yahweh's ways. They had refused the gentle waters of Shiloah. This was why they were now melting in fear before the Kings of Syria and Israel.

7. Because Ahaz was now calling on heathen Assyria to rid Judah of the menace of Syria and Israel, an evil flood would be let loose over the land of Judah. It would be as if the mighty River Euphrates, which waters Assyria, was to be transported across and bring a flash flood over Judah. The King of Assyria and his mighty armies would invade and ravage the land.

8. These waters would "reach up to the neck" – but no further! This may imply that the Assyrians would devastate the land of Judah and even besiege Jerusalem, but

nothing more. They would be unable to capture the city. So there *was* some hope. The damage done by Assyria would be immense, and it would be inflicted on the land of Immanuel, but for Immanuel's sake many people would be spared.

9. Isaiah defiantly addresses all the godless nations. They were to make alliances with each other, and be dismayed. They were to get ready, and be dismayed.

10. They were to seek each other's advice, but in vain. They were to speak out, but their words would have no effect. Why? Because God was with his people. This is a strong echo, perhaps an obvious quotation, of the name Immanuel, which as we have already seen means *God-is-with-us*.

11. This (v 9-10) was how Yahweh spoke to Isaiah and his followers. "His hand was strong upon me": it was a vivid prophetic vision. Godly people are sometimes deeply wrought upon and their impressions can then be exceptionally significant, although they need to be tested (1 Jn 4:1-3). Are they in harmony with the balance of God's will as revealed in scripture? Here Yahweh warned Isaiah and his followers "not to walk in the way of this people".

12. Isaiah and his followers were to reform their whole way of thinking. They were to reserve the word "conspiracy" for the ultimate conspiracy, formed by people who were united in their rebellion against God. They were not to fear what godless people feared, namely the spent armies of Rezin and Pekah. Unlike the godless people, they were not to live in dread.

13. Yahweh of the armies was to be at the centre of their thoughts. Isaiah and his followers were to treat Yahweh's name as holy (Mt 6:9), and to fear him alone (Mt 10:26-28). His presence was to induce a sense of awe in them (Mt 17:5-6).

14. For those in Judah and Israel who trusted in him, Yahweh was their sanctuary, which means a place of absolute protection. He was a stepping-stone which they could depend on. But for those in Judah and Israel who did not trust him, Yahweh would be their stumbling-block, a trap and a snare for the ungodly people of Jerusalem. This verse, taken in conjunction with 28:16, would be quoted by the Messiah and referred to in the New Testament (Mt 21:42-44, 1 Pet 2:8).

15. Many who considered themselves to be followers of Yahweh would stumble and fall, and be broken. They would be caught in a trap they had themselves sprung, and would be taken away into exile.

Meditation: The Signs of true Godliness

In verses 11-15 we have Isaiah's beautiful description of the qualities of godliness that the Lord looks for in his people. Isaiah felt Yahweh's hand heavy on him as he saw the vision of what true godliness looks like. To be godly involved being very different from the people who were nominally followers of Yahweh (v 11). It is the same today. Many churchgoers in the 21st century are likely to be dependent on their emotions, and will sometimes be dominated by various kinds of fears. They may see conspiracies everywhere, and if so they will miss the real conspiracy, which is the one directed by the godless world against the holy God and his Son Jesus Christ (v 12). Isaiah was given three ways in which he and his followers should think of God.

First of all, Yahweh was to be *regarded as holy*. One of the two most important attributes of God is his holiness (and the other is his love). Jesus Christ addressed God the Father as holy (Jn 17:11) and taught his followers to begin their prayers by hallowing God's name (Lk 11:1-2). Isaiah and the godly remnant of true believers wanted to put God first in their lives, and they did so by training themselves to remember what God was like. They wished to regard him as holy.

Secondly, they were to *fear Yahweh*. The idea of fearing God is so out of fashion nowadays that godly people are rebuked if they give voice to it in the course of a Bible study or discussion group. Nevertheless, it is there in the Bible, certainly in the Old Testament (which surprises no one) and equally certainly in the New (which does surprise Christians). In the Old Testament the essence of wisdom is fearing God. "The fear of Yahweh is the beginning of wisdom" is an idea that appears repeatedly (Job 28:28, Ps 111:10, Prov 1:7, 9:10, Mic 6:9). The people of God are instructed to fear him. They are commended when they do so, and condemned when they don't.

The New Testament takes up these ideas and develops them in various ways. One of Jesus's sayings is of special interest: "I tell you, my friends, do not fear those who kill the body, and after that can do nothing more. But I will warn you whom to fear: fear him who, after he has killed, has authority to cast into hell. Yes, I tell you, fear him!" (Lk 12:4-5, and see also Mt 10:28). Until two thirds of the way through the twentieth century, a *God-fearing person* was a synonym for a godly person. This phrase is no longer used nowadays. Nevertheless, God's holy remnant are to fear God. Isaiah was told, "Let [Yahweh] be your fear". Yahweh was to be the fear of Isaiah as he had been the fear of Isaac (Gen 31: 42, 53). Not only was Yahweh to be Isaiah's fear; he was also to be Isaiah's dread (v 13).

Thirdly, God was to be a *sanctuary* for Isaiah and his followers. They would be safe in him. Like their former King David, they could pray, "[Yahweh] will hide me in his shelter in the day of trouble; he will conceal me under the cover of his tent; he will set me high on a rock" (Ps 27:5). In v 14 the image is that God is like a large stone on the ground. When proper use is made of it, it can be a stone that one may stride on with confidence, a stepping-stone that will help one attain a good objective. But this stone can also be wrongly or carelessly used, and then it will prove to be a stumbling block, a trap and a snare for those who lack trust in God. Whether the stone who is God proves a help or a hindrance depends on faith: as Isaiah was to put it later in his prophecy, "One who trusts will not panic" (28:16). Jesus picked up the idea, comparing himself to a large and heavy cornerstone that could hold a building together, or else fall on someone and crush him (Mt 21:42-44). In his first epistle, Peter in turn quoted Jesus (1 Pet 2:8).

Those of us who follow Jesus Christ should focus on the *holiness* of God and learn to *fear* him, and then we shall find ourselves increasingly trusting him as our *sanctuary* and as our *stepping-stone*.

XVIII

8:16-22 Isaiah instructs his Disciples

What seems to be happening in this section is that, by persistently turning away from the light of Yahweh's word in the *Torah* of Moses and in the oracles spoken by the prophets, the rebellious people of Judah were entering into a very dense darkness, in which the only communication they had from God was the signs proffered by Isaiah and his curiously named children. Otherwise the land was in a state of spiritual famine – a famine of the word of God (Amos 8:11).

16. Isaiah takes responsibility for the preservation of the messages that Yahweh has revealed to him. They constitute a testimony of immense value, which needs to be bound up and stored away. The scrolls on which they were written were to be rolled up and carefully conserved in jars, which were then sealed and kept by the disciples of Isaiah. These disciples were those who had listened humbly to Yahweh's word and understood it. Unlike the great majority of Isaiah's hearers, they had turned away from their pride and disobedience and returned to God. They were forgiven and healed (6:10).

17. Isaiah himself would have felt crushed by the haughty indifference of King Ahaz. He withdrew from public life and dedicated himself to "waiting for Yahweh", an activity that renewed his strength (41:30-31). Though Yahweh was "hiding his face from the house of Jacob", Isaiah rested his hope in him. Was Yahweh finished with Judah? Isaiah's hope was that he would persevere with them. Was Isaiah's ministry to the high and mighty a thing of the past? No; Yahweh was always there, and so there was hope. Isaiah waited for Yahweh.

18. Isaiah was aware that he and the children that God had given him – not only the children he fathered with the long names, but also the other disciples who responded to his teaching – were "signs and portents from Yahweh of the armies, who dwelt on Mount Zion". The names of some of these people were significant: Isaiah means *Yahweh-is-the-saviour*, Shear-jashub means *A-remnant-shall-turn*, Maher-shalal-hash-baz means *Quick-pickings-Easy-prey*, and the name of the royal child Immanuel means *God-is-with-us*. But it was not merely that Yahweh performed signs and portents through his godly people: something much more wonderful was taking place. Isaiah and his followers *were* signs and portents to their unbelieving generation, and perhaps also to subsequent generations. The first part of this verse is quoted in the New Testament (Heb 2:13) as typical of a model church gathering, with disciples that are teachable, expectant and faithful. A steady faith in the Lord God was then, and still is today, a very powerful sign for those who do not believe in him.

19. In contrast to Isaiah, some of the religious teachers were spiritualists rather than prophets. They neither taught nor reasoned, but instead spoke gibberish. They idolatrously worshipped several gods. They were mediums who consulted the dead. They were leading God's people astray into what was occult and forbidden. Isaiah's denunciation is very powerful: why consult the dead on behalf of the living? Seeking out occult ways is particularly abominable in God's eyes (Deut 18:9-14). Two godly kings of Judah, Hezekiah and Josiah, worked hard to try and exterminate these aspects of religious apostasy.

20. Those who taught like this or were instructed in this way would be plunged into ever deeper darkness and ruin. It would not be like nightfall, for they would have no dawn to look forward to.

21. They would not have a life. They would "pass through the land", possibly on the way to exile, existing rather than living. They would wander meaninglessly, suffer terrible distress, and starve because of the famine of the word of God. In their hunger they would curse their king and their gods.

22. Whether they looked up at the sky or down to the ground, they would see nothing but distress and darkness. All would be gloom and anguish. They would continue to penetrate into ever thicker darkness. Isaiah has painted a grim picture of the fate of the godless. It would find its initial fulfilment between 734-732 B.C., when the northern kingdom of Israel was overrun by the Assyrian army under Tiglath-Pileser III. They invaded in great numbers, their troops were well equipped, and although they deported some prisoners, they also impaled others on stakes or flayed them alive, and then severed their heads and piled them up in heaps. The Assyrian army conquered the people of Zebulun, Naphtali and Galilee (9:1), and deported many of them to Syria and beyond.

Meditation: The godly Remnant

There is something wonderful and deeply encouraging about verses 16-18 of Isaiah 8. Isaiah and his very few followers had been rejected and dismissed by Ahaz, King of Judah. It is likely that Isaiah himself, who was possibly of noble birth and a friend of people in high places, was then ostracised in court circles. He would have become *persona non grata*, being forced to retreat from public life. But Isaiah could not react bitterly and resentfully. Yahweh was so real in his experience that he would find comfort and sustenance in him.

Isaiah remembered well the visions and oracles he had received from Yahweh. He had committed them all to writing, in order to ensure that the memory of them would not be lost. As John Skinner has pointed out, there is something in the heart of a true prophet that will not allow the truth of God to perish. Disowned by proud men and driven in upon himself, Isaiah found in the truth of his rejected prophecy an indissoluble link of communion between himself and God. In the midst of all his tribulations and the scorning of his life's work, he knew that he was supremely blessed. Yahweh, the Holy One of Israel, had spoken to *him* and received *him* into his fellowship. And in his individual response to the voice of God there was a first fruits of that instinctive relationship with the One who reveals himself, which he knew constituted the abiding essence of personal religion.

Isaiah felt great pity for those who had once been his friends but now no longer cared for his company. He knew that their personal animosity against him was a symptom of their deep-seated rebellion against Yahweh. He could discern where their attitudes and intentions would lead them. It was all very disheartening.

But Isaiah did not just sit and feel sad. He had a tiny group of followers that included his wife and young children. He formally bound them together into a little band that he referred to as "[his] disciples". We may think of them as "the school of Isaiah". They would look after and preserve a priceless treasure, the scrolls inscribed with his prophetic oracles. God had spoken, and his word was eternal: it would never pass away. This was perhaps the first case in history of a religious community that was not based on family or nationhood. It was the birth of something quite new. It was the prototype of the Christian church, the first step in the separation of religion from political or national life. Similar small groups of people would keep emerging in the Old Testament, and they reappeared in the New. They were the godly remnant.

Part of their *raison d'etre* was to look after the precious deposit of God's word. Sometimes they had to bury it, like hidden treasure, to protect it from those who would gladly have destroyed it. At other times they preserved it by living out its message, that God is holy and implacably opposed to sin, and also loving and intent on restoring sinners who would trust him to do this for them. The godly remnant has never been fashionable. Very few of its members ever had friends in high places. Isaiah was an exception, and he suffered for it.

Barry Webb writes that something profoundly important has been happening in this section, 8:16-22. "There has been a marked sharpening in the demarcation between the faithful and unfaithful within the visible community of God's people, between those who respond to the word of God with obedient faith and those who do not, between the true and the false. This will happen more and more as the book runs its course until it becomes a major strand of its message in [chapters 28-39]. Often the difference between the true and the false is difficult to discern. Wheat and tares, sheep and goats, can look very much alike to the untrained eye. But the divine judge sees the difference clearly, and the [tests] of life increasingly distinguish them from one another. On the last day, of course, the separation will be absolute and permanent. The line that was being drawn in Isaiah's day is still being drawn today, with the same ultimate issues at stake".

What kept Isaiah going? Quite simply, a quiet, subtle and altogether invaluable sense of God's presence with him. Yahweh was hiding his face from disobedient people, but he would not hide his face from Isaiah and the godly remnant. And so the prophet waited for Yahweh, and placed his hope in him. To "wait for the Lord" sounds, to our rushed and harassed generation, like a waste of time. We shall see what it entails in due course; it is in fact one of the most important and profitable activities that fallen men and women may engage in. To place our hope in God is to live as if God means everything to us, and as if doing his will is the top priority in our lives.

XIX

9:1-7 The Dawning of the Messiah

1. The people of Zebulun, Naphtali and Galilee were in anguish during the years of their defeat by Assyria in 734-732 B.C. and later during their exile. This was "the former time" when Yahweh brought them into contempt. But a "latter time" would come, around 28 A.D., when the glory of God would be seen on the way of the Sea and the land beyond the Jordan – Galilee of the nations. The gospel writer Matthew quotes Isaiah 9:1-2 as he begins his narrative of the ministry of Jesus the Messiah (Mt 4:12-17).

2. A huge sense of relief is prophesied for the people who walked in darkness; they will see a great light. They may have plumbed the depths of darkness, but it is on them that the light will shine. "For it is the God who said, 'Let light shine out of darkness' (Gen 1:2-3), who has shone in our hearts to give the light of the knowledge of the glory of God in the face of Jesus Christ" (2 Cor 4:6).

3. This would make Galilee great. There would be much joy there. There would be gladness and thanksgiving to God, as there is when the harvest is good, and when treasure or plunder is obtained and shared.

4. The terrible yoke on Israelite shoulders would be broken. The bar that held them would fall off. The rod of their oppressors would be no more. God himself would set them free, as he did through Gideon when the Midianites oppressed them (Judg 6:1-7:25).

5. The implements of war having been shattered, the boots and clothing of the enemy would likewise be burnt in the fire. The longed-for deliverance would finally have arrived, but who would the deliverer be?

6. The deliverer or saviour is a humble little child, who has been born for us. He is a son, a very special son, who has been given to us. To him great authority has been granted, and it rests gently on his humble shoulders. His name is Wonderful Counsellor, Mighty God, Everlasting Father and Prince of Peace. Each of these titles is divine, and each is worthy of having a book written about it.

Isaiah's watchword for the child up to now has been Immanuel, which means *God-is-with-us*. But here this name is expanded, and we shall continue to learn more about the greatness and the humility of the child as the prophecy of Isaiah continues its course. The half has not yet been told us.

7. The child's authority would grow until it was all-encompassing (Mt 28:18). He would give his peace to his followers (Jn 14:27). He would be a King in the line of David (Mt 1:1). He would establish and uphold his kingdom with justice and righteousness, and his kingdom would last forever (Rev 11:15). How could this possibly happen? How could a humble little child be a divine king? "The zeal of Yahweh of the armies [would] do this".

Meditation: The Child that would be born

After conquering and destroying Syria (which was then called Aram) in 732 B.C., King Tiglath-Pileser III of Assyria marched his army south to Israel and subdued most of the territory around Lake Galilee, taking most of the people into exile. It was the darkest hour for the land of Zebulun and the land of Naphtali, "Galilee of the nations". It was at this time that Isaiah spoke out a magnificent prophecy about them. The part of Israel that had just been devastated would eventually be the first to see the glory of the Messiah (v1). Verses 2, 6 and 7 are justly celebrated in churches throughout the world at Christmas time, and Handel included them in his greatest oratorio, *The Messiah*, which he composed in 1741.

Strangely enough, the Messiah of Jewish expectation would in fact be born not in Galilee but in Bethlehem of Judaea, as Isaiah's fellow prophet Micah had prophesied (Mic 5:2). This being so, why did Isaiah focus on despised Galilee as the region where the divine deliverer would make himself known in his glory? The answer is that the child would leave Bethlehem soon after his birth, and after a brief sojourn in Egypt he would go to Galilee. There he would be brought up and begin his ministry, in Galilean villages like Nazareth, Cana and Capernaum and in the surrounding countryside. He himself would be known as a Galilean. People would refer to him as *Jesus of Nazareth*. Some of them would marvel that anything good could possibly come out of that region (Jn 1:46, 7:41).

What an unimaginable honour this would be for despised "Galilee of the nations", where foreigners had settled on "the way of the sea", the trade route from Damascus to the Mediterranean. Galilee was a place for foreigners and merchants and fishermen. It was not a place for kings, still less for great King David's greater Son. When he eventually arrived, the long-expected child would turn darkness into light, shame into glory, distress into joy and oppression into peace.

This child that would be given to Galilee would also be given to the world. Verse 6 is amazing. He would not only be the Messiah of Old Testament expectation. He would not only be the great liberator of all who are oppressed and enslaved. He would be much, much more than just an extraordinary man. Supreme and all-encompassing authority would be placed on his shoulders, and yet he would be humble and caring. His loving governance would be marked by four qualities: counsel, might, fatherhood and peace.

He would be for us the Wonderful Counsellor, whose matchless teaching would be a reliable guide for all who followed him (28:29). He would be none other than Mighty God, to whom the godly remnant would return (10:21). He would be the Everlasting Father, who is our redeemer from of old (63:16). He would be the Prince of Peace, through whose passion and death all who turn humbly to God would find peace with God (53:4-6).

Verse 7 speaks of how his glory would grow. After appearing in despised Galilee he would reign on David's throne, surpassing the greatest kings of the past. His kingdom would be established, from Israel down to Judah and then outwards to reach every nation on earth. He came from despised "Galilee of the nations", and his rule would finally embrace *all the nations*, for the hope he would bring would not be for Jews alone, but for Gentiles also. "His authority shall grow continually and there shall be endless peace".

This remarkable prophecy about the beginning of the Messiah's ministry would go unheeded at the time of its fulfilment. One of Jesus's first followers would ask, "Can anything good come out of Nazareth?" (Jn 1:46). The chief priests and the Pharisees would declare, quite incorrectly, that "No prophet is to arise from Galilee" (Jn 7:52). In fact, Both Elijah and Jonah had come from Galilee, and as the Evangelist Matthew pointed out, quoting Isaiah 9:1-7, a great light would arise for the people who sat in darkness in Galilee (Mt 4:12-17).

XX

9:8-10:4 The Sins that God will judge

God's retribution was going to strike, principally against the northern kingdom of Israel, for generations of rebellion, idolatry and misrule. It would also impact the land of Judah, because of the proud rejection of Yahweh on the part of King Ahaz. It is likely that this passage originally had 5:24-30 attached after 10:4. Once it is reunited, it forms another of Isaiah's striking poems, with a haunting refrain that appears five times: "For all this his anger has not turned away; his hand is stretched out still".

8. The first stanza of the poem (v 8-12) tells of God's judgement on the pride and arrogance of the northern tribes. His punishment would be to inflict on Israel further losses of territory. The Lord God sent his word against all of them.

9. The northern kingdom of Israel (also known as Ephraim or Samaria) knew very well what was wrong. Nevertheless, they maintained their pride and arrogance of heart, and answered back.

10. Their bricks had fallen, for most of their cities had been destroyed, but in their bravado they spoke of rebuilding some settlements with dressed stones. Their sycamore trees had been uprooted or chopped down, but their response would

be to plant some cedars instead. The people said, "God is angry, let us wait a little; God is appeased, let us do as we did previously".

11. Because of this proud response, Yahweh would raise up adversaries against them and stir up their enemies.

12. Syrians would ravage them on the east and Philistines on the west. Israel would be devastated. But this was not all; worse was to come.

13. The second stanza (v 13-17) is about God's judgement on ungodly leaders, as well as on those who have been led astray by them. The divine punishment was defeat and widespread slaughter in war. In their pride, the people of Israel did not return to God, not even after his initial judgement on them.

14. Picturing them as fawning dogs, Yahweh cut off their heads and their tails. Picturing them as palm trees, he lopped off their branches at the top and their reeds at the bottom.

15. The elders and members of the court were the head, and the false prophets who taught them lies were the wagging tail.

16. The leaders of Israel had misled them, and they had together gone astray. The teaching of the false prophets had left them confused and lacking in conviction.

17. Derek Kidner writes pithily, "Judgement begins with leaders but does not excuse those who follow". The Lord is known as the one who looks after the weak and the vulnerable (1:17), so in this case why would he not spare their young, nor show mercy to the orphans and widows? Because "*everyone* was godless and an evildoer. *Every* mouth spoke folly". The whole nation shared the guilt of their rulers. But this was not all; worse was to come.

18. The third stanza (v 18-21) tells of God's judgement on the disunity of his people. His "punishment" would be internal anarchy. George Adam Smith makes the observation that there are times when we cannot tell what is due to human sin, and what is due to divine judgement. The evil actions of all the people would be like a blazing fire that would consume thorn-bushes and set thickets aflame. Clouds of smoke would spread over the land.

19. Because of the holy and righteous anger of Yahweh of the armies, the sin of the people inevitably led them to anarchy, and they began to vent their fiery rage on one another, like the abandoned children in *Lord of the Flies*. Other people were just fuel for the fire. Nobody had mercy on anybody else.

20. Their destructive behaviour was like that of beasts who gorge themselves and devour without ceasing, for nothing would stop their madness. They would inflict judgement on each other, but it was ultimately God's judgment.

21. The Israelite tribes attacked one another. They vented their fury on their brothers and sisters. The people of Manasseh slaughtered those from Ephraim, and the Ephraimites those of Manasseh. Together the northern Israelites attacked their southern relatives from Judah. But this was not all; worse was to come.

10:1. The fourth stanza (v1-4) describes God's judgement on injustice. His punishment was a final warning about captivity and exile. Israel did not heed this warning (given around 732 B.C.) and they would be utterly destroyed ten years later. The government of Israel was notorious for its iniquitous decrees and oppressive statutes. These inevitably favoured the rich at the expense of the poor.

2. The needy were deprived of justice, and the poor of their rights. Advantage was taken of widows and orphans. The weak and vulnerable suffered needlessly.

3. Where would the rich despoilers go in the day of disaster, when everyone would be affected? There would be no one to help them, and their ill-gotten fortune would be of no use either to them or to anybody else.

4. The wealthy and the carefree would end up lying in the streets with the other dead bodies. But this was not all; worse was to come. It would be worse because this time it would be God's judgement on *Judah* rather than on the northern kingdom of *Israel*. Much of northern Judah would be destroyed by the well-trained and ruthless Assyrian army at its fearsome worst. The final stanza is to be found in 5:24-25. It is followed by a description of the darkness that was already encroaching in 5:26-30. We have already studied the end of the poem. There is no repetition of the refrain at the end: Yahweh's anger has finally turned away, and his hand is no longer stretched forth.

Meditation: Justice will be meted out in full

This section (9:8-10:4) was originally followed by 5:24-30. At some stage in the process of editing and compiling the book that we know as "Isaiah", the latter part was displaced. It is helpful to read the whole passage out aloud, 9:8-10:4 followed immediately by 5:24-30. The latter ends with a stanza of unusual power and majesty, telling of the terrifying might and destructive power of the Assyrian army. These were the allies that King Ahaz was seeking instead of trusting in Yahweh.

The Lord sent a word against Jacob, and it fell on Israel:
And all the people knew it, Ephraim and the inhabitants of Samaria,
but in pride and arrogance of heart they said:
"The bricks have fallen, but we will build with dressed stones;
The sycamores have been cut down, but we will put cedars in their place".
So Yahweh raised adversaries against them, and stirred up their enemies,
the Arameans on the east and the Philistines on the west,
and they devoured Israel with open mouth.
　For all this his anger has not turned away;
　His hand is stretched out still.
The people did not turn to him who struck them, or seek Yahweh of the armies.
So Yahweh cut off from Israel head and tail, palm branch and reed in one day:
Elders and dignitaries are the head, and prophets who teach lies are the tail;

for those who led these people led them astray,
and those who were led by them were left in confusion.
That is why the Lord did not have pity on their young people,
or compassion on their orphans and widows;
for everyone was godless and an evildoer, and every mouth spoke folly.
> For all this his anger has not turned away;
> His hand is stretched out still.
For wickedness burned like a fire, consuming briers and thorns;
it kindled the thickets of the forest, and they swirled up in a column of smoke.
Through the wrath of Yahweh of the armies the land was burned,
and the people became like fuel for the fire; no one spared another.
They gorged on the right, but still were hungry,
and they devoured on the left, but were not satisfied;
they devoured the flesh of their own kindred;
Manasseh devoured Ephraim, and Ephraim Manasseh,
and together they were against Judah.
> For all this his anger has not turned away;
> His hand is stretched out still.
Ah, you who make iniquitous decrees, who write oppressive statutes,
to turn aside the needy from justice, to rob the poor of my people of their right,
that widows may be your spoil, and that you may make the orphans your prey!
What will you do on the day of punishment,
in the calamity that will come from far away?
To whom will you flee for help, and where will you leave your wealth,
so as not to crouch among the prisoners or fall among the slain?
> For all this his anger has not turned away;
> His hand is stretched out still.
Therefore, as the tongue of fire devours the stubble,
and as the dry grass sinks down in the flame,
so their root will become rotten, and their blossom go up like dust;
for they have rejected the instruction of Yahweh of the armies,
and have despised the word of the Holy One of Israel.
Therefore the anger of Yahweh was kindled against his people,
and he stretched out his hand against them and struck them;
the mountains quaked, and their corpses were like refuse in the streets.
> For all this his anger has not turned away;
> His hand is stretched out still.
He will raise a signal for a nation far away,
and whistle for a people at the ends of the earth;
here they come, swiftly, speedily!

None of them is weary, none stumbles, none slumbers or sleeps,
not a loincloth is loose, not a sandal-thong broken;
their arrows are sharp, all their bows bent,
their horses' hoofs seem like flint, and their wheels like the whirlwind.
Their roaring is like a lion, like young lions they roar;
they growl and seize their prey, they carry it off and no-one can rescue.
They will roar over it on that day, like the roaring of the sea.
And if one looks to the land – only darkness and distress;
and the light grows dark with the clouds.

XXI

10:5-19 The Assyrian Scourge will also be judged

These verses are about God's control of history in tumultuous times, both in the world in general and with special regard for his chosen people. The successes of godless people such as the pagan Assyrians will be seen to have furthered God's purposes. Their victories, even at their most cruel and unjust, will have served the ends of divine justice. But their personal glory was shallow, and their pride would not be permitted to go unpunished.

5. Assyria was just the rod of God's anger. The weapons they wielded against the nations (including Israel and Judah) were expressions of the judgement of God. But although the Assyrians were fulfilling God's will, they did so arrogantly. They would not be absolved of their moral accountability. The sovereignty of God and the responsibility of flawed people are in tension here. God's supreme control and our free will are both in view – at the same time.

6. God sent godless Assyria against godless nations, to defeat peoples with whom he was angry. They would take great spoils and seize valuable plunder. They would trample on those they conquered as if they were mud in the streets.

7. The Assyrian warriors did not set out to fulfil God's purposes. God did not figure in their plans. They were out to destroy some nations and to cut off others.

8. The King of Assyria boasted that his commanders were as powerful as kings.

9. As far as he could see, there was no difference between Calno and Carchemish, or between Hamath and Arpad, or between Samaria and Damascus. Different nations, different cities – what did it matter to him? His army was invincible.

10. The king of Assyria, possibly Sargon who reigned from 722-705 B.C., had conquered kingdoms whose gods had more impressive images than those which were worshipped in Jerusalem and Samaria, the capitals of Israel and Judah.

11. Sargon complacently believed that he would subdue Jerusalem and her idols just as he had done with Samaria and her images. Verses 9-11 suggest that this

passage should be dated between 717 and 701 B.C. In 717 Carchemish fell and was incorporated into the Assyrian empire, and in 701 the massed Assyrian armies invaded and subjugated Judah, and proceeded to besiege Jerusalem.

12. It was in fact Yahweh who had been making use of the Assyrian army for his own purposes! Once it had accomplished his will in Jerusalem, Yahweh would "punish the arrogant boasting of the king of Assyria and his haughty pride".

13. The Assyrian king believed that all his destructive military exploits were due to the strength of his hand, and had come about by his wisdom and foresight. It was because he, Sargon, wished it, that nations had been born or ceased to exist, and it was he that had plundered their treasures. The Assyrians used to worship idols shaped like bulls; like a raging bull Sargon had brought other kings down and humiliated them.

14. It was Sargon's hand that had gathered the plunder of other peoples. It was he who had helped himself to the riches of his enemies, like a child gathers the eggs left behind by a mother bird. No mother birds ever moved or chirped to stop *him*!

15. Isaiah is devastating in his dismissal of Sargon's pride and arrogance. Like the other Old Testament prophets, Isaiah was sustained by his humble faith in the one true God, Yahweh, who was the Holy One of Israel. He dwelt with those who were humble and contrite (57:15), but he opposed the proud and would pass judgement on them (2:5-22). This arrogant pagan king was a mere tool in the hands of Yahweh, like an axe or a saw. And yet he considered himself superior to the one who made use of the tool. Can a rod hold the man who holds it in his hand? Can a staff lift up a real human being?

16. Therefore the Lord, Yahweh of the armies, would destroy the mighty Assyrian army with a devastating sickness. The glory of Yahweh would light a fire.

17. Yahweh would himself be the fire that would consume the Assyrian army, "his thorns and briers", in a single day. This is an extraordinary prophecy. How could it possibly be fulfilled in a single day? We shall read about the amazing fulfilment later on, when we reach chapters 36 and 37 of Isaiah.

18. In a way, the Assyrian army was glorious, like a forest or a fruitful land. Yahweh would destroy it, soul and body, through sickness and fire. The mighty Assyrian men would be like invalids wasting away on their deathbed.

19. A few survivors might arise, as from the ashes of a great forest fire – but they would be so few that a child could count them.

Meditation: The Proud deceive themselves

In the Middle Ages theologians wrote about a tree of vices. They considered the seven deadly sins to be the seven branches of this tree. They were labelled anger, avarice, envy, gluttony, lust, sloth and vanity. But the root of the tree of vices was the cardinal sin, namely pride.

In a similar way, the medieval theologians wrote about a tree of virtues. It too had seven branches, which were labelled love, faith, hope, prudence, fortitude, justice and temperance. These seven virtues were the union of the three Christian graces (1 Cor 13:13) and the four classical virtues. At the root of the tree of virtues was the cardinal virtue, namely humility. Both trees, the one of the vices and that of the virtues, used to be depicted in diagrams of trees.

This view, that humility was the greatest virtue and pride the greatest vice, was widespread in mediaeval Europe. In England it persisted long after the Middle Ages had ended: indeed, it was still widespread two thirds of the way through the 20th century. Proud people were considered disagreeable, and humble people delightful. When applying for a job, it was a tricky thing to write a *Curriculum Vitae*. How could you present your achievements and credentials to others while remaining modest and self-effacing?

Inherent in this old European world-view is the fact that glory and honour belong to God, and become unseemly when arrogated by any person, however exalted. The prophet Isaiah has given us the pen portrait of a pagan king who considered that a great deal of the world's glory and honour was his own. Sargon's pride and arrogance were overweening. Like his predecessors Tiglath-Pileser III (king of Assyria from 745-727 B.C.), Shalmaneser V (727-722 B.C.) and his successor Sennacherib (705-681 B.C.), Sargon (722-705 B.C.) thought of himself more highly than he should have done (Rom 12:3). He reckoned that he was the disposer supreme and the judge of the earth. His decisions would determine the fate of nations. Isaiah makes it clear that God has nothing but scorn for such people. For God himself is humble, as is his Son Jesus Christ (Mt 11:29).

God has appointed a day against all who are proud and lofty and who lift themselves high (2:12), yet he delights to dwell in the hearts of those who are humble and contrite in spirit (57:15). Pride is an exceedingly ugly human quality. Pride leads to boasting. The proud person can easily become domineering, and derive satisfaction from bullying those over whom he has power. He who is proud eventually deceives himself into thinking that he is better than others and that God's approval rests upon him. Isaiah leaves us in little doubt that the opposite is the case. Sargon was not the most fortunate person in the world, greatly to be envied by everyone else. He was in fact one of the most unfortunate, and greatly to be pitied. It would have been far better for him if he had never been born. His end would be like a wasting sickness and a devouring fire.

XXII

10:20-34 The Repentance of the Remnant

20. On the day when God would punish the Assyrians for their pride, a small remnant of the northern kingdom of Israel together with the survivors from Judah would no longer depend on Assyria, as King Ahaz had done with such dogged persistence. Instead they would put their trust in Yahweh, the Holy One of Israel, and they would do so sincerely.

21. A remnant would return. This was the meaning of the name of Isaiah's oldest son, Shear-jashub: *A-remnant-shall-turn*. The prophecy contained in the name would be fulfilled. Some would repent and return to their "mighty God". In 9:6 this was a title ascribed to the coming Messiah; here it refers to God.

22. The people of Yahweh had become very numerous, but only a remnant would return. The destruction of the majority of the descendants of Abraham had been decreed. There would be an exterminating judgement which would reduce the large population of Judah to a tiny group of survivors. This is not presented as an act of savagery on Yahweh's part. It was a tragedy for his rebellious people. It would be allowed in the overruling providence of God as a punishment for their disobedience. It would be a convincing proof of Yahweh's judicial righteousness (1:27), and of the moral and social ideals on which his government of the world is based. Its result would be a people who were godly and righteous.

23. Yahweh would be placing a full stop in the middle of the story of his people, and by doing so he would give them a new beginning. Isaiah repeats that this was Yahweh's deliberate decree. The results would not only affect the land of Judah and Israel, but also the whole wide world.

24. Therefore Yahweh, God of the armies, appeals to his people who lived in Jerusalem not to be afraid of the Assyrians when they came to intimidate them, like the Egyptians had done, with their superpower status and weaponry.

25. God's displeasure with the people of Jerusalem would not last long. When it came to an end, his anger would be directed to the destruction of the Assyrians. God has used in the past (and still uses today) the destructive actions of evil people in order to accomplish his purposes, but this does not mean that these evil people are not accountable to him.

26. In the past Yahweh had struck the Midianites at Oreb (Judg 7:25), and lifted his staff against the Egyptian chariot-drivers (Ex 14:15-29, etc.) The people of Jerusalem were urged to remember his love for them on these occasions. There would be a repetition with Assyria.

27. The great day would come when the Assyrian burden on their shoulders would be lifted, and the yoke on their necks would be destroyed.

28. Isaiah now imagines the Assyrians descending on Jerusalem from the north. In verses 28-32 he describes the route that they might take. It is the natural one from the north. Assyria did eventually invade Judah, destroy its towns and besiege Jerusalem in 701 B.C. When they did so, they in fact came from the south, having just campaigned against Lachish (36:1-2). So the oracle that includes verses 28-32 was not written after the event. This was a prophecy spoken in advance of what it predicted, probably written 10-15 years before it happened. Isaiah is describing

poetically the intimidating invincibility of the Assyrians. He is imagining what it was going to be like to be invaded and besieged by them. They might begin their invasion at Rimmon in Assyria. From there they would go to Aiath, then pass through Migron and store some luggage at Michmash.

29. Then they would cross the mountain pass. This is the pass of Michmash, where Jonathan had famously overcome a garrison of Philistines (1 Sam 13:23-14:15). After crossing the pass, the Assyrians would lodge for the night at Geba. Nearby towns would faint with fear, like Ramah, or flee, like Gibeah.

30. Isaiah can almost hear the people of Gallim as they cried aloud, and doubtless those in Laishah would listen in terror. The dwellers of Anathoth would perhaps try and comfort them.

31. Those in Madmenah would take flight, as would the inhabitants of Gebim.

32. On that day the Assyrian army would halt at Nob and shake their fists at the mount on which Jerusalem was built. In this way they would seek to intimidate the citizens of Zion.

33. The people of God need not panic. On that very day an amazing divine rescue would take place. That very day would be the promised day of retribution against Assyria. Yahweh, Sovereign over all armies, would wield his axe in terrifying fashion against the forest of pagan warriors. Branches would be lopped off, the tallest trees cut down, and the proud would be humbled and brought low.

34. Entire thickets would be felled, and the tallest cedars of Lebanon would come crashing down. The people of Jerusalem need not be afraid!

Meditation: In Whom do we place our Trust?

In this section Isaiah explains more clearly what he means by *the remnant*. The remnant would consist of those who would be spared in Yahweh's great act of judgement (v 20). Their returning (v 21) or repenting will be marked by the way in which they turned away from their fatal policy of trusting in earthly power, and instead adopted the attitude of relying quietly and humbly on Yahweh alone. The requirement of any follower of Yahweh to depend on him above all else is one of the recurring themes in Isaiah's prophecy. As far as this prophet is concerned, to trust in Yahweh was a very important matter.

He was not alone. Throughout the Old Testament we find the call to depend on God. Abraham was approved because he trusted God enough to believe in his promises (Gen 15:6). Moses was approved because he nearly always did exactly as God told him (e.g. Lev 16:34). King David was approved because his heart was true to Yahweh his God (e.g. 1 Ki 11:4, 15:3). In one of the psalms attributed to him he wrote, "For God alone my soul waits in silence; from him comes my salvation. He alone is my rock and my salvation, my fortress; I shall never be shaken" (Ps 62:1-2). In another he put it at its simplest: "In God I trust" (Ps 56:11). These words were pluralised to "In God we trust", which became the official motto of the United States of America in 1956. A quick look at a concordance will multiply the list of examples.

In the New Testament there is a similar emphasis on the importance of trusting God. The only difference is that because Jesus Christ is God's Son, who has made God the Father known to people (Jn 1:18), faith in Christ is equivalent to trust in God. We are therefore exhorted to believe "into" Christ (Jn 3:16), and there are numerous other expressions that present the same truth (Jn 1:11-13, 2:5, 3:36, 4:13-14, 5:24, 6:35, 7:37-39, 8:31-32, 9:35-38, 10:27-28, 11:25; 12:44-45, 13:8-10, 14:6, 15:5, 16:28, 17:3, 18:37, 19:30, 20:30-31, 21:24-25). These are a few of the references in John's Gospel; there are many more in the New Testament.

The names of God will help us to put our trust in him. Yahweh was God's "family name" for his Old Testament people, and Jesus Christ is God's "family name" for his New Testament people. When God chooses to make himself known to people, he discloses various aspects of his nature to them through his name. God loves to approach his children in a fatherly and familiar way. We relate to God not as some abstract and aloof spirit, but as someone whom we may get to know and love. For those who knew him in the Old Testament days he was *Yahweh*, the great "I am". For those who have known him or will know him in our New Testament days, he is *Jesus Christ*, our great Saviour and King.

In whom do we ultimately put our trust? Whom do we rely on when everything goes wrong? In whom do we believe? There are basically four options:

(a) We may trust in **an object** or in **our possessions**. Many of God's people in Isaiah's time trusted in man-made images or idols (2:18-20). One or two may have been "good" idols, like the famous bronze snake made by Moses (Num 21:4-9, Jn 3:14-15), which King Hezekiah would have to destroy (2 Ki 18:4). Most were heathen idols. Isaiah points out how absurd this idolatry was (44:9-20). God created us; we created our idols; we can know God who is full of goodness and life; our idols are lifeless and we cannot relate to them. Are we more sensible today? What are our idols? What possessions do we love above all else? Jesus Christ pointed out that "One's life does not consist of the abundance of possessions" (Lk 12:15). Have we taken note of this?

(b) We may trust in **ourselves**. This is the inevitable consequence of pride. The proud will be condemned by God on the last day, if not before (2:12-17). Those who profess to be his people will be condemned if they are proud and trust in themselves (9:8-12). Those who do not know him will also be condemned if they are proud and trust in themselves (10:12-19).

(c) We may trust in **other people**, especially those we perceive as powerful. This was the sin of Isaiah's enemy, King Ahaz. Yahweh was strong enough to look after his own people. Ahaz preferred to have the security afforded by an alliance with Assyria. This alliance was costly in terms of the tribute paid by the vassal nation to their protectors. When in due course the cost became prohibitive and Judah stopped paying the tribute, Assyria would set out to subdue them.

This trust in people was condemned by the prophets. Thus says Yahweh, "Cursed are those who trust in *mere mortals* and make *flesh* their strength, whose hearts turn away from Yahweh. They shall be like a shrub in the desert, and shall not see when relief comes. They shall live in the parched places of the wilderness, in an uninhabited salt land. Blessed are those who trust in Yahweh, whose trust is Yahweh. They shall be like a tree planted by water, sending out its roots by the stream. It shall not fear when heat comes and its leaves stay green; in the year of drought it is not anxious, and it does not cease to bear fruit" (Jer 17:5-8).

We likewise long for security, and this involves trusting other people for it. If we are being provident and making appropriate sacrifices for our futures and those of our dependents, this is responsible and godly behaviour. It can, however, be the result of a lack of trust in God. There is a form of security which is idolatrous. Its pursuit will have a harmful effect on our relationship with God. We should ask ourselves who it is that we ultimately trust.

(d) We may trust in **God** and in **his Son Jesus Christ**. Then Yahweh will keep us in perfect peace (26:3-4).

XXIII

11:1-5 The Humility of the Messiah

This is a most influential passage. It concerns not only the lowliness of the Messiah but also the way in which God's Holy Spirit would fill him and equip him for his mission. It is arguably the most important passage about the Spirit of God in the Old Testament, and because of its Trinitarian implications it is of great interest for any follower of Christ. For some reason it is rarely preached upon nowadays. This is strange, since today's church is characterised above all else by its desire to know and understand the Holy Spirit's work. At any rate, because this passage is not considered to be of the first importance, quite a few church members miss out on a particularly edifying part of God's word.

1. We have just seen that the forest of Assyria is to be felled, never to grow again (10:33-34). Judah too would be felled, but in this case a shoot will be seen growing from the fallen tree of Jesse, who was the father of King David. After emerging from Jesse's roots, the shoot would become the Branch, whom we have already encountered (4:2, 6:13). The Branch is the coming Messiah.

2. Davidic descent is only one of the qualities required for Messiahship. The Branch must also be equipped for his office by the Spirit of God, who will rest on him and remain with him during the three years of his ministry. The book of Isaiah lays great store on the fact that the Messiah would have the Spirit resting upon him (42:1, 59:21, 61:1). The Spirit is described as sevenfold in his operation, and

this idea of the sevenfold Spirit of God would later be picked up in the New Testament (Rev 1:4, 3:1, 4:5 and 5:6).

(**a**) He is the Spirit of Yahweh, for the promotion of godliness.

(**b**) He is the Spirit of wisdom, for just and discerning government.

(**c**) He is the Spirit of understanding, for empathy with all people.

(**d**) He is the Spirit of counsel, for the edification of the needy.

(**e**) He is the Spirit of might, for warfare against evil and deceit.

(**f**) He is the Spirit of the knowledge of Yahweh, for the growth of the church.

(**g**) He is the Spirit of the fear of Yahweh, for the cultivation of humility.

3. The delight of the Branch would be in the fear of Yahweh. His life on earth would be marked from start to finish by his humble dependence on, his reverence for and his adoration of God his Father. The Messiah's greatest longing would be to please his Father. His fear of God would totally eliminate the possibility of disappointing or disobeying him in any way. How different this was from the fear of King Ahaz, which impelled him to seek security in powerful people rather than in Yahweh. The Messiah would give the highest priority to fearing God (Mt 10:28) and would always depend on God his Father for guidance (Jn 5:19-20). Moreover, he would (in the words of John Skinner) "be quick to recognise [the fear of God] in others and take delight in it whenever he found it".

So closely would the Branch depend on his heavenly Father that his judgements would not be inspired by what he saw, but by the impressions that the Spirit of his Father communicated to him. Other people might look on the outward appearance, but the Son of God would, like Yahweh, look on the heart (1 Sam 16:7). Nor would the Branch make hasty decisions on the basis of what he heard. He would possess divine spiritual insight into other people's hearts, and would distinguish between the appearance and the reality.

4. He would be the guide of the poor and disadvantaged, assessing them with perfect justice. He would decide with equity for the meek. Being himself meek and humble, he would love to be with people who were meek and humble. The words he breathed out would have great authority, setting free those who were imprisoned and bringing down those who had oppressed them.

5. He would be an example for his people, being clad with righteousness around his waist and faithfulness around his loins. All his doings would be good and worthy of his followers' trust.

Meditation: The Sevenfold Spirit of God

So far, Isaiah has portrayed the coming Messiah in four ways. First, he is the child Emmanuel or *God-is-with-us*, who would be with his people in the time of their oppression (7:14-17, 8:5-8). Secondly, this child would be brought up in Galilee and he would then embark on a divine rescue mission: he would be seen to be *Wonderful Counsellor,*

Mighty God, Everlasting Father and *Prince of Peace* (9:6-7). Thirdly, he would be a *Branch* that would sprout from the stump of Jesse (6:13, 11:1). Curiously, he would also be the *root* of Jesse (11:10). How can the Messiah be both the root and a shoot of the same tree? We shall find out later. Fourthly, he would be *wonderfully endowed with the Spirit of God*. God did not give the Spirit "by measure" to his Messiah, but in all fullness (Jn 3:34). What is the Spirit like? What can he do for a person? The answers are there in verse 2.

(a) The Spirit is the Spirit of **Yahweh**, for the promotion of godliness. God is loving and God is holy. This is his dual nature. His Spirit is the Holy Spirit and he is the Spirit of love and compassion. When the Messiah began his ministry, he would be so wrought upon by the Spirit of God that both the love and the holiness of God would shine through him. He would be "full of grace and truth" (Jn 1:14, 17). His character would be perfectly balanced, just like God's.

(b) The Spirit is the Spirit of **wisdom**, for just and discerning government. In his ministry the Spirit-led Messiah would encounter people in positions of leadership and people who were the servants of others. He would deal with each according to their station in life, as far as possible obeying those in power and encouraging the poor to keep the law. He would seek justice and equity for all people.

(c) The Spirit is the Spirit of **understanding**, for empathy with all people. His mind sharpened by the Spirit, the Messiah would know how to meet every person at his or her point of need. Quoting words of Isaiah (35:4-6, 61:1), he would be able to tell doubters that through his ministry "the blind receive their sight, the lame walk, the lepers are cleansed, the deaf hear, the dead are raised and the poor have good news brought to them" (Mt 11:4-5).

(d) The Spirit is the Spirit of **counsel**, for the edification of the needy. The words of the Spirit-filled Messiah were wonderfully positive and had an unprecedented moral and edifying persuasiveness. Troubled minds were set at peace by his words of authority (Mk 5:1-15). People who had previously been promiscuous had their lives completely turned around, and were instructed on how to become pure (Jn 4:5-26, 39-42).

(e) The Spirit is the Spirit of **might**, for warfare against evil and deceit. The Messiah would be given heroic energy. After being tempted, he would be "filled with the power of the Spirit" (Lk 4:14). Among his many mighty restorative acts, he would heal people from their diseases and deliver those who were oppressed by evil spirits. He would libe-rate the captives, and set free those in bondage to evil thoughts.

(f) The Spirit is the Spirit of **the knowledge of Yahweh**, for the growth of the church. Knowing the will of Yahweh, the Messiah would broadcast the salvation that would be available to anyone who personally trusted in him (Jn 3:16). He would define eternal life as being one and the same thing as knowing God and his Son Jesus Christ (Jn 17:3). People would get to know Yahweh and his Messiah in ever growing numbers, and their lives would be transformed.

(g) The Spirit is the Spirit of *the fear of Yahweh*, for the cultivation of humility. The Messiah would always find his fulfilment in accomplishing Yahweh's will (Jn 4:34). He would live a life of perfect submission to God his Father (Jn 5:19-20, 30, 36). He would always wait for God's will to become clear, and then he would speak or act accordingly. So great would be his longing to please his Father at all times, that he would be distressed at the very possibility of deviating from his Father's will in any way. He would be afraid of displeasing God. Before his Father he would always be humble. This is what the fear of Yahweh means. The person who fears God does not cower away from him in petrified terror. On the contrary, his fear of God releases him from all other fears and facilitates his perfect obedience of God. The hymn-writers Tate and Brady gave us some helpful words: "Fear him, ye saints, and you will then have nothing else to fear".

In today's church believers are urged to seek all kinds of manifestations of the Spirit of God. In fact, there are seven which are more important and more useful than any of the others, both for the one who has been given them and for those with whom he or she comes into contact. They are the seven that the Messiah was so wonderfully endowed with. And the last of these seven is the most important and useful of all.

Concerning the Messiah, we read in 11:3a that "His delight [would] be in the fear of Yahweh". This was what he prized most of all. He loved his heavenly Father so much that to walk in the fear of him was his ongoing delight. Indeed, the Hebrew phrase may be translated "He will inhale or draw his breath in the fear of Yahweh". In his commentary on Isaiah, George Adam Smith wrote that this "is a most expressive definition of sinlessness – sinlessness which was the attribute of Christ alone". Do we aspire to live a perfect life? It is quite possible that the best way to draw near to perfection is to delight in fearing God.

XXIV

11:6-16 Life under the Messiah

This passage describes what life will be like in the future, when the Messianic Kingdom arrives and the Messiah reigns supreme. In verses 6-9 we catch a beautiful glimpse of the next life, when discord and evil will no longer exist. Verses 10-16 describe the great homecoming, when the people of Yahweh, exiled because of their rebellious disobedience, would return to their land and begin life afresh. Widespread reconciliation would take place, and the people of God would enjoy peace. While verses 6-9 look ahead to heaven, verses 10-16 are a prophecy of the return of the Jews to their own land, which has been fulfilled twice.

6. Isaiah looks forward to the new world that will come into being at the end of the age. It will be altogether pleasant and peaceful, because the Prince of Peace will be in charge. Reconciliation will be visible everywhere. Wolves and lambs will pasture together. Leopards and kids will lie down next to each other. Calves and

lions will play with a fatling. A little child will run around with all of them.

7. There will be perfect concord. Cows will graze with bears. Their young will rest beside each other. Lions will be vegetarian, eating straw like the oxen.

8. Trust will reign supreme, for there will be nothing to mistrust. Young children will play over the holes of asps, and newly weaned infants will search into the dens of adders without needing to be risk-assessed. The whole of creation will be renewed, and every hope and longing will be fulfilled.

9. Pain and suffering will no longer exist. No creature will ever be hurt by another. No creature will ever be destroyed. The whole earth, referred to as the mountain of God, will be a holy place. Nothing bad will ever happen there. Why? Because "the earth will be full of the knowledge of Yahweh as the waters cover the sea". Every person and every creature will know and love Yahweh. The Spirit of the knowledge of Yahweh will fill them all.

10. Before that, there would be a day when the Messiah would bring salvation to all the nations, who would be prompted to make inquiries about him. They would be attracted to the true God and to his anointed servant, the Messiah, who would be the greatest of all the religious teachers, and would speak with great authority (Mt 7:28-29). Truth has an in-built attractiveness, especially for those who sought after it in the pagan nations. We have already met this idea in 2:2-4.

    It is interesting that the one who would be the *shoot* of Jesse (v1) is here called the *root* of Jesse. A root brings forth a tree; the tree then brings forth a shoot – so how can the root be the same as the shoot? The Messiah is a divine being who was God's agent in the creation, yet he would be descended from David's father Jesse. He who created both Jesse and David would become a man, and he would be born from their family line. This may help us to answer the riddle set by Jesus Christ: David calls the Messiah his Lord, so how can the Messiah be the son of David? (Mk 12:35-37; see also Ps 110:1).

11. Before that, there would be a day when God would form his new Messianic community by gathering in Jewish people from every part of the world. The survivors of his people would return to the Promised Land. The remnant, who were in faraway places like Assyria, Egypt, Pathros or Upper Egypt, Ethiopia, Elam in Susiana, Shinar in Babylonia, Hamath in Syria and the islands of the Mediterranean Sea, would finally end their exile. God would "recover" them. He would bring them back home.

12. God would raise a signal or banner. It would be better than the one that was raised in 5:26 to bring down the Syrian and Israelite armies against Jerusalem. Because it is a better signal, people from all the nations would turn to God. To begin with, the remnant of Judah and Benjamin (the southern kingdom) would return, and also the remnant of the ten tribes of Israel (the northern kingdom). But the nations of the world would soon follow (49:22-23).

13. The Jewish people would themselves be reconciled, and the old feuds and wars between Judah and Israel would be a thing of the past.

14. The reunited kingdom of the Jews would flourish and become very strong. It would attract Philistines from the west, and Edomites, Moabites and Ammonites from the east. Isaiah believed that one aspect of the Messiah would be his power as a warrior, so he sometimes uses the language of warfare. These enemies, who had formerly sniped at God's people, would one day say, "If you can't beat them, join them". The force before which these nations would be forced to capitulate would be the gospel, and their incorporation into the people of God would be the fulfilment of Israel's call to be a light to the nations.

15. A greater exodus would result (35:1-2 and 48:20-21). The Gentile nations, excluded from God's people until now, would be set free from their slavery to idols, and a way would be made for them to come and know Yahweh, who is the one true God.

16. There would then be a highway from Assyria to Israel for the remnant in Assyria. Indeed, a highway would be made ready for believers from every nation to enter and inherit a place in the Promised Land. It is not yet clear what Isaiah is referring to, but later on we shall learn more about this universal way back to God (19:23-25, 35:8-10, 40:3-5, 42:17-20, 49:8-12, 57:14-19 and 62:10-12).

Meditation: A Chapter full of Hope

Chapter 11 of Isaiah presents us with three wonderful prophecies about the future. Each of them has a partial fulfilment in this life, and each will be wholly fulfilled in the new life that awaits God's people beyond the grave. The first prophecy concerns the perfect indwelling of our humanity by the Spirit of God (v1-5). The second is about the peace and communion of all nature when it is covered by the knowledge of God (v6-9). The third is about the meaning that will be brought to all the events of history as they contribute to the divine purposes of redemption and lead on to their marvellous fulfilment (v10-16). Together, these prophecies sum up the Judeo-Christian hope which we have for the future.

Hope is one of the three Christian graces; the others being faith and love (1 Cor 13:13). The greatest of these is love, but the most neglected is hope. We all need the hope of the wonderful events that lie ahead. This hope will help us look ahead to our future lives in the renewed heaven and earth, where we shall spend eternity. The writer of the epistle to the Hebrews declared that "We have this hope, a sure and steadfast anchor of the soul, a hope that enters the inner shrine behind the curtain, where Jesus, a forerunner on our behalf, has entered" (Heb 6:19-20).

In the New Testament times in which we live, the promise of the Holy Spirit is for *all* of God's people, not just a selected few (Joel 2:28-29). The Spirit endows *every person* who knows and loves God with wisdom and understanding, with counsel and might, and with knowledge and fear of God (v2). With these invaluable gifts, God's people may go about their everyday lives in ways that are just, compassionate, good and reliable (v4, 5).

Isaiah then writes about how beasts will live in harmony. This is not an allegory about alienated people who will be reconciled: Isaiah is referring to the animal world. St Paul would echo this prophecy in his epistle to the Romans (Rom 8:19-23). George Adam Smith put it like this: "The curse of conflict and mistrust between man and his fellow-creatures is due to man's sin, and [will] only be done away by man's redemption. For man is to blame for the wildness of the beasts, and it is through his sanctification that they may be restored to sympathy with himself". When the Messiah rode into Jerusalem in triumph, he would ride on the colt of an animal that had never been ridden previously. This would be a foretaste of the future, when beasts would not only live in friendship with each other but also with humans. Isaiah prophesies that the Spirit of knowledge and fear of Yahweh (v 2) would so radiate from the Messiah to other people, that the earth would be full of the knowledge of Yahweh (v 9), just as the waters cover the sea.

Finally, there is to be a great ingathering of God's people, who will return to God and find themselves fully reconciled with him and with one another. The glorious hope of God's people is of a renewed world where they will be cared for by the Messiah himself, the perfect prophet, priest and king.

One of the most striking features of this passage is the description of the coming Messiah as being both the *shoot* and the *root* of David. The Messiah would indeed be a *shoot* of David, being descended from David both in the royal line (Mt 1:6-16) and in a line of direct descent (Lk 3:23-31). But to call God's anointed one the *root* of David introduces quite a different factor into the equation. It means that Jesse sprang from him. The Messiah was the root and origin of the Messianic family into which he would be born. He is more than just God's special emissary, sent by God to carry out God's rescue plan for his fallen world. The Messiah is himself *God*. Everything came into being through him (Jn 1:3). This includes all people, and all people includes Jesse and David. The *shoot* of Jesse was also the *root* of Jesse.

There are some magnificent prophecies in chapter 11 of Isaiah, and it will be helpful and encouraging for us if we look forward to their complete fulfilment and consummation in the life to come. But one little-known prophecy in this chapter has already been fulfilled in all its glory.

The Messiah would think about the signal or banner which, according to Isaiah's prophecy, would be raised or lifted up (v 12). The Messiah was probably thinking of it when he said, "And I, when I am lifted up from the earth, will draw all people to myself" (Jn 12:32). He had doubtless meditated on the names of God in the Old Testament, one of which is "Yahweh is my banner" (Ex 17:15). The Messiah was himself Yahweh (9:6). He would himself be the ultimate banner that would be raised and lifted up on a cross. His self-sacrifice would have a magnetic power of attraction, and countless people from all the nations and peoples of the world would be drawn to him. They would all get to meet him face-to-face on the final day, and then they would enter into his bliss and glory.

XXV

12:1-6 The Song of the Saved

Just as the Israelites under Moses paused to sing a song of salvation after Yahweh had delivered them from slavery to their Egyptian oppressors (Ex 14:30-31, 15:1-18), so each and every person whom God has delivered from slavery to sin may sing this delightful and refreshing song of thanksgiving and praise. It is an echo of Isaiah's transformational call, which he described in chapter 6.

1. God's anger had remained over his people. Isaiah has haunted us with the sense of what it must have felt like with his refrain "For all this his anger is not turned away; his hand is stretched out still" (9:12, 17, 21, 10:4, 5:25). But now at last the divine anger is turned away! It has been replaced with the sweetness of God's comfort. Our raging spiritual thirst, which is that heavy and crushing sense of alienation and estrangement from him, is no more. Here, to comfort means to save, and true comfort or salvation can only be found by escaping into the everlasting arms of the God whose anger we have culpably stirred up.

2. The paralysing fear and the sense of utter weakness are also gone. They have been replaced by a quiet trust in *Yah Yahweh*. This title for God appears only here and in 26:4. The abbreviation *Yah* was first used by Moses to celebrate God's salvation during the Exodus, and often appears in the Psalms as part of the exclamation "*Hallelujah!*" The Lord God is the strength of those who love him and the saviour of those who look to him in faith. The second half of this verse is an echo of the song of Moses (Ex 15:2). There is a wonderful paradox here, and blessed is the one who understands it. There are times when a sense of alienation and isolation comes upon us. This stems from God's anger. In the end, the only source of comfort is the same God who was previously angry!

3. Our raging spiritual thirst is now being satisfied by living water from the wells of salvation (Jn 4:13-14). Those who have been saved may draw this living water at will from God's inexhaustible supply of salvation. This verse is a little known Messianic prophecy. During their annual Feast of Tabernacles, the Jewish people commemorated the occasion when water poured out of a rock after Moses had struck it (Ex 17:1-7). The High Priest would receive a large jar full of fresh water, and he would pour it out prodigally on the altar. As he did so, the crowd would sing this verse, "With joy you will draw water from the wells of salvation". When the Messiah came, he would on one such occasion cry out in a loud voice, "Let anyone who is thirsty come to me, and let the one who believes in me drink. As the scripture has said, 'Out of the believer's heart shall flow rivers of living water'" (Jn 7:37-38). The living water symbolises the salvation that can be ours thanks to the Messiah. He would fulfil verse 3 by purchasing our salvation at the great cost of his own life blood, as we shall see when we get to chapter 53.

4. The people of God will say to one another that it is not enough to thank God and call upon his great name. Worship is the immediate response to God's saving deeds, but worship must then lead to witness. The deeds of God are worthy of being proclaimed to the nations, to people who have not yet encountered him. Such people need to hear that God's name is exalted. The name of God means his nature. God is at the same time radiant in holiness and warm in love.

5. Psalms of praise are to be sung to him, for he has displayed the splendour of his glory in his acts of salvation. This should be made known in all the world.

6. The people of Jerusalem are to shout aloud and sing for joy because of their great king. God is ever present in power with his people. He delights to save them from evil, and to restore them fully. He is great *in our midst*. He is indeed the Holy One of Israel, who has resolved to dwell in the midst of sinners. How can this be? Isaiah has yet to show us that the saviour of the world is none other than the Holy One of Israel.

Meditation: a Song of Wonder and Joy

When the sheer wonder of God's salvation is unfolded, the person who is saved instinctively longs to burst into song. The natural reaction to God's amazing grace is to sing about it, so Isaiah rounds off the first section of his book by providing us with a short psalm of praise. It was written so that ordinary people like you the reader of this commentary, and I the writer, might learn it and treasure the truths we find in it, and perhaps sing it out aloud. This song of the saved is brief and concise, and it is a gem of the first water. From beginning to end it sparkles with the joy and amazement of God's wonderful salvation.

The song has a simple structure. It features two reasoned exhortations for us to praise God for his saving deeds (v1-2, v 4-6). They are separated by a prophetic word of promise in v 3, "With joy you will draw water from the wells of salvation". The theme throughout is the wonderful salvation wrought by God.

Verses 1-2 are a beautiful poetic restatement of Isaiah's call in 6:1-7. On the one hand, God's anger has vanished and been replaced by his comfort (v1). On the other, Isaiah's dread of God has vanished and been replaced by his joy at having trusted the God of his salvation (v2). Moreover, just as God moves from forgiveness in 6:7 to commissioning and proclamation in 6:8-10, so those who drink from the wells of salvation (v3) move from giving praise to God (v1-2) to the proclamation of his name among the nations (v4-5).

In the midst of the singing, those who are saved pause for a moment. With great joy they draw water from the wells of salvation, and proceed to drink it. Their thirst for the living God is once again satisfyingly quenched, and they enjoy the deep satisfaction of his presence as he re-creates them and makes everything new.

God is himself the very centre of this song. He relates to the singer (v1, 2). He is known both by his covenant name Yahweh (v1, 2, 4, 5), and by his title *the Holy One of Israel* (v6). His deeds have given him great glory and fame (v4, 5).

This first section of Isaiah (chapters 1-12) has emphasised the holiness of God and his determination to rescue his people from the penalty, the power and the very presence of their sins. God will succeed in his plan, and Isaiah loves to look forward to the new life that those who know and love God will enjoy once their salvation has been consummated. *The Holy One* will then dwell in the midst of his people, the redeemed Israel (v6). Great in their midst shall he be! Nothing could be better than this! Blessed are those who have received the salvation of God and who exult in the God of their salvation.

PART 2 – LORD OF THE NATIONS

XXVI

13:1-16 Babylon's Day of Reckoning

Chapters 13-23 of Isaiah contain messages for the different nations of the world. The central truth that they enshrine is that Yahweh is the King of *all* the nations. These messages were given during various periods of Isaiah's life. Some are dated (e.g. 14:28 and 20:1), others can be dated, and a few are impossible to date. They form a prelude to Isaiah's Apocalypse (chapters 24-27), which is followed by oracles concerning the onset of the Assyrian crisis (chapters 28-39), as prophesied in Part 1 (chapters 1-12). The first of the heathen nations to be addressed by Isaiah is Babylon, the great future oppressor.

1. This oracle about Babylon is attributed to Isaiah, the son of Amoz (1:1). He was able to foresee that Babylon, a distant nation which in his time was a vassal-state to Assyria, would one day appropriate Jerusalem's treasures (39:5-6). Assyria would be defeated between 612-609 B.C. In 605 B.C. the Babylonians would take over from the Assyrians as the world superpower. They would then become the scourge of many countries, including Judah.

2. This is like the beginning of an epic war film. Up on a bare hill a signal is raised in order to recruit an army, and cries sound out. Soldiers are waved in. They enter through noble city gates in order to assemble for their enrolment and training.

3. Isaiah warms to his theme. Unbeknown to the soldiers, it is Yahweh himself who has given the order and summoned them. The soldiers are not holy; far from it. Yahweh refers to them as his *consecrated ones* because they are set apart so as to fulfil his purposes. As they exult in their pride, little do they know that their *raison d'etre* is to execute Yahweh's will and thereby placate his righteous anger.

4. From the mountains comes a throbbing sound. It is the tumult of a vast crowd of people. Kingdoms are in uproar and nations have gathered together. Yahweh of the armies is bringing together a vast army to fight a battle for him.

5. The soldiers have come from faraway lands, as distant as the heavens. They are at the beck and call of Yahweh, armed with his weapons in order to satisfy his indignation. They will destroy the whole kingdom of Babylon.

6. People should wail, for the day of destruction appointed by Yahweh is near. Isaiah's warning is plain: "It will come like destruction from the Almighty!"

7. People will be paralysed by terror. Their hands will be feeble, and their hearts will melt inside them. They will be unable to think or act.

8. They will be filled with dismay. Sharp pangs of pain will overcome them. Their agony will be inescapable, like that of a woman in labour. They will look at each other in a state of shock, their faces reddened and feverish with shame.

9. The great and terrible day of Yahweh has arrived. We must wait until v 19 for confirmation that it is the Babylonians who are its objects (v1, v 19). For them it is a cruel day, a day of wrath and anger, when their land will become desolate. Sin must be punished and sinners will be destroyed.

10. There will be portents in the stars of heaven and in their constellations. The sun will be darkened and the moon will not give its light. This darkness speaks of the withdrawal of the vision of God, and of the approach of divine retribution.

11. There is a moral purpose behind all this. Yahweh declares that he will punish the world for its *evil* and its *iniquity*. What is it that lies at the heart of their evil deeds and Yahweh's consequent anger? What is their chief sin that he so hates? Yahweh tells us: "I will put an end to the *pride* of the *arrogant*". Those who will be laid low are extremely proud; they are insolent tyrants.

12. There will be a shortage of people left alive. In Babylon even the finest gold will be more plentiful than the very scarce survivors.

13. The heavens will tremble and the foundations of the earth will be shaken on account of Yahweh's wrath, for the day of his fierce anger is cosmic in its scope.

14. The despair of the Babylonians on the day of their doom will be like that of a hunted gazelle or of a sheep with no one to protect it. There will be no escape. They must flee from everything, but there is nowhere to flee to.

15. Any Babylonian who is found will immediately be put to the sword.

16. Their young boys and girls will be seized by the legs and have their heads dashed against a rock, as the exiled Jews longed for in Ps 137:9. Their houses will be plundered and their wives raped before them. No mercy will be shown. The Babylonians will be destroyed. On the day of Yahweh (v 9) the forces of evil, sinful people included, will be Yahweh's instruments of retribution on those whose pride has led them to commit atrocities against their fellow human beings. There is an unforgiving spirit here, but Isaiah is not advocating revenge. He is allowing room for God's wrath (Rom 12:19). In fact, the fall of Babylon would duly prove to be a peaceful one. The final accounting suggested here would occur much later, on the final day, the great day of Yahweh (2:10-21).

Meditation: From Babel to Babylon

Isaiah begins his oracles about the heathen nations by prophesying the downfall of Babylon. The Babylonians had a long history, going back to a great grandchild of Noah called Nimrod (Gen 10:6-8). He became a mighty warrior and founded a town called Babel (Gen 10:9-10), before moving on to Assyria and building its capital, Nineveh (Gen 10:11). Later on, the settlers at Babel attempted to build a tower that would reach to the heavens (Gen 11:1-9). Although they were thwarted in their ambition, they became notorious for their pride and self-sufficiency. The tower of Babel would be an everlasting symbol of the worldly arrogance and pomp of those who choose to rebel against God and go their own way. The Babylonians were the descendants of the settlers at Babel, and they inherited their worldly and godless pride.

Babylon had already become a great kingdom under Hammurabi as early as the 18th century B.C., and they would reach their zenith under the leadership of Nebuchadnezzar. He inherited the Babylonian throne in 605 B.C. and for 43 years led what was perhaps the mightiest superpower in history, until he died in 562 B.C. Isaiah lived long before Nebuchadnezzar, but he foresaw and was concerned by the rise of Babylon. As far as this Jewish prophet was concerned, Babylon would in due course rise very high. Because it was the nation that *par excellence* had defied God, it would also fall just as surely as it had risen.

How did Babylon fall? According to surviving contemporary records, Cyrus took possession of the city peacefully in 539 B.C. The prophecy of Isaiah was fulfilled in essence but not in detail. This suggests that chapter 13 was probably written by Isaiah himself over 150 years in advance, rather than by a later writer after the fall of Babylon had taken place. Isaiah chose to dress up his foretelling of the fate of the proud and godless city with terminology normally reserved for the final day of Yahweh. Was he right to do so? George Adam Smith writes that "There may be periods in man's history when, in opposition to man's unholy art and godless civilisation, God can reveal himself only as destruction"

Isaiah was rightly captivated by his vision of the day of Yahweh. God's justice, and ours, demands that on the final day every wrong should be seen to have been put right. We shall be judged according to what we have *done*. This is a humbling thought for everyone to ponder. Thanks be to God that he has appointed a means whereby we may escape the ultimate consequences of our actions. Our salvation must depend on righteousness. Thanks be to God that the righteousness on which our salvation depends is in fact that of another person's perfect life. However, for the clearest revelation of the good news of salvation in the whole of the Old Testament, we must await Part 5 of the book of Isaiah, namely chapters 40-55.

XXVII

13:17-22 The Overthrow of Babylon

17. Yahweh would call the Medes to deal the death blow to the city of Babylon. It would be a tranquil overthrow. The Medes were the major power in the Medo-Persian Empire led by Cyrus. They captured Babylon without a struggle in 539 B.C. and later overthrew the Babylonian armies. The Medes were not a covetous people. They are described here as having no regard for silver, and not delighting in gold. They were not out to enrich themselves with the city's fabulous plunder. All they wanted to do was to conquer it and subjugate its peoples.

18. The army of the Medes would have been capable of the merciless slaughter of men, women and children described in this verse, and no doubt they dealt harshly with any Babylonians who resisted them. But the city of Babylon itself surrendered without a struggle and its citizens were spared the sword. According to the Greek historian Herodotus, "Owing to the great size of the city, the outskirts were captured without the people in the centre knowing anything about it. There was a festival going on, and they continued to dance and enjoy themselves until they learnt the news the hard way". How did the Medes capture the city of Babylon? It was completely impregnable, with a wall surrounding it that was 60 metres tall and 45 miles in circumference. The great River Euphrates flowed through the city, entering and exiting it through two huge tunnels under the wall. According to some historical sources, Cyrus, King of the Medes, ordered a canal to be dug and diverted the entire river before it reached Babylon. The course of the Euphrates dried up, and Cyrus and his army marched through the muddy tunnel into the city, which was taken completely unawares. It fell in one night.

19. Verses 19-22 describe a process that was only completed centuries later. In 275 B.C. Seleucus Nicator decided to build his new capital Seleucia on the Tigris 40 miles from Babylon, which was then largely abandoned. After that the city did indeed gradually become a ruin, though it still had some inhabitants in the first century A.D. By then the celebrated hanging gardens were gone forever, but when the last dwellers moved away, the imperial glory and the splendour and pride of the Chaldeans did revert to barren desert, just like Sodom and Gomorrah.

20. Babylon would remain a perpetual ruin, forever abandoned. No-one would ever live there again, not even passing nomads. Sheep would not be allowed to graze there. The great city would be regarded as an accursed and uncanny place.

21. Only wild beasts would make their home there, and they would be sinister howling animals. Ostriches would walk there, and goat-like satyrs would dance.

22. Hyenas would cry out from the high towers, and jackals from the palatial residences. The time did indeed come when all this was fulfilled. The days would run out for Babylon the great.

Meditation: The Doom of godless Civilisation

Nineveh, the capital of Assyria, would fall to the Babylonian army in 612 B.C. In the following three years the rest of Assyria would be completely subjugated or overthrown. The new superpower would not, however, be an improvement on the old. The same arrogant spirit of cruelty and selfish ambition would find a new expression. While the Assyrians delighted in brute force and destructive military power, the Babylonians would revel in boundless wealth and luxury.

Neither of them would think twice about slaughtering an entire nation. In some cases they opted to resettle the people in a different land, where they subjected them to slave labour. Assyria proceeded in this way with the northern kingdom of Israel in 722 B.C., exiling the ten tribes to a number of different faraway lands. The Babylonians did the same to the southern Kingdom of Judah in 597 and 586 B.C., exiling the citizens of Jerusalem to the dry plains of what is now Iraq. Several other nations received the same treatment. The Assyrian emperors loved to boast of their conquests and resettlements (10:5-11, 37:10-13). The Babylonian emperors preferred to boast of their riches and plunder (Dan 4:28-30).

The Assyrians were uncultured. Their art glorified military victory, and their sport was to humiliate and torture the peoples they had overthrown. The Babylonians were different. They were highly civilised. They cared more for their brain than their brawn, and they became very resourceful. But in their civilised culture there was no place for the living God. They had their idols of silver and gold, but were not attracted to Yahweh who was both caring creator and loving saviour. They achieved their aim, amassing vast wealth and living in undreamt of luxury, and they were immensely proud of their selfish achievements.

Their fall came because they became increasingly able to achieve their ends with money instead of the exercise of military power. As George Adam Smith wrote, "With money the Babylonians did all they wished to do, and believed everything else to be possible. They subsidised kings, bought over enemies, and seduced the peoples of the earth. The foe whom God now sent them was impervious to this influence. From their uncorrupted highlands came down upon civilisation a simple people, whose banner was a leather apron, whose goal was not booty nor ease but power and mastery, who came not to rob but to displace". And so the prophecy rang out, "See, I am stirring up the Medes against them, who have no regard for silver and do not delight in gold" (v 17).

We may learn two truths from all this. The first is that civilisation is not the same thing as godliness. The present writer spent forty years of his life teaching in an institution renowned for its culture and learning. The academic environment and the collegiate approach did not foster unselfishness and social concern. A spirit of selfishness was gradually imparted to most of those who spent a few years there before moving on to places of higher learning. It was a difficult environment in which to follow Jesus the Messiah, although a small remnant did flourish by God's grace. The second lesson is that exalting civilisation or culture is just another manifestation of the primeval sin of pride, which God hates.

XXVIII

14:1-11 The Proud will be brought low

Verses 1-2 are an important statement about the ongoing faithfulness of Yahweh towards his people. Then in verses 3-23 the oracles against Babylon are resumed with a taunt against its mighty ruler. In Alec Motyer's opinion, "No translation can reproduce the sweep and surge of this truly magnificent poem. It is the work of a master. Among known Bible writers, none but Isaiah could be its author".

1. This verse and the next anticipate chapters 56-66 and look ahead to a time when Israel would again be a people to be reckoned with. In spite of the sins of his people, Yahweh would have motherly compassion on them, and would again bless them with his grace and undeserved favour. He would resettle them in the Promised Land. Foreigners would be so impressed with them that they would attach themselves to Israel and convert to the worship of Yahweh (56:6-8).

2. A reversal of roles would take place. After the foreign nations had re-settled the people of God in the Promised Land, they would serve Israel once again, as in the glory days of David and Solomon. The ultimate fulfilment of this prophecy would have to wait until the Messiah had completed his work, when his followers would delight, like St Paul, to be slaves of Jesus the Messiah (Rom 1:1).

3. Yahweh would not only restore his people to their ancestral land, but also give them rest from the pains of their slave-labour while in exile. The deepest experiences of rest did not come during David's reign (2 Sam 7:1), nor during Solomon's (1 Ki 8:56). They would come later with the Messiah (Mt 11:28-30).

4. Then the people of God would be able to sing a song taunting their formidable oppressors. The most formidable would be Nebuchadnezzar, King of Babylon. The song begins by proclaiming the end of the oppressor. His insolence is ended. Once again, as in 1:21, both phrases begin with "How".

5. The staff or sceptre of a ruler is a symbol of his power. Yahweh has taken away all power from the wicked ruler who was addicted to it and revelled in it.

6. Some of the Babylonian Emperors used to strike down whole people groups in malevolent fury, raining blow after blow upon them. They would rule nations in anger, never ceasing to make people's lives even more difficult. Nebuchadnezzar in particular was an extremely powerful despot and dictator.

7. The world would sigh in relief at the passing of the King of Babylon. Turmoil would give way to rest, clamour to quiet. People everywhere would sing for joy.

8. Even the trees would be glad when this empire passed on. In contemporary accounts of the exploits of certain Assyrian Kings, they were described as fellers of giant trees. It was the same with the Babylonian Emperor Nebuchadnezzar. Tall cypresses and huge cedars would exult, for his demise assured their survival.

9. Sheol is the abode of the dead. In Old Testament belief, life continues after death.

Without the resurrection of the body life will, however, be shadowy and spectral. Sheol is consequently described as a gloomy and ghostly place. On the arrival of the King of Babylon it will bestir itself and rouse its inhabitants. The dead who dwell in Sheol are called *shades*, for their existence is shadowy and insubstantial. The *leaders* and the *kings of the nations* are equally ghostly, but they will recognise the newcomer and rise to greet him. Mighty they once were, but now they are feeble and Sheol itself must raise them from their thrones.

10. The shades welcome the King of Babylon with the crushing news that he is now as weak as they are. From now on he too will be nothing more than a shade!

11. It was the hedonistic pomp of this powerful ruler that led to his downfall. The sound of harps would no longer please his ear, for there was nothing in Sheol that could feed his pride or give him pleasure. Instead the Babylonian despot would lie on a bed of maggots and cover himself with a blanket of worms. Clearly Sheol is not equipped with the comforts of a five-star hotel. Hedonists would miss the standards of luxury that they once delighted in. Their self-importance and self-indulgence would be over. Death will leave no room for pride, and the previous pampering of the body will be remembered as what it was, an empty vanity.

Meditation: The Bully who made it to the very Top

The King of Babylon is presented to us here as a diabolically proud tyrant. He is the personification of worldly arrogance, being more civilised and cultured than his Assyrian counterparts, but nevertheless defying Yahweh and crushing other people in his insatiable greed for riches, luxury and power. His downfall means the downfall of malicious and oppressive bullying. It is good and right if we find satisfaction in the exposure and punishment of such ugly and cruel qualities.

Barry Webb writes that the personality of the King of Babylon "lies at the heart of every evil for which particular nations will be indicted in the following chapters. It also lies at the heart of all the horrendous acts of inhumanity which human beings and nations still commit against one another today. That is why the tone of this song should not cause us any embarrassment. This is no cheap gloating over the downfall of an enemy, but the satisfaction and delight which God's people rightly feel at his final victory over evil. The same note of celebration is heard [towards the end of the Bible (Rev 18)] where, once again, Babylon is a cypher for all that opposes God and his purposes".

Who was the King of Babylon mentioned in verse 4? The likeliest candidate may well be Nebuchadnezzar, for it was he who would conquer and destroy Jerusalem in 586 B.C., even though this would be over a century after Isaiah wrote this poem taunting him. The Bible gives us a mixed review of him. The prophet Jeremiah, a contemporary of King Nebuchadnezzar, seems to suggest that Yahweh longed for him to repent and for Babylon to be healed. Some attempts may have been made to bring this about (Jer 51:8-9).

In the book of Daniel (chapters 2, 3 and 4) a vivid picture is painted of the pride and despotism of King Nebuchadnezzar. Nevertheless, we read here that God was at work in his heart. This led the King of Babylon to suffer a fit of insanity which lasted seven years, after which he recovered his mind and praised God. He then acknowledged him as the Most High, saying "I, Nebuchadnezzar, praise and extol and honour the King of Heaven, for all his works are truth, and his ways are justice; and he is able to bring low those who walk in pride".

Did Nebuchadnezzar repent? Most theologians no longer consider the first half of the book of Daniel to be a historical account. His insanity is not mentioned in contemporary writings, although we are told that in his final years he began to behave irrationally, paying no attention to his sons or daughters, and becoming very suspicious of his sons. It is tempting to speculate whether Nebuchadnezzar may have been humbled in some way that left its mark in the narrative of Daniel. If so, this would explain the unexpectedly merciful end of the city of Babylon in spite of the terrible prophecies of its destruction. For Yahweh did promise that he would meet a humble and repentant sinner more than halfway (Jer 18:7-8, Ezek 18:21-23, 2 Chron 33:10-13).

XXIX

14:12-23 The Day Star falls from Heaven

12. Here are two further exclamations beginning with "How", as in v 4. The King of Babylon is taunted by those he once used to intimidate. Great is the fall of him who had been *Lucifer*, the Day Star and the son of Dawn! Greatly has he been brought down, he who had once laid low the nations!

13. Not only had he been an oppressive bully, he was also driven by selfish ambition. In his heart he had aspired to the highest position in heaven, above the very stars, seated amidst the very greatest. The *mount of assembly* is Mount Zaphon, where the Canaanite gods were said to meet, rather like the Greek gods on Mount Olympus. The King of Babylon worshipped a multiplicity of gods who were not God, and he fondly imagined himself to be one of them. There is a close link between Babylonian ambition and the idea of storming heaven. In Genesis 11:4, the builders of the tower of Babel laboured in order to reach the uttermost heights of God's space. Their consuming ambition was to make a name for themselves, so that they would not be nobodies scattered across the earth.

14. The King of Babylon wished to climb above the clouds and become like the Most High. The way he went about this was by exalting himself. There is a right way of being God-like, but it is not a question of self-aggrandisement or self-exaltation. Instead it involves self-sacrifice and self-giving (Phil 2:5-11).

15. Now the proud one has been brought very low, not only to Sheol but to its very depths. Such is the consequence of the "vaulting ambition that o'erleaps itself" (Shakespeare, *Macbeth*, Act 1, Scene 7). It was thought that there existed different degrees of unpleasantness in Sheol. This idea was later developed, and Jesus seemed to endorse it (Lk 12:46-48). In medieval times it was extended to hell, and Dante's *Inferno* famously described the nine circles of hell. The first was Limbo, and the other eight were for the besetting sins that characterised the damned (lust, gluttony, greed, wrath, heresy, violence, fraud and treachery).

16. Those who saw the dead body of the King of Babylon would marvel. Was this the man before whom the earth trembled? Was it he who shook kingdoms?

17. Was it he who turned green lands into deserts? Who overthrew cities? Who permanently exiled those who had held back their tribute?

18. Other kings lay in state in their own tombs, but not the King of Babylon.

19. He was utterly cast out, banished even from his grave. He was like putrid flesh rotting away at the bottom of the Pit, as if he had fallen in battle and been trampled underfoot. His covering would consist of other rotting corpses. This utter squalor was the consequence of his self-exaltation. Anyone who glories in his or her self will become completely repulsive, fit only for rejection.

20. The King of Babylon would not be joined with others who had died and been entombed. He would be forever alone, for he had destroyed his own land and killed his own people. A curse would be upon him; his very name would perish.

21. His descendants would inherit his guilt. They would not inherit the earth, nor would they rule over cities. Yahweh promised that such a destructive and proud royal line would not continue to perpetuity.

22. Yahweh would rise against his posterity. They would be completely cut off from Babylon. There would be no future for them.

23. Babylon itself would become swampland and the home of the hedgehog. The broom of Yahweh would sweep the final vestiges away, leaving only ruins.

Meditation: The diabolical Son of the Dawn

The second half of this poem has a cosmic element to it. This led the early church fathers to see in it a symbolic description of the revolt and fall of Satan. For this reason, *Lucifer* came into use as an alternative name for the devil. Together with Ezekiel 28:11-19, this passage seemed to provide an understanding of Satan's origins, and to answer a question which has been asked not only in medieval times but also in our own. Who created the devil? How could an altogether evil and devious being like him have come into being?

The answer suggested by Isaiah 14:3-23 and Ezekiel 28:11-19 is that Satan was originally Lucifer. Lucifer was one of the two archangels, the other one being Michael. They were supreme among all the creatures made by God, superior even to humans.

Michael and Lucifer occupied the second place among all living beings. Only God himself was greater than them.

Michael was perfectly happy with his position. He was humble before God and aspired to do well the jobs that God assigned to him. Lucifer, on the other hand, yearned to improve himself. Life was pretty good being number two behind God. But might it not be even better if he were to lift himself up to number one?

According to our passage, Lucifer therefore said in his heart, "I will ascend to heaven; I will raise my throne above the stars of God" (v 13). He went on, "I will ascend to the tops of the clouds, I will make myself like the Most High" (v 14). In our passage these blasphemous feelings are attributed to the King of Babylon (v 4), but on account of their cosmic nature they sound as if they might have been uttered much earlier by a being of a different type. Angels and archangels were already around in the primeval stage of creation, before God created the universe and other living creatures such as humans. It is not implausible to argue that it was Lucifer who spoke to himself in this way. And it was Lucifer who fell as a result, for he was brought down to Sheol, to the depths of the Pit (v 15).

Similar impieties are ascribed by the Prophet Ezekiel to the Prince of Tyre. *Thus says Yahweh: Because your heart is proud and you have said, "I am a god; I sit in the seats of the gods in the heart of the seas", yet you are but a mortal, and no god, though you compare your mind with the mind of a god (Ezek 28:2). Therefore thus says Yahweh: because you compare your mind with the mind of a god, therefore . . . strangers from the most terrible of the nations . . . shall thrust you down into the Pit, and you shall die a violent death in the heart of the seas (Ezek 28:6-8). Thus says Yahweh: You were the signet of perfection, full of wisdom and perfect in beauty. You were in Eden, the garden of God; every precious stone was your covering, carnelian, chrysolite, and moonstone, beryl, onyx, and jasper, sapphire, turquoise, and emerald; and worked in gold were your settings and your engravings. On the day that you were created they were prepared. With an anointing cherub as guardian I placed you; you were on the holy mountain of God; you walked among the stones of fire. You were blameless in your ways from the day that you were created, until iniquity was found in you. In the abundance of your trade you were filled with violence and you sinned; so I cast you as a profane thing from the mountain of God, and the guardian cherub drove you out from among the stones of fire. Your heart was proud because of your beauty; you corrupted your wisdom for the sake of your splendour. I cast you to the ground . . . I brought out fire from within you; it consumed you . . . You have come to a dreadful end and shall be no more forever* (Ezek 28:12-19).

The interpretation that these are the thoughts and words that led to Satan's fall is not unattractive. Some of these thoughts and words, attributed to the King of Babylon and the Prince of Tyre, are more suggestive of a fallen archangel than of powerful despotic men. This interpretation also gives us an answer to the difficult question about the origin of the devil. Furthermore, it seems to agree with certain New Testament texts such as Luke 10:18 and Revelation 12:9.

However, there are several commentators who suggest that the cosmic references are inspired not by Yahweh's heavenly council but by a heathen Canaanite Pantheon. They also point out that when the Bible speaks about Satan's fall in other passages, it seems to be referring to the eventual final defeat of his present evil regime rather than to a hypothetical previous fall from grace. If this is so, perhaps the old medieval interpretation about Satan's origin is not authoritatively taught in the Bible. The cosmic grandeur of v 12-14 may point to Babylon as being symbolic of the proud, worldly and despotic city, as in the final book of the Bible (Rev 18:1-24). This tidies everything up very neatly, but we are left with an unanswered question. Who created the devil?

XXX

14:24-32 The Fate of Assyrians and Philistines

Isaiah has described worldly pride and power, as symbolised by Babylon, and he has made it clear that God will condemn it. Now the prophet turns to the other nations. The two short oracles in this section were delivered at different times during Isaiah's ministry. The one in verses 24-27 concerns Assyria. It reiterates the threat hanging over Judah because of the treaty that King Ahaz had forged with Assyria in 735 B.C. (see 10:5-34), and it dates from a year or two after this. The Assyrian power would be broken in the land of Judah. The one in verses 28-32 was written later, and refers to the Philistines. They came to King Hezekiah in 716 B.C. to propose a joint rebellion against Assyria.

24. Yahweh has given his word. Isaiah stresses that the designs which God has decided upon will happen. They will come to pass exactly as he planned them.

25. The Assyrians would be broken by a crippling blow – and this would happen in the land of Judah, at a time when God's people were at their most vulnerable. The corpses of the Assyrians would be trodden on in the mountains of Judah. The yoke and burden of Assyria would be taken away from the land of promise – for ever. Not infrequently God's mightiest manifestations of power seem to take place when his servants are at their weakest (Acts 4:27-31).

26. The plan concocted by the mighty Assyrians was one thing (10:12-13). The King of Assyria thought that it would have earth-shattering ramifications. In his opinion, it was his own hand that controlled the destiny of nations. His aim was universal empire, and surely nothing could come in his way.

27. The plan devised by Yahweh was altogether different (10:15-19). What *he* had purposed would certainly not be overruled by any man. Once *his* hand had been stretched out, no one could possibly turn it back. Isaiah knew that Yahweh ruled over the world in absolute sovereignty. He was working out his plans. Nothing could frustrate Yahweh's purposes, and the events of history would gradually confirm Isaiah's words, and reveal the wonderful and grandiose details of God's great master plan.

28. We now switch forward to the year 716 B.C., just after King Ahaz had died. It was he who had forged an alliance with Assyria 19 years earlier. The oracle that follows came to the Prophet Isaiah.

29. At that time Assyria was experiencing certain difficulties with some of her more powerful neighbours, notably the Babylonians, and her mighty army no longer looked invincible. The Philistines were then involved in an anti-Assyrian alliance with some other small nations and Egypt (see chapter 20, especially v 1: Ashdod was in Philistia). The Philistines were delighted at what seemed to be an unexpected vulnerability among the Assyrians. They therefore sent a delegation to King Hezekiah of Judah to urge him to join them in a revolt against Assyria (see v 32). But the rod that had struck them in the past was not yet broken: worse was yet to come. Because the mighty King Shalmaneser of Assyria had died six years earlier, in 722 B.C., it looked as if the snake might have been rendered harmless. But from its root came an adder in the shape of the new King, Sargon. He would prove to be a flying fiery serpent.

30. The rejoicing of the Philistines was unfounded. True blessings come not from this world, nor from its power and its riches, but from God. The poorest of the poor would enjoy the rural life, and the needy of Judah would lie down in safety. It was Philistia that was now doomed. Their stock would be wiped away by famine, and their remnant would be killed by the Assyrians.

31. The gates of the Philistine cities would wail, and the cities themselves would cry. The people of Philistia would melt in fear at what was coming. The dust was already rising in the north. Myriads of brutal Assyrian soldiers were on the march. Several Philistine cities would be destroyed in 715 B.C.

32. King Hezekiah was facing a very demanding test, just as his father had 19 years earlier (see 7:1-17). Should he trust Yahweh or enter into military alliances? What answer should he give to the Philistine delegation? Isaiah urged the King of Judah not to enter into intrigues, but to trust in God. Hezekiah decided that the prophet was right: "Yahweh has founded Zion, and the needy among his people will find refuge in *her*".

Meditation: The Reiteration of basic Lessons

In this section Isaiah returns to two of his favourite and recurring themes. The first is that nothing can frustrate Yahweh's sovereign purposes. The second, that it is possible to live in peace and security, with no fear of being overrun by bullying neighbours, provided that we ourselves fear God and trust in him.

In verses 24-27 there is a remarkable prophecy about Assyria. Their vast army, which would pose a growing threat to God's people, would be decisively crushed in the mountains around Jerusalem, and this event would be witnessed by the people of that city. We have already encountered the prophecy that the Assyrian army would be devoured by a wasting sickness in a single day (10:16-19). We are now informed that this would happen in the uplands of Judah. And it did actually happen there, on the mountains around Jerusalem. The prophecy was fulfilled in history. This act of God, attested and verified by witnesses, would be a demonstration to the world that the rule of Yahweh extended to all the nations, and that his purposes were being worked out among all the peoples. This is one of the lessons we learn from the prophecies concerning the heathen nations in chapters 13-23. Clearly God is concerned for his people: that is obvious. But here we learn that he is concerned for everyone else in the world *as well*. God wants all people to learn that when they are in real trouble and are looking around for someone to help, they should look to *him*. Because he is both powerful and loving, he is both able and willing to help.

Then in v 28-32 we have the short oracle about the Philistines. They had sent an embassy to King Hezekiah in Jerusalem in 716 B.C. to ask him to join in an alliance against mighty Assyria. Egypt was the strong card in the pack: with Philistia and Judah as partners (among others), she might defeat the Assyrians, who were then busy holding off the growing Babylonian menace. It was just as well that Hezekiah decided not to join Philistia and Egypt in their anti-Assyrian alliance. Soon the Assyrian army would mass itself against the enfeebled Philistines. They would utterly crush them in 715 B.C., and so fulfil the prophecy of v 31. Later on Egypt would likewise be defeated by the Assyrians. Judah did not take part in the rebellion, and was therefore spared – for the time being. The weakness of Assyria in 716 B.C. was only temporary. Rumours of their imminent demise were simply not true. Once they had repelled the army of the Babylonians, the Assyrians would attain the zenith of their power, first under Sargon and later under Sennacherib.

The only sure refuge for God's people was, and still is, Yahweh himself. If only they trusted in him, there would be no need for them to panic (28:16). Hezekiah was a godly King, but the son of Ahaz was sorely tempted to follow in his father's faithless footsteps. It needed considerable prophetic encouragement on the part of Isaiah for Hezekiah to keep trusting in Yahweh. He did so – just!

XXXI

15:1-9 Moab will be defeated and must flee

This oracle concerns Moab. Moab himself was the son of one of Lot's daughters. He was therefore related to Abraham (Gen 19:36-37). All the Moabites were his descendants. Ruth the Moabitess was a grandmother of King David. Despite these family ties with Israel, the Moabites did not worship Yahweh. Sometimes they led God's people astray (Num 25:1-5), or rebelled against them (2 Ki 3:4-7). The oracle can be dated to 718 B.C., three years before the destruction of Moab in 715 B.C. by a regiment of the Assyrian army sent by Sargon.

1. Ar was the capital of Moab and was located on its northern border, on the banks of the Wadi Arnon (Num 21:15, 28; Deut 2:18). Kir was Moab's chief stronghold Kir-hareseth or Kir-heres (16:7, 11). Once Kir had been laid waste in one night, all would be lost for the Moabites. The earlier loss of Ar, their main city, would have plunged every Moabite into despair.

2. Those who dwelt in Dibon would go to their little "temple" on the high places, where they used to worship their idols. These idols would now prove useless to them. Their wailing would be the cries of despair of people with no hope, who had put their trust in false idols rather than in the one true God worshipped by their distant relatives. Dibon, Nebo and Medeba were small settlements in Moab, north of Kir, all placed on the King's Highway (Num 21:21-30).

3. There would be mourning in the streets. People would wear uncomfortable and itchy sackcloth, thinking that God might hear their cries if they inconvenienced themselves in this way. They would wail loudly in the village squares and on the housetops, shedding many tears.

4. Heshbon, Elealeth and Jahaz were also on the King's Highway, north of Kir. They, together with three other settlements mentioned in v 2, would depend on Kir to resist the invasion. Once Kir fell, all hope would be lost for Moab.

5. Zoar was to the south in Edom, near the Dead Sea (Gen 19:20-22). Eglath-Shelishiyah is unknown. Luhith and Horonaim were also south of Moab. The fact that those who dwelt in Kir would flee to the south suggests that the invaders would come from the north. They would be a regiment of the Assyrian army, sent by Sargon, King of Assyria, to destroy Moab and either slaughter or resettle its people. The anguish described by this verse is intense, and a similar grief is conveyed in 16:7, 9 and 11. It was rare in those days to lament the ravages of war, and even rarer to express sadness for the fall of an enemy, but there are numerous examples of these sensitive reactions in the Old Testament. Here the speaker is Isaiah, and he speaks for God: "My heart cries out". The spokesman of Yahweh reveals Yahweh's heart. It is God himself who laments the plight of the Moabites.

6. The site of Nimrim is also unknown to us, but Isaiah grieves because of the destruction of their water supply and the consequent desertification of the fields.

7. The refugees carry their treasured possessions with them as they flee. In hope mixed with despair they cross over the Wadi of the Willows. This may be the Brook Zered that marked the frontier between Moab and Edom.

8. A cry of utter grief and hopelessness is heard throughout Moab. The wailing is heard from Eglaim to Beer-Elim, two locations at either extreme of Moab, their equivalent of the Israelite "Dan and Beersheba".

9. Much blood stains the waters of Dibon, which are red. But even more grief will come to Dibon. This time we hear the words of Yahweh himself. The remnant that escaped the massacre would have to face "a lion". The ferocious Assyrian army would destroy both the fugitives and the remnant who remained in Moab.

Meditation: God weeps as he smites

It occasionally happens that I see a person who has wronged me in the past embarking on a course of action that will lead to his unhappiness or disaster. How should I react? I cannot just sit back and be happy that he is about to be receive divine retribution. Love cannot rejoice when disaster befalls an enemy, for love is always positive: it rejoices not in the misfortunes of others but in what is good and right for them (1 Cor 13:6-7). So what can I do? I may try to warn this person, knowing full well that because of what happened in the past anything that I now say to him will be counterproductive, and my warnings will probably settle and establish him in his wrongdoing. Perhaps it might be better if I prayed for him, that God might intervene in some way that would bring him to his senses.

Wisdom says, "Do not rejoice when your enemies fall, and do not let your heart be glad when they stumble" (Prov 24:17). St Paul says, "Rejoice with those who rejoice, weep with those who weep" (Rom 12:15). What does Isaiah say?

Isaiah and the people of Judah would have been well acquainted with their distant relatives from Moab. In spite of historical disagreements and a few lingering grudges, not all the Jewish people would have rejoiced at the news that a severe judgement was about to be meted out to their neighbours. Isaiah was deeply moved by the vision he saw of what would happen to Moab. His sympathy is evident. He wished he could have helped the Moabites in their time of great need, but he and his followers were powerless and could not intervene. Maybe this oracle would have been read out to some of the Moabites in order to warn them of their future downfall. If so, a few of them may have responded by fleeing to Judah in good time, prior to the arrival of God's judgement in the form of the destructive Assyrian army.

The tone of this lament is different to that of 14:3-23. There the King of Babylon was at least in part a representative figure, standing for the evil and pride that lie at the root of every sin. His punishment is symbolic of God's final defeat of evil. As Barry Webb writes, it should be possible "to rejoice in God's victory over evil without taking pleasure in the death of any individual or nation". Isaiah would not and did not gloat at the downfall of Israel's distant relatives in Moab.

In verses 5-9 we read of the desperate straits to which the Moabites were going to be reduced. Isaiah's grief implies that the suffering and despair of the Moabites affected God deeply. Alec Motyer memorably writes that Yahweh "weeps as he smites", and that "the grief of the judge of all the earth is one of the striking truths of this oracle". This profoundly moving fact cannot be put across without using clearly anthropomorphic language. God is holy, so he must judge and punish. God is also loving, so as he judges and punishes there are tears in his eyes.

For Yahweh there was no contradiction between loving the people he had created and warning them clearly of the judgement to come. Because he loved the people of Moab, he had to warn them and carry out his promises of judgement. Because he had to judge and punish evil, he forewarned the Moabites of certain disaster unless they turned to him by coming to live in Judah (16:4).

XXXII

16:1-14 Moab's Hope, Pride and Fall

1. The Moabite refugees would try to settle at Sela, which was in Edom by the fords of the Wadi Arnon (v2). Here they would perhaps consider whether to seek their home in Judah and become vassals of God's people. They were sheep-raisers, so Isaiah urges them to send some lambs as tribute, via the desert path, to King Hezekiah who lived on Mount Zion in Jerusalem.

2. By the fords of the Arnon they would feel homeless and insecure, like fluttering birds or scattered nestlings. Their hearts would be restless, for they had never found their rest in Yahweh.

3. Isaiah imagines God's people as they respond to the plea of some Moabites for refuge in Judah. He urges the people of Judah to be welcoming and caring towards these refugees. They should advise them where to settle, deal justly with them, and provide them with shelter in their fiery trial. Far from betraying them to the Assyrians, they should protect them from any further attack. The Land of Promise was not for the exclusive use of the Israelites. It was also for those from heathen nations who came to it for refuge. They were to be granted a secure place in it.

4. Isaiah urges the people of Judah to allow these outcasts to settle in God's land, and thereby protect them from being destroyed by the Assyrians. The time would come, says Isaiah, when every oppressor would depart and all destruction would be a thing of the past. No more marauders would seek plunder in the ravaged lands. Judah would be able to offer Moab a peaceful future, characterised by righteousness. Isaiah does not say how long this would take. Alec Motyer writes, "The promises of God do not offer immunity from earth's trials, and the Bible does not entice by unreal expectations. It is the way of faith to accept life as it comes and to see behind it the hand of God".

5. In the ideal future revealed to Isaiah the Messiah would be enthroned. His kingdom would be marked by steadfast love. The Messiah would be a descendant

of David. He would rule faithfully and seek justice. He would speedily do what was necessary to put right whatever was wrong. When the Moabites came to Judah in their despair and great need, they would unconditionally be offered the best that Judah had. They would be invited to join in the Messianic kingdom. This is a reminder that the Messiah's blessings were not confined to Judah and Israel.

6. Only now does Isaiah reveal the reason why Yahweh had decided to judge and punish Moab. It does not surprise us to read that it was because the Moabites were extremely proud. Their manner was arrogant and insolent. In particular, they loved to boast, but their boasts were empty and false.

7. It is on account of the pride of her people that Moab must now wail, and others would also wail for them. The Moabites would be wiped out, and the celebrated raisin-cakes that they used to produce in Kir would be a thing of the past. Never again would the Moabites enjoy them.

8. No more raisins would be available because there would be no more Moabite vineyards. Their fields in Heshbon and Sibmah would languish. Those fields once produced huge clusters of grapes, which were used to make wine that was drunk in large quantities by rulers of the surrounding nations. Moabite wine was famed in adjacent lands across the desert, as well as in more distant lands across the sea.

9. Isaiah weeps for the wine of Moab, which would be missed by many. Other nations would join the regions of Moab in lamenting the demise of their wine industry. The Moabites would no longer loudly celebrate their annual vintage.

10. The fruitful fields would no longer be acclaimed with joy and gladness, and songs would no longer be heard in the vineyards. Those who used to tread the grapes would no longer do their work in the presses, and the vintage shout would be replaced by the pitiful silence of those who had been visited by disaster.

11. Isaiah was deeply upset by the sadness of it all. His heart throbbed for Moab, and his very soul mourned for the loss of their stronghold at Kir. From the brash and heady heights of boasting, the Moabites had plummeted down to the deepest troughs of despair and destitution.

12. There is a pun in this verse. We might say, when the Moabites *arrived* and *writhed* at the high place of prayer, all the prayers that they prayed there would be useless. The gods of Moab were no gods. They were utterly incapable of saving Moab in their day of great need.

13. In the past similar prophecies had been spoken about Moab.

14. But now Yahweh sets a time limit for their repentance. Moab has three years in which to join the people of Judah and worship the Holy One of Israel. These "three years of a hired worker" would pass by very quickly, for hired workers counted the days of their hire and did not labour for a single day more than the

contracted period specified. When those three years were up, the great majority of Moabites would be brought into contempt. Now they were a multitude; then only some survivors would remain, and they would be "very few and feeble".

Meditation: The timeless Nature of God's Word

Isaiah's prophecy concerning the Moabites has a remarkably contemporary feel about it. It has much to say about two growing trends in the 21st century: our inclination to leave the poor to their own fate, and our tendency to be proud of what we believe to be our own personal achievements.

In verses 1-5 we have the Bible's answer to the question, what can we do to help people who are refugees or are in some other way lost and leading a purposeless existence? The Moabites were like fluttering birds or scattered nestlings (v 2). Their land had been ravaged, their homes destroyed, and their fields laid waste. They were in despair about the future. They were perhaps considering whether to seek asylum in neighbouring Judah (v 1). How were God's people to react to their overtures and their despairing cries for help?

Isaiah proclaims Yahweh's words for this eventuality. First of all, God's people were to offer practical help and hospitality to the refugees: "Give counsel, grant justice; make your shade like night at the height of noon; hide the outcasts, do not betray the fugitive; let the outcasts of Moab settle among you; be a refuge to them from the destroyer" (v 3-4a). Secondly, they were to introduce the Moabites to the God who alone could meet their deepest needs, namely Yahweh. A future time was on its way "When the oppressor [would be] no more, and destruction [would have] ceased, and marauders [would] have vanished from the land" (v 4b). A new order would come into being. "Then a throne shall be established in steadfast love in the tent of David, and on it shall sit in faithfulness a ruler who seeks justice and is swift to do what is right" (v 5). The Messiah, who would be a descendant of David, would one day be the great King. He, unlike every ruler before him, would rule with perfect justice and always do what was right.

The duty of the followers of the Holy One of Israel towards the refugee was very *challenging*, not least because in this case the refugee had been a long-term enemy. They were to offer practical help, as far as they were able, and also share the good news of the God whom they knew and loved, who would send his Messiah to rescue them from their troubles and give them a future. For this same God would declare to them and to those they had helped, "I know the plans I have for you, says Yahweh, plans for your welfare and not for harm, to give you a *future with hope*" (Jer 29:11).

The problem the Moabites had, and which all modern people seem to have also, was the problem of *pride*. Isaiah exposed it starkly; "We have heard of the pride of Moab – how proud he is! – Of his arrogance, his pride and his insolence; his boasts are false" (v 6). What exactly was it that the Moabites were so proud of? From the context, it would appear to have been *their exceedingly good export wine* (v 7-11). They were like some people today who proudly boast that they are great *connoisseurs* of wine, who own bottles of rare and excellent vintages, or who own vineyards that yield superlative grapes for wine-making. But even though their excellent vineyards were a gift from God, the Moabites boasted about them as if the wine was their own achievement. They might have been brought to their senses by some questions posed some 770 years later. "For who sees anything different in you? What do you have that you did not receive? And if you received it, why do you boast as if it were not a gift?" (1 Cor 4:7).

It is interesting that in a later oracle about Moab, the Prophet Jeremiah returned to the theme of viticulture: "Moab has been at ease from his youth, settled like wine on its dregs; he has not been emptied from vessel to vessel, nor has he gone into exile; therefore his flavour has remained and his aroma is unspoiled" (Jer 48:11). For a long time Moab had had an easy existence, but this was a fatal ease. Sheer cliffs provided them with good defences; sheep and vineyards brought them great wealth. The problem was that shelter and wealth can breed complacency. To be continually undisturbed may be good for wines but it is not necessarily good for people. Sometimes to be emptied from one vessel to another can bring both a new holiness and a long-term fruitfulness to the lives of Christians who have never previously been through the mill.

What happened when Sargon's troops mercilessly overran Moab in 715 B.C.? Perhaps a very small number of refugees would have heeded Isaiah's oracle and escaped to Judah. Most of the Moabites would have been killed or exiled. Most of those who escaped would have gone up to their high places. There they would have prayed to their heathen gods and their idols, but their prayers would have been in vain (v12). As Alec Motyer put it, "The way of faith is the way of realism, of facing life as it really is. To reject the way of faith for the way of self-confident pride and boasting is to retreat into a dream world, except that its consequences are far from dreamlike". Outside of Yahweh's promises there can be no salvation. Pride is deadly because self-reliance inhibits a spirit of trust in him.

XXXIII

17:1-14 Damascus and the Northern Tribes

In this passage we return to Isaiah's early ministry in the years around 735 A.D. The Syrians had formed an alliance with Israel (meaning the northern ten tribes). They had attempted to force King Ahaz of Judah to join them in a hopeless revolt against Assyria (7:1-9). Ahaz decided to join the enemy instead. Judah became a vassal state of Assyria. Rather than rely on Yahweh to protect Judah from small enemies like Syria and Israel, Ahaz had linked hands with the superpower of his time. This would bring great hardship to God's people in future years.

1. Syria (known then as Aram), and in particular her capital Damascus, is briefly informed of the fate that awaits her people (v1-3). Damascus would cease to be

the city of the Arameans, for Aram would cease to be a nation. Her towns would be turned into heaps of ruins when Assyria destroyed them, and Damascus itself would fall after a lengthy siege in 732 B.C., and become just an administrative centre of an Assyrian province.

2. The smaller towns of Aram would become desolate and deserted places where flocks of livestock could come and lie down in peace, unmolested by people.

3. The ten northern tribes, which were referred to as Israel or as Ephraim (their largest tribe) until their destruction in 722 B.C., now receive an extended rebuke. The very fact that they are linked together with Aram, and classed among the heathen nations, is eloquent in itself. Ephraim would lose its fortress in Samaria, and Damascus would no longer be part of the kingdom of Aram. Both prophecies are mentioned in the same breath. Also mentioned together are the two remnants: the sad and scanty survivors of Aram, and what would remain of the former glory of ten of Jacob's sons.

4. The glory days would be over. "On that day", the day appointed by Yahweh for the humbling of man's pride (2:9-12), the glory of these ten tribes would be brought low. Few would survive the coming judgement. The ten fat tribes would, as it were, be struck with skeletal leanness. Their proud beauty would be replaced by the despair of utter destitution.

5. Their land would be subject to depredation, and all its richness would be taken away. Their people would be put to the sword. Those who were spared would be exiled. Only a few, the gleanings after the reapers had passed by, would be left.

6. Their people would also be like an olive grove whose trees had been beaten hard and only a handful of olives remained. The survivors would be two or three from one tribe, four or five from another. This was Yahweh's word.

7. These gleanings, however, would fulfil God's purpose for the northern tribes. Although only a tiny number would be left, "on that day" they would *at last* worship their Maker instead of the idols they had made. This did duly happen (2 Chron 30:10-12, 25), and it was a remarkable encouragement for the godly King Hezekiah. The "ten lost tribes" would not be lost in their entirety.

8. No longer would the Israelites look admiringly at their incense altars or their poles for the worship of Asherah, who was the consort of their chief Canaanite god El. They had made the poles and the altars with their own hands, and then proceeded to worship them. But no good had ever come their way on account of their idolatry. The people would finally realise the folly of worshipping idols made by their fingers, instead of Yahweh who had made *them* (v7).

9. "On that day" the strong walled Israelite cities would all be captured and destroyed, just as the Israelites themselves had captured and destroyed the walled cities of the Hivites and the Amorites when they conquered the Promised Land. Once again the result would be desolation.

10. Why did this tragedy befall the Israelites? What Syria had done was bad enough: her people lived in God's world without God. But the ten tribes began to indulge in blatant idolatry as soon as they seceded from Judah and Benjamin (1 Ki 12:25-33). From the beginning, they followed the way of Jeroboam the son of Nebat, who caused Israel to sin. This distracted them from following Yahweh with a single mind, and led them into convenient alliances (such as the one with Syria) instead of simply trusting in their God. Now Yahweh rebukes them, saying, "You have forgotten the God of your salvation, and have not remembered the Rock of your refuge". They had deceived themselves by planting "pleasant plants" and setting out "slips" (i.e. cuttings) "of an alien god". This was an ancient rite they had learnt from the Canaanites who dwelt there before they moved in and dispossessed them. Plants and slips alike were taken to a hilltop shrine (such as the gardens of 1:29), and were induced to grow and blossom at an artificially rapid rate. The speed of growth would have been associated with the power of fertility of the heathen god worshipped at that shrine. But this god was no God, and what the Israelites had done was abandon their God, who was Yahweh, the one true God.

11. So the Israelites planted their exotic plants, force-feeding them with excessive compost and too much exposure to the sun. The initial growth was remarkable, but the plants would soon wither and perish. This could have dampened the hope of the heathen worshippers and discredited the idol they worshipped at that shrine. It did not. Idolatry was like rot: it set in and continued. As a result, when the day appointed by Yahweh duly arrived, it would not be just these harvests in the high places that would "flee away in a day of grief and incurable pain". The Israelites themselves would also be forced to attempt flight so as not to be struck down.

12. God's instrument for punishing the ten tribes would be the mighty Assyrian army. Verses 12-14 confirm the prophecies of 7:8 and 8:4. Isaiah returns to the simile of a vast river in flood, as in 8:7.

13. This time Isaiah likens the Assyrians to the roaring of many waters, to huge waves that overwhelm and kill everyone in their wake. But Yahweh would rebuke them, and those waters would then be like chaff that is chased by the wind. Thus far God would allow them to come, but no further. Their master was not the King of Assyria but Yahweh. He would use them and later he would discard them.

14. In due course, the day of Yahweh would also come for the Assyrian army. One evening sudden terror would grip them. One by one they would fall down, mortally ill. By the next morning 185,000 would have died. This would be the fate of those who had despoiled and plundered the northern tribes of Israel in 734 B.C. and 722 B.C. It was a few years later, in 701 B.C., that the extraordinary event would take place. It would be witnessed by Isaiah and by the citizens

of Jerusalem. One day their besiegers were intimidating them, completely in control, and the next day they were all dead (37:36).

Meditation: The Folly of heathen Cuttings

Verses 10 and 11 of Isaiah chapter 17 are obscure but repay close attention. The "pleasant plants" planted by the northern Israelites were pots of flowers that grew and withered quickly. The Canaanites used to place them in the high places where they worshipped their heathen gods. There are indications in ancient writings that the god known to the Greeks as *Adonis* and to the Hebrews as *Tammuz* was also known by the name *Naman*, which is here translated "pleasant".

The Israelites chose plants that would germinate and grow quickly. There would be observable growth "on the day", and blossoming "in the morning" that they were sown (v 11). This unnaturally rapid growth was a form of imitative magic. The Canaanite gods were more like impersonal forces than personal beings, so they could not be influenced by ordinary prayers. Because of this the worshippers would perform an action that in some way matched what they wanted their god to do, hoping in this way to prompt him into action. They believed that the sexual rites of Baal worship might succeed in rousing him so that he might bring fertility to the land, to the animals and to the people. Likewise the planting of "pleasant plants" and the setting out of cuttings "of an alien god", which resulted in quick germination, might succeed in prompting Baal to act quickly.

Isaiah made the point that however successful their enterprise may have seemed in its early stages, it was doomed to failure in the long run. This was primarily because Baal and the other Canaanite deities were *not* the one true God (v 7, 8). They were worshipped in the form of idols, and those idols were made by man. Yahweh was the great creator who made man. He therefore was the one true God, worthy of being worshipped by his creatures. He was also the God of Israel, who promised to look after his people. He was the *Holy One of Israel*, whom most of the northern Israelites had abandoned in favour of heathen idols.

The northern Israelites had been given a big clue about the falsehood of their idols. They may have succeeded in making their pleasant plants and their slips of an alien god grow very quickly. But they would also have seen the consequence of force-feeding and over-heating their plants. They withered away as quickly as they had grown and blossomed. Their rapid growth was not a harbinger of potent fertility, but of death. Up in the high places the harvest would always "flee away" (v 11). This pointed not to Baal's potency but to his utter incompetence to bring fertility. And the Israelites would reap the consequences of their false and foolish worship. They would reap a harvest of death. They would flee away – "in a day of grief and incurable pain".

Why would they have to suffer like this? Because they had forgotten the God of their salvation (v 10). In Hebrew "the God of your salvation" is one word, *Yesha*, which was very close indeed both to Isaiah's own name, and to the name that would be given to the Messiah when he was eventually born in 5 B.C. "The God of your salvation" is a great name for God. God is a God who saves: this is one of his greatest attributes. As Alec Motyer points out in his commentary, Israel could never say, "Ah, but he will not save now", for he is ever the saving God. Nor could they say, "Ah, but he will not save us now", for he is "your" saving God. Had they placed their faith in *Yesha*, they need never have been visited by a day of grief and incurable pain.

Alec Motyer also points out that the non-Biblical religions invariably encourage *human initiative* in a way that seeks to manipulate and thereby bring about a divine response. The Judeo-Christian religion of the Bible tells of the *divine initiative* and presents the character and intentions of God in a way that seeks to bring into being responsive faith and intelligent prayer. Because it is impossible to manipulate God, the only alternative is to trust him.

XXXIV

18:1-7 The Destiny of Ethiopia

1. The text mentions Cush, which was also called Ethiopia, but the words "beyond the rivers" point to what is now Sudan, just beyond the Atbara and Blue Nile rivers. This is a land where insects abound, hence the "whirring wings".

2. In 715 B.C. Piankhi, ruler of what was then Ethiopia but is now Sudan, took control over Egypt, founded the twenty-fifth dynasty, and began to assert himself on the world stage. He sent envoys from Sudan to all the Palestinian nations, promising them Egyptian aid if they rebelled against Assyria. The envoys sent to Jerusalem travelled along the Nile, on which they sailed in vessels made of papyrus. The people of Cush were tall and smooth, and their reputation was fearsome. And yet Yahweh had made it clear that the envoys had no business in Jerusalem. Through Isaiah, his mouthpiece, he dismissed them: "Go!"

3. God's people were not to enter into foreign alliances that might involve the worship of foreign deities. Yahweh's will was that they should wait for *him*. Isaiah now invites all the peoples of the earth to observe the just retribution that Yahweh has in store for Assyria. Her mighty army would reach the mountains around Jerusalem. At that desperate moment Yahweh would raise a signal, and the nations would see. The trumpets would sound, and the peoples would hear.

4. In the meantime Yahweh would work out his purposes behind the scenes. From his dwelling he observes the actions of men with immense calmness, "like clear heat in sunshine, like a cloud of dew in the heat of harvest". He is present but unseen, quiet but purposeful. He provides the warmth and dew that are necessary for a great harvest. When his own appointed time arrives, he reaps it.

5. The moment when Yahweh would reap would be when the blossom was over, and the grapes were ripening. The Assyrian army would succeed in surrounding the city of Jerusalem, but when their victory was certain, they would be cut down. It would be as when the reaper of the vintage cuts off shoots with pruning hooks, and hews away any branches that are spreading.

6. Suddenly, at the moment when they were about to consummate a magnificent triumph, the foreign invaders would all die. The soaring birds of prey and the animals of the land would take it in turn to consume their corpses.

7. When the right moment came, the Ethiopians – tall and smooth, feared near and far, mighty and conquering – would be welcome in Jerusalem. They would bring acceptable gifts for Yahweh. They would come once again from their own land to Mount Zion. The second time round they would not be trying to negotiate an alliance against Assyria. Their purpose then would be to get to know Yahweh, the Holy One of Israel. They would bring gifts in homage to him. Perhaps the meaning of this is that they would themselves be the homage gifts.

Meditation: No to political Scheming

Speaking around 705 B.C., Isaiah had a warning for the Egyptian-Cushite nation. The anti-Assyrian alliance that their envoys were seeking to form was bound to fail, and they would be ravaged by the Assyrian army. But Assyria would not be allowed to continue their depredations and devastations. Yahweh was quietly taking note of events. He would wait until Assyria was ripe for destruction. When the moment came, Yahweh would raise a signal and have trumpets blown. The Cushites would see and hear the sudden miracle. They would then send a tribute-gift, possibly themselves, to Mount Zion, which was the place of the name of Yahweh, the Lord of the armies.

This mysterious passage is also "An oracle concerning Egypt" (19:1). It comes in a section (chapters 18, 19 and 20) on the role of Egypt in God's purposes. It also looks back to the previous three verses (17:12-14), repeating the prophecy about the destruction through deadly sickness of the entire Assyrian army.

Assyria and Egypt were the leading players in an ongoing battle for control of the Fertile Crescent, which encompassed the territory from the Nile to the Euphrates. The small nations in between them included Philistia, Moab and Judah (also in earlier years Syria and Israel, before they were destroyed by Assyria). These countries were all too weak to stand up to either of the main powers. They were consequently always eyeing up alliances, either led by Assyria against Egypt, or (in this case) led by Egypt against Assyria. Some concerted diplomatic activity was being carried out. Envoys travelled long distances in order to cement these alliances. Egypt had already got Philistia on their side (14:28-32), and now a delegation of Cushites had arrived in Jerusalem in order to try and bring the people of Judah on board too. Would they succeed? If so, it would begin to be a sizeable alliance.

In this oracle, Isaiah provided clear guidance for King Hezekiah as he pondered whether to join an anti-Assyrian alliance led by Egypt. The word of Yahweh was "No". The envoys must be told to "Go" (v2). The people of God were not to join in alliances with or against superpowers. There were three reasons for this.

The first reason is that the trust and confidence of God's people should be placed not in powerful men but in God. Once they were steadily and consistently relying on God, those who did not know God would be drawn to them and, through them, to God himself (v7). This theme recurs in the book of Isaiah. We have already seen it in 2:3 and 11:10. It would be repeated in greater detail in chapters 60, 61, and 62. It is a theme that is also found elsewhere in the Old Testament. It is joyfully expressed in some of the Psalms (e.g. Ps 68:31-35 and Ps 87:1-4).

The second reason why God's people should not be drawn into an alliance with Egypt was that such an alliance would undoubtedly fail against the might of Assyria, which was still unbroken. This is why this oracle begins with "Ah" or "Woe" (18:1). Even with the help of the Egyptian army, the alliance had no chance. As we shall see, Egypt would be soundly defeated.

The third reason was that when the time came for foolhardy Assyria to attack Judah, she would take on not only the weakness of Judah but also the unbeatable might of the Almighty. Isaiah was convinced that Assyria's pride would come before a mighty fall. Time after time he prophesied the doom of the Assyrian army. How right he was we shall see in due course.

XXXV

19:1-15 The Folly of Egypt

The chapters on Egypt illustrate the great truth (stated in so many words in 19:22) that God strikes in order to heal. Egypt would be broken down, but she would later be remarkably renewed. The people of God kept on hankering after Egypt, despite the fact that they had been slaves there. Perhaps Egypt stands for the worldly spirit that fascinates and at times recaptures Christians. "All that is in the world, the desire of the flesh, the desire of the eyes, the pride in riches" (1 Jn 2:16) constitutes a huge temptation, and chapters 18-20 give us a graphic picture of the consequences of being lured away by it. But Egypt was also part of the world that would need to be saved through the Messiah who would be sent by Yahweh. Egypt's restoration is prophesied in 19:18-22, and is a clear sign of the universality of Yahweh's love and concern.

1. Isaiah uses a poetic image to suggest rapid and swift action: "Yahweh is riding on a swift cloud and comes to Egypt". The inner resources of the Egyptians would rapidly crumble. Their idols would tremble and their hearts would melt with fear: both their beliefs and their morale would be dealt a shattering blow.

2. Their fragile man-made unity would be broken by a damaging civil war, person against person, friend against friend, city against city, and northern kingdom against southern kingdom.

3. Their creativity and drive would be lost. Their wisdom would be confounded by Yahweh himself. They would resort to every type of superstition, consulting idols, forbidden spirits of the dead, ghosts and familiar spirits. This is a catalogue of pathetic non-beings that could not help them, but which might possess a certain evil reality that could deceive them and cause them great harm. In the New Testament we are taught that idols are powerless, unless those who have dealings with them believe that they have power (1 Cor 8:4-13). Then that power becomes a different type of power, which will proceed to destroy them.

4. The Egyptians would also lose their freedom. Hard masters and fierce kings would enslave them and then lord it over them. Their decay would lead to tyranny. This was a divine word from the Sovereign One, Yahweh of the armies.

5. The lifeline of the Egyptian people was going to be taken away from them. A terrible drought would visit them, and then the source of Egypt's fertility, the plentiful waters of the Nile, would dry up.

6. The Egyptian canals would be stagnant and stink. The branches of the Nile would become completely dry. The reeds and rushes, so necessary for some of their cloth industries, would rot.

7. Bare mud flats would appear instead of water. Seeded fields would be scorched.

8. The fishing industry, at the heart of their food supply chain, would collapse. Anglers would mourn and lament. The net-fishers would stand by and be idle.

9. The workers in flax would be in despair. The carders and the loom-workers who wove linen cloths would turn pale and feel faint. The textile industry would quietly come to a halt.

10. Those who wove the rushes into mats would cry in dismay. Each wage-earner would be given grief instead of wages. The material prosperity of every Egyptian depended on the industrial and financial sectors, which would cease to be viable and could no longer function.

11. Chaos and anarchy would reign. The wisdom of the princes would turn out to be folly. Pharaoh's counsellors would talk nonsense. They would be reduced to jockeying for position. They would boast that they belonged to the "wisdom caste", and therefore were the possessors of ancient wisdom.

12. If any of them had been truly wise, they would have understood the signs of the times and worked out that this was all Yahweh's doing. He had planned it and it was part of his ultimately corrective purpose.

13. The princes at both the current and the previous capital cities would all be stultified, unable to give good advice. The pillars of the establishment would lead the nation even further astray.

14. A spirit of bewilderment and dizzy confusion would take over. This would be mortifying for a country that in the previous two millennia had prided itself on the education and training of its officials.

15. Isaiah used a similar saying to describe the discomfiture of Israel and Syria on a previous occasion (9:14). Egypt would be the victim of so many insoluble disasters and problems that nobody, from Pharaoh down to the most humble worker, would be able to do anything about them.

Meditation: Why rely on the Unreliable?

The first part of this chapter (v 1-15) is in poetry and deals with Yahweh's judgement on the Egyptians. The second (v 16-25) is in prose and concerns their repentance and Yahweh's consequent promise of salvation for them. It is not clear which particular conquest of Egypt these prophecies are referring to. Perhaps Isaiah was looking ahead to the destructive Assyrian invasions by Esarhaddon in 671 B.C. and Ashurbanipal in 667 B.C. The first of these was decisive, and the second dealt ruthlessly with the few remaining pockets of resistance.

In verses 1-15 Isaiah focuses on Egypt's toxic religion (v 1-4), her absolute dependence on the River Nile (v 5-10) and her false and worldly wisdom (v 11-15). The religion was idolatrous and different gods were worshipped at different centres. As a result the nation could not be united, and civil wars kept brewing up (v 2). The Nile was the lifeline of most Egyptians. When it dried up, all the life-sustaining industry ceased (v 5-10) and the desert encroached and devoured vast tracts of land, leaving hundreds of people homeless. The wise men were all fools (v 11). They had no insight into Yahweh's plans and, when disasters began to befall them, they had no helpful suggestions to offer (v 12-15).

The whole passage is reminiscent of the exodus of the Israelites, when Yahweh demonstrated on a previous occasion the pitiful powerlessness of the Egyptian deities, the vulnerability of the Nile on which Egypt was so dependent, and the almost comic stupidity of the wisdom of the Egyptian sages.

How different it would have been if the Egyptians had known Yahweh! The Holy One of Israel is powerful and purposeful (v 1). Those who continually trust in him are happy and lack for nothing (Ps 84:11-12). And his wisdom is on a totally different plane to that of men (55:8-9, Rom 11:33-36).

The immediate application for God's people is, of course, to reiterate their need to keep trusting in Yahweh. From around 715 B.C. onwards, Egypt had become the potential ally of every country in the Fertile Crescent that was disaffected with its role of being a vassal state to Assyria. It was very tempting for King Hezekiah to join forces with Egypt in order to try to escape from the stifling Assyrian yoke. This oracle would remind Hezekiah and the other politically ambitious princes in Jerusalem that Egyptian affairs were always liable to be disrupted by disunity, economic collapse and the stupidity of their counsellors. At that time Egypt was incapable of being more than an extremely unreliable ally.

It is always better to rely ultimately on the God who created us and loves us than on fallible men who are liable to fail, and who cannot keep their promises of help.

XXXVI

19:16-25 The Repentance of Egypt

The phrase "on that day" occurs six times in these ten verses. Isaiah is looking ahead to a "Day of the Lord", perhaps not the final day of judgement, but certainly a series of climactic days of great importance for the Egyptians, which will finally result in their conversion and restoration. The prophet carried with him a vision of the widespread future conversion of the Gentiles, and here it is at the forefront of his mind. In this passage Isaiah takes the Egyptians, who once oppressed the Jews, as the representatives of the Gentile world.

16. The first stage in the conversion of these heathen people would be *fear*. "On that day" the Egyptians will "be like women and tremble with fear" before the hand of Yahweh of the armies, as he raises it against them.

17. Not only will the Egyptians fear God; they will also fear God's people. The land of Judah will become fearsome to them. The mere mention of it will strike fear into Egyptian hearts. This is because of the plan that Yahweh has devised against Egypt, which we have already studied in verses 1-15. What is the reason for this emphasis on fear? Perhaps it is because "The fear of Yahweh is the beginning of wisdom" (Ps 111:10). It is a necessary step towards restoration.

18. "On that day" fear will lead to *submission*. In these verses Isaiah speaks out a most remarkable prophecy. He states that "on that day" the Hebrew language will be spoken in five Egyptian cities, whose people would swear allegiance to Yahweh's name. One of these cities would be the so-called City of the Sun, previously the centre of the worship of the sun-god Ra, which is also called *On* in Egyptian and *Heliopolis* in Greek.

19. "On that day" submission would result in *access* to Yahweh. There would be an altar to him in central Egypt, and a pillar dedicated to him at the border. Jews from Egypt would follow their ancestors Abraham (in building an altar, Gen 12:8) and Jacob (in erecting a pillar, Gen 28:22).

20. The altar and pillar built in his honour would be a sign and witness to Yahweh in the land of Egypt. They would symbolise the fact that some of his people dwelt in Egypt, and their presence there meant that the whole land was consecrated to him. Like the Israelites under the judges, they would sometimes cry to him because of their oppressors or persecutors. Yahweh would then send them a saviour (Judg 3:9, 15, etc.) and thereby defend and deliver them.

21. In a wonderful way Yahweh would "make himself known to the Egyptians".

"On that day" access to God would lead to *knowing* him. Like the Israelites, they would worship Yahweh with sacrifices and burnt offerings. If they made any vows to him, they would keep their word and perform them.

22. Although Yahweh would have struck Egypt a terrible blow, the reason he had struck them was in order to heal them (Hos 6:1). As a result of being brought low, the Egyptians would turn to Yahweh and put their trust in him. He would "listen to their supplications and heal them".

23. "On that day" there would be a *highway* joining Egypt to Assyria. There would be contact and interchange between the two peoples. In former times the bitterest of enemies, they would now worship Yahweh together. The deep wounds resulting from ancient hostilities would be healed as the warring parties forgave one another and worshipped the one true God. This echoes the promise of a highway in 11:16 for the heathen nations to travel to Zion.

24. "On that day" Israel, Egypt and Assyria would be *equal parties* in bringing God's blessing to "the midst of the earth".

25. The Gentiles would be blessed together with the Jews. Yahweh would then address each of them in a similar way. Egypt would be *his people*. Assyria would be *the work of his hands*. Israel would be *his heritage*. The downfall of the people of Egypt and Assyria would lead to a spiritual revival among their descendants. No vision of the incorporation of the Gentiles among God's people could be as inclusive, as universal and as mission-centred as this. The most bitter and cruel enemies of God's people would one day be numbered with them!

Meditation: Prophecies and their Fulfilments

Different prophecies are fulfilled in different ways. In this passage some of the early verses (v 18, 19) have been fulfilled to the letter, but the later ones (v 23-25) are either still awaiting their fulfilment, or else they have been fulfilled in a way that is symbolical rather than literal.

Let us begin with the five cities mentioned in v 18. At various times after the deportations of 597 B.C. and 587 B.C., if not earlier, Jewish colonies were formed in several Egyptian cities, and in some of them there were more Jews than Egyptians. Hebrew became an important language in them. There was an important Jewish community in Alexandria, where the Hebrew Old Testament began to be translated into Greek in the third century B.C. and the work was completed before 130 B.C. Another important Jewish centre at that time was the city of On, better known to us as Heliopolis, "the City of the Sun". Three others might have been Migdol, Tahpanhes and Memphis (Jer 44:1), which had been colonised by Jews in the sixth century. So it is not difficult to locate five cities that accord with verse 18. At various times between 597 B.C. and 175 B.C. there would have been five cities in Egypt which fulfilled what Isaiah said.

Then there are the altar and pillar mentioned in v 19. Some scholars believe that it is pointless to try and link the building of the altar and pillar in this passage with concrete historical events, but is this so? Altars would have been found in temples: were any Jewish temples built in Egypt after Isaiah wrote? Yes, there were. Sometime in the middle of the sixth century B.C. a colony of Jews built a small temple in the Egyptian city of Elephantine. It was destroyed in 411 B.C. by the local Egyptian authorities. Around 170 B.C. a large temple, which became a strong rival to the one in Jerusalem, was built at Leontopolis by the legitimate heir of the Jewish High Priesthood, called Onias IV. He did so in the belief that he was fulfilling verse 19. As for pillars, it is not unlikely that some were built on the Egyptian border with Judah. Pillars were not as long-lasting as temples.

It is a matter of opinion, if not of controversy, whether or not the latter part of the prophecy in verses 23-25 has been fulfilled. There has never been a highway joining Egypt to what used to be Assyria, passing through Israel on the way. But in the Christian era some of the earliest churches were set up in all these regions, and the Christian believers, some of whom were the descendants of the people who lived there in Isaiah's time, would have enjoyed an equal status as Christians with their fellow-believers in other parts of the Fertile Crescent. So some of the Christians in Assyria, Egypt and Judah would have got to know one another and worshipped together. This unity and fellowship between people who previously were sworn enemies would have fulfilled the prophecies of these verses.

In a similar way today, in some exceptionally disunited regions such as the Balkans, the church is the only institution that has succeeded in uniting people from opposing factions. After centuries of hatred and the murders of family members, individuals are forgiving one another, and a real measure of closure is being attained. This can only happen at the foot of the cross. Through his envoy, the Messiah, God would reconcile the world to himself, and at the same time effect a reconciliation between those who were at odds with one another.

The blessing of God himself closes this chapter. "Blessed be Egypt my people, and Assyria the work of my hands, and Israel my heritage". It is the people of God, formed by his providence and fully in union with the Messiah, who worship him in truth and are the beneficiaries of his blessing.

XXXVII

20:1-6 The Crisis of Ashdod

An inscription from the time of the Assyrian King Sargon provides us with the background for this incident. It took place three years after the events of 14:28-32. The Philistine city of Ashdod had revolted against Assyria in 713 B.C. The Assyrians immediately deposed Azuri, King of Ashdod, and appointed his brother Akhimit in his place. The people of Ashdod then removed Akhimit and appointed a new leader called Yamani, who was determined to carry on the hopeless struggle. He was promised support by the Egyptian-Ethiopian coalition, and he also approached Edom, Moab and Judah for further help. Isaiah's advice to Hezekiah, King of Judah, and to the people of Jerusalem, was not to join in the revolt against Assyria.

1. The year in question was 711 B.C. The city of Ashdod, part of Philistia, had revolted against Assyria the best part of three years earlier, refusing to pay the annual tribute due from vassal states of the Assyrian empire. Sargon, King of Assyria and the mightiest ruler in the world, duly sent his army to sort out the problem. The Assyrian commander-in-chief or *turtanu* did so in ruthless and characteristic fashion. The city of Ashdod was turned into a heap of ruins, and its citizens were either put to the sword or led into captivity.

2. At the start of the crisis Yahweh had instructed Isaiah to remove his sandals and even the sackcloth tunic which, like other prophets, he regularly wore (2 Ki 1:8). He was to walk around barefoot and naked apart from his loincloth, like a captive being led into exile.

3. When Ashdod fell, Isaiah uttered an oracle from Yahweh. He, Isaiah, had been walking like a conquered and humiliated captive for three years. This was a sign and a portent – but it was not principally against Ashdod. It was against Egypt and Ethiopia, and it was invested with special divine significance.

4. In the same way that Isaiah had been walking around Jerusalem, Sargon would lead away as his prisoners and exiles not just the people of Ashdod (anyone could have foreseen that) but also the fearsome Egyptians and Ethiopians. Young and old alike, they would march as captives to a distant land, naked and barefoot, with bared buttocks, to their great shame and disgrace.

5. History tells us that Egypt and Ethiopia were indeed finally subdued by Assyria 40 years later, when Esarhaddon came and conquered them in 671 B.C. But Isaiah's sign and portent spoke to many people whose hopes were set on Egypt, including the citizens of Jerusalem who had witnessed the prophet's strange self-exposure. They realised that what had happened to Ashdod would also happen to them if they allied themselves with the Egyptians.

6. The coastland mentioned here is Palestine; the inhabitants were the Philistines, the Edomites, the Moabites and, in particular, the people of Judah. The first three of these had joined the rebellion led by Egypt against Assyria. Egypt would be of no help to them, and furthermore would lose face in a most humiliating way. Their turn would come to be overrun and subjugated. The people marvelled at the future trouble that lay in store for the Egyptians, in whom they had trusted for help and deliverance. If their strong ally was impotent to help itself, how would *they* possibly escape? Isaiah's answer would have been that a world crisis is not to be faced by courting the protection of strong enemies, but by looking in simple trust to God.

Meditation: The naked Prophet as a Sign

It was not unusual for the prophets of Israel and Judah to behave in ways that were striking and weird, if not actually improper. The prophet Jeremiah, for example, was told to walk all the way to the River Euphrates and hide a loincloth in a cleft of a rock by the riverside. After a lengthy period he was to walk all the way back to that same spot and retrieve his loincloth, which he found to be, unsurprisingly, ruined by the elements. Yahweh then revealed to him a message for the people of Judah and Jerusalem: their pride would be ruined just like the loincloth had been, and they would be seen as being good for nothing. They would then cling to Yahweh as a loincloth clings to a body (Jer 13:1-10).

The prophet Hosea was told by Yahweh to marry a prostitute and have children by her (Hos 1:2-3). She would later leave him, but in spite of this he was to seek her out and take her back as his wife (3:1-3). This merciful but shocking marriage would be like an acted parable about the spiritual unfaithfulness of God's people towards Yahweh.

Of all the prophets, the one who behaved most weirdly was Ezekiel. Exiled to Babylon, he experienced a number of surreal visions (e.g. Ezek 1:1-28). He also acted out a number of curious little dramas in front of his fellow exiles (e.g. Ezek 4:1-17, 5:1-17). For several years he was struck with fits of ritual dumbness, when he could not speak (Ezek 3:26, 33:22). He also prophesied the death of his wife a few hours before it happened (Ezek 24:15-27).

By comparison with Ezekiel, Isaiah was a relatively normal person, although he did give his sons some extraordinary names ("Hello, Ahaz, this is my son *A-remnant-shall-turn*"). The most bizarre aspect of his ministry took place during the crisis of Ashdod. He walked semi-naked around Jerusalem, like a beggar or captive. This behaviour must have brought forth both the astonishment and the derision of the respectable citizens of Zion. They saw him wearing nothing but a loincloth, day in day out, for the best part of three years.

We may find this behaviour quite incomprehensible, but it is clear that he was under orders from Yahweh to act as he did. It must have been very embarrassing for him to obey Yahweh and degrade himself in public to such an extent. His task was to startle both the ruling classes and the common people of Judah, and to convince the two groups of the futility of joining the anti-Assyrian alliance led by Egypt and Ethiopia. The Egyptians were a proud and blustering people, and it was a strong temptation for smaller states to trust in Egypt's assurance of military support and their promise of a speedy deliverance from the Assyrian tyranny. The godly King Hezekiah must have been sorely tested. He was encouraged to join in the Egyptian alliance by his courtiers, but he was also strictly forbidden by the Prophet Isaiah from doing so.

Isaiah's wandering about naked was a powerful sign that must have spoken to the common people of Jerusalem and, in the end, persuaded Hezekiah to say no to Yamani. The message of this sign and portent did come across, to the King, to his court, and to the whole nation. Thanks to Isaiah's brave humiliation, the people of God were, for the time being, spared from attack by the brutal Assyrians. The northern kingdom had already been destroyed and its peoples scattered in a way from which they would never fully recover.

The prophet's advice was good and Hezekiah did well to heed it. After three years of naked self-exposure, Isaiah was vindicated. What happened was that the Egyptians did not come to Ashdod's aid. Instead they left its people to defend themselves. Ashdod was harshly subjugated by the Assyrian army. Their rebel leader Yamani then fled to Ethiopia, but the Assyrians demanded that he be handed over to them. The Ethiopians opted for prudence. They decided that the better part of valour would be to hand Yamani over to what Derek Kidner euphemistically calls "the Assyrians' tender mercies". By so doing they proved themselves unworthy of trust as an ally in the international goings-on.

XXXVIII

21:1-10 Babylon, the Wilderness of the Sea

The subject of this oracle is the eventual fall of Babylon (v9), still in the distant future. It was a vision (v2) which affected Isaiah emotionally (v3, 4). He saw himself as no more than a watchman, whose duty it was to be faithful and to report clearly what he saw (v8-10).

1. Isaiah announced his subject in a cryptic way: he was going to speak about "the wilderness of the sea". This suggests an untamed nature that is uncontrollable. Like a whirlwind in the Negeb, it came through the desert, from a terrible land. Jeremiah would later express the divine retribution that would come to Babylon in similar terms (Jer 51:42-43).

2. Isaiah described his vision as a stern one. He saw the Babylonians as being treacherous and destructive. They were both betrayers who betrayed, and also destroyers who destroyed. Isaiah then heard Yahweh as he commanded the Persians (Elam) and the Medes to attack Babylon. Yahweh had decided that the time had come to bring to an end all the sighing that Babylon was causing.

3. Isaiah was inwardly shaken by what he saw. He was in anguish, and his pain was like that of a woman in labour. He was so overwrought that for a while he was unable to face the vision. His agitation was not unlike the deep emotion that Jeremiah would experience over a century later (Jer 4:19-22). The difference is that while Jeremiah would grieve for the people of Judah who were the victims, Isaiah seems to have grieved for their tormentors on the day of God's retribution. The experience of the few true prophets, as opposed to the many false ones, is invariably painful, uncomfortable and unpopular.

4. Isaiah wanted to see the twilight of Babylon, the evil city that had been the cause of much sighing. But the twilight he saw in his vision was dark and terrible, so

much so that he was horrified and appalled. His mind was reeling and his body trembled. What exactly was it that he had seen?

5. When the Persians and the Medes attacked Babylon, over 150 years after the vision that Isaiah saw, they caught the troops that defended the city unprepared, enjoying a feast (as in Dan 5:1-4, 30-31). They had prepared the table with victuals, spread out comfortable rugs around it on which they reclined, and then proceeded to eat and drink. Suddenly they were barking out orders to one another to rise up and prepare for battle. They hastily oiled their shields so that arrows would glide off them. But it was too late. It was not just a case of the enemy being at the gates. They had already entered the city.

6. Yahweh told Isaiah to post a lookout, who would announce what he saw. This is a prophet's job: prophets *are* watchmen (Ezek 33:1-9, Hab 2:1-3).

7. The lookout would also listen diligently. When he saw lots of riders on horses, donkeys and camels, he was to listen very carefully before making his report. His objectivity is emphasised. He was charged with reporting what he saw and heard: nothing more, nothing less.

8. As the watchman calls out to Yahweh, his identity becomes clear: he is none other than Isaiah himself. While he was being given the vision, the prophet may have been in an ecstatic condition in which he temporarily had an *alter ego* or a split personality. In v 6-8 he was able to see his prophetic consciousness on the watchtower, and to talk about himself in the third person. There he was, standing at his post, waiting patiently through the night, waiting for the vision to come.

9. Suddenly he saw the cavalcade. "There they come, riders, horsemen in pairs!" He realised their significance. It was the end for mighty Babylon. Then Yahweh replied, confirming the prophet's intuition: "Fallen, fallen is Babylon; and all the images of her gods lie shattered on the ground". This cry, "Fallen, fallen is Babylon the great!" is taken up in the final book of the New Testament (Rev 18:2-24), where Babylon symbolises the pride and ungodliness of worldly people.

10. Finally Isaiah communicated the content of his vision to the people of Israel. He described it as what he *heard* from Yahweh. He addressed his nation tenderly as "My threshed and winnowed one". The people of Jerusalem would suffer a lengthy and agonising ordeal at the hands of the Babylonians. And yet, even in the dark night of their soul there would be hope. In Isaiah's time the hope of God's people was not yet well formed. Isaiah's contribution to its development was twofold. The day would come when the account books would be settled and wrongs would be put right. And a remnant would survive and enjoy the new life.

Meditation: Babylon – the Reality not the Symbol

This oracle is not without its difficulties, and it raises two questions. First of all, why are we given another oracle about Babylon after the extended one in chapters 13 and 14? And secondly, since it appears to predict the conquest of Babylon by the Medes and Persians which actually happened in 539 B.C., could it have been written by the prophet Isaiah himself over 150 years earlier?

Why another oracle about Babylon? As the eighth century B.C. drew to a close, Hezekiah began to look to Babylon instead of to Egypt in his search for a possible political ally of Judah against Assyria. This is implied by the warm welcome that Hezekiah gave to the envoys from Babylon in 39:1-4. In the vision of 21:1-10, Isaiah saw that Babylon, like Egypt, was destined to be overrun by other nations. There was to be no comfort for Judah from that quarter, only a warning that she would eventually suffer at Babylon's hands. The earlier oracle about Babylon in chapters 13 and 14 was a taunt; this one is full of foreboding. To some extent, the Babylon that Isaiah denounced in chapters 13 and 14 may have been symbolic of any proud or ungodly people; here it does mean the nation that bore that name.

Babylon was in continuous rebellion against Assyria between 721 B.C. and 648 B.C. The city was overrun by Sargon in 710 B.C., by Sennacherib in 702 B.C. and 689 B.C., and by Asshurbanipal in 648 B.C. Its final conquest by Cyrus in 539 B.C. was relatively peaceful. The most painful defeat it suffered was the one that took place in 689 B.C. Sennacherib recorded that he filled the streets with corpses, destroyed the temple of the local deity Marduk, and carried its image away to Assyria. After each of its Assyrian visitations Babylon was rebuilt, and its great army was reassembled and rearmed. Eventually Babylonia took Assyria's place as the most fearsome superpower on earth. In 597 B.C. and 586 B.C. the Babylonians overran Judah. They destroyed Jerusalem after a long siege (588-586 B.C.) and took many Jewish captives into exile. The end came for the proud Babylonians when they were conquered by the Medes and Persians led by Cyrus the Great in 539 B.C.

Does the oracle in 21:1-10 refer to Babylon's temporary defeat by Sennacherib in 689 B.C. or to their final subjugation 150 years later? Verses 2 and 5 suggest it was the latter. The prophet correctly foresaw that Babylon would one day fall to the Medes and Persians, and he also foresaw that the army commanders would be feasting when the invaders forced their way in. At the same time, the prophecy was clearly given before the event, for the prophet's extreme discomfiture (in v 3-4) incorrectly suggests, as do chapters 13 and 14, that Babylon's fate would be terrible, perhaps involving the torching and destruction of the city and the killing of its people. We know that Babylon surrendered peacefully in 539 B.C.

The main question about this oracle is, did it come from Isaiah himself, in which case it might have been spoken around 705-700 B.C., or was it a later prophecy from the time of the Babylonian exile? The reception given by Hezekiah to the Babylonian envoys in 39:1-4 suggests that it was Isaiah himself who uttered it, in order to dissuade Hezekiah from rushing into an undesirable alliance with Babylon (39:5-8). Hezekiah partly heeded Isaiah's warning. Although he had to face the fact that Judah and Jerusalem would one day be overrun by the Babylonians, he comforted himself with the thought that at least this sad event would not happen during his days (39:8). This was a selfish sentiment by a godly man, similar to 21st century thinking about global warming, which will affect our grandchildren far more than ourselves.

XXXIX

21:11-17 Dumah and Arabia

These two short oracles are somewhat impenetrable, and remain among Isaiah's most difficult and mysterious writings. There is an indication in the text (see the comments on v 16) that may allow us to date them to 716 B.C.

11. Seir was the principal town, and Dumah a small settlement, in Edom. Perhaps Isaiah chose to entitle his oracle on Edom after *Dumah* because this name means "silence", and Isaiah foresees that the Edomites will have to suffer in silence. The question, "What of the night?" means "How long must the night go on? When will morning arrive?" The people of Edom were about to be plunged into a time of great suffering, compared here to a dark night. The Assyrian army would ravage their land and wreak havoc with their settlements. A voice from Seir is asking the sentinel or watchman, the prophet Isaiah, how long this would last.

12. The prophet's reply is, at first sight, discouraging. The morning *will* come, but it will itself be followed by another night, and so on. There will be respites, but they will be temporary. Further nights would follow. But the prophet urges the questioner to persevere in his quest for light. He should come back with further inquiries. Maybe he will ask the right question in due course?

13. The "desert plain" is "Arabia", which has the same consonants as the word "evening". The prophet continues to write cryptically, and we who read his words must try to decipher his meaning. The evening, like the night in v 11, represents a season of suffering that would befall the people of Arabia, once again at the hands of the Assyrians. The Arabian tribespeople were desert nomads, who were difficult to reach. They probably thought that their inaccessibility would protect them from the Assyrian army. Here Isaiah addresses the nomads from Dedan, who used to wander with their caravans around the scrublands and desert plains, and in the next verse he speaks to the more settled people of the land of Tema. Both of these tribes lived towards the south of Arabia, but their northern relatives from Kedar were about to receive a most undesirable visitation.

14. The Dedanites and the people of Tema would encounter some destitute people who were refugees. Isaiah urges them to share their bread and water with these hungry and thirsty people.

15. The refugees were from Kedar (v16, 17), and they would be fleeing from the Assyrian troops into the wilderness. Terrified of the mortal swords and the lethal arrows, they would try to run away from the stress of battle.

16. God the Almighty had spoken to Isaiah: in less than a year's time the glory of Kedar would be no more (see the comments on 16:14 for the meaning of "years of a hired worker"). These peace-loving nomads of northern Arabia would not be spared by the Assyrians.

17. There would be few survivors, and their weapons would be scanty. Yahweh, the God of Israel, had decreed this and made it known through his prophet. The matter was absolutely settled. It would definitely happen. It did. Sargon had an account written about his invasion of Arabia in 715 B.C.

Meditation: Questions and their Answers

Suffering raises difficult questions. Some of them have no answer, some have an answer that is difficult to understand, and some have answers which are positive and practical. Sometimes the answers, where they exist, will involve hard work for people who would prefer not to knuckle down to it.

The Edomites lived in rocky fortresses. They were a proud people, confident of their invulnerability (Obad 3, 4), but they would prove to be no match for the all-conquering Assyrian army. After a harrowing and desolating visitation, the few Edomite survivors would have had some agonising questions to ask.

For some of their questions, the answer would be at best an unhelpful *silence*. "What can you tell me?" "I can tell you nothing". "Will things change?" "Wait and see". For certain other questions the answers would be like a slap on the face. "How long will the night go on?" "Until the morning comes". "Will we be secure then?" "Yes, but only until the following night arrives".

What questions might the Edomites have asked that Isaiah would have loved to answer? "Will a time ever come when all will be well?" "Yes, but it is reserved for those who know and love Yahweh". "Is there anything I can do now that will be helpful?" "Yes, wait for Yahweh".

There is hope, but hope is the preserve of God's people. The writer of Proverbs put it like this: "The way of the wicked is like deep darkness; they do not know what they stumble over. But the path of the righteous is like the light of dawn, which shines brighter and brighter until full day" (Prov 4:19, 18). Those who walk in the light that God has provided for them (the "righteous"), will be given *more* light and *more* hope. Those who ignore or reject the light that God has provided for them (the "wicked"), must endure the *silence* of the night.

Sometimes things seem to go on as they always have done (Eccl 1:8-11, 2 Pet 3:4). Day and night come from nowhere and duly disappear to nowhere. The light of God's glory is wonderful when it comes (12:1-2), but it seems remote for those who are waiting for it (21:11).

God is both an inscrutable observer from afar and a kind friend close by (57:15). The end will come and the end is not yet. Hope lies in the unknown future. Hope is certain even though its details are uncertain.

The people of Kedar dwelt in tents and had a nomadic life in northern Arabia. If the watchword for Edom was *silence*, for Kedar it was *evening*. When the night arrived, there would be silence. By now it was evening: the shadows were lengthening and night was drawing in. The time would soon come when the glory of Kedar would come to an end, said Yahweh. Then the people of Kedar would be few. These few would be destitute. They would be traumatised into silence. They would not be able to ask any questions.

Perhaps their neighbours from Dedan and Tema would ask a question about them. "Is there any practical thing we can do to help our brothers?" "Yes, bring water to the thirsty, meet the fugitive with bread". "This would be inconvenient. Why should we do this for them?" "Because they have fled from the swords: from the drawn sword, from the bent bow, and from the stress of battle".

Sometimes the answers to difficult questions leave people of good will with hard work on their hands. Hopefully they will undertake it gladly. Perhaps at least they will go ahead and offer *some* help, even if initially they do so with mixed feelings. Maybe some will not help, and instead go on with their busy lives.

The godless world hates having to solve the huge problems that keep on arising. It would really prefer to pretend that those problems did not exist. Maybe the times when it is confronted with impossible problems are precisely the times when a prophetic voice is saying, "Wait for God" (Mt 25:40, 45).

God's purposes are being fulfilled in all sorts of ways. Sometimes through great dramatic events (v9), sometimes in the long and silent periods of time when nothing seems to be happening (v12), and also during those times of crisis when disaster strikes hard (v13-15).

XL

22:1-14 The Valley of Vision

1. It is now Jerusalem's turn to be included among the heathen nations. The Jewish capital, slightly elevated, lies in the midst of a valley (Ps 125:2). With their privileges as God's people, the people of Zion should have had a clear vision of their God and his purposes. The city should have been like a *valley of vision*. We shall soon see how clear or blurred its vision was. To have been chosen by Yahweh would not exempt them from his judgement (Amos 3:1-2).

   Although John Skinner came close to doing so, Derek Kidner may have been the first commentator to conjecture that the people of Jerusalem had just witnessed the most stupendous deliverance in their history, in 701 B.C. The entire

Assyrian army lay dead around them, and Sennacherib had retreated in abject defeat (37:36-37). The besieged men and women then climbed onto the rooftops of their houses in order to celebrate. Isaiah was deeply shocked and hurt.

2. Isaiah proceeded to paint a stark contrast between the triumphalist jollities that they were enjoying in the present, and the grim fate that lay in store for them 115 years in the future. They were shouting in exultation, but in his mind's eye the prophet could see the day when their descendants would be decimated by a siege of 18 months (2 Ki 25:1-3). The resulting famine would lead to many casualties.

3. The details of this verse would be fulfilled to the letter. The King of Israel and his chief ministers would attempt to escape from the surrounded city. In the middle of the night they would ride through the encircling Babylonian troops, but they would soon be followed and eventually captured (2 Ki 25:4-7), and the King of Babylon would then pass judgement on them.

4. For Isaiah the present revelling of the citizens of Zion was sheer escapism that amounted to the deepest rebellion against Yahweh. Although the destruction of the Assyrian army marked the summit of his career, he was appalled. He asked the people to leave him alone, and wept bitterly. He would not be comforted by them, for what he was seeing was a vision concerning their destruction.

5. Isaiah declared that the sovereign Lord had a day planned for the "valley of vision". It would be a day of tumult and trampling and confusion. The walls of Jerusalem would first be undermined and eventually battered down. Cries for help would go unheeded and echo in the surrounding mountains.

6. By 588 B.C. the people of Elam would be loyal vassals of Babylon. The location of Kir is not known; it is not the same Kir as the one in Moab (15:1). The archers, chariots and cavalry of Elam, together with the foot-soldiers of Kir, would unite with the Babylonian army so as to capture and destroy Jerusalem.

7. The valleys that encircled Jerusalem were well-known to its people. They would be full of chariots. The enemy cavalry would stand by the city gates. The siege would be tightly drawn and escape would be out of the question.

8. The defenceless nature of the city would be exposed. The people had access to some weapons, but they would be woefully inadequate. The House of the Forest had been the armoury of Jerusalem since the days of King Solomon (1 Ki 10:17).

9. There were breaches in the city's defences which would require and receive attention. Two kings of Judah to whom Isaiah brought the word of Yahweh, Ahaz and Hezekiah, had both attended to the water supplies of Jerusalem (7:3, 2 Ki 20:20). Further attention would need to be given to the underground conduit by later kings at the beginning of the sixth century B.C.

10. Here are further prophetic details that might well have been fulfilled. The houses in Jerusalem would be examined. Some of them would have to be broken down, so that their bricks could be used to fortify the city wall (Jer 33:4-5).

11. A reservoir would be built where the city walls on the south-eastern hill converged; an extension to them would allow room for two pools (2 Ki 25:4). The people of Jerusalem would work hard, but their labour would be in vain. Their activism did not *stem from* their faith. It amounted to *a denial of* their faith. They may have toiled away, but they persistently refused to look to Yahweh in simple trust. Yahweh, who is the author of everything, had long ago planned in detail what would happen, but they just ignored him.

12. The prophets had urged the rebellious people of Yahweh time and again to turn back to the Holy One of Israel. They should have wept and mourned for their sins, shaved their hair and put on sackcloth. But they did not wish to face the one who had created them, and had now spectacularly redeemed them. They opted for their own forms of escapism: hard labour that might lead to self-sufficiency, and partying that would provide excitement. Both amounted to a refusal to repent.

13. The people of Jerusalem were already deeply alienated from Yahweh. Their unforgivable sin was to shut Yahweh out of their lives. They turned to pleasure rather than to him, saying, "Let us eat and drink for tomorrow we die". Because Yahweh was not real to them, there was no *future with him* for them to look forward to (1 Cor 15:32). Yahweh's own people should have been full of hope, yet *they had no hope*. They might easily have died at the hand of the Assyrians; within a few more years they would die of old age. So they thought that they might as well binge and get drunk. They wanted to have what the world could offer them before they died. This was their attitude, even though Yahweh had just intervened with an amazing miracle on their behalf.

14. Yahweh's message came to Isaiah like a voice in his ears. The iniquity of his people would not be forgiven. It would call down death.

Meditation: The unforgivable Sin of Jerusalem

John Skinner writes: "The key to this passage – the most pessimistic of all Isaiah's prophecies – is the discordance between the mood of the prophet and the state of public feeling around him. In a time of universal mirth and festivity he alone is overwhelmed with grief and refuses to be comforted. In the rejoicings of the populace he reads the evidence of their hopeless impenitence and insensibility, and he concludes his discourse by expressing the conviction that at last they have sinned beyond the possibility of pardon. The circumstances recall Christ's lamentation over Jerusalem on the day of his triumphal entry" (Lk 19:41-44).

Isaiah was bitterly disappointed by the spiritual results of the most extraordinary divine saving action in all of Jerusalem's history. Surrounded by the terrifying army of Sennacherib, the city was being subjected to a siege that might lead to its utter destruction. Then, in one single night, "the angel of Yahweh set out and struck one hundred and eighty five thousand in the camp of the Assyrians; when morning dawned, they were all dead bodies. Then King Sennacherib of Assyria left, went home, and lived at Nineveh" (37:36-37).

Isaiah was hoping that the people of Jerusalem would react to this great salvation by giving praise and glory to God for their amazing deliverance. The prophet was fully expecting them to put on sackcloth and – at last – become part of God's remnant by repenting of their social injustice and lack of faith. This and only this would be an appropriate response by the people of Yahweh to the extraordinary exploits of their wonderful God.

John Skinner continues: "Bitter must have been [Isaiah's] disenchantment when he saw that the crisis had come and gone, and left the temper of the nation as frivolous, as secular, and as insensible to the divine as it had been before". Deliverance from the potentially deadly siege should have acted as a call to serious reflection and penitence. In fact it prompted everyone to raid the city's plentiful food reserves for lasting the siege, and then overeat and get drunk.

It was especially sad from Isaiah's point of view that this had happened in the "valley of vision", where he had received most, if not all, of his visions. He must have been mortified when he realised that what for him was a visionary place was for the people just a low-lying swamp of blindness. Their persistent sins and their ill-timed frivolity seemed to have sealed their fate. The failure of the people to discern the hand of God in the events that had befallen them was the crowning and incontrovertible proof of their unbelief, and so the "valley of vision" was now destined to become for their descendants a vale of tears.

Worst of all, Isaiah had heard Yahweh solemnly declare to him: "Surely this iniquity will not be forgiven [them] until [they] die" (v14). Some sins are mortal and it is pointless to pray for those who have committed them (1Jn 5:15-17). One sin that is mortal is the one Jesus called "the blasphemy against the Holy Spirit". In its context, this appears to be that extreme state of hardness of heart in certain people which causes them to attribute to the devil the good works wrought by or through Jesus the Messiah (Mk 3:22-30).

We learn from this passage that another mortal sin is for religious people to persist for decades in selfish and self-sufficient living and then, when an absolutely amazing miracle of salvation takes place, to plunge into gluttonous feasting and binge drinking while saying, "Let us eat and drink, for tomorrow we die". Other public expressions of contempt for God's rule may in a similar way plunge the speakers into mortal sin. In the Middle Ages it was common for people to fear God, and yet even then there were some who would complacently say, "Let us eat and drink for tomorrow we die" (v13). A distinguished eleventh century poet expressed his attitude as follows: "Some there are who tell of one who threatens to toss into hell the useless pots that marred as he made them. Rubbish! He is a good fellow and all will be well" (the Persian poet Omar Khayyam, in his *Rubaiyat*).

XLI

22:15-25 Two senior Officials are found wanting

Shebna was a high official in the royal court, the equivalent of the Foreign Minister in King Hezekiah's cabinet. He will appear again, with Eliakim (v 20-25) in 36:3, 11 and 37:2. It is likely that he was the leader of the pro-Egypt party (see chapters 30, 31), against which some of Isaiah's preaching was directed. He may have been the chief negotiator when envoys came to Jerusalem to arrange international alliances. Here Yahweh utterly dispenses with his services because of his arrogant love of status symbols and his proud self-importance.

15. Yahweh of the armies spoke to Isaiah: "Go to this steward". As *Master of the King's Household*, Shebna was in charge of the national finances. Through his mouthpiece Isaiah, Yahweh had scornful and terrible words for Shebna. He would be cut down to size because of his pretentious ostentation.

16. What exactly had Shebna done? He had built himself a very costly mausoleum at the nation's expense. Although he was not from a noble family, he had carved out his resting place in the rock "on the height", where the royal family and other dignitaries were buried. Because of this, Isaiah asked him, "What right do *you* have here? Who are your relatives here?" In other words, "Just who do you think you are?" A large tomb-lintel of a senior official has been found in Jerusalem. It describes the intended occupant of the tomb as "over the Household" (v 15). It may have come from Shebna's tomb, but a mortice hole has destroyed the name.

17. For this outrageous exhibition of the lust for power and recognition on the part of a *nouveau riche*, Isaiah informed Shebna that Yahweh was "about to hurl [him] away violently": he would first "seize firm hold on [him]".

18. Yahweh would then "whirl [him] round and round, and throw [him] like a ball into a wide land; there [he would] die". Shebna had also assigned to himself some chariots of a particularly splendid type, the Rolls Royces of his time. These trappings of office meant the world to him, which is why he was about to lose his own soul. So much for his love of the insignia of the wealthy and powerful. "There your splendid chariots shall lie, O you disgrace to your master's house!"

19. Shebna would be thrust down from his high office, and he would be stripped of his post. This appears to have happened by 701 B.C., when he was downgraded to being secretary of the new Foreign Minister, Eliakim (36:3, 37:2).

20. Eliakim at first sight appears to be a much better person. He is initially described as Yahweh's "servant", for he would serve God.

21. He would inherit Shebna's robe and sash of office. Shebna's authority would be invested on him, and he would be like a father to the people of Jerusalem and the land of Judah. Eliakim would serve the people as well as God.

22. On his shoulder would be "the key of the house of David". In those days keys were large and made of wood. They would literally be carried on the shoulder. In this context, however, the key was a symbolic one: Eliakim would be given great authority over the people of God. The opening and shutting describe the power to make decisions that only the king could override. Such a responsibility was God-given and intended for the good of all. In this verse we have the background for the Messiah's commission of Peter (Mt 16:19) and of the church (Mt 18:18). Ultimate authority, however, belongs to the Messiah himself (Rev 3:7, 8).

23. If Shebna was as unreliable as a ball (v18), Eliakim should have been as dependable as a peg. Yahweh would "fasten [him] like a peg in a secure place". Peg and wall would be stable. The problem could still arise that too much weight might be hung from the peg: then the peg would break. Eliakim would receive great honour: he would "become a throne of honour to his ancestral house". This may be a euphemism. It appears to mean that Eliakim would use his position to help members of his family to advance in dignity.

24. On Eliakim the whole weight of "his ancestral house" would rest. All of his family would look to him for advancement, from the noblest to the most humble. This would prove to be too much.

25. "The peg that was fastened in a secure place would give way". Sadly, Eliakim would in the long run prove unworthy of the honours conferred on him. Even when exercised in kindly fashion, nepotism constitutes an abuse of office. Great privileges are accompanied by great responsibilities (1 Sam 2:30). The peg "will be cut down and fall". Not only Eliakim would suffer; so would his relatives who had benefited from his patronage. "The load that was on [the peg] will perish, for Yahweh has spoken".

Meditation: No Privileges without Responsibilities

If verses 1-14 were about the faithlessness of the people of Jerusalem, then verses 15-25 are about the faithlessness of their leaders. The main lesson to learn is that although leadership does bring certain privileges, these privileges will always be accompanied by their corresponding responsibilities.

Shebna found his *raison d'etre* in the worldly benefits of his office, and attempted to secure a place in history by his own efforts. He loved to show off ostentatiously (splendid chariots, v 18), and he wished to perpetuate his memory by being buried in a magnificent tomb (v16). Eliakim, by contrast, ran the risk of becoming a person to whom family and friends would look for advancement and promotion (v 23b-25). He would be in a position to help, and would be expected to do so.

Together, they display two subtle alternatives to the way of faith. It is possible for any of us to be like Shebna. We can aim for self-sufficiency by creating our own *persona* and then adorning the self-image we have put together. We can begin to focus primarily on ourselves, instead of worshipping the living God. This may boost our ego in the short term, but God is not fooled. In the end disaster will strike. We shall be like a cricket ball that God hits for an almighty six.

It is also possible for any of us to be like Eliakim. We can aim to help other people, perhaps even to *love* other people, in such a way that we *possess* them, and they begin to form part of *our* small but increasing kingdom. When Eliakim reached the top, he attracted the attention of certain family members. They began to look to him for help in finding a good job or position. Not only was this an example of nepotism, it was also a case of placing one's faith in people rather than relying on the Lord. Its end would be calamitous. It would prove to be a tragedy for Eliakim, who was foolishly expanding his own kingdom in this way instead of looking for God's kingdom. "The peg [would] give way". It would also prove to be an absolute disaster for those who found their security in him. We are told that they would "perish".

As Alec Motyer wisely pointed out, "Human beings are neither self-sufficient (Shebna) nor sufficient for others (Eliakim). In each case there is a fatal usurpation of the place fit only for God. Isaiah reiterates the message of 2:22, 'Stop trusting in man'".

What must it have been like for Isaiah to deal with these two people and to record their failings for posterity? There are some indications in the passage (22:15-25) that Shebna was the leader of the pro-Egyptian party and was as a result an enemy of the prophet, but that Eliakim favoured Isaiah's stance of trusting in God and preferred to keep clear of political alliances.

In his commentary, John Skinner entitled this passage "A philippic against a *parvenu* politician". He wrote, "It is likely that Isaiah found in [Shebna] the most astute and resolute opponent of the policy which he advocated. This opposition, together with his hearty contempt for the character of the man, is the occasion of Isaiah's only invective against an individual. Eliakim, who is designated as his successor (v 20), was probably the leader of the party favourable to Isaiah's views, and the substitution of one minister for the other was equivalent to a radical change of policy on the part of Hezekiah".

Verses 16-19 are almost comic in their vituperative nature. Did Isaiah lose his cool? Did his channel of communication with Yahweh become hazy for a while, so that his words were motivated by anger and hatred? Or did Yahweh command him to express great loathing, in which case we would be more than well advised not to imitate Shebna's example? The dismissal of Shebna from his very senior post seems to have been effected in a humane fashion. We are told that, far from being projected as an inter-continental ball-shaped missile, he was simply relegated to the post of secretary. He would have lost face, but not his head.

There is a distinct change of tone in verses 20-25. Eliakim is initially presented as a very good replacement for Shebna. This would fit in with his being a supporter of Isaiah's views. Skinner believes that verses 24-25 were a later addition, possibly by Isaiah himself. If the prophet did live to witness and record Eliakim's fall from grace, he would have been extremely disappointed that the man he had written up so positively ended up by being found guilty of nepotism, and was then publicly disgraced.

XLII

23:1-18 Tiresome Tyre, destroyed and restored

Better known as the Phoenicians, the people of Tyre, Sidon and other nearby ports on the Mediterranean were renowned for their commercial wealth. They were the wealthiest traders in the world. They had dealings with nations from England to India. In the New Testament, Isaiah's oracles about Babylon and Tyre (chapters 13, 14, 23; see also Ezekiel chapters 27, 28) are combined to form a picture of worldly powers as the seducers and oppressors of God's people (Rev 17 and 18).

1. The news reached the Tyrian ships at the Phoenician colony of Tarshish on the Spanish Mediterranean coast, where they arrived from Cyprus. There they were told that the great fortress of Tyre had been destroyed. According to Alec Motyer, the "ships of Tarshish" were the largest class of merchantmen in ancient fleets.

2. The Tyrians from the coast and the merchants of Sidon are bidden to be still and to reflect on their past glories. Their commercial agents used to cross the sea, in order to replenish their large coffers, but now a great hush descended on them.

3. They once traversed the mighty waters as the greatest international merchants. Their imports used to include grain from Shihor, which was the Nile delta.

4. The Tyrians and Sidonians were now left homeless. The sea itself bewailed the loss of the fortress of Tyre, declaring that it was now like a childless mother who had forgotten that she ever had children.

5. The Egyptians would be greatly distressed when they heard the news of Tyre's destruction, for they had always had many ties with Phoenicia (see v 3).

6. Some of the surviving Tyrians, after bewailing their great loss, would attempt to find a new base for themselves in the colony of Tarshish.

7. They would be asked about their formerly exultant city. Its origin had been in ancient times, and it had always produced explorers and colonisers.

8. Who could have destroyed Tyre? Their people had founded many states, their merchants were wealthy princes, and their traders were internationally renowned.

9. It was Yahweh of the armies who had planned the deed! This was not because of Tyre's wealth but because of their self-deifying pride. God had purposed to humble all worldly pride and glory, and to shame those who had been greatly honoured on earth. Once again, Isaiah declares that of all the evils that exist, human pride is the most odious to Yahweh. The pride of man must give way to the humility of God. It will fade away and perish before it (2:10-21).

10. The ships of Tyre would now have to be permanently based in Tarshish. The harbours of Tyre were no longer open and available.

11. Yahweh had dealt a huge blow to Mediterranean commerce. This would be worse than a huge stock market crash. It would shake many kingdoms. Yahweh had decreed it: the fortresses of Tyre and Sidon, and other Phoenician ports on the coast of Canaan would all be destroyed.

12. Yahweh tells these immensely wealthy merchants that their time of glory is over. He advises the people of Sidon to move across to Cyprus, but warns them that even there they would be unable to find rest and security. True peace is not to be found in a geographical location, but in trusting the one true God (26:3).

13. Which nation was it that would subjugate Tyre? Isaiah states that on this occasion it would not be Assyria. It would be the Babylonians, also referred to as the people of Chaldea. "They erected their siege towers, they tore down her palaces, and they made her a ruin". This looks ahead to the longest siege in history – it would go on for a mind-boggling twelve years, from 585-573 B.C. But although, humanly speaking, it was the Chaldeans that brought Tyre to its knees, the primary cause of Tyre's fall was Yahweh (v 9).

14. The lament of verse 1 is repeated word for word. The ships that from now on would have to dock in Tarshish must wail. Their fortress had been destroyed.

15. Tyre was destroyed and subsequently rebuilt on several occasions. Isaiah prophesies that after this particular destruction, Tyre would be forgotten for a period of "seventy years, the lifetime of one king". After that, it would "happen to Tyre as in the song about the prostitute".

16. Isaiah spells out the words of the song. Tyre would be like a forgotten harlot who would take a harp, make sweet melody and sing. Then at last she would be remembered once more.

17. After seventy years Yahweh would revisit Tyre, and it would again become a great trading centre. But its people would return to their old ways, prostituting themselves with all of the kingdoms of the earth. Material things are always seductive and will never cease to be tempting. In this life the love of money will always be a root of all kinds of evil (1 Tim 6:10).

18. In the final verse of this oracle Isaiah claims back earthly treasures for their rightful use. In some future age the merchandise and wages of Tyre would be dedicated to Yahweh. Her profits and her wares would no longer be hoarded, but would supply abundant food and fine clothing. This would be distributed among those who lived in the presence of Yahweh. The Messiah would put it like this: "Blessed are the meek, for they will inherit the earth" (Mt 5:5). And eventually, all the nations that had drunk the wine of the wrath reserved for the harlot would one day present their glories and their treasures to God in the New Jerusalem (Rev 18:3 and 21:24).

Meditation: Yahweh, the Lord of the Nations

In the light of the fact that Isaiah addressed his messages primarily to his own people, why did he speak at such length about the nations of the world? Eleven of the first 39 chapters of Isaiah (13 to 23 inclusive) is a high proportion of his literary output, amounting to 28% of the total. Perhaps consciously following in his footsteps, Jeremiah, Ezekiel and Amos also included among their writings extensive prophecies about the foreign nations. Three of the Minor Prophets wrote exclusively about one heathen country or city: Obadiah about Edom, and Jonah and Nahum about Nineveh. There was certainly among most of the prophets what one might call an international interest.

The Old Testament prophets thoughtfully considered the nations of the world in order to demonstrate that Yahweh was the Lord of *all* peoples, not just of Judah and Israel. This was only natural for a monotheistic people like the Jews. If there is only one God, then he rules over all, not just those to whom he has chosen to reveal himself in a special way. He therefore has something to say about the history and the destiny of them all. Whatever Yahweh purposed for the future of Israel, and this included judgement and a new beginning for a remnant that would be rescued by a Messiah-king, he also had his purposes for those who did not yet know him and acknowledge him.

Here is a brief summary of ten of the principal ideas that Isaiah put forward in these eleven chapters about the nations:

1. God will humble those who are proud. This includes cultured tyrants (13:11) and abusers of God's people (17:12-14). It includes those who are proud of their mercantile skill and their riches (23:8-9), those who show off their tomb or their means of transport (22:15-19), and those who are experts at viticulture (16:6-10).
2. People from the heathen nations will be given an opportunity to share in God's salvation (14:1-2, 16:4-5, 18:7, 19:23-25, 23:18).
3. There is nothing that can frustrate God's purposes for the nations (14:24-27, 17:7, 21:16-17).
4. Peace and security are possible, but only for those who fear God (14:32).
5. God weeps as he smites. He will punish people if and when he must, but it saddens him to have to do so (15:5, 16:9-11, 22:4).
6. God smites in order to heal. As far as possible, he acts positively (19:22).
7. Those who know God should not rely on unreliable people or nations, but on the One who is reliable (19:1-17).
8. Those who know God should help refugees (16:3-5). Those who do not know God should also help refugees (21:14).
9. Idolatry and the worship of foreign gods are forbidden to God's people. These activities will ruin their lives if they indulge in them (17:7-11).
10. The prophets of God should make their points clear and ensure that God's message gets through somehow. They may write prose, poetry, lament, taunt or bitter invective, but they should consider God's punishments with tears in their eyes, and in a spirit

of empathy. They may occasionally be called to shock people by behaving in extremely unconventional ways (20:1-4).

Part 3 – Yahweh's Plans

XLIII

24:1-13 The World in Chaos

The section that includes chapters 24-27 is sometimes referred to as Isaiah's Apocalypse. The prophet no longer has individual nations in view. Now it is the whole world: the word "earth" features 25 times in these chapters. Chapter 24 is mainly an announcement of the day of judgement, but also a pessimistic survey of the state of the world. In chapters 25-27 we shall read that death will be swallowed up forever (25:8), and come across one of the two clear Old Testament references to bodily resurrection (26:19). In all this the prophet centres his vision on Jerusalem. Some of the other nations – Moab, Egypt and Assyria – still make an appearance (25:10-12, 27:12-13). Yahweh will intervene in judgement, but after the devastation joy will not only be restored but will prevail.

1. An apocalyptic time has arrived. Yahweh will lay waste the whole earth, and make it desolate (as in Jer 4:23-27). There follows a powerful word play: he will twist or scour its surface, scattering its inhabitants.

2. Life will become horrible for *everyone*. All ranks and classes will be affected by a common destruction. Not only will the majority suffer who are irreligious, but also the minority who are godly. Not only will the many be traumatised who are labourers or workers, but also the few who are managers and chief executives. Not only will those who wait on others eat humble pie, but also those who bossily order them around. Not only will shoppers be disappointed and downhearted, but also salespersons and shop owners. Not only will those who have borrowed lose out, but also those who have lent. Not only will debtors feel the burden of their debts, but also their creditors, for they will not be paid back.

3. The earth will be laid waste, and chaos will reign. The world will be utterly despoiled, and nothing beautiful will remain on it. All this will most certainly take place, for Yahweh has decided it and has made it known.

4. A terrible drought will come. The earth will dry up and wither. Water will be scarce and many will suffer thirst. The world will languish and wither. People will not feel like working. Needs and tasks will multiply; it will all be too much. The heavens will languish together with the earth. The sun will be stifling and life will lose its zest. A profound unhappiness will descend over everyone.

5. What is the reason for this world-wide devastation? Why is Yahweh destroying his beautiful creation? Because "the earth lies polluted under its inhabitants".

Is this a "green" statement? Yes, but it is very much more than that. The physical pollution of the earth echoes the moral pollution of its inhabitants. Yahweh pinpoints the heart of the problem. The people "have transgressed laws, violated the statutes, and broken the everlasting covenant". They have violated the most important dictates of morality. They have done what they knew was wrong. The heart of the human problem is always the problem of the human heart.

6. The earth, not surprisingly, is under a curse because of the selfishness of its people. They are guilty before God, their maker and saviour, and they suffer on account of their guilt. Populations dwindle, but there is a ray of hope in this verse. "Few people are left". "Few" is better than none, especially if the remnant are godly. This fleeting flash of light will repeat itself in verse 13.

7. Wine (v7) and music (v8), the usual means of social enjoyment, will cease. Those who love to party will be left alone, sighing. When people choose "the fleeting pleasures of sin" (Heb 11:25), real joy can no longer be part of their lives.

8. The sounds of joy will no longer be heard. Timbrels and lyres will lie unused, and those who were jubilant will now be alone. They will lose the will to live.

9. People will try every means to escape from being engulfed by darkness. They will seek to drown their sorrows, but will be unable to do so. They will try strong wine and singing, but the drink will taste bitter in their mouths and further enhance their deep-seated resentment and sense of grievance. As Alec Motyer observes, "To want nothing but this world is to end up with nothing but want".

10. "The city of chaos" (in Hebrew *tohu*) is unnamed but typical. Its chaos is the result of sin, which returns us to the original entropy of the universe before the Spirit hovered over the "formless (*tohu* again) void" (Gen 1:2). Sin always has a regressive effect. It returns to formlessness the order instilled by God. The most damaging sin is to live in God's world without God, and every attempt to found a godless city will result in meaningless *ennui*, however civilised it may pretend to be. Its houses will end up by being "shut up so that no one can enter". It is lonely and scary to live in the city of chaos. It is best to live alone there. There is no community. It is as if everyone decided to self-isolate perpetually.

11. There will be protests because of the lack of wine. The times of joy will, to all intents and purposes, be over. That lovely sense of pleasure and satisfaction which we call gladness will be banished from the earth.

12. The cities will be left desolate. Their gates will be battered into ruins. There will be no protection or security then.

13. Isaiah foretells the almost complete extermination of the human race. But there is another ray of hope; did you notice it? After the grapes of wrath have been harvested (Rev 14:17-20), "the gleaning" will still be there. A few good grapes will remain. A few godly people will be left, as in verse 6. We have met this idea before, with the same metaphor being used to describe the fate of the

ten northern tribes (17:6). Once again we are being presented with the godly remnant (10:20-23).

Meditation: The Fall and Rise of Planet Earth

"Now Yahweh is about to lay waste the earth and make it desolate, and he will twist its surface and scatter its inhabitants" (v 1). The prophet here announces the imminence of the Day of Judgement. Yahweh is about to do this; he could do it at any moment. Two happenings will characterise that great day. God will execute his judgement, which will be devastating (v 1-13, 17-22). And Yahweh will be exalted and praised amid tremendous joy, expressed in song (v 14-16).

Why will God judge the earth? The reason is clearly spelt out in verse 5b. God's laws, written in the consciences of every man and woman, have been broken. His statutes, the standards of right and wrong which are known to all people without exception, have been violated. His everlasting covenant, whereby every person in the world knows that they are answerable for their actions before the God who loves them, has been broken. And so the divine judgement must come.

The Hebrew of verse 1 is particularly vivid. Yahweh will take up the earth as you or I would pick up a filthy bowl. He will turn it upside down, scrape out unwanted remains, and then scour it clean. This is what God has to do, and he will do it because of people's selfishness and disobedience. He is holy and must clean up the futility and impurity of the world. What he created as very good, we have contrived to spoil. Nowhere does the Bible teach that matter is evil. When God had created all things, "he saw everything that he had made, and indeed, it was very good" (Gen 1:31). On the other hand, at various points the Bible declares that the ground is cursed, but it is made abundantly clear that this cursing is on account of people's sin (e.g. Gen 3:17).

This is the background to verse 5a: "The earth lies polluted under its inhabitants". It is evident that there is something wrong with the environment in which we live. When we speak of a few locations in the countryside nearby as being "unspoilt", we imply that most of the rest of the planet has been spoilt, and that we ourselves are guilty of spoiling it.

George Adam Smith writes eloquently about this: "The flood, the destruction of Sodom and Gomorrah, the plagues of Egypt and other great physical catastrophes happened because people were stubborn or foul. Matter was thus convulsed and destroyed, not only for the purpose of punishing the moral agents, but because of some poison which had passed from them into the unconscious instruments, stage and circumstance of their crime. According to the Bible, there would appear to be some mysterious sympathy between humankind and nature. People not only govern nature; they infect and inform her. As the moral life of the soul expresses itself in the physical life of the body for the latter's health or corruption, so the conduct of the human race affects the life of the universe to its farthest limits in space. When people are reconciled to God, the wilderness blossoms like a rose (chapter 35); but the guilt of men and women sullies, infects and corrupts the place they inhabit and the articles they employ; and the destruction of matter becomes necessary not for the punishment of people, so much as because of the infection and pollution that has been transmitted to matter".

This principle is to be applied to the whole planet on the final day. What happened to Sodom and Gomorrah because of the notorious sin of its people (Gen 19:13, 24-25), what happened to Jericho on account of the sin of the Canaanite residents (Josh 6:1-26), will on the day of judgement become the fate of the whole world. Isaiah's prophecy (v6) will be confirmed in the New Testament. "The day of the Lord will come like a thief, and then the heavens will pass away with a loud noise, and the elements will be dissolved with fire, and the earth and everything that is done on it will be disclosed" (2 Pet 3:10).

The results will be wonderful for the planet itself. It will be recreated as it once was, but it will be freed from the pollution that spoilt it. It is almost as if the earth will welcome its destruction and subsequent restoration, when the sea and the hills will sing (Ps 98:7-9). Isaiah has already prophesied about this: "the earth will be full of the knowledge of Yahweh as the waters cover the sea" (11:6-9).

The Apostle Paul also wrote on this theme. "The creation waits with eager longing for the revealing of the children of God; for the creation was subjected to futility, not of its own will but by the will of the one who subjected it, in hope that the creation itself will be set free from its bondage to decay and will obtain the freedom of the glory of the children of God" (Rom 8:19-21). People were put in charge of the lower creation, and through the fall they infected it with a bondage to decay. But in God's plan, the Messiah would break the result of the fall, not only for men and women, but also for the creation which is dependent on them.

There is more on this later in the book of Isaiah. We must wait until the book's penultimate chapter to learn about God's future creation of "new heavens and a new earth" (65:17).

XLIV

24:14-23 Godly Praise lightens the Gloom

The judgement of God is both terrible (for the lost, v 1-13 and 17-22) and glorious (for the meek who have been wronged, for whom every wrong will be put right, v 14-16, 23). After the stilling of worldly singing will come the increasingly loud and joyful songs of the remnant.

14. The scattered remnant (verses 6, 13) will lift up their voices and sing with joy. They will shout from both the west (this verse) and the east (v15). The cause of their joy is the *majesty* of Yahweh.

15. They also rejoice because they can *give glory* to Yahweh. The rejoicing will spread to the islands of the Mediterranean Sea near to the land of Israel. It will be good when humble people glorify the *name* of Yahweh, the God of Israel. The name sums up the person, so the name of Yahweh means what he is like: majestic, holy, righteous, just, generous, kind and loving.

16. Once all of Israel is singing Yahweh's praises, the worship spreads out to all the Gentile nations. From the ends of the earth songs of praise can be heard. Glory will be given by all the godly, whether Jewish or Gentile, to the Righteous One. He will ensure the triumph of good over evil and will put to rights every wrong that has ever been committed. But the prophet is deeply troubled, and cannot share in such a positive outburst of praise and delight. He declares that he is pining away and feels under a curse. "Woe is me!" he says, "for the treacherous deal treacherously". He then corrects himself, because things are even worse than that. In fact, the treacherous deal *very* treacherously.

17. We are back to the Day of Judgement. Terror, pit and snare are much alike. All of life seems a series of traps to catch out the unwary inhabitants of the earth.

18. If a person flees at the sound of terror, he will fall into the pit. And if he is fortunate enough to climb out of the pit, he will be caught in the snare. The Prophet Amos, who preached to the ten northern tribes, was older than Isaiah. He used a similar progression to illustrate the inescapability of God's judgement: the day of Yahweh would be "as if someone fled from a lion, and was met by a bear; or went into the house and rested a hand against the wall, and was bitten by a snake" (Amos 5:19). Once "the windows of heaven are opened" it will be like the judgement of the great flood. The foundations of the earth will tremble.

19. The earth will crack open. It will be torn apart into fragments. It will be shaken violently.

20. The earth will stagger like a drunkard, swaying to and fro like a building about to topple in a hurricane. The earth will be loaded with guilt. Great will be its fall. The old polluted planet will never rise again.

21. The judgement will not be confined to the evils on earth. It will be cosmic in its scope. The host of heaven means "the rulers, the authorities, the cosmic powers of this present darkness, the spiritual forces of evil in the heavenly places" (Eph 6:12; see also Rom 8:38-39, Col 2:15, Rev 12:7-9). These forces of evil will be punished in heaven, just as the kings of the earth will be punished on earth.

22. They will all be gathered together in a pit. They will be imprisoned there, and after a long period of time they will be punished (2 Pet 2:4, Jude 6). Their torment with its everlasting consequences (66:24, Rev 20:10) will be a perpetual reminder to godly men and women of what they, by grace, have been utterly saved from. They will welcome God's judgement as the ultimate triumph of good over evil, and of right over wrong.

23. The end will be dazzling glory. The moon and even the shining sun will pale by comparison. The most radiant One, Yahweh of the armies, will reign as King

in the holy city, for the prophet cannot help but think of Jerusalem as the ultimate dwelling place of the holy remnant. A similar vision rounds up the New
Testament (Rev 21:22-27).

Meditation: The Subject no one may talk about

The great Bible truth that there will be a final judgement is out of fashion today, but that
is not all. We have reached a point where to mention the judgement is the ultimate *faux
pas*, the supreme pinnacle of poor taste. When absolutely pressed on the matter, many
nominal Christians would reply, "Of course we believe in it! But please do not mention it
in public. We would rather not think about it".

Barry Webb writes that the message of God's judgement "needs to be sounded
clearly today, when the church has grown squeamish about the truth of divine retribution". Verses 17-22 make it clear that escape will be impossible for those whom God
will judge. They will be like animals who are fleeing from a mighty hunter who has laid
down an endless series of traps for them, and they will not be able to escape him for
long (v 17-18). As they continue to run away from the heavenly hunter, the ground they
are stepping on will break up under their feet (v 19-20). Like captive rebels, they will be
cast into prison, together with the dark forces they have followed, and there await their
final punishment (v 21-22).

There will be no escape for impenitent rebels who have persistently ignored and
disobeyed God. Indeed, God has already "fixed a day on which he will have the world
judged in righteousness by a man whom he has appointed, and of this he has given
assurance to all by raising him from the dead" (Acts 17:31) – the man in question being,
of course, the Messiah.

The purpose of the judgement is wholly positive. It will bring inner cleansing and settled
holiness. It will glorify God, who will be seen to be in the right, and whose radiance will
out-dazzle even the heavenly luminaries (v 23). A vital constituent of God's glory is his
grace. There will be great rejoicing among the humble, the poor and the godly all over
the earth (v 14-16). God will have done what is *right*. He will be exalted as King of kings in
the city of God (v 23, which recaps 2:1-5). He will manifest his glory before his *elders* – for
every member of the godly remnant, however humble their calling or their gifts, will be in
a position of responsibility and oversight in the new life (Lk 19:17, 19).

It is not only the 21st century church that dislikes any mention of the coming judgement. The prophet suffered fits of despondency after preaching about it. He was considering the positive side, speaking of the joy of the godly remnant as they praised Yahweh
for his majesty and his righteousness (v 14-16). Suddenly he was enveloped in deep
gloom. He felt himself wasting away. It was not easy to come to terms with the fate that
awaited certain people, however much they may have deserved it. "But I say, I pine
away, I pine away. Woe is me! For the treacherous deal treacherously. The treacherous
deal very treacherously" (v 16).

We have encountered this same pattern of behaviour a number of times. In 21:3-4 Isaiah, in spite of longing for God's retribution to be visited on Babylon, went into a state of shock when he realised what was coming to them: "Therefore my loins are filled with anguish; pangs have seized me, like the pangs of a woman in labour; I am bowed down so that I cannot hear, I am dismayed so that I cannot see". In 22:1-2 and 12-14 Isaiah was astonished that the people of Israel were overeating and getting drunk immediately after being dramatically rescued by God in one of the most amazing miraculous visitations of all time, and in 22:4 he was inconsolable, saying, "Look away from me, let me weep bitter tears; do not try to comfort me for the destruction of my beloved people". In 22:25 Isaiah must have been very upset when he discovered that someone whom he had trusted and who had attained high office had been found guilty of nepotism.

Here in v 16 a particular sin committed by a few people had deeply upset him: "I pine away. Woe is me! For the treacherous deal treacherously. The treacherous deal very treacherously". The immoral and unreliable world just goes on in its selfish ways. There is no stopping it. The Bible suggests that certain sins, which people are hardly aware of committing, are potentially damnable. Unclean speech (6:5) is one. Deceitful treachery is another. It is a horrible sin (Jn 13:21-30).

XLV

25:1-12 The great Deliverance

1. Another song is heard. We must wait until v 4 to find out who the singers are. They are wholeheartedly praising Yahweh because he is *their* God. They exalt him and praise his name. What he has done causes them to marvel. His purposeful plans, which he formed long ago (22:11), reveal his faithfulness and his resolve.

2. The enemies' fortifications are toppled and their worldly city (Nineveh) collapses in ruins. Great palatial dwellings have been destroyed. They belonged to presumptuous people, alien to God's purposes. They will never be rebuilt.

3. The word *ruthless*, occurring three times in three consecutive verses, tells of the special suffering of certain people who were poor and needy. The nations that oppressed them were strong and ruthless, but they have been brought to their senses by Yahweh of the armies. They now fear him, even in their cities.

4. We are told that it is the *poor* who are singing this song. They have found a refuge in God. When they were needy and in great distress, Yahweh was there for them. He sheltered them from evil, from stormy rain and searing sunshine. There were times when the ruthless battered them like a winter rainstorm.

5. The noisy aliens were relentless, like heat in a dry place. Then Yahweh subdued the enemies, like a cloud when it covers up the heat of the sun.

6. "This mountain" refers to Mount Zion, i.e. Jerusalem (24:23). There Yahweh would provide for people from all nations of the world a celebratory feast of rich food and vintage wines. The food would be nourishing, with tasty marrow, and the wines would be clear in spite of their age. According to John Skinner, "This passage (v 6-8), standing out as it does from a gloomy background of judgement and terror, is one of the most remarkable and fascinating in the Old Testament".

7. There, in Jerusalem, Yahweh would destroy the shroud that for so long had covered the peoples and the sheet that for so long had been spread over the nations. This shroud and sheet could be one used for mourning in a time of great wretchedness (v 8). Here it probably refers to a veil that kept many people in a state of blindness, unable to recognise their God and saviour (2 Cor 3:15-16).

8. In this verse we have a promise which, according to Derek Kidner, "is one of the glories of both the Old and the New Testaments". The prophet states that Yahweh "will swallow up death forever". This was picked up by the Apostle Paul when he wrote that "Death has been swallowed up in victory" (1 Cor 15:54). After his wonderful triumph over death, the Lord God "will wipe away the tears from all faces" (quoted in Rev 7:17). As if this were not enough, he will also remove all the disgrace of his people, who have been derided throughout the whole earth. This is certain to happen, "for Yahweh has spoken". In one truly magnificent verse, the last enemy is gone, the last tear is shed and the last cause of shame is obliterated. But one undesirable thing still remains to be destroyed.

9. On that great final day the godly will say that they had waited expectantly for God's salvation. They had patiently looked to Yahweh to save them fully. The day of their salvation finally arrived! They quietly and joyfully urged each other to be glad and to rejoice in God's wonderful salvation.

10. Yahweh's hand would rest on Mount Zion. But what of the impenitent? The Moabites are introduced as the embodiment of pride (v 11, see 16:6). They were not a great people, but they were *so very proud*. What would happen to their pride, that very undesirable thing? They themselves would suffer great indignity, being trodden down like straw in a dung-pit. Isaiah has already wept about their fate in 15:5 and 16:7, 9, 11. He is not unfeeling about his distant relatives.

11. Even if they tried to swim away through the swill, employing the breast-stroke, they would not escape. "Their pride will be laid low".

12. To symbolise the downfall of their arrogance, the high fortifications of their walls would be demolished, "laid low, cast to the ground, even to the dust". As the Messiah would later say, "all who exalt themselves will be humbled" (Lk 18:14, see also Isa 14:14-15).

Meditation: What the next Life will lack

We try to think of the next life in terms of what it will hold in store for us. The Bible, however, often presents it to us in terms of what will *not* be there (Rev 21:8, 22-27). Here in chapter 25 the prophet informs us of five things that will be completely absent once God has intervened to wind up this current age. They are: the shroud or veil, the last enemy, the tears of pain or sorrow, the disgrace of being God's people, and the root of all evil which is pride.

(a) "And he will destroy . . . the shroud" (v7). The shroud or veil that keeps us from seeing God clearly will be removed. No longer shall we have periods when we are blind to him, or "see [him] in a mirror dimly" (1 Cor 13:12), or "see the glory of the Lord as though reflected in a mirror" (2 Cor 3:18). Instead, we shall see God *clearly*. "When he is revealed, we will be like him, for we will see him as he is" (1 Jn 3:2). In the interim, we may continue in our efforts to perceive God and his Messiah more clearly in spite of the veil. We have our priceless hope of glory. "And all who have this hope in him purify themselves, just as he is pure" (1 Jn 3:3). We will be encouraged as we continue to be "transformed into [his] image from one degree of glory to another" (2 Cor 3:18).

(b) "The last enemy to be destroyed is death" (1 Cor 15:26). In this life, the reality is that one out of one die. Death opens its mouth and swallows people up, one by one. There is a relentlessness about death that depresses us all. Death is the terror of kings and the king of terrors. But on the final day, it will be God's turn to open his mouth, and "he will swallow up death forever" (v8). The words, "he will swallow up death forever", contain the clearest expression of the hope of eternal life to be found in the prophetic writings. There will be no more death!

(c) "Then the Lord God will wipe away the tears from all faces". We have all seen a very minor disaster occur when a child falls down and bursts into tears. The father or mother will pick their child up, and with their hand they will gently and lovingly wipe away the tears. The Lord God, our heavenly Father, will wipe away our every tear (Rev 21:4). John Skinner comments that "Perhaps no words have ever been written that have sunk deeper into the aching heart of humanity than this exquisite image of the divine tenderness".

(d) "The disgrace of his people he will take away from all the earth". Towards the end of their stay in Egypt, the Israelites lived as slaves, and their existence was miserable. Likewise in our own days, the people of God suffer disgrace for the name of Jesus Christ. They are hindered in their mission by circumstances and by sin – the sin of worldly people and their own sin. They are unable to live according to their true dignity as sons and daughters of God. This state will be completely changed. Their new nature will be fulfilled in a perfect environment where everything will point towards love and holiness (Phil 3:20-21).

(e) "Pride will be laid low". The pride of people is exceedingly ugly and it will destroy them in hell. In the lake that is full of pigswill proud people will not cry out for God to save them. Instead, they will try to save themselves. This will not work. They will eventually get exhausted from breast-stroking. They will then begin to sink. They will drown in unspeakable filth. That filth which fills the lake will consist of the pride of all the people who persisted in clinging onto it.

It is wonderful to think what we have been saved *for*. We shall enjoy God and worship him forever. We shall spend the numberless years of eternity trying to grasp fully the unreachable depths of God's love, the self-giving deeds and words of the Messiah, and the beauty of the endowments given to us by God's Spirit.

Equally, it is wonderful to think of what we will be saved *from*. A future in which our vision continued to be blurred and we could only see dimly, a future in which death went on destroying, a future marked by tears of grief and shame, a future full of the reproaches of other people, and a future where everyone was scarred by selfish pride – this would not be a future. It would be hell.

XLVI

26:1-13 The City of God will endure

1. It is time for another song. This one is being sung by the godly remnant in the land of Judah. They (and we) have a city, Jerusalem, and it is strong. Its strength comes from the living God, who alone gives it victory. It is not meant to be a city of chaos (24:10), nor to be greatly fortified (25:2), nor to be ruthless (25:3), and when God has finished his restorative work there, it will not be lofty (v5).

2. Its gates will open wide to welcome people of other nations, but only if they are righteous and keep faith.

3. This verse is short, but its advice is priceless. It could be translated, "You will keep those people in perfect peace, whose mind is focused on you, because they trust in you". The godly are those who have learnt to rest in God. They know how to "wait for Yahweh" (40:31). They will be kept by God in perfect peace, which is not just the absence of strife, but also positive well-being and wholeness. "Peace" here is "*Shalom Shalom*", and *Jerusalem* literally means "Foundation of double peace". Those who live with God in his city will have peace. Genuine believers are often given deep peace at times of crisis and even at death.

4. Therefore the prophet urges us to trust in *Yah Yahweh* (12:2) forever. In him we have an "everlasting rock". God is always dependable. He will not give way, like shifting sand. To build the edifice of our lives on him is a guarantee that we will be kept perfectly safe (Ps 18:2, Mt 7:24-27). A famous hymn by Augustus Toplady begins, "Rock of ages, cleft for me, let me hide myself in thee".

5. What is lofty must be levelled. Yahweh is a humble God, and he cannot endure his people if they are proud. So he brings low the inhabitants of the proud heights. He lays low the lofty city, casting its pride to the dust.

6. The poor and needy have no need for exploits stemming from loftiness and pride. On the day of Yahweh their feet will trample over such exploits.

7. The righteous walk on a level and straight path. It is absolutely right for them in every detail (Ps 84:6). It does not always feel like an easy path, but the Just One will somehow ensure that for the righteous, it will prove to be a smooth one.

8. In this world the people of God have to spend periods of time waiting for him. Sometimes we wait for him "in the path of [his] judgements". We may need to wait in order to find out when we should do something, and as we do so we learn about his timing for us (Ps 37:5). The more we learn about him, the more our heart's desire is for the spread of *his* name and *his* fame (Mt 6:9, Ps 57:5, 11).

9. We can wait for God in the night. Sometimes he gives us sleepless periods so that we may wait for him. Sleeplessness can be pleasant and constructive if we know how to wait for God. As we long for *him*, we find ourselves praying for the peoples of the world to learn righteousness from his judgements.

10. We may wonder how the rich and proud can learn God's righteous ways. Having received the favour of God, they often respond perversely. They remain indifferent to his majestic holiness, and they refuse to learn his righteousness.

11. Yahweh's just hand is lifted up against the rich and the proud, but they do not see it. We long that they might see God's zeal as he purifies his people. It is dangerous to resist him. We long that he might burn away whatever it is that impedes the rich and the proud from learning his ways. We dread the thought that he might have to destroy them.

12. We look to Yahweh to ordain peace for us. We can do nothing without his help (Ps 90:17, Ps 127:1-2). All our achievements are thanks to his grace.

13. Ungodly people have lorded it over us. It is a feature of life in this world. When we were placed under the lordship of the proud and the unsympathetic, we found ourselves unsatisfied and unfulfilled. It is only Yahweh who brings deep satisfaction, for he is our God!

Meditation: A profound Psalm born of Experience

In this section the prophet gives us a psalm to sing aloud or to think about quietly. Some of its thoughts may not immediately be clear or helpful, but as we meditate on it we shall begin to realise how deep it is as a summary of reality, both now and when it was written. The psalm in these verses is structured like a chain. A word or idea is taken up from one verse, and suggests a new thought for the next. It is a helpful exercise to retrace our way through it.

In v 1 the psalm or song is introduced. The theme of this verse is that we, as God's people, have a strong city. Its strength is not human but divine. If God is for us, who is against us? (Rom 8:31). God's strength is as good as any bulwarks or walls. The mention of city *walls* brings to mind city *gates*.

In v 2 the command is given to open the gates of the city of God. All are welcome, whatever their nation or people group, provided only that they keep the faith. The mention of *faith* prompts the prophet to explain carefully what *faith* means.

In v 3 we sing about faith. The most important thing that we can do is to trust in God. Our mind should be steadfast and fixed. Our focus must be on God himself. He will give us his peace even in the midst of turmoil. It is a question of whom we *trust*. This immediately causes us to declare who it is that we *trust*. With faith, it *is* possible to please God (Heb 11:6).

In v 4 we urge one another to trust in Yahweh forever. He is our God and in him we have a totally dependable rock that will continually hold us up. This rock of ours is everlasting. The *everlasting* nature of God leads us to think about what we might depend on that is undependable and *fleeting*.

In v 5 we reflect on the fall of the city of man. It is full of proud people, but those who walk in pride, God is able to bring low (Dan 4:37). The city is haughty and lifts itself up, but it will be laid low by God, and cast to the dust. This *dust* reminds us of dusty *footpaths*.

In v 6 we think of the poor and needy, whose steps will trample on the dust that was once a proud city. These people are often identified by the prophet with the *righteous*, so our thoughts turn to the humble and *righteous* people of God.

In v 7 we think about the path of the righteous. It is a level path. This does not mean it is an easy path: the opposite is often the case. But the Just One will make smooth the way of the righteous. The thought that God is *Just* leads us on to think of his *judgements*.

In v 8 we reflect that the path of Yahweh's judgements sometimes involves waiting for him. Our soul's desire is for his name to be hallowed, for his kingdom to come, and for his good and perfect will to be done. As we think of waiting for God and of our *longing* for him, we think of our *nocturnal thoughts*.

In v 9 we remember those sweet hours in the middle of the night when we yearned for God. Our inner being longed for him, for when he stirs the nations and judges of the earth, *worldly* people may begin to learn righteousness. Many people are *wicked*, how will they learn?

In v 10 it occurs to us that the wicked will never learn righteousness from the good times in life. Were they to come into the city of God and see uprightness, they would deal perversely as is their wont. They would be *blind* to Yahweh's majesty. What might they be able to *see*?

In v 11 we are pessimistic whether anything could change them. Yahweh's hand raised in punishment? They would not see it. What if they saw Yahweh's zeal as he transforms his people into those who are holy and *humble*? This ought to make them feel ashamed. If it does not, their *pride* makes them fit for destruction.

In v 12 we cast away any thought that might make us proud of what we have done. We remind ourselves that anything good that we have done, Yahweh has done for us. It is so good to humble ourselves before him in this way (1 Pet 5:6). It restores our vision and helps us to walk humbly with *our God* (Mic 6:8). It is only *Yahweh* who can ordain peace for his humble people.

Finally, in v 13 we declare that in Yahweh alone there is true joy and peace to be found. We have toiled under ungodly lords. They did not bring us joy and peace. From now on it is only Yahweh whose name we shall acknowledge!

This method of interpreting a passage is suitable when dealing with many of the Psalms. It involves untangling the train of thought of the original writer. It is interesting to see how he or she was led from one idea to another, often by means of a word. This same technique of writing was used in novels by authors like Marcel Proust, James Joyce and William Faulkner in the first half of the twentieth century. It was termed "Stream of Consciousness" and was considered the last word in *avant-garde* writing. It was in fact invented over two and a half millennia earlier by some wise Hebrew men. They used it as a means to describe how they and their readers could profitably talk to God about their lives and his purposes.

XLVII

26:14-21 Waiting for the Resurrection

The prophet changes the direction of his psalm. His thoughts turn to the "shades" that inhabit Sheol. We have encountered them briefly before (14:9-11, 15-20). God's people sometimes have to "wait for Yahweh". The shades in Sheol are also "waiting" – and their long wait will not be in vain. Little do they know that what they are waiting for is the resurrection of their bodies.

14. The prophet thinks of those who have died. His first thought is that his previous oppressors (v 13) no longer live, for the shades do not rise from Sheol. Yahweh must have punished and destroyed them. Indeed, so much is this the case that the very memory of them has perished (Ps 9:6; Ps 37:10, 20, 35-36).

15. Yahweh has replaced the godly departed with their children and successors. He has increased the nation, and so brought glory to himself, enlarging its borders.

16. The prophet reminds Yahweh that the godly departed used to seek him. When his punishing hand was heavy upon them, "they poured out a prayer".

17. The prophet aligns himself with the godly people among the shades: he is, as they once were, similar to a woman about to give birth. Life is not easy for the godly, so he and they would writhe and cry out in their birth pangs. This agony that they suffered was on account of Yahweh and his mysterious designs.

18. They were in labour; they writhed in pain. Would something great come out of this suffering? Sadly, instead of a child, all they could produce was wind! They had no glorious victories to remember, and nobody would live long enough to enjoy the new life forever. This did not make sense, unless it was, as Barry Webb

suggests, "an acute crisis of faith which must issue in either despair or a break-through to a new understanding of God's ways".

19. It is at this moment of absolute perplexity that Yahweh shouts out his reply. It is a magnificent promise of new resurrection life. It is a New Testament promise uttered over 500 years ahead of its time. It is one of only two texts in the entire Old Testament that promise bodily resurrection. God declares that the dead shall live, that their bodies shall rise, that the earth will give birth to these shades after many years of death, and that those long dead will awake and sing for joy. The divine dew will fall on them and awaken them. It is a "radiant dew", a dew of light, for it brings the freshness of dawn (Ps 110:3b).

20. The judgement of Yahweh is on its way, so God's people are to enter into their rooms and shut the doors. They are to hide until the wrath is past. This is not unlike the occasion when God shut Noah up in the ark (Gen 7:6-16), or when the Israelites on the eve of their exodus from Egypt were told to take refuge from the destroying angel (Ex 12:22). God's people are to "hide [themselves] for a little while until the wrath is past". It will not take long for God's judgement to fall. It will be better for them to hide away, so terrible will it be. Could this hiding away refer to death? God's people will be shut up in the grave, safely waiting for the destruction of this present world and the emergence of the new one.

21. On that dreaded day "Yahweh [will come] out from his place to punish the inhabitants of the earth for their iniquity. The earth will disclose the blood shed on it, and will no longer cover its slain". Every bit of bloodshed, every malicious action, will be disclosed. Every crime ever committed will be accounted for, even those "perfect crimes" about which nobody was ever supposed to find out. The guilty will be seen to be guilty, and their bloodshed, their pride and their selfishness will finally reap the reward that they deserve.

Meditation: An extraordinary new Insight

There is going to be a glorious new world. Everything there will be perfect. It will be like the old world, but gloriously renewed, with neither pride nor selfishness nor sin to mar it. The prophet was glad to proclaim this good news, but it was greeted with a troublesome question: who would enjoy the perfectly renewed earth? Presumably it would be those who were still alive when it happened. Everybody else would have died. Even those who were alive then would not enjoy the new world for very long. They too would die. As a result, this was not a very inspiring hope. At best, it consisted of a fleeting glimpse of a wonderful world peopled by perfect men and women. Death is always an incongruity, and in a perfect world death would be all the more incongruous. There had to be some way around the problems raised by the irreversibility of death.

But death will be no more. The prophet has already declared (25:8) that Yahweh of the armies will swallow death up for ever. So those of God's people who are alive in the final day would live for ever in God's new world. That sounded better, but a problem remained. What about those of God's people who died or would die before the final day? It was unfair that they should miss out on eternal life.

But wait a moment. Yahweh had something further to say through his prophet, and it was amazing. Isaiah 26:19: "Your dead shall live, their corpses shall rise. The earth will give birth to those long dead". Christians have declared for nearly two millennia that they believe in the resurrection of the body. The prophet anticipated them, and said as much over 500 years before the first Christians believed in the Messiah. The prophet was way, way ahead of his time. How did he come to this belief?

It was a giant leap of faith-prompted thinking. If Yahweh was such a great saviour God, it just had to be so. If God was going to renew the heavens and the earth (11:6-9, 65:17-25), there would have to be some people to enjoy it. The promises of God were for his godly people. They would not get much enjoyment if death still existed – but Yahweh would swallow up death forever. But why should all the godly of past generations not partake as well? Why must they continue their endless existence as shades in Sheol? This was surely unjust and unfair. It would be a dark stain on Yahweh's perfect designs. As the prophet wrestled with what seemed an intractable problem, one day the truth burst in upon him. It was another oracle from the Holy One of Israel. Yahweh spoke it forth; Yahweh shouted it! "Your dead shall live, their corpses shall rise. O dwellers in the dust, awake and sing for joy! For your dew is a radiant dew, and the earth will give birth to those long dead".

The great truth of the resurrection of the body, trumpeted loudly and clearly in the New Testament, would only be anticipated on two occasions in the Old. The certainty of our future resurrection is signed and sealed by the resurrection of the Messiah from the dead. The followers of the Messiah have a wonderful living hope. And the first gleam of this hope is recorded here, in Isaiah 26:19. It shines as brightly as any of the prophecies in this wonderful book.

The other Old Testament text that promises bodily resurrection is Daniel 12:2. It adds two further insights. First, there will be a resurrection not only of the just but also of the unjust. Secondly, the resurrection will be followed by everlasting life for the just, and by shame and everlasting contempt for the unjust.

XLVIII

27:1-13 The Root, the Shoot and then the Fruit

1. As in 14:21, the judgement of God will not be confined to the evils on earth. Its scope will include the evil beings in heaven, including the fleeing and twisting serpent Leviathan, also known as Satan (Rev 12:9), and the dragon that is in the sea, also known as the beast (Rev 13:1). These will be killed by Yahweh, who will make use of his cruel, great and strong sword.

2. The theme of God's vineyard (5:1-7) is taken up once more. This time the end product is in view, and it will be wonderful. The vineyard is now a pleasant one, and it is good to sing about it.

3. It is hardly surprising that it has turned out so well. Yahweh joyfully informs us that he has appointed himself as its keeper. He confides to us certain details about the loving care that he lavishes on it. He continually waters it. He guards it night and day. He makes sure that nothing will harm it.

4. Yahweh has no wrath against his vineyard any more. His anger is directed against the potential thorns and briers, against the enemies of his people. These he will do battle against if necessary; these he will burn up and destroy.

5. Even the thorns and briers might be spared by Yahweh. He would rather be reconciled to his enemies than have to destroy them. He longs that they might draw near to him for protection. Twice he gives voice to his wish that they might make peace with him. The ball is in their court.

6. The order, in horticulture as in spiritual growth, is: the root, the shoot and then the fruit. "In days to come" God's people would first of all take root by feeding on God's fertilising word, then they would blossom and put forth shoots by obeying his will, and finally they would fill the whole world with their good fruit, which is justice and righteousness (5:7). Notice the contrast between God's vineyard in 5:1-7 and here: it is no longer the world that devours the vineyard, but instead the vineyard takes over the world and fills it with fruit.

7. In verses 7-11 the prophet contrasts, on the one hand, the constructive hardship that would make and refine the true people of God (v 8-9), and on the other, the utter destruction that would befall the enemies of God (v 10-12). Both parties would be struck down; both would in some cases be put to the sword. But there would be a world of difference between them.

8. God's people would be refined through the bitter hardship of exile. A blast of wind from the East, sharp but not lasting, would remove them from their land.

9. There was a double link between God's people renouncing their idolatry and his blotting out of their sin. Not only would the first be the condition of the second ("by this"), it would also be the ongoing consequence of the second ("the full fruit of"). Yahweh would help his people to destroy their old stone altars and sacred poles. Even if this meant their exile, it would constitute an important start, and it would put his idolatrous people on the right road.

10. As for the nation that subjugated God's people and took them into exile, utter disaster would befall them. In the end, their fortified city (Nineveh, as in 25:2) would be a deserted ruin, a wilderness in the wilderness. Calves would graze there, and playfully strip the branches of its formerly loved trees.

11. Once the boughs were dry, women would break and burn them in a warming fire. The enemies of God's people are a nation with no understanding about

the true God. Therefore their maker would have no pity on them; the one who formed them in their mothers' wombs would show them no favour. Because they had been pitiless with the weak, no pity would be shown to them.

12. After the harvest of judgement is over, Yahweh would thresh from Assyria to Egypt in order to gather in the valuable gleanings, namely his people. Yahweh would collect them together one by one and restore them to their land of promise. Not a single one would be lost out of those who relied on Yahweh.

13. "On that day" a great trumpet would be blown (18:3), summoning God's people in exile in Assyria and Egypt. They would return and worship him again on the holy mountain, Mount Zion in Jerusalem. God's final triumph is depicted here not as a new creation, but as the gathering in and bringing home of God's people. This idea lies, of course, at the heart of redemption (Rev 7:9-17).

Meditation: An Apocalypse written ahead of its Time

George Adam Smith made the observation that commentators find it very difficult to date Isaiah's Apocalypse (chapters 24-27). The disaster envisaged in chapter 24 cannot be applied to Judah and Jerusalem alone. Its scope is worldwide and it seems to usher in a new world in which everyone gives praise to God.

In chapters 25-27 there are historical references, but they contradict one another and leave both readers and students perplexed. They suggest certain historical circumstances that pertained before the exile, others that point to the exile itself, and yet others that only applied after the exile. Among the pointers to a pre-exilic date is the guilt incurred by Judah on account of the idolatry of its people (27:9). The mention of Assyria and Egypt (27:12-13) is also strongly suggestive of this, as is the absence of any mention of Babylon. To a lesser extent, the reference to Moab (25:10-12) makes more sense if it was written before the exile.

Secondly, there are other clues which suggest that Isaiah's Apocalypse was composed during the exile. God's people appear to be immersed in a heathen environment (26:9, 10), and the prophet urges them to withdraw from it and enter into the privacy of their chambers (26:20, 21). On various occasions there are prayers and promises of deliverance from the oppressor (24:22, 25:4-5, 26:11-13). Furthermore, hopes are expressed of the establishment of Zion and the repopulation of the Holy Land (24:23, 26:7-8).

Thirdly, some verses imply that the speaker has already returned to Zion (26:1-2). There are mentions of Yahweh's actions "on this mountain" (25:6-10). He is said to have increased the nation and enlarged its borders (26:15). There is a looking back to an expulsion and an exile (27:8). There is a hymn celebrating a restoration that has taken place (25:1-5).

How then should we date this apocalyptic section of the book of Isaiah? How can we explain the catchwords and the living experiences that stem from three distinct periods? The present author has already written on the authorship of the book of Isaiah (see the Introduction, p.6-8). In common with many others, he believes that there were three main authors, Isaiah and two later members of his school. The third of these was a prophet who arose after the return from exile. Like the two prophets who preceded him, he was a gifted poet. In addition, he was a capable editor. He wrote chapters 56-66, and then edited the entire Isaiah *corpus*. He gave final shape to the apocalyptic section (chapters 24-27), including in it some earlier material written by his two predecessors, and unifying its style.

Perhaps his greatest contribution to theology is to be found in the two songs of praise which form chapters 25 and 26. If indeed he wrote them around 530-520 B.C., he was centuries ahead of his time. It would be difficult to exaggerate how much he contributed to the hope of godly people by two of his statements. The first is that God "will swallow up death forever" (25:8). The second is "Your dead shall live, their bodies shall rise. O dwellers in the dust, awake and sing for joy! For your dew is a radiant dew, and the earth will give birth to those long dead" (26:19). The godly need not fear death, or the dust that follows it. The divine and refreshing dew will one day moisten that dust and they will come back to life.

XLIX

28:1-13 So simple! Anyone could understand it

In much of chapters 28-33 Isaiah takes on the temporal and spiritual leaders of Jerusalem in the period 710-701 B.C. He challenges them to face the realities of history, truth and God's sovereignty. Isaiah preached consistently and insistently against an alliance with Egypt against Assyria. God's people were to trust in Yahweh himself for protection from Assyria, and not in the Egyptian army.

1. Ephraim, another name for the northern kingdom of Israel, takes us back in time to before 722 B.C., when it was destroyed by the Assyrians. Ephraim is cited here as an example of what could easily happen to Judah in later years. Its leaders had been proud, like a garland of fading flowers. Bloated with rich food and overcome with wine, the glorious beauty of those who were once God's people was rapidly disintegrating. They had sunk to being "the drunkards of Ephraim".

2. The northern Kingdom was under threat. The Lord had "one who is mighty and strong". This is a reference to the King of Assyria who, together with his highly trained army (5:26-30), would be descending on the capital Samaria. He would be like a tempestuous and destructive hailstorm, and also like a devastating flood.

3. The proud garland of the drunkards of Ephraim would be trampled underfoot.

4. The fading flower of their once glorious beauty, which was on the heads of those bloated with rich food, would be like a first-ripe fig. It would be seized by the hand of a hungry army and swallowed up. This is a vivid word-picture, for the

first-ripe figs, which appear at the end of June, are twice as large as the seasonal figs in October, and they were considered a great delicacy.

5. The dark clouds of judgement part for a moment and we are allowed to see true beauty. It will adorn *the remnant* of God's people "in that day". It will be a garland of glory and a diadem of beauty. It will be Yahweh of the armies himself!

6. Because Yahweh will sit in judgement, there will be both a spirit of justice and a perfect sense of right judgement in all things. Thanks to Yahweh's strength, those who were battling at the gate would be able to turn back any invaders.

7. So much for the drunkards of Ephraim. They got what was coming to them. But what of the princes and courtiers of Judah in the days of the good King Hezekiah? They "also reel with wine and stagger with strong drink". What about the religious leaders? "The priest and the prophet reel with strong drink, they are confused with wine, they stagger with strong drink". And what about their vision of Yahweh? "They err in vision, they stumble in giving judgement".

8. Isaiah confronted these leaders on several occasions. He describes their state of drunkenness very vividly. It must have been disgusting to see the temple chamber where they met. "All tables are covered with filthy vomit; no place is clean". Yahweh's representatives had vomited on the hallowed temple furniture.

9. It is these intoxicated leaders whose words we now hear in v 9-10. They taunt Isaiah for his clear message, and for the simplicity of his words. "Whom is Isaiah lecturing as if they were children? To whom is he spelling out his message? What he says is basic. It is fit only for babies, whether weaned or still breast-feeding".

10. The drunk priests and prophets resented being treated like children, and went on ridiculing Isaiah. "His method is so simple! Precept upon precept, precept upon precept. So tedious! Line upon line, line upon line. No sophistication! Here a little, there a little. Even little children could understand what he is saying!" The Hebrew is a string of repetitions of very similar sounds: "Zaw lasaw zaw lasaw, kaw lakaw, kaw lakaw". J. B. Phillips translated it like this: "Are we just weaned? Must we learn that the law is the law is the law; the rule is the rule is the rule?"

11. The answer is that this is how Yahweh *will* communicate with them: "Truly, with stammering lip and with alien tongue he will speak to this people". Yahweh would speak to them through the harsh rhyming accents of uncouth Assyrians.

12. Isaiah had presented them with a simple but vital truth. What these weary priests and prophets needed was very simple: to enter into God's rest and peace. This and only this would be true repose (see also 30:15). Yet they did not wish to hear him! The idea of finding peace with God was, in their opinion, *just too simple*. Had the Messiah himself appeared to them in person and offered them rest and peace, they would probably not have been interested (Mt 11:28-30).

13. Because of their refusal to listen, God's clear word would become gibberish to the temporal and spiritual rulers of Jerusalem. Yahweh had spoken to them simply,

so that they could easily understand. For them, it rightly was, "Precept upon precept, precept upon precept, line upon line, line upon line, here a little, there a little". But they just turned God's sense into nonsense, hardening their hearts until they became incapable of understanding straightforward truths. Because they had despised words that were intended to save them, similar-sounding sentences uttered by Assyrian soldiers would spell out their doom. They would not take steps forward but instead would fall back. They would not enjoy wholeness but instead would be broken and snared. Finally they would lose their God-given freedom and instead be taken captive.

Meditation: Keep it simple and clear

I (the present author) used to know a former Archbishop of Canterbury, Lord Donald Coggan. One Sunday Lord Coggan was preaching at the local cathedral, and I was unable to go. A few days later I met a Canon of the Cathedral, and asked him if he had been at the service. "Yes, I was there", he said. I asked, "Lord Coggan is an amazing preacher, is he not?" He was embarrassed and replied, "Well, that is a matter of opinion". So I asked, "What did *you* think of him?" He said, "I am afraid I found him rather pedestrian. Everything he said was simple and clear. *Even a child* could have understood his sermon".

That was an unforgettable verdict on a scholarly and distinguished preacher. It is alarming to think what the Canon would have regarded as a good sermon! He would probably not have made much of Lord Coggan's many books. They were scholarly, well researched, clear and straightforward. They appealed to thoughtful Christians who wanted to delve deeply into the Bible.

When Isaiah preached he spoke engagingly but clearly. In his prophetic oracles he combined wonderful poetry, lucid argument, intriguing parables, penetrating analyses of character, convincing links between sin and judgement, wise retorts and epigrams, scornful invective, and numerous other oratorical devices. He was completely faithful to Yahweh, and did not flinch from expounding the basic truths about God and mankind: God's holiness and our sin, God's love and our need of rescue, and God's inevitable judgement for those who firmly persisted in rejecting his plan of salvation. He lived at a time of great spiritual rebelliousness, and many in the religious establishment did not like his teaching. They bitterly resented being told that they, the cream of the theological cream, needed to repent of their sins. They declared that it was *not so simple*. It could not be! Why did Isaiah have to go on saying the same things in all manner of different ways? Why couldn't he move on to *deeper* things?

What the priests and prophets mocked was exactly what Isaiah aimed to achieve, and it was also the worthiest goal of any preacher or teacher. Isaiah captured in words and then eloquently shared the essential simplicity of revealed truth. When he preached, he engaged in a carefully crafted exercise of edification.

One of Isaiah's emphases was the need to place one's trust in God and then to stay one's mind on him. This was the only way that anyone could find that deep experience of peace and rest that was the essence of knowing God. With his emphasis on rest, Isaiah reminded the national religious leaders of their duty to set an example and to minister humbly. They were to enter the place of rest themselves, and then encourage others to follow their example. Isaiah would spell out the idea of entering into God's rest in 30:15. It was the same message that Isaiah had already preached to King Ahaz in 7:4, 9. Alec Motyer commented that "Trusting the Lord is not only an interior exercise of the soul in the calm of a Sunday, but also a repose of the soul during the hard pressures of a Monday".

It was *this very message* that the religious establishment just could not stomach. They hated it. They derided Isaiah for putting it across clearly and persuasively. They poured scorn on him and humiliated him.

George Adam Smith writes that a passage like this has an application for other times than its own. "The truths are relevant to every day in which luxury and intemperance abound, in which there are eyes too fevered by sin to see beauty in simple purity, and minds so surfeited with knowledge or intoxicated with their own cleverness, that they call the maxims of moral reason commonplace and scorn religious instruction as food for babes".

L

28:14-29 Foundation Stone or stumbling Block?

14. Yahweh's word now comes to these scoffers who were the leaders of God's people in Jerusalem.

15. Some of them had returned from Egypt with their wonderful piece of papyrus, proclaiming "We shall have peace in our time!" Isaiah destroys their illusions. They had chosen the wrong kind of security. Their latest secret alliance with Egypt was quite simply a contract with death and an agreement with Sheol. They believed it would keep them safe when the overwhelming Assyrian scourge passed through, but in fact they had no hope for future peace and safety. As far as God was concerned, it was as if they had said, "we have made lies our refuge, and in falsehood we have taken shelter".

16. To provide them with a real hope, Yahweh gave them a rock-solid promise on which they could rest their weight. This promise, together with the one in 8:14, is quoted twice in the New Testament (Rom 9:33 and 1 Pet 2:6). It concerns an architectural keystone: a foundation stone or cornerstone. In 8:14 the stone the building will rest on is the Lord himself, but here in 28:16 it is the Lord who lays it. What is the answer to this riddle? Simply that the stone is the Messiah who

has been sent by the Lord, and the Messiah is also Lord. And what does it mean to build on this "sure foundation"? It means to trust fully in God and in his Messiah, for "One who trusts will not panic". To trust God means to wait for him (49:23b). It is the opposite of panic, which leads to sending couriers to Egypt hastily and shamefully. The foundation stone was there; it was up to them how they would treat it. If they wished, they could use its promise as the foundation of their lives, and then they would find out how solid it was. Alternatively, they could neglect the stone, and then it would become for them a stumbling-block (8:14).

17. This promise was very important because of Yahweh's high standards. Perfect justice is where he draws the line, and perfect righteousness is his plummet. Yahweh would therefore send strong hail to sweep away the peoples' refuge of lies, and irresistible floods to overwhelm their shelter of falsehood.

18. Judah's contract with death was null and void, and its agreement with Sheol was broken and useless. Egypt would not rescue Jerusalem when Yahweh sent his overwhelming scourge, the Assyrian army. Only Yahweh could help them. Would his people trust in him?

19. The coming judgement would be like an extended visitation. From the same scourge would come repeated and persistent blows, raining down and wreaking havoc. It would be too late then to understand and act upon "the message". *Now* was the time to respond and find rest and refreshment. Later – only terror.

20. Egypt would prove to be a miserable and useless resource, like a bed that is too short and whose covering is too narrow to guarantee warmth in a cold night.

21. Yahweh would rise up again like a bursting flood as he did when he gave David victory over the Philistines at Mount Perazim (2 Sam 5:20). He would rage as he did when David struck down the Philistine armies in the valley of Gibeon (1 Chron 14:16). God had in the past swept away David's enemies; now he would sweep away the remains of David's Kingdom. To punish his own people would be a strange deed for Yahweh to perform. Such a task would be an alien work for him to undertake.

22. Isaiah therefore urges the scoffers not to scoff, or the bonds that bound them would become even stronger. The prophet has heard a decree of destruction from the Lord God, which would affect the whole land.

23. Isaiah follows this up with a parable about the farmer's wise labour.

24. Farmers do not keep on ploughing a field once it has been ploughed, nor do they keep opening up and harrowing the soil. Ploughing and harrowing are not ends in themselves, but means to an end. That end is fruitfulness.

25. Once a field is levelled, they scatter seeds of dill and cumin, and they plant wheat in rows. They plant barley in the right place, and make a border of spelt.

26. They are well instructed, for they have learnt their craft from God himself.

27. At the harvest, dill is not threshed with a threshing sledge, nor is a cart wheel

rolled over cumin. Dill is beaten out with a stick, and cumin with a rod.

28. Grain is crushed so as to make bread, and it is therefore best not to thresh it. A cart wheel and horses may be driven over it. Not too much, lest it be pulverised.

29. This wisdom comes from Yahweh of the armies; he is a great teacher and wise in his own doings. Just as a farmer treats different soils in different ways, and uses different instruments for threshing different types of seed, so Yahweh will patiently pursue his purposes for good, both through his kind actions and his strange work of judgement. This combination of the kindness and the severity of God (Rom 11:22) is perfectly suited to the people that he has to deal with. Notice the description of Yahweh as "wonderful in counsel"; likewise one of the names of the Messiah would be "Wonderful Counsellor" (9:6).

Meditation: God's strange and alien Work

There are a number of ways in which Christians respond to the Bible's teaching that God will judge all people. Some *shy away* from it completely. Quoting texts like John 3:17, they like to emphasise that the Messiah came primarily to save us. This means that they neglect the context of his salvation, which is to save us from *perishing* (Jn 3:16). They also forget the fact that the Messiah is not only the saviour of the world but also the One whom God has appointed to judge us all on the last day (Mt 25:31-46, Jn 5:22-29, Acts 17:31).

Some Christians feel compelled to *emphasise* the judgement of God. They mention it at every opportunity. This may cause them to lose sight of the positive side of the good news (most of John 3:16, Isaiah 4:2-6, 11:6-9, and so on). They may come across to others as being themselves judgemental, and however realistic their message may be, it will seem unattractive.

The best approach to difficult concepts like the future judgement is to work out what the balance of scripture is. If we read the Bible regularly, we are promised that we *will* know the truth (Jn 8:31-32). We shall be in a position to see through any unbiblical over-emphases, and steer clear of them. We shall want to present God as *both* holy *and* loving, and his Messiah as *both* judge *and* saviour.

What insights does our passage have to offer on God's coming judgement?

(a) It is right to trust in God for salvation, but foolish to rely on people (v 15).

(b) It is right to rely on the precious cornerstone that God has provided (v 16). If we construct the edifice of our whole lives on the Messiah, our trust in him will keep us from panicking in difficult times. Instead, it will bring us peace.

(c) If we put our trust in anyone or anything other than God or his Messiah, it will be as if our bed was too short and our blanket too narrow (v 20). We shall be cold and anxious, and suffer nightmares instead of enjoying true rest. As Augustine famously put it, our hearts remain restless until they find their rest in God.

(d) It is helpful to realise that judgement is God's *strange* work. It is foreign to him to punish people (v 21b). He must do so, but this is not something that he likes to do. The great German reformer Martin Luther reflected on this verse, and he found comfort in the fact that although judgement is God's strange work, salvation is his *proper* work.

(e) There are many lessons to learn from God's beautiful creation around us (v 23-26). A ploughman does not go on breaking up the fallow ground forever; he only does so until he has a good seed bed, on which he proceeds to sow. Likewise, God isn't going to punish his rebellious people for ever, but only until they are ready to fit into his good purposes. The judgement on the nation will last as long as it has to, but it will not go on for ever.

(f) When it comes to threshing, a farmer has to be careful about which instrument to use (v 27-29). If he uses a threshing sledge on small seeds like dill, or a cart wheel on cumin, he will destroy his seed. He should use a stick or a flail. Of course, when it comes to threshing grain, a cart wheel is good, but even then he must not over-thresh and pulverise the grain, or it will be useless. Farmers thresh, but they do so in a limited way so as not to damage the seed or the grain. God likewise threshes appropriately, taking due care not to cause his people lasting or unnecessary damage.

(g) What God is saying to people is this. For your pride, for your drunkenness, for your inability to accept my word, I am going to plough you up – but only in order to be able to sow good seed. I will bring a thresher over you, but only to separate the good seed from the husks. God is "wonderful in counsel, and excellent in wisdom" (v 30). He has a plan for his people. The plan will include suffering or punishment for the purposes of purifying us, or helping us to bear good fruit. God's chastisement is exactly right for each individual person.

LI

29:1-8 A miraculous Reprieve for Jerusalem

1. Ariel is Zion or Jerusalem (see end of v 8). The word *Ariel* means the altar hearth that was in the Temple (Ezek 43:15). It was a large square altar, with horns at the four corners. Inside it a fire was kept burning and the smoke rose up. Its meaning here must be something like "God's special hearth and altar". Isaiah is about to prophesy that the whole city of Jerusalem would become a consuming fire. Jerusalem was also the city where King David settled, and where the various festivals instituted by Yahweh took place at their appointed times, year by year.

2. In spite of its glorious past, Yahweh is about to distress Ariel. There would be moans and laments. Jerusalem would itself become an altar hearth. Yahweh would light up a consuming fire there, and the city would be burnt to ashes, with every expectation that its people, the people of God, would be exterminated.

3. Just as David had once camped around Jerusalem, besieged it with towers and raised siege-works against it, now it would be David's descendants who would

be at the receiving end. All the epic tales from the past would not help them. Nor would the endless ongoing round of religious festivals (v 1b). Neither a godly heritage nor the externals of religious observance can protect people when God lights a fire of judgement. Any false religion will attempt to make God our servant instead of acknowledging that we are his servants.

4. When the judgement came, the pride of Jerusalem would be turned into the most abject weakness and helplessness. Her citizens would speak like the shades from Sheol. Their voices would be wraith-like, and their speech like a whisper.

5. And yet when all seemed lost, Yahweh would suddenly intervene. The multitude of enemies would become like dust. The bullies and tyrants would be like chaff.

6. There would be a divine visitation. Yahweh himself would come to the rescue! He would be clothed with thunder and clamorous earthquake, he would breathe out a whirlwind and a tempest, and he would wield a flame of devouring fire.

7. The nations had gathered together to fight against Jerusalem and her citadel, the Temple of Yahweh on Mount Zion. But they would vanish like a dream.

8. In the moment of their victory they would be frustrated. They would be like a hungry person who dreams that they are eating, but then wake up still hungry. They would be like a thirsty person who dreams that they are drinking, but then wake up fainting with thirst. This, says Isaiah, is what it will be like for those who fight against God's people. John Skinner observed, "A more vivid representation of utter disenchantment can scarcely be conceived".

Meditation: God is committed to his People

Isaiah reiterated on several occasions this promise of a miraculous and divine delive-rance for Jerusalem. There was a threefold content to his prophecy: (a) The people of Jerusalem were ready for judgement because of their social injustice and idolatry, (b) Yahweh would send the Assyrian army to devastate Judah and initiate an apparently deadly siege of Jerusalem, and (c) Just when the Assyrians had the city surrounded and were thinking about storming it and destroying it, Yahweh would intervene miraculously and destroy the Assyrians.

So far, Isaiah had spoken this prophecy on six occasions. In 10:5-19 he declared that although Assyria was the rod of his fury, Yahweh would also proceed to punish the arro-gant boasting of the Assyrian king. In v 16 Isaiah provided the detail that Yahweh would send a wasting sickness on the Assyrian army. He repeated the prophecy immediately in 10:24-27 and 33-34, asserting that in a short time Yahweh would direct his anger to the destruction of Assyria. In 14:24-27 Isaiah said that Yahweh would "break the Assyrian" in his, i.e. Yahweh's, land. In 17:12-14 Isaiah supplied the detail that the destruction of the entire Assyrian army would be accomplished in a single night (17:14). In 22:1-2 and 12-14 Isaiah foresaw what the consequence of God's deliverance would be, and he was appalled that the response of the citizens of Jerusalem would be gluttonous and drunken bingeing. And in the present passage, 29:1-8, Isaiah repeated that the mighty Assyrians would be reduced to dust, and become like a dream.

These prophecies are particularly impressive as they are interwoven almost casually into the text. It is inconceivable that they were inserted later, after the event had taken place. They had their dramatic historical fulfilment in the year 701 B.C. (37:33-37). We shall see exactly how the details were fulfilled in history in Part 4. For the moment two points need some further thought.

The first point concerns the unusual and universal language of the passage we are studying, 29:1-8. A number of commentators, including Derek Kidner, believe that the gathering of *nations* (v 7-8), the *siege-works* (v 3), and the *spectacular signs* of v 6, are suggestive of a future struggle, one that will be even more dramatic than the immediate fulfilment in 701 B.C. This future struggle is also the subject of later prophecies in the Old Testament (e.g. in Zech 14:1-5), and it is even echoed in the New Testament (e.g. in Rev 19:17-21).

The nations will mount a bitter and deadly attack on the followers of the Messiah. They will do great harm to the people loved by God, but they are destined to be disappointed (Isa 29:7, 8). We have already seen many occasions when worldly leaders like Hitler in Germany, Mao in China, Ceausescu in Romania, and Hoxha in Albania have attempted, unsuccessfully, to destroy the church. There will be further and worse attacks in the future. We are still to see the final concerted attack, in which no mercy will be shown.

The second point to be noted is that those who attack God's people are attacking God, for he is deeply committed to those who are followers of the Messiah. If any reader of these words is anxious about the increasing hostility of worldly people towards the followers of Christ, let him or her take courage. We are not to fear those who kill the body, but who after that can do nothing worse. We are to fear God, who after he has killed, has authority to cast into hell (Lk 12:4-5). As the hymn by Nahum Tate and Nicholas Brady puts it, "Fear him, you saints, and you will then have nothing else to fear". The Messiah himself has promised to intervene, and he is committed to saving his people.

LII

29:9-24 The Darkness deepens and is dispelled

9. In v 9-12 Yahweh has inflicted a judicial stupidity and blindness on the people of Judah and Jerusalem. They chose to stupefy themselves, so they are in a stupor. They chose not to see the prophetic word, so they have become blind (Jn 9:39-41). They are drunk, but not from wine. They stagger, but not from strong drink. Self-will has its own punishment: it gets its own way – but at what cost!

10. Yahweh poured out on them a spirit of deep sleep. Their spiritual lethargy is such that they can no longer react to him. He has closed the eyes of false prophets so that they can no longer see visions, and he has covered the heads of seers so they

can no longer see anything (1 Sam 3:1). The trouble is that, "where there is no prophecy, the people cast off restraint" (Prov 29:18).

11. The prophetic vision has become like a sealed document. Those who are readers will not read it, for it is sealed and they cannot be bothered to open it.

12. Those who are unable to read will likewise not be able to do so, even if the document was to be unsealed, but they do not care. God's will had become to the people of Jerusalem like a closed book. But their inability to read was judicial. It was their expressed wish not to know God's will (30:10).

13. Here we have the very definition of formal and insincere religion. It is to draw near to God with the right words, and to honour him by what we say, when all the time we are just pretending, because our hearts are far from him. True worship is impossible if we are in this state, for our "worship" would then be no more than a human commandment learnt by rote. The Messiah would one day quote these words to a group of Pharisees who valued human traditions more than the word of God (Mt 15:6-9, Mk 7:5-8). True worship is a very positive activity (Jn 4:23, Heb 13:15) and some church people miss out on it.

14. Because the people of Jerusalem were like this, having the form of religion but denying its reality, the Lord God declares that he will do amazing things with them, confounding their speech. The wisdom of those who considered themselves to be wise would perish. The discernment of those who were reputed to be discerning would be hidden. Without reality and depth, wisdom and discernment are just unhelpful manifestations of self-centred cleverness.

15. Isaiah mocks the furtiveness of the pro-Egyptian party. They were very proud of their plans for an anti-Assyrian alliance, which they tried to keep secret. They thought they were wiser than Yahweh, and they reassured each other that their scheming was invisible and unknown. But Yahweh saw and knew.

16. Isaiah tells the leaders of the pro-Egyptian party that they have turned things upside down. He confronts them with some unanswerable questions. Is it the potter or the clay that is in charge? Can the pot say to the potter, "You are not my maker"? Can the creature say to the creator, "You have no understanding"?

17. It is ridiculous to make plans against Yahweh, for he is the God who will bring about great reversals. He will speedily turn the wilderness in Lebanon into good land. Any land that was already good will become much better, so that land that used to be deemed fruitful fields will later be classed only as scrubland.

18. "On that day" a truly wonderful reversal would be brought about by God with the deaf and the blind. The deaf would then be able to hear words from a scroll, now unsealed. The blind would begin to see out of their gloom and darkness.

19. The meek and the needy had endured terrible suffering, but God always had them in his mind's eye. The meek would find themselves rejoicing in Yahweh, and the needy would exult in the Holy One of Israel (Hab 3:17-18).

20. The tyrant who used to bully the meek and the needy, and the scoffer who so arrogantly used to despise the godly, shall be no more. Anyone whose mind was set on doing evil would be cut off from the land of the living.

21. The practitioners of injustice would likewise be cut off. There would be no more false witnesses in lawsuits, no more bent lawyers to confound honest ones, and no more corrupt judges to deny justice to those who were clearly in the right.

22. In the light of the reversals that he would implement, Yahweh, who redeemed Abraham by calling him out of pagan idolatry, has this to say concerning the descendants of Jacob. The day would come when Jacob would no longer turn in his grave because of their behaviour.

23. The Patriarch would look at his children, formed by Yahweh, and he would see them hallowing Yahweh's name (Mt 6:9). They would hallow the Holy One of Israel, magnifying and praising his wonderful life-bringing holiness. They would rightly fear God (11:2, 3), and stand in awe of him.

24. Even the most imperfect people of God are to be perfected. Those who used to err in spirit would now be able to understand; those who previously grumbled would now accept instruction.

Meditation: The Challenge of Isaiah's Words

This section (29:9-24) is quoted five times in the New Testament. The Messiah himself used v 13 to rebuke the Pharisees who considered human traditions to be more important than the word of God (Mt 15:6-9, Mk 7:5-8). The Apostle Paul made use of verses 10, 14 and 16 to confront the stubborn unbelief of certain people in his day (Rom 11:8, 1 Cor 1:19, Rom 9:20). This is consequently a challenging passage. We who are Isaiah's readers should ask ourselves whether we sometimes draw near to God with our words and lips, while our hearts are far from him. Do we sometimes doze off in a spiritual stupor? Has our wisdom, such as it once was, disappeared, and have we taken our discernment and hidden it away? Do we sometimes think that we are wiser than God, or that our way is better than his? The lesson of verses 9-16 is that if we are hypocrites, God will judge us by handing us over to our own puny little wisdom, and we shall end up as the proud purveyors of our own blindness and stupor.

In some ways the vision of the future in verses 17-24 is even more challenging. God is going to bring about a great reversal. He will humble the proud in order to jolt them out of their deception. "On that day" (v 18) the deaf will hear the word of God, and the blind will be able to read it. The meek and the needy will take delight in Yahweh and exult in the Holy One (v 19). All forms of evil will cease (bullying, mocking, despising, and perverting the course of justice in any way). It is striking and instructive that the people of God will hallow God's name. They will stand in awe of him and fear him.

If this is what God's ideal is going to be like, we should aim for it now, in this life. We should repent deeply of our pride, which is the sin that God hates above all others.

We should gaze at Yahweh, as he is portrayed in the book of Isaiah, and learn to be meek as we compare ourselves with him. We should realise our great need. Once we see ourselves as we are, we shall be numbered among the meek and needy – and great will be our delight in the Lord (Ps 37:4). We should turn away from any evil or injustice that mars our lives. We should hallow God's name, and thereby begin to pray the Lord's Prayer aright.

Most important of all, we should fear God (v 23). When Isaiah first encountered God's holiness, his reaction was to lament his own lack of it. "Woe is me! I am lost, for I am a man of unclean lips, and I live among a people of unclean lips" (6:5). He was later instructed to think of God as follows: "[Him] you shall regard as holy; let him be your fear, and let him be your dread" (8:13). Isaiah learnt to fear God. He became a God-fearing man.

How did he learn to fear God? He had seen the majestic and glorious holiness of Yahweh. "My eyes have seen the King, Yahweh of the armies!" It was the first lesson he learnt about God. God was fearfully holy. The second lesson about God would follow later: God was a loving God. This is implicit in much of Isaiah's teaching in chapters 1-39, but only in 16:5 is it explicitly mentioned, and then as a quality of the coming Messiah. We have to wait for chapters 40-66 to learn the principal lessons in the book of Isaiah about God's love. If we wish to present a faithful picture of God, we must emphasise both his holiness and his love. How do these two attributes feature in what we think and say about God?

In the Middle Ages Europe was a very Christian continent. Most people feared God. They had little knowledge of God's love, however, and there was little joy in their lives. From the writings they left us, it seems that few of them delighted in God. This imbalance impoverished their Christian lives: they knew God and they feared him, but on the whole there was little ardour in their worship.

We may consider ourselves fortunate not to have lived in the Middle Ages, but are we in the 21st century church any better at presenting a balanced picture of God? In our stress on the love of God we have over-reacted to the imbalances of the medieval church. It is now the case that never before in its 2,000 years of existence has the church sunk so deeply into superficiality and irreverence. God's Messiah is celebrated in one song as "my mate", which is very far indeed from Isaiah's teaching. It is no good to proclaim that God loves us if at the same time we carefully omit any references to God's holiness. Why is God's love so amazing? Mainly because we do not deserve it one little bit. And yet the negative side, namely our own sin and guilt and God's consequent righteous judgement, is seldom mentioned in sermons nowadays. It is no wonder that so few Europeans in our day fear God. Sadly this includes most Christians.

Who is to blame for this? Barry Webb believes it is the leaders of the church: "It is truly astounding what depths of inconsistency religious people are capable of, especially in positions of leadership, where backroom decisions and policies all too often belie the faith in God that is professed in the pulpit". The supreme concern of many church leaders today is never to offend sinners. They are terrified in case they should give the impression that the God they believe in is holy and will punish our sins. So they present us instead with a God who is like a large pink fluffy cushion. We are urged to let go and fall into his arms with absolutely no sense of awe or fear, and bask in his comforting love.

What the church must do in order to reverse this trend and return to hallowing and fearing God is to rediscover its roots. It must return to a commitment to personal and corporate study of the Bible. In churches where there is not much heart-worship (v 13) the people will not be able to endure much Bible study. They will say, "I'm afraid the Bible is a closed book to me" (v 11, 12). May God effect a great reversal in today's church, so that God's people once again become hearers of God's word (v 18).

LIII

30:1-17 Our Reliance should be on God

1. The pro-Egyptian party were about to forge an anti-Assyrian alliance with Egypt. Once again Isaiah castigated the secretive politicians of the pro-Egyptian party. He declared that Yahweh saw them as rebellious children who were carrying out a plan contrary to the one he had suggested. They had been forging this alliance against his will, and because of this they were adding sin to sin.

2. The year was 702 B.C. In a little over a year the terrifying crisis would come. Isaiah had dissuaded God's people from forging an alliance against Assyria nine years earlier (20:1-6), and had continued to preach that they should trust in God rather than in Egypt (28:14-22). But now opinions had become polarised. Judah's envoys were on their way to Egypt to formalise the forbidden alliance. Isaiah told the pro-Egyptians that they had ignored the wishes of Yahweh. In their longing for protection from the mighty Assyrians they had decided to trust in Pharaoh's protection and to seek shelter in Egypt's shadow.

3. Because of their lack of trust in God, the pro-Egyptians would inevitably end up by being disappointed by those in whom they had trusted. All that they would receive from Pharaoh was shame. The only thing that Egypt's protecting shadow would bestow on them was humiliation.

4. The faithless alliance would be signed in Zoan, near Tanes which was the nearest Egyptian town to the border with Judah.

5. Everyone would come to shame, for the Egyptians could not profit their allies (19:1-15). Nothing but shame and disgrace would result from this alliance. Certainly no help or profit would be forthcoming from Egypt.

6. Isaiah describes the envoys from Judah on their way to Egypt. Their journey through the Negeb, a troubled and distressed land, would expose them to danger from wild beasts and snakes. They would carry on donkeys and camels the riches

and treasures that constituted the price of the alliance. It would be a waste of their waning resources. Much of the money would be used to purchase a few of the celebrated Egyptian horses, which would not prove helpful to them (v 16).

7. Rahab was a name for Egypt, (used also in Ps 87:4, 89:10). Egypt's help was worthless and empty, so Yahweh had called their people "Rahab who sits still", translated by Moffat as *Dragon Do-nothing*.

8. Isaiah was told to write this nickname of Egypt, *Dragon Do-nothing*, on a tablet and in a book. He was to placard the tablet around Jerusalem. This would be a clear message for the people of the city, unlike the cryptic one in 8:1 which would have perplexed them until it was explained.

9. In verses 9-14 we have one of the clearest statements in scripture of the logic and reasonableness of God's judgement. The people of Judah and Jerusalem were rebellious. They did not have a trusting faith in Yahweh. They were like stubborn children who just would not listen to good teaching.

10. Isaiah knew from his own experience of them that they were fickle with regard to prophecy. They would say to the prophets, "Do not tell us your doom-laden visions. Do not tell us what Yahweh says is right. Make your teaching easy and smooth. Tell us what is nice and pleasant".

11. They would go on, "Leave the hard path you are on; find an *easy* way. Stop talking to us about God's *holiness*. That would upset us". The real prophets like Isaiah, however, knew very well that what is true and right was vital to their communities, just as soundness and accuracy are vital to a building (v 13).

12. The people of Jerusalem were wrong, because *God is holy*. Therefore Yahweh said that he would judge them because *they rejected his word*. Instead of trusting in him, they were trusting in their power to oppress the poor and needy, and were relying on their deceitful foreign alliances.

13. Their wrong attitudes and their evil actions had made them like a high wall with a break in it. The wall was bulging out and would soon collapse. Its crash would come suddenly, and would only take an instant.

14. They would disintegrate so completely that they would be like a large pot that has been smashed to smithereens. No big fragments would remain, which could be used for scraping ashes from the hearth or dipping water from the cistern.

15. Again the Lord Yahweh, the Holy One of Israel, spoke. Again he gave his people an opportunity to turn to him in faith and be rescued from their enemies. The challenge was typical of Isaiah's preaching (26:3). It was by returning to *Yahweh* in heartfelt repentance, and finding *his* rest instead of rushing around in indecent haste (v 16), that they would be saved (28:16). It was by quietly trusting in him that they would find strength. But they refused!

16. Because they thought that they could escape on Egyptian horses, they would be forced to try to escape. Because they insisted on riding swift horses, they would

find that their pursuers were even swifter than they. It was all such a rush. They lived in a constant hive of activity. And all their rushing was to no avail.

17. Their strength would evaporate. A few enemies would overcome a crowd of God's people. The old blessing would be reversed (Lev 26:8), for Yahweh had given up on them (Deut 32:30). They would be publicly disgraced: their weakness would be paraded like a flagstaff on top of a mountain, plain for all to see.

Meditation: Activism or quiet Waiting?

King Ahaz had forged an alliance between the Kingdom of Judah and Assyria in 734 B.C. As a result, the annual payment of tribute money to their Assyrian overlords was bound to prove a demoralising experience for the people of Jerusalem. Year after year a large part of the annual budget had to go to the King of Assyria, and the people of Judah could not shake off their vassal status.

At an early stage in the proceedings, the good King Hezekiah did forge a brief alliance with Egypt, thereby rebelling against Assyria (2 Kings 18:7). He was not punished because the King of Assyria was then intent on destroying the northern Kingdom of Israel (2 Kings 18:9-12). Hezekiah realised that Judah would not be able to withstand an Assyrian invasion, so he resumed the payment of tribute to his Assyrian overlords. But there would be a continuing wish to shake off the heavy Assyrian yoke, and the only way to do so was to join with Egypt and some other nations in an anti-Assyrian alliance.

During these years of pro-Egyptian intrigues the message from Yahweh spoken by his mouthpiece, the prophet Isaiah, was, "Do not put your trust in Egypt. Do not put your trust in horses. Put your trust in me, and I will protect you".

The pro-Egyptians refused to listen to this. They thought that the years between 710-702 B.C were propitious for an alliance with Egypt, because the Assyrians were busy dealing with their most dangerous enemy, the Babylonians. They failed to realise that the Assyrian army would eventually subdue Babylon, and then turn to the south-western front. They could not understand that the Egyptians were no match for the Assyrians, and could not be relied on for help.

Until 702 B.C., Isaiah just about managed to keep King Hezekiah on the right course, trusting in Yahweh for help rather than in Egypt. But in the end the pro-Egyptians got their way, and went to Egypt to sign a treaty of alliance. Isaiah strongly rebuked them (v1-5, 8-14). He used an architectural illustration to make his point. The rebellious people of Judah were like a faulty high wall that was bulging out and whose collapse was certain.

Other prophets had used architectural illustrations to make similar points. Amos was a bit older than Isaiah, and he compared God's judgement to a plumb line which measured holiness. God would use his plumb line to check the wall that his people were building. In fact he was measuring people with it, to see if they were upright and straight (Amos 7:7-9). We like to effect an easy repair on a shaky wall by "papering over the cracks". In ancient times they would whitewash a wall rather than put an extra layer of wallpaper on it. Ezekiel, who lived much later than Isaiah, prophesied to a colony of Jewish exiles in Babylonia, telling them that God was angry with the way they "whitewashed their wall", and he would send wind and rain and hailstones to destroy the wall (Ezek 13:8-16).

John Skinner makes an apt comment. "The slight beginnings of transgression, its inevitable tendency to gravitate more and more from the moral perpendicular, till a critical point is reached, then the suddenness of the final catastrophe – are vividly expressed by [Isaiah's] magnificent simile. First unbelief, then secret intrigues; lastly open rejection of the divine warnings – these are the stages by which the breach between Yahweh and his people gradually widens, until it ends in the irreparable collapse of the state".

Isaiah himself persevered with his basic point. With v 15 he repeats Yahweh's requirement for the umpteenth time. His people should not put their trust in Egypt or in horses. They should trust God. They should return to him and find his calmness and rest. They should not rush around madly, but quietly trust God.

In his comment on this great text (v15), John Skinner aptly writes, "The first pair of expressions describes the external policy, the second the attitude of mind, demanded by the occasion. On the one hand, averseness to war, renunciation of earthly help and a calm neutrality in international affairs; on the other, restful trust in Yahweh: in this last, the prophet says, they would have manifested the truest strength or courage". Sadly, they refused.

LIV

30:18-33 Future Blessings and purifying Fire

The people must have been dazed by all the sombre and difficult prophecies of judgement. Realising their fragility, Isaiah rekindles their hope. This is one of the loveliest passages in the book. For those who trusted in Yahweh there would be wonderful blessings *in this life*. This would include both spiritual blessings (v18-22) and material ones (v23-26), though in the case of the latter the prophecy goes beyond the events of 701 B.C. to the final apocalypse and the end of the age.

18. Yahweh was waiting to be gracious to his people; at the right moment he would eagerly rise up to show mercy to them. The people were reminded that he is a God of justice (5:15-16). Because Yahweh is just, they would most certainly be blessed by him if they humbled themselves and in their turn waited for him. There must be waiting on both sides. We wait for God; he waits to bless us, like the father of the prodigal son. The waiting, the quiet seeking, the resting in his presence – these are important lessons for God's people to learn (8:17, 64:4). The fact that God in turn waits patiently for us is a little known fact about him.

19. Isaiah assures the people of Jerusalem that their weeping would not go on forever. As soon as he heard their cry, Yahweh would immediately be gracious to them. He would answer their longings for restoration and blessing.

20. In this life, because of the tendency to pride, people will benefit from times when they are fed with the most meagre necessities of existence, "the bread of adversity and the water of affliction". These were siege rations. Yahweh is not only our Lord, who disposes our circumstances, but also our teacher. As our teacher he will no longer hide himself from us. Instead he will give us clear guidance concerning his will. Our inclination will change and we shall become increasingly teachable. In our mind's eye we shall see his teaching.

21. In this life we who are God's people continually go astray. When we make a wrong decision and deviate from the straight path of righteousness, choosing to go either to the right or to the left, we shall hear a voice behind us, that of a father walking behind his children, saying, "*This* is the way; walk in it".

22. In this life, we will reach the point when we willingly destroy our idols. They may or may not be costly, they may or may not be made of gold and silver, but we will throw them away as if they were "filthy rags", i.e. used sanitary towels (64:6). As we discard them we will gladly say, "Away with you!"

23. The welfare of God's people was intimately bound up with their land. So after speaking of the restored relationship between them and Yahweh, Isaiah goes on to describe the restored fruitfulness of their land (v 23-26). There would be abundant rain for the seed that was sown, and it would yield a bumper harvest. There would be ample pasture land for their cattle. What a contrast this would be to "the bread of adversity and the water of affliction".

24. The working animals, oxen and donkeys, would be strong because they would eat the best fodder – fine silage winnowed with spades and forks.

25. The very cosmos will be transformed: there will be bubbling brooks of refreshing water on every mountain and high hill. But this will only happen after "a day of the great slaughter, when the towers fall". This part of the prophecy suggests something that is still in the future. Barry Webb comments that "The world must be purged of its evil by God's judgement before, finally and for ever, the sun of righteousness shall rise, with healing in its wings" (Mal 4:2).

26. The luminaries will be dazzling in their luminosity. The moon will shine as brightly as the sun, and the sun will become seven times brighter. This will happen on the day when Yahweh "binds up the injuries of his people, and heals the wounds inflicted by his blow". In chapter 1 Isaiah saw the land of Judah as it was being devoured by aliens, and the people of Jerusalem were left bruised and bleeding (1:7-8). Now a wonderful reversal takes place: the wounds of the people are bound up and their land is restored. It is a very beautiful vision.

27. In verses 27-33 it is the fate of the Assyrians (v 31) that is primarily in view, but most commentators also see an application to the eventual winding up of the present age and the final judgement. Yahweh is depicted as an angry warrior, and this is perhaps what is meant here by his *name*. He is a warrior, just as he was

in the Exodus. He comes from afar, unannounced, and he is in warlike mood. He is extremely angry with those who have tormented his people. His lips pronounce his indignation, and his tongue is a devouring fire.

28. His breath is a rising and overflowing tide, reaching up to the neck. One day the godless nations will find themselves caught in it, and they will be dragged by God's bridle (37:29) towards "the sieve of destruction".

29. For God's people the destruction of evil will be final and complete liberation. They were told to celebrate it in two ways. First, they were to sing a song, similar to the ones sung in their annual holy festival, the Passover. Secondly, they were to sing gladly, as when people set out in procession to their rock, Mount Zion, accompanied by the sound of a flute.

30. Yahweh would raise his majestic voice, which would be like thunder, and cause it to be heard by all. He would rain down blows on the enemy, and these blows would be plain and visible. He would give vent to his settled opposition to all that is evil, and would destroy it like a devouring fire, accompanied by a cloudburst and a tempest and hailstones.

31. The Assyrian army would be terror-stricken when Yahweh struck them. Their destruction in 701 B.C. would anticipate God's final victory at the end of the age.

32. This is a difficult verse. The Hebrew is particularly obscure. As it stands it does not harmonise easily with Isaiah's usual generous tone. It says that as Yahweh the warrior fights against evil with a brandished arm, every blow of his judgement will be seen to be part of the triumph of good over evil. Therefore it will be accompanied by the music of timbrels and lyres, just as Miriam's song was after the destruction of the Egyptian army (Ex 15:20).

33. The "burning place" is *Topheth*, the place of final destruction for the lost, which the Messiah called *Gehenna* (or, as we translate it, hell). Elsewhere in the Old Testament we are told the dark story of how it got the name *Topheth* (Jer 7:31-33). We may think of it as having a vast funeral pyre in its midst, which will become the final destination of the King of Assyria. There was no need for the people of Jerusalem in Isaiah's time to fear this Assyrian ruler. He was greatly to be pitied, for he would end up being devoured in the fires of hell.

Meditation: Grace upon Grace from God's Fullness

This is a passage that is full of comfort and hope.

First, we discover that God waits for us to wait for him (v 18). If God does not bless us immediately, it may be because he is a God of justice who waits until we have repented and begin to trust him again. He is more than willing to give us time to turn to him, but we must make time to wait quietly for him.

Secondly, we discover that God is a compassionate teacher. He disciplines his people (v 20a), hears their cries and answers them (v 19), reveals himself to them in their hour of need (v20b), and shows them step by step how to live in order to please him (v21). In the midst of our greatest adversity he manifests himself in such a way that we immediately recognise him as our teacher, and then we respond by being his willing, if occasionally errant, pupils.

Thirdly, we discover the blessing of God's guidance (v21). This comes as we walk forwards along his path. When we begin to stray to the right or to the left, we shall hear a voice pointing us to the right way. "The voice behind you" is close by, and implies a newly rediscovered intimacy between God and ourselves.

Fourthly, we discover the freedom and joy that come from wholeheartedness. The old idols and images are gladly thrown away (v22). Previously there had been divided loyalties; now there is a longing to obey the first commandment, "You shall have no other gods besides me" (Ex 20:3, margin).

Fifthly, we discover what it is like when the windows of God's grace and goodness are opened to us one after another (v23-26). We are given here a bountiful depiction of plenty, a bright depiction of sunshine, a satisfying depiction of enough food and water, and a wonderful depiction of ample blessing.

Sixthly, we discover that God will finally triumph over evil. The destruction of the King of Assyria prefigures God's final victory. The people of God were to celebrate it in song (v29). An important question arises: should the people of God today celebrate God's triumph over evil? The mention of burning fire and streams of sulphur (v33) may shock us. Will God really do that to his enemies? There are some difficulties here, but we may come to terms with them by rediscovering the logic of the Bible's teaching about God's judgement:

(a) Isaiah has used poetic language to describe something appalling, the judgement and destruction that awaits every person who proudly rebels against God and who persistently ignores and disobeys him.

(b) The King of Assyria was one such person. There have been, there are and there will be many others. The lost will include some who are well-known and others who are relatively unknown. The lost will be "many", while those who find eternal life will be "few" (66:16, Mt 7:13-14).

(c) God's final retribution, however, will be seen to be absolutely right. Nobody will wish to disagree with it. It is presented in this section as the third feature of God's grace towards us. He pours out spiritual blessings on us (v18-22), he wonderfully renews the world we live in (v23-26), and he will one day destroy all our enemies (v27-33).

(d) There is an extraordinary free offer of salvation made to all people by God. Those who accept the offer will be saved, and they will end up in glory.

(e) Those who refuse God's offer of salvation, not once but many times, will have to face the consequences. God gave them their free will and he cannot override it. He will therefore judge them for their refusal. Without divine judgement, the future glory would be tainted by disobedience and rebellion.

(f) Each of us has a choice. The warrior is determined to deliver us, but if we persistently refuse him he will have no alternative but to destroy us.

LV

31:1-9 On Whom do we depend?

1. Isaiah reiterates the main parts of his message. First of all, Egypt's help would be worthless. Alas for those who looked there for help! It was the height of folly to rely on horses. It was out of place for God's people to trust in chariots (because they were many) and in horsemen (because they were very strong). God's people should trust in God. They should have looked in trust to the Holy one of Israel. But instead of consulting Yahweh, they followed their own wisdom (5:21).

2. Yahweh also is wise. But his wisdom is beyond understanding, for sometimes he brings "disaster". This word really means *evil*. God has so constituted the way things are that he allows evil to exist and even to flourish – for a while (45:7, Amos 3:6). In spite of this, God is also utterly dependable: "he does not call back his words". He will always keep his promises – unlike the Pharaoh of Egypt. He will rise against "the house of evildoers" (the people of Judah), and against the helpers of those who "work iniquity" (the Egyptians).

3. In Isaiah's view, there was all the difference in the world between people and God, between flesh and spirit. What *needs* life but does not have it is one thing; the God who *is* life is quite another. Many people in Judah would have disagreed. Because of this, Yahweh would stretch his arm against both Egypt the helper, who would stumble, and against Judah who was being helped. Both would perish.

4. It was foolish to look to Egypt for help, and the second part of Isaiah's message was that Yahweh was the avowed saviour of his people. He is compared to a growling lion in this verse and to birds in flight in v 5. Like a lion, Yahweh is strong and determined. Like a lion, he is not daunted by mighty opponents, and he will prove a formidable protector. It is always best to have him on your side.

5. Like birds hovering overhead, Yahweh would be solicitous and caring. He would encircle Jerusalem. He would protect it, deliver it, spare it and rescue it.

6. Isaiah therefore tenderly urges the people of Yahweh to "turn back to him whom [they had] deeply betrayed". To the prophet, the repentance and conversion of his people were more important than their deliverance from the great threat.

7. To return to Yahweh would mean putting him first and having no other gods besides him (Ex 20:1-4). The people of God would throw away their idols of silver or gold which their own hands had made (see 2:8, 2:20, 17:8, and 30:22). It was precisely these idols which typified their betrayal of Yahweh.

8. If the people of Jerusalem did this, then the Assyrian army would fall. The sword that would subdue 185,000 warriors would be no ordinary sword: it would be superhuman. Sennacherib himself would be forced to beat a very hasty retreat, and the people of Jerusalem would not need to lift up a weapon in anger. Isaiah is declaring that if God's people repent, they will be protected by God's power.

9. The rock of the Assyrians was far from being dependable and immovable (Deut 32:31), unlike the rock of the people of Judah (26:4). The Assyrian officers would be in such a panic that they would desert their standard. Yahweh's fire was in Jerusalem, but his burning holiness would not necessarily be comfortable (33:14).

Meditation: What an extraordinary God!

At some time before 701 B.C., probably a year earlier, the "good" King Hezekiah showed himself to be less than good. He stopped obeying Isaiah's strictures to have nothing to do with Egypt. After the alliance with Egypt was forged, he took the bold step, encouraged by his pro-Egyptian courtiers, of telling the King of Assyria that Judah would no longer be a vassal state of Assyria, and that the annual tribute would no longer be forthcoming. Sennacherib would have been infuriated and given orders for his army to begin its march southwards. At that stage Egypt forgot the promises made in the alliance. Sennacherib destroyed the walled towns of Judah, exiling thousands of Jews (2 Ki 18:13). He then proceeded to "invest" the city of Jerusalem, encircling it with Assyrian soldiers and laying siege to it. Would Yahweh also forget his promises to the citizens of Zion?

This is probably the moment when Isaiah spoke the oracles in the passage we are looking at. Isaiah wished to give Hezekiah and the people of Jerusalem a new vision of what God was like, before urging them to repent of their lack of faith. So he presented them with three unusual descriptions of God.

(a) **Yahweh is like a wise man** (v 2). The pro-Egyptian Jews were also wise – in their own eyes. Yahweh had his plans and purposes. To bring them to fulfilment, he might allow evil to prosper, and disaster to strike. Judah would suffer and so would Egypt. Yahweh could use anything from a proud Assyrian army to a new virus to teach his people a lesson and thereby help them to repent. If he promised evil, he would bring evil to happen. He said, "I form light and create darkness, I make welfare and create woe; I, Yahweh, do all these things" (45:7).

(b) **Yahweh is like an unabashed lion** in his work of salvation (v 4). He is imperturbable in his sovereignty. Picture the grim lion who has seized his prey – a lamb. The lamb represents Judah and Jerusalem. A band of shepherds – pro-Egyptian courtiers and politicians – is called out against the lion; they make noises against it. Does the lion care? No; Yahweh the lion "will come down to fight upon Mount Zion and upon its hill". George Adam Smith noticed that "there is something majestic in that picture of the lion with the shouting shepherds, too afraid to strike him. Yahweh persistently frustrated their plans for 'the salvation of the state'. He looked like a lion, delivering Jerusalem to destruction". But the lion had not come to destroy, for he is a saviour. He is not, however, a comfortable saviour or a safe saviour. In fact, he is like a fire (v9). C.S. Lewis wrote similarly about the Christ-lion Aslan, "Aslan is a lion – the lion, the great lion. Who said anything about safe? He is *not safe*. But he *is good*. He is the King, I tell you".

(c) **Yahweh is like a protective bird** looking after her young. Imagine a number of birds who are feeding their little fledglings. One day the birds fly up from the trees and hover nervously above their nests. Why? A hawk is in the sky. Until it flies away, the birds will hover, full of motherly anxiety. "Like birds hovering overhead, so Yahweh will protect Jerusalem; he will protect it and deliver it, he will spare it and rescue it". Seven centuries later the Messiah would use a similar metaphor as he wept over the same city, saying, "Jerusalem, Jerusalem! How often have I desired to gather your children together as a hen gathers her brood under her wings, and you were not willing!" (Mt 23:37).

Hezekiah would have thought about these three pictures of what God was like. Then Isaiah asked him, together with the other people of Jerusalem, to repent. "Turn back to him whom you have deeply betrayed, O people of Israel" (v6). When we reach the historical section and see what happened next (chapters 36, 37) we shall discover that Hezekiah did turn back to Yahweh with all his heart.

LVI

32:1-8 The honourable King and his Subjects

This is another oracle about the future Messiah, following on from 7:14-17, 9:1-7 and 11:1-5, etc. Derek Kidner believes that it "shows [the Messiah's] greatest triumph, in the flowering of his own qualities, given by the Spirit of Yahweh, in the character of his subjects, from his office-bearers downwards".

1. "See, a king will reign in righteousness", says Isaiah. Great advances in God's kingdom have often begun with a single person, and this king is none other than God's anointed one, the Messiah. As a result of his perfect leadership, princes will rule with justice. These princes, while subordinate to the king, will be in powerful positions, and they will use power just as God uses it – with justice.

2. Each prince who works for the Messiah will be a source of security and refreshment for needy people. They will protect them from calamity, encourage them and provide welfare for them, and so imitate Yahweh himself (25:4, 26:4).

3. Ordinary people who serve the Messiah will fulfil the purpose for which they were created. Like him, they will use their gifts of vision and listening to focus on what is good and true and wholesome (unlike those who speak in 30:10-11). They will then be able to assist the needy in their times of difficulty (50:4).

4. They will find themselves transformed so that they think aright (29:9, 18) and surprise themselves by the quality of their sense of judgement. They will discover how to speak in a way that is wholesome and apt.

5. A new sense of discernment will be widespread. People will be able to tell the difference between those who are true and those who are out to deceive. They will distinguish between, on the one hand, amoral fools and unscrupulous villains, and on the other, those who are noble and honourable. Derek Kidner writes, "Above all, truth will have ousted the fictions under which vice takes shelter".

6. In verses 6-8 we have Isaiah's commentary on verse 5. First of all the fools are atheistic (Ps 53:1). Their words are blasphemous, their minds work independently of God, their practices are ungodly, and they speak untrue words about God. The people who are spiritually hungry are unsatisfied by what they say, and those who thirst for the refreshing water of the wells of salvation remain thirsty (12:3).

7. Likewise the villains do what is evil, and plan to ruin the poor with deceitful traps. They will even take advantage of the vulnerable nature of their victims.

8. But the noble ones plan benevolent and beneficent actions, and take their stand on what is good and true and helpful (Phil 4:8).

Meditation: The Messiah

When Isaiah began to prophesy, many of the people of Judah believed in a future glorious king. This was based in part on Yahweh's promise to David that he would perpetuate his dynasty (2 Sam 7:4-17). People were therefore longing for another king like David to arise. This looking forward to a great king linked itself to another strand of Old Testament expectation, which concerned the coming prophet similar to Moses, whom God would raise up in the future (Deut 18:15-18). A further strand of expectation focused on the great high priest from the order of Melchizedek who would purify the people of God in preparation for the end of the age (Gen 14:18-20, Ps 110:4, Zech 6:12-13, Hebrews chapters 7-10). By the beginning of the first century A.D., the godly Jews were awaiting the arrival of a great deliverer who would combine all three roles of Prophet, Priest and King.

When Isaiah received his call, Yahweh spoke to him about a terrible judgement on his people, which would be like a tree being burnt until only a stump remained. That stump would be "the holy seed" (6:13). This idea of a holy seed, a tiny remnant that would get smaller and smaller until it was represented by a single person, captivated Isaiah. In his mind the stump became a branch, which was going to be beautiful and glorious (4:2a). The branch was a person. He was one and the same as "the fruit of the land", who would be the pride and glory of the survivors of Israel (4:2b).

Then came years of opposition from King Ahaz, who "did not do what was right in the sight of Yahweh his God" (2 Ki 16:1-4). Ahaz refused to ask for a sign, but Isaiah gave him one anyway. A woman would give birth, and a child called Immanuel would be born (7:14). This name means "God is with us". Immanuel is represented as someone who would be a helpless and innocent sufferer. George Adam Smith wrote that "Before this child arrived at years of discretion, not only would Syria and Ephraim be laid waste, but Yahweh himself would devastate Judah. The child's hopes and aspirations would be dissipated by the sins of others, and he would be born only to share his people's poverty" (7:15-25, 8:5-8). Here is the first hint in the book of Isaiah that the Messiah would be a suffering servant of Yahweh. He would not only be "God with us", but he would also suffer for sinful people.

The sufferer then metamorphoses into the deliverer. The child Immanuel would indeed be born as one of God's people. He would be a son given to Israel. He would be given great authority and would reign on David's throne, establishing his kingdom and upholding it with justice and righteousness forevermore (9:6-7). His name would be fourfold and it would have divine resonances: Wonderful Counsellor, Mighty God, Everlasting Father, and Prince of Peace.

The next stage is that the shoot or branch that came out of the stump of Jesse would have the Spirit of Yahweh resting upon him. The Spirit would endow him with all the gifts and abilities that he would need for his work. He would be like Yahweh, full of wisdom, understanding, counsel, and might. He would know Yahweh and he would fear Yahweh. He would judge the poor with righteousness and decide with equity for the meek of the earth. Righteousness and faithfulness would be his belt (11:1-5).

Finally, the Messiah is presented to us as the king who would reign in righteousness. So amazing would be his reign that his subjects would be made righteous also. His wonderful qualities would take root and flower in his subjects, whether they were leaders or those who were led (32:1-8). The eyes of everyone would contemplate the king in his beauty (33:17).

This is a summary of the evolution of Isaiah's thinking about the Messiah. It is a bold and remarkable portrait. The Messiah would be the stump, the holy seed, the branch, and the fruit of the land. He would be "God with us" and suffer for his people. He would be the great deliverer who would establish David's kingdom and who would be called Wonderful Counsellor, Mighty God, Everlasting Father and Prince of Peace. He would be the one on whom the Spirit of Yahweh would rest, and who would delight in the fear of Yahweh. He would be the beautiful king who would reign in righteousness and whose followers would become like him. Isaiah contributed greatly to the expectation that the Messiah would be a wonderful king in the line of David.

There is more to come in the book of Isaiah about the Messiah. The pioneering thoughts of the prophet may have inspired some of the later developments, but these should be dated over a century after his time. His own thinking about the Messiah prompted the holy remnant to look out for his coming. When the Messiah eventually arrived, godly people recognised him and received him. One of them said, "We have found him about whom Moses in the law and also the prophets wrote, Jesus son of Joseph from Nazareth" (Jn 1:45).

LVII

32:9-20 True Peace does not come easily

9. We have come across the pampered ladies of Jerusalem before (3:16-4:1). In Isaiah's day the members of the high society had an escapist mentality (22:13, 28:14-15). Here he summons the women to rise up and listen to him. Why? Because they were *at ease* and *complacent*. These are the same words as those which in verse 17 are translated *peace* and *quietness*. Perhaps we may learn from this that the neutral quality of serene contentment can turn into either the vice of ease or the virtue of peace, and likewise that a sense of stability can turn into either smug complacency or the thoughtful quietness that waits for the Lord. There are two paths along which those who are by nature serene and stable may walk. One is bad and leads to destruction. The other is good and leads to life.

10. The year was 702 B.C. King Hezekiah had just refused to pay the annual tribute to Assyria. In little over a year an apocalyptic crisis would engulf Judah and threaten the complete destruction of Jerusalem. The Assyrians would take all the 46 lesser walled cities of Judah before surrounding the last and greatest one, the capital. They would destroy the vineyards and orchards belonging to these women, who had previously been complacent but would now shudder.

11. For the third time in three verses Isaiah calls these women complacent. This time he urges them to shake off their false ease and instead tremble with fear. They were to strip off their expensive designer clothing and instead put some cheap and itchy sackcloth on their loins.

12. They were to mourn, beating their breasts, because of what would happen to their pleasant fields and their fruitful vines.

13. The curse of the good fields being infested with thorns and briers would visit the homes of all the landowners who lived in Jerusalem, leaving them joyless.

14. The palace would be abandoned and Jerusalem deserted; the landmarks would become dens of animals or pastures of flocks – for a very long time. This disaster, and the glory in v 15 that would reverse it, went beyond the tribulations that befell God's people in 701 B.C. and in the following years of recovery. This may be a prophecy that looks further forward, to a time when Jerusalem would no longer be the central focus of God's people. This idea recurs in verse 19.

15. In the same way this great text, which resonates of Pentecost, may point to a much later time when God's people would be sent out to all the Gentile nations. The impulse for them to do so would come when "a Spirit from on high [was] poured out on [them]". When they set out on their mission, God's people would see time and again the wilderness of this godless world turn into a fruitful field, so much so that what used to be deemed fruitful fields would now be classed as scrubland (29:17). There would be an extraordinarily fruitful time.

16. This suggests that God's peace cannot be forced onto a corrupt society. The ground must first be cleared and re-sown with *righteousness*, which will then bear the good fruit of peace (v17). We would like to have peace first, and then seek for righteousness, but Isaiah had worked out that it has to be the other way round. For this to happen, the working of the Spirit of God is vital (v15). After the pouring out of the Spirit, justice and righteousness, which are the foundations of the social order (1:21, 1:26-27, 28:17), would be established everywhere.

17. The consequence of this establishment of righteousness would not be false ease but peace. It would engender not complacency but quietness and trust in God, which would last forever. Verses 9-20 form a neat unit: false security leads to disaster, disaster results in restoration, and restoration brings true security.

18. God's people would dwell in homes that are peaceful, secure and quiet. They would find true rest (Mt 11:28-30). We have already seen that peace and security stem from a penitent and believing relationship with Yahweh (30:15).

19. This is a difficult verse. It may be a corrupted reading, or a displaced saying that was originally elsewhere. If we take it in this context, its meaning might be that the ideal life, as described by Isaiah to the people of Judah, would have the peace and quietness we associate with the countryside, with rural and pastoral living. There would be no forests, because crops cannot grow there, and no cities, because they are overcrowded and lack the beauty and peace of the countryside.

20. Isaiah pronounces a blessing on the people, for they would all sow on fields that were adjacent to streams, and their livestock would be free to range wherever they wished. These pictures of a secure and well-watered land look ahead to the renewed world that God would cleanse from evil and then transform. It is an idealised representation that combines all that is best in ordinary everyday life.

Meditation: Waiting for the Holy Spirit

There is no short cut to the ideal world where justice, righteousness and peace prevail, and where there is perpetual quietness and trust before God. The renewed life can only come after God's people have deeply repented, perhaps after God has painfully judged them (v9-14). Also, it cannot come without the outpouring of God's Spirit (v15).

Let us wind forward about 730 years. After the crucifixion and death of the Messiah, the small group of his followers who made up the holy remnant were devastated. But quite rightly the cords of death were not able to hold on to God's anointed One, and on the third day he rose from the dead in accordance with the scriptures (Ps 16:9-11, Hos 6:2, Jonah 1:17). In the next few days his followers were bewildered by the unexpected meetings they had with him, and then after some weeks came his departure. Just before he left them, he told them to remain in Jerusalem and wait for the promised Spirit of God.

Ten days later came the Day of Pentecost, the Jewish feast of the first-fruits. The 120 followers of the Messiah were gathered together in the Temple early that morning.

Suddenly one of Isaiah's great prophecies was fulfilled right where they were: "A Spirit from on high [will be] poured out on us, and the wilderness [will become] a fruitful field, and the fruitful field [will be] deemed a forest".

There was a remarkable transformation in those 120 men and women. They were all filled with the Holy Spirit. Tongues of fire rested on each of them. They knew that they were being sent out into the world to live and work to God's praise and glory. On that very day they brought forth some of the fruits of the gospel, and the 120 followers of the Messiah became 3,120 (Acts 2:1-42). That was just the beginning!

The Holy Spirit has been poured out again and again since that unforgettable initial baptism of the church on the feast of Pentecost in 30 A.D. The Spirit of God has been poured out on individuals and on groups of people. Each time the result has been a revival that brought glory to God, whether it took place in a single believer, or in many of them. These revivals were and continue to be notable, for many reasons. Those involved repent deeply; they have a new love for the Messiah and a determination to extend his kingdom; they humbly and obediently delight in God's word; and they pray with great ardour and zeal.

How can we speed up a future revival by the Holy Spirit, in our own lives, and hopefully in the lives of others as well? George Adam Smith wrote that "Isaiah speaks here (v16-20) of human conduct and human effort, righteousness and labour, being necessary to fill up the blessedness of the future. But together with all the prophets he, first and indispensably, places the Spirit of God".

First, and there are three requirements, we must continue to live out the truths that we know about God. It would not be right for us to withdraw from ordinary life. We should continue to promote justice, and work to help the needy (Micah 6:6-8). Our conduct and our effort will help to fill up future blessings.

Secondly, we should set aside some time in which we can wait quietly for the Lord. The Messiah's last words to the holy remnant were to *wait* for the promised Holy Spirit of God. He was echoing one of the most repeated and emphasised lessons in the book of Isaiah. Throughout its pages we, its readers, are urged on various occasions to "wait for Yahweh" (8:17, 26:8, 30:18, 33:2, 40:31, 49:23, 64:4). And this leads us very naturally to the final requirement.

Thirdly, we must acknowledge that God's blessing will only come when "a Spirit from on high is poured out on us". This is why we *must* wait for the Lord. How do we wait for him? We continue in the lives where God has placed us, working and praying for God's name to be honoured, for his kingdom to come, and for his good and perfect will to be done here on earth as it is in heaven. But we are painfully aware that we need a fresh touch from God. We need a divine miracle so that our hearts are set on fire with love for him and for the Messiah. This can only come from a visitation by the Holy Spirit. So we wait for God, longing for his Spirit to be poured out on us. We humble ourselves before him, casting aside every form of human pride. We ask God to visit us afresh with his salvation, and long that he may enter into our trembling hearts (57:15).

LVIII

33:1-16 From Impenitence to Terror

This chapter depicts the mood in Jerusalem when Sennacherib's army was at the gates, and at the eleventh hour God's people began to repent and return to him. The whole of chapter 33 has been compared to a psalm. It features changes of mood and of speaker, and may have been written for use in future emergencies. God's people are in desperate straits and try to focus on him (v 1-9). God himself addresses the enemy, who will self-combust (v 10-12). There is dialogue between God and his people (v 13-16). The ending is full of hope (v 17-24).

1. Isaiah begins by castigating some people who are treacherous destroyers. To whom is he referring? He does not tell us, which means that his denunciation is applicable in all ages including our own. It is likely that he is referring to the King of Assyria, Sennacherib. This man was certainly a destroyer, and he was also treacherous. Having happily accepted the tribute money that Hezekiah belatedly realised he had to pay him (2 Ki 18:13-17), Sennacherib attacked Jerusalem *anyway*. He was later dealt with treacherously, because two of his sons eventually assassinated him (37:37-38). It was not the only time in the book of Isaiah that treacherous machinations had proved to be deeply upsetting (24:16).

2. Isaiah moves from denunciation to entreaty. As Jerusalem's spokesman before Yahweh, he declared that only Yahweh could help them now. Yahweh should be trusted, because he is the God of grace, who bestows undeserved blessings. His arm would be strong in the mornings, when the Assyrians might launch an attack on the besieged city. Yahweh would bring salvation in times of trouble.

3. Yahweh would manifest his glory in a way that would convulse the enemy, causing such devastation and panic that those who remained were forced to flee. The heathen nations could only scatter before Yahweh's terrifying majesty.

4. The people of God would gather the enemy's spoil like caterpillars gathering food. They would pounce on it and seize it like leaping locusts.

5. Isaiah moves on to praise. Yahweh is exalted on high. He would once again fill Zion with justice and righteousness so that the nations would go there to learn to walk in the paths of Yahweh (2:2-3).

6. Yahweh would be the stable rock that his people needed. He would grant them abundant salvation, wisdom and knowledge. Isaiah once again urged the people to fear the Lord. This, said Isaiah, was Zion's treasure. It was the key that could unlock all the good things that God has for his people.

7. Isaiah lamented the treachery of the King of Assyria. So appalling was it that even the bravest were raising a cry. Some envoys of King Hezekiah had just returned from Lachish, where they had presented Sennacherib with the tribute he had demanded. They brought back the alarming news that the Assyrians,

violating every consideration of honour, were insisting on the surrender of the capital.

8. The deserted highways echoed the days of the Judges, when caravans ceased and travellers kept to the byways (Judg 5:6). It was a desperate situation that went on until Yahweh raised up Deborah to bring victory to Israel over the Canaanites. Would there be a repeat performance? The Assyrians had broken the promise they had made to the people of Jerusalem. They had despised the oath they had given. They had disregarded their obligations. God's people were in despair.

9. The land of Judah around the capital was wasting away, having been ravaged by the merciless Assyrian army. Lebanon had been overpowered; the green land of Sharon had become a desert; Bashan and Carmel had lost their natural beauty.

10. God answers! He begins by telling the enemy that he would arise *now*. He would stand up in order to act. He would exalt himself. The moment had come.

11. The Assyrians thought they could pulverise the nations, but their violence was like a self-consuming fire. Vain pursuits and aggressive attitudes bring about self-immolation. We have met the self-destructive aspect of sin before (1:31, 30:13).

12. In the end, the mighty Assyrians would be burnt down to lime in Yahweh's white heat. They would be like thorns as they burnt and crackled in the fire.

13. The news of the divine intervention would spread. It would be a great demonstration to all the world of the omnipotence of almighty God.

14. The people of God in Zion knew that they were sinners, and God's mighty rescue had filled them with terror and trembling. They had realised at last what Yahweh is like, and they asked themselves how they could live with his holiness, which was like a devouring fire with unchanging flames (31:9). The devouring fire refers to God's righteous displeasure with sin, and also to the sinner's inbuilt system of self-destruction (v 11). The profound heart-searching in verses 14-15 is similar to that in certain Psalms (15:1-5, 24:3-6). It may have been part of an admission liturgy that was carried out in sanctuaries, especially in the Temple, and it probably dated back as far as King David (2 Sam 6:9).

15. It is only the righteous and the upright who will not be touched by Yahweh's devouring fire. Righteousness and uprightness are described negatively, for the pursuit of good implies the avoidance of evil. Minor habits of twisted thinking and the occasional viewing of impure images constitute powerful temptations for our imaginations. Purity of speech, financial probity, freedom from the love of money, rejection of gossip and the avoidance of the second (and lustful) look are important. Deeds of shame are always preceded by thoughts of shame. The people who denied themselves in the ways described here would be specially favoured by Yahweh. They would be given a new vision of his beauty (v 17).

16. These people would dwell in absolute security. Yahweh would prove to be a rocky fortress for them. They would never lack food to eat or water to drink.

Meditation: The consuming Holiness of God

Chapter 33 of Isaiah plunges us into the middle of the most dramatic events in the prophet's life. It contains one extraordinary detail which we should not overlook, namely the people's discovery of the consuming holiness of God. The year is 701 B.C. The people were cooped up in Jerusalem in what we might euphemistically describe as a lock-down. The city was surrounded by Assyrian soldiers who had invested it and who were preparing for a siege of several months. God's people were facing a long time of waiting, increasing hunger, and then a holocaust and utter destruction. Isaiah may have written this, one of his final oracles, in two parts: the first (v1-12) on the eve of the great deliverance, the second (v13-24) on the morning after, when salvation had arrived.

Isaiah shares in the sense of outrage at the treachery of the King of Assyria (v1), before leading his fellow citizens in humble prayer as they wait for Yahweh, the God of grace (v2). He then anticipates the *dénouement*: a terrible tumult, fleeing soldiers, the gathering of spoil (v3, 4). He worships God as their saviour and highlights the importance of fearing him (v5, 6). Isaiah then returns to the plight facing God's people, for they were dealing with a treacherous enemy (v7) and the surrounding countryside had already been taken and destroyed (v8, 9).

Only God could help them now. He chose to do so. Isaiah boldly proclaimed the words of God himself. Yahweh declares that he would rise up like a consuming fire to burn the Assyrian hordes down to lime (v10-12). And then – it was bed-time. Whether anyone else snatched any fitful sleep that night is not recorded, but we may assume that Isaiah slept in perfect peace (26:3-4). The next morning, the terrible threat had gone, but another terror had entered the lives of the people.

The holiness of God is like an all-pervading atmosphere that burns away anything that is unholy. When Yahweh arose, the Assyrians had no chance (30:33). Whatever killed them had left them all lifeless. The life had been fully burnt out of them, burnt to lime. And when God's people looked out over the city walls that morning and saw all the Assyrians lying dead on the ground, they had mixed feelings. They were hugely relieved because the siege was over, and they would not be destroyed. But they also realised that there was much that needed to be burnt away in themselves, and that they would be unable to withstand the fire any better than the Assyrians. Was not Jerusalem the dwelling-place of Yahweh, and Ariel the special hearth and altar of his consuming fire? And so they cried out, "Who among us can live with the devouring fire?" (v14).

God was Immanuel, God was with them. His salvation would protect them and his love would enfold them. But his holiness would burn away the stubble in them (4:4), and his judgement would prompt them to throw away all their beloved idols (2:20, 31:7). He would strive with them until his justice and his righteousness characterised their lives. Isaiah had told them who could survive the unchanging flames. "Those who walk right-eously and speak uprightly, who despise the gain of oppression, who wave away a bribe instead of accepting it, who stop their ears from hearing of bloodshed and shut their eyes from looking on evil" (v15). Only they could live in the heights with Yahweh (v16). Since he alone was the giver of life, what could exist beside him except what was like him? The will that longs for the best in others, the heart that is pure, and the character that is transparent – only these might dwell with the unchanging flames. Only these would be like the bush that Moses saw, ablaze but not consumed. For God, in whom we live and move and have our being, is a consuming fire.

The question we might well ask is, were all the people of Jerusalem able to face up to the holiness of their God? Did all of them repent of their sins? Did all of them throw away their idols? We have been given some hints, and we shall try and puzzle out the answer to this question in the meditation of section LXVII (p. 202-203).

LIX

33:17-24 The Land of the Forgiven

Isaiah speaks not only of the blessing of deliverance from the Assyrians but also of the blessing that will be Zion's when Yahweh's purposes for her are finally fulfilled. Barry Webb writes that "The one is a foretaste of the other, and the two are merged in Isaiah's prophetic vision".

17. The Messiah would one day teach that the pure in heart would be blessed, for they would see God (Mt 5:8). Isaiah had just told God's people to shut their eyes from looking on evil (v 15), and now he tells them, "Your eyes will see the king in his beauty". It is, therefore, the eyes of the pure in heart that will gaze at this very satisfying vision. The pure would see Yahweh (v 22) – or perhaps it is the Messiah once again (32:1). He would be seen in a spacious and panoramic landscape, wonderfully restored after the ravages inflicted by the enemy.

18. The pure in heart would no longer think of the almost unbearable trials they had to go through. They would even struggle to remember the treachery of their enemies, who had counted and weighed the tribute, and had then counted the towers of their besieged city to make an inventory of buildings for demolition.

19. The pure in heart would never again listen to insolent people, whose proud speech was incomprehensible and whose arrogant statements were unpleasant. There would be no room for pride in the new world of the humble.

20. The pure in heart would see Zion, once again a tranquil place of pilgrimage. It would be like an immovable tent (4:5-6). It would be the end of their journey.

21. There they would see Yahweh, for it is he that is the beautiful king (v 17) – or is it the Messiah (32:1) who is so closely identified with him? He would be the source of the broad rivers and streams that would flow through the New Jerusalem (Ezek 47:1-12, Rev 22:1-2). No galley with oars or stately ship would be able to go there, for the rivers of the city of God would provide secure defences, unlike the Tigris had done for Nineveh or the Nile for Memphis (Na 3:7-8).

22. Yahweh would also be their Lord. Many of his people had once shied away from his authoritarian titles, *judge*, *ruler* and *king*, but now they would gladly confess them, for in them were to be found the bases for all the beauty and security of their lives.

23. So secure would the city of God be (v 21) that the unrighteous people who tried to enter into it on sailing ships (lawless Gentiles or the sinners of Zion, v 14) would find their rigging going awry, their mast toppling and their sail sagging. The prey of these ungodly people would be plundered, and even the lame in God's city would walk about collecting the plunder.

24. God's people would never again suffer sickness, for all who lived in his city would be forgiven people, their iniquities washed clean (Ps 103:3). John Skinner writes, "In the conception of the Messianic community, the abolition of sickness, the chief evil of life, is the indispensable pledge that guilt is taken away".

Meditation: Twelve Blessings of the New Jerusalem

Who is the King of verse 17? It could be the Messiah, as in 32:1. The statement that "Yahweh is our king" (v 22) suggests that it is Yahweh. Whether it is God the Son or God the Father makes little difference, because God is one (Deut 6:4 mg). In the New Jerusalem that God is preparing for his people, the pure in spirit will live with God and they will see him (Rev 21:3, 22:3-4). This section (33:17-24) once again focuses on the glorious future of God's people. As they realised the great blessings that lay in store, their hope would be rekindled and renewed. This was true of the godly in Isaiah's day and it is also true of the godly now.

(a) They will see the king – meaning either God himself or the Messiah – in his beauty (v 17a). Some paintings are beautiful. So are some pieces of music. So are some people. But nothing or nobody is as beautiful as God and his Messiah. There is no beauty akin to spiritual beauty. There is nothing as beautiful as divine holiness, divine humility, divine self-giving and divine love (64:4).

(b) They will live in a beautiful land that stretches as far as the eye can see (v 17b). Forget about this world's beauty spots. They are little more than a dim reflection of the perfect beauty of the place that God is preparing for those who love him (1 Cor 2:9, which quotes 64:4 and slightly modifies it).

(c) They will barely remember the terrors of this life, and if they do, they will muse on them (v 18). There will be no more treachery, no more deceit, and no more broken promises. They will be healed of all their bad memories (Rev 21:4).

(d) They will no longer be surrounded by insolent people, whom they cannot understand (v 19). Everyone will be holy and kind. The company will always be very pleasant. All the people will be at one in their love and worship of God – Yahweh, the Messiah and the Spirit of God.

(e) They will have reached their final destination – the New Jerusalem, the city of God (v 20), where everything is right and in order. This particular tent will never need to move again, its stakes will never be pulled up. None of its ropes will be broken. There will be no more anxiety, for all that is necessary will have been accomplished and finished (Jn 19:30). It is an amazing thought – nobody will ever need to feel anxious again. Subjunctives will become redundant!

(f) The river of the water of life will flow through the city (v 21). On each side of the river will be the tree of life with its twelve kinds of fruit, and the leaves of the tree will be for the healing of the nations (Rev 22:1-2).

(g) Our beautiful God will be our judge, ruler and king. His judgements will be just, his rule gentle and benign, and his kingdom righteous and peaceful (v 22a).

(h) God will save us (v 22b). In the past he saved us once and for all from the *penalty* of sin (we were justified), in the present he is saving us from the *power* of sin (we are being sanctified), and in the future he will save us from the very *presence* of sin (we shall be glorified).

(i) We shall dwell in complete security (v 23a). God promises a certain security in this life for those who follow him wholeheartedly: nothing can separate us from the love of God in the Messiah (Rom 8:38-39). But in the next life we shall no longer need to be on our guard against evil, for we shall be absolutely secure.

(j) There will be bounty for us – spiritual, physical, intellectual and relational blessings – which each person will receive and share (v 23b). We shall be content, and we shall be rich beyond measure. Above all, we shall have God in his beauty!

(k) We shall never be ill again (v 24a). We shall be the possessors of new bodies that are imperishable, glorious, and powerful (1 Cor 15:42-43). We shall be freed from every infirmity and weakness that blights this life.

(l) All of us will have been fully and freely forgiven by God (v 24b). Until a person meets God, his or her greatest need is to be forgiven by him. A great barrier separates us from him (59:1-2). As we shall learn in Part 5 of this book, God sent the Messiah to provide the only effective solution for the problem of our sin. Are you forgiven? By the astonishing grace of God, I am. How wonderful it is to be forgiven by God. It brings a new joy and happiness to life (Ps 32:1-5).

LX

34:1-17 The universal Judgement

Chapters 34 (on the universal judgement) and 35 (on the flowering wilderness) are no longer concerned with the Assyrian crisis and the partial restoration that followed it. Instead, like chapters 24-27, they point towards cosmic events. Like chapters 24-27, they may have been written after Isaiah's time.

1. The prophet summons the heathen nations to listen to Yahweh's verdict on their lives. The peoples of the world must give heed, the whole earth must hear. Every person in every nation is called to attend to Yahweh's judgement.

2. This verse and the next do not make for easy reading, but they are corrective to a view of God held by many in today's church. God is not bound to forgive the impenitent. There is such a thing as the holy anger of God against injustice and sin. God is committed to condemn those people who persistently refuse to repent and instead continue in their rebellion against him. He "gives them over" for destruction because they have refused all his overtures of reconciliation.

3. Their dead bodies will be cast away and the stench will be terrible. Their blood will flow downhill. It is a grim and gruesome picture.

4. The first half of this verse would be quoted by the Messiah (Mt 24:29, Mk 13:24-25) and later echoed in Revelation 6:12-14. As a prophecy, it points forward to the eventual return of the Messiah to wind up this present age. Then those who are doomed, described here as stars or planets in the sky, would wither away like an old leaf or an unpicked fruit.

5. Edom is now singled out for judgement, just as Moab was in 25:10-12. Having raged throughout the heavens, at this point the storm arrives and remains over Edom. In the Bible Edom symbolises those who are godless (Heb 12:16) and those who always persecute the godly in the spirit of Antichrist (Obad 10-14). The Edomites were not only the principal adversaries of God's people, but also the nation that was diametrically opposed to their views. For this reason they were doomed to judgement. The spirit of Edom had to be expunged before the new heavens and the new earth could be formed.

6. This verse and the next describe a sacrificial slaughter. Yahweh's sword is red with blood and greasy with fat. The godless people of Edom are being butchered as if they were sacrificial animals. Lambs, goats and rams stand for different strata of society in Edom. There would be a terrible slaughter. Alec Motyer points out that "In the sacrificial system, the blood and the fat were exclusively for God" (Lev 7:23-27). The point being made by the prophet is that it is God's prerogative, not ours, to judge and to avenge. "Vengeance is *mine*; I will repay, says the Lord" (Lev 19:18, Rom 12:19).

7. The whole nation is doomed. The wild and untamed dwellers of the heights, those with young blood and the leading citizens would all be struck down. Another equally gruesome picture of the judgement meted out by the Messiah on Edom will appear in the final part of the book of Isaiah (63:1-6).

8. The day of vengeance on the enemies of God's people coincides with the year of release and vindication for Zion (see also 35:4, 61:2, 63:4 and Jer 50:28, 51:6). Why does Yahweh bring retribution in this way? Because he has resolved to make sure that justice is done and seen to be done on this earth. Because he has resolved to make sure that righteousness is seen to triumph over evil.

9. The final doom of Edom is now represented by two images. The first (v 9-10) is of a perpetual conflagration, the second (v 11-15) of a dreary solitude inhabited by sinister creatures. The first echoes the fate of Sodom, and the second, that of Babylon. We are told that the waterways of Edom would carry pitch and sulphur, and the pitch would be burning.

10. Day after day would pass and the fire would not be quenched. Its smoke would continue to rise forever and ever (Rev 14:11). It would remain as waste land throughout the generations, and nobody would ever travel through it.

11. The only inhabitants of this dreary wasteland would be hawks and hedgehogs, owls and ravens. The *confusion* and *chaos* in this verse are the same rhyming words (*tohu* and *bohu*) as *formless* and *void* in the second verse of the Bible (Gen 1:2). Here (as in Jer 4:23) they imply an undoing of the work of creation and a return to meaninglessness, shapelessness, instability and emptiness. The line and plummet were used to demolish buildings. The use of these instruments gives the destruction undertaken by God a precise and scientific character.

12. Once creation is undone, nothing would be left. "No Kingdom There".

13. Its strongholds and fortresses would be covered with thorns, nettles and thistles. Jackals and ostriches would dwell there.

14. Wildcats and hyenas would bump into each other there. Goat-demons (13:21) would converse with each other. Restless *Lilith* would rest there; this is a word derived from Babylonian demonology for a nocturnal creature or a demon.

15. Owls would nest and hatch there, and buzzards would gather there and mate. The last state of Edom is a parody of the first, grisly and ongoing.

16. The prophet emphasises that each of these creatures would be found in the ruins of Edom, each accompanied by its mate. This was written in "the Book of Yahweh", which may be the collected sayings of Isaiah and his school (8:16).

17. God had decided on the punishment for sin. He would apportion it with perfect justice. The judgement would be severe. It is not clear whether it would involve extinction, but in any case its consequences would be everlasting.

Meditation: The last Thing that People talk about

Judgement belongs to God, not to us (Mt 7:1-2). God himself finds it a strange and alien task (28:21). Nevertheless, the idea of God's judgement is central to the Bible. God is a king (33:22). A good king rules his people. If his people are set on rebelling against him, he must put down their rebellion.

God is slow to anger, and this lulls many people into a false sense of security. They ask, "What about his promise to return? It has not materialised, has it? The world ticks on much as usual. There are a few scares here and there, but it does not look as if the great universal judgement is going to happen" (2 Pet 3:4).

Isaiah consistently declared that God's just and righteous anger against our sin is a reality that we must all come to terms with (33:14-15). God will not tolerate rebellion for ever. People who persistently ignore his clear warnings will one day get a terrible surprise.

God's wrath is written up in the newspapers every day. He gives people up to their wrong beliefs. He allows them to sow the seeds of selfishness and to reap their inevitable harvest of discord. The poor and the needy are not the only ones who suffer. Everyone suffers. In the 21st century the people of the world are paying a very high price for their rejection of God. And things will become worse, much worse. Barry Webb writes: "This is nothing compared with what is to come; it is like the tremors that precede an earthquake. And the earthquake itself, the final shaking of everything, is what Isaiah sets before us".

It will be absolutely awful. The language of this chapter is graphic. Slaughter, the stench of rotting corpses, streams of blood, the skies rolling up, planets and stars withering – it will be unimaginably terrible and terrifying. Yahweh is a king and he is also a *warrior* (30:27-28). His sword kills and drinks its fill (v5). It is sated with blood and gorged with fat (v6). And in the end, that sword will deal with all of God's enemies. It will descend upon those who consistently set themselves against the godly. Part of the purpose of the judgement is to vindicate the people of Zion (v8). Some of the retribution meted out on the great Day of Judgement will be an expression of God's favour on behalf of those who are his people.

When God began the job of choosing his own people and educating them about his purposes, he started with one man, Abraham. He made the following promise to him: "I will make of you a great nation, and I will bless you, and make your name great, so that you will be a blessing. I will bless those who bless you, and the one who curses you I will curse" (Gen 12:2-3). Those who were not among the descendants of Abraham would therefore be judged according to how they reacted to those who were. If they blessed God's people, God would bless them in turn. If they cursed God's people, God would curse them in turn.

The final points made in this chapter about the universal judgement are that it is inescapable and that its consequences are everlasting. No one who will be slain by God's sword will survive. Their homes will become burning pitch, the air thick with sulphur. The only living beings that will survive the conflagration will be ghostly creatures of the night. The die will be cast by God. He will decide, and his decision will be perfectly just. His judgement will be severe, but it will be seen by all to be perfectly right. Whether it will be eternal punishment or painful annihilation is not completely clear, but in either case the consequences will last forever. In this passage, the evident absence of survivors among the lost suggests that it may be the latter. We may have thought through this subject and we may have reached certain convictions about it, but it is such a difficult matter that it is probably best not to be dogmatic, nor seek to share our views with others.

LXI

35:1-10 The flowering Wilderness

We now move from the terrible judgement of God to the tender restoration of his people. The attractive gentleness of this chapter is enhanced by its position as an oasis of greenery and calm between the devastation of judgement in chapter 34 and the historical accounts of war, sickness and selfishness in chapters 36-39. There is a similarity between the imagery used in this beautiful picture of Israel restored and that which we shall find in chapters 40-55.

1. The desert road is full of joy, carpeted with spring flowers. After a time of rain, deserts can indeed be transformed in an extraordinary way.

2. There is an abundance of crocuses in blossom, and the desert road rejoices in song. It is shaded with great cedars of Lebanon, and decorated with the plants and flowers that adorn Carmel and Sharon. Why is there all this beauty and promise of new life? The answer is, because Yahweh himself will pass by in his glorious majesty. He will lead his people back to their land after their years of exile.

3. Some of God's people are elderly and weak, and others just need to stiffen their resolve. The prophet asks that their hands may be strengthened and their knees made sturdy for the journey home. Such encouragements are still needed today (Heb 12:12-13), both in our struggle against sin and in our endurance of the trials that come our way. They strengthen our godly hope, which is "a sure and steadfast anchor of the soul" (Heb 6:19), and help us to keep going.

4. The prophet asks that those who are apprehensive about the coming journey should be comforted and encouraged. They are not to be afraid, for their God is coming to bring them restitution and vindication. He will save them completely.

5. We are told that Yahweh is coming, that God is on his way. Perhaps the main fulfilment of verses 5-6 would be in the ministry of the Messiah (61:1-2, Lk 4:16-21). He would quote these verses so as to encourage his forerunner to trust God even in imprisonment (Mt 11:5, Lk 7:22). He would open the eyes of the blind (e.g. Mk 10:46-52, Jn 9:1-41), and unstop the ears of the deaf (e.g. Mk 7:31-37).

6. Thanks to the Messiah the lame would leap like a deer (e.g. Mk 2:1-12), and the tongue of the dumb would sing for joy (e.g. Mt 9:32-34). How could this be? We are told that waters would appear in the wilderness and springs would break forth in the desert (41:17-20, and see also 30:25 and 33:21). In the Bible there is a link between fresh water and health (2 Ki 5:10, 14 and Jn 9:7). The wilderness would not only be transformed into a garden: it would also become a healing spa.

7. Everywhere water and greenery will spring up. The hot sand will become not a mirage but a real pool, the thirsty ground springs of water, the home of jackals a swamp, and instead of yellow grass there will be reeds and rushes.

8. The desert road becomes a royal highway. It is called the Holy Way. Nobody who is unholy may travel on it, only God's people. It is for those who have chosen to live a holy life and have renounced what is worldly and sensual. It is a road where encouraging progress is made. Once a traveller is on it, the way ahead is clear. Even a fool will not wander off and go astray.

9. The Holy Way will be a safe highway. Wild beasts will be unable to get onto it, but the redeemed will walk there.

10. Those whom Yahweh has ransomed (Mk 10:45) will return home. They will resettle in Zion. This would be partially fulfilled by the return of the Israelites to their land in 539 B.C. Its greatest fulfilment will be when all of God's redeemed people will arrive in the New Jerusalem in the age to come (Rev 21:1-8). Their entry and their residence there will be full of endless joy. This verse is either copied from or was copied in 51:11, which is identical to it, word for word.

Meditation: The Wonder of returning Home

The chapter is addressed to a people who are in captivity. It speaks about the fulfilment of their longing to see the glory and majesty of Yahweh their God (v 2). It announces their salvation (v 3-4), and the miracles that would take place both in themselves (v 5-6a) and in the desert on their way home (v 1, 6b-7). It describes the special highway that God would build (v 8a), and promises them security and progress as they walked along it (v 8b-9). It tells of the joy that would be theirs when they finally arrived in Zion (v 10). Then, at last, their hunger for home and their longing to be close to God would be satisfied. They would have reached their final destination. Sorrow and sighing would be a thing of the past.

This much is clear, but who exactly was the prophet addressing these words to? There are at least four ways in which Christians have interpreted this prophecy. Some carry more conviction than others. Isaiah's prophecies seem to be multi-layered. It is part of their divine inspiration that they may be interpreted correctly in different ways at different times in history.

The first interpretation, believed by many, is that this passage was written as an encouragement to the exiles in Babylonia to help prepare them for their eventual return to Jerusalem. It was probably written during the exile (586-539 B.C.), by the author of chapters 40-55 of the book of Isaiah. He foresaw that after the fall of Babylon Cyrus the Great would decree that the Jews would be allowed to return to their own land and rebuild their Temple. The return would be arduous and the Jewish people would face many obstacles on their arrival in Jerusalem. Their resolve would need strengthening. The purpose of the passage was to give them hope and help them to look ahead to their journey home. There is no doubt that this is why the passage was written in the first place, but much of its exalted language does not tally with the experience of the returning exiles. They made their way to Jerusalem gladly enough, but the re-settlement of Jerusalem would prove an arduous mission, as the books of Ezra and Nehemiah make clear.

The second interpretation is that this passage is a Messianic prophecy. When the Messiah came, he would come as a saviour and vindicator of his people (v4). His ministry would be attended by miracles (v6-7), and the spiritual vision of his followers would be like a desert that was blossoming (v7). He would show the people of God the Holy Way and urge them to get on it. This too has been widely accepted as a correct interpretation.

The third interpretation, believed by some in our own day, is that this passage is a prophecy that was fulfilled when the Jews returned to their land and the state of Israel was proclaimed in May 1948. A few years later the Negev was irrigated and burst into blossom (v1-2, 7), and highways were built in the desert (v8). But sadly there seems to have been little change in the spiritual outlook of the Jewish people as a result of their repatriation. Even if the current return to Israel was a definite fulfilment of prophecy, this would not justify the Jews maltreating other ethnic groups in order to achieve it. As with Jesus' crucifixion and those whose actions brought it about, the fact that the re-occupation of the land by the Jews since 1948 can be viewed as having been foretold in scripture in no way justifies the actions of those Jews who are maltreating Palestinians in the present day in order to fulfil the re-occupation. For these reasons this interpretation has found less favour than the others.

The fourth interpretation is that the passage points forward to the followers of the Messiah in the Christian era. The Messiah is "your God" who has come to vindicate and save his people (v4). It is he who has redeemed (v9) and ransomed (v10) them from their selfishness. It is he who strengthens his followers and gives them hope (v3-4). They have embarked on a journey that will take them from their present state as exiles to their final home in the renewed Jerusalem (v10). As they wander through the spiritual desert of this present life, it is he who makes their journey fruitful (v1-2) and refreshing (v7). It is he who through the witness of his people continues to open the eyes of the spiritually blind. He continues to enable the spiritually dead to hear. He continues to restore those who are crippled by their sin. He continues to put a new song in the mouths of the defeated (v5-6). We who are his followers need to be constantly reminded that we are walking along the Holy Way (v8a). When we are foolish enough to stray, the Messiah will bring us back to the Holy Way (v8b) because he is absolutely committed to us, and sometimes the process of our restoration may be quite rough. However, provided that our focus is on him, he promises us that no enemy will be able to deflect or harm us (v9).

It is really good to walk on the Holy Way and it will be wonderful when we finally arrive home. We shall then be at rest and full of joy in the company of God himself. This is where we have always wanted to be. For the time being we are exiles (1 Pet 1:1-2) and our hearts cry out for home (2 Cor 5:1-9). We are like the prodigal son in the parable, on the way home. Unlike him, we know the welcome that awaits us. The Holy Way is proving to be a wonderful highway. True, there are not many people on it (Mt 7:13-14), but there is something special about our travelling companions, and this also inspires us to keep going. This beautiful chapter of the book of Isaiah rekindles our hope and helps us to persevere.

This fourth interpretation of the passage is the present author's favourite.

Part 4 – In God we Trust

LXII

36:1-12 The Tactics of Intimidation

Chapters 36-39 are unusual in the book of Isaiah, being a historical account that is written mainly in prose. They mostly coincide almost word for word with 2 Kings, chapter 18:13, 17-37 and all of chapters 19 and 20, and it is possible that they were copied from this source. In chapters 36 and 37 the political crisis that had been developing during the years of Isaiah's ministry finally reached its nail-biting climax. The narrative is sober and restrained, and moves inexorably towards the culminating moment of Isaiah's life and ministry.

1. There is a problem about these events taking place in the fourteenth year of King Hezekiah. The sixth year of his reign coincided with the fall of Samaria in 722 B.C. (2 Ki 18:9-10). The invasion of Judah related here took place 21 years later, in 701 B.C., and so we would expect this to be the twenty-seventh year of Hezekiah's reign. A possible cause of this error is that originally some different material came just before chapters 36 and 37: certainly the events narrated in chapters 38 and 39 happened before those in 36 and 37. If so, the initial phrase, "In the fourteenth year of King Hezekiah", might originally have introduced much earlier events, prior even to those in chapter 38. It was probably kept as the beginning of the whole section when the order of the chapters was altered, so it originally referred to events prior to Hezekiah's illness in chapter 38.
   The Assyrian invasion described here was a devastating blow for Judah. The King of Assyria, Sennacherib, captured many fortified towns, as well as numerous villages. An enormous number of God's people were taken captive into exile.

2. After some diplomatic moves by King Hezekiah designed to save Jerusalem from being conquered by the Assyrians (2 Ki 18:14-16), Sennacherib decided in his ruthless and treacherous way to go ahead with the siege regardless. He sent a great army to invest Jerusalem. One of his most senior civil officials, the Chief Cup-bearer or Rabshakeh, came from Lachish as his representative, and stood by the conduit of the upper pool (7:3). He spoke to Hezekiah's senior officials. He had a message from the king of Assyria for all the people of Jerusalem.

3. We have already come across two of the senior officials of King Hezekiah mentioned here (22:15-25). Eliakim now occupies the position previously held by Shebna although, in the end, both of them were found wanting. Nothing more is known about Joah.

4. The Rabshakeh proceeded to teach all subsequent tyrants the technique of subversion. Both of his speeches (v 4-10 and v 13-20) are diabolical examples of how to humiliate and intimidate those who are in a position of weakness. His most deadly ploy was to sow unbelief and despair by subtly twisting the truth. He began by declaring that he spoke in the name of the great king. He asked Hezekiah to account for the bravado that had led him to rebel against Assyria.

5. It could not have been mere words of wisdom that lay behind Hezekiah's rebellion. He must have been depending on some other ally. Alec Motyer notes that Isaiah had told the pro-Egyptians that if they refused to heed his prophecies, they would hear exactly the same message from foreigners (28:9-11) – and here was an Assyrian speaking and making use of Isaiah's own words: confidence, rely, trust and power. His question, "On whom do you now rely?" would in fact make an excellent title for a sermon on Isaiah's most reiterated plea, that our ultimate trust should be in God. The answer that we give to this question will, of course, determine the course of our lives.

6. The Rabshakeh stated that if Egypt was Hezekiah's ally, then it would prove to be an unhelpful alliance, like a staff that pierces the hand of anyone who leans on it. Pharaoh would not keep his promises. Here the Rabshakeh was speaking the truth. Isaiah himself had likewise prophesied about the unreliability of the Egyptians (e.g. in 19:14-16, 28:15, 30:1-7, 31:1-3).

7. The Rabshakeh then proceeded to argue that not only was Hezekiah without earthly help, but he had also forfeited the protection of his own god. The King of Judah had committed what in the eyes of the heathen nations was sacrilege, by abolishing the local sanctuaries and insisting that Yahweh should be worshipped only in the central sanctuary in Jerusalem. This argument showed how closely the Assyrians kept a watch on the internal affairs of the other countries. Hezekiah had indeed reformed the worship in Judah, clearing away the worship of images and false gods (2 Ki 18:3-6). This reform, however, had not brought Hezekiah the disapprobation of Yahweh, but his approval. So the Rabshakeh was mistaken, his basic premise being false. Yahweh had not utterly forsaken his people. What Yahweh had done was to bring them to a position where they had to trust in him.

8. The Rabshakeh taunted the people of Jerusalem with a wager. He would give them two thousand horses if they could find riders for them. This would have been galling for the pro-Egyptian party in Judah, who had been very conscious of their weakness in cavalry (30:16, 31:1-3, and v 9 of this chapter). Even with this large equine gift, however, the people of Jerusalem would have lost to Assyria.

9. If Hezekiah was relying on Egypt, his power would not have matched that of any of the Assyrian captains. How then could he defy the great king?

10. The Rabshakeh then claimed that Yahweh himself had sent the Assyrians. As a matter of fact, Isaiah had taught this very truth (5:26, 7:18-20, 10:5-7), but his

standpoint and his presuppositions were completely different. Coming as it did from the Rabshakeh, it was an arrogant, incorrect and blasphemous statement. It was nevertheless persuasive because it was partly based on the truth.

11. The Rabshakeh was probably making his wishes known in Hebrew ("the language of Judah") with the help of an interpreter. Eliakim, Shebna and Joah were concerned that his words might unsettle the people of Jerusalem, so they pleaded with him to speak to them in Aramaic instead, which both he and the three of them understood, but which would be incomprehensible to the others.

12. The Rabshakeh immediately seized his advantage and sought to stir up disaffection among the people. His answer was insulting and humiliating. He declared that Sennacherib's message was for all the people of Jerusalem. The siege that was about to begin would result in their bread and water running out, and they would then have to eat their own excrement and drink their own urine.

Meditation: The Half-truths that are hurtful

The first verse of this chapter is reproduced in 2 Kings 18:13, but the immediate sequel to the invasion, which is amplified in the record of the Kings (2 Ki 18:14-16), is not in the book of Isaiah. The King of Assyria, Sennacherib, also describes this invasion in his records, which have survived. He laid siege to forty-six walled towns in Judah and captured them. He also captured many villages. He claimed to have taken over 200,000 prisoners into exile. He also claimed to have shut up King Hezekiah in Jerusalem "like a bird in a cage".

His invasion was prompted by the fact that the King of Judah had reneged on the annual tribute payment the previous year. Ever since Ahaz had formed an alliance with Assyria in 734 B.C. the Kingdom of Judah had been a vassal state of Assyria, and the annual tribute that had to be paid was a crippling burden. After the ruthless invasion and subjugation of Judah, Hezekiah realised that he had made a mistake in joining the Anti-Assyrian alliance led by Egypt. He sent envoys to Sennacherib at Lachish and sued for peace, promising to pay whatever the King of Assyria asked for. Sennacherib's price (according to 2 Ki 18:14) was three hundred talents of silver and thirty of gold. This tallies quite well with Sennacherib's records.

King Hezekiah raided the Temple and his own royal treasury for the silver (2 Ki 18:15), and then stripped the gold from the doors and the doorposts of the Temple (2 Ki 18:16). He sent the silver and gold to Sennacherib at Lachish. In this way, King Hezekiah, after losing nearly all the land and people of Judah, managed to pay the tribute with interest. Having fulfilled the demands of Sennacherib, he was confident that Jerusalem would be spared. He had not counted on Sennacherib's perfidious treachery. What happened next was that "The King of Assyria sent the Rabshakeh from Lachish to King Hezekiah at Jerusalem, with a great army" (v2). Sennacherib was demanding the immediate surrender of Jerusalem.

Did the people of Judah and Jerusalem deserve this terrible punishment? On many occasions Isaiah had said that they did. For four decades he had prophesied that God was angry with their social injustice and their idolatrous worship. Their show of religion in the Temple, far from impressing him, was abominable in his eyes (1:10-17). Isaiah had even predicted that Yahweh would use the Assyrians as the rod of his retribution and as a scourge to bring the people of Judah back to him.

Sennacherib was an exceptionally arrogant and unholy agent of Yahweh, but even he had reasons for what he did. Judah was a vassal state of Assyria and Hezekiah had reneged on the tribute payments that were due to the sovereign nation. Isaiah had warned Hezekiah not to put his trust in Egypt for protection, but in the end the King of Judah had given way to his pro-Egyptian courtiers. The rebellion had taken place, and severe reprisals followed.

The land of Judah was destroyed and the enemy was surrounding the city of Jerusalem. Yahweh had promised that his people would be judged, and now it was happening. The Rabshakeh was ranting away. His arguments were scoring points because they possessed a measure of truth. And he hadn't finished yet.

LXIII

36:13-22 The Meekness of the Bullied

13. The Rabshakeh boldly resumed his verbal assault, speaking loudly in Hebrew so that the common people of Jerusalem could hear him. Throughout his address he pointedly avoided addressing Hezekiah as king. Instead he urged everyone to hear the message of Sennacherib, the "great king, the king of Assyria".

14. The Rabshakeh asked the common people not to be deceived by Hezekiah, who was helpless and completely unable to deliver them.

15. He told the people of Jerusalem that they would be unwise to heed Hezekiah's request that they should rely on Yahweh. He imagined Hezekiah saying to them, "Yahweh will surely deliver us; this city will not be given into the hand of the king of Assyria".

16. The great Sennacherib's message was that, instead of heeding Hezekiah, the people should accept the Assyrian terms for peace. If they surrendered meekly, they would be allowed to eat their own grapes and figs, and have access to their own water cisterns.

17. Such normality would only go on for a certain period of time, however. The ingenious Rabshakeh had worked up for the occasion a parody of Yahweh's promise to lead the people of Israel into a land flowing with milk and honey (Lev 20:24). Eventually, according to the Rabshakeh, Sennacherib would come and deport the citizens of Jerusalem, taking them into exile and resettling them in a land like their own, with grain and wine, bread and vineyards.

18. Any declaration that Yahweh could or would save them would be misleading, said the Rabshakeh, for none of the other national gods had been able to save their people from the Assyrians.

19. The gods of Hamath and Arpad, two major Syrian cities (see 10:9), were now in the pantheon in Nineveh, as were the gods of Sepharvaim, whose location is unknown. Nor had the gods of Samaria been able to protect their people.

20. Just as these gods had failed, so would Yahweh. He would be unable to save Jerusalem from Sennacherib's hand. These words of the Rabshakeh were high blasphemy, and they were heard by Yahweh (37:6). The pride and arrogance of the Assyrians were known to God, and detested by him (10:5-19).

21. The people of Jerusalem were not easily swayed by tyrannical subversion. They had been told by King Hezekiah not to answer a word, and they gladly obeyed. There are times when it is best to keep silent. Even the Messiah would in his day amaze people by the dignified silence he sometimes maintained (53:7, Mt 27:14, Lk 23:9, 1 Pet 2:23). There is something impressive about the humility with which the people took all the verbal abuse. Some of what the Rabshakeh had said earlier on had opened old wounds, but towards the end of his second speech he overplayed his hand. The inconsistency he showed between claiming to have been sent by Yahweh (v10), and the contempt with which he later spoke about him (v18, 20), would have been obvious to all his hearers. As for the Rabshakeh's placing Yahweh, the one true God, their covenant God, on the same level as the gods of the nations – this was too much! Nothing could have been more counter-productive. It moved the people to trust in the only One who could deliver them.

22. Hilkiah, Shebna and Joah then tore their clothes, as a sign of their repentance and submission to Yahweh. They then returned to Hezekiah and told him what the Rabshakeh had said, and the King of Judah heard their report.

Meditation: A terribly clever Man

George Adam Smith wrote that in the whole Bible there is not a single person to be found who is cleverer than this Rabshakeh. In order to fulfil his purposes he spoke very eloquently. He was an expert on the language and religion of the tribe of Judah, and was familiar with the demands made by Yahweh on his people and their failure to fulfil them. He had the spirit of Satan in his make-up, combining both accusation and temptation in his speeches. He clearly thought very highly of himself, and was no stranger to the pride and power of the mighty Assyrians.

As an accuser he pointed out Hezekiah's failings (v4-6) and his consequently weak political position (v14-16, 18). As a tempter he made skilful use of the truth. He equipped himself with a number of unanswerable facts, such as the unreliability of Egypt (v6) and the failure of the heathen gods (v19). He used mockery (v8), threats (v12b) and cajoling (v16-17). He perverted good theology to serve his own cause, misrepresenting the reforms of Hezekiah (v7), selecting from Isaiah's preaching (v10, see 10:6, 12), and drawing misleading conclusions from false religions (v18-20). The Rabshakeh's objective was not to seek the truth but to manipulate and domineer. Because of this Hezekiah was right to say to the people, "Do not answer him" (v21).

This incident from the time of Jerusalem's siege by Sennacherib has something to teach us in our own day, when true religion and the knowledge and fear of God are under constant and insidious attack. It becomes ever more difficult to resist the plausibility of worldly arguments, the temptation to be self-indulgent and satisfy our every wish, and the possibility of abusing other people's trust and the power that they have entrusted to us. Occasionally we shall come across someone like the Rabshakeh, and be tempted to doubt the correctness of the lessons we have learnt from God and from Scripture. Are we right to shun certain cultural pursuits because of their ungodly basis? Is it good to deny ourselves the tasty morsels of gastronomy? Must we keep on humbling ourselves before God and suppressing the feeling of pride in our achievements?

In our day, culture often looks down haughtily on simple faith in Christ. Its offer of comfortable selfishness, unchecked by habitual discipline or the fear of God, is not easy to turn down. Its patronising tone, its appearance of having a superior understanding of the workings of the human mind, its apparent tolerance which contrasts with the apparent intolerance of Biblical Judeo-Christian religion, are all remarkably similar to the blasphemous cajoling of the Rabshakeh. Sometimes we shall have nothing to say in reply, and that is not a bad sign. It will give us a special insight into the occasional silences of the Messiah.

All of these arguments of the world, the flesh and the devil (Eph 2:1-3) are easily seen through if we keep studying the Bible. One of the main differences between today's church and that of 50 years ago is that the study of the Bible is not widely encouraged as it used to be. What little Bible study and exposition there is to be found in today's church is based on carefully chosen extracts from the Bible that lack some of its most important truths. The seriousness of sin, our guilt before God, the simple good news of the cross and the resurrection, the importance of knowing and fearing God, the need for boldness in personal sharing of the good news, the vital nature of self-discipline and the use of the means of grace, the future judgement, the fact that heaven is not the only destination after death – all these great truths are rarely preached about nowadays.

If the people of God are not well grounded in the scriptures, today's descendants of the Rabshakeh will have little trouble in leading them astray.

LXIV

37:1-13 Man proposes but God disposes

1. King Hezekiah's response to this intimidating message was a model of how faith can overcome despair. Like his three officials, he too tore his clothes in a demonstration of repentance and faith. He also put on sackcloth to underline his utter humiliation before Yahweh, and went to seek God in the Temple. Hezekiah knew he was far from perfect. He was in desperate straits, but they were partly of his own making. Now he cast himself on Yahweh and on Yahweh's prophet.

2. He sent Eliakim, Shebna and the senior priests, all covered with sackcloth, to see the prophet Isaiah. He knew he had to be reconciled with the prophet, who had always opposed alliances with Egypt and rebellion against the Assyrians.

3. The deputation informed Isaiah that Hezekiah had said that it was a day of distress, rebuke and disgrace: distress because of the people's adversity, rebuke because he was chiefly responsible for it, and disgrace or contumely because of the shame brought upon God's good name. The King of Judah used a metaphor about birth. It was as if children were ready to be born, but the mother had no strength for the labour. By this Hezekiah meant that he remembered Isaiah's prophecies about the destruction of the Assyrian army, but he lacked the faith and the right standing with Yahweh to pray for their fulfilment.

4. Hezekiah knew that Yahweh would have heard the blasphemies uttered by the Rabshakeh, who had been sent by Sennacherib to "mock the living God". This being so, Hezekiah hoped that the blasphemers would get the punishment they deserved, and he asked Isaiah to pray for the godly remnant that remained (10:20-21), that it might return fully to Yahweh at that momentous time. We should recall that Isaiah had named one of his sons *A-remnant-shall-turn* (7:3).

5. The two officials and the priests went to see Isaiah, who had already prayed and was in possession of Yahweh's message for this crisis.

6. Isaiah replied without any rancour to the two officials and the priests, some of whom had previously opposed his preaching. He asked them to pass on a word from Yahweh to the king: he was not to be afraid on account of the words with which the servants of the king of Assyria had reviled him.

7. Yahweh himself would cause Sennacherib to hear a rumour that would distract his attention from the siege of Jerusalem. The king of Assyria would then return to his own land, where in the course of time he would be assassinated. This was Yahweh's word, and it would not return to him empty, but it would accomplish the purpose for which he sent it (55:10-11).

8. The Rabshakeh went back to Sennacherib and found him fighting against Libnah, having already completed the utter destruction of Lachish.

9. At this juncture Sennacherib heard a rumour about a possible attack on his forces by some Ethiopians who had set out to do battle with him, and he promptly sent a message to Hezekiah. There is a problem concerning the identity of the Ethiopian king in question, since Tirhakah reigned from 693-671 B.C. and the events of this chapter took place in 701 B.C. Recent scholarship has shown that

Tirhakah would have been in his twenties in 701 B.C., and perhaps he was already co-regent with the ailing and elderly Ethiopian monarch.

10. Sennacherib sent a message to Hezekiah telling him not to trust in Yahweh. He was not to believe Yahweh's word that Jerusalem would be protected.

11. Sennacherib candidly reminded Hezekiah that the kings of Assyria had utterly destroyed all the nations they had fought against.

12. The gods of those nations had not delivered Gozan, Haran, Rezeph and the people of Eden who were in Telassar from destruction by the Assyrians. All these places were in the region of the upper Euphrates.

13. The kings of the Syrian towns Hamath, Arpad, Sepharvaim, Hena and Ivvah had all succumbed to the kings of Assyria. By implication, Judah had no chance: Hezekiah would be killed and Jerusalem would be razed to the ground. The pride and misplaced confidence of Sennacherib knew no bounds.

Meditation: The Word of Man and the Word of God

There were three important differences between the messages that King Hezekiah received from Sennacherib (first via the Rabshakeh, and then through a letter) and from Yahweh (via Isaiah). One difference between them was that the first was destructive of faith and fostered despair, while the other belittled despair and created faith. Another difference was that the first came from a proud heathen king and his arrogant official, while the other came from a humble God and his lowly prophet. There was also a third difference between these messages, which we shall return to later.

Sennacherib was driven by his overweening pride. Isaiah had taught that human arrogance is the worst sin; it is the sin that God hates (2:10-17). Pride is defiance against the benevolent rule of God. It is pride that expels God from the throne of a person's life. It is pride that usurps that throne, and then proceeds to make life horrible by its twisted wishes and imperious demands. It is pride that demands the number one position. It was pride that lay behind the original sin that Adam and Eve committed (Gen 3:4-6). It was pride that prompted Lucifer to commit the primal sin before them (14:12-15). Pride is the preliminary sin from which all other sins are engendered. It was the besetting sin of the king of Assyria, "the great king". In the past Isaiah had made known "the arrogant boasting of the king of Assyria and his haughty pride" (10:12). He had declared Yahweh's intention to punish the warriors of the king of Assyria because of it (10:16). Now Isaiah revealed that Sennacherib would receive what he deserved for his pride and the deceit and violence it had spawned. The punishment would fit the crime. The king of Assyria would "return to his own land", and in due course Yahweh would "cause him to fall by the sword in his own land" (v 7).

It was pride that prompted Sennacherib to crush Hezekiah and destroy Judah and Jerusalem when the King of Judah withheld the tribute in 702 B.C. It was humility that led Yahweh to forgive and restore Hezekiah after the King of Judah had disobeyed him and gone against the advice of his prophet. It was pride that would lead Sennacherib to his eventual destruction, but it was humility that led Yahweh to limit the judgement he was bound to visit on his people, and to persevere with them until, as the holy remnant, they turned back to him.

And this leads us to the third and most important difference between the two messages, that of Sennacherib and that of Yahweh, for King Hezekiah. The word of Sennacherib would not prevail, but that of Yahweh would. God's word is creative, humble and everlasting. How foolish many people are to ignore it.

LXV

37:14-20 The Prayer of King Hezekiah

Finally, buoyed by Yahweh's creative word, Hezekiah prays – and what a prayer it was! This was Hezekiah's finest hour. Never before or since has an earthly king risen to the occasion and helped his people in such a magnificent way.

14. Sennacherib had decided to pursue his war of nerves against Hezekiah until the bitter end. After reading his letter, the King of Judah was wise enough neither to dismiss his threats, nor to despair on account of them. He returned to the Temple and spread the message out in front of Yahweh.

15. Then the King of Judah addressed the King of kings.

16. Hezekiah began his prayer by focusing on who God was. He was Yahweh, Lord of the armies, the God of Israel. He was enthroned above the cherubim in the Most Holy Place in the Temple, and he ruled from his "house" in Jerusalem, which was the earthly extension of his heavenly throne. He alone was God, and he was God not just of Israel but of all the kingdoms of the earth. It was he who had created heaven and earth. Hezekiah's heart must have thrilled as he realised afresh the incomparable majesty and surpassing glory of his God.

17. Hezekiah then asked God to attend to the crisis by hearing and seeing what had taken place. It was Yahweh whom Sennacherib had blasphemously mocked.

18. Prayer must be real, and the King of Judah was realistic. The kings of Assyria had so far succeeded in all their destructive campaigns, cruelly laying waste the nations and destroying their lands. Their army was, humanly speaking, invincible. Now they encircled Jerusalem and, barring an unprecedented miracle, would duly take the city and utterly destroy it. The outlook for Yahweh's people was, from all points of view bar one, absolutely hopeless. Their end was imminent.

19. The false gods of the people they conquered had proved useless. Some had been taken to Nineveh as prized trophies of war, but most, as the King of Judah realised, were consigned to the flames. Hezekiah confessed that they were no gods

but simply the work of human hands, made of wood or stone and therefore completely lifeless and incapable of helping anybody.

20. It was inconceivable that Sennacherib would destroy the people of Yahweh as he had destroyed the heathen whose gods were no gods. Therefore Hezekiah prayed that Yahweh would save Jerusalem from the hand of the king of Assyria. In that way all the kingdoms of the earth would know that he alone, Yahweh, was the one true God. And so this prayer, which began by focusing on the honour and glory of God, ends on the same note.

Meditation: How can the Prayerless pray?

At first Hezekiah could not bring himself to pray. He sent a message to Isaiah (v 2) and went to the Temple to try and sense God's presence, but we are not told that he prayed straightaway. The burden of guilt that he carried must have been crushing. The rest of the land of Judah was destroyed, two hundred thousand of his people were deported, and now his capital was surrounded and besieged. He was to blame, for he had disobeyed Yahweh's word through Isaiah. Instead of relying on God for protection, he had put his trust in a notoriously unreliable nation, and rebelled against his overlord, the king of Assyria. He had disobeyed his God, the God who had revealed himself to Israel and to him, and whose worship he had sought to reform and purify. And now, at first, he could not even bring himself to pray "Yahweh my God", but instead sent a message to Isaiah in which he speaks of "Yahweh *your* God" (v 4), and asked the prophet to pray for the holy remnant to turn back to him.

Isaiah's reply consisted of Yahweh's creative word for Hezekiah (v 6, 7). It brought new faith and trust into the King of Judah's mind and heart. Because Yahweh would cause Sennacherib to return to his own land and to die by the sword there, there was hope after all. Hezekiah took courage, and began to see some light at the end of what was a very long and dark tunnel.

We may learn from this that, on those occasions when we are so crushed that we cannot pray, when there are no words to pour out to God, we can turn to the Bible and read (quietly or out loud) a passage with God's words. There is something powerful and eternal about the words in God's book. They have a germ of life in them. They are a little seed of faith that can transform our prayerlessness into real and life-changing prayer.

It was at this stage that the letter from Sennacherib arrived (v 9-13). This time Hezekiah did not turn to Isaiah. He went straight to Yahweh. He went in the full confidence that the prophecies concerning Yahweh's protection, proclaimed during many years by his mouthpiece Isaiah, would be fulfilled. He spread out Sennacherib's letter before Yahweh and then he poured out his heart in prayer.

This time Hezekiah found that he could pray. And how he prayed! With a godly confidence, the King of Judah was emboldened to address the King of kings. He did so humbly, focusing on Yahweh's incomparable majesty and splendour. But he also did so boldly, because he knew he was addressing a very great God, and because it was Yahweh's character and reputation that were at stake.

Barry Webb wrote that "Hezekiah's prayer was magnificent because it arose from a deep and true understanding of who God is, and was fundamentally an act of worship. Such prayer lifts people out of themselves and into the presence of God. In that context, present problems are not lost sight of; they are just seen from a new perspective, and the cry for deliverance becomes a cry that God's kingdom may come and his will be done. If only we could learn to pray like this, what times we would have on our knees, and what a difference we would see in the progress of the gospel in the world".

Like Hezekiah, we may learn to magnify God in our prayers. Instead of presenting him with our usual list of requests, we may pray that he might so act and work out his purposes in the world that the people around us would see his glory and know that he alone is God.

Prayer is not overcoming God's reluctance but taking hold of his *willingness*. Prayer does not prepare us for greater work; prayer *is* the greater work. Prayer is what happens when weakness *leans on omnipotence*. Prayer can *succeed* when all else has failed. When we work, *we* work; when we pray, *God* works.

LXVI

37:21-32 The Promises of the living God

Isaiah somehow knew about Hezekiah's prayer, and he sent him another message from Yahweh. It is an extended oracle, which begins by considering the pride of Sennacherib and his imminent humiliation. It continues with reassurance for King Hezekiah concerning the future years. It ends with a specific prophecy that would be fulfilled "that very night" (2 Ki 19:35).

21. Yahweh now speaks to Hezekiah, because Hezekiah had just spoken humbly to him about the king of Assyria (Ps 50:15). This is how it sometimes is: because someone has prayed, God steps in and the whole course of history is changed.

22. In verses 22-29 we have a taunting triumph song – given to the victors in advance of their triumph! This verse imagines the appropriate reaction of the people of Jerusalem to the Assyrian threats. They despise and scorn them. The Assyrians would retreat, and Zion would still be a "virgin" fortress.

23. Here is Yahweh's reply to the Assyrian challenge, "On whom do you now rely?" (36:5). His answer is a reciprocal question, "Whom have *you* mocked and reviled?" On receiving the news of what was about to be fulfilled that very night, Sennacherib would realise that he had made a very big mistake in raising his voice and haughtily lifting up his eyes against the Holy one of Israel.

24. Through his high official the Rabshakeh, Sennacherib had *mocked* the Lord. The king of Assyria had also been guilty of *boasting*. His boasting was not in the

one true and living God, but it was selfish boasting, that he had crossed high mountain passes with his chariots, that he had felled tall cedars and cypresses in Lebanon, and that he had explored very remote heights and dense forests.

25. He had also dug up wells and drank their waters. By diverting some branches of the River Nile, he had thought of drying up many of the waterways of Egypt, bringing financial ruin to the industries of that country (19:4-10).

26. Yahweh now taunts Sennacherib, telling him that he does not know the meaning of his own career. Yahweh had determined its course long ago! (10:5-19; see also 22:11 for a similar expression concerning the people of God). It was Yahweh who had decided to use Sennacherib as an instrument of judgement, prompting him to make fortified cities collapse into heaps of rubble.

27. The Assyrians considered the peoples of the cities they conquered as existing for their benefit, like the plants of a field. These people were like tender grass, weak and unable to offer resistance. They were transient and insignificant, like the grass that appears and then disappears on the rooftops, blighted by the sun. Because the Assyrians despised the people they conquered, they also despised Yahweh who had created all people in his own image.

28. Yahweh knew all about Sennacherib: about his rising up and his sitting down, about his comings and his goings, and about his ranting and raging against him.

29. Because of Sennacherib's arrogant raging, Yahweh would drag the king of Assyria, like a beast, back to his own land. Sennacherib would be humiliated, just as the Assyrian kings had humiliated other rulers. Esarhaddon's relief at Zenjirli shows Pharaoh Tirhakah of Egypt and King Baalu of Tyre, each with a ring in his nose, with an Assyrian conqueror holding the cords that passed through the rings. Now it was going to be Sennacherib's turn to taste the flavour of humble pie.

30. Isaiah assured Hezekiah that the land of Judah would recover, even though the harvests would be poor for the first two years. The effects of the mass invasion and depopulation of Judah meant that normal agricultural activity could not be resumed immediately. This prophecy would be a sign and a promise for King Hezekiah, reassuring him that God would continue to prosper and protect him.

31. Good would come from this crisis. The remnant is mentioned again (10:20-22). Trust, which is the necessary condition for God to intervene, was now active (30:15) and deliverance would inevitably follow (31:4-5). To take root downward and bear fruit upward is a vivid form of words which means to enjoy security and prosperity. It also suggests laying down invisible roots (praying and walking with God) and thereby bearing good fruit (justice and righteousness).

32. From Jerusalem there would emerge a holy remnant who, after surviving the Assyrian crisis, would begin life all over again, seeking to please God. This would happen thanks to the zeal of Yahweh on behalf of his people: a zeal that chastises and reforms his people, but does not destroy them.

Meditation: A fine Prayer gets a wonderful Answer

Prayer changes things. Prayer moves the hand that moves the universe. It was because Hezekiah had prayed to him that Yahweh now spoke to Hezekiah, reassuring him that he, the Holy One of Israel, was about to intervene on behalf of his people. We may observe how God's response is perfectly adjusted to the prayer that prompted it.

In the first place, Hezekiah magnified God (v 15-16). He did not focus on the catastrophe that seemed to be in store for the people of Jerusalem. He focused on Yahweh, the Lord of the armies and the protector of his people Israel, who in great humility had chosen to be enthroned above the cherubim in the Most Holy Place in the Temple of Jerusalem. He was the God of all the nations, but he had chosen to reveal himself in the first place to Israel, in the hope that the Israelites would be a light that would in turn enlighten the Gentiles. He alone was the creator of heaven and earth. In his response, Yahweh told Hezekiah that he had determined the course of history long ago. In days of old he had planned what he was now bringing to pass (v 26). So the King of Judah could relax. God, his God, was utterly in control. Hezekiah could learn from this what Isaiah had tried to teach him in the past, that God would keep in perfect peace any person whose mind was steadfastly resting on him, because that person was trusting in him (26:3). Hezekiah's strength would be in quiet trust (30:15).

Secondly, Hezekiah brought to God's attention the proud words spoken by the king of Assyria, initially through his emissary the Rabshakeh, and later personally through his message (v 17). Sennacherib had said that Yahweh would prove to be useless, just as the idol-gods of the nations had been useless. The king of Assyria and his army were invincible. This sort of arrogance amounted to blasphemy. In his reply to Hezekiah, Yahweh declared that he was well acquainted with the ranting and raving of Sennacherib. He knew how this man loved to boast about what he had done and about what he would like to do (v 23-25). He also knew about every occasion when he had sat down or stood up, and about every time he had gone out or come back in. Because Sennacherib had behaved in this proud and selfish way, Yahweh would put a hook in his nose and a bit in his mouth, and lead him back to where he had come from (v 28-29). Hezekiah could learn from this that even the very successes that feed human arrogance proclaim the sure sovereignty of God.

Thirdly, Hezekiah had asked God to save the people of Jerusalem in such a way that all the kingdoms of the earth might know that he alone, Yahweh, was the true and living God (v 20). God would certainly do this. He promised Hezekiah that the king of Assyria would not enter Jerusalem, nor shoot an arrow there, but instead would return to his place (v 33-34). He, Yahweh, would protect the city of Jerusalem for his sake and for King David's sake (v 35). He even gave Hezekiah a sign of his favour, promising him enough food for all the people of Jerusalem until they could get back into the rhythm of cultivation (v 30). He would provide a new start in life for the remnant that had survived (v 31-32). And as we shall see, God did all this. He was about to work a miracle so extraordinary, that people from every land who have read about it have concluded that Yahweh alone is God. The only true and living God is the Holy One of Israel!

LXVII

37:33-38 God fulfils his Promises

33. Yahweh promised Hezekiah that the king of Assyria would be unable to come into the city of Jerusalem. His warriors, massed around the city, would be unable to fire an arrow in anger, nor would they approach it with a shield, and nor would they cast up a siege ramp against it. The details about their inability to fire arrows or make use of shields is of interest, and provide us with a clue as to the exact nature of their fate.

34. Sennacherib would return to his own land by the same way that he came. Yahweh reiterates his assurance that he would not come into the city.

35. Yahweh declares his commitment to defend and save the city. He would do this for his own sake and for the sake of King David – which perhaps involves the Messiah, who was David's seed.

36. Instead of *Then*, 2 Kings 19:35 has *That very night*. The fulfilment of the prophecy of protection and deliverance in Isaiah's oracle (v 33-35) took place during the night that followed its utterance by Isaiah (see 17:14 and the comments at the beginning of the meditation in section LVIII, p. 177). The description of what happened is precise and concise. "The angel of Yahweh set out and struck down one hundred and eighty-five thousand in the camp of the Assyrians; when morning dawned, they were all dead bodies". For some reason Sennacherib did not include in his records his account of what happened, preferring to concentrate on his siege and destruction of Libnah, so we are dependent on the Biblical account for the number of casualties. It has been conjectured that never before or since in wartime have so many died in such a short period. The total number who died on the days when the atomic bombs fell on Hiroshima and Nagasaki together added to around half of the 185,000 mentioned in this verse.

37. This devastating blow forced Sennacherib's hand. He departed and returned to Assyria, where he lived the rest of his days in Nineveh.

38. Nineteen years later, the king of Assyria was duly assassinated while he was worshipping in the temple of Nisroch. It was two of his own sons, Adrammelech and Sharezer, who put him to the sword, and then escaped to the land of Ararat. Sennacherib was succeeded by another son, Esar-haddon. There is a poignant irony in the difference between Hezekiah and Sennacherib when presented as men of prayer. The King of Judah prayed to Yahweh in the Temple of Jerusalem, and Yahweh promptly worked an extraordinary miracle and saved him from a

fate worse than death. The King of Assyria prayed to the idol Nisroch in its temple, and Yahweh promptly visited him with the righteous judgement that he deserved.

Meditation: How did God do it? Did People repent?

First question: *how* did God do it? In what way did the angel of Yahweh strike down 185,000 Assyrian warriors? We possess two clues. The first comes from the Greek historian Herodotus, writing around 450 B.C. He states that at one stage in their campaign of 701 B.C., part of the Assyrian army had marched against Egypt. On their journey, these warriors had passed close to a very insalubrious area near Pelusium, which was swampy and prone to pestilence. There they had unknowingly been joined by some field mice, who found their way into the carts that carried their provisions and their weaponry. The rodents nibbled their way through the strings of their bows and damaged their equipment in various ways. This is all in the account of Herodotus.

George Adam Smith noted that "The Serbonian bog, between Syria and Egypt, was a place terrible for filth and miasma. The plagues, with which this swamp several times desolated the world, were first engendered among the diseased and demoralised populations, whose villages festered upon its margin. A Persian army was decimated here in the middle of the fourth century B.C." In his *The History of the Decline and Fall of the Roman Empire*, Edward Gibbon wrote that "The fatal disease which depopulated the earth in the time of Justinian and his successors (541 A.D. and following) first appeared in the neighbourhood of Pelusium, between the Serbonian bog and the eastern channel of the Nile". Later the crusaders also suffered from the infection to the north of the bog.

It is not unlikely that this section of Sennacherib's army subsequently rejoined the rest of the warriors in the siege of Jerusalem. At that stage the field mice began to have contact with the soldiers. The mice were carriers of a very nasty form of bubonic plague which may have been made all the more deadly by being conjoined with both pneumonic plague and septicemic plague. There was no social distancing, and the deadly infection spread very quickly. Then came that terrible night with much wailing and terrible cries of despair in the Assyrian camp, and men began to drop dead in their thousands. Those who were yet unaffected were ordered to dig mass graves and bury the dead, and then the contagion would have spread to them too. As the new day dawned those who were still alive took flight, most of them dying as they fled from Jerusalem. By morning many dead bodies could be seen in the Assyrian lines. Most of the dead had been stuffed into mass graves, saving the people of Judah from the perilous task of burying a vast multitude. When it came to dead bodies, the Israelites were sticklers for their rules on sanitation, and they would have avoided any contact that might have "made them unclean" and passed the infection on to them.

Did you notice the other clue? It comes in verse 33. "[Sennacherib] shall not . . . shoot an arrow there, [nor] come before it with a shield". Bows are of no use whatever without bow-strings, and nor are shields without shield-straps. Hungry mice love to eat fibre and leather.

Second question: did the people of Jerusalem repent? The answer is yes and no. Yes, they did repent *at that time*. When their city was surrounded by Assyrian soldiers, they finally realised that Isaiah had been right all along. The only thing they could do then was to trust in Yahweh. Isaiah had been urging them to do this all along, until the final act of the drama. With death staring at them in the face, and certain that God had brought the calamity upon them because of their unbelief in him, they repented. They feared Yahweh. They humbled themselves before him, and he heard their cry. There can be no question about it. They all repented, each and every one of the citizens of Jerusalem.

But that is not the full story. Yes, they did repent, but no, their repentance was only skin deep. It had no love for God in it, only fear. Fear had seized the godless, and they cried out, "Who among us can live with the devouring fire? Who among us can live with everlasting flames?" (33:14). The people had no choice but to put their faith in God, but theirs was the faith of demons. They could not endure the presence of the holy God they had turned to.

Some of them began to turn back to their old lives straightaway. Isaiah has left us a haunting picture of how he came out of his house that morning after Yahweh's deliverance. He asked people, "What do you mean that you have gone up, all of you, to the housetops, you that are full of shouting, tumultuous city?" (22:1-2). He later reflected, "In that day Yahweh of the armies called to weeping and mourning, to baldness and putting on sackcloth; but instead there was joy and festivity, killing oxen and slaughtering sheep, eating meat and drinking wine. 'Let us eat and drink, for tomorrow we die'" (22:12-13).

Some years later, Hezekiah died and his eldest son Manasseh began to reign. "He did what was evil in the sight of Yahweh. He rebuilt the high places that his father Hezekiah had destroyed; he erected altars to Baal, made a sacred pole, worshipped all the host of heaven, and served them. He built altars in the house of Yahweh. He made his son pass through fire. Moreover Manasseh shed very much innocent blood, until he had filled Jerusalem from one end to another, besides the sin that he caused Judah to sin, so that they did what was evil in the sight of Yahweh" (2 Ki 21:2-4, 6, 16). By tradition, the death of Isaiah took place in the middle of this carnage. Manasseh had him "sawn in two" (Heb 11:37). Things got better under Manasseh's son Josiah, but the people of Judah seemed unable to cement a true repentance. In the end, 115 years after Sennacherib failed to do so, God finally allowed Jerusalem to be taken and destroyed by the King of Babylon, Nebuchadnezzar.

How about us? Have we repented? If so, was it a deep and true repentance?

Oh Holy One of Israel, Yahweh of the armies, only by returning to you and resting upon you can we be saved, and only by quietly trusting in you can we be strong. Reveal our selfishness to us in all its ugliness. Enable us to resist its pull and instead to look to you. Prompt us to say no to the lust of the world, the lust of the flesh and the pride of life. Help us to be still and to know that you alone are God.

LXVIII

38:1-8 The Illness of King Hezekiah

The episode of Hezekiah's illness related here precedes the Assyrian crisis of 701 B.C. because it took place before the arrival of the embassy sent to Jerusalem by Merodach-Baladan of Babylon (39:1), and this embassy must have been sent by 702 B.C. at the very latest (see the comments at the beginning of section LXX, p. 208).

1. Although King Hezekiah had reformed the religious practices of Judah and Jerusalem, there were other aspects of his rule where he had been unfaithful to Yahweh, for example on the controversial matter of international alliances. When he was in the prime of life he became ill, and it seemed as if he was going to die. He was suffering from a malignant boil or carbuncle (38:21), a symptom of a potentially deadly form of plague. In his time this was often fatal. Isaiah came to see him with a prophetic word from Yahweh. The king was to set his affairs in order. He would not recover his health, but would die.

2. Hezekiah was upset by Isaiah's prophecy, and when the prophet had left, "he turned his face to the wall and prayed to Yahweh". At this bitter moment Hezekiah must have felt as if he was alone with God. It was no help being the King of God's people. Leaders are human like other people, and it can be very lonely at the top. But Hezekiah knew that God was very close by.

3. He asked God to remember the days when he had walked before him faithfully and wholeheartedly, and had carried out some magnificent religious reforms. But he was realistic. In great distress because he was about to die, he wept bitterly.

4. At that very moment Isaiah was given another prophetic word for Hezekiah. He did an about turn and returned to the king's chamber (2 Ki 20:4-5).

5. He told him that Yahweh, the God of his ancestor David, had heard his prayer and seen his tears. Yahweh made no mention of Hezekiah's presumed good works and wholeheartedness. But because of his prayer and his tears, Yahweh would add fifteen years to his life. If the illness occurred in 702 B.C., that would imply that Hezekiah's death would take place in 687 B.C. This is the year in which most scholars date it.

6. Yahweh also promised to deliver and defend the king and his city from a future Assyrian invasion. There would be a reprieve for Hezekiah: he was given another fifteen years of life. There would also be a reprieve for Jerusalem. Both were just that: reprieves. Hezekiah would not live forever, nor would Jerusalem remain inviolate in perpetuity.

7. Yahweh also gave King Hezekiah a sign, to assure him that the prophetic word would be fulfilled.

8. A miracle would take place. The shadow cast by the sun on the dial of Ahaz would turn back ten steps. Perhaps this was something that Hezekiah was able to see

from his sickbed. We are told that it happened just as Yahweh had promised. The sun turned back ten steps. Perhaps the dial of Ahaz was a sundial, and the steps were little notches on it. Some commentators have conjectured that there was a strange disturbance of the atmosphere or a special alignment of clouds, and this caused an unusual phenomenon of refraction of the sunlight to take place. John Skinner comments that "The retreating shadow, miraculously lengthening the day, was a pledge of the postponement of that 'night in which no man can work' (Jn 9:4), which had almost overtaken Hezekiah".

Meditation: Why God changes his Mind

In this section we have an example of God granting a second prophecy that overrules an earlier one. Yahweh had sent Isaiah to see the ailing King Hezekiah with the sombre message, "You shall die; you shall not recover". The king, in despair, turned to prayer and wept bitterly. Because of his prayer and his tears, God spoke again to Isaiah, who returned to the king with the new message, "I will add fifteen years to your life".

This is by no means the only case recorded in the Old Testament of God changing his mind. There is a memorable one in the book of Jonah. After a few initial misadventures involving a great fish, Yahweh finally persuades his recalcitrant prophet Jonah to go to Nineveh. There he is charged with preaching doom to the evil Assyrians. Jonah's message is brief to the point of being laconic: "Forty days more, and Nineveh shall be overthrown!" When the people of Nineveh heard it, they all repented and put on sackcloth. As soon as they had done so, "When God saw what they did, how they turned from their evil ways, God changed his mind about the calamity that he had said he would bring upon them; and he did not do it" (Jon 3:10).

Another example, from the book of Isaiah, concerns the contrast between the terrible fate prophesied for Babylon and the relatively peaceful capitulation of the city to the Medes under Cyrus (See chapters 13 and 14, and the meditation in section XXVIII, p. 89-90). The explanation may be that Nebuchadnezzar, the evil king of the Babylonians, had repented of his ways. If so, God would have then adjusted the judgement that would be visited on him, and later on his city, so that the terrible predictions in 14:11, 13:15-16 and 19-20 were no longer binding.

We learn from this that God can and does change his mind. He can and does "repent". Just as we can change our minds and reverse a decision we have made, so can God. Indeed it is precisely when we repent and change our mind about evil that God follows suit and repents of what he was going to do about it.

The clearest text on this is in the book of Jeremiah. Yahweh is speaking, and he says, "At one moment I may declare concerning a nation or a kingdom, that I will pluck up and break down and destroy it, but if that nation, concerning which I have spoken, turns from its evil, I will change my mind about the disaster that I intended to bring on it. And at another moment I may declare concerning a nation or a kingdom that I will build and plant it, but if it does evil in my sight, not listening to my voice, then I will change my mind about the good that I had intended to do to it" (Jer 18:7-10).

The same moral principle applies even if there has not been a prophecy (Ezek 18:21-24). A wicked person may repent and begin to do what is good; that person will not suffer for previous sins but will live. A righteous person may turn to evil and do what is wicked; that person's righteous deeds will not be remembered but he or she will die. Where a prophecy has been proclaimed, that prophecy acts as a warning. If the warning is heeded, the judgement promised in the prophecy will not be forthcoming, but if the prophecy is ignored, judgement will follow. It is interesting that those who heard Ezekiel's declaration said that Yahweh's way was unfair. In fact the very opposite was the case (Ezek 18:25-29). Sometimes human estimates of God's justice are far off the mark.

LXIX

38:9-22 King Hezekiah prays for Healing

9. After he recovered from his illness, King Hezekiah wrote a psalm for public use. In it he described his bitter feelings, his subsequent joy and desire to praise God, and what he learnt from his experience. In verses 10-16 he describes his anguish at the prospect of death, and in verses 17-20 his joy and gratitude when he was assured of his recovery.

10. He begins by lamenting that he would be cut off in his prime. He would be reduced to being a shade, imprisoned within the gates of Sheol.

11. He would no longer enjoy worshipping Yahweh in the land of the living, nor would he be able to interact any more with other mortal people.

12. He uses vivid metaphors. His fragile dwelling would be removed from him like a nomad's tent that was being rolled up. Like a weaver finishing her pattern on a particular cloth, his life would be decisively cut off from the loom and then rolled up. Like a day that turns to night, he would come to an end.

13. Like Job, Hezekiah complains that he was impotent against God. He spent his nights weeping. Hostile and strong like a lion, God was breaking all his bones. God was bringing his life to an end swiftly, like a day as it turns to night.

14. Hezekiah cried out in prayer like a swallow or crane, he moaned like a dove. His eyes looked up to God until they became weary. He was oppressed and longed for the security of God-given health.

15. The thought that Yahweh had told him that he would die left him speechless. Sleep was out of the question. His heart was full of bitterness.

16. He realised that he, like all people, had taken many things for granted, which were the substance of life. How he longed for health to be restored to him!

17. At this stage light begins to enter his being. "Surely it was for my welfare that I had great bitterness". Any maturity he had did not come from the good times in his life but from the bad times. Furthermore, he had an assurance that Yahweh would keep back his life from the Pit. Then a liberating truth dawned on him: he was forgiven! He could not understand this but he knew it was true, and he said, "You have cast all my sins behind your back".

18. He was filled with gratitude and knew he was not heading for Sheol, for Sheol never gives thanks. His heart was full of praise, and death is incapable of praise. He had a new hope for the future, based on Yahweh's faithfulness, so he was unlike those in the Pit. He felt as if he was being given a new life.

19. It is the living who give thanks to God, and now he was once again one of the living. Like a father with his children, he would make known God's faithfulness.

20. Yahweh would save King Hezekiah, and then the whole congregation would sing about this, accompanied by stringed instruments, in the Jerusalem Temple.

21. Isaiah had earlier told Hezekiah's servants to apply a poultice of figs to the boil that was the symptom of Hezekiah's serious illness. Yahweh can use medical treatments and other natural means to effect a cure, just as the Messiah would do during his earthly ministry (e.g. Mk 7:33-34, Jn 9:6-7).

22. Hezekiah had also asked Isaiah for a sign, and the prophet gave it to him. Verses 21-22 are misplaced; they ought to appear between verses 6 and 7 (as in the equivalent passage in 2 Ki 20:5-11).

Meditation: Death had not yet been swallowed up

At first Hezekiah felt numb. Yahweh, his faithful covenant God, had just told him that he would certainly die and not recover (v 10). He was not just shattered, he was also shocked and angry. His fragile life would be decisively cut short, and all its pleasures and delights would be no more (v 11-12). Tearful and exhausted, he could not think straight. God, who had been his greatest friend and companion in times of need, was now like a hostile lion (v 13).

He did not stop looking upwards, and this helped him. He was trying to lift his eyes to heaven, to focus on Yahweh (v 14). Yet it was he who had struck him. It was difficult to pray to the only One who could help him, since it was he who had allowed the mortal illness to afflict him (v 15). This was the cause of his anger, but as he prayed further, it became also a reason for gratitude.

Suddenly he could see clearly. Everyone took so much for granted, including all the things by which they lived (v 16). He had suffered bitterness, like everyone else – but now he saw that it had always been for his own good. Sometimes it is only when people look backwards and upwards at the same time that they realise that the most undesirable commodity in the world, suffering, is the means that God uses to teach them the lessons that really matter.

Hezekiah realised that, having brought him to the edge of the Pit, Yahweh was now holding him back from falling into it. He had a fresh realisation of the grace of God. Yahweh had forgiven him all his sins! It was as if he had cast them behind his back (v 17). No wonder that his heart was filled with praise. He wanted to thank and praise Yahweh (v 18-19), and he wanted others to join him as he did so. That is why he composed this Psalm to be sung in the Temple (v 20).

The book of Isaiah has the prophecy that Yahweh would swallow death up for ever (25:8), but this had not yet happened. This is why Hezekiah believed that when he died, he would not only be separated from people, but also from Yahweh. Like everyone else in his day, he believed that death would prevent him from seeing God in his beauty (v 11). Death would separate him from Yahweh's loving welfare, from his protection and from his forgiveness (v 17).

It is very different for us who live after the ministry of the Messiah. "To be or not to be?" In answer to this question, those who follow the Messiah can say that to live is very good, but to die is even better (Phil 1:21). To live on in this world is good, because it means fruitful labour (Phil 1:22), but to depart and be with the Messiah is far better (Phil 1:23). The words of the Messiah to a dying man two millennia ago, "*Today* you will be with me in Paradise", continue to resonate in our time. When the time comes for the Messiah to be revealed in his glory, his followers will be astonished to discover that they will be like him. To have such a hope is a huge blessing, which purifies those who have it (1 Jn 3:2-3).

There is, therefore, a great difference in the attitude to death of King Hezekiah in 742 B.C. and of a follower of the Messiah today. The latter might be glad that the time had come to be taken, but Hezekiah was thankful to be left behind.

What is the reason for this great difference? It is, quite simply, the resurrection and ascension of the Messiah. It is he who has achieved the transformation, by abolishing death and bringing life and immortality to light (2 Tim 1:10). This makes the achievement of Hezekiah and other Old Testament saints all the more remarkable. They faced death in its utter horror, and yet triumphed. On dying, they inherited dignity and unending bliss. Their hearts are now at peace and their faces suffused with glory. They walk in a radiant procession of worship before the throne of Yahweh, their covenant God, throughout all eternity.

LXX

39:1-8 The Pride of King Hezekiah

Merodach-Baladan (or Marduk-Baladan, i.e. *The god Marduk has given me an heir*) was king of Babylon between 721–710 B.C. and for nine months in 703-702 B.C. It was almost certainly in the later period of his rule that he sent some envoys to King Hezekiah of Judah. The aim of the embassy may have been to flatter Hezekiah in the hope that Judah would become an ally of Babylon against Assyria. It is not unlikely that Hezekiah came to a preliminary agreement with the Babylonians, since at the time he was also about to join the anti-Assyrian alliance led by Egypt.

1. The envoys arrived in Jerusalem with letters and a present for Hezekiah. The king of Babylon had heard about his illness and his remarkable recovery, perhaps through reading a copy of his poetic memoir (38:9-20). The parallel passage in 2 Chronicles 32:31 is of great interest. It tells us that it was the Babylonians' scientific curiosity about the miraculous sign of the sun-dial that prompted the embassy. Furthermore, it tells us that when Hezekiah met the envoys, "God left him to himself, in order to test him and to know all that was in his heart". When we meet important people we may in turn be exposed to temptation.

2. Hezekiah welcomed these envoys gladly, and gave them a guided tour of the treasury in his palace. His indiscretion seems to have been prompted by vanity and a desire to show off. He showed them the silver, the gold, the spices, the precious oil, the armoury, and all that was in his storehouses. In short, he showed them *everything*. Sadly it would seem that Hezekiah's faith and prudence both dissolved in the face of flattery. The world with its strong bias against the one true God is somehow very alluring for nearly all of God's people.

3. After the envoys had taken their leave, Isaiah appeared before King Hezekiah and asked him what these men had said and where they had come from. Hezekiah answered the less embarrassing part of the question, saying that they had come from afar, from Babylon.

4. Isaiah then asked what these men had seen in Hezekiah's palace, and the King of Judah replied truthfully. They had seen everything; there was nothing that he had not shown them.

5. Isaiah then prophesied with a word from Yahweh. The price of disloyalty to the Holy One of Israel is high, and because of this God would have his say. John Skinner wrote that, "The reception of an embassy from the sworn enemies of the king of Assyria was in itself an act of rebellion likely to precipitate a conflict which Isaiah had striven to avert; and the childish vanity displayed by Hezekiah, his pride in earthly resources, and his readiness to enter into friendly relations with the powers of this world, were tendencies against which Isaiah's ministry had been a continuous protest. All these tendencies sprang from a single root, the lack of that absolute faith in Yahweh as the all-sufficient guide and protector of the nation which was the fundamental article of Isaiah's political programme".

6. God's message to King Hezekiah was a sombre one. The day would come when all the riches in his palace and all the treasures stored up by his ancestors would be taken away to Babylon. Unlike the Assyrians, the Babylonians would succeed in taking Jerusalem. Nothing would remain.

7. This was not all. Some of Hezekiah's descendants would be taken to Babylon, where they would be emasculated and live as exiled vassals in the royal palace of

the king of Babylon. What a rebuke this was for Hezekiah, for having gloried in human wealth and human patronage.

8. Amazingly, Hezekiah found comfort in the postponement of God's judgement, and told Isaiah that the prophecy he had spoken was good. The prophet probably read his thoughts, and would have been appalled by the catchphrase Hezekiah had coined: "Peace and security in my days". A similar slogan, "Peace for our time", would later be coined, just as misguidedly, by the British Prime Minister Neville Chamberlain on the 30th of September, 1938. It too would prove in retrospect to have been unhelpful in the long run.

Meditation: Extraordinary Prophet, but flawed King

Under the inspiration of Yahweh, Isaiah predicted that one day the Babylonians would conquer Jerusalem and carry away all the treasures of the kings of Judah to their heathen land. It was a remarkable prophecy. At that time, Babylon was not yet a superpower. Ninety-three years would have to pass before they finally conquered Assyria in 609 B.C. In Isaiah's day all that Babylon could do was to mount regular challenges on Assyrian rule, distracting their neighbours from their imperial ambitions. In a flash of God-given insight, Isaiah foresaw that the Babylonians would replace Assyria as the number one superpower, and then conquer Judah and Jerusalem, proceeding to confiscate all their treasures. This actually happened in 586 B.C., 116 years after Isaiah predicted it in 702 B.C.

There was something special about Isaiah. He was a godly man. He tutored the King with great love and patience, and at the same time he was unbending and holy. He must have prayed for Hezekiah on innumerable occasions.

Hezekiah knew and loved Yahweh, but there were flaws in his character and his faith was frustratingly up-and-down. Here is a brief review of his career.

He began with an UP. "In the first year of his reign, in the first month", he began a wide-ranging and resolute reform of the national religion by cleansing the Temple (2 Chron 29:3-36). He followed this with a nationwide celebration of the Passover (2 Chron 30:1-27), a thoroughgoing destruction of the pagan shrines (2 Chron 31:1) and a reorganisation of the priestly system (2 Chron 31:2-19). The chronicler sums up his activity by writing that "Hezekiah did this throughout all Judah; he did what was good and right and faithful before Yahweh his God. And every work that he undertook in the service of the house of God, and in accordance with the law and the commandments, to seek his God, he did with all his heart: and he prospered" (2 Chron 31:20-21).

He continued with a DOWN. He found it difficult to trust in Yahweh's promise to protect his people, and instead he considered forging international alliances, just as his father Ahaz had done. Early in his reign he rebelled against Assyria (2 Ki 18:7) but got away with it because the Assyrians were waging other battles. At one stage it seemed increasingly likely that he would go against the wishes of his mentor Isaiah and join with

Egypt in a major rebellion against Assyria (28:7-22, 30:1-7). Just then, Hezekiah was visited with a mortal illness (38:1).

Next came an UP. Hezekiah prayed earnestly to Yahweh, who heard his prayer and healed him, gave him a sign and promised him protection from Assyria for the city of Jerusalem (38:2-8). Hezekiah was so grateful that he composed a wonderful psalm relating his experience of bitterness followed by joy (38:9-20).

Next came a DOWN. The chronicler described it like this: "Hezekiah did not respond according to the benefit done to him, for his heart was proud. Therefore wrath came upon him and upon Judah and Jerusalem" (2 Chron 32:25). Some envoys from Babylon visited him, and Hezekiah showed them all of his treasures and his weaponry (39:1-4). He was unrepentant when Isaiah came and explained to him the consequences of his indiscretion (39:5-8). Shortly after this, Hezekiah sealed an alliance with Egypt against Assyria, and reneged upon his payment of tribute to the king of Assyria (31:1-6). Isaiah had warned him that this would have very serious consequences. The Assyrians duly invaded and destroyed the land of Judah, and then laid siege to Jerusalem (36:1-3).

Next came an UP. Hezekiah spoke to Isaiah about the treachery and the extremely intimidating words of the king of Assyria, both via his envoy the Rabshakeh and in a letter to the King of Judah (36:4-37:13). And then Hezekiah prayed, and it was a fine prayer indeed (37:14-20). His prayer once again received an immediate answer from Yahweh, who first reassured him and then proceeded to fulfil his own promises and purposes (37:21-38). In the words of the chronicler "Hezekiah humbled himself for the pride of his heart, both he and the inhabitants of Jerusalem, so that the wrath of Yahweh did not come upon them in the days of Hezekiah" (2 Chron 32:26).

That brings us to where we are. After this Hezekiah went down and up.

There was a DOWN with regard to Manasseh, the son and heir of Hezekiah. In the years 701- 687 B.C. Manasseh grew up from childhood and eventually became co-regent with Hezekiah. It does not appear that Manasseh was taught by his father to love and fear Yahweh. After Hezekiah died, Manasseh became a monster of evil, reversing all his father's good reforms and immersing himself in idolatry and the worship of false gods. He even sacrificed one of his sons to a heathen god. His actions plunged Judah into the darkest years of its history. The rebellion against Yahweh that took place during his long reign was so serious that it was irreversible, and Yahweh declared that Judah would have to be destroyed (2 Ki 23:26-27). The means of Judah's destruction would be the Babylonians. Hezekiah seemingly did not do enough to influence his son Manasseh for good.

Finally there was an UP. We read that "God [gave] him very great possessions" and that "Hezekiah prospered in all his works". His further "good deeds" were written up by Isaiah (2 Chron 32:29, 30, 32).

From this it may be seen that Hezekiah was godly but flawed. He was like all of us a strange mixture of good and evil. But at heart he knew and loved Yahweh. He was someone in whom God began a good work, and persevered with him until its completion (Phil 1:6).

It is time for us to say good-bye to this good King of Judah. His adventures have captured many peoples' imaginations. We must also say good-bye to the greatest of the prophets, Isaiah the son of Amoz, though we shall return briefly to him in Appendix 2 at the end of this book (p. 361-362). Much remains of the book named after him, but it was probably written by his spiritual successors, the first of whom may also have been called Isaiah. We shall turn now to this man's writings, and refer to him as II Isaiah, a shorthand for "Second Isaiah".

PART 5 – A NEW BEGINNING

LXXI

40:1-11 A Herald of good Tidings

We emerge after a century and a half has passed by. The year is around 550 B.C. Jerusalem was taken some thirty-six years earlier and razed to the ground. Its people were deported to Babylon, its treasures were confiscated, and its Temple destroyed. The exiled Jews had done a lot of thinking, and were being helped by two remarkable prophets of the exile, the priest Ezekiel and II Isaiah. Very little is known about the latter, although we shall endeavour to deduce a few facts about him from the scanty clues that he has left for us. As we begin this part of the book of Isaiah, expectancy is in the air. The Babylonians are displaying signs of military weakness, and a man called Cyrus is growing in power as king of the Medes. Could he be the one who would finally overthrow Babylon and be the great liberator that God's people had been waiting for?

1. Someone gently urges that God's people should be comforted. The repetition of the opening word is a feature of II Isaiah's style. The speaker is God himself. His people are crushed, but he will give them a new start. The first thing they need is *comfort*; they are starved of reassurance.

2. The speaker continues, Speak *tenderly*. Speak to their *hearts*. Speak to Jerusalem: not to the city, which is in ruins, but to its people, exiled and servants in a foreign land. *Cry* to them. There is good news. They have served their term. Their penalty is paid. Yahweh has already repaid them *double* for their sins! Their exile is drawing to an end. They can now begin to look ahead to their return.

3. A voice cries out that Yahweh's highway is to be made ready in the desert. There are already spiritual and supernatural forces in motion which will bring about the return of the captives to their ancient abode.

4. The exiles must prepare themselves for the return to Jerusalem. The valleys of false humility had to be lifted up, and the mountains and hills of pride flattened. The uneven ground needed to become level, and the rough places a plain. Then the highway would be ready for the journey to freedom, for the return home.

5. There and then the glory of Yahweh would be seen. All the peoples of earth would line the highway and see it. This would be so, for Yahweh had spoken it.

6. A voice says, "Cry out!" and II Isaiah replies, "What shall I proclaim?" The answer is, he should declare that all the peoples are like grass. They are weak and perishable, with as little power as flowers in a field (Ps 103:15-16).

7. Grass withers and the flower fades when Yahweh breathes on them the hot winds of the Near East. The godless people of the world are like that, transient. Yes, the people are certainly like grass!

8. Grass withers, the flower fades, but the word of Yahweh our God, spoken through his prophets, will stand for ever. Why is this? Because Yahweh's word announces his unchangeable purposes for the world, which constitute the one permanent factor in human history. Verses 6-8 are a picture of II Isaiah's personal call to be a prophet. They highlight the eternal nature of God's word, reinforcing the first Isaiah's emphasis on faith (7:9, 26:3-4, 30:15, etc.) They are quoted in the New Testament, where the word of God is contrasted to the transience of people. The word of God is also the cure for this transience (1 Pet 1:23-25). Since it stands forever, so will the people of God who feed on it (Deut 8:3, Mt 4:4).

9. The people of Zion, that is Jerusalem, are told to climb a high mountain and to proclaim loudly the good tidings to the towns of Judah: "Here is your God!" The word for *glad tidings* is the Hebrew basis for the word *gospel* or *good news*.

10. The Lord Yahweh is coming together with his people, with great might and a strong arm, as in the first exodus from Egypt. He brings with him his reward and recompense. He would bestow the blessings of salvation on his people, and the sufferings of the exile would then vanish away like a bad dream.

11. Yahweh will care for his flock like a good shepherd. He will gather the lambs in his arms and carry them in his bosom. He will gently lead the sheep. He will be there with them, as they set out on the long journey back to Jerusalem.

Meditation: Something amazing was going to happen

The deportation of God's people to Babylon and their seemingly endless years in exile were a very dark period in the history of the Jews. In the first deportation in 597 B.C. the cream of God's people were taken to the Babylonian plains and settled in acceptable conditions in encampments that gradually became small towns. The exiles of the second deportation in 586 B.C. were not so fortunate, and many of them were forced to become builders of Nebuchadnezzar's cities and palaces. It was to the earlier deportees that II Isaiah prophesied. Nearly fifty years had gone by since they had been led away from their beloved Jerusalem. Nearly all the original exiles had died, and it was their children and grandchildren who now fed on the prophetic words of the past, which they kept carefully and treasured.

That divine word was their life. It meant so much to them. It contained the ancient memories of Yahweh and the amazing deeds he had done, liberating them from captivity in Egypt. It told them of the way he had spoken to them through the prophets, who had urged them to trust in him alone. In some of those prophetic words there were hints that Yahweh was full of grace and forgiveness, but for them there was only a dark time of captivity in a flat foreign land. How they missed the hills around Jerusalem! How they missed the worship at the great Temple! But there was one thing above all others that some of those captives were thirsty for, and this was Yahweh's word. They waited for it more than those who watch for the morning (Ps 130:6). They hungered for it. What they wanted – and how they wanted it – was for Yahweh to speak to them.

One day, around about the year 550 B.C., the word of Yahweh broke the long silence. They recognised it at once. The speaker was *their God*, and they were *his people*. This new word from God began by assuring them of this. Comfort *my people*, says *your God*. The word then went on in an unexpected way. They expected to hear about their term of punishment, about their guilt and about their sins. What they heard must have brought tears of disbelief to their eyes. Their term was *served*, their guilt was *paid*, and they had received from Yahweh *double for all their sins*. They were forgiven. But that was not all. There was something they had to do now. They needed to prepare for the long journey home. They had to make *themselves* ready for it. They had to *want* to go home.

It was all unbelievable. It was good news to be proclaimed from the housetops. It was all about Yahweh, about his undeserved kindness to people who knew that they did not deserve it. It was something to be spoken about. "Then the glory of Yahweh shall be revealed, and all people shall see it together" (v 5). Everything that was human might perish. Practically no one was still alive who remembered Zion. The day of the Israelite kings was past. Even their greatest prophet Isaiah was no more. But they had *the word spoken by Yahweh*. Gone were the Temple and the Ark. Their leaders might fall; all the signs of authority might be taken away. But Yahweh had *spoken to them*. His word remade them. It energised them. With Yahweh speaking to them, they had a hope to live for.

John Skinner wrote that "The first proclamation of glad tidings to Zion (see 41:27) is a passage of singular beauty, breathing the spirit of new-born hope and enthusiasm with which the prophet enters on his work. The announcement of a miraculous restoration of the exiles to their own land is the central theme of his prophecy, and the point round which all the ideas of [chapters 40-55] crystallise. As yet the historical fact is but dimly outlined, the writer's mind being occupied with its ideal significance as a revelation of the glory and the gracious character of Yahweh (v 5, 10-11). His state of mind borders on ecstasy; his ears are filled with the music of heavenly voices telling him that the night is far spent and the day is at hand; and although his home is with the exiles in Babylon, his gaze is fixed throughout on Jerusalem and the great divine event which is the consummation of Israel's redemption".

This passage speaks of wonderful good news. In some ways it is the forerunner of the New Testament gospel, just as the last of the Old Testament prophets, John the Baptist, was the forerunner of the Messiah. Indeed, all four gospel writers quote verse 3 as finding its fulfilment when John the Baptist first appeared in the wilderness of Judea (Mt 3:3, Mk 1:3, Lk 3:4, Jn 1:23). The exiles in Babylon lived in a foreign wilderness, and John the Baptist used the wilderness of Judea for the work of heralding the arrival of the Messiah (Mt 3:1). The coming of the Messiah would take an unexpected form (Mt 3:13-15), as would the exodus he would accomplish (Lk 9:31), but for the Jews exiled in Babylonia what came suddenly and unexpectedly was the good news of their coming exodus and their return to Zion.

LXXII

40:12-20 Yahweh of Israel, incomparable God

After a wonderful beginning (v1-11), this chapter gets even better. Verses 12-31 contain one of the greatest poems ever written about God, in which II Isaiah smiles at the smallness of our theological ideas and of our faith, just as God did in his challenge to Job (Job 38-41). In this hymn of praise II Isaiah portrays God as our creator (v12-20), as our supreme disposer (v21-26) and – provided we wait humbly for him – as the One who will empower us (v27-31). In verses 12-20 inanimate matter (v12), human minds (v13-14) and the earth's resources (v15-17) are all put into their proper perspective by being compared to the One who created them all. This should not be misunderstood. It does not render them meaningless. Instead it shows that their meaning derives from their Creator.

12. II Isaiah draws out the greatness of Yahweh as the creator by asking a series of unanswerable rhetorical questions. These will both humble the pride of his hearers, and raise their thoughts, as they contemplate the true nature of God. What sort of being must he be who measured the oceans in the hollow of his hand? How could he mark off the heavens with his span? (This is the distance from the tip of his thumb to the tip of his little finger when the hand is open). How could the dust of the earth fit into the pint pot in his kitchen? And what must his instruments be like if he could weigh the mountains in his scales and the hills in a balance?

13. In this verse and the next the prophet moves on to consider the perfection and self-sufficiency of Yahweh's knowledge and wisdom. Who else adjusted God's intelligence to make it right? Who was ever his official counsellor and instructed him? This verse was quoted in the New Testament by Paul in Rom 11:34.

14. Who else did Yahweh consult so as to be given insight? Who taught him how to deal with perfect justice? Who else imparted knowledge to him, and provided him with a discerning mind? The questions in these two verses do have an answer: nobody did! Nevertheless, the thinking needed to answer them was put to good use. Once again the conclusion is that Yahweh is incomparable.

15. In verses 15-17 II Isaiah focuses on the insignificance of all that exists when it is compared to Yahweh. The nations are only a drop in his bucket, whose loss would hardly be noticed. They are like dust particles that do not turn his scales. He can pick up the islands as if they were tiny particles of fine dust.

16. Morally, there is not one person in the world who is in the right before God. If a burnt sacrifice was required to atone for our sins and propitiate Yahweh, all the giant cedars of Lebanon would not provide enough fuel for it, nor would all the livestock in Lebanon suffice as a sacrifice.

17. Likewise, the heathen nations are as nothing in his sight. He could add them all up and the result would be less than nothing, just emptiness.

18. The thought of Yahweh's immeasurable greatness and majesty as compared with man's suggests the puny and unreal nature of idol-gods and the consequent folly of idolatry. Yahweh is the incomparable creator; the genesis of idols is that they are the creations of human workmen. God's view of his creation will show up the absurdity and perversity of man's created gods. II Isaiah's view is echoed, albeit with less eloquence, in the New Testament (Acts 17:29).

19. To demonstrate the absurdity of worshipping idols, II Isaiah takes us on the first of several guided tours of a Babylonian idol factory (see also 41:6-7, 44:9-20 and 46:1-7). Some idols are made of cast brass which is then gilded and provided with chains. This is to keep them from toppling, for they are unable to keep upright on their own, and when they fall they cannot stand up again.

20. Other idols are made not of metal but of wood. Mulberry and other hardwoods are good because if they become moist they will not rot. Once you have the wood, you need to find a skilled carver who can devise an image that will not topple. Nor, of course, will it do anything else! The result is described ironically as a gift.

Meditation: The intractable Problem and its Solution

When II Isaiah saw his fellow exiles, he saw men and women who were longing for God. They were captives in a foreign land, unable to deal with their plight. They had been forgotten by God, and said "My way is hidden from Yahweh, and my right is disregarded by my God" (v 27). And the prophet had to reply, "Your God is too small!" He proceeded to teach them that the Holy One of Israel was majestic, great beyond their wildest imaginings.

His teaching begins with God, because everything else follows from God. All the oracles that would follow, all that interpreted the history of their day or pointed forward to the day of the Messiah, the facts and the promises, the appearance of Cyrus, the fall of Babylon and the redemption of God's people, their mission to the ends of the earth, the conversion of the heathen, the accomplishments of the servant of Yahweh – all this and more stemmed from God. Once their vision of God was corrected and expanded, the people of Israel would have a fresh vision, both of Yahweh and of their destiny, and armed with new hope they would be able to learn further lessons and prepare to be restored to their own land.

God himself was at the heart of everything that II Isaiah wanted to say. His style stemmed from his brilliant monotheism. It was thoughts of God that everywhere fired his imagination. His greatest passages occurred when he soared to some lofty vision of Yahweh's glory in creation or history. From those heights were born his critical and corrective complaints. He often poured his sarcasm and scorn on those who worshipped idols and those who had a small view of the creator. George Adam Smith wrote that, "The breadth and the force of his imagination, the sweep of his rhetoric, and the intensity of his scorn may all be traced to his sense of God's sovereignty, and are the signs to us of how absolutely he was possessed by this as his main and governing truth".

Like many other Old Testament prophets, II Isaiah considered that the prophetic word had more power to transform people's lives than the work of the priests, more even than the Temple rituals and the whole sacrificial system. In any case, with the Temple lying in ruins, there had to be some other approach to the one true God than through animal sacrifices. Perhaps this is why II Isaiah made no mention of his fellow prophet of the exile, Ezekiel, who had been brought up as a priest and whose prophetic oracles were quite different.

II Isaiah voiced his reservations about the sacrificial system in verse 16. Even the most gigantic sacrifice imaginable would be unable to take away the sin of fallen humanity. There was not enough wood nor were there sufficient animals for any sinner to sacrifice and thereby atone for the seriousness of their selfishness and their sin. The prophet Hosea had proclaimed the word of Yahweh to the northern kingdom of Israel: "I desire steadfast *love* and not sacrifice, the *knowledge of God* rather than burnt offerings" (Hos 6:6). The first Isaiah had voiced similar reservations about the worship in the Jerusalem Temple (1:10-17).

This must have set II Isaiah's mind thinking. There *had to be* an answer to the human predicament. There *must* be a just and righteous atonement for human sin. There *must* be something in history or in the universe that would make it not only possible but also right for Yahweh to forgive the sin of humanity. But the problem was so serious that it seemed intractable. Someone put it very well: "The heart of the human problem is the problem of the human heart".

As II Isaiah wrestled with this most demanding of all problems, he thought about God and his purposes for the world. Starting again with God and with the prophetic word that had been given in previous centuries, he slowly inched his way to the correct solution, which was a fusion of two distinct thoughts. One was that sin deserved and must receive its due judgement and punishment. The other was remarkably original: the Messiah, whom he called the servant of Yahweh, would suffer as he served. We must wait a while longer before II Isaiah shares his most important and abiding insight with us.

LXXIII

40:21-31 The Disposer who can also Empower us

The titanic similes and comparisons of this great poem continue, first telling of God as the supreme disposer (v 21-26) and then describing how we may get to know him as the one who empowers us (v 27-31).

21. Once again a series of questions begins a new section of text. Their message is equivalent to the exclamation, "Surely you know this!" The truths about God's greatness are basic. Everyone has come across them. They are intuitive and have been known "ever since the creation of the world" (Rom 1:20). Even children know them. They can be deduced from nature (v 12-20) and history (v 21-26).

22. Men propose, but someone else disposes. Who is it? It is the One who sits above the horizon (Ps 113:5-9), from where the inhabitants of the earth seem like tiny grasshoppers (Num 13:33). In the beginning he created the heavens as easily as we would close a thin gauze-like curtain, and then he spread those heavens out as easily as we would put up a tent.

23. It is Yahweh who brings down princes and reduces mighty rulers to nothing. There is a contrast between his permanence and the transience of the potentates.

24. No sooner are the princes and rulers established in their rule that he blows upon them and they die. They are like plants that have been sown and taken root, but the hot wind withers them, like the grass and the flowers of verses 6-8, and the tempest carries them off like stubble. This being so, why live in fear of the tyrants? "Fear him, you saints, and you will then have nothing else to fear".

25. Two further unanswerable questions are asked of us by the Holy One of Israel. As we reflect on them, we come to the conclusion that he is the incomparable One, the God of heaven and the one true God.

26. We are urged to lift up our eyes and look at the stars. There is a great lesson to be learnt by looking up at them. Who created all the stars? It is someone who numbers them and calls them out by name, one by one. He made them all and not one is missing. The vastness of his creation does not speak of God's absence but of his precise control over every particle of the universe. How then can he, the God of Israel, be accused of forgetting his people?

27. And yet the people feel Yahweh has abandoned them. The aim of this hymn about God's greatness will now be made clear. The prophet is aware of the pessimism and unbelief of his fellow exiles. They complain that their way is hidden from Yahweh, and their right has escaped his notice. II Isaiah longs to counteract their faithless thoughts. Instead he wants to inspire them with a vision of the incomparable greatness of God. It is not, of course, a question of Yahweh being too great to care for them. Rather, because the God of Israel is so great, he cares very much for his people and will intervene to save them.

28. Two more questions emphasise that what follows is basic and should have been well learnt by the people of God. Yahweh is eternal, the creator of all that exists, infinite in his power and inscrutable in his wisdom. God is too great to fail his enfeebled people; at no point will any circumstances get on top of *him*.

29. God not only exercises his majestic power; he also *imparts* it. He is an inexhaustible source of strength to those who have none in themselves, if only they follow the appointed way to appropriate it.

30. Natural strength is soon exhausted. Even those who are young and strong run out of energy. This reminder of our human frailty clears the way for our trust in God and his ability to transcend natural resources.

31. Here is the goal towards which we have been building since verse 12. Human imaginings (v 18) and doubts (v 27) can now give way to the humble expectancy that is urged upon God's people throughout the book of Isaiah. If we wish to be empowered by God, then we must *wait* for him. The way he empowers us is by *renewing our strength*. The Hebrew words mean *change our strength*, as one might change into fresh clothes after having a shower. We shall then be able to soar upwards on wings of faith and hope. We shall be able to run the race marked out for us without getting weary. We shall be able to persevere, walking steadily day by day, fulfilling the tasks that God appoints for us without fainting away.

Meditation: Waiting – so easy and yet so hard

The idea that people should *wait* for God is put forward eleven times in the book of Isaiah (8:17, 25:9, 26:8, 30:18, 33:2, 40:30-31, 42:4, 49:23, 51:5, 60:9, 64:4). In one sense, waiting is one of the easiest activities anyone can do. But because we all live busy lives, we find it strangely difficult. It is frustrating when we have to wait ten minutes in the queue at the Post Office. It is nerve-wracking when a bus or a train is delayed by 20 minutes. It is intolerable when we have to wait four hours to be treated at A & E. Our gut feeling about waiting is that it is a waste of time, and time is a precious commodity in our ultra-busy 21st century. In spite of this, we may transform our times of waiting into wonderful and creative occasions, provided that we are *waiting for God*. What are the reasons why, according to the book of Isaiah, we should spend time doing this?

First of all, it is good to *wait for God* during the difficult periods of our lives. We all live through times when, for reasons that are not clear to us, God seems to be far away. At those times we can imitate the first Isaiah, who said, "I will *wait for Yahweh*, who is hiding his face from the house of Jacob, and I will hope in him" (8:17). At other times it is far worse, and we may feel as if we are being punished for our sins or our lack of faith. Then we may *wait for God* and pray, "In the path of your judgements, Oh Yahweh, we *wait for you*; your name and your renown are the soul's desire" (26:8). There are also times when a particularly troublesome problem may seem insurmountable. Then our prayer could be, "Oh Yahweh, be gracious to us; we *wait for you*. Be our arm every morning, our salvation in the time of trouble" (33:2).

Secondly, it is a help and strength to *wait for God* in the ordinary times, when our routine is going well. When no major problems are besetting us, it is easy to become spiritually dry. At such times we often need a fresh touch of God's free and undeserved grace. "Yahweh *waits* to be gracious to you", and because of this "blessed are all those who *wait for him*" (30:18). God promises us that "Those who *wait for me* shall not be put to shame" (49:23). When this proves true in our lives, we shall join those who can say, "From ages past no one has heard, no ear has perceived, no eye has seen any God besides you, who works for those who *wait for him*" (64:4).

Thirdly, some people who do not know God are *waiting for him*. We shall learn more from Isaiah 2 about our mission to these people. He often referred to the heathen nations as "the coastlands". Although they did not know Yahweh, some of them were nevertheless *waiting for him*. God says that "The coastlands *wait for me*, and for my arm they hope" (51:5). In II Isaiah's writing, the arm of Yahweh often means the Messiah. Those who do not know God need to hear about his Messiah, for "There is salvation in no one else, for there is no other name under heaven given among mortals by which we must be saved" (Acts 4:12).

There are two reasons why some who do not know God are *waiting for him*. The first is that they know that perfect justice is only to be found in the Messiah. We read of him that "He will not grow faint or be crushed until he has established justice in the earth; and the coastlands *wait for his teaching*" (42:4). The second reason is because they wish to join the people whom God has chosen and blessed. "For the coastlands shall *wait for* [*Yahweh*] . . . because he has glorified you" (60:9). It is quite a thought that among those who do not yet know God, there are some who are *waiting patiently for him*. This is all the more reason for those of us who do know him to do likewise.

Fourthly, there will be times in our lives when we lose hope and feel that God has simply forgotten about us. This is what the Jewish exiles felt like in Babylon. Their lives were bearable but they were without hope. It was for believers who had lost hope that II Isaiah wrote chapter 40 of the book we are studying. The chapter builds up to a magnificent climax, where the great secret of how to regain divine strength is revealed. "Even youths will faint and be weary, and the young will fall exhausted; but those who *wait for Yahweh* shall renew their strength, they shall mount up with wings like eagles, they shall run and not be weary, they shall walk and not faint" (40:30-31).

Blessed indeed are those who *wait for God*. There will come a time in the future when they will be able to say, "Lo, this is our God; *we have waited for him*, so that he might save us. This is Yahweh for *whom we have waited*; let us be glad and rejoice in his salvation" (25:9).

LXXIV

41:1-7 God challenges the Nations

1. We find ourselves in a vast judicial debating chamber. With his call for silence Yahweh himself opens the proceedings. He will challenge the heathen nations (the *coastlands*) to answer the question as to who it is that is shaping history, but first he suggests that they should renew their strength, for the war of words would be tough. At the right time they might approach the bar and put forward their case (v 21-29). Then, together, they would reach a judgement.

2. The court case concerns a victor from the east. His formal identification will be made in 44:28, but he is Cyrus. Already king of the Persian city of Anshan, in 549 B. C. he became king of the Medes after a victorious three year campaign. He was a rising star and his ambitions clearly included becoming the emperor of all Persia and, following that, conquering the Babylonians. Who was it who had raised him up and was using him in his service? To whom was Cyrus delivering the nations? The fact that he was pulverising them with his sword and bow implied that he was the person chosen by God for the task of liberating his people.

3. Cyrus was divinely protected as he pursued his enemies, and so swift were his movements that his feet scarcely seemed to touch the ground.

4. Who had brought this to be? Who had worked towards this end throughout the generations? It could only be one being. Yahweh himself answers in front of all who are gathered: "I, Yahweh, am first, and will be with the last" (Ex 3:13-15). He already was before the first people appeared, and he would be there with the last of them. He was working out his actions in the light of his eternal purposes. He is not only the God of creation, but also the God of history. The attribute of eternity claimed by God would later be claimed for himself by the Messiah. After he had finished the work that God had given him to do, he returned to God and called himself "the first and the last" (Rev 1:8, 17; 2:8; 21:6, 22:13).

5. The nations were fully aware of Cyrus. They found his progress terrifying. In their consternation they attempted to get the better of Yahweh by manufacturing new and better idols in order to arrest the new conqueror's progress.

6. They worked together and helped each other. They encouraged one another by saying, "Do not be afraid of Cyrus or of Yahweh. Be courageous!"

7. The various artists and workmen also tried to lift up each other's spirits. The artisan encouraged the goldsmith, and the workman with the hammer encouraged the one with the anvil. They applauded each other's contribution, saying, "It is good". Then they fastened the idol in an upright position with nails. It would have been altogether unacceptable if their new and improved idol had toppled before Yahweh, like the Philistine god Dagon had done (1 Sam 5:1-5).

Meditation: Specific Prophecies versus vague Auguries

Chapter 41 is presented to us as a legal dispute. It concerned the question as to who was the true God. Everyone was agreed that the true God was the one who was in complete control of history. Whoever determined the course of history would be able to predict the future course of events. The participants in this trial would be asked to weigh the specific prophecies of Yahweh – some of which had already been fulfilled and some that were about to be fulfilled – against the vague and futile auguries of the idols and the oracles of that time.

In 585 B.C. a triple alliance had been formed between the three most powerful nations in south-west Asia: Babylonia, Lydia and Media. It lasted until each of the three in turn fell to the new name, Kurush of Anshan, known to us as Cyrus the great of Persia. He was not only a victorious conqueror but also dealt kindly with those he conquered. He repatriated many peoples to their original land, and encouraged them in the worship of their own god. He was a benevolent hero – "le plus sympathique de l'antiquité" according to the French historian Halévy.

He sprang from the Persian city of Anshan, to the east of Babylon – hence the direction indicated in verse 2, "Who has roused a victor from the east?" But after he became the king of Media in 549 B.C. his base was north of Babylon – hence the new direction in verse 25, "I stirred one up from the north, and he has come". It was in 549 B.C. or soon after that II Isaiah wrote chapter 41. Media was taken, which land would be next? Apprehensive because of the new conqueror, the nations turned to their idols and commissioned new ones (v 5-7).

Croesus, the immensely wealthy king of Lydia, had special reasons to fear that Cyrus would next set his sights on him. According to the Greek historian Herodotus, he resolved to find out in advance the results of a possible war with Cyrus. He wrote to seven oracles near and far that claimed to possess superior knowledge, asking a test question to which he knew the answer. Two of the oracles, at Delphi and at Amphiaraus, sent back the correct reply.

Croesus opted for the Delphic oracle, and offered a huge number of sacrifices to the gods at Delphi, namely 3,000 of each type of animal. He melted down hundreds of golden treasures, and made 117 solid golden bricks, each six palms long, three palms wide and one palm high. He sent them all to Delphi, together with a golden lion that weighed ten talents, two large mixing bowls that weighed eight talents each, one of gold and the other of silver, and numerous other treasures. By this gift, he hoped to get a favourable reply to the question that consumed him: who would win a conflict between Cyrus and himself?

Back came the oracle's reply. It was, unfortunately, ambiguous. "If you go against Cyrus, you shall destroy a great empire". The oracle did not commit itself as to which empire Croesus would destroy – that of Cyrus, or his own. So the king of Lydia wrote again requesting clarification, and asking if he would enjoy a long life. The reply this time was not only ambiguous, but also cryptic.

This insight into the preparations that Croesus was making for a possible war with Cyrus gives us a glimpse into the excited activity of the national leaders and their priests and idol manufacturers in those uncertain days. The irony of II Isaiah in verses 5-7 is severe, but the imbecility of the heathen idolatry deserved it.

Amidst all this ferment, there was one religion in the world whose oracles gave a clear message and whose God claimed Cyrus for his own. The appearance of this conqueror was proof that Yahweh presided over the destinies of nations. It was he and he alone who was sovereign over history. When, in II Isaiah's imaginary trial, the nations appeared before him, they tried hard to resist the inevitable conclusion. They devised a plan. They would collaborate in the production of a new super-idol. Might it perhaps be able to thwart Cyrus' progress?

LXXV

41:8-20 Reassurance for God's Servants

The scene in court is interrupted until verse 21 as Yahweh, with great warmth, turns to reassure his people. He offers them the strength to be able to persevere in spite of the opposition of their enemies. In particular, he promises them two invaluable assets, namely his presence (v10) and an inward refreshment that will transform their lives (v17-20). These are two of the most wonderful promises in the Bible, and it is no surprise that they are greatly prized by believers.

8. By calling his people by the names of two of their patriarchs, Yahweh assures them that they are his servants, his chosen ones and his friends.

9. Yahweh tells them that he will take them back from Mesopotamia, "the ends of the earth", for he has called them from "its furthest corners". He again declares that they are his servants and that he has chosen them. He has a special task for them, and therefore he has not cast them off. As the theologians put it, his election and call are irrevocable. Here in verses 8 and 9 is the first mention of Yahweh's "servants". At the moment the reference is plural, to all the people of Israel, but in some passages in the following chapters II Isaiah will speak of *the* servant of Yahweh, meaning one person in particular.

10. The first promise is fivefold. God's people were not to fear anyone else, for *he was with them*. They were not to look around in dismay, for *he was their God*. He would *strengthen them* when they were weak. He would *help them* when they were in need. He would *uphold them and give them victory* when they were facing opposition in the mission he had given them to do.

11. Yahweh would also scatter their enemies. Anyone who was angry with them would be ashamed and disgraced. Morally speaking, anyone who fought against them would perish and disappear from sight.

12. They would look for those who had opposed them, but they would not be able to find them. Yahweh would make such an impression on those who were warring against them that their hostility would come to nothing.

13. How could this be? It was because Yahweh their God was holding their right hand. He could tell them not to fear, for he would be alongside them to help.

14. God's people might feel like worms, just as Jacob did when, full of fear, he was reunited with his brother Esau. But they were not to fear their opponents. Yahweh promised them his help in overcoming all the difficulties that would come their way. He would be their Redeemer, for he was the Holy One of Israel. Here the word for redeemer is *Go'el*, the kinsman-redeemer (Ruth 3:12-13, 4:1-12) who was charged with buying back the property of a next-of-kin, of avenging his death, and in general, of assuming all of the next-of-kin's needs as his own. In chapters 40-66 of Isaiah the word is used twelve times, always referring to Yahweh, and its associated adjective is used a further six times, likewise always about Yahweh. It implies that Yahweh would reclaim and rescue his own people who were alienated or lost. It was a word that was rich in meaning for the exiles, and knowing that God was their *Go'el* would have brought new hope to them.

15. A threshing sledge was a solid object, made of heavy boards and armed with teeth, for it was studded with flints. It would be dragged over reaped corn to break open the ears. These were then winnowed by being tossed up in the air with a pitchfork, so as to allow the breeze to blow away the husks. The people of God were about to face many difficulties, some of which would seem as formidable as mountains and hills. But the solidity and grinding power of a threshing sledge would be theirs. They would crush the mountains and reduce the hills to chaff.

16. The metaphor continues, for God loves it when his people leave a good imprint on the world. They would winnow their difficulties and the wind would carry them away, or maybe even scatter them if it was a gale. Then they would rejoice in Yahweh and glory in the Holy One of Israel.

17. Verses 17-20 should not be taken literally. They are a promise of inward refreshment and empowering that *would be seen by other people*. With touching pathos II Isaiah describes the miserable condition of God's people at that time. As captives and aliens in a foreign land, they had little to look forward to. They were like destitute people whose throats were parched with thirst, but they had no way of getting water. At that period of time, in their extremity of need, Yahweh would answer them. The God of Israel would not fail them.

18. Did they need fresh water? Yahweh would open rivers on bare hills, and make springs appear in the dry valleys. The wilderness would become a pool of water, and everywhere around them the dry land would be well watered.

19. The desert that signified their barren sun-baked lives would be transformed into a grove of beautiful shady trees. Yahweh would place there cedars, acacias,

myrtles, olives, cypresses, planes and pines. They would grow together, and transform the sandy waste into a canvas full of variegated greenery and coolness.

20. The scale of the restoration would be extensive and full of splendour. Yahweh would not forsake his own people, but instead he would carry out the promises he had made to them. In this way he would vindicate publicly the ancient word he had given through his prophets. The whole world would be made aware of this, and by reflecting upon it they would realise that it was Yahweh's creative power that had brought about the extraordinary transformation.

Meditation: Two wonderful Promises

God's people were losing hope. Their lives in exile had been bearable but purposeless. They were languishing in captivity and in despair they yearned for God's love and acceptance. God heard their voice and spoke to them. His words were exactly what these exiles needed to hear. It would be impossible to think up any message that would have been more suited to their needs and aspirations.

In this passage God comforted his people with three word-pictures that tell how he would make a difference in their lives, and also gave them some promises which are wonderful beyond description. The three word-pictures are as follows: they were his servants, whose enemies he would overcome; they were like a worm that he would transform into a threshing-sledge; and they were desert travellers whose desperate need for water and shade would be amply provided.

There were numerous assurances of divine help and power. These would prove to be reliable, because they all came from Yahweh (v 13, 14, 16, 17, 20) who was also the Holy One of Israel (v 14, 16, 20), their Redeemer (v 14) and their covenant God (v 8-10, 13, 17). He is able to provide those who believe in him with an inexhaustible supply of whatever they might need. He is a fountain of grace, which for the Babylonian exiles meant undeserved favour, opportunity and power. We who are followers of the Messiah today are God's people just as the Old Testament Israelites were. God can likewise be a fountain of grace for us.

There is one prohibition, for them as for us. God's people are not to give way to the fear of man, for fear will harm their faith and threaten their whole relationship with God. It used to be said by some preachers that the command not to be afraid comes 365 times in the Bible, and therefore we should obey it every day of the year. Leaving aside the fact that the number of references is much lower than 365, such exegesis is evidently incorrect since it leaves us in the dark concerning February 29th on leap years. As this is a command from God we shall wish to heed it every single day, including February 29th. The command comes three times in our passage (v 10, 13, and 14) and appears frequently elsewhere in the book of Isaiah (e.g. 7:4, 8:12, 35:4, 40:9, 43:1, 43:5, 44:2, 44:8, 51:7 and 54:4).

The two promises in verse 10 and verses 17-20 are marvellously encouraging and worth committing to memory. They point forward to the Messiah's double promise to his followers of his presence and his peace (Jn 14:18-21, 27). They are also similar in their purpose to the Messiah's description of the Holy Spirit's ministry to his followers (Jn 14:26). The Holy Spirit would be another Comforter, just as Yahweh's two promises in verses 10 and 17-20 of this passage are comforting. They provide us with comfort in both senses of the word, for they not only reassure us of God's presence and help, but they also com-*fort* us or *fort*-ify us, for God will provide us with inner *strength* to keep us persevering in doing what is good.

The reason we need not be afraid is because of Yahweh's promise that he is with us (v 10). He is our God, so there is no cause for us to be dismayed. He also gives us his assurance that he will strengthen us in our weakness, help us in our difficulties and uphold us with his right hand of victory.

Yahweh hears and answers the cries of the needy (v 17a). He renews their lives so that what was previously a meaningless desert existence without his presence now becomes, with him, a purposeful life of service with refreshing oases to be seen all around (v 17b-18). The original fulfilment of this prophecy concerned the return journey of the exiles in 539 B.C. and their reestablishment in Jerusalem in the years that followed. Like many of the prophecies in Isaiah, this one is also applicable to our own journey as pilgrims in an alien world. When we walk in a dry desert and are desperately thirsty for God, he will draw near to refresh us with living water (12:3; Jn 4:10, 13-14; Jn 7:37-39). He will provide us with shady trees to cool us down in the heat of the day (v 19). And the world will see and notice, it will consider and understand, and it will realise that it is *the hand of God* that has done this and made such a difference.

LXXVI

41:21-29 The Futility of Idols

Yahweh renews his challenge to the nations, and this time he asks them to bring their idols to the courtroom, so that they too may speak, and the content of their pronouncements may be compared to that of Yahweh's prophecies.

21. Yahweh, the King of the children of Jacob, asks the coastlands to bring their idols so they may expound their case and produce their evidences and proofs.

22. Before considering the future the idols may also refer to recent events of history and explain them, and suggest how they will impact the future. Then they may declare "the things to come", prophesying what will happen in the future.

23. Yahweh now addresses the idols. If they are able to predict future events, they will indeed be gods. If they can tell what the future will be, whether it be good or bad, they will be worthy of awe. Foreknowledge is the test of divinity.

24. Unfortunately for the heathen defendants, their idols and gods are nothing. They are utterly incompetent. They have nothing whatsoever to say. Now comes

a serious charge by Yahweh. Anyone who chooses to worship dumb nonentities instead of the living God who speaks and acts is an *abomination*.

25. It is Yahweh's turn to state his case. He has called a new name to come from the north, who has responded to Yahweh's bidding. Everyone is talking about Cyrus. He will come from the Media in the *north*, but he hails from Anshan in the *east* (v2), "from the rising of the sun". He was summoned by name, for Yahweh raised him up to do a particular job. He would displace powerful rulers as if he was treading them on mortar, or as potters tread clay.

26. Who out of all the idols prophesied the coming of Cyrus? Which of them got it right from the beginning, so that everyone might know in advance? Which of them predicted it in advance, so that everyone might say that "he was right"? The answer is that none of the idols did so. None of them proclaimed the coming of Cyrus; none of the idols was heard to say anything.

27. Yahweh, on the other hand, did declare it to the exiles from Zion. He gave them "a herald of good tidings", Cyrus of Persia, who would sign the decree authorising the exiles to return to Jerusalem.

28. Yahweh looks around at all the idols once again. None of them gives good counsel. None of them can supply a proper answer to a question. When it was paid a vast quantity of gold, even the Delphic oracle failed to deliver, giving a word that was ambiguous. The mighty Croesus, ruler of Lydia, was told that if he was to attack Cyrus, he would destroy a mighty kingdom. In the end he chose to do this, and thereby destroyed his own kingdom.

29. Yahweh has the last word, but the conclusion is inevitable. All idols are a delusion. They can do absolutely nothing. Their images are empty wind.

Meditation: The God who controls Events

It was, of course, an imaginary challenge. Yahweh did not actually confront the coastlands and their idols in a large courtroom. Nevertheless it is an imaginative and instructive courtroom scene. We cannot help picturing it in our minds. Thousands of idols are carried into the arena by the priests that control them. They are dazzling in gold and silver, flashing with gems of the first water, and clad in gorgeous robes. Having positioned them in orderly rows, their acolytes swing high their censers, the priests mumble their repeated supplications, and silence is proclaimed so that the idols may speak out what is in their minds.

It was a great challenge. Come and be tested by the facts! History is in the making, so give us your own interpretation of it. Prove your divinity by divining the future. We don't want vague or ambiguous phrases. We are not interested in your ability to produce ingenious or enigmatic epigrams. Tell us something that is clear-cut, be it good news or bad, and tell it clearly so that anyone will understand exactly what you are getting at. Yahweh is insistent on the need for clarity: set forth your case, bring proofs, so that we may consider, so that we may know, so that we may know again (v 21-23). But not a single idol or worldly oracle could rise to the challenge (v 24, 28-29). They did not speak forth their minds, because they did not have a mind, nor were they capable of speech. They were nothing.

Therefore Yahweh answers his own challenge. He explains recent history, and claims that he himself was behind what was happening (v 25). He has no problem in interpreting present events, because it was he who set them in motion. For him it is a trivial matter to provide a clear and definite forecast of their issue, for he knows exactly what their purpose is. The heathen religions were totally baffled by the arrival of Cyrus on the world scene, and they had nothing whatsoever to say about the future results of the great events stirred up by Yahweh through the Persian. On the other hand, Yahweh had told his people (40:1-11) the meaning of these events. They would lead to the restoration of the Jews to their own land in 539 B.C. He had given "to Jerusalem a herald of good tidings" (v 27).

We should note that Yahweh is not God simply because he can predict. Here he demands predictions from the heathen idols, because forecasting the future is part of what God can do. If you are God, this means that you have planned the future and therefore already know it, but God is infinitely more than that. God is, as a matter of fact, omniscient, but he is even more than that. God is very great, and his majesty leaves all people speechless. We have read about his sovereignty as the creator and supreme disposer of all people, and as the one who strengthens those who wait for him (40:12-31). God is glorious in his power, in his control and in his faithfulness. He created the heavens and the earth, he is the supreme director of history, and he is unfailing as he saves and renews his people. It is a lack of faith that prompts some to say that he has forgotten his people. The fact is that nobody who puts their trust in him will be disappointed.

Why did Isaiah enlarge upon the utter uselessness of idols? From early times the people of God had a weakness for idol worship. When they took possession of the Promised Land, they adopted some of the idolatrous practices of the people they displaced. Idolatry became widespread and ingrained in their outlook. From the first, Yahweh had forbidden idol worship; his people were to worship him alone (Ex 20:1-3). He warned the Israelites what the consequences of their idol worship would be. They persisted, and this duly resulted in their exile to Babylon. Once settled there they would have encountered the mindless idolatry of the Babylonians. II Isaiah was determined to stamp out any trace of idolatry in God's people prior to their return home. It would appear that he succeeded, to judge by the silence on the subject of idolatry among most of the post-exilic writers. His success stemmed from the way in which he described the one true God in his prophecies. In them Judeo-Christian monotheism reached its most absolute and enduring expression. Never before or since had the sovereign power and the kind character of God been portrayed together to such good effect.

As we shall see later, there are various reasons why idolatry is abominable (v 24) to the one living God. The choice of whom to worship is really the ultimately important choice in the lives of all people. If they get it right, they will know and love God, and his wonderful promises will be fulfilled in their lives. If they get it wrong and worship a lie, they will sink into the darkness of unreality, and in the end they will deceive themselves.

LXXVII

42:1-9 The first Servant Song

Enter the servant of Yahweh. This time the reference is not to the superhero Cyrus, who had been enlisted, probably unaware of the fact, in Yahweh's service (41:2). Nor is it a reference to Israel, the chosen but faithless nation, described as Yahweh's servant (41:8). This is about *the* servant of Yahweh.

II Isaiah wrote four remarkable passages about the servant of Yahweh: 42:1-9, 49:1-7, 50:4-9 and 52:13-53:12. (There is a fifth, 61:1-4, which is also very much in II Isaiah's style, but it does not appear in the chapters attributed to him. There is even a sixth that is quite different from the others, as we shall see). The four passages are often referred to as "the four servant songs of Isaiah". They were not written as songs, but are very beautiful and evocative poems that prophesy the coming of a humble and godly person, the Messiah.

We now turn to the first servant song. Compared to the overpowering depiction of Yahweh in chapters 40 and 41, this passage is as gentle as the person it describes. Verses 1-4 were quoted by the gospel writer Matthew (Mt 12:17-21).

1. Being his *servant* and his *chosen*, the servant of Yahweh is associated with the people of Israel (41:8), who were likewise God's servants and chosen by him to be lights for the heathen world. But the servant would succeed where Israel failed, and thereby fill Yahweh's soul with delight. We are given some reasons for his success. The first is because Yahweh had put his Spirit on him. The endowment of the Spirit was a feature of the Davidic King-Messiah, as we saw in 11:1-5. This is no coincidence, for the servant *is* the Messiah. Because he has the Spirit of God, he begins to stand out. His divine perfection would place him on an entirely different plane to the rest of God's people. He would have a universal ministry, bringing *justice* to all the nations. The Hebrew word translated *justice* is *mishpat*, which here means both the revealed principles of true religion and the putting right of all that is wrong.

2. The servant of Yahweh stands out by being unobtrusive and unassertive. He likes to work in a low-key way and prefers to avoid the limelight. His quiet influence has been compared to God's "still, small voice" (1 Ki 19:12, Authorised Version), that spoke so tenderly to the exhausted Elijah.

3. The servant of Yahweh is a beautifully humble person who is gentle and tender with the weak and inadequate, with whom he is glad to associate. The two

metaphors are phrased negatively. The servant would not break the bruised reed, nor would he quench the dimly burning wick. Instead, he would heal the reed by splinting it at the bruise, and he would fan the wick back into flame with his breath or spirit. Instead of crushing the dying elements of goodness in people, he would strengthen and restore them. This is how he would bring forth *justice* or true religion, and he would stick to his task faithfully until he achieved his wish. He wanted to see that the reed was strong, and the wick was burning brightly.

4. The words for *grow faint* and *be crushed* are closely related to the words for *dimly burning* and *bruised* in the previous verse. We could translate the first half of the verse as *He will neither burn dimly nor be bruised.* The servant of Yahweh would possess adequate inner resources and be resilient. He would not burn low or take insults to heart until he had accomplished his task of establishing *justice* or true religion throughout the world (as in v 1, 3). His light would never be extinguished, and he would never allow himself to be crushed. This perseverance is another reason for his success. The heathen nations, dissatisfied with and unfulfilled by their religious systems, were waiting for the servant's *teaching*, which would purify their beliefs and bring them new life.

5. From speaking *about* his servant in verses 1-4, Yahweh now speaks *to* him in verses 5-7. He speaks as the creator (41:12-17). He it is who made heaven and earth, and stretched them out like a large map. He it is who gave breath and spirit to men and women. Breath and spirit both have the same meaning, they are the divine principle of life breathed into people at their creation (Gen 2:7).

6. Yahweh declares that he has called his servant *in righteousness*, i.e. with a proper and decided purpose. He has sustained and appointed him for this purpose. The purpose is twofold: he has given his servant both as a covenant to his people and as a light to the nations. Both phrases are pregnant with meaning. The servant will be *a covenant to the people* not only because he was their promised Messiah, but also in the sense that he would be the means by which the people would enter into a *new covenant* with Yahweh. He would also be *a light to the nations.* This term would be quoted by the saintly Simeon when he saw the Messiah as an infant (Lk 2:32), and later used as a formative motto for the church (Acts 13:47). God's people are chosen not in order to make them feel special, but because they are to show the way of God to those who do not know it (Jn 14:6).

7. In other contexts blindness and imprisonment could be a reference to the Babylonian captivity, but in this passage something universal is being revealed. Alienated from God because of their sin, people are spiritually blind and locked up in the dungeon of their selfishness. By means of the new covenant people would receive the vision of God and be liberated from their bondage to sin.

8. After addressing his servant, Yahweh now speaks about himself. On account of his name, because of who he is, what he has announced would most certainly

be fulfilled, for his word always proves true. He does not share his knowledge of the future with pretenders, nor does he allow idols to tell out the praiseworthy mission of his servant. His wish is that his glory would manifest itself as and when his light is spread throughout the world.

9. "Former things", such as the appearance of Cyrus, had already come to pass (41:26). This revelation about the servant is a new thing that is being declared. Here is the outline of something quite new. It concerns the servant of Yahweh, who would be a humble and gentle liberator.

Meditation: New Things I now declare

In chapters 40-55 II Isaiah wrote about three servants. The first was Cyrus, the world conqueror, whose first mention as a servant of Yahweh comes in 41:2, but he disappears from view after 48:15, by which time he was fulfilling the mission God gave him. The second was Israel, the chosen but disobedient nation, whose first mention as being Yahweh's servant comes in 41:8. The third is *the* servant par excellence, the Messiah, who makes his entry here at the beginning of chapter 42, but will reappear in subsequent chapters. There is much about him in our passage. What truths have we learnt about him?

First of all, the servant was both chosen and greatly delighted in (v 1). In his case, *electio* would finally coincide with *dilectio*. We can almost sense the pure and radiant divine joy, the joy of the Father whose Son brought him nothing but sheer delight. Every other servant of Yahweh had failed him in minor or major ways, but here was *his* servant, the one who would bring him *nothing but pleasure* (Mt 3:17, Mk 1:11, Lk 3:22). What about God's servants today? If we love God, we shall long that he will be able to delight in us. This possibility will capture our imaginations and inspire us to do and to say what is good, for *his* glory and not for ours.

Secondly, the servant is humble by nature and avoids publicity (v 2). How very different from Cyrus! Cyrus would perform the task Yahweh had assigned to him, but he would be practically unaware of doing so on account of the fuss and noise that he would be stirring up at the same time. His life would be filled with the glamour of worldly success. Amid the dazzling luxury, would he be able to listen to the one who had lifted him up to the dizzying heights of fame? Would he be interested in knowing and loving the one true God? How does this apply to us? Is it our number one priority to set aside time for quiet and stillness in our lives? Do we wait for God? Do we long for his holy and loving presence?

Thirdly, the servant would teach God's truth that would transform the world (v 4). The Hebrew word for *teaching* used here is *torah*, used for the entire body of teaching delivered by Moses. Moses had prophesied that God would one day raise up a new prophet like him, into whose mouth God would put his own words that the prophet would speak at God's command (Deut 18:15-18). II Isaiah is saying that the servant of Yahweh would be this prophet just like Moses.

There was a great difference between Cyrus and the servant of Yahweh. Cyrus was primarily interested in military warfare, while the servant would be primarily interested in teaching the truth that sets people free (Jn 8:31-32). The best that Cyrus could do would be to sign a decree authorising the return of the Jewish exiles in Babylonia to their promised land. The servant, on the other hand, would leave behind a new body of teaching. Because of its divine origins it was the truth, and because it was true, it would transform the world.

We should realise the importance of this. In his essay *God in the Dock*, C.S. Lewis comments that people often wish to know whether the Christian faith works, whether it is good or not. But that is not the right question to ask about it. The real question, the question they should ask, is this: *Is it true?* In our subjective and utilitarian age we are in danger of losing our concern for absolute truth. In church discussions the big questions are: *Will it work? Is it relevant? Will people like it?* The question of truth is no longer considered important.

Since C.S. Lewis made these comments, there has been a further polarisation. Because of the trend to be "inclusive" about the opinions held by different people on moral matters, some of the truths taught in the Bible *may no longer be expressed in public* in the 21st century. Even if put across with gentleness and sensitivity, even if backed up by weighty reasons, they are not to be voiced, not even in church. The present author is writing this in 2020. Certain moral matters must not be discussed, period. Other related matters, such as the true requirement to fear God, or the Biblical truth about the judgement of God, are also increasingly frowned upon when they arise in church discussion groups. How could anyone be so imprudent as to teach those truths? Some people would find them offensive! The trouble is, that because they are true and may not be aired abroad, the judgement of God will be visited on our generation. Might that judgement include the temporary closure of churches worldwide, because some of them have caved in to contemporary inclusiveness and thereby excluded those who would dare to criticise that inclusiveness on Biblical grounds?

Fourthly, the servant would be a covenant to the people of God (v6). The prophet Jeremiah had prophesied that there would be a new covenant (Jer 31:31-34), different from the old covenant set up by Moses. As a result of the new covenant, three amazing things would happen. God would write the servant's new teaching in the hearts of God's people (Jn 14:26, 16:13). All of God's people would know God because they would know his servant (Jn 17:3). And God would forgive and forget all their sins (1 Jn 1:9).

Fifthly, this revelation about the servant is a new thing that is being declared (v9). Yahweh's foretelling of Cyrus and what he would achieve was prophesied some ten years in advance of its fulfilment. That was sufficient to reduce all of the world's idols to stunned silence. This prophecy about Yahweh's servant, taken in conjunction with the other three "servant songs", is of an altogether different order. It was spoken some 577-580 years before the servant engaged in his ministry. The rounded picture that it gives of the servant's achievements and character is breath-taking in its detail and its scope. It should reduce *anyone* who reads the four "servant songs" to awestruck silence.

LXXVIII

42:10-17 Praise to the Lord Almighty

"New things" (v9) may inspire new songs, and in verses 10-12 II Isaiah presents us with a song in which the creation is called to celebrate Yahweh's glory. Occasional outbursts of song suddenly appear in these chapters (e.g. in 44:23, 49:13, 52:9-10), as they do in the Isaiah apocalypse in chapters 24-27. The one we have here may have inspired certain passages in the Psalms.

10. A new song of praise is to be heard from "the end of the earth". The sea and its creatures roar, as do the heathen nations. The first half of this verse is similar to Psalms 96:1-3 and 98:1, the second half to Psalms 96:11 and 98:7. Why do nature and also the heathen nations burst into song? It is on account of their sheer joy at the liberation which the servant of Yahweh will bring them. The whole world will be brought into a new covenant with God (v6) and in due course nature itself will be set free from its bondage to decay (Rom 8:19-22).

11. Even Israel's bitterest enemies Kedar (Ps 120:5-7) and Sela in Edom (16:1), whom we have encountered as being under Yahweh's judgement (21:16-17, 34:5-17), are invited to participate in God's grace by raising their voice or perhaps shouting. There were two types of tribesmen in Kedar (a region of Arabia). Some were nomadic and wandered in "the desert", others were settled in "the villages". Some commentators suggest that Sela may be the town that was later called Petra.

12. The words *glory* and *praise* are an echo of verse 8. II Isaiah longs that even the enemies of Israel may give Yahweh the glory that is rightly his due, and that the heathen nations may declare his praise.

13. Yahweh is a fountain of grace for undeserving people who repent and turn to him. This does not mitigate his wrath against those who refuse to respond to him. Yahweh can be like a soldier, full of terrible fury towards his enemies. His cry of anger will petrify them, and then they will see his power wielded against them.

14. Yahweh is slow to anger, but when he is persistently provoked the moment eventually arrives when his anger flares up. Then he will no longer hold his peace and restrain his zeal to put right wrongs that cry out for redress (Lk 12:49-51). With a loud cry like a woman giving birth, he will gasp and pant, and his hot breath will be released. A titanic effort is needed to accomplish redemption, and the accompanying judgement will be devastating for the impenitent.

15. His angry breath will convert pleasant and well-watered mountains and hills into a wasteland. It will dry up the plantations of idolaters. Their rivers will turn

into parched land and their reservoirs will dry up. This is the exact opposite of what Yahweh will do for the poor and needy who cry to him for help (41:17-20).

16. Even while he is angry with the impenitent, Yahweh remains tender and faithful towards the poor and needy, who are the helpless victims of evil. When they cannot see their way ahead, he will gently lead them in new ways and guide them in paths they have not travelled on. He will flood their dark moments with his own light, and remove the obstacles that prevent their progress. Yahweh will proceed with his mysterious purposes, but he will on no account forsake his own.

17. God cannot be a saviour without being a judge as well. Those who will face his terrible final judgement will not benefit from the salvation he makes possible for those who repent. Some people do not turn to him, but persist in idolatry. They will be turned back and utterly put to shame. If one may compare God to a coin with two sides, then the first "servant song" reveals one side and verses 13-17 the other. Later we shall study II Isaiah's greatest oracle, the fourth "servant song". It will likewise reveal one side of the coin, while 63:1-6 will reveal the other.

Meditation: When parallel Lines meet

Yahweh's commissioning of his servant is marked by a hymn of praise (v 10-12). Its theme is the incomparable grace of God, which is available to everyone and everything, to God's enemies as well as his people, and to the creation itself. But although the commissioning centres on the servant, the hymn and the subsequent oracle of judgement (v 13-17) concern Yahweh himself. In the first "servant song" (v 1-9), the work of redemption is being entrusted to a humble man. In the passage that follows (v 10-17), the work of redemption is undertaken by God, and it involves him in costly and sacrificial labour. This is an example of the two strands of prophecy that can be found throughout the book of Isaiah.

In one of the strands, God will achieve the salvation of Israel (and with the help of Israel, of the whole world) through an extraordinary human personality, presented sometimes as a child, at other times as a king, and now as a servant. In the other strand, God himself will come visibly to deliver his people and to reign over them. These two lines of prophecy run throughout the Old Testament like parallel lines. As mathematicians will be quick to tell you, parallel lines never meet. In fact this is incorrect. They do meet if they are the same line, and then they meet at every point!

But how can a humble man be the same being as the one and only God? This was something the Jews could not have worked out, but their holy scriptures are full of tantalising hints. No one got closer to solving the ultimate riddle of theology than II Isaiah with his four brief glimpses of the One whom he referred to as the servant of Yahweh.

Verses 13-17 are remarkable for the way in which II Isaiah depicts God as being clothed with human passion and agony. The language is both anthropomorphic (soldier, warrior, cries out, shouts aloud, woman in labour, gasps, pants) and anthropopathic (stirring up fury, holding his peace, keeping still, restraining himself). God is likened to a man both physically and emotionally. If God can be like a man, then a man can be like God. There is no difficulty here, for God made man *in his own image*. But the solution to the ultimate riddle is more than this. It is to affirm that God *is* a certain man, the Messiah, and that the Messiah *is* God. It is not a question of likeness, but of identity.

It would have been quite impossible for one of the prophets, or for any of the Jewish people, to stumble on the truths of the Trinity and the Incarnation. They are and will continue to be the two great mysteries of the *Christian* faith. The Messiah was God made man. The Messiah is both fully God and fully man. How could this be, when one of the prophets had declared that Yahweh had said, "I am God and no mortal" (Hos 11:9)? Our prophet will likewise quote Yahweh as saying, "My thoughts are not your thoughts, nor are your ways my ways" (55:8). And yet, as George Adam Smith observed, it is in the writings of II Isaiah that "we find some of the most remarkable ascriptions to God of personal effort, weakness and pain". This commentator explained the paradox as follows:

The highest goodness does not belong to the distant and absent leader but to the sympathetic and agonising servant. If God was the creator and the righteous judge of all people *and nothing more*, we would be unable to say that God is love. We would have to say instead that his martyrs and his prophets were more admirable than he. The soldiers who serve their country on the battlefield or lay down their lives for their people are more admirable than the King or Prime Minister who sent them forth. But what if God is someone who does not break a bruised reed, nor quench a dimly burning wick, but instead mends the reed and fans the wick into a flame? This begins to be a different matter (42:3). And if he is "despised and rejected by others, a man of suffering and acquainted with infirmity" (53:3), even better. Best of all, if "he [is] wounded for our transgressions, crushed for our iniquities", if "upon him [is] the punishment that [makes] us whole, and by his stripes we are healed" (53:5), then this makes all the difference. *That* is a truly wonderful God! *That* is a God of love! It is almost a case that God *had* to become a servant and suffer in order to demonstrate his love to us.

LXXIX

42:18-25 When the Blind lead the Blind

In these chapters there is an ongoing tussle between the reforming grace of God and the wilful disobedience of his people. *They* seem bent on selfish rebellion; *he* is equally tenacious in his attempts to turn them from their evil ways.

18. Yahweh speaks harshly in his frustration with Israel. As a people they are deaf, for they will not listen. They are also blind, for they never look up at him.

19. The people of Israel are meant to be Yahweh's servants and messengers, but Yahweh asks if anyone is as blind and deaf as them. He is so exasperated with them that he repeats the questions. Some commentators believe that the Hebrew word translated *my dedicated one* is better rendered *he who is at peace with me*. If this is so, it highlights God's problem. His people, whose default position is to be at peace with him, simply will not respond to his pleas for repentance. As a result, they will lose their invaluable gift, peace with God.

20. The people of Israel can and do see many things, but they remain basically unobservant. Their ears are open and they can hear, but choose not to do so. They can find out God's will, but have no desire to do so. Their inability to register the truths God has revealed about himself and mankind is a very serious disability.

21. It was pleasing to Yahweh "to magnify his teaching and make it glorious". This does not necessarily mean that he went to great pains to make it engaging, compelling and interesting, although that is true. Most commentators believe, in the context of these chapters, that Yahweh wished to magnify the *scope* of his teaching by making it available to all the nations, and not just to Israel.

22. Yahweh is aware of the limitations placed on his people by their exile. They were robbed and plundered when the Babylonians took Jerusalem. As captives it was as if they were trapped or incarcerated. They were despoiled victims with no one who would help them or restore them.

23. Yahweh invites the people of Israel to heed what he has just said. There is a terrible contrast between their ideal calling to enlighten the nations and their present predicament in captivity. He asks if any of them will learn from the past and resolve to attend and listen to him concerning their future restoration.

24. Yahweh imagines what his people might wish to say if they came to their senses. They might confess that it was God who had handed them over to their captors. They might acknowledge that God had done this because they had sinned against him, refusing to walk in his ways and to obey his laws.

25. Yahweh had therefore poured on the Israelites "the heat of his anger and the fury of war". This was not in order to destroy them but to teach them, but they remained unresponsive. The flames engulfed them, but it made no difference. They were severely burnt, "but [they] did not take it to heart". So far, the bitter lesson of exile had been lost on them. They had felt their calamity deeply, but they had not seen it as a visitation by Yahweh, inflicted on them for their sins.

Meditation: The right Question to ask

This passage interrupts the positive outlook. The conqueror Cyrus has appeared in order to facilitate a return of the Jewish exiles to their land. The servant of Yahweh would appear in due course to provide a solution to the greatest problems of the world. It remained then for the people of Israel to prepare for their mission to be the servants of God himself, to be a light that would enlighten the heathen nations. But right here another great problem arose. Israel was unfit for the task ahead. What would befall the needy world when God's people proved to be just as needy as the world,

and appeared to have forgotten all about the means of salvation? This is an important matter for the church in every age, for the church perennially fails to live up to its
calling and instead lapses into forgetfulness. Instead of serving, its members desire to
be served. Instead of bringing glory to God who created and redeemed them, they
want the spotlight to shine on themselves.

In these verses the people of God, the church, are described as blind and deaf
to the truths of God (v 18-20). They possessed the greatest treasure in the world, the
glorious teaching of God himself (v 21). But they had neglected and rejected it so often
that they were now captives. They were "a people robbed and plundered, all of them
[were] trapped in holes and hidden in prisons; they [had] become a prey with no one
to rescue, a spoil with no one to say, 'Restore!'" (v 22). It was time for some searching
questions to be asked.

The church often asks the question, "Why?" It would do well to ask the question
"Who?" The question asked by God in three of these verses is "Who?" (v 19, 23, 24).
We find it easier to ask the question "Why?" which is often prompted by our pride. Our
pride is quick to claim that we did not deserve whatever it was that happened to us,
and to assume that our reasoning will be sufficient to explain the mysterious turns that
life takes. But there are always aspects of the human condition that are not subject to
human logic, and sometimes the answer to the question "Why?" will not provide any
comfort to our troubled heart.

The first question God asked was "Who is acting as if they were blind and deaf?"
(v 18-20). The right answer is, "It is God's people. In particular, I myself. It is out of order
for me to be blind and deaf to God. I am supposed to be his servant! I am dedicated to
him and at peace with him. How then can I ignore what he says?" The second question
God asks is, "Who among you will give heed to this, who will attend and listen for the time
to come?" (v 23). Maybe the answer is, "I will". God frames the third question for us: it is
we that ask it. "Who allowed my selfishness to take its course and arranged for its rightful
consequences to be visited upon me?" (v 25). The right answer is, "God did, and it was
one of his many attempts to make me in reality what I am in theory, namely his servant".

Will it really help to ask "Who?" and get back to God, and have dealings directly
with him? The Bible's view of history is that God is the first cause. He is the main agent
behind all the events that take place. This does not deny the existence of secondary
causes, but it does emphasise the importance of the first cause. Every member of the
church, which is the body of the Messiah, needs to realise that God does not abdicate
his sovereignty when he uses tyrants or viruses or fallen and flawed people in the church
to work out his purposes. Through all the changing scenes of life it is always he that we
must deal with in the first instance. We may examine secondary causes as well if we
wish, but God is to come first.

With verse 25 we are back to where we started: the unfitness of Israel to fulfil the
tasks God has given to them. Israel cannot pretend to be servants like Yahweh's servant

in 42:1-7. Their lack of spiritual perception (v18-20) has resulted in divine chastisement (v25). This is a sad picture of the church. Is there no hope, then, for the body of Christ on earth? Yes, there is. Some church members may ask the question "Who?" They may then realise the heights from which they have fallen, and confess their sins to God (v24). A revival may then begin. The members of the church may then realise what they are, namely God's dedicated ones who are at peace with him. They have been dedicated to God in order to serve as his servants and messengers (v19).

LXXX

43:1-13 Grace for God's disobedient People

In verses 1-7 Yahweh, having just castigated his people Israel for their spiritual blindness, proceeds to assure them that in spite of their wilful sins he has not cast them off. With some of the most tender words that were ever spoken by a father to his sons and daughters, he promises them that nothing in the world would separate them from either his care (v2) or his love (v4, see also Rom 8:38-39).

1. "But now" – The "but" signals the switch from Yahweh's exposure of Israel's unresponsiveness to his assurance that he will persevere in the task of bringing them back to himself. Yahweh speaks tenderly of how he created and formed the Israelites (Ps 139:13-16). They are not to fear (41:10) for he is about to *redeem* them (the perfect tense indicates the certainty of what he will do). He addresses them as those who are familiar and dear to him, for they *are his.*

2. His anger had set them on fire (42:25) but now he is with them and they would not be harmed by the extreme perils of waters and rivers, or of fire and flames.

3. He was Yahweh their God, and also the Holy One of Israel. He would proceed to save them. The way in which he would become their saviour is best explained by the metaphor of *ransom.* Great nations, Egypt, Ethiopia and Sheba would fall to Cyrus and his descendants, to recompense them for allowing Israel to return to their land (Prov 21:18). At the same time, of course, it is true that in the long run all the nations would gain more from Israel than they would lose, for Israel would be a light to them (42:6). It is also true that Israel's ultimate ransom would be of an altogether different sort, but that must await our study of the fourth "servant song" (53:8-9, Mk 10:45, 1 Pet 1:18-19).

4. Here is the heart of the matter. Yahweh *loved* Israel: they were precious to him and he honoured them: he would even give nations in exchange for them. He loved his people in spite of their ingratitude, disobedience and spiritual blindness. This message of God's love for unworthy people who keep on rejecting him was the principal theme of the prophet Hosea's preaching to the ten northern tribes (Hosea 11:1-9). It was a message that Hosea was to exemplify in his own life.

He was instructed to marry a prostitute, for that was precisely what Yahweh had done in pledging himself to his faithless people (Hosea 1:2).

5. His people were not to fear. Yahweh would also gather together the Israelites from the dispersion. This is a reference to the ten tribes, exiled to various different parts of the world when Assyria overran the northern kingdom in 722 B.C.

6. He would call upon Mesopotamian lands and Egypt to release the descendants of the dispersed Israelites. He would adopt them as his sons and daughters. Fire and water, heathen peoples and enormous distances would not prevail: anyone whom Yahweh called *mine* (v 1) would arrive home safely.

7. Because every single Israelite was a son or daughter of Yahweh, created for his glory, formed and made by him, the honour of Yahweh's name was at stake.

8. Having reassured his people in this way, Yahweh proceeds to convene another court hearing. The idolatrous nations had produced dumb witnesses, but Yahweh now gives the order to bring forth witnesses of his own – his flawed but much loved people. They are *blind*, yet have eyes; they are *deaf*, yet have ears (42:18-20). But they are not dumb. He despaired of them in 42:18-25. But now, after calling them his own, he restores to them their task of being his *witnesses*.

9. Next, Yahweh summons all the nations to gather and assemble at his hearing. Which of them had prophesied events that were now beginning to take place? Which of them had foretold the "former things"? Did any of them have the sovereign capacity to determine the course of history in advance, and then bring their vision to pass? They were free to bring witnesses who would listen to them and then corroborate them. But they all remained silent.

10. In spite of their failures, Yahweh held his people to the high calling he had given to them. They were still his witnesses and his chosen "servant". They would give testimony as to Yahweh's deity. This would not only be for the instruction of the world, but also so that they themselves might know and believe Yahweh. They would realise that he is God. There was no other god apart from him in the past, and there would not be another god apart from him in the future (v 11, 13). Being a witness is edifying. It is not a heavy burden, but a liberating privilege.

11. Yahweh now testifies about himself. He and he alone was God. There was no other saviour. II Isaiah had perceived that his ability and desire to *save* was the attribute above all others that marked Yahweh out as being God.

12. He, Yahweh, had declared the salvation of his people in advance, and then accomplished it. No "strange god" had done this. His people were witnesses of this fact and could testify about it.

13. Yahweh winds up the proceedings with the final decision of the court. He, Yahweh, was God. The deliverance he would bring would mark a new stage in his revelation of himself as the saviour of his people. He was resolutely set upon

their salvation, and nobody would be able to snatch his own out of his hand (Jn 10:28-29). He *would* work, and who could possibly hinder him?

Meditation: When Grace meets Disobedience

If we consider these last two sections together, they provide us with a remarkable insight as to how God regards his people. There are three different and almost irreconcilable aspects to his thinking. First of all, he is appalled and angry at his people's spiritual blindness and their disobedience of his teaching (42:18-25). Secondly, he loves them and they are so precious to him that he will not let go of them, for they are his (43:1-7). Thirdly, in the important work of mission, he will entrust them with the vital task of being his witnesses (43:8-13). Why does he persevere with them when they persist in rebellion and ignore his words?

The answer is, because he loves them (43:4). Why does he go on loving them when they are altogether unlovable? Because he loves them (Deut 7:7-8). But when he goes on loving them, do they then respond to his love and start obeying him? No, they do not, they just keep on disobeying and ignoring him. Does he then give up on them? No, he keeps on loving them!

This is one of the most marvellous truths about God. It is almost unbelievable. At our best, we are his unprofitable servants (Lk 17:10). But once he has taken us on as his servants, God stays loyal to us even though we do not remain loyal to him. He created and formed us, he redeemed us and called us by name, and we are his (43:1). If we follow him and his Messiah, he will speak to us in the wonderfully tender words of 43:4, "You are precious in my sight. You are honoured by me. I love you". It does not depend on our being good servants. If we have done a few tasks well for him, and begin to think we are quite good servants, we have missed the point. It is all thanks to his grace, to his undeserved love and favour for us, and to the strength that his Spirit freely gives us. He does not accept us because of a few merits we may think we have, nor because of one or two good things in our make-up. He accepts us *in spite of everything*. He loves his unprofitable servants! He loves us because he is love (1 Jn 4:8, 16). This is what God is like.

The call to be God's witnesses (43:10) fitted the Israelites comfortably in the context of God's wonderful encouragement and reassurance. In spite of their flaws and weaknesses, the people of God could and would be his witnesses. They would even bring glory to him (Jn 17:10). Truth was on their side, and as they rose to the occasion and declared it, the truth would fire their imaginations and build them up. Witness is not only the sending out of truth into the world, but also the means for strengthening the witnesses in their faith, hope and love.

For all their disobedience and lack of faith, God treated them as capable of giving evidence. Though they had made little progress in getting to know their great God, they nevertheless knew more about him than any other nation on earth, and they could speak forth wisdom that the profoundest heathen thinkers had missed. If the imagined courtroom scene had actually taken place, the witnesses would have come up to the witness box and might have spoken as follows:

Question: "Give us some examples of Yahweh foretelling former things and whether or not they happened". **Answer:** "Yahweh told our ancestor and progenitor Abraham that his descendants would spend a lengthy period in bondage in Egypt, and that afterwards they would depart from there after many judgements, loaded with plunder, in order to dwell in the land you are in now. All this was fulfilled" (Gen 15:13-16). "Yahweh also spoke through his prophet Isaiah to our good King Hezekiah after he had shown the envoys of the King of Babylon his treasures. He told him that all those treasures would end up here in Babylon and that we ourselves would become captives in this land. This too was fulfilled and remains true this day" (39:5-7).

Question: "Give us an example of Yahweh foretelling something that is in the process of being fulfilled in our own day". **Answer:** "Yahweh told us that he would rouse a victor from the east who would deliver nations to him and trample kings under foot. So it is happening with Cyrus of Anshan to the east of Babylon. He will in due course liberate us and return us to our own land".

Question: "Give us an example of a new thing that Yahweh has told you that he will do in years to come". **Answer:** "Yahweh told us that he would send us his servant and put his Spirit upon him. This servant will be a humble man who will be very gentle with the broken and the faint-hearted. He will persevere until he has established justice in the earth, and the nations are waiting for his teaching".

"Thank you, you may step down. No more questions".

Like Yahweh before him, the Messiah said to his followers, "You shall be my witnesses" (Acts 1:8). If we are one of his followers, we too may witness to a love that never gives up. We too may testify about a purpose that never falters. We too may declare that God's salvation always satisfies in the long run.

The people of the Lord, in spite of their vicissitudes, were and continue to be his witnesses and his chosen servants. The history of Israel and our own history are in themselves a powerful testimony for God. When grace meets disobedience, grace perseveres and, in the end, it wins.

LXXXI

43:14-28 Provident God, indifferent Israel

14. Yahweh, the Redeemer and the Holy One of Israel, is about to act in favour of his covenant people. He will send some people to Babylon (presumably the Persian army) and break the bars that were holding his people captive. The proud clamour of the Babylonians would then be turned to cries of lamentation. This is the first mention of Babylon since 39:1-8.

15. The one who would do this is none other than Yahweh, their Holy One. He created the people of Israel, and he was their King.

16. In verses 16-17 Yahweh reminds the Israelites of their original exodus from captivity in Egypt. He made a way of escape for Israel in the Red Sea, creating a path for them in the middle of the waters (Ex 14:21-22).

17. He brought forth the Egyptian army, warriors on horses and chariots. They followed the Israelites into the sea, but the waters engulfed them and drowned them. (Ex 14:23-29). Like a wick that is squeezed, they were totally extinguished.

18. The exodus from Egypt was a "former thing" from of old. The exiles could forget about it, for its wonders would be surpassed by what was about to happen.

19. Yahweh was about to do something quite new. It was just beginning to appear. Perhaps the Israelites might soon perceive it. Yahweh would create a way through the wilderness so that his people could return to Jerusalem. He would make rivers in the desert to provide them with refreshment along the route. The implication is that these miracles would rival those in the Red Sea during the Exodus (v 16-17).

20. Even the wild beasts, jackals and ostriches would honour Yahweh for the provision of water. It is indeed a wonderful thing when rivers appear in a desert.

21. Yahweh would supply this provision for his chosen people, whom he had formed, making them just as they were for himself, to declare his praise.

22. "Israel's devastating response to the divine ardour is a yawn of ennui", as Derek Kidner memorably put it. No rebuff could have been more offensive. Far from calling on Yahweh (Ps 50:15), his people were weary of him. They may have kept up appearances, but they had again given their God the cold shoulder.

23. In past days the people had showed Yahweh the same bored indifference in their Temple sacrifices (1:10-17). In Babylon they were not able to sacrifice sheep in honour of him. He in turn had not burdened them by demanding sacrifices, nor had he wearied them by requiring incense offerings.

24. In Babylon God's people had not been able to give him thanksgiving offerings or the fat of sacrifices. Yahweh had taken this burden from them. In fact Yahweh continually bore all their burden (46:3, 4), but they just added further sins to it. Moreover, their weary reaction to Yahweh was wearisome to him.

25. Israel were not using the means ordained by God for the forgiveness of their sins, and they kept adding further sins to their account, so Yahweh would undertake in person the work of atonement. He would blot out their transgressions for his own sake, and no longer remember their sins (Jer 31:34). Barry Webb wrote that "This word of forgiveness totally dominates its context, like a shaft of brilliant light piercing a night sky. The dark sayings around it simply serve to throw it into sharp relief". II Isaiah would disclose later how this forgiveness would be accomplished (53:4-6).

26. Once again Yahweh offers to prove his case against his people in a court of law. He summons them to present their side of the argument to him (as in 1:18). They might wish to claim certain merits, or to urge certain pleas.

27. Their problem of rebellious sinfulness went right back to their first ancestor, Jacob (later called Israel). Also implicated were their "interpreters", the religious establishment, most of whom transgressed against Yahweh.

28. Because of this, Yahweh had allowed the profanation of the priests (the "princes of the sanctuary") when Jerusalem was taken and the Temple destroyed. He had also delivered his people Jacob or Israel to *utter destruction*. The Hebrew word used here is *herem*, reserved for such objects of judgement as the city of Jericho or the Amalekites, with whom there was to be no compromise; they were *devoted* to destruction. It was the strongest term of opprobrium in the language. It meant that Yahweh had placed his people under a curse.

Meditation: The God who takes the Initiative

These chapters keep coming back to certain important truths, one of which is the sovereignty and absolute authority of God. Everything that God undertakes has its origin in his eternal purposes, is assured by his power, and happens exactly when he takes the initiative for it to do so.

Here is a selection of some of the sayings attributed to him. "I, I am Yahweh, and besides me there is no saviour" (43:11). "I am God, and also henceforth I am he; there is no one who can deliver from my hand; I work, and who can hinder it?" (43:13). "I am about to do a new thing" (43:19). "I, I am he who blots out your transgressions for my own sake, and I will not remember your sins" (43:25). "I am the first and I am the last; besides me there is no god" (44:6). "Is there any god besides me? There is no other rock; I know not one" (44:8). "I Yahweh, made all things" (44:24). "I am Yahweh, and there is no other; besides me there is no god" (45:5). "I am Yahweh, and there is no other" (45:6). "I form light and create darkness, I make weal and create woe; I Yahweh do all these things" (45:7). "Who declared it of old? Was it not I, Yahweh? There is no other god besides me, a righteous God and a Saviour; there is no one besides me" (45:21). "Turn to me and be saved, all the ends of the earth! For I am God, and there is no other" (45:22). "Only in Yahweh, it shall be said of me, are righteousness and strength" (45:24). "Even to your old age, I am he, even when you turn grey I will carry you. I have made, and I will bear; I will carry and will save" (46:4).

All these sayings are from chapters 43-46, and there are others that are similar in their tone. They all indicate the absolute authority of God. The first person singular pronoun plays an important part in God's revelation. Indeed the covenant name of God in the Old Testament, Yahweh, means something like "I am who I am". Each successive part of that revelation is given by the initiative of "I am". Revelation at its most creative and enriching is not the publication of truths about God, but the personal presence and communication to people of God himself. The most important thing in life is not knowing *about* him but knowing *him*. In this section of the book of Isaiah there is an abundance of phrases with "I am" or "I am he". There is a recurring refrain: "no other god besides me". All this is an invitation and an incentive for us to get to know him.

The history of religion (including the Judeo-Christian religion) is full of errors and unhelpful tendencies. Some people look to the revelation primarily for intellectual ideas (knowing about God, "What good deed must I do to have eternal life?" Mt 19:16), others for material benefits (the prosperity gospel, "Teacher, tell my brother to divide the family inheritance with me", Lk 12:13), and others for power over other people (the spirituality of manipulation, "Grant us to sit, one at your right hand, and one at your left, in your glory", Mk 10:37). The prodigal son completely missed the target when he said to his father, "Give me the share of the property that will belong to me", but later scored a bull's eye when he said, "I will get up and go to my father" (Lk 15:12, 18).

If we read the Bible, that is good. It is the best book to read. Why are we reading the Bible? This is a very important question. If our prime objective is to find some new history, philosophy, theology, morality, spirituality, reassurance, challenge, insight, satisfaction or stimulation, we may well succeed, but it will do us little good unless God opens our minds to understand what we are reading. The reason we should read the Bible is in order to encounter and get to know the living God, and to receive his grace, forgiveness and restoration. As we get to know him, we shall know that we are precious, honoured and deeply loved (43:4), and that we have eternal life (Jn 17:3). If we have this, we have everything. A mother was pushing a pram with her new-born child in it. A friend of hers came up to the pram and said, "Oh, how lovely – what an absolutely marvellous thing – you are so fortunate – this is the most beautiful pram I have ever seen". This did not go down very well with the mother!

The present author believes that the best part of the New Testament is John's Gospel, and the best part of the Old is the book of Isaiah. These are the books of the Bible that he would recommend other people to read first. Ambrose, who was Bishop of Milan from 374-397, found himself with an exceptionally bright convert to baptise and look after in 386. This convert, whose name was Aurelius Augustine, would become one of the most important Christian writers in history. He had been converted by reading St Paul's epistle to the Romans, and Ambrose wanted to recommend some further good reading. What would you have advised? Ambrose told him to read the prophecies in the Book of Isaiah, particularly the second half, beginning at chapter 40. Augustine did so. It was good advice.

LXXXII

44:1-8 God will richly bless his People

1. As in 43:1, the "But now" announces a switch from Yahweh's anger with Israel on account of their unresponsiveness to his assurance that he will succeed in the task he has taken on of perfecting them. How wonderful it is when present gloom is suddenly lit up by the promise of a brilliant future. Once more Yahweh speaks positively to his people: he repeats that they are his "servant" and his chosen ones.

2. Yahweh reminds his people that he made them, intricately forming them in their mother's womb. He would help them, they need not fear. He addresses them tenderly, calling them his chosen and his servant. He addresses them as both *Jacob* ("deceiver") and *Jeshurun* ("upright"). Moses used *Jeshurun* (Deut 32:15, 33:5, 26) which, like *Israel*, is derived from *Jashar*, ("upright", Josh 10:13).

3. Yahweh would pour water on the thirsty land and create streams on the dry ground. Because of the accompanying promise of the Spirit, this must have a figurative meaning. Anyone who was thirsty for God could go to him and drink from his "wells of salvation" (12:3). The Messiah would make the same promise. He likewise would declare that the water that he would provide would be the Spirit of God, and that anyone who drank it would be greatly blessed (Jn 7:37-39). Here Yahweh promises with lavish generosity to "pour" both his Spirit (the cause) and his blessing (the effect) on the descendants of his exiled people.

4. The offspring of Israel would indicate the ever widening flow of God's living water (Jn 4:10, 13-14). Like green tamarisks and willows planted by the side of flowing streams, they would flourish. But who would these offspring be?

5. Among the offspring of Israel would be some of the Gentiles. The declarations of allegiance in this verse would come from them, as they expressed their longing to share the blessing poured out on the community of Yahweh's people descended from Jacob. Some would call themselves after Yahweh or Jacob, others would proudly tattoo the name of Yahweh on their hands – anything to become part of the privileged people of God. Gentile proselytes who took up Judaism were rare in Old Testament days (Ps 87:4-6). This verse is looking forward to a time when many people from the heathen nations would follow the Messiah. They would thereby get to know God and join the people of Israel (Acts 11:16-17).

6. Verses 6-8 reiterate the essence of II Isaiah's prophetic teaching. The various titles ascribed to Yahweh declare that he is the King and the Redeemer of his people, and the God of the armies. He is the first and the last (41:4). Besides him there is no god. This constitutes the clearest possible expression of monotheism.

7. Nobody is like Yahweh, for if they were, they would have declared themselves to him and would have predicted the future just as he had done.

8. In spite of being exiles in a foreign land, the Israelites were not to be afraid of the future tumults. Did Yahweh not declare them in advance? They would resolve themselves and lead to their return to Jerusalem. They themselves were witnesses of the prophecy. Yahweh then asks, is there any god besides him? We know the answer to that one. There is no other rock. Even Yahweh does not know one.

Meditation: A Promise for our Times

The old covenant was the contract between God and his people that we find in the Old Testament. There would also be a new covenant between God and his people, which would supersede the old one. It would be introduced by God through his Messiah. We find the details of this contract in the New Testament. The word *covenant* means a legal disposition or *testament*; the two divisions of the Bible detail the two covenants. The new covenant was foretold by the prophets in the Old Testament, and the outpouring of God's Spirit would be one of its features. We find a description of the new covenant in Jeremiah 31:31-34, while the promise of the pouring out of the Spirit on all of God's people is set out in Isaiah 44:3, Ezekiel 36:26-27, 37:11-14; Joel 2:28-29; and Zechariah 12:10.

Some passages in Isaiah, including chapter 35, 40:3-5, 41:17-20, 43:18-21 and 44:1-5, promised blessing and protection for God's people in their exodus from captivity and their resettlement in Jerusalem after the fall of Babylon in 539 B.C. But the journey back and the new beginning in their own land were not easy times. The blessings poured out seemed modest, even after the Temple had been rebuilt (Hag 2:3). God indeed accompanied and empowered them, but their return could hardly be compared to deserts turning into green and pleasant lands.

The real fulfilment of these passages would come as a result of another *exodus* or departure, the one which the Messiah would accomplish in Jerusalem (Lk 9:31). During the last evening before his death, he gave his followers some instructions about his memorial service. He broke some bread and gave it to them, saying "This is my body, which is given for you". Then he poured some wine into a cup and gave it to them to drink, saying, "This cup that is poured out for you is the *new covenant* in my blood" (Lk 22:19-20). By these words, the Messiah was saying that the new covenant, prophesied by Jeremiah some 625 years earlier, was about to be established. The forgiveness of sins, promised as one of the blessings of the covenant, was about to be available, and the sacrifice to ratify the covenant and secure its blessings would be, as it had been in the first covenant, a blood sacrifice. In this case, the sacrifice would not be an ordinary lamb but the Messiah himself, whose blood would be shed in his death.

After he had died and been brought back to life, and just before he returned to God, he gave his disciples a great commission, to "Make disciples of all nations" (Mt 28:18-20). The disciples had to wait for the Holy Spirit to be *poured out* on them, which duly happened on the day of Pentecost, and then they set out on their great adventure, empowered to pass on the good news of the Messiah in the power of the

Holy Spirit. As they did this, they lived in the light of the teaching they had received from both the Old Testament prophets and the Messiah (Jn 8:31-32). They duly discovered that what the prophets and the Messiah had taught them was true.

The great blessings of the promises in verses 1-5 of our passage were fulfilled in the careers of the Messiah's followers as they obeyed him and persevered in what they had learnt. They proved in their lives that the language of deserts turning into watered groves with lush green growth was realistic and not exaggerated. And what was true for them has also been true for successive generations of the Messiah's followers, including those of us who follow him today.

What could be more surprising than a desert that turns to a green landscape? It is a beautiful picture of fresh growth, of green shoots and buds, of lots of colourful blossom and flowers, and of well-watered fertility. And God has a curious way of appearing by surprise in the most unusual places: prisons, hospitals, refugee camps and war zones. He does so at the most surprising times: in international crises, at those dark times when people are thinking of ending their lives, during pandemics and at the most embarrassing moments. He specialises in transforming the wilderness of our messed-up lives into beautiful gardens with tidy borders and pleasing lawns. Who is like him? Is there any god besides him?

LXXXIII

44:9-28 The Ridiculous and the Sublime

Among the recurring themes in these chapters are the scornful passages about idols and their devotees (40:18-20, 44:9-20, 45:20, 46:1-7). The exiled Jews had little to look forward to in captivity, but their occasional visits to the craftsmen who made the idols would always bring forth a chuckle or two. Tears of laughter would come to their eyes, and their minds would boggle at the absurdity of it all.

9. The makers of these idols are themselves futile (*tohu*), and the gods that they form cannot profit them. Idols can neither see nor think, so they will not help their worshippers to do so. Those who worship them will therefore be put to shame.

10. There is no point in fashioning an image that will do no one any good. The makers think they are creating a god, but it is just a meaningless image.

11. The adherents of the idols will be put to shame. The artisans who make them are just ordinary men, incapable of creating a god. If the idolaters were to face up to Yahweh, they would be terrified and all of them would be put to shame.

12. The manufacture of idols is now described in minute detail. A lot of human strength and ingenuity is wasted in the production of these useless deities. The worker in iron forms an idol over a fire, shaping it with hammers and forging it with muscle power. As a result he is hungry and thirsty, weak and faint.

13. The carpenter marks out the dimensions of the idol on a block of wood. He then gives it shape with planes, and carves it with a sharp piece of metal. The idol is fashioned as a human, with beautiful features, and will be set up in a shrine.

14. The very material of which the idols are made is selected from the trees of the forest, and might equally have been used to cook the idol-maker's food. Cedars, holm trees or oaks may be used. A forester plants them, then the rain nourishes them, and when they are full-grown he cuts them down.

15. The carpenter uses part of the wood to warm himself and bake his bread. Then he takes the rest, makes an idol, and bows down before it in order to worship it!

16. Half of the wood he burns in the fire, partly so as to roast meat over it, which he then eats, and partly so as to warm himself. Having fed himself, he then feels inwardly satisfied and pleasantly warm.

17. With what remains he makes an idol, before which he then bows down and worships. Amazingly, he prays to it, saying, "Save me, for you are my god".

18. With biting satire II Isaiah depicts the inability of the idol-makers to realise what they have done. Their eyes are plastered and cannot see, their minds are closed and cannot understand. John Skinner writes that "They are incapable of applying the most rudimentary principles of reason to their own actions".

19. None of them is capable of discerning what they have actually done. They are unable to face up to it. They burn half the wood so as to bake bread, cook meat and eat. Then they fashion the other half into an abomination, and proceed to prostrate themselves before a block of wood.

20. Their minds are deluded. They have gone astray and cannot save themselves. Better the ashes of the burnt wood than the fraudulent result of their creativity!

21. In verses 21-28 we turn to the sublime from the ridiculous. Yahweh bids Israel to remember the lessons he has taught them so far. Once again he addresses them as both Jacob the deceiver and Israel the upright one. They were Jekyll and Hyde at the same time. Twice Yahweh reminds them that they are his "servant". Because he had formed them in the womb, he would not forget them.

22. Yahweh would sweep away their sins. Like a transitory cloud of mist, they would vanish away. This truth about forgiveness is the same as the one in 43:25, but the metaphor is new. If any of Yahweh's people had given way to idolatry, they could return to him and he would redeem them from their sins.

23. This God, who is real and does act on behalf of his worshippers, is worth singing about, and II Isaiah calls on the heavens above and the depths of the earth beneath, and on the mountains and the trees, to sing the wonder of his redemption. The redemption is as good as done, and Yahweh will be glorified in Israel.

24. The one who speaks is Yahweh, who formed the people of Israel in their mothers' wombs. He created all that exists: he and he alone stretched out the heavens and spread out the earth; no one else helped him.

25. Yahweh frustrates the forecasts of lying diviners and makes fools of them. He likewise makes the wisdom of the sages look foolish. Many oracles addressed to Babylonian kings in the period 587-539 B.C. have survived. All of them are messages of hope. There is not even one forecast of the doom that would follow.

26. Yahweh now repeats the prophecies of restoration, but in greater detail. He confirms his previous words about the Israelites, who are his servants and messengers. Jerusalem would be built up again into an inhabited city, and the ruined walled towns would be rebuilt.

27. Once again Yahweh reminds the Israelites of the great exodus from Egypt. He could say to the watery deep of the Red Sea, "Be dry", and it happened. Remembering this, the faith of the Jewish exiles would be strengthened. Since Yahweh had done that, he could work these new wonders as well.

28. Yahweh reveals the name of the one he will use to overthrow Babylon and facilitate his people's release. It is Cyrus. He was Yahweh's *shepherd*, because he would lead Yahweh's sheep from Babylon. He would fulfil Yahweh's purpose. He would decree that Jerusalem was to be rebuilt, and that the foundations of the Temple were to be laid down.

Meditation: When the Godly become scornful

A visit to a Babylonian idol factory would have provided a party of exiled Jews with considerable comic relief from their uncongenial surroundings. They were monotheists and their enemies were worshippers of idols. George Adam Smith has argued that monotheism, even in its most primitive forms, raises people intellectually. There is a world of difference between the thinking of idolaters and that of people who serve the one true God, Maker and Redeemer, with their mind as well as their heart and strength. The Jews in captivity were conscious of this, and they could be very scornful of the idolatrous ways of their captors.

In verses 9-20 of our passage there is an evident tone of superiority as well as of scorn. The Jews were amazed at the crass stupidity of the Babylonian idolaters. "They do not know, nor do they comprehend; for their eyes are shut, so that they cannot see, and their minds as well, so that they cannot understand. No one considers, nor is there knowledge or discernment" (v 18-19a). Are these verses describing the idolaters or their idols? It is in fact the former, but it could equally be the latter. The point is that we become like the one we worship. If we worship mindless and dumb idols, we shall eventually be the same as them, unable to think aright on spiritual matters, and with little of any use to say to anyone.

Our inability to see the utter futility of idol-worship is both ancient and modern. In our own day we just will not face up to it, because we think that idolatry means the worship of human-shaped statues made of metal or wood. In fact it includes the worship of heroes, whether political or sporting or artistic. It also includes the worship of inanimate objects like cars, computers, or worldly treasures. Idolatry is the worship of the creature rather than the creator (Rom 1:25).

In our day sensualists worship in the temple of Venus, feeding on the ashes of physical gratification. Men of the world worship money, rank and high office, and are prepared to sacrifice everything else, turning it to ashes in order to win worldly power and feed on it. The followers of fashion worship the opinions of their peers and feed on the ashes of human applause. Agnostic and atheistic scholars worship in the austere halls of academia, and feed with the ashes of human recognition an appetite designed to be nourished by eternal truth.

Idolatry is deceptive. A certain idol catches our eye or begins to form itself in our mind. We spend our money purchasing it, or else we spend our mental energy designing its final details and incorporating them within the shadowy recesses of our imagination. At the end of this process, we finally take our idol and hold it, either with our hands or in our minds. Or at any rate, we think that we are holding it. The truth is that it is now holding us, and it will take a miracle if we are ever to free ourselves from its grip.

LXXXIV

45:1-13 God and the pagan Cyrus

In verses 1-8, Yahweh tells of his calling and control of Cyrus, presented to us in the context of the true God's worldwide revelation of himself (v 6), his absolute sovereignty (v 7), and his desire to establish righteousness (v 8).

1. Yahweh speaks to Cyrus and addresses him as his *anointed* or special one, whose right hand he holds. Because he was divinely controlled and directed in this way, Cyrus would be able to subdue nations and strip kings of their robes and their power. Yahweh himself would open barred doors for him. Once opened by God, these doors could not be shut by men.

2. Yahweh promises Cyrus an uninterrupted career of victory, and enlarges on the Persian Emperor's successes. Yahweh would go ahead of him to facilitate his task, levelling mountains, breaking bronze doors and cutting through iron bars.

3. The *treasures of darkness*, like the riches hidden in secret places, are the ones that were most carefully concealed, because they were the most precious. Cyrus had already acquired the fortune of Croesus, and when he added to this the loot of Babylon, he would be fabulously wealthy. By this serendipity Cyrus would be expected to realise that he had been called by Yahweh himself, the God of Israel. He had been summoned by his name so as to fulfil God's purposes for Israel.

4. It was for the sake of his servants and chosen ones, the people of Israel, that Yahweh had called Cyrus by name, and surnamed him with appellations like *my shepherd* (44:28) and *my anointed* (v 1). He had done this even though Cyrus *did*

not know him. In antiquity Cyrus was widely regarded as a favourite of the gods because of his unbroken string of military successes. Isaiah 2 modified this view: he was a chosen servant not of *the gods*, but of *Yahweh*, the one true God.

5. Again Yahweh proclaims his own uniqueness. There is no other like him. Apart from him, there is no God. He was equipping Cyrus for his service, even though Cyrus *did not know him.* Cyrus entered into his path of conquest unaware of the true God who was prospering him.

6. The ultimate purpose of Cyrus's victories was that "they", the heathen lands from east to west, should know that Yahweh was the one and only true God.

7. This is a remarkable saying by Yahweh. It is a typically Hebraic expression with two parallel pairs of opposites, *light* and *darkness*, *weal* and *woe*. Some commentators think it means that God created all that exists, but this empties the saying of much of its power. Could it mean that God created evil as well as good? For the moment, we may if we wish study and ponder Psalms 17, 44 and 73, and Amos 3:6. Later we shall explore this verse further in Appendix 1 (p. 359-361).

8. As his hearers think ahead to the blessings that will follow the triumph of true religion, Yahweh calls on the heavens to rain down heavenly righteousness. He then asks the earth to drink in this heavenly blessing, so that a double fruit created by him may spring up, of salvation and earthly righteousness.

9. Some of the Israelites found it difficult to come to terms with the idea that the chosen agent for their restoration was a heathen conqueror. How could Yahweh, who is holy, think of using such a person to bring good to Israel? It would mean that they would be in a subordinate position to a heathen emperor. But Yahweh was sovereign, and he told them that they were wrong to quibble with their maker, just as a clay pot would be wrong if it quibbled with the potter. The clay is simply not in a position to ask the potter, "What exactly are you up to?", or to comment on the overall shape of the resulting pot.

10. By questioning God, they were committing an impropriety, like a person who rudely intrudes on parents about to have a child, asking the father what sort of creature would result, and the mother what the outcome of her labour would be.

11. Therefore Yahweh speaks to the Israelites as the Holy One and the Maker of Israel. He makes it clear that it is inappropriate of them to ask about his dealings with his children, or to dictate to him what the work of his hands should be like. They are his twice over, by creation and redemption, but they must not presume.

12. Yahweh did, after all, make the earth and create the people on it. He repeats the argument about how his hands stretched out the heavens and how he placed myriads of stars on them (40:26-28). Yahweh knows what he is doing, and it was he who had called Cyrus to carry out a mission for him.

13. He had raised up Cyrus with a consistent, straightforward and right purpose. It was Cyrus who would bring about the rebuilding of Jerusalem, and he would do

so by liberating the exiles and restoring them to their own land. Cyrus would do this from an inward impulse given to him by Yahweh, and not with an ulterior motive. It is true that Yahweh would recompense him for what he did (43:3), but there was no question of this being an inducement.

Meditation: Called and successful – but responsive?

In his earliest references to Cyrus (41:2-4, 27) II Isaiah did not mention his name, though his hearers would have realised who he was talking about. He finally names him in 44:28. From there until 45:13 Cyrus takes centre stage. The ultimate scope of his mission is made clear. He would set the exiles free, providing them with the means to rebuild Jerusalem and lay the foundations of the new Temple. The far-reaching moral result of his generosity to Israel would be the universal conviction that Yahweh, the only God, is a saviour.

The term *anointed* which Yahweh applies to Cyrus (v 1) is *masiah*, the Hebrew word for someone who is anointed, and which we transliterate as *Messiah*. In the Old Testament it was used principally in referring to God's anointed kings (e.g. Saul in 1 Sam 24:6). Here the title simply designates Cyrus as one consecrated and set apart by Yahweh to be his agent and representative. From this we may infer that Cyrus was appointed and equipped by God for a supreme task, and that his more spectacular military victories would merely be the prelude to it.

When II Isaiah wrote this passage, Cyrus did not know Yahweh (v 4, 5). It is likely that he never got to know him. The action that was to be the climax of his career (the release of Israel from Babylonian captivity) would have been a very minor episode as far as he was concerned, for human valuations can be way off the mark (55:8). He did acknowledge Yahweh (Ezra 1:2-4), but then it was his custom to honour the deities of the nations he conquered, including those of Babylon. This is quite clear in his records, where he diplomatically attributes his victories to the gods of the people he conquered, including Marduk in Babylon. Cyrus could well have recognised the existence and influence of Yahweh (v 3b), but it was quite a different matter to know him personally. In the context of these chapters, to know Yahweh would have implied acknowledging that he was the only God (43:10, 11; 44:6, 8; 45:5, 6, 21, 22), and this is something that Cyrus, as a lifelong polytheistic idolater, would probably never have even considered.

We need not infer from this passage that Yahweh made a personal revelation of himself to the mind of Cyrus. Cyrus could (and should) have learnt that Yahweh had called him and enabled him to be a world conqueror (v 3). But like everyone else, it was up to him to work out that Yahweh was the only true God (v 6). God's use of him did not interfere with Cyrus's free will. This applies throughout the Bible. People may do certain actions with a malicious intent, but these actions are part of God's plan and purposes, and can be overruled by him so that good comes out of them. Two examples are the sale of Joseph into slavery (Gen 50:20) and the crucifixion of the Messiah (Acts 4:27-28).

Cyrus was only a temporary shepherd and anointed one whom God used for a very specific mission in order to further his divine and inscrutable purposes. It is the servant whom we met in 42:1-9, and whom we shall encounter again on three occasions, who would prove to be the much greater deliverer and saviour that the people of God and the nations of the world so desperately needed.

George Adam Smith summed it up pithily: "Cyrus is acknowledged as an elect servant of Yahweh. But neither in his closeness to God, nor in his effect upon the world, can Cyrus be compared for an instant to *the* servant".

LXXXV

45:14-25 The Nations come to God

In a magnificent passage these verses look beyond the restoration of Israel, to a time when Gentile nations would call on Yahweh and find their salvation in him.

14. The Gentiles mentioned here, Egyptians, Ethiopians and Sabaeans, had never been part of Israel's empire. In spite of this they would come over and meekly surrender themselves and their treasures to the people of Yahweh, pleading to be allowed to join in his worship. They would testify about the God of Israel, saying, "God is with you alone, and there is no other; there is no god besides him".

15. The people of Israel are astonished and declare that their God and saviour is truly "a God who hides himself". He had hidden himself from the Gentiles who found Yahweh altogether inscrutable, and his ways past finding out (Rom 11:33).

16. Any who persisted in shameful idolatry would be confounded. All those who manufactured idols would end up together in utter disgrace.

17. God's people, on the other hand, would be saved. Yahweh would rescue them for ever. Never would they be ashamed or confounded, "to all eternity".

18. Yahweh declares that, far from being inscrutable, he had revealed himself to everyone as the great divine creator of the heavens, and the one who formed and established the earth. He had proved his good will towards all people by the way in which he did not form the earth as a chaos (*tohu*), but instead made it with a clear purpose in mind, namely to be inhabited. It was Yahweh who did this, for no other god could have done it.

19. Yahweh had revealed himself to Israel more fully than to the Gentiles. He had shown himself to be understandable, clear and truthful. He had not spoken darkly, but had instead provided light to make the way plain for those who walked in the darkness. He had not declared himself cryptically, but perspicuously in order to be found. He had spoken the truth with complete uprightness, and there was no small print in his offer of salvation.

20. The survivors of the great judgement are asked to assemble themselves and draw close to Yahweh. They are not to be like those who do not have knowledge, who carry their wooden idols into battle and pray to gods who cannot save them. The very fact that they carry their idols means that idols are powerless, and it is a pointless exercise to pray to them for salvation.

21. Once again Yahweh issues a challenge, this time to these Gentile survivors, to present their side of the argument. Yahweh asks them who foretold the rise of Cyrus and his conquests. Was it not him? There is no other God apart from him. He is a God who is interested in what is right, and he is a saviour. Where else can a saviour like him be found? Nowhere, for there is none.

22. Yahweh tells the Gentile nations stretching to the ends of the earth to turn to him and be saved, for he alone is the true God, and there is no other.

23. Yahweh has sworn by his own name (for there is no greater name), and has declared rightly a word that would not return to him empty (55:10-11). It is that before him every knee would bow and by him every tongue would swear. This statement would be quoted in the New Testament, where it would be applied, not only to Yahweh (Rom 14:11), but equally to the Messiah (Phil 2:10-11).

24. Only through Yahweh can people emerge victorious from the world crisis. The Gentiles would say this. Only in him are righteousness and strength to be found. Those who previously reacted angrily to him will come to him in shame.

25. In Yahweh all the offspring of Israel, including the Gentiles who worship the God of Israel, will find victory. They will all glory in him.

Meditation: The God who hides himself

In 1996 a retired missionary called H.H. (Bert) Osborn wrote a book on Christian apologetics, in the style of C.S. Lewis, with arguably the most curious title ever given to a Christian book. He entitled it "God and the Antelope in the Bush". It is a clearly reasoned book and the present writer recommends it.

The book begins with an imaginary walk by two people in the bush country in Africa. One of them spots an antelope in front of a bush on the other side of a clearing. His companion cannot see it. It is perfectly camouflaged by the bush behind it, which is the same colour as its skin. The antelope is there all right, but the strange thing is that one person can see it and the other cannot. God is like that antelope, writes Bert Osborn. He hides himself. He camouflages himself. As a result, you can find two people talking about God: one is absolutely certain that he exists, and the other equally certain that he does not.

II Isaiah wrote, "Truly you are a God who hides himself, O God of Israel, the saviour" (v15). Assuming that this is so, it raises two important questions. First, *why* does God hide himself? Secondly, in what ways does God *reveal* himself?

To answer the first question we must first think about the particular way in which God created the members of the human race. It could have been very different. He could have created a race of robots who always unquestioningly obeyed him and did what was right. This would have resulted in a perfect world where everything was blissful, but existence would have been predictable and boring.

Instead God decided to create humans in his image, able to think for themselves, *having free will*. This was risky. At some stage these humans might choose to disobey him and go their own way. This is in fact what happened. The virus of selfishness infected people from the start, and the contagion spread to every man and woman. The cost in terms of human suffering was incalculable. Was it worth it? God must have reckoned that it was. It meant that in the end, after many adventures and misadventures, God would have what he had longed for from the start – some people who were *his* people out of choice, who followed him *willingly*, not because they were coerced. They had exercised their free will, and decided to follow and obey their creator. Somehow, this meant a lot to God.

In order to respect their free will, God hid himself. He had to. If he had always been visible, his presence would have been proof that he existed, and constituted an unsubtle reminder to people to obey him – or else. People would have carried out God's will unwillingly and the result would have been an embittered race of rebels kept in check by a strict schoolmasterly God. This would have been a most unhappy arrangement. That is why God elected to camouflage himself.

What about the second question, how does God reveal himself to people? The best answer can be found in Psalm 19. God reveals himself through his creation in the natural world (Ps 19:1-6), through the Bible (Ps 19:7-10) and through our consciences (Ps 19:11-14). Of these three, the second is the most important.

The wonders of the natural world intuitively suggest a creator (Rom 1:20), but they have nothing to say about God's grace and mercy for the penitent.

Our consciences are unstable and do not always work properly. At best, they may persuade us that we need a Saviour God to rescue us from our selfishness, but they cannot tell us what God is like or how to find him.

The scriptures are the primary means God has chosen to reveal himself. This idea takes some getting used to. Why did he choose a book, a collection of ancient writings, to make himself known to men and women? Partly because a book is an accessible object. Most people can read, and those who cannot can listen to a person who can. Partly because a book is a good place to hide in. It is not an obvious place to look for God. Of course, there have to be indications for seekers of where to look, and there are – but they are in the book itself, in the Bible.

This creates a circular argument. Those who know the one true God want to show other people how to find him. Where should they look? In the Bible. How do they know that this is the place to look for him? Because it says so – in the Bible. The inevitable circularity of this argument gives people who wish to avoid God a good excuse. They will not look at the Bible, because the argument for looking there is a circular one. This means that God has chosen his hiding place very well. He does not overwhelm people with the evidence for his existence, for that would be to violate their free will. The evidence pointing towards God is very strong, but it is neatly tucked away in a book, which people need not open.

"Truly, you are a God who hides himself, O God of Israel, the Saviour".

LXXXVI

46:1-13 The helpless Gods of Babylon

As the future events in Babylon begin to be foretold in greater detail, the gods of the city are now mentioned by name. *Bel* means Lord (like the Canaanite *Baal*) and was the alternative name given to *Marduk*, the chief Babylonian deity. *Bel's* son *Nebo* was the god of learning, an activity greatly valued in Babylon. The kings were named in honour of them, e.g. *Bel*shazzar and *Nebu*chadnezzar.

1. The idols would often be carried in processions, but here they are depicted as massive refugees, stooping as they are taken out of their temples. The plan was to take them out of Babylon during its overthrow by the Persians. They would have to be carried on oxen, and they were proving too heavy for the poor beasts.

2. The idols stooped once again on their way back into their temples. They were too heavy a burden to be saved. They would become captives of the Persians.

3. While an attempt was being made to *bear* these overweight idols away in shameful flight, Yahweh declares to Jacob and Israel, to Hyde as well as Jekyll, that he is the *bearer* of his people. He had *borne* them since before their birth.

4. Yahweh would continue to bear his people's burden, even to their old age, when their hair would turn silvery. Because he had made them, he would always bear them, and those he carried he would also save. What a contrast to the idols: they could they not save their devotees. In fact, they were such a burden that they could not even themselves be saved.

5. Yahweh again asks to whom he is being compared. Is he, the God who bears his own people, like the false gods, too heavy to be borne by their devotees?

6. Not only were the false gods a heavy burden to carry, they were also a burden to those who worshipped them in terms of their cost. Those who commissioned them had to take a lavish quantity of gold and silver to a goldsmith, who would create the image of a god. Then people would fall before it and worship it.

7. They would then bear the idol to its appointed place, from which it was unable to move. How pointless it was to cry for help to an image made of precious metal! No reply would be forthcoming. Idols cannot save.

8. Once again we have the theme of prediction as the proof that Yahweh alone is God. The people were rebellious at the idea of a heathen liberator, so Yahweh urged them to think about how he had carried them, and to bear this in mind.

9. They were to remember how Yahweh had dealt with them throughout history. This would demonstrate that he alone was God; no other god was like him.

10. Yahweh could declare the outcome of historical events right at their very beginning. Long before they happened, he had predicted future events. They were certain to take place, so as to further his purposes and fulfil his intentions.

11. An example, being fulfilled as they waited, was the calling of Cyrus to set them free from their captivity. Cyrus was a predator ("a bird of prey") but also predestined ("the man for my purpose"). Yahweh had spoken this, and he would bring it to pass. He had planned it, and he would fulfil it. Yahweh was sovereign.

12. Yahweh urged his stubborn people to listen. They were far from being what they ought to have been. The word "righteousness" is here rendered *deliverance*. It means what is right or is "as it should be". It includes the ideas of uprightness, justice and putting right what is wrong. In these chapters it is sometimes the latter sense that predominates (as in v 13), but here (v 12) it would have been better rendered as *being righteous*.

13. God would bring near his deliverance and hasten his salvation. It would be seen in Jerusalem itself when Israel, who was Yahweh's glory, returned there.

Meditation: The Carriers and the Carried

In this passage II Isaiah reiterated several truths that he had already expounded, but he also outlined a new insight which was relevant then and is relevant now. It applied to people in ancient times, who made idols and worshipped them. It applies now to God's people, when they are more concerned about keeping up the forms of their faith than about allowing God to sustain them. It makes all the difference to a believer how he thinks of his faith: is it something *he has to carry*, or is it something *that will carry him*?

This arises from the description of the idols (v1-2, 5-7) in this passage. Because they were made of metal, they were immensely heavy. It was impossible to carry them away from Babylon; they had to remain in their temples. They had also cost a fortune to produce. In every way they had proved to be a very heavy burden. What a contrast to Yahweh! With him it was, it had to be, the other way round: not a matter of his people carrying *him*, but of *him* carrying his people.

John Skinner commented that "The profound insight into the nature of true religion which is characteristic of this prophet is nowhere more clearly exhibited than in this striking and original contrast". His words to the Babylonian exiles speak to us with great tenderness, just as they spoke to them: "Listen to me, O house of Jacob, all the remnant of the house of Israel, who have been borne by me from your birth, carried from the womb; even to your old age I am he, even when you turn grey I will carry you. I have made, and I will bear; I will carry and will save" (v 3-4). We will be *his* burden throughout our lives.

How does God carry us? The answer is, he gives us a steady moral ground on which to base our thoughts, words and actions. He has taught us his moral truths in the Bible, and while we walk on them we are on safe ground and will not be moved. The trouble arises because the church in the 21ˢᵗ century, under attack from certain pressure groups, has given way on some of the grounds of morality. Some actions, previously considered wrong by believers, are considered wrong no longer. As a result, some believers have had the firm ground taken away from under their feet. Other believers have been taught, in church, that they should no longer take the morality of the Bible as binding. Any believers in such a position will be able to find solid ground only in scripture, and when they treat it again as the word of God they will be borne aloft once more.

Even when the ground is rocky we are liable, in our selfishness and waywardness, to wander away from its stability. When we sin, our conscience is aroused and we cease to experience that undefinable sense of God's presence with us which turns our routine existence into the life that is truly life. Any believers in this position may return to God, repenting of their sin and confessing it, and they will then find something wonderful. God has *borne away* those sins! As we shall soon discover, it is the servant of Yahweh who "has *borne* our infirmities" (53:4). As Yahweh himself puts it, "The righteous one, my servant, shall make many righteous, and he shall *bear* their iniquities" (53:11). It is the same verb as is used in 46:3-4 when Yahweh says that he *bears* and carries his people.

The God who bears us when we have fallen into sin is also the God who will carry us in seasons of fierce temptation. It is not uncommon for experienced believers to be sorely tempted and to try and resist temptation on their own. This can be a huge burden to bear, especially when they give way, perhaps saying, "God will forgive me, he is merciful". Everything then begins to go wrong, and the burden of their sin becomes intolerable. Why? Simply because "this is the will of God, your sanctification" (1 Thess 4:3). Even then, when we stray into the path that leads to destruction, we shall find him saying to us, "The eternal God is your refuge, and underneath are the everlasting arms. He will drive out your enemy before you, saying, destroy him!" (Deut 33:27, New International Version). God keeps bearing us at those times when we are discouraged and stop walking alongside him. He will puzzle out how to bring us back to himself.

Ever since the exodus from Egypt, God has been carrying his people (Ex 19:4 Deut 1:31, Hos 11:3-4). He promised to carry the exiles in Babylon back to Zion (40:11). He would do so by giving them solid ground to walk on, by bearing away their sins, and by holding on to them even when they strayed from him. What folly it is to try and carry the burden of our faith ourselves. If we do this, we shall be like those foolish idolaters. If we do this, we may become a heavy burden for our pastors whose job it is to look after us (Num 11:11-15). It is best to allow God to bear our burdens of faith. He is able to carry the heaviest loads.

LXXXVII

47:1-15 The inevitable Doom of Babylon

This is another taunt-song against Babylon (like 14:3-21). The city is doomed. No mercy will be shown to her, for she herself was merciless (v 6, Jas 2:13). The description is not pitiless. This is not only about the triumph of justice, but also about the tragedy of the unredeemed sinner.

1. Dust and toil, nakedness and shame, silence and darkness (v 1-5) all symbolise the final condemnation of Babylon, personalised as a young royal princess. She is told to sit, no longer on a throne but on the dusty ground. She would no longer receive the treatment of someone who was so tender and delicate that "she does not venture to set the sole of her foot on the ground" (Deut 28:56).

2. The luxurious lady would be forced to perform the duties of the lowliest slave in her household, and grind meal in order to make bread. She would have to take off her veil and her robe, and endure great humiliations.

3. Her body, previously her private possession, would be exposed to public view. Yahweh would repay those who had similarly humiliated his people on their way to Babylon. None of the oppressors would be spared from this retribution.

4. The fall of Babylon would be for the sake of the exiled Jews. It had been decreed by their redeemer God, Yahweh of the armies, the Holy One of Israel.

5. Babylon, capital of a great Empire, had taken for granted her prerogative of wielding imperial power. Now she must sit in the silence of judgement and enter into the darkness of doom. She would no longer be the mistress of kingdoms.

6. Yahweh had been angry with the people of Judah and Jerusalem, and had given them over to Babylon for chastisement. But Babylon had shown them no mercy. Her men had laid on all the Jews, even on the frail and elderly, an exceedingly heavy yoke. These men were now charged with having been pitiless and inhuman.

7. The explanation of their cruelty lay in their enormous pride. They thought that their supremacy would be everlasting. They never considered that there would be a day of reckoning, nor that their evil actions would meet with retribution. The philosophy of Nazi Germany was remarkably similar. There is also evidence that many of the leading Nazis, like the Babylonians, relied on occult advice. "Earth's proud empires pass away", as John Ellerton wrote in his hymn.

8. The punishment of the Babylonians would be made all the more bitter by their memory of the self-indulgent luxury that they had enjoyed in the past, and which was now gone forever. They had sat securely because of their scholarship and wisdom. The envy of other nations, this had silenced their consciences. Worst of all, in their heart of hearts they had said, "I am, and there is no one besides me", thus usurping God's autonomy (45:5, 6, 21, 22). They had been complacent, thinking that they would always be well provided for, and their future was secure.

9. Two great misfortunes would be heaped upon them on God's appointed day, loss of fortune and of security. They would suffer them "in full measure". Their sorceries and powerful charms would prove useless in warding off their just retribution. II Isaiah regarded their spells as having "great power". There are serious warnings in scripture about such practices (Deut 18:10-12).

10. In spite of their wickedness they had sat securely because they thought no one could see them. They were wrong, because Yahweh saw everything. What led them astray was their wisdom and knowledge, which from the context may refer to their knowledge of occult practices like sorcery and enchantments. They ended up by saying in their heart, "I am, and there is no one besides me". They thought they were the captains of their fate and the masters of their soul.

11. Evil would visit them, resisting their charms. Disasters would befall them, which they could not ward off. Ruin would come on them suddenly, out of the blue. It would constitute a horrible surprise to these wealthy Babylonians.

12. They had placed their trust in their many enchantments and sorceries. They would now prove useless. They thought occult practices would lead them to success and also inspire terror in their enemies. The historical records of Babylon confirm the profusion of magical rites in use there (v 9-12, see also Ezek 21:21).

13. Not only did the Babylonians use charms and sorceries, they also consulted astrologers. These people studied the heavens and predicted events on earth from the motion of the moon and stars. Such vague notions wearied the Babylonians and kept them from knowing the true God. There would be no salvation for them from astrologers. They saw the stars but were too weary to see what was coming.

14. With regard to the coming fire of judgement, the astrologers would be like stubble. Unable to deliver themselves, they would be consumed by it. That would be an unwelcoming fire; one would not come to it in order to warm oneself!

15. Their old associates, the merchants from other nations, would vanish into the undergrowth, like "fair-weather friends". No one would be left who could help them. Nobody would save them from the judgement.

Meditation: Babylon – great but evil

The Old Testament does not have anything good to say about Babylon. It does not have a single word of praise about its famous hanging gardens, which were one of the Seven Wonders of the World. It does not mention its culture or its commerce. It says nothing about the strength of its walls that were 80 feet wide and 320 feet tall, or of its 250 defensive towers, which made the city itself absolutely impregnable. But neither earthly glory nor culture, neither wealth nor raw power make for happy living. Poison was at work in Babylon's heart.

For all her glory, Babylon was a kingdom divided against itself, which would not stand. Many of her people were, to all intents and purposes, slaves. They had contributed to her rebuilding and they hated their rulers. Her traders, who brought her great fortunes, stayed with her only as long as she was profitable to them (v15). Her priests were at odds with her rulers. Above all, her religion was a burden, not an inspiration. In spite of all this she felt secure, and she was very proud.

Babylon's pride showed itself in the inhuman exploitation of her captives (v6), in her disregard of moral values (v7), in the way she dismissed the possibility of retribution (v10), in her assumption that she was immune to misfortune and had a natural right to the good things in life (v8), and in the way she used religion to manipulate other people (v9, 12). Babylon's pride, coupled with her idolatrous godlessness, put her under a special curse.

The religion of Yahweh was unique in those days for its absolute intolerance of all auguries, divinations, charms and sorceries. They marred the moral sensitivity of their devotees. The randomness of fate stifled their faith in a benevolent providence, and the regular consulting of horoscopes made them weary (v13).

II Isaiah saw no virtue in Babylon, but there is pity and pathos in his presentation of the princess reduced to servanthood (v1-3), and in the way in which he speaks of the futility of Babylonian science (v8-13). Perhaps there was a corresponding pity in the heart of God. In spite of Babylon's impregnability, Cyrus took the city effortlessly in one night, and by morning every citizen of the empire had become a Persian. Painful reprisals would have been meted out on the Babylonian leaders and their pampered ladies, but on the whole the old order disappeared without needless bloodshed under the just but merciful hand of God.

By diverting the city's main water supply into a nearby reservoir, the Persian troops entered the city through a low-lying canal. The king was having a party. The Babylonian soldiers were on duty up in the walls and did not notice anything untoward until it was too late. The city lived on under new management, but it gradually fell into irreparable decay. Its ruins are now dust and stones, but Babylon is not dead. Her pride lives on. So does her godlessness. So does her inhumanity to her fellow human beings. She thought it her right to perpetrate outrages. She said, "I am, and there is no one besides me". In spite (or is it because?) of her many false gods, she was a godless city. Her godless pride lives on after her fall and will only be eradicated when the Messiah returns in glory to put an end to the old order.

John the Seer spoke of Babylon, probably referring to Rome, but he calls the evil city Babylon. It represents the evil attitudes prevalent in Babylon towards the end of its "great" period. These evils are still prevalent in today's world and we are urged to avoid them (Rev 17 and 18). The eventual downfall of evil is celebrated in song (Rev 19:1-8 and Handel's Hallelujah Chorus).

To be hard on those who are down is Babylonian. To use the weaknesses of others as fuel for our pride or gossip is Babylonian. To think we are all right because of our wealth or our gifts is Babylonian. It is dangerous enough to say, "I am", and utterly perverse to go on,

"And there is no one besides me". We may wish to heed the voice from heaven that says, "do not take part in her sins", and so avoid having to "share in her plagues" (Rev 18:4).

LXXXVIII

48:1-22 God's Love for the Unlovely

In this chapter various themes which have already been dealt with, in some cases more than once, make their final appearance. Among them are a reference to the victories of Cyrus, a prediction of the fall of Babylon, an appeal to prophecy, a mention of "former things" and "new things", and the appellation of Israel as the servant of Yahweh. These themes, together with the scorning of idols and the stress on Yahweh being the only God, will now disappear from II Isaiah's radar.

1. Yahweh calls for the attention of certain Israelites, all from the tribe of Judah. They profess allegiance to him, but it is shallow. They invoke their God, but in a formal and insincere way. There is no reality in their prayer.

2. They call themselves the people of "the holy city" Jerusalem. They depend on Yahweh, their God, but it is only a show.

3. Yahweh had in the past declared the "former things", such as the exodus from Egypt, well in advance. Then he suddenly "did" these things, and they happened.

4. This was because he knew they were obstinate, stiff-necked and hard-headed.

5. We now learn that several of the Jewish exiles had taken to idol-worship in Babylon. Their talk was pious enough (v 1, 2), but their hearts were focused on their idols. They were hardened hypocrites (v 4, 8). The argument from prophecy, meant for the heathen, is now directed at them. Yahweh had spoken about Cyrus in advance, so that they would be unable to credit the predictions to the idols.

6. They had heard Yahweh and could bear witness to his reliability. Now he would declare new things, previously hidden and which they had not known.

7. They were not old news, but new, in the very process of gestation. They had not heard these things before. They could not say that they already knew them.

8. They had not heard Yahweh's word in the past. Their ears were tightly shut. They did not want to know. Yahweh knew that they were treacherous people, rebellious against him from their birth.

9. Yahweh was angry, but his decision was to defer his anger. He did so for the sake of his *name*, so that people might know that he is a gracious God. He would show restraint, and would not cut them off. God's patience with his rebellious people was amazing: it was undeserved (v 9), constructive (v 10) and resolute (v 11).

10. He had begun to refine them in the furnace of adversity, but they were not yet as pure as refined silver.

11. He had resolved to keep persevering with them for the sake of his *name*.

12. Having outspokenly exposed the idolatry of his own people, Yahweh now reaffirmed his call. He it was who had called them. He is the first and the last.

13. With his hand he had laid out the foundation of the earth as we would lay out a map. With his hand he had also spread out the heavens. When he summoned the stars, they stood at attention.

14. Yahweh asked the Israelites to gather and listen. Nobody else had said what he was about to say. Yahweh chose Cyrus. It was he who would fulfil Yahweh's will concerning Babylon and be strong in his opposition to the Babylonians.

15. Yahweh had called Cyrus to do this. He had brought him over and would prosper him in his attack on Babylon.

16. Yahweh told the Israelites that he had not spoken in secret. He had always been there, interpreting and guiding the course of history. But who spoke the last line of this verse, "And now the Lord Yahweh has sent me and his Spirit"? It could not be Yahweh, for Yahweh had sent him. It must be his servant whom we first met in 42:1-9. We are about to study the second of the four "servant songs", but here the servant of Yahweh makes a brief cameo appearance. Yahweh would send him (42:6), and the Spirit of God would be upon him (42:1).

17. In verses 17-19 we have a plea from Yahweh that is full of unusual pathos and depth of feeling. He is their Redeemer, the Holy One of Israel, and their God. He teaches them for their own good, and leads them in the right way.

18. If only they had paid attention to his commandments! If only they had listened! On many occasions they had been entreated to hear or listen, four times in this chapter alone (v1, 12, 14 and 16). They did occasionally hear, but did they ever *listen*? Notice how "You have heard" (v6) is quickly followed by "You have never heard" (v8). If only they had truly listened, they would have prospered like a proper river instead of drying up like a *wadi*. They would have persevered without ceasing, like the waves of the sea.

19. Their children would have been as numerous as the grains of sand, and their descendants even more so. Their name would never have been cut off.

20. The command to go forth from Babylon is liberating, but it would need to be echoed later (49:9, 52:11, 55:12, 62:10), for many of the exiles would be reluctant to undertake the long journey back. II Isaiah puts a song of praise for this great redemption in the mouth of the exiles, to be heard to the ends of the earth.

21. The miracles of the exodus would be repeated on the trip back to their homeland. Yahweh would provide a steady supply of water in the desert.

22. For those who refused to listen, the price of self-will would be loss of peace and ill-health of soul. The sad realism of this verse will reappear (57:21), and the book of Isaiah will come to a humbling end on a similar note (66:24).

Meditation: When God captures your Imagination

What sort of man was II Isaiah? Because his writings were added to the book of Isaiah of Jerusalem, he was probably a member of "the school of Isaiah" (8:16) and thus acquainted with Isaiah's writings, "the book of Yahweh" (34:16). He adopted a few of his teacher's literary traits, the most significant of which was the appellation of God as "the Holy One of Israel". But their styles were different. The master's was forceful and concise; the pupil's profuse and flowing, with amplifications and repetitions. The pupil was influenced by his master in a number of small ways, but even so he was his own man.

There are no autobiographical glimpses of II Isaiah in the chapters he wrote (40-55), and he did not use the first person singular pronoun to refer to himself. If we wish to find out more about him, we shall be reduced to searching through his oracles for some clues about his personality and background.

II Isaiah was capable of a wide variety of emotions. Tenderness and awe come together in chapter 40, and the conflict between Yahweh's love of his people and his holy anger with them on account of their sins is a motif that recurs on several occasions. In the passage we are studying, II Isaiah's description of Yahweh's sadness in verses 17-19 is deeply moving. "Oh that [they] had paid attention to [his] commandments!" (v18). But the people of God ignored God's benevolent wishes, and so failed to receive many wonderful divine blessings.

The favourite themes of II Isaiah were: (a) God's majesty and greatness, (b) Salvation both in terms of the liberation of the exiles by Cyrus and their inward spiritual transformation by Yahweh and his servant, (c) Forecasting the future as a criterion for distinguishing the true God, and (d) The plain statement that Yahweh was the only God in contrast to the utter futility of the idols.

Yahweh himself was at the heart of everything that II Isaiah wanted to say. It was by thinking about God that his imagination was fired and his quill was activated. II Isaiah's greatest flights of eloquence took place as he took off and soared to some lofty vision of Yahweh's glory in creation or history. God's sovereignty seems to have been his principal and governing truth. At the same time, II Isaiah often depicted God as being clothed with human passion and agony. He likened God to a man both physically and emotionally.

His greatest prophetic achievements were the four "servant songs". The insight into human nature that he displayed in his portrayals of someone who would be perfect man were amazing. Many authors have tried to describe human perfection in words, but only II Isaiah and the four gospel writers have succeeded. II Isaiah's description is a perfect prophecy and summary of the life, ministry, death and resurrection of the Messiah in the four gospels. What might the sources of his inspiration have been? We will leave aside the influence of divine inspiration, and concentrate on the prophet's possible strengths and weaknesses.

II Isaiah must have struggled in his own life to attain certain standards of morality and godliness. Somehow he knew that what counts is a combination of unusual qualities, like a strong sense of social justice, a humble low-key approach, gentle dealings with those who are hurting, and being a persevering teacher (42:1-4).

He must have been aware of the value of reading and studying the word of God in the Prophets and other early Old Testament writings, and he may have become a student of God's word early in life. The words that are spoken reflect the inner heart of the speaker, and for one's mouth to be like a sharp sword, much prayerful study of scripture is needed. The fruit borne by this discipline will in any case seem scanty in comparison with the expenditure of time it takes, and yet it will be worthwhile if it is done *soli Deo Gloria* (49:1-4).

Another thing II Isaiah would have cultivated is the gift of speaking in an encouraging way. His daily study of scripture would have enabled him to sustain with a word those who were weary. He would have learnt to hear God prompting him to speak to this person, but not that one. Even so, the reaction to his words would sometimes be discouraging, and occasionally even violent. He had learnt to trust in Yahweh regardless during such times, and Yahweh would of course see him through them (50:4-9).

At times II Isaiah would have failed his God. He would have gone through the bitterness of sinning, wandering away from God, realising the gravity of what he had done, repenting and returning to God, being forgiven and restored, and recapturing that elusive but invaluable sense of God's presence with him. And he would have wondered how God could forgive and accept an unreliable man such as himself to be his mouthpiece. The answer to this question probably came to him in an instant, out of the blue. There would be a man – the Messiah (whom II Isaiah called *the servant of Yahweh*) – who, like II Isaiah, would be sensitive and responsive to the needs of others and who would respond gently and humbly to those needs. He would, like II Isaiah but to a greater degree, allow the scriptures to mould his view of God and people, and would walk humbly with his God, depending on him for guidance in his everyday life. Unlike II Isaiah and every other person who has ever lived, he would live a sinless life, always pleasing God by his actions, his words and his thoughts. Because of this he would be "despised and rejected by others, a man of suffering and acquainted with infirmity" (53:3). And the purpose of his life would be to die for the sins of others (53:5), for Yahweh would lay on his innocent person the iniquity of them all (53:6). He would be stricken for the transgression of his people (53:8). His life would be a sin-offering (53:10). He would bear the sin of many (53:12). *That* was why Yahweh could forgive and use II Isaiah. *That* was why Yahweh kept persevering with his people in spite of their extreme rebelliousness. *That* was why Yahweh's eternal purpose was to perfect for himself a people who would love and obey him from the heart.

LXXXIX

49:1-13 The second Servant Song

1. The servant now steps out of the shadows and speaks. In this part of the book of Isaiah, the speaker of the discourses in the first person singular is always either Yahweh or the servant of Yahweh. By implication the servant is being closely identified with Yahweh, and this anticipates the Messiah's close identification of himself with God the Father (Jn 10:30). In this second "servant song", the servant addresses the *coastlands* or faraway nations of the world, and urges them to listen. Together with Israel, the Gentiles will feature in the servant's mission (v 6, 7). He declares that Yahweh called him while he was still in his mother's womb (Jer 1:4-5, Lk 1:42). He also received his name before he was born. In fact he would receive two names while in his mother's womb: one would be *Son of God* (Lk 1:35) and the other *Yeshua*, which is transliterated as *Jesus* (Mt 1:21) and means *Saviour* or *God is my Saviour*.

2. The servant says that Yahweh has made his mouth like a sharp sword. There were various types of sword in antiquity: some were short-bladed like a dagger, with the blade in the shape of a tongue. The words of the servant would be life-giving and incisive, sharper than any sword, cutting away at the selfish character of his hearers and discerning their innermost thoughts and intentions (Heb 4:12). The servant himself was like a polished arrow, which could not fail to fly straight to the bull's eye in the target. It is interesting that both the sword and the arrow are said to be *concealed*. The sword is hidden in the shadow of Yahweh's hand, and the arrow in Yahweh's quiver. The servant's preparation was unseen.

3. There is a paradox. Israel (v 3) is sent to Israel (v 5). No Old Testament prophet, priest or king was great enough to bear the name of *all* of God's people. It is only the Messiah, who is outlined in this passage and who would be the central figure in the New Testament, who is worthy to be known as *Israel*. He would be the fulfilment of everything that Israel always longed for, and could never reach, the incarnation of all that Israel should have been, but never was. He would glorify God. The radiant holiness and ardent love of God would be seen as the Messiah made him known to people (Jn 1:18).

4. The servant would face strong opposition (v 7), and this would tempt him, as it tempts all people, to discouragement. He would wonder whether his lengthy preparation had been in vain and his work fruitless, yet he would not yield. He knew that his cause was Yahweh's cause, and that his God would reward him. By looking to God he overcame the temptation (Heb 2:18).

5. Yahweh himself is about to speak (in v 6). He formed his servant in his mother's womb. And now the two "servants" of chapter 42 (42:1, 19) are brought together.

One of the bearers of the name *Israel* (v 3) is entrusted with bringing the other, the nation of Israel, back to God.

6. Yahweh tells *the* servant that the salvation of Israel would be too easy a task for him. Yahweh's greater purpose for him was that he should make salvation available to the ends of the earth (42:1, 4; Lk 2:32; Acts 13:47). Perhaps the difficulty of the task he undertook, to reach *all* the nations, explains the extent of his preparation: thirty years, for three years of ministry. God is patient. When he calls someone to do a task for him, he prepares that person very thoroughly.

7. Yahweh, the Redeemer and Holy One, now encourages his servant, who is "one deeply abhorred by the nations". This note of rejection and suffering (see also v 4) will begin to recur in further descriptions of the servant. Here we learn that he would be "deeply despised" and "the slave of rulers", and so it proved. The Messiah would be handed over to the political authorities of his time and treated unjustly. But among the Gentiles, there would be kings who would stand before the servant-Messiah, and princes who would bow down before him. He would receive worldwide glory, which was his rightful due.

8. Again Yahweh addresses himself to his servant. At a certain moment Yahweh would intervene and he would both answer and help him. He would "keep" him from death's grip (Acts 2:24-28). The first part of this verse was quoted in the New Testament as fulfilled after the death and resurrection of the Messiah (2 Cor 6:2). The servant would also be a *covenant* to the people, for he would be the means by which the people would enter into a new covenant with Yahweh (42:6).

9. Verses 9-12 might have an immediate application to the Israelite captives as they returned to Jerusalem, but the sheer wonder of the promises points to a spiritual fulfilment rather than a physical one. Physical exile, Babylonian captivity, restoration and return to the Promised Land are all "types" of the stages that God's people will go through when the servant delivers them. Cyrus was a deliverer on a physical level, but the servant would be a deliverer of another kind, on a different level. Captives are urged to emerge from the darkness. There would be a process whereby they would be fed like a flock of sheep in their pasture.

10. They would not suffer hunger or thirst. Extreme conditions would not crush them. God's restoring work is beautifully described: "He who has pity on them will lead them, and by springs of water will guide them".

11. Their paths would be levelled, so that they would not involve so many tiring "ups" and perilous "downs".

12. People from distant lands would join God's people. Syene is Aswan on the Nile, where a Jewish colony already existed in II Isaiah's time.

13. Heaven and earth are to sing for joy. Yahweh has comforted his own people, and he will have compassion on his suffering ones.

Meditation: Aspects of Servanthood

It would take Yahweh *thirty years* to prepare his servant for his life's work. We are an impatient generation. We find it hard to do the easiest thing, which is to wait for God. The church is impatient and looks for quick results. When he was twelve years old the Messiah may have been itching to begin his ministry (Lk 2:49), but it was Yahweh's will that he should wait eighteen more years, like a sharp sword hidden in the shadow of his hand (v 2). In his spare time, he studied the scriptures and spent time waiting for God.

The servant was also like an arrow, hidden in Yahweh's quiver (v 2). How did Yahweh polish this arrow? In the same way that he polishes his arrows today. He used the rough sandpaper of irritating tempers and vexing circumstances, and the small-grain sandpaper of small annoyances and the fretting of daily life.

The result was that the servant's mouth was like a sharp sword and his speech like a polished arrow. This is a picture of his inner life of communion with God, which was kept hidden from other people. The servant would later constantly depend on God for guidance and wisdom in his ministry. His manner would be humble and gentle, as we read in the first servant song. But there would be moments when God would wield his sword and fire his arrow in order to defeat evil and release desperately needy people from bondage.

It would never be easy for the servant. He would often wonder if the work he did was worth all the preparation and effort (v 4). At what stages in his ministry would the servant have experienced such despondency? Alec Motyer wrote, "There are moments in the gospels where Jesus faced ill-minded rejection, blind unbelief, prejudice and misunderstanding; when people and disciples were caught up in the glamour of signs and wonders, and the primary task of preaching was threatened (Mk 1:37-38); when he cried, 'How long!' (Lk 9:41); when he could only sigh over continuing failure to understand (Mk 8:21); and when he foresaw the falling away of the inner group (Mk 14:27)". In spite of this, however, however disappointing the results were, however frightening the threats, however hostile the circumstances, the servant did not lose heart. He persevered as though he was seeing him who is invisible (Heb 11:27). His cause was with God, his recompense in God's hands.

In the end, the servant who was "deeply despised and abhorred among the nations" would be acknowledged by many, even among the mighty of this world (v 7). One example of the many kings and princes who would acknowledge the servant was Napoleon. During his period of quiet and meditation at the end of his tumultuous career, he wrote movingly in his *Memorial* from St Helena that the glory of the Messiah would surpass his own. "Everything in Christ astonishes me. His spirit overawes me, his will confounds me. Between him and anyone else in the world, there is no possible manner of comparison. The nearer I approach, the more carefully I examine, everything is above me – everything remains grand, of a grandeur that overpowers".

The "servant Israel" (v 3) was the representative of the nation Israel (v 5), and stood for all that was good in the people of God. The contracting of the nation Israel to a single person, the servant Israel, is not unlike the idea of the remnant in the earlier chapters of Isaiah, which contracted from the godly portion of Israel and Judah to one person, the Branch, who was also the royal Messiah.

Henri Blocher quotes a 19th century German scholar called Franz Delitzsch, who wrote, "As the history of salvation proceeded, the scope of God's redemptive dealings with man seemed to grow narrower and narrower. God started, as it were, with the whole human race, first at the time of Adam, and then again after the flood. Then one line of the human race was chosen: God made his covenant with Abraham and his descendants. But he did not make it with all of Abraham's descendants: only Isaac and his line were chosen – Isaac, not Ishmael. Even among Isaac's children, only one – Jacob, not Esau – was chosen. And then, getting narrower, the prophets made it clear that not all those who descend from Israel (i.e. Jacob) are truly Israel. Only a remnant will inherit the promise.

But where is this remnant when we look for it? When God looks for a man to intervene and establish justice in the land he finds none (Isa 59:16, Ezek 22:30). Ultimately only one person remains after the sifting process, only one is truly Israel, in whom God is glorified. And this man said so. He said quite clearly, 'I am the true Israel'. He used the Old Testament's most common symbol for Israel, the vine: 'I am the true vine' (Jn 15:1-5; see also Ps 80:8-16, Isa 5:1-7, Jer 2:21 and 6:9, Hos 10:1). In him the pyramid reached its vertex.

The lines, however, did not stop there. Starting from Christ, there is a symmetrical broadening. In him, the true Israel, the true vine, are the branches that feed on his life and are purified by him. Those who find salvation in him inherit the promise which belongs to the true remnant. To them also, in a secondary sense, the name Israel truly belongs (Rom 9:6-8, Gal 3:6-9 and 6:15-16, Phil 3:3). All the Gentiles who have faith in Christ are incorporated into this community. So this new Israel, the Israel of God, is a new humanity, spreading over the whole earth. The second servant song states that the servant is 'a light to the nations, that my salvation may reach to the end of the earth'. What a perfect symmetry in God's plan!"

LXXXX

49:14-50:3 God comforts Zion and her People

The poetry of this passage is celebrated for its beauty and is profoundly moving. Zion is the personification of her former inhabitants, and is bereaved and barren. But Yahweh has not forgotten her, and a wonderful surprise lies in store (v 21).

14. Yahweh has just said that he "will have compassion on his suffering ones", but Zion, who represents all the exiles, says that Yahweh has abandoned her.

15. She is not really abandoned, because Yahweh cannot forget her. Mothers do not forget their suckling infants, they cannot stop loving them. Yet even a *mother's* pity might conceivably fail – but Yahweh *cannot* forget his people.

16. Yahweh has a picture of Jerusalem inscribed on the palms of his hands. He looks at his hands and sees the walls, which will need rebuilding. This is one of the boldest anthropomorphisms in the Bible.

17. Yahweh comforts Zion by saying that her future builders will outnumber their past destroyers, and the latter are now far away from her.

18. Zion should take a good look: her people are about to return! Yahweh swears by himself (as in 45:23) that, like a bride, she will wear them like an ornament.

19. After decades of being a ruin, Jerusalem now has her best days before her, for her new family will overflow her boundaries, and her enemies would be far away.

20. The newcomers would complain that the city was overcrowded, and put in a request for more room for living.

21. Zion will ask how it could be that she was once again the mother of many children. Her previous children were exiled and she was bereaved and left all alone. The promises of Zion's repopulation are repeated by II Isaiah (54:1), and taken up in the New Testament where they are applied to the city of Jerusalem that is above, to the universal church in heaven and earth (Gal 4:25-27).

22. Yahweh says that he will give his signal to the nations, who will then bring Zion's children back to her in the large pocket in the front of their garments, where little children used to be carried.

23. The Gentile leaders are described as bowing down to Zion's children in abject surrender (45:14). II Isaiah uses an extravagant but very Oriental metaphor for self-humiliation. Its significance here is then spelt out. The restoration of God's people will be a sign to them from Yahweh that those who waited for him would not face disgrace. Again, the importance of simply *waiting for God* is implied.

24. A question is asked as to whether a predator can be forced to disgorge its prey, or a tyrant to release his captives.

25. Yahweh's answer is yes. The promise he makes is remarkable: "I will contend with those who contend with you". Yahweh would save his children.

26. The enemies of Zion would engage in internecine warfare and consume one another. The images used are brutal. The outcome of this would be that everyone, Jew and Gentile, would know that Yahweh was the saviour and redeemer of his people, and would show his might on their behalf.

50:1. At this point another question is asked. Has the covenant between Yahweh and his people been broken beyond any possibility of renewal? If so, there would be a bill of divorce making the separation absolute and final. Had Yahweh sold his children into slavery? If so, there would be a contract of sale. Neither of these documents existed. The true explanation of the slavery of the children and the divorce of mother Zion was the fact that the children had sinned.

2. Yahweh expresses his surprise at the very lukewarm response to his offer of restoration. At first nobody seemed to be interested. Yahweh asks if his power to save is in doubt. He is able to dry up a sea by rebuking it. He can dry up rivers, leaving the fish to die. He did so during the exodus from Egypt.

3. He can bring darkness over the land. He also did this during the exodus.

Meditation: Has God given up on his People?

There was a huge amount of pain felt and expressed among the exiles. Why had Yahweh given them up to the Babylonians? Why were his people in exile? Had Yahweh abandoned his people altogether?

The truth was that God was like a mother towards them, incapable of forgetting her suckling children (v15). He loved them so very much that he had made an engraving of them in his hands (v16). He wanted Zion to be like a bride, decking himself with them (v18). He wanted them to be happily settled, if a bit cosy and overcrowded, with Zion as their mother (v19-21). This passage has been of help to the people of God down the ages when things have not gone well and they are in distress. They may then ask three questions, which are answered here.

Question 1. Does God remember them in their pain? When the years go by and hope fades, has he not indeed forgotten them? II Isaiah answers this twice over. In the first place, God is like a mother suckling her child at the breast. Can she forget her child? Surely not, though in some appalling and extreme cases, it might be possible – but Yahweh cannot forget his people. He says, "I will not forget you" (v14-15). Secondly, God has inscribed them on the palms of his hands. The verb inscribed is sometimes described as "tattooed", but neither of these carries the force of the original Hebrew. "I have engraved you on the palms of my hands" is more like it (v16). The engraving on the hands is made using a sharp piece of metal, such as a burin, or a flint tool with a chisel point, or a rusty nine-inch long Roman nail.

Question 2. Even if God does remember his people, what hope do they have? They were in the grip of terrible circumstances. "Can the prey be taken from the mighty, or the captives of a tyrant be rescued?" (v24). The answer is "Yes, definitely" (v25). II Isaiah gives two reasons. In the first place Yahweh, being God, is stronger than the mighty and the tyrants. He will contend with those who contended with his people (v25). Secondly, the oppressors of God's people are a house divided against itself, and in due course they will attack each other (v26). In any case, the reality is that those who choose their own way will in the end destroy themselves if they do not destroy each other. It is part of the justice with which God rules the world that this must be so (Mt 7:13-14, 1Jn 5:11-12).

Question 3. Has God given up on them altogether? Year after year of hardship goes by, and there is no hope. This is what it was like for the Jewish exiles in Babylon. What does God have against them? The relationship between God and man is like a marriage, but it seems as if God has divorced them. The relationship is like that between a father and his children, but it seems as if God has sold his sons and daughters into slavery (50:1). The answer that II Isaiah provides is again twofold. First of all, where is the evidence for the divorce or the sale? There is none. There is no bill of divorce and no receipt for the sale into slavery. God cannot divorce or sell as slaves those whom he has once taken into covenant with himself. They may backslide, rebel and lose faith, but they are nevertheless still his. Secondly, although God still loves them and is planning the best for them, he did allow them to go through the furnace of suffering. What does he have against them? The fact that they sinned against him (50:1b).

The passage ends with two questions posed by Yahweh. The first is, why is there such a poor response to his appeal? He is calling his people out of their exile and suffering, so why do they want to live on in bondage? The second is, is his mighty hand so shortened that he cannot redeem? If they really believe that their God, the almighty, has no power to deliver, let them do some hard thinking, some remembering. We in our turn may ponder his past deliverances, not only as recorded in scripture, like the exodus from Egypt, but also in our own lives. The practice of keeping some kind of spiritual diary may prove helpful.

LXXXXI

50:4-11 The third Servant Song

4. The servant is the perfect learner, whom Yahweh has instructed morning by morning by awakening his *ear*. As a result, the servant is the perfect teacher, whose speech is finely tuned to meet the needs of his listeners. With an apt word he is able to help the weary to keep going forward. Both his listening ear and his speaking tongue have been *taught*. He listens in the early morning, he teaches during the rest of the day. First a humble disciple, then an authoritative teacher, that is the correct order.

5. The servant is so teachable that his obedient response to Yahweh's teaching will lead him into difficult paths. He will encounter the active spite and fury of evil. Yahweh had opened his ear and the servant did not turn backwards. In no way did he rebel. He faced what was coming to him meekly and willingly.

6. There is a general rule that everyone who is godly will face opposition and persecution. This would be true of the servant of Yahweh. It has been true of all God's servants in the past and it is true of all God's servants now. The servant of Yahweh would have his back brutally scourged. He would present his face to be abused both verbally and physically by his adversaries. To pull someone's beard was an extreme insult in antiquity, for the beard was a symbol of dignity.

7. The servant was aware of Yahweh's help. He knew he would not be disgraced. Because of this he set his face "like flint" as he went on his way to face opposition and rejection. He knew that in the long run he would not suffer shame.

8. Yahweh would in due course vindicate his servant. In any case Yahweh was always near him and would strengthen him in the hour of suffering. Therefore

the servant courageously resolved to enter into a final and decisive confrontation with those who felt threatened by him, even though the odds would be stacked against him. In this verse and the next we have another imagined legal hearing. The servant and his enemies are described as standing up in a hearing in a court of law. One party is completely innocent but faces false accusations from the other.

9. If Yahweh, the God of all, is helping the servant, who will be foolhardy enough to declare him guilty? The Apostle Paul asked a very similar question (see Rom 8:33-34). So may we when accusing fingers are pointed at us. Those who wrongly judge or condemn the innocent (51:6) are like a garment that wears away and perishes. They are helpless, like a cloth that is being eaten away by moths (51:8).

10. The exiles who listened as II Isaiah uttered these words were presented with an ultimate choice, just as we are if or when we read them today. The words of faith we have just heard from the servant are a matter of life or death. They may be to us an inspiration which we shall try to live up to. We will then be among those who fear Yahweh and obey his representative the servant. When dark times come, we will walk in the darkness without artificial light. We shall trust in the loving nature of Yahweh and rely on him to see us through.

11. Those who do not take to heart the servant's words will also go through dark times, but they will create their own light by kindling fires and lighting firebrands. This is an image of living in God's world as rebels against God, and of trusting in man-made schemes instead of in God. Yahweh declares that such people will receive from him the doom of having to lie down in torment. It is a paradox that those who trust in God sometimes have to walk in darkness, while those who are self-sufficient always walk in light, although it may be light that they themselves have created. Some paradoxes are true to life. This one certainly is.

Meditation: The Teachability of the Servant

Very few people nowadays are happy to be disciples of God. Throughout the world there is a hunger for education, but the education that is sought after is all about discovery and creativity. Students are urged to develop their own theories rather than uncritically adopt those of their teachers. Very few students today are "students of the book", focusing primarily on the text of the Bible. Henri Blocher wrote that in our day, "It is difficult for us to assume the Biblical attitude of discipleship, which conflicts with man's tendency to self-affirmation".

Perfect teachability would only be attained by the servant of Yahweh, who would say, "Very truly, I tell you, the Son can do nothing on his own, but only what he sees the Father doing; for whatever the Father does, the Son does likewise" (Jn 5:19). Although the servant would not claim creative originality, no teacher ever presented his material in such a fresh way. He would assume the position of a disciple as he studied the scriptures day after day. There would have been a day when he would have read about himself in the passage we are studying!

The result of his being taught by Yahweh was that the servant always had the right word to say at the right moment to whoever he spoke to. It is not enough to speak the right word: it must be spoken at the right moment, or it will be in vain. Very good words have fallen at the wayside and been devoured by the birds, while the same words, spoken on other occasions by other speakers, have proved to be God's healing balm and his fortifying syrup. The tone of voice and the smile in the eyes are often more important than the words themselves. It has been written that the touch of the comforter must be that of the nurse on the fractured bone, or that of the mother with her frightened child.

To be teachable does not mean that one is passive or weak in character. The servant himself combined teachability with courage. He knew he was going to be put to death. With everyone else, death is the closing up of life; with the servant, it was the object of his life. We all die because we were born; the servant was born in order to die. Knowing he would die, in his final journey to Jerusalem he would set his face "like flint" (v7, and see Lk 9:51, Mk 10:32). He did not allow his face to look weak even though, like all people, he shrank from suffering. How different the servant's courage was from stoic resignation, which is a blend of self-sufficiency and feigned indifference to suffering.

Yahweh, who would vindicate the servant, was always near to him. Some would say that the servant was the friend of tax-collectors and sinners; Yahweh would justify him by making it clear that he associated with them in order to restore them and then transform them into godly people. Others would say that the servant was beside himself; Yahweh would justify him by giving him teaching to impart that was of such superb quality that it has never been equalled. Some would say that the servant had a demon; Yahweh would justify him by giving him power to cast out demons and deliver those who had been oppressed by them. A few would say that the servant was guilty of blasphemy, equating himself with God; Yahweh would justify him by raising him from the dead and exalting him to the right hand of power (v8).

Where are those who would copy the servant's example of faith, in some cases at the cost of their lives? Resting with him from their labours, awaiting the great day when they will be given new bodies, so as to live with him in the new earth which he would prepare for them. Where are those who would go their own way and kindle their own fires? Lying down in torment (v11), awaiting the terrible day when they will have to render an account of their lives to the servant, who will then say, "I never knew you. Go away from me, you evildoers" (Mt 7:23). Where are those who would condemn the servant and never repent of having done so? Their innermost beings are wearing out like a garment; the moths are eating them up (v9). And what would happen to the servant? Yahweh would exalt him, indeed he has already done so. He has given his servant the name that is above every name. To him every knee shall bow, and every tongue will confess that the servant of Yahweh is Lord, to the glory of God the Father (Phil 2:9-11).

LXXXXII

51:1-16 A Hope that rekindles Faith

By now Babylon is under Persian rule and Cyrus is deciding the conditions upon which the exiles of various nations will be allowed to return to their homelands. Deliverance is very near, and II Isaiah wants to strengthen the faith of the Jews. Faith comes from messages that are *heard* (Rom 10:17), so the prophet nourishes the faith of the godly exiles with a number of messages that confirm the previous prophetic call to trust in Yahweh (50:10).

1. Only a fraction of the exiles had any desire to return to Jerusalem. Yahweh addresses himself to the few who did. They pursued the right course and sought after Yahweh, so Yahweh deals with their fear that they would be too few. He urges them to look at the rock and quarry from where they emerged.

2. They all descended from one man, Abraham, and his wife Sarah. Abraham was "but one" when Yahweh called him, but Yahweh blessed him and "made him many". The day of small things is not to be despised (Zech 4:10), for when God is involved, modest beginnings can lead to extraordinary accomplishments.

3. Yahweh would comfort his people. Jerusalem would be changed from a rubble mountain to a clean and attractive city. It would be like a desert being transformed into a divine garden characterised by prelapsarian innocence. People there would speak with joy and gratitude in their eyes; they would be glad and sing.

4. Yahweh again urges his people, his nation, to listen to him and heed his words. There would be a universal extension of true religion. The teaching and justice of Yahweh would reach and enlighten all the peoples.

5. There would also be swift deliverance and salvation among all the peoples. Yahweh will embrace them in his arms and rule over them with righteousness. The Gentile nations would be waiting for him. Their hope was in his intervention.

6. Not only will the religion of Yahweh be universal, it will also be eternal. Things that are seen (the heavens and the earth) will vanish or wear out, and the ungodly will perish like gnats. Yahweh's salvation, by contrast, will last forever, and the effectiveness of his rescue and restoration will never come to an end.

7. For the third time, Yahweh urges the righteous to listen (v1, 4, 7). They had Yahweh's teaching in their hearts. Therefore they need not fear the reproaches and humiliations that might come their way.

8. The mortality of the ungodly echoes the servant's words in 50:9. Here it is contrasted with the eternal quality of God's interventions. Moths and worms eat up garments and wool. That is what it would be like for those who opposed God's people. By contrast, Yahweh's deliverance and salvation would last for ever.

9. The hope of the godly exiles is now rekindled and they respond to Yahweh. The short and staccato lines in verses 9-10 indicate their enthusiasm as they look

ahead to their return to Jerusalem. They entreat his "strong arm", a phrase which may refer to the servant of Yahweh, to intervene on their behalf, just as he did "in days of old" during the exodus. Rahab and the dragon are nicknames of Egypt and are themselves symbolic of chaos.

10. Yahweh had dried up the Red Sea, making a way for the Israelites to escape from Pharaoh. It must have been encouraging for the exiles to know that he would be with them during the difficult times that lay ahead.

11. II Isaiah now speaks forth part of another oracle, 35:10. It is a most beautiful promise which bears repetition. So wonderful would Yahweh's help be as the Jews returned home from Babylon, that their difficulties would not only fade into the background, but would be transformed into occasions for great rejoicing.

12. In response to the appeal of his faithful people in verses 9-10, Yahweh again speaks to them with words of comfort (in both senses, to reassure and also to strengthen). "I, I am he". God himself is the ground of comfort, for he is the disposer (v 12), the creator (v 13) and the God of the covenant (v 15, *your* God). His people need not fear the opposition of transient mortals who would perish.

13. The faithful had forgotten God, in the sense that they had lost sight of the fact that he was the omnipotent creator of heaven and earth. Because of this they suffered from constant anxiety. They thought their oppressors would be furious and bent on destroying them, but their fury was a little thing, almost nothing.

14. The oppressors would speedily release the oppressed. The Jews would not die but would return to their homeland. They would not suffer hunger on the way.

15. Yahweh was *their* covenant God. His commitment to them was absolute even if theirs to him was not. He would stir up the waters of the sea once more if it were necessary. After all, he was Yahweh of the armies.

16. The first part of the verse recalls the charge to the servant in 49:2. Yahweh had entrusted to his people the invaluable treasure of his words, and he had hidden them in his hand during their years of exile. Indeed, it was by being the bearer of Yahweh's words that Israel fulfilled an important part of her calling to be his people. She had been engaged in the task of putting into writing the final form of the Old Testament and carefully preserving it for the future use of God's people. Israel had done much more besides, but we may be forever grateful to her for this "gift beyond price".

Meditation: Hope will ward off Discouragement

The Messiah would one day teach that "Whoever does not receive the kingdom of God as a little child will never enter it" (Mk 10:15). The two most typical marks of a happy child are trust and hope. Trust (or faith) prompts the child to depend on his mother for nourishment and on his father for support. Likewise hope (or expectancy) makes the child look forward to future surprises that will leave him open-eyed with wonder. As

Donald Coggan has written, "A child has a minimum of life to look back on. He has everything to look forward to. So his capacity for anticipation is high; he has a thirst for the future that can hardly be satisfied. Watch his eyes when he is promised a visit to the circus, the zoo, or whatever. Listen to him as he cries, 'I can't wait!' Tell him about Christmas or the holidays, and he will count the days. Expectation – anticipation – the attitude of the tip-toe – hope. These are the marks of any normal child".

Yahweh was preparing his people (or at any rate the godly remnant of them) for freedom and for the journey back to Jerusalem. He wanted to quicken their faith and arouse their hope. To do this he spoke to them through his prophet II Isaiah. In this passage he had some delightful answers to five of their anxieties.

First anxiety: "We are so few". Answer: those true-hearted believers in Babylon began as one solitary man, their ancestor Abraham. They should therefore take courage in spite of the fewness of their number, for the same blessing that rested on Abraham also rested on them. Yahweh would transform the dusty ruins of Zion into a new and thriving city which would be full of joy and gladness. There they would enjoy delightful times with Yahweh, as Adam and Eve did in the Garden of Eden (v1-3).

Second anxiety: "It will be hard work, and then we shall die – what is the point?" Answer: a glorious future belongs to those who wait for Yahweh's salvation. It will be full of purpose, reaching out to the nations who have never heard the teaching of Yahweh. Also, even if heaven and earth were to pass away, their great salvation would continue, for it was imperishable and eternal (v4-6).

Third anxiety: "It is so discouraging because other people oppose and insult us". Answer: it was because they lived pure and upright lives that they were ridiculed. They were afraid of those who despised their godliness. They should realise that the reproach they feared was that of frail and short-lived mortals, while the salvation they hoped for would endure to all generations and for ever (v7-8).

Fourth anxiety: "Yes, we are willing to have a go, but how should we pray?" Answer: They should challenge Yahweh to reveal his power as in the past (v9-10), and then they should sing the song of the ransomed of Yahweh (v11). This is the kind of prayer Yahweh loves to hear from his people. In our prayers we may remember Yahweh's mighty acts of salvation in the past and look for repeat performances in the future. If we have the privacy to do so, we may also sing joyfully. The book of Psalms and the church hymnbook could be a helpful source of familiar and unfamiliar songs for us.

Fifth anxiety: "This is all very well and we agree with it, but we find it hard to focus on what lies ahead". Answer: their primary focus should be on Yahweh! It was he and he alone who was strengthening them for their task. They need not fear the fury of their opponents. If they looked at Yahweh they would laugh and say, "What fury?" Yahweh was their maker and their God. He would judge their enemies. He had put his words in their mouths. He had hidden them in the shadow of his hand, and they were now safe from extreme dangers.

How would those who were seeking for Yahweh respond to his encouragement? It seems that these answers to their anxieties did the trick. Their hope was fanned back into flame. In 539 B.C. 42,360 of them set out for Jerusalem after the decree of Cyrus (Ezra 1:2-4, 2:64).

LXXXXIII

51:17-52:12 Rescue is on the Way

In verses 17-23 Yahweh speaks to Jerusalem, who patiently awaited the return of her exiled children. The season of her degradation was about to end. In 52:1-10 the tone changes: there is good news of peace. Finally in 52:11-12 the Jewish exiles are urged for their own good to make a clean break from Babylon.

17. II Isaiah urges Jerusalem, the personification of her people, to rouse herself. She had drunk from Yahweh "the cup of his wrath", and was therefore intoxicated and staggering. The cup of Yahweh's wrath is a symbol of God's judgement on sin. It was destined to change hands, from Jerusalem to her tormentors (v 22-23).

18. The pathos and brutality of the downfall of Jerusalem are vividly described with the pictures of her groping with no one to take her by the hand (v 18), of her trapped as an antelope in a net (v 20), and of her humiliating prostration (v 23).

19. Two calamities have befallen Jerusalem: devastation and destruction on her buildings, and famine and sword on her people. There is no one to comfort her.

20. On every street the people of God lay dying, as if they had fainted (Lam 2:11-12, 19, 21). They had struggled to get free like an antelope trapped in a net. They had drunk to the dregs the wrath of Yahweh.

21. Jerusalem had served her term and her penalty was paid (40:2). Wounded and drunk with the wine of Yahweh's wrath, she is commanded to pay attention.

22. Her sovereign is Yahweh. He is her God, who intercedes for her people. He now speaks to her. Yahweh's message is simple. He has removed the "cup of staggering" from her hands. She will no longer drink from it.

23. Instead, Yahweh will place the cup into the hands of her tormentors. These were the Babylonian soldiers who, at the fall of Jerusalem in 586 B.C., had told the Jewish people to lie down on the ground so that they could walk over them. This was the custom in antiquity when one nation had conquered another.

52:1. Yahweh's reply to his people's cry that *he* should "Awake, awake" (51:9) is to call *them* to "Awake, awake" (as in 51:17). The Messiah would also make a similar rejoinder during his ministry (Mk 9:22-23). Yahweh tells Zion to emerge from her dazed state. She is to dress herself in her best garments. She is the holy city, and her unholy enemies will no longer live beside her.

2. She is to pick herself up and dust herself down. She may remove the bonds from her neck. Captive she has been, but not for much longer.

3. Yahweh makes it clear that his redemption is not a commercial transaction. The Babylonians were not Yahweh's creditors (50:1) but his agents, and they were not themselves guiltless (47:6-7). This idea of being "redeemed without money" would be given fresh meaning in the New Testament (1 Pet 1:18-19).

4. The Babylonian oppression was similar to Israel's stay in Egypt, which was willingly accepted at first but later resulted in their enslavement. It was similar to the oppression that came from Assyria, inflicted without reasonable cause.

5. Yahweh's question would be better rendered as "And what do I find here?" The Babylonian oppression was excessively harsh. The oppressors had taken God's people into exile and then howled at them. They attributed their captives' misery to Yahweh's inability to help them, thereby despising Yahweh's name.

6. Yahweh's people would know his name or character. He was a saviour and his salvation would bring honour to his holy name (Ezek 36:21). When Yahweh took them back to Jerusalem, they would know that he had spoken the truth. His intolerance of any further punishment being meted to his people is remarkable.

7. II Isaiah imagines the day when Jerusalem first heard the news that her people would soon return to her. How blessed (as well as blistered) were the feet of the messenger who had walked for months to bring this good news! He was sent to bring to the city of God good news of peace and salvation (Rom 10:15). Her God would establish his kingdom.

8. The sentinels or watchmen on the city walls were "looking for redemption" (Lk 2:38). Without them the message would have fallen on deaf ears. They sang for joy at the prospect of seeing Yahweh's return to the city where he dwelled.

9. The ruins of the city burst into a psalm-like song (v 9-10), for Yahweh had comforted his people and had redeemed their city.

10. Yahweh had wrought salvation in holiness and this was seen by all the nations.

11. II Isaiah again urges the Jews to avail themselves of this opportunity to flee from sin by leaving Babylon. They were not to touch any "unclean thing", leaving behind every object that might be tainted by heathen idolatry. They would not walk out bearing spoils from Babylon, as when they left Egypt (Ex 12:35-36). The priests were to purify themselves and process carefully as they left the evil city, carrying the valuable holy vessels. Their departure from Babylon symbolises the withdrawal of the church from the embrace and judgement of the world, so as not to have to share either the world's sins or its plagues (Rev 18:4).

12. Unlike the exodus from Egypt, the departure from Babylon would not be hasty but deliberate, not in flight but in perfect security. The Jews would have a divine escort protecting them (Ezra 8:21-23). He would be both their vanguard and their rear guard.

Meditation: Yahweh, Judge and also Redeemer

In this passage we learn about how Yahweh is both the judge and the redeemer of all people. In each case we are given a remarkable insight into the way he deals with his human creatures.

(a) **Yahweh is to be our judge.** This is made clear by the metaphor of the cup, which II Isaiah puts to good use. The people of God, personified by Jerusalem, are described as having drunk at the hand of Yahweh "the cup of his wrath". They have drunk to the dregs the bowl of staggering (v 17). The due apportionment of the wrath of Yahweh for each and every person is blended into a cup, which those who are guilty of sin must drink. This cup is also a bowl that will make them stagger. This does not refer to ordinary alcoholic drunkenness, but to the final stages of *delirium tremens*. The intoxication is deadly. The doublet of cup and bowl provides emphasis, as it usually does in Hebrew poetry.

The people of God are later described as being drunk, but not with wine. II Isaiah returns to the metaphor of the cup (v 21), which contains the requisite quantity of wrath but has not yet been drained to its dregs. Yahweh then takes the cup out of their hand and hands it to someone else to drink instead, the one who trod on them so cruelly (v 22). The poor intoxicated drinkers see that the cup has been taken from their hand. They will drink from it no more, ever again. Their days of heavy drinking from the cup of God's wrath are now over.

In several Old Testament passages the cup of Yahweh is a symbol of the righteous anger or wrath of God against the rebelliousness, selfishness and sin of all people (Job 21:20, Ps 75:8, Jer 25:15, Ezek 23:33-34, Isa 51:17, 21-23). The same figure of speech recurs in the New Testament in the book of Revelation, where the wicked "will drink of the wine of God's wrath, poured unmixed into the cup of his anger" (Rev 14:10), and the judgement of God is described as the pouring out on the earth of the seven bowls of God's wrath (Rev 16:1-21).

The cup must be drunk by the guilty, and for them to drink it will be death and destruction. The only alternative is for someone else to drink it instead. In our passage it was the oppressors who had tortured God's people who would drink it instead of them. This substitution would perhaps have helped the Jewish exiles to understand the way in which God could somehow forgive and save them. Their cup had been taken from them and given to someone else. That was a helpful insight. It did not, of course, resolve all the underlying problems. The oppressors would drink the cup that their own oppression of the Israelites had earned. Who could worthily drink the cup of God's wrath against the Israelites because of the Israelites' own sin? There existed only one solution to this problem, and it was God's solution. It was through II Isaiah that it was revealed to the world (52:13-53:12). The prophet will expound the divine solution in the fourth of his "servant songs", which we shall study in our next five sections.

(b) **Yahweh is our redeemer** as well as being our judge. He buys us back for himself "without money and without price" (55:1). Our salvation will cost us nothing. It is free.

It is sheer undeserved grace. "You were sold for nothing, and you shall be redeemed without money" (52:3). It cost us nothing to get into sin. Getting out of it will either cost us everything or it will cost us nothing. If we opt for Yahweh's redemption, it will cost us nothing, because the cost was paid in full by the servant of Yahweh. Some people find it difficult to receive a salvation that costs them nothing. They are proud, and they would rather pay. "Very well", says Yahweh. "It is your choice. If you want to pay, pay, but it will cost you everything. You would be better off with my free offer, which costs you nothing. But it is up to you". Yahweh's way of redeeming us is through his servant, and it is explained in the fourth "servant song". To this great passage, the highlight of the Old Testament, we now turn.

LXXXXIV

52:13-15 The great Surprise

We shall now devote five sections to the fourth "servant song". It is the heart of the book of Isaiah, the pinnacle of its theological themes of righteousness and sin, judgement and grace. If this book's theology is a golden crown, then the fourth "servant song" is the jewel in the crown. It begins in 52:13 and goes on until 53:12. It is divided into five stanzas of three verses each. The first line of each stanza sets the theme for the rest of the stanza. The stanzas gradually increase in length, and fill up the picture that they reveal. The language is deeply poetic. The passage deals with the unparalleled sufferings of the servant of Yahweh, and the effect that they produce on those who find out about them. Yahweh himself is the speaker in the first stanza. He introduces us to his servant, and looks ahead to his future exaltation, which would contrast strikingly with his earlier abasement.

13. *'See, my servant shall prosper'*. This is the theme of the first stanza and also of the fourth servant song as a whole. It is about a servant who eventually reaches the top, even though along the way he plumbs the lowest depths of degradation. The word *prosper* also means *deal wisely*. Indeed, in the long run wise dealing usually leads to prosperity. Wise dealing was thought of as one of the features of the coming Branch or Messiah (Jer 23:5). This opening theme of final success will be repeated in the last verse of the passage (53:12); it is an example of a literary device called an *inclusio*.

'He shall be exalted and lifted up, and shall be very high'. The Jewish Old Testament commentary *Midrash* gives the following meaning of this clause: "[The servant] shall be exalted above Abraham, he shall be lifted up above Moses, and shall be higher than the angels that minister". The servant's career would in the end be crowned with total success. The three steps up in this clause describe a dignity beyond all of the rewards available in this world. For Christians they correspond

to the servant's resurrection, ascension and exaltation at the right hand of Yahweh on high. The words used of the servant are the same as those applied to Yahweh himself elsewhere in the book of Isaiah: "High and lofty" (6:1, 57:15). This establishes a very close connection between Yahweh and his servant.

14. *'Just as there were many who were astonished at him'*. The astonishment was because of the spectacle of his exceptional misfortunes. According to the next clause, these would turn him into an object of repellence and contempt for some people, although later he would be revealed to them in his true dignity.
'So marred was his appearance beyond human semblance, and his form beyond that of mortals'. Physical blemishes disqualified a person from priesthood (Lev 21:16-21), and possibly from active kingship as well. But here the blemishes inflicted on the servant by others constitute an inevitable part of his mission.

15. *'So he shall startle many nations'*. The word translated *startle* means *sprinkle* elsewhere in the Old Testament. It is used of the action of a priest in the rituals of sacrifice and purification (Lev 4:6, 8:11, 14:7). II Isaiah may have intended to convey the truth that the servant of Yahweh is not only the Messianic King and the unequalled prophetic teacher, but also the great High Priest.
'Kings shall shut their mouths because of him'. When the kings of the earth gaze at the suffering servant, they are faced with the foolishness and weakness of God (1 Cor 1:22-25). They are speechless. They have nothing to say.
'For that which had not been told them they shall see, and that which they had not heard they shall contemplate'. The moment comes when the kings realise that the servant was from the start the most important person they ever encountered or heard of. His scarred and contorted form hid the fact that he was the saviour of the whole world, and the one to whom all authority in heaven and on earth would be given. The kings also understand that, by being repelled by his appearance and by ignoring him, they have missed out on his salvation and on all that is good.

Meditation: The great Reversal

The fourth servant song is an extraordinarily powerful passage. One of its striking features is the way in which the servant of Yahweh is not named, and he is only identified as "my servant" twice (52:13 and 53:11). Otherwise we just read "he", "him" or "his". He is presented as other-worldly, almost spectral. He never speaks for himself, not even when severe suffering is inflicted upon him. We do not really see him, although some seeing does take place: those who caused him great suffering will later see him in retrospect as he really was. He casts a shadow on their faces and a dark cloud on their hearts. He likewise haunts us as we read the book of Isaiah. He is mysterious and he remains aloof.

We begin with a peep at the end of the story. Yahweh's servant will deal wisely and prosper. This is a story with a wonderful ending. But prior to that there will be great bodily disfigurement and untold suffering. The middle three stanzas will spell this out. At the end, there will be a great reversal, which will astonish and surprise many people. The last they saw of the servant was a terribly contorted form, barely human, marred beyond belief. His head was punctured and stripes of blood flowed down his face, his back was terribly lacerated with deep scars, his side had a large fresh wound, his hands and feet were pierced, and his form was out of joint with his rib-cage bulging out.

Will those scars still be visible in the next life? Will they form part of "that which had not been told them" and that which "they shall see"? The followers of the servant have speculated about this. If the scars are visible, they will be radiant with glory. The nations will be startled by them, and kings will be dumbfounded. That which is most abhorrent and undesirable in this life will be what is most glorious in the next. Every sacrifice made for the sake of the servant or of his God will prove to have been infinitely worthwhile. Even a cup of water offered to a thirsty soul for the servant's sake will receive its rightful reward (Mk 9:41).

What will be most astonishing to the high and mighty is that the servant will finish up in the highest place, far above them. Those myriads of people who ignored him and paid no attention to his words will be left speechless. The great reversal that has taken place will seem inconceivable to them, and yet they will know full well that it was absolutely right. They will ask questions like "What did people do to him? How could I have just ignored him? Why has he been lifted up so high? Why did so many of us not realise what was going on?" This is how the song begins: it starts off by describing people's shock at its ending.

Another song or poem was written about this great reversal a few years after the servant's earthly life. It names the servant and urges his followers to have the same attitude of mind as he did. It also highlights the change in his fortune:

"The Messiah Jesus, though he was in the form of God, did not regard equality with God as something to be exploited, but emptied himself, taking the form of a slave, being born in human likeness.

And being found in human form, he humbled himself and became obedient to the point of death – even death on a cross.

Therefore God also highly exalted him and gave him the name that is above every name, so that at the name of Jesus every knee should bend, in heaven and on earth and under the earth, and every tongue should confess that Jesus the Messiah is Lord, to the glory of God the Father" (Phil 2:6-11).

LXXXXV

53:1-3 The great Suffering

Now it is II Isaiah's turn to be the speaker, and he takes up the servant's story from his early childhood up to the final days of his ministry. In this stanza the prophet speaks of how other people reacted to the servant, and of the acute mental and spiritual pain which their constant barrage of selfishness and lack of empathy must have caused him.

1. *'Who has believed what we have heard?'* The second stanza begins with an exclamation of wonder at the unbelief of the people, and it goes on to consider the insensitivity and unbelief of those who saw the servant's suffering but did not realise its cause. The message about the suffering servant of God is foolishness to ungodly people (1 Cor 1:18). Where the gospel has not been heard for a long time, its first proclamation is often received with polite or impolite disdain. Henry Ellison, a former missionary, wrote that "Even in Christian circles ridicule generally awaits the person, at least at first, who strips the veneer of respectability from the gospel and preaches it with all its offence". Who would believe the message of the fourth "servant song"? Not many people. Kings and nations would indeed be speechless in the future, but how many are dumbstruck now? Very few. They have not believed what we have heard, and the arm of Yahweh has not been revealed to them.

   And to whom has the arm of Yahweh been revealed?' The arm of Yahweh is his servant, who powerfully intervenes in the affairs of mankind (51:9, 52:10). The servant's power is most clearly made known through what appears to be folly and weakness. It is a divine saving power to bring everlasting good to the poor and needy of this world. This power is not visible to the many, who are proud and haughty. This is why the story of the servant baffles them. Its meaning is disclosed to the humble who are crushed by heavy burdens. The servant delights to reveal himself to people like them (Mt 11:25-30).

2. *'For he grew up before him like a young plant, and like a root out of dry ground'.* He was born on ground that was dry and barren from God's point of view. There was little deep spirituality, little care for the poor and needy, little love for and delight in Yahweh.

   'He had no form or majesty that we should look at him, nothing in his appearance that we should desire him'. The servant was not physically attractive by the world's standards. He did not have the handsome features of the Hollywood actors who played out his role. Some commentators wondered if he suffered from a facial disfigurement. It is also possible that his identification with those who were hurt or vulnerable may have given him a sorrowful look, though his eyes would have been lively and full of love. In any case, it was not just the servant's features that were disliked; the whole of his life constituted an offence to the high and mighty of this world. His lowly birth, his upbringing as a carpenter's son and apprentice, his self-education in the Old Testament scriptures, the fact that his followers were chosen from among the poor and the rebels of society, and his self-identification with human sin (v4), all earned him the world's scorn.

3. *'He was despised and rejected by others'*. Henri Blocher wrote that the servant would have gone through "the subtle, almost hidden psychological pain of *contempt*. The need for acceptance, esteem and acknowledgement is one of the basic hungers of the human personality, especially of such a sensitive and open personality as the servant's. How agonising to be starved of them!" The people of Jerusalem despised the servant because he came from Galilee. The people of Galilee despised him because he came from Nazareth, a Galilean village with a bad reputation. The people of Nazareth despised him because there was a question mark about whether he had been born out of wedlock (Mk 6:3). Other people preferred not to associate with him. He was not welcome in their cliques. He had associated with the lowly, and that was perceived to be a fault.

'A man of suffering and acquainted with infirmity'. The inner suffering of the Messiah would make an interesting book; it has not yet been written. On one occasion he was so tired that he fell into a deep sleep in a boat on a stormy sea (Mk 4:37-38). On another he was so weary of giving out to other people that he entered a house and did not want anyone to know it (Mk 7:24). Another time, full of exasperation, he wondered how much longer he would have to put up with faithless people (Mk 9:19). Once he felt very lonely and apprehensive, and looked to his friends to encourage him, saying "I am deeply grieved, even to death" (Mk 14:33-34). And once he was submerged in such bitter anguish that for several hours he was deprived of the sense of Yahweh's presence with him (Mk 15:34). The servant was associated with griefs and sorrows, but they were not his own. They were the griefs and sorrows of the needy people he encountered.

'And as one from whom others hide their faces he was despised, and we held him of no account'. He could have echoed the words of Job, "[God] has made me a byword of the peoples, and I am one before whom people spit" (Job 17:6, and see also Job 19:19, 30:10).

Meditation: The great Rejoicing

In verse 2 we are told that the servant "grew up before [God] like a young plant, and like a root out of dry ground". This is sublime poetry, and it tells us how God saw his servant. The dry ground was the desert that God saw when he looked at the innermost hearts of the men and women that peopled the earth. As they were born he wondered in each case, "Will he do what is right? Will she please me?" Every time the answer was "No". Even among his own people he was forced to conclude, "There is no one who does good; no, not one" (Ps 53:3). Not even among the holy remnant; not a single soul was completely unselfish. Both morally and spiritually the whole world was a barren and infertile wilderness.

God had created the earth in order to people it with men and women who would be part of his family, who would reciprocate his love for them by loving him and delighting in him, just as a child loves his parents. What did God get for all his pains? Dry ground. He got a race of selfish sinners who rebelled against him and persistently ignored and disobeyed him. He gave them a beautiful environment to live in, but they spoilt it. He gave them health and strength, but they abused their appetites and did not respect their own bodies. He presented them with a great purpose to live for, but they ignored it. He made them in his own image, but their response to him was either faint-hearted or hostile. He looked down on the earth, and he saw dry ground, no growth, nothing that pleased him.

Until the servant was born. He grew up before God like a green plant, and like a root out of dry ground. The servant was a tender shoot, whose root was full of life and love. And so the little baby grew up. He became a boy and later a man. And God watched his every step, enthralled. God was so pleased! He was so full of joy! For the first time he had a plant growing in the barren wilderness. The servant pleased him in every way. The servant's life was altogether beautiful.

This was the great rejoicing: It was God who rejoiced because of his servant. This is why this meditation is entitled *The great Rejoicing*. But it could equally have been entitled *The great Rejection*. On the whole, the people of this world did not react to the servant in the same way as God did. God was delighted with him; the great majority of people were not.

The servant was not born with a silver spoon in his mouth. He did not enjoy a privileged life. Even while he was a vulnerable infant, his first resting place was a manger for livestock, his life was under threat, and he became a refugee. His parents were from the peasant class and lived on the bread-line. Poverty was his constant lot. His followers were mostly humble and uneducated fishermen, who were slow to learn and flawed in many ways. One of them would betray him and another would disown him; the rest would abandon him and flee on the occasion of his arrest. There were a few women who supported his itinerant ministry: their faith was in some cases stronger than that of the men who followed him, but even they were far from perfect. He had to undergo an unjust trial and was sentenced to an agonising and protracted death. He was abused verbally and physically. Two terrorists were his companions in execution. From all sides bar one he met with imperfect responses, including misunderstanding, humiliation, bitter hatred and contempt. The sole exception was God himself. God's opinion of his servant was very different to the opinion people had of him.

The servant had no form or majesty that people should have looked at him. There was nothing in his appearance that they might have found desirable. When he walked around in Galilee or Judea, there was nothing out of the ordinary about him. Nobody would have imagined for a moment that he was anyone special. God did not give him the advantage of physical handsomeness. He was not one of those ever-cheerful people who always smiled. He was carrying the griefs and sorrows of others, and his compassion for others would have tinged his features with a wistful sadness. Those who knew him well would have agreed with the saying that "he was despised and rejected by others, a man of suffering and acquainted with infirmity". This type of person is not popular. The servant should have been admired because of his concern for the poor and the needy, but most people shrank from his realism, preferring to focus on fleeting pleasures. Being with him aroused their consciences in alarming ways, and they were accustomed to walking through life in a complacent frame of mind. Some even felt threatened by his loving care, especially those in the religious establishment.

While God continued to gaze at the servant's life and to love what he saw, people were thinking that, "as one from whom others hide their faces he was despised, and we held him of no account". Such was the difference of opinion regarding the servant's life and ministry. God rejoiced in him, but people rejected him.

LXXXXVI

53:4-6 The great Substitution

This stanza is presented to us as spoken by the people of God. They have suddenly realised what II Isaiah must have realised when he wrote this servant song. The servant was going to die for *their* sins. This middle stanza brings us to the heart of the servant's mission. He did come to live a humble life and to encourage those who were weak or burdened. He did come to teach as no one had ever taught before or since. He did come to heal the sick and to deliver those in the grip of evil spirits. But supremely, he came to take personal responsibility for people's sins, for their selfishness and for their rebellion against God. He would do so by willingly bearing the guilt of those sins and the punishment that they deserved on his own innocent person.

4. *'Surely he has borne our infirmities and carried our diseases'*. The third stanza begins with the admission by the people that it was *their* woes that befell the servant. It is easy to read the accounts of the Messiah delivering many people who were brought to him with a word and curing many who were sick (Mt 8:16), without realising the human cost involved to him (Mt 8:17). In fact he removed demon-possession and sickness, which are the occasional accompaniments of sin, by somehow bearing and carrying *to himself* their sinful cause, and so getting rid of them. This is a picture of what he did with our sins, which are at the root of every evil. He bore them away when he was put to death by his enemies.

   'Yet we accounted him stricken, struck down by God, and afflicted'. The people of God assumed that when the servant was arrested and treated harshly by the authorities it was because God was striking him down for having sinned. The most basic moral judgement, which all of us sometimes make without thinking, is that when people suffer, it is their fault, and they suffer because God is angry with them. This is how God's people first reacted to the suffering of the servant of Yahweh. But after thinking through the matter, they realised they were wrong.

5. *'But he was wounded for our transgressions, crushed for our iniquities'*. The word *wounded* is best translated *pierced*, which is its usual meaning in the Old Testament. Here the people are suddenly brought short by the realisation of what was really happening. Previously they thought that he was being struck down and afflicted by Yahweh. But now they suddenly saw the connection between the servant's suffering and their own sins. Their sins, our sins, were heaped upon this innocent servant who had always delighted to do things in God's way. He bore our sins as he was put to death. All of our hatred, our malice, our spite and our vindictiveness were laid upon him. In his own body he bore all of our wilfulness, our selfishness, our pride and our rebelliousness. He died for our slanders, our thefts, our adulteries and our coveting.

   'Upon him was the punishment that made us whole, and by his bruises we are healed'. The connection between the servant's suffering and the people's sins was a reciprocal connection. On the one hand, the servant suffered on account of their sins. On the other, the people were restored and their sin was taken away by his suffering. The servant suffered, the people were forgiven. The servant was punished and bruised, we received his wholeness and his health.

6. *'All we like sheep have gone astray, we have all turned to our own way'*. Verse 6 begins with *All we* and ends with *us all*: the two pairs of words are identical in Hebrew, and sin is perfectly answered by grace. The people realise that their misfortunes were the outcome of the inconsiderate selfishness in which they lived, following their own impulses and interests, and of their wilful propensity to go their own way and thereby end up alienated from God and humankind.

   'And Yahweh has laid on him the iniquity of us all'. The central truth of chapter 53 is that by the initiative of God himself, the servant atoned for the sins of all people by penal substitution. This means that he suffered the punishment for sin that we deserved, he was our substitute. This is expressed eleven times in the chapter (twice in v 4, four times in v 5, once in v 6, v 8, v 10, v 11, and v 12).

Meditation: The great Replacement

We are told in the New Testament how the servant prepared for his final ordeal. "[He] offered up prayers and supplications, with loud cries and tears, to the one who was able to save him from death, and he was heard because of his reverent submission. Although he was a Son, he learnt obedience through what he suffered; and having been made perfect, he became the source of eternal salvation for all who obey him" (Heb 5:7-9). Shortly before his passion and death he was so wrung with anguish that he was in some danger of dying from a broken heart before his execution. If the anticipation of what was coming to him was so heart-rending, how much worse must the reality have been!

Sin leads to suffering. Sin deserves to be punished. The person who sins shall die (Ezek 18:4), unless God provides a substitute. "We accounted him stricken, struck down by God, and afflicted. But he was wounded for our transgressions, crushed for our iniquities". The people now see that he suffered greatly, but was himself innocent. He was in fact suffering vicariously. He was their substitute, bearing the punishment that was due to their sins and the sins of mankind.

In his book The Cross of Christ, John Stott wrote helpfully about this. "The concept of substitution may be said to lie at the heart of both sin and salvation. For the essence of sin is man's substituting himself for God, while the essence of salvation is God substituting himself for man. Man asserts himself against God and puts himself where only God deserves to be. God sacrifices himself for man and puts himself where only man deserves to be. Man claims prerogatives which belong to God alone; God accepts penalties which belong to man alone".

Substitution was a very familiar concept for the Israelites. It was written into the Torah or Law of Moses. The book of Leviticus (chapter 4) taught that if a sinful man, under the wrath of the holy God, wished to approach God, he had to sacrifice a spotless victim in his place. This was how atonement could be achieved. This was at the heart of the institution of sacrifice. God had decreed that sin was so serious that anyone who sinned had to die, unless a sinless substitute died in their place. And so, ever since that law was given to Israel, spotless lambs and other unblemished animals had been sacrificed in place of sinners.

The sacrificial system, however, was insufficient. It was impossible for Yahweh to overlook wilful sins. The entire sacrificial system was designed to take away ceremonial sins, sins committed mainly by accident, and perhaps sins of moral failure – but they had to be unintentional (Lev 4:13, 22, 27). The system could not cope with high-handed sins, or sins deliberately committed. An animal sacrifice would not be enough in that case. There was no provision for intentional sins in the law. For intentional or deliberate sins, only a person could be a substitute for a person. The ultimate Lamb of God would have to be, not an animal, but a human being: one who was both spotless before God and yet fully identified with sinners in their condemnation. The sacrifice of a perfect man was needed to complete and fulfil the Old Testament sacrifices and render them valid.

The servant made himself an offering for sin. He offered not another life, but his own, as a sin offering. Since he offered this sacrifice, he was the priest; since he offered himself, he was also the sacrifice. He himself was the Lamb of God who takes away the sin of the world (Jn 1:29).

The sacrificial system was both educational and efficacious. It foreshadowed the true sacrifice. In the days prior to the coming of the servant, this still lay in the future. The Old Testament sacrifices were pointing ahead to the one sacrifice that would complete them and truly effect forgiveness for anyone who trusted Yahweh or his servant. In the middle stanza of the fourth servant song, the people of God realise that the old principle of substitution was finally at work in a real way. This was good news, but its cost was huge.

Some people have objected to substitutionary atonement on the grounds that it is not just. How can justice be served if an innocent party suffers in place of the guilty? This objection to the justice of vicarious suffering is removed when the one who suffers does so voluntarily as well as vicariously. Indeed, this helps to highlight the justice of God (Rom 3:21-26, especially v 25). It suggests that the pinnacle of human achievement is to bear the sins of someone else in the way that only the servant could have done. It also suggests that the corresponding pinnacle of human achievement for flawed and fallen people like ourselves is to forgive those who have wronged us. This is a mark which often distinguishes professing believers from others after a tragedy or a crime.

There was a terrible separation between Yahweh and his servant while the servant was bearing our sin. This separation was willingly accepted by both Yahweh and his servant, and it was due to our sins and their just reward. There is, of course, no question of the servant having been a loving third party who came to rescue mankind from the wrath of an angry God who was not keen on the rescue. The fourth servant song makes it clear that the whole initiative in the great plan to rescue mankind from the consequences of wilful sin was due to Yahweh (v 10). Somehow, in a way that we can never fully understand, God was both in the servant, reconciling the world to himself, and at the same time making the servant, who knew no sin, to be sin for our sakes (2 Cor 5:19, 21).

LXXXXVII

53:7-9 The great Silence

II Isaiah is the speaker again in the fourth stanza. The emphasis is now on the meekness and submissiveness of the servant during his undeserved sufferings. The stanza describes a procession (v 7), an execution (v 8) and a burial (v 9). The willing servant is led out to die, he is put to death by unjust and uncaring people, and he is buried in the tomb of a rich man instead of being cast into the common grave reserved for criminals. As in the second and third servant songs, there is an emphasis on the servant's masterful and perfect control of his tongue, both in his silences and in his words.

7. *'He was oppressed, and he was afflicted, yet he did not open his mouth'.* The fourth stanza begins by stating the servant's meek acceptance of his sufferings, and will go on to develop this theme. People subjected the servant to acts of violence and severely afflicted him in the cruellest manner imaginable. In spite of this, he remained silent (Mt 27:14, Mk 14:61). "When he was abused, he did not return abuse; when he suffered, he did not threaten; but he entrusted himself to the one who judges justly" (1 Pet 2:23).
   'Like a lamb that is led to the slaughter, and like a sheep that before its shearers is silent, so he did not open his mouth'. The servant had defeated the priests and religious leaders in argument when they had their debates in the Temple precincts. During his trials, however, he said nothing in defence of himself. He had been born in order to die, and he resisted the temptation of trying to walk away free.

We are left marvelling at the silence of the Lamb.

There had been another famously gentle lamb, the prophet Jeremiah, but he spoke out vigorously for divine retribution to be visited on his oppressors (Jer 11:18-20, 12:1-3). The Lamb of Yahweh was different, praying for the forgiveness of his oppressors (Lk 23:34), but otherwise remaining silent towards them.

Henry Ellison comments that "In the long history of human crime and wrong there has always remained one solace to those who have been wrongfully accused and condemned. In the hour of judgement and death they have been able to proclaim their innocence and to call on God to vindicate and avenge them. But even this last solace is not an option for the servant. He will pray for his murderers but not against them, he will cry to God but not to men. So perfectly had he identified himself with the father's will that there was neither murmur nor complaint". He left us an example, that we might follow in his steps (1 Pet 2:21).

8. 'By a perversion of justice he was taken away'. He was put to death without any opposition or objection from any quarter, and in defiance of justice. The death of the servant was tantamount to judicial murder.

'Who could have imagined his future?' It would have seemed inconceivable that the servant, so cut off from human love and care, would have had such a vast posterity. There would be "a great multitude that no one could count, from every nation, from all tribes and peoples and languages, standing before the throne and before the Lamb, robed in white, with palm branches in their hands" (Rev 7:9).

'For he was cut off from the land of the living'. The servant-Messiah was put to death. He really died. To make sure of this, his side was pierced with a spear and at once blood and water came out (Jn 19:33-37). Then he was buried (v 9).

'Stricken for the transgression of my people'. It had been costly for the first Isaiah to know that he was forgiven and accepted by Yahweh, the holy One of Israel (6:1-7). II Isaiah must have longed for the same assurance that he was forgiven and that his sins were covered. For that matter, he must have wondered how any Israelite could be forgiven by Yahweh in a way that did not compromise his holiness. One day, as II Isaiah meditated on these great themes, the answer was revealed to him. The servant would be stricken for the transgression of my people and, indeed, for the transgression of all peoples.

9. 'They made his grave with the wicked'. The prophetic vision is remarkable throughout, but here it goes into extraordinary detail. The Messiah was unjustly convicted of sedition and put to death as a criminal. His rightful burial place would have been in the common grave that was ignominiously reserved for criminals. But God overruled so that this did not happen.

'And his tomb with the rich'. In fact the Messiah would be buried in a tomb belonging to a wealthy man (Mt 27:57-60). This detail has surprised many seekers after the truth. The French philosopher Blaise Pascal wrote that "Prophecies are the greatest proof of Jesus Christ" (see also Appendix 3, p. 362-365). For some people fulfilled prophecies may be the clinching argument in their journey of faith. If this particular prophecy had not been fulfilled, its meaning would have remained utterly elusive forever.

'Although he had done no violence, and there was no deceit in his mouth'. This declaration of the servant's innocence and of his moral perfection is repeated in the New Testament. "He committed no sin, and no deceit was found in his mouth" (1 Pet 2:22). II Isaiah has given us the image of the lamb led to the slaughter, and statements about the servant's freedom from deceit and his patient resignation to the will of God. This implies that the prophet thought of him as someone who was completely without sin.

Meditation: The great Restraint

James 3:2 declares that "Anyone who makes no mistakes in speaking is perfect, able to keep the whole body in check with a bridle". The servant's mouth was like a sharp sword or a polished arrow (49:2). His words struck home with the power of life and death: life for those who accepted them and found them to be life-changing, and death for those who rejected them and hated him for having spoken. His tongue was the tongue of a teacher, able to sustain the weary with a word in season (50:4). His speech was always transparently straightforward: "there was no deceit in his mouth" (v9).

Throughout the Bible, both in the Old Testament and the New, our speech is presented as having a great potential for both good and evil. The tongue is described as dangerous and difficult to control (Job 5:21, Jas 3:6), but also as a fountain of blessing (Prov 12:14, 1 Pet 3:10). Straightforward and truthful speech is encouraged (Prov 22:21, Mt 5:37), but lying is forbidden (Lev 19:11, Col 3:9).

Speech reveals what the innermost heart of a person is like (Mt 15:18). Speech can be a sign of two-facedness or double-mindedness (Jas 3:9-12). Speech will be a criterion for weal or for woe on the Day of Judgement (Mt 12:36-37). Perfect control of one's speech, both in one's silences and in one's spoken words, is a proof of the perfection of one's personality (Jas 3:2). By declaring that there was no deceit in the servant's mouth, II Isaiah is ascribing moral perfection to him.

When people were crucified in antiquity, the extreme pain that they experienced would loosen their tongues, and they would shout curses and declare their hate and vengefulness until they drifted off into madness. Then they spoke gibberish and their words made no further sense. When the innocent servant was crucified, he did not curse, nor did he speak a single hateful word, nor did he pray for divine retribution for those who had treated him unjustly. His restraint was remarkable. He was a man who could control his mouth, and "anyone who makes no mistakes in speaking is perfect, able to keep the whole body in check with a bridle" (Jas 3:2). But although he was silent towards his enemies as he was dying, he did speak seven times. The seven wonderful and deeply moving sayings which he spoke during his final moments have been cherished by his followers ever since, and have been a source of great blessing for many. They were cries of forgiveness, restoration, provision, dereliction, thirst, accomplishment and commitment.

The servant forgave his torturers, his mockers and his executioners. He accepted and restored a dying criminal and assured him of eternal life with himself. He made provision for his earthly mother, who would otherwise have been destitute when he died. He cried out in the anguish of dereliction because there was a real separation between Yahweh and himself on account of the sins of mankind. After his spiritual agony he was thirsty, not only physically but also for the living God from whom he had been separated by our sins. Just before he died he knew that he had completed the task that Yahweh had entrusted to him, and he said so: "It is finished, accomplished! – the sins of the world are paid in full" (Jn 19:30). His work completed, he then surrendered his life, committing it to Yahweh.

The fourth servant song is concise, indeed laconic, in what it says about the words spoken by the servant as he was dying. It tells that he was silent as regards retribution for his enemies. It also tells that his speech throughout his life had been completely free of deceit. This was very striking. It meant that the servant of Yahweh was no ordinary man. He had perfect control of his tongue, and therefore he was morally perfect. He was well qualified to be the perfect and sinless Lamb of God that would take away the sin of the world. "He committed no sin, and no deceit was found in his mouth" (1 Pet 2:22).

LXXXXVIII

53:10-12 The great Spoils

In the final stanza II Isaiah speaks first, and Yahweh takes over halfway through verse 11. We are told of the glorious future in store for the servant as the reward of his obedience, which included his willingness to die for people, bearing their sins and making them righteous. The servant would see his offspring and prolong his days, which means, by implication, that he would be raised from the dead and would share his great reward with the many and the numerous.

10. *'Yet it was the will of Yahweh to crush him with pain'*. The fifth stanza begins with a reminder that behind the servant's suffering lay the will of Yahweh who is a holy God. This is an unexpected statement. We tend to think that the servant suffered because of the weakness, the pride and the ill-will of his contemporaries, but here it is stated plainly that the first cause of his suffering was the will of God. This must be tempered by the fact that Yahweh was suffering side by side with his servant. Both the Old Testament and the New are balanced on this matter, teaching that it is possible for people to perform evil actions which will be overruled by God so that good may come from them (Gen 50:20, Acts 2:23-24).

'When you make his life an offering for sin'. The servant was going to be a sin offering, the Lamb of God who takes away the sin of the world (Jn 1:29). He was also a guilt offering (this is the meaning of the word used here), and would deal comprehensively with the consequences of sin. Those who would trust in him would find that the burden of their guilt was taken away from their shoulders.

'He shall see his offspring, and shall prolong his days'. This prophecy looks ahead to the resurrection. After he was raised from the dead, the servant would have the satisfaction of seeing that his labour had not been in vain.

'Through him the will of Yahweh will prosper'. This places the servant on the same level as Yahweh. Both Yahweh and his servant had a common purpose. This was that the servant's death would establish a renewed covenant between God and people of all nations, by which eternal salvation would be granted to those who followed the teaching of Yahweh and his servant.

11. *'Out of his anguish he shall see light, he shall find satisfaction through his knowledge'.* The older Revised Standard Version had "He shall see the fruit of the travail of his soul and be satisfied". The thought here is profoundly moving. If you, the reader of this commentary, and I, its writer, are followers of the servant-Messiah, we are a small part of the fruit borne by the travail of his soul. His pain was the pain of childbirth. It was so great that it penetrated into the depths of his innermost soul, and the servant died. We are the children of those agonising birth pains. Was it worth it? He who gave his life for us now looks on us, the fruit of the travail of his soul. What does he think? He sees light! He is satisfied! He is very pleased! This is extraordinary and life-changing.

'The righteous one, my servant, shall make many righteous'. It was only the one who was completely righteous who could *make* many righteous (2 Cor 5:21). The followers of the servant have an honourable part to play in the divine mission. Our part is to lead others into the righteousness that has been purchased for them by the servant. A beautiful Old Testament prophecy states that "Those who lead many to righteousness [will shine] like the stars forever and ever" (Dan 12:3).

'And he shall bear their iniquities'. Alec Motyer writes that "Verse 11 is one of the fullest statements of atonement theology ever penned. The servant knows the needs to be met and what must be done. As Yahweh's servant he is fully acceptable to the God whom our sins have offended, and he has also been appointed by Yahweh to his task. As righteous, he is free from every contagion of our sin. He identified himself personally with our sin and need. The emphatic pronoun *he* underlines his personal commitment to this role. He accomplishes his task fully: negatively, in the bearing of iniquity; positively, in the provision of righteousness".

12. *'Therefore I will allot him a portion with the great'.* The word *great* is translated as *many* elsewhere in the Old Testament, including four occasions in the fourth "servant song" (52:14, 15 and 53:11, 12). It would also be better translated as *many*

in this clause. Yahweh himself has the last word about the servant. He declares that he will vindicate the servant, and that his career will end in a triumph, the fruit of which will be shared by many. After his earthly mission had come to its victorious end, he has had increasingly many followers in every age who have marvelled at his moral beauty, at the dignity and majesty with which he accepted injustice, and at the wonder of the salvation that he achieved for all those who put their trust in him.

'And he shall divide the spoil with the strong'. Cyrus, servant of Yahweh, with his outstanding God-given might, failed to save the world though he did succeed in the mission that Yahweh assigned to him, the liberation of the Jewish captives in Babylon. Israel, servant of Yahweh, with her privileged status, failed to reach out and save the world, though she did succeed in putting into writing and then preserving the Old Testament scriptures, with which a small remnant nourished themselves, and out of whose stock came the Messiah. The Messiah himself, servant of Yahweh, in spite of having all the odds stacked against him, did save the world. He won a great spoil, which he would share with the *strong*. This word may also be translated *numerous*. It would then echo the word *many* in the previous clause. The servant received great booty after his great victory, and he would generously share it with many who suffered scarcity on his account.

'Because he poured out himself to death'. The servant was marked by his self-giving. He gave himself for the spiritually and materially poor and needy people of this world. He kept on giving himself and pouring himself out. In the end, he poured himself out to death. One of his early followers wrote, "[He] loved me and gave himself for me" (Gal 2:20).

'And was numbered with the transgressors'. The servant did not just die for the evildoers of this world. He identified with them. To all intents and purposes, he was one of them in his death, for he was executed in the company of two of them, one of whom he was able to restore (Lk 22:37, 23:32-33 and 39-43).

'Yet he bore the sin of many'. He had said during his ministry that he would die as a ransom for the sins of people: "[He] came not to be served but to serve, and to give his life a ransom for many" (Mk 10:45)

'And made intercession for the transgressors'. Real intercession is prayer for others coupled with intervention on their behalf. The servant's life was full of his intercessions and his interventions, and he also fulfilled this clause during his execution (Lk 23:34).

Meditation: The great Reward

The servant's presence in this great passage haunts us. He does not materialise in it, but is a spectre that astonishes us and leaves us speechless. The reason why the servant seems somewhat wraith-like is because this passage is a *prophecy*. At the time when the prophecy was fulfilled, however, the servant was perfectly real. The portrait of him in the four "good news books" that were written about him is extraordinarily lifelike. Those of us who have got to know him through reading those four books have found him to be more real in our experience than many of the people around us, some of whom seem quite unreal by comparison.

The servant was born around 525 years after the prophecy was written, and he died some thirty-five years later. His name was Jesus of Nazareth. He answered the questions that the prophecy left unanswered. The correspondence of the details in the four "servant songs" and those of his life, ministry, death and resurrection as recorded in the four "good news books" is remarkable.

Who was responsible for the death of the servant? Was it the religious authorities of his time, who subjected him to an unjust trial and condemned him to death for blasphemy because he equated himself with Yahweh? Was it the Roman rulers of his time, who gave in to local pressure and condemned him to death for sedition because he claimed to be a king? Was it the crowds, who were easily led to cry out for his execution? Was it his followers, one of whom betrayed him, another of whom disowned him, and the rest of whom deserted him? Was it you and I today, whose sins he bore? Ultimately it was none of these. *Yahweh* was responsible. It was his master plan for our salvation that his servant should die for our sins. It was the servant's wish to give himself for us.

Was it worth it? The servant would later remember his travail, his labour pains. He had seen with his eyes the timid oppressed by the strong, and the bereaved lamenting the loss of those deeply loved. He had heard with his ears the wailing of the world's sorrow, and the screams of those being tortured. He had sighed over the blind, the deaf, the dumb, the lepers and the possessed. He had retreated before the rejection and contempt of those he had come to save. All of these experiences, added together and multiplied by the incalculable number of needy people, had broken his compassionate heart. "How much longer?" he had asked.

These elements of emotional pain were part of what he suffered, but the much greater part was the indescribable agony he went through as the substitute and sacrifice for human sin. He poured himself out to death (v 12). The physical pain of crucifixion was in the background as he took upon himself the punishment that made us whole, and received the bruises by which we are healed (v 5). He tasted death for every one of us. He so identified himself with our sins, their shame and guilt, that he declared himself forsaken by God. This was perhaps the most terrible of all his many sufferings.

These were agonising "labour pains". And yet, "He shall see the fruit of the travail of his soul and be satisfied". Was it worth it? He won an eternal salvation for us. His triumph yielded great spoils, which he shared with the many, with numerous people who were spiritually poor and needy. We know from our experience that the best times in life are those in which we have been able to bless, to give joy, to encourage, to build up someone who was broken and in need. Sadly, our capacity and our opportunities to do this are limited by our human imperfections and weaknesses. But with the servant-Messiah this was not the case.

All power in heaven and earth has been given to him. He can use the power for the pure benefit of the many whom he ransomed from sin and shame. He shares not only his spoils with them, but also his portion. He calls us his friends – more than that, his brothers and sisters. And we may copy him, sharing our portion of human gifts and worldly goods with those he brings across our path. He will then look again, and once more see the fruit of the travail of his soul and be satisfied. This chain reaction of good, of self-giving, of sharing the Messiah's blessings with those who are poor and needy – this all stems from his passion and death. Surely *this* is his greatest reward. It was not enough to redeem a vast multitude. He then proceeds to share with them all the blessings he has rightly been awarded. God could not give, nor the servant ask for, a reward greater than this.

Worthy is the Lamb who was slaughtered to receive power, wealth, wisdom, might, honour, glory and blessing! We thank you, Lord Jesus, servant-Messiah, for all that you went through for us. Our remaining days in this life, and the numberless years of the next, will not suffice for us to praise you and worship you adequately – but we shall give it a go. Yours be all the praise, for ever and ever, for the honour of your great and worthy name. AMEN.

LXXXXIX

54:1-17 Yahweh and his People reconciled

This chapter's sense of peace, security and progress may be thought of as the consequence of the servant's sacrifice that we have just considered. In Christian terms, the atonement (52:13-53:12) is followed by the primitive church (chapter 54) and the preaching of the gospel message (chapter 55).

1. Jerusalem is addressed as a barren and desolate woman. She is told that she now has more children than before, and therefore she should burst into song. Paul linked this verse with the story of Sarah and Hagar (Gal 4:27), seeing in the New Jerusalem a picture of God's true people, born from above (see 49:14-23).

2. Jerusalem is asked to extend her tent in order to be able to fit in all her new children (49:20-21). There would be strains on the old structures (Mk 2:21-22).

3. The new community would spread out, taking over Gentile lands. There would be a worldwide expansion of the knowledge of Yahweh.

4. The people of God should not fear or be discouraged. The shame of Jerusalem's youth would be wiped out by her reconciliation to Yahweh, who was her maker and her husband. The distressing events that had led to their original separation would be forgotten. History was history; a glorious future was beckoning.

5. The people of God now had a husband who acknowledged them as his proper wife, and wished for very close and tender relations with them. He was their Maker, Yahweh of the armies, the Holy One of Israel, their Redeemer. He was far from being a mere tribal god, for he was the one true God, the God of the whole earth.

6. Yahweh had called back his erring wife. The metaphor picks up the thought in 50:1. The estrangement of a "wife of a man's youth when she is cast off" is acutely painful but need not be long-lasting. It is not the guilt of the estrangement but its pain that is being highlighted and dealt with. The guilt had already been borne away by the servant (53:4-6).

7. Jerusalem's rejection was only a temporary withdrawal of Yahweh's favour towards her. With great compassion Yahweh would win her back for himself.

8. In a moment of great anger Yahweh hid his face from Jerusalem. Then a change came over him, brought about by the servant's work (53:10). Yahweh ceased from wrath and instead showed grace, mercy and kindness. His reconciliation with Jerusalem is described in verses 8-10, and is full of tenderness. Yahweh's love is everlasting, so the restoration was final. Jerusalem was redeemed!

9. The permanence of the new relationship is illustrated by the covenant Yahweh made with Noah, whereby a universal flood would never happen again (Gen 9:11) Therefore the anger of Yahweh against Jerusalem was now a thing of the past; never again would Yahweh be angry with his people or rebuke them.

10. The permanence of the reunion is confirmed by the unchanging mountains and hills. Even they may depart and be no more, but the steadfast love of Yahweh will never depart, nor will his new covenant of peace ever be removed. This great promise stems from his compassion: it is undeserved, and also unconditional.

11. Verses 11-17 are a picture of the future people of God, the church, to whom some wonderful promises are being given. Yahweh declares that Jerusalem is afflicted and storm-tossed. She has not yet been comforted. Strength (mortar could be made from antimony) and beauty (various precious stones) would combine to make her a luxurious treasure-city. This picture would be picked up and developed in the New Testament (Rev 21:9-21).

12. The foundations, pinnacles and walls of the New Jerusalem would be made of precious stones such as blue sapphires and red rubies.

13. In the New Jerusalem there would be city-wide discipleship. The teaching of Yahweh (8:16) would be passed on from adults to children. The result would be righteousness and prosperity for all the citizens. The servant-Messiah would quote this text; he would be the teacher provided by Yahweh (Jn 6:45).

14. To hear Yahweh's teaching would bring about righteousness. The result of being righteous would be that the people of God would be established. Their position would be unassailable, for Yahweh would be at their side to protect them from enemy oppressors and from anything that might cause them fear or terror.

15. If any man tried to stir up strife with the people, it would not be Yahweh who had sent him. Furthermore, he would fail in his evil intent, because God's people were righteous, and Yahweh would back their cause.

16. As for any weapons produced for use against Jerusalem, it was Yahweh who had created both the blacksmith who had made those weapons, and the trouble-maker who wished to destroy the city of God. Who was in control? His people need fear no one else. It was only Yahweh himself whom they should fear.

17. Yahweh promises that no weapon fashioned against his people would prosper. They would be able to confound any satanic tongue that rose against them with false judgements or accusations. The New Jerusalem would be impregnable, unlike Babylon with its colossal walls and towers. She would of course suffer attacks of various sorts, as would the servant of Yahweh, but Yahweh would give her, as he would give his servant, the unanswerable weapon of truth (Lk 21:15). This would be the heritage and the vindication of all who were Yahweh's servants: peace, security, righteousness and victory over enemy opposition.

Meditation: What a great Salvation!

It is important that we should distinguish between the natural and the punitive consequences of wrongdoing. Suppose a man drinks too much and then behaves in a drunk and disorderly fashion, and is arrested. There will be two results. First, he has broken the laws of his country and must pay the penalty. He may have to spend the night drying out in a police cell, and then he may also be liable to a fine. These are the punitive consequences of getting drunk. Once he has paid the penalty, his standing is restored with regard to the law. But he may also suffer from a hangover and lapse into a depressed state, from which it may take him some time to recover. These are the natural consequences of getting drunk.

Some sins, by their very nature, have lasting natural consequences, even though their punitive consequences may be postponed to the next life. Suppose Mr Smith walks out on his wife and disappears, leaving Mrs Smith distraught with two young children to feed. The years go by. Mr Smith misses out on relating to his children as they surmount their difficulties and grow into adulthood. After a long time he returns home. Mrs Smith in saintly fashion welcomes him back and they are reconciled. But the two Smith children want nothing to do with him. He will forever be their unfaithful father who walked out on their mother. There is nothing he can do to win them back; he has missed out on the joys of parenthood.

If, after committing a sin, we confess it to God and turn from it in repentance, longing to do better in the future with God's help, we shall be forgiven and fully cleansed (1 Jn 1:9). Are the natural consequences of our sin removed? Sometimes they are – by the grace of God, and if those we have sinned against forgive us. At other times they are not, and we may have to live many years, if not the rest of our lives, with the consequences of the wrong things we have done in the past.

Think of an immensely costly Old Master painting. A vandal hammers some nails into the panel that supports it and scratches the paint. The art restorers can remove the nails. Maybe with painstaking care they can do a good job and restore the painting to much of its original glory. It has lost a great deal of its value, however, because it was damaged and then restored. It is no longer in its original condition. The saving work of the servant of Yahweh (53:4-6) is like that. After confessing our sin, we may be restored, forgiven, and fully accepted by God himself. But the natural consequences of our sin remain, and they may prove to be costly, or may cause us trouble and sadness for the rest of our lives.

Like many other prophecies in the book of Isaiah, the one in chapter 54 can be interpreted on at least three different levels. In the first place, it had an immediate fulfilment when the Jews who were exiled in Babylon returned to Jerusalem in 539 B.C. In our passage Yahweh promised them a new beginning. He assured them that his presence would accompany them, both during the journey and later, when the city was being rebuilt. He also promised to protect them from their enemies, who might attack them physically with violence, or emotionally and spiritually with verbal accusations.

Secondly, the prophecy may refer to the rebuilding of the city of God which has been ongoing in the days of the new covenant. God is at work edifying and restoring his people against a background of constant pressure and increasing opposition. The divine architect is watching over his people as he builds the renewed city (1 Pet 2:5). Each follower of the servant-Messiah is a living stone in the building. In this context, it is interesting to think about how these stones came into being. All of them are said to be precious gemstones: sapphires, rubies and other such jewels: how are these gemstones formed?

Gemstones are an ordinary mineral, often corundum mixed with other elements, which has been subjected to great heat and compression. These external pressures lead to the formation of these stones, which are very precious and of great beauty. The gates of the New Jerusalem are said to be great pearls (Rev 21:21). Pearls are formed when a tiny piece of grit falls into an oyster, causing it such pain and distress that it surrounds it with layers of calcium carbonate in crystalline form, so that the grit will lose its sharp bite. Instead it turns into a pearl. God's pearls and gemstones are formed through painful pressures and irritations.

Thirdly, the prophecy we are studying seems to be promising us an even greater redemption in the future, when even the natural consequences of our sins will be forever wiped out in the new start that we shall be given. The city of God that is built of priceless jewels is clearly not the present Jerusalem, built of bricks, rocks and cement. We shall live in the heavenly city, with our dark past fully forgotten. There we shall suffer no more shame or disgrace (v 4), we shall be loved eternally (v 8, 10), and never again will God be angry with us (v 9). We shall be taught perfectly (v 13), be established in righteousness (v 4), enjoy freedom from strife (v 15) and live happily with God, forever safe from any further physical attack or any accusation from a judgemental tongue (v 17).

The promise of salvation is of abundant forgiveness and protection in this life, and of full and perfect redemption from sin in the next life, including deliverance from all the natural consequences of sin. When we first trusted in the servant of Yahweh, we were saved from the *punishment* of sin. As we continue to trust in him, we are being saved from the *power* of sin. And when the great day arrives when we begin the new life in the New Jerusalem, we shall even be saved from the *presence* of sin. All this is thanks to the servant, who is glad to share his spoils with us. Hallelujah, what a saviour!

C

55:1-13 Invitation to Live

This passage, in which II Isaiah makes his bow, is a gem of the first water. As an invitation for those who are thirsty to come to God for salvation, it is outstanding. There is nothing else that surpasses it, not even in the New Testament. Verses 1-5 are about God's abundant grace, available as part of the benefits of the New Covenant. Verses 6-13 speak of the need for repentance, the urgency of accepting God's offer, and the great deliverance that will be accomplished.

1. The word *come* occurs three times in this verse, and once more in verse 3. It is addressed to those with a deep, unsatisfied thirst (as in Eccl 1:3, Jn 4:13, Jn 7:37-39). The offer is for the wistful and thirsty individual, as well as for the crowds who are spiritually poor and hungry. The Messiah claimed that he would himself fill up the inner void in people's hearts (Jn 6:35). The Bible draws to an end with an echo of this grace-filled offer (Rev 22:17). There is a delightful paradox at the end of the verse: "Buy . . . without money and without price". Salvation is beyond price, but it is available free of charge. What cost the sinless servant of Yahweh everything, costs us sinners nothing. Under grace, assured possession and total dependence are combined (Heb 4:16). This is a juxtaposition that most people find difficult because it strikes such a deadly blow to their pride.

2. Some of the exiled Jews had picked up the very Babylonian skill of making money through trade and business. They were in danger of losing their religion and their souls through their newly acquired devotion to materialism. Yahweh urges them not to waste their money and energy on something that could not satisfy them. What would be the point of gaining the world if the cost was their own souls? (Mk 8:36-37). Instead they could listen to Yahweh, receive his free offer, and delight themselves in what was richly nourishing and satisfying.

3. In this verse the invitation becomes fully personal. It engages the mind and will of those who are invited, and draws them into God's *new covenant* which is based on the servant's teaching and work (42:6, 49:8). The mention of David implies

that the Davidic Messiah prophesied by the first Isaiah is one and the same as the servant of Yahweh prophesied by II Isaiah.

4. When David was King of Israel, he conquered various heathen countries. As he became the "leader and commander" of these subject peoples, a knowledge of his religion, however fragmentary, spread among them, and by this means he became, in effect, "a witness to the peoples".

5. Likewise, the Jews to whom II Isaiah was preaching would in turn attract the attention of various heathen nations. They would be drawn by what Yahweh was doing for his people, and would be eager to learn from them about Yahweh and his servant, great David's greater descendant, the Messiah. This was a measure of how greatly Yahweh would bless them through his servant.

6. God's threefold calling of the sinner (v1) needs to be reciprocated by the sinner's calling of God. There is an urgency here. It is wonderfully possible to seek Yahweh – but only *while he may be found*. Anyone may call upon him – but only *while he is near*. The prophet might have added, "O that *today* you would listen to his voice! Do not harden your hearts" (Ps 95:7-8). The day of salvation is always *today*, if we hear God's call and reciprocate it with our own. Tomorrow we may be too busy, and we may be deaf towards God. If we continually refuse his call, he may conclude that there is no point in continuing to call us.

7. Any person who is inwardly hungry and needs that hunger to be satisfied, is also a wicked rebel against God and needs salvation. This verse provides an excellent definition of repentance. It is a challenge both for the will (*forsake their way*) and for the mind (*their thoughts*). It calls for a radical U-turn, from disobeying God to *returning* to him. It involves aspects that are both negative (*forsake*) and positive (*return*, i.e. turn towards). It is personal (*to Yahweh*) and specific (for *mercy*). Its appeal is backed up by the shortness of the time (v6) and also by the abundance of the promise (v7). It is paradoxical that the wicked and unrighteous come to God *just as they are*, but they also come in order to be transformed from what they are *into people who are pleasing to God*.

8. Yahweh explains why these truths might seem amazing to his people. It is because his thoughts and ways are different from theirs.

9. God's thoughts transcend the thoughts of men and women, just as heaven is higher than the earth. The thoughts of Yahweh are about his eternal purposes of redemption, and are therefore too vast and too sublime to be measured by the narrow conceptions of our flawed human minds (40:27-28, Jer 29:11, Mic 4:12).

10. Yahweh compares his word to rain and snow. These two forms of water come down from heaven and moisten the earth, bringing fertility and nourishment. Their work is slow and silent, but effective and essential.

11. Yahweh's word that he reveals through his prophets is both far-reaching and fertile, containing his purposes about salvation. His word is very powerful and

effective; one might say that "it is the power of God for salvation to everyone who has faith" (Rom 1:16). It does not return to Yahweh without accomplishing its purpose. It always succeeds in the mission on which he sent it. His word works invisibly, under the surface, unseen by other people (see Mk 4:26-29 – a neglected parable that expresses the Messiah's confidence that the Kingdom of God would prevail. Isaiah chapter 55 expresses the same certainty).

12. His word goes beyond us and our own circumscribed little world. Yahweh decrees life! The exiles will be liberated, and they will then be able to return safely to Jerusalem. Nature itself will rejoice at the salvation of God. Mountains and hills will sing, and trees will clap happily (35:1-10, 40:3-5, 41:17-20). This is Yahweh's redemption.

13. There will be a healing of the natural consequences of sin. The thorns and briers of life will be transformed into cypresses and myrtles. The resulting new world, eternal as a result of its renewal, will be both a living memorial and an everlasting sign to Yahweh and to his servant, the twin architects of this great salvation.

Meditation: A fruitful Conversation

This chapter is so logically built up that its genesis may go back to a conversation between II Isaiah and some Babylonian exiles shortly before their liberation. Here is a summary of that conversation, and with it we say good-bye to II Isaiah and prepare to meet his successor, the third prophet who made a major contribution to this great book, and who may also have been the person who edited the book of Isaiah into its present form. We shall refer to him simply as *the prophet*.

II Isaiah: I have an invitation for you. It is from Yahweh himself. He says, Come to me, you who are thirsty, and drink my vintage wine and double milk. Come to me, you who are hungry, and eat the rich food that I will give you.

Exiles: You make it sound very appealing. But what is the small print? How much will this top-class fare from Yahweh cost us?

II Isaiah: It will cost you nothing. The bounty on offer is indeed very costly, but its price has been paid in full by Yahweh's servant. For you, it is completely free.

Exiles: We are people who value the things we pay for. If what Yahweh offers is completely free of charge, what is the point in our receiving it? How can it be valuable to us if it costs us nothing?

II Isaiah: You have spent your life labouring for money. Has this satisfied you? No, you think you need to make more money. When you have all the money in the world, will that satisfy you? No. Stop labouring for what cannot satisfy you. Instead, come to Yahweh and delight yourselves with what he offers freely, and then you will be satisfied. Yahweh will make a new covenant with you, which will last for ever. You will at last be able to fulfil his world-wide mission.

Exiles: We are David's children, and we await great David's greater son, the Messiah, whose kingdom will embrace all the nations.

II Isaiah: You are absolutely right in saying this. You are beginning to realise that your primary role in this world is not to make lots of money but to witness to the nations. Once Yahweh is at work transforming your lives, these nations will run towards you like iron filings rushing to a magnet, because you will then have something wonderful that they do not have. Therefore, come to Yahweh today!

Exiles: You have convinced us. Yes, we will come to Yahweh, but in our own way and in our own time. We will first think about what we can do to transfer our money to the Jerusalem bank, and then we will come to Yahweh.

II Isaiah: No. Seek Yahweh *now*, while he may be found. You have admitted that he is near, so call upon him at this very moment. You may never again have such a good opportunity to return to your God.

Exiles: All right, all right. We get your point. We are coming to him. Obviously we must sort this out *now*. What exactly do we need to do?

II Isaiah: The most important thing you need to do is *repent*. Up to now you have been running away from Yahweh. You must do a U-turn and begin to run towards him. Put behind you your ungodly ways and your selfish thoughts. Return to God as best you know how. Beg him for mercy and he will be merciful. Confess your sins to him and he will freely forgive you. You will then start again from scratch. Yahweh will give you a clean sheet. He will forget all your past sins.

Exiles: We will, we will. Just one quick question. We believe what you are saying to us, but we find it difficult to understand. We are used to earning our way to the top. The way of Yahweh seems very strange. How can all our sins be forgiven?

II Isaiah: The reason why this is so difficult for you to understand is because Yahweh's thoughts and ways are much higher than your thoughts and ways. Think of it like this: heaven is much higher than earth. Therefore Yahweh's thinking is much higher than yours.

Exiles: That makes sense. After all, he made us. But we are businessmen. We are in the money-making world. It is a funny world with its own quirky little rules, but it is what we identify with, it is what makes us click. In what way will things change for us who inhabit this strange world?

II Isaiah: The best business in the whole world is the business of spreading the word of Yahweh. In this business you will possess a guaranteed long-term prosperity. Yahweh has made the most amazing promise, which will really take hold of your imagination. He sends forth from his mouth his word, his message, and – listen – it *never* returns to him void! It *always* accomplishes his purposes. It *always* succeeds in achieving his objective.

Exiles: Why does he send forth his word?

II Isaiah: First, to change people, and then, to feed them. His word is like rain and snow. Rain and snow come down from heaven, they water the plants and trees, and they provide grain and vegetables and fruit for your nourishment. It is true that at first the word of Yahweh is like a sword – it pierces your heart and brings about a radical change in your life. But after that, it is like food – you will need it in order to grow and become godly people, the sort of people you really want to be, and the people whom you were made to be.

Exiles: This sounds really good. In fact, it is getting better and better. What sort of changes will happen to us, what will we notice?

II Isaiah: It will be like your walks through the hanging gardens of this city, except more natural and much more beautiful. There will be abundant lush growth, watered by Yahweh. The trees will suddenly burst into applause because of what Yahweh is doing in you. The weeds will go; there will be no more thorns and briers. Instead – more trees, more plants, different varieties, lots of flowers, everything flourishing and fulfilling its potential. Every year that passes, things will get better and better. And then, one day, the kingdom of Yahweh will arrive in all its fullness. Yahweh's servant will be the King. The whole world will be wonderfully renewed. This will be a memorial for Yahweh, an everlasting sign that will never be cut off. You cannot imagine the wonder and the joy of it!

Exiles: Yahweh, Holy One of Israel, we surrender ourselves to you now. We have heard many things about you in the past, but now we come to you. We are undeserving and sorry. We thank you that your servant will save us from all our sins. We place our trust in you and in him. Accept us, O God our Redeemer. From now on, we are yours. AMEN.

PART 6 – THE FUTURE IN STORE

CI

56:1-8 Yes to Outcasts, No to corrupt Leaders

The third main author of the book of Isaiah wrote most of chapters 56-66 and then edited the whole book into the form that it has had until our own day. We shall refer to him as *the prophet*. His style is similar to that of II Isaiah, but his concerns were the welfare of the returning exiles and the problems of opposition and corruption that would arise back in Jerusalem. Once these exiles arrived back and began to resettle, they would live through times of great expectations and great difficulties. The prophet declared that Yahweh would rescue his people from their troubles and make them into a crown of beauty in his hand (62:3).

1. The captive Israelites were about to be set free by Cyrus. He would allow them to return to Jerusalem. They would soon set out, but who exactly would go? The prophet has some surprises in store for us. He begins with another oracle in which Yahweh extols the virtues of justice and righteousness. These are the qualities he demanded from his people; it was their responsibility to live like this. Yahweh's side of the deal was to provide salvation and deliverance. These would soon be forthcoming when Cyrus signed his edict and set the Jews free (Ezra 1:2-4).

2. Yahweh pronounces a benediction on those who maintain justice and do what is right. He picks out one area of concern, the keeping of the Sabbath. This had lapsed during the exile, for Babylon was a city of business: trade took place seven days per week. Many of the Jewish exiles had become important men of business, and they broke the Sabbath. They ignored the command to keep special one day in seven and reserve it for rest, recreation and worship. Yahweh's response was to declare blessed anyone who kept the Sabbath and did not profane it.

3. There were two groups of people who wondered if they would be allowed back. They were the Gentile converts to Judaism and the eunuchs. The former thought that Yahweh would separate them out from among his people, and the latter knew that they could not have children and were therefore barren, "a dry tree" unable to contribute to the procreation of the Israelites.

4. To the eunuchs, Yahweh said that what mattered was not their mutilation. They would not be barred from membership of his people on that account. The law may have given the opposite impression, but it was probably enacted to exclude those who had mutilated themselves as part of a heathen rite, and were continuing in their heathen ways (Deut 23:1). What was important was

whether eunuchs kept the Sabbath, thereby obeying God's covenant and choosing what pleased him.

5. If they did obey the terms of the covenant, Yahweh would provide a monument for eunuchs in his Temple, and they would be better off than if they had borne sons and daughters. He would give them an *everlasting* name among his people. The point of the law (Deut 23:1) was to make emasculation abhorrent in Israel.

6. To the foreign converts, Yahweh spoke in a similar manner. Their nationality was unimportant (Ex 12:48-49). What mattered was whether they worshipped Yahweh and loved being his servants, and – again – whether they kept the Sabbaths and did not profane them, thereby keeping his covenant.

7. Yahweh would bring these Gentile converts to Jerusalem, to his holy Temple. There they would rejoice, and their burnt offerings and sacrifices would be accepted on his altar. The Temple of Yahweh would be known as "a house of prayer for *all peoples*". Sadly the Messiah would be disappointed 568 years later, for this was not the case then. He would take action to restore the court of the Gentiles for the use of those for whom it had been intended (Mt 21:13).

8. Yahweh here declares that he would gather in the *outcasts* of Israel – eunuchs *and* Gentile converts. He also promises to gather in yet *more* outcasts. Yahweh loves the people whom the world rejects. This verse is a beautiful promise. Little-known among Bible readers, it would be familiar to the Messiah (Jn 10:16).

Meditation: God's Ways are not our Ways

The exiled Jews were getting ready to return to their homeland. Some wished to remain in Babylon and make lots of money; that was their decision. Those who wanted to leave would be free to do so – or would they? Two groups of people, eunuchs and Gentile converts, wondered if they would be eligible.

When people groups were taken captive in antiquity, their conquerors would emasculate some of the boys, to prevent their people group from growing too rapidly. The Jewish eunuchs would have included some who were descended from King Hezekiah (39:7), and because they could not propagate their family lines they wondered if they would be considered useless within the restored Israel. Not at all, said God. He did not look on their physical condition or their outward appearance. He looked into their hearts (1 Sam 16:7). If they were eager to please him and held on firmly to his covenant, he would not only welcome them back, but he would also give them a memorial that would last much longer than any sons or daughters would have done: he would give them an everlasting name!

The Gentile converts had been won over by the holy and pure religion of the Israelites. On being circumcised, they could join in the Sabbath worship that went on in the gatherings or synagogues that cropped up all over Babylon. But would these Babylonians or people from other foreign nations be considered to be God's people and allowed to join with the returning Jews? Once again, God said a clear yes! Provided that they loved him and worshipped him, they could go and live in Jerusalem, and they would even be eligible to enter the Temple precincts. There would be special place in God's house for them. They could offer sacrifices and rejoice in God's goodness like the rest of God's people.

In other words, those who were true Israelites because they loved God and wanted to live lives that were pleasing to him would be eligible, even if they could not contribute to the propagation of the Israelite race, and even if they were foreign converts. God wanted to gather the outcasts of the world and include them in the ranks of his own people. His ways are not our ways.

It may seem surprising to us today that for these two groups, as for everyone else who wished to return, one of the criteria of righteousness was whether or not they observed the Sabbath faithfully. Several of the Jews in Babylon evidently did not. Those who were in the money industry would have had to work every day of the week, and they could not have kept the Sabbath. They would have missed out on corporate worship, and they would probably have become liable to burn-out for failing to observe their maker's instructions (Ex 20:8-11). But we might well ask, why has the prophet included this emphasis on observing the Sabbath?

The same emphasis will reappear in 58:13 (see also Ezek 20:12-17 and 22:8, 26). Although it was one of the most ancient of Israel's religious institutions (Ex 20:8, Deut 5:12-15, Amos 8:5), the Sabbath acquired its special significance during the exile. In Babylon the ordinances of Temple worship had to be suspended, and the Sabbath and circumcision became the chief external signs of faithfulness to the covenant. The Sabbath was all about rest and worship. Rest for masters, rest for servants, and rest for their animals. It recalled the rest of Yahweh after he had completed his work of creating the heavens and the earth (Gen 2:2-3). It looked forward likewise to a time when his work of re-creation would also be complete. Then all his people would enjoy a Sabbath rest in the new earth that he would create for them to live in (66:22-23). Informal corporate worship was observed on the Sabbath in a manner that would later give way to synagogue worship. The Sabbath was not an end in itself, but a sign that the Israelites loved their God and wanted every part of their lives to be lived in submission to him. The observance of the Sabbath seems a strange custom in the 21st century, but it would have been taken for granted by the Jews. It should not seem strange to Christians today.

In the early days after the coming of the Messiah an event took place that showed God's concern for the outcasts of this world. The conversion of the Ethiopian eunuch (Acts 8:26-40) is a beautiful example of the gathering in of the outcasts (v 8) that began in earnest after the Messiah's life and ministry on earth. This Ethiopian court official was *both* a Gentile *and* a eunuch. It is interesting that the scroll that he happened to be reading when Philip the evangelist met him was from the book of Isaiah. It was, in fact, the fourth "servant song". That was the scripture that led to his conversion. He was the first fruits of a wonderful harvest of souls in the great continent of Africa, which is still going on today.

CII

56:9-57:13 Old Evils are to be avoided

The prophet now makes use of old material, probably from the reign of the evil King Manasseh, who was King of Judah from 696-642 B.C. In one of the darkest passages of the whole book of Isaiah, the prophet describes the evil ways of the Israelites in those days. These old evils were errors very much to be avoided in the future, especially in the new start that Yahweh was about to provide for his people. On arrival in Jerusalem, they were not to revert to the evil ways of their ancestors, lest the fate that befell those ancestors should be repeated.

9. The prophet addresses himself to "the wild animals in the forest". These were heartless people who preyed on the innocent and vulnerable in order to deprive them of their money or their innocence. He tells them that they could come and devour God's people, for there was no one competent to come to their defence.

10. The *sentinels* or watchmen were the religious leaders of Israel – priests and prophets – in the days of King Manasseh. They should have been on the lookout for "the wild animals", so as to give good warning of their approach to the people of God. But they neglected their duty. They were *blind* dogs, and had no vision. Therefore they were *without knowledge*, and as a result they were *silent* dogs that could not bark, priests with no message. Instead of preaching, they lay down and *dreamt*, indulging themselves in day-dreaming.

11. Finally, these religious leaders pleased themselves: their appetite was mighty, like that of dogs who *never had enough*. The *shepherds* were the rulers of Israel. If anything, they were worse than the religious leaders. They were mindless, and during the reign of King Manasseh they all did their own thing. They lived for the sake of their own gain.

12. They drank too much wine and strong drink, and in the end one day would be followed by another, all of them "great beyond measure", because their lives consisted of an endless series of alcoholic binges.

57:1. During his reign, King Manasseh "shed very much innocent blood, until he had filled Jerusalem from one end to another" (2 Ki 21:16). The righteous people of Jerusalem perished as a result. Those who were devout were "taken away from calamity". Their murders may have spared them from worse things to come. The prophet laments the fact that no one took these atrocities to heart, nor did any one understand the significance of what was going on. But Yahweh saw and knew. "Because King Manasseh of Judah has committed these abominations, thus says Yahweh, the God of Israel, I am bringing upon Jerusalem and Judah such evil that the ears of everyone who hears of it will tingle" (2 Ki 21:11-12).

2. Those who were upright entered into *peace* and *rested* on their "couches", meaning their tombs or biers (2 Chron 16:14, Rev 14:13). Once they were murdered, no further

distress or harm could befall them. In a time of disaster it is far better to die and to *rest in peace* with Yahweh than to live on in terror and anxiety. For the wicked leaders who had oppressed them there would be neither *rest* (v 20) nor *peace* (v 21).

3. The prophet bids any Israelites who may be harbouring any of these old sins in their hearts to draw near to him and receive a severe dressing-down. He calls them the "children of a sorceress", the "offspring of an adulterer and a whore".

4. They loved to mock the godly, despising them with abusive gestures. They were difficult to deal with, disobedient and insincere, "children of transgression, the offspring of deceit".

5. The Israelites had learnt idolatrous ways from the Canaanites whom they had displaced when they took over the Promised Land. Two of their cults are referred to here. The fertility cult was associated with evergreen trees as a symbol of life, and it was expressed in orgiastic cults. The cult of Molech went further, involving child sacrifices. The first Isaiah had preached against these kinds of idolatry, with their ugly sexual practices and dark associations (1:29, 17:8-11). After the godly King Hezekiah died, the people of Judah returned *en masse* to their old idolatry, which was ingrained in their hearts (2 Ki 21:1-5). They even slaughtered their sons, imitating their King, Manasseh, who had burned his own son as a sacrifice to the pagan god Molech (2 Ki 21:6). They carefully chose desolate and secluded spots for the performance of these odious practices.

6. In verses 6-13 *you* is consistently feminine. The prophet warns the returning exiles to steer well clear of the false gods that many of their ancestors worshipped. These practices prompted him to compare them to a harlot. This figurative use of harlotry is common in the Old Testament. Ezekiel developed the comparison at length in his prophecy (Ezek 16:1-58 and 23:1-49). Before the exile the people of God would descend to the *wadis* to pour out drink and grain offerings to their idols and false gods. Yahweh refused to be appeased after such behaviour.

7. On the mountain tops they would build a bed in order to perform sexual rites. There they also offered sacrifices to idols.

8. Behind their doors they would set up their phallic symbol, a carving of a male or female genital organ. They worshipped false gods or idols, and indulged in sexual orgies. In this way they were unfaithful to Yahweh, the Holy One of Israel, to whom they were wedded by covenant. He was their rightful "husband", but they uncovered their bed and made it wide in order to "sleep around" with other gods. Because there was a strong sexual aspect to this cult, and because the Israelites "loved their bed", the charge of spiritual adultery stood.

9. They made special pilgrimages to the shrines of the heathen god Molech, taking with them special perfumes to anoint themselves during the rituals. They also sent envoys to other nations in an attempt to forge alliances, instead of trusting in Yahweh to protect them from enemy invasions.

10. They persisted in these manifold idolatries to the point of weariness. They got no lasting satisfaction from them, but nevertheless went on and on. They refused to recognise that what they were doing was "useless". Every so often their desire was rekindled and off they went again. There is an observant eye behind this picture of grim but weary determination.

11. Behind their addiction to idols the prophet detects a complete lack of the fear of Yahweh. They lived a lie, pretending to follow Yahweh, but they never thought of him nor remembered him. It was as if Yahweh had kept silent and closed his eyes – but he had not! Their infatuation would inevitably lead to disillusion.

12. Yahweh would concede that they performed their Temple rituals and paid lip service to him, but this outward righteousness would not count in their favour. Correct religious practice is no guarantee of its authenticity.

13. When the going got tough, they would naturally cry out to their idols, and it would be a futile waste of breath. Idols were spiritually insubstantial and would soon be gone with the wind. On the other hand, those who took refuge in Yahweh would soon repossess the land and inherit the holy Temple mount.

Meditation: The severe Warnings of God

The passage we are studying is firmly set in the mountainous country of Judah with its valleys, rocky outcrops and streams (57:5-7). It details the false worship of the people of Judah in the days of the evil King Manasseh, who restored idol worship after the reforms of his father, the godly King Hezekiah (57:6-10). Manasseh also made his son "pass through the fire" as a sacrifice to the terrifying heathen god Molech. His government was corrupt because of cronyism, and the religious leaders were no better (56:9-12). Manasseh instituted a purge of the few who were really godly, putting them to the sword or causing them to disappear. At least this meant that they were spared further atrocities (57:1-2).

The people of Judah were exiled because they ignored Yahweh and disobeyed him in a way that the prophets likened to adultery. They, as the people of God, were spiritually married to God, but by their idolatry and worship of false gods they had committed adultery. Now, after suffering many indignities and pangs of conscience during the exile, they were about to return home. It was essential that they did not lapse into their former idolatrous ways, so the prophet reminds them of what their ancestors used to be like and describes the evils of false religion as starkly as he is able. He gives the returning exiles four good reasons why they should remain faithful to Yahweh and avoid false worship like the plague.

First, the social results of false worship would be so appalling that in some cases it would be better for a godly person to die and rest in peace with God than to live on in an evil and adulterous generation (57:1-2).

Secondly, false religion is often an excuse for indulgence in sexual practices that are harmful and forbidden (57:7-10). Excessive sexual activity is debilitating. Not only is it physically draining, but the fact that it is forbidden by God and therefore wrong is damaging to the consciences of those who indulge in it (57:3-4).

Thirdly, the addiction to sex or the worship of false gods is very unsatisfying. This type of worship promises much but delivers nothing more than a fleeting sense of gratification. It leads to an addiction to sex. It may promise freedom, but it leads to enslavement. It ultimately fails to deliver what it promises (57:10).

Fourthly, when the storms of life come, as they surely will to everyone (Mt 7:24-27), false gods and idols will be utterly useless. They will then be seen to be what they are, less substantial than the wind or even a fleeting breath (57:13).

In his devotional commentary on Isaiah entitled "Straight to the Heart of Isaiah", Phil Moore makes the following comment: "The Lord allowed the people of Old Jerusalem to wear themselves out with their religion, just as he allows churches to wear themselves out today chasing church growth through the latest paperbacks and conferences. He brought them to the end of their strength so that they might lay hold of him, yet tragically they refused". Here is a comment from a 21ˢᵗ century church leader in the modern charismatic tradition who has realised the difference between true and false worship. True worship engages with the living God who is both holy and loving; it involves personal study of scripture; it aims through its preaching to declare the whole counsel of God; and it is both fulfilling and satisfying. False worship in the churches of the 21ˢᵗ century involves the cult of a God whose sentimental love appears to override his holiness; it fails to engage with the Bible and all the problems that it raises; it aims through its services to maintain the worshippers on a constant emotional "high"; and it proves wearying and unsatisfying in the long run.

CIII

57:14-21 The God of Grace speaks

The gracious offers of Yahweh in this passage contrast with the warning tone of verses 1-13, which we have just studied. The elevated language of the second half of chapter 57 is quite different from the stark, down-to-earth language of the first half. It would seem that there are times when Yahweh has to rebuke and punish his people, but he does so only in order to proceed to reassure and restore them.

14. The exodus from Babylon has begun. Yahweh speaks, but his tone is full of grace: "Build up, build up; prepare the way, remove every obstruction from my people's way". Every obstacle that blocks the progress of God's people needs to be cleared away. Yahweh is determined that they will grow in grace and in their knowledge of him. His teaching and his resourcefulness will do the trick.

15. Grace condescends. Yahweh describes himself as "the high and lofty one who inhabits eternity, whose name is holy". *High* and *lofty* are adjectives that aptly describe the great being who is almighty God, the creator of heaven and earth. These adjectives have already appeared together in descriptions of him in 6:1, and of his servant in 52:13. He inhabits eternity. There he sits enthroned for ever. Because his name, i.e. his essential being, is *Holy*, he dwells in the high and holy place. His abode is at present inaccessible to us. He "dwells in unapproachable light, whom no one has ever seen or can see" (1 Tim 6:16). But that is not the only place where the living and true God dwells. He is a humble God, and he dwells with those who are contrite and humble in spirit. Why does the high and lofty one stoop so low in his choice of alternative accommodation? It is because he purposes "to revive the spirit of the humble, and to revive the heart of the contrite". The condescending God descends into humble hearts.

16. **Grace gently forbears.** Yahweh is forbearing, which means that he patiently abstains from being over-severe in his dealings with his disobedient people. The motive for his divine clemency is his compassion for the frailty of his creatures. Were he to prolong his legal claims and his righteous anger, he would do them more harm than good. He does not want the spirits of his people to grow faint.

17. **Grace sometimes has to punish.** Before the exile (Jer 6:13) and after it (Neh 5:1-13) covetousness was a common sin among the Israelites, especially among the wealthy. They were avaricious and did not attend to the needs of the poor (56:11). Therefore, Yahweh was angry and punished them. He also withdrew the sense of his presence from them, but they just kept going back to old sins.

18. **Grace reclaims the undeserving and unpromising.** Yahweh is perfectly aware of the faithless disobedience of his people. Nevertheless, when they rebel against him, his first thought is of how he will heal them, lead them and repay them good for evil. He hopes that in due course they may mourn their sins and bring forth "good fruit" from their lips (Hos 14:2, Heb 13:15). God always punishes sin, yet he will not abandon the sinner. Somehow, his anger turns to salvation (12:1).

19. **Grace offers peace to those who are far and those who are near.** This verse was quoted by the Apostle Paul, who referred it to Gentiles and Jews (Eph 2:17).

20. **Grace is persistently refused by some people.** They are the wicked. Their fate is ongoing restlessness; they will not find peace. The image used here of a restless tossing sea was taken up by Jude in his epistle (Jude 13).

21. It is the choices people make which will determine whether they have "Peace, peace" (v19) or "No peace" (v21). The wicked have free will and are entitled to choose. They will realise that choices, like actions, have consequences. This has been well written as follows: "No God, no peace. Know God, Know peace".

Meditation: The dwelling Places of Almighty God

Isaiah 57:15 is a prime candidate for the accolade of being the most wonderful verse in the whole book of Isaiah. Taken in context, against the dark background of 56:9-57:13

and the wonderful outpouring of grace in verses 14-19, it is a deeply encouraging text that will both repay memorisation and inspire private worship. It deals with the two dwelling places of the Holy One, his principal residence and his second home.

The verse begins with the self-revelation of who God is. We could not work this out for ourselves: God had to reveal it to us. He refers to himself as the high and lofty one, transcendent and above all. These two adjectives, "high" and "lofty" can only be used to describe one being, and that is God himself in his various persons: Yahweh or the Father, the Messiah or servant of Yahweh, and the Spirit of God. No one else is high and lofty. No fallen and flawed person is high and lofty. Some may act as though they were high and lofty, and when they do this they are stealing the attributes of God and attempting to pass them off as their own. In particular, the proud of this world love to think of themselves as high and lofty. In the end, this will only earn them the judgement of God. It is worth reminding ourselves of what the day of judgement will be like. It is described in 2:10-21, and 2:12 is particularly worthy of note, "Yahweh has a day against all that is proud and lofty, against all that is lifted up and high".

God is the high and lofty one, whose name is Holy (the Holy One of Israel). He inhabits eternity, and dwells in the high and holy place. That is the only place that is clearly fit to be his habitation. The Israelites all knew this. It was true that in a symbolic sense his presence dwelt with his people in the Temple, which was "the house of God". The inner room of the Temple was called the "Holy of holies" and there, on the gold cover above the ark, was the mercy seat for the divine presence. But God himself dwelt in the highest heaven.

King Solomon emphasised that God's dwelling place was in heaven during his prayer of dedication for the newly built Temple of Jerusalem. "But will God indeed dwell on the earth? Even heaven and the highest heaven cannot contain you, much less this house that I have built" (1 Ki 8:27). Solomon repeated the truth that God dwelt in heaven a *further eight times* (1 Ki 8:30, 32, 34, 36, 39, 43, 45 and 49). He could not have put it more clearly. God's people might pray towards the Temple, which symbolised his presence with them. But God himself did not live there. He dwelt in heaven. The Temple itself was not inviolable; the time would come, in 586 B.C., when it would be destroyed.

So much for the first half of Isaiah 57:15. The high and lofty one dwells in the high and holy place. But the verse goes on to reveal to us something else which we could not have worked out for ourselves. God has a second home here on earth. It is more modest in size and comfort than the Temple built for his presence by King Solomon. God also dwells "with those who are contrite and humble in spirit, to revive the spirit of the humble, and to revive the heart of the contrite".

The consequences of this are awe-inspiring, but they are wonderfully and gloriously true. The Holy One, the Almighty God who made heaven and earth, is so humble that he gladly and willingly comes and dwells in the innermost beings of those who are contrite and humble. For us, to be contrite is to be broken-hearted on account of the sins we have committed and their consequences. For us, to be humble is to realise our smallness and insignificance when compared to God. God comes in the person of his Holy Spirit and dwells in the hearts of people who are both contrite and humble. Our bodies become the Temple of the Holy Spirit. They are no longer our own. They were bought by the blood of the servant-Messiah. Therefore we aim to glorify God in our bodies (1 Cor 6:19-20).

Isaiah 57:15 is strikingly paradoxical. The holiness of Yahweh places him at an unapproachable distance from human pride and greatness, and at the same time his love brings him very near to the humble in spirit (Ps 138:6, and see also Ps 113:5-6). Israel had learnt through the discipline of the exile that God was both utterly exalted and utterly condescending. Peace with God was attained through humility, by recognising that God was perfectly holy and they were not.

CIV

58:1-14 Worship - hypocritical or true?

By now the exiles had begun to settle in Jerusalem and in the surrounding land. Outwardly they were worshipping Yahweh, and they even seemed to delight in him. Nevertheless, something was going wrong. Their prayers were not being answered, and Yahweh pointed out the reason. Their worship was just an act. It lacked sincerity. It was not real. It was contradicted by their behaviour, which was displeasing to God and opened them up to the charge of hypocrisy.

1. Yahweh urged his prophet to raise his voice to the full as he confronted the people with their rebelliousness and their sins (Mic 3:8). They had lapsed into sin once again, but they tried to hide their sins behind good religious practices.

2. The people did indeed seek Yahweh. They acted as if they were a nation that followed his ways and did what was right. You could not have told whether they were being righteous or whether they were wandering away from Yahweh's good path. All the signs were very good. They kept asking Yahweh for direction, and they were glad as they came to him. The big question was whether their religiosity was accompanied by action.

3. The people complained that they did indeed fast, but the efforts they made in order to humble themselves seemed to go unseen by Yahweh. In his reply, he in turn asked them if the kind of fasts they practised could possibly be pleasing to him (v3b-5). He began by pointing out that on fast days they looked after their own interests and oppressed their labourers by forcing them to work, and so break the Sabbath. Their social insensitivity was an ugly thing (Jas 5:1-5). God would have found it nauseating (1:15-17).

4. Their fasting made the people of God irritable and quarrelsome. Occasionally they would even lapse into violence. Such thoughtless and insensitive fasting

meant that their prayers were not heard by God on high, let alone answered. "My words fly up, my thoughts remain below; Words without thoughts never to heaven go" (Shakespeare, *Hamlet*, Act 3, Scene 3).

5. Yahweh asks whether true fasting consists merely of public self-humbling, stooping like a bulrush and wearing sackcloth and ashes. Was it a public show of discomfort such as this that the Israelites considered to be a fast?

6. Yahweh now drops a bombshell. He redefines fasting so that, in contrast to a hypocritical outward show, it includes justice for the oppressed (v6) and loving care for the destitute (v7). First of all, it must lead to the restoration of servants and slaves, who should be treated with justice and no longer oppressed (Neh 5:5). Whoever seeks mercy from God must show mercy to his fellow humans.

7. Furthermore, fasting involves sharing food with the hungry, providing shelter for the homeless, and donating clothing to the destitute. This task must begin with the poor who live nearby, but it will also involve the poor who are far away.

8. When Yahweh's people understood what true religion was and complied with its requirements, he would pour upon them one blessing after another (v8-12). Their *light*, meaning their salvation, would break forth like the dawn. Their ailments would rapidly be healed. If they were wronged, they would be vindicated by a show of Yahweh's favour. Yahweh's glory would always follow them.

9. Then Yahweh would hear and answer their prayers. This is Yahweh's reply to their moans about unanswered prayer (v3a, 4b, see also Jas 4:3-10). If trouble came, they could cry to him and he would be right there with them. The section from verses 9b to 12 may be summed up by the Messiah's saying, "The measure you give will be the measure you get" (Mt 7:2). They were to stop oppressing people. They were not to point at them with contempt, nor to malign them.

10. They were to feed the hungry and relieve the needs of the afflicted. Then their salvation would appear, and their problems would melt away.

11. Then Yahweh would guide them continually, and satisfy their hunger for him in the difficult times. He would strengthen them inwardly and they would be as fresh and as fruitful as a watered garden. They would bring refreshment to others like an unfailing spring of water. The attractive image of our lives being like a watered garden was first introduced by the prophet Jeremiah (Jer 31:12).

12. Their rebuilding projects in Jerusalem would be successfully completed, and their new buildings would last for many generations. They would succeed in the repairs of their city wall, and they would be enabled to restore the streets of the city to their former evenness. Most of the book of Nehemiah (Neh 1:1-7:4) consists of an eyewitness account of how the rebuilding was achieved.

13. Yahweh continues with instructions about how the Sabbath was to be kept. He desired an observance that was both unselfish and also full of gladness and gratitude. They were to forget about going their own way or pursuing their own

interests on that day. They were to honour the Sabbath and make it delightful. Their hearts were to be so thrilled with Yahweh that the day set apart for him would be a source of joy from start to finish.

14. Then they would take delight in Yahweh (Ps 37:4) and he would carry them triumphantly over all the obstacles in their path. They would enjoy the heritage of their ancestor Jacob (also called Israel). It would have proved worthwhile for them to have kept the Sabbath as a special day, for Yahweh in turn would keep his promises and shower blessings upon them.

Meditation: Yahweh and his Servant agree

In this passage the people of God, freshly returned from exile, are urged to repent of their religious wrongdoing. There were four acts of piety which they either neglected or else practised in the wrong way: almsgiving, prayer, fasting, and keeping the Sabbath holy to God. As a result, their religion looked devout when in fact it was hypocritical, and lacked reality and spiritual truth.

The problem is expressed very clearly in verses 2-3a and 4b. Day after day the people went through their religious duties. They tried hard to please God, to the extent that they pretended to delight in drawing near to him. But it was all pointless: they fasted but God did not see, they humbled themselves, but he took no notice, and they prayed, but their voice was not heard. What was wrong?

(a) **Their almsgiving was wrong.** They did not care about the poor and needy. They did not feed them, nor did they shelter them, nor did they provide clothing for them – not even for the poor and needy that were their close relatives (v7).

(b) **Their prayers were wrong.** They met regularly for worship. They prayed and read their scriptures. They enjoyed practising their religion. They delighted to draw near to God (v2). They thought God would be very pleased – but they were completely mistaken. God does not care for ritual without righteousness. To attend a thousand services will not do anyone any good if he or she is disobeying God at the same time. The servant-Messiah would say to the people of his day who heard his word but did not act on it, "Why do you call me 'Lord, Lord', and not do what I tell you?" (Lk 6:46-49). The prayer of the impenitent sinner bounces off the roof (59:1-2), but the prayer of the righteous is powerful (Jas 5:16).

(c) **Their fasting was wrong.** They fasted in an attempt to manipulate God into blessing them. Their purpose was not to draw near to God but to serve their own interests (v3b-4). Their motive was to put on a show of self-sacrifice that might impress God (v5). Before they fasted, they should have made sure that their servants and slaves had the same freedom to fast as they had (v6). True fasting must include self-denial, dealing with others rightly, and delighting in God. We refuse to eat one of this world's meals in order to feast on the Bread of Heaven.

(d) **Their Sabbath observance was wrong.** They set aside its principles; they pursued their own interests on that day instead of God's; for them it was not a delightful day of rest and worship to look forward to; and they dishonoured it even though it was firmly established as one of God's institutions (v 13).

Sabbath-keeping is much disregarded by God's people in the 21ˢᵗ century. But as an institution it is ancient, independent of geographical place and historical time, and it has twice survived the disappearance of other aspects of its religion (in the exile and in the shift from Judaism to Christianity). It is an essential component of a spiritual religion and of a just social morality. It has more than proved its divine origin and its indispensability to humanity.

The servant-Messiah would teach his followers that the first three of these, almsgiving, praying, and fasting, were to be done in secret, in order to avoid the possibility of hypocrisy (Mt 6:2-4, 5-6 and 16-18). The general principle he gave was, "Beware of practising your piety before others in order to be seen by them; for then you have no reward from your Father in heaven" (Mt 6:1).

On the subject of Sabbath-keeping, the practice would become so riddled with petty legalisms that it would turn into a burden too heavy to bear. No believer could delight in it or look forward to it. The servant-Messiah would urge the people of his time to return to the standard set in verses 13-14, teaching that "The Sabbath was made for humankind, and not humankind for the Sabbath" and that he, "The Son of Man, [was] Lord even of the Sabbath" (Mk 2:27).

What are the blessings that will come our way if we practise our piety in the right way? This writer has counted nineteen in this passage: four in verse 8, two in verse 9, one in verse 10, five in verse 11, four in verse 12 and three in verse 14. The ones in verse 11 are particularly attractive: day-by-day divine guidance, needs satisfied in difficult times, inner strength, unfailing fruit-bearing, and inner refreshment that we can share with other thirsty people.

How could the problems of hypocritical or unreal religious practice be sorted out if they recurred in today's church? The answer is in our passage, in verse 1. Today's preachers are called by God to shout out and not hold back. They are to lift up their voices like a trumpet. What is it they are to proclaim? As part of their message, they are to announce to God's people their rebellion and their sins. They are to urge the people to repent. They are to warn the people that if they continue as they are, their prayers will not be heard and their piety will be unreal. Equally, they are to assure the people that if they repent and come back to basics, God's blessing will come upon them in extraordinary abundance.

CV

59:1-15a God will deal with Injustice

Once again there is a problem with unanswered prayer. But while chapter 58 describes true piety and the blessings that accrue to those who practise it, chapter

59 paints a picture of sin (v 3-8) and its distortion of all good values (v 9-15a). Its end is anarchy and chaos, when life is no longer worth living.

1. The people think that the obstacle to their salvation must be the impotence or indifference of God. But his hand is strong to save, and his ear can hear very well.

2. The true reason for God's seeming silence and inactivity is the *separation* that our sins have created between him and us. They have formed a barrier. This is because sin separates. Guilt causes the alienation between people and God.

3. The hands and fingers of God's people were like the hands and fingers of Lady Macbeth, stained with guilt. Their lips and tongue uttered wickedness. In verses 3-8 we see the effects of sin as it spreads. Our fellowship with God cannot survive it, nor does society. The whole community becomes infected with guilt, and the moral law is breached.

4. The justice system becomes corrupt. Legal procedure is abused, and lawsuits are conducted with an absolute disregard for justice and truth.

5. The *adders' eggs* represent the poisonous influence of sinful people, which has a toxic effect on others. The attempts made by the righteous to stamp it out only seem to propagate it all the more.

6. The *spiders' web* (introduced in v 5) speaks of the futility of relying on the policies or promises of sinful people: they are flimsy. Their works are malicious and their hands perpetrate violent deeds. Alec Motyer sums up the significance of the adders' eggs and the spider's web as follows: "There is a constant factor in us as sinners which is a menace to others and which makes us continually ineffective in what we do for ourselves. Sin is a contagion and a frustration".

7. Evil men are quick to do what is wrong, even to the extent of murdering the innocent. Their thoughts of shame precede their deeds of shame. The Apostle Paul used verses 7-8 in his argument to prove our universal guilt (Rom 3:15-17).

8. They have no desire for peace, and their ways are unjust. They are crooks through and through, and those who follow them forfeit their peace.

9. The word *therefore* ushers in the progressive consequences of having chosen evil. The sorrow and dejection of the people is depicted in verses 9-12 in striking and pathetic images. It is a picture of their better side. They long for salvation, denoted here by the words *justice* and *righteousness*. They are weary because of its ongoing deferment, which is caused by their failure to repent, and they feel like weaklings. They are reduced to waiting in darkness for the light to come.

10. The groping of the blind and the stumbling in broad daylight is a metaphor for the judgement of God. When people are visited by it their way of thinking is affected and they walk in darkness. The opponents of the Messiah would court the judgement (Jn 3:19) and later suffer its blinding (Jn 9:39-41, 12:35-40).

11. The people vainly long for deliverance and peace. They growl like captive bears and coo like mournful doves. They must continue to wait.

12. The people finally confess their sins, which have caused them such misery (v 12-15a). Like David who sinned before them, they cry out to God, "For I know my transgressions, and my sin is ever before me" (Ps 51:3).

13. There follows a list of the general sins which they know they have committed: they have overstepped the mark laid down by God and gone beyond it; they have disowned him by their idolatries; they have deviated from the morality that God has laid down for them; their talk has been about oppressing others and revolting against authority; and they have devised untruths and spoken them from the heart.

14. Justice, righteousness, truth and uprightness are now personified. Three of the four have been barred from participation in society, and one, truth, has stumbled. In godless times all of the virtues suffer. Many are simply excluded, but truth is often the first casualty, in this case in the market square. Two sets of weights were in use: those for purchases were too light; those for sales were too heavy.

15a. Truth has fallen and is no more. Those who are decent are victimised because they are the only ones who are out of step. It is not only public justice that has gone awry; so has public opinion (Amos 5:13).

Meditation: Sin spoils, Sin spreads, Sin separates

In the old days, when sermons used to be preached about our sins and their consequences, there was an often repeated but nevertheless very good three-point sermon, whose headings were entitled: sin spoils, sin spreads and sin separates. Various passages of the Bible could be expounded with integrity by using these three points, and our passage today is one of them.

(a) Sin spoils. There is abundant evidence of this. We are sinners like Lady Macbeth, and we cannot wash off the bloodstains from our hands. Even after being forgiven, some sins continue to haunt us with their natural consequences. Our words cause distress to others, and we cannot control our tongues (v3). Our sins are shameful and they are like clothing that cannot be hidden – except that the clothing is thinner than gossamer and is quite useless as a result (v6). The sinner loses the ability to remain calm, and knows no peace (v8). We wait for God's blessing, but in vain – there is nothing but inky darkness (v9) and increasing blindness (v10). We lament and mourn (v11), until in despair we finally confess our sins to God (v12-13).

(b) Sin spreads. We all agree that justice is now greatly flawed and its rulings are flawed – especially if they affect us (v4). Our sins are like poison for other people, and sometimes we cannot eradicate them: any attempt to do so proves counter-productive and they spread all the more (v5). We begin by cultivating shameful thoughts, which lead to a harvest of sinful actions and eventually to a network of sinful habits or highways (v7). Virtues that we have cultivated in the past begin to be absent from our speech and actions, and in some cases they even die away (v14). We vent our frustrations on anyone who dares to make a stand for good, because we feel shown up for what we really are (v15a).

(c) Sin separates. There it is, in verses 1-2. Because of our sin, there is a barrier between us and God. We cannot see him because there is a great dark roof hanging in the air between him and us, the barrier of sin. He is therefore hidden from us, and without his gentle presence accompanying us, our faith becomes unreal and we begin to doubt the goodness or the power of God, sometimes even his very existence. We feel alienated and anxious; life loses its zest.

Because of our sins, there is only one thing we can do, and that is to lament them. They have brought us nothing but misery. They have spread and infected other people. They have created a barrier between us and God, effectively hiding his face from us. Public lamenting of sin is out of fashion in today's church. In the Church of England there is a General Confession. It was once widely used in the service of Holy Communion, but this is no longer the case. Here are its words:

"Almighty God, Father of our Lord Jesus Christ, Maker of all things, Judge of all people: We acknowledge and bewail our manifold sins and wickedness, which we from time to time most grievously have committed, by thought, word and deed against your divine majesty, provoking most justly your wrath and indignation against us. We do earnestly repent, and are heartily sorry for these our misdoings. The remembrance of them is grievous unto us, their burden is intolerable. Have mercy upon us, have mercy upon us, most merciful Father; for your Son our Lord Jesus Christ's sake, forgive us all that is past; and grant that we may ever hereafter serve and please you in newness of life, to the honour and glory of your name, through Jesus Christ our Lord, Amen".

This bewailing of sins committed is what we have in verses 9-15a. There are numerous communal laments like this in the Old Testament, including several of the Psalms (e.g. numbers 12, 44, 60, 74, 80, 85, 90). These prayers are prayed (or rather, used to be prayed) in deepest contrition, with tears in the eyes of those who prayed. There was no more pretending that everything was all right, or that one could keep on coping. People had come to the end of themselves. They knew they could not deliver themselves. They cried loudly to their God.

Already in post-exilic times, some 2,550 years ago, such public confession and bewailing of sins was beginning to be unpopular and to go out of fashion. "Truth is lacking, and whoever turns from evil is despoiled" (v15a). Even in church circles, anyone who is out of step with the current trends is sidelined. In the year 2020, when the present book was written during the Corona Virus lockdown, most Church of England worship services included only an unsatisfactory and very superficial confession of sins. The present author's stated concern for the poverty of the wording of the services and the Biblical imbalance of most of the preaching has been dismissed by several members of the clergy.

Is it any surprise that the quality of most of the Christian literature published in the 21st century is so disappointing? Those who were brought up on the great Christian books and commentaries of old say that "The old is better". The old-fashioned Christian books were much better at presenting a balanced view of God, declaring both his holiness and his love.

CVI

59:15b-21 The solitary Saviour

What could possibly bridge the chasm between the shame of Zion and the glories which are to follow in chapter 60? There is only one answer: Yahweh himself. He is described as a warrior who arms himself for the confrontation with evil, and then undertakes his work of salvation which will have worldwide consequences. The chapter ends with a promise of the new covenant. It confirms the gift of the Spirit and the word of God to his people for ever.

15b. The existing situation was hopeless. It could only be resolved by the personal intervention of Yahweh. He was well aware of the depths to which his people had sunk, and he was displeased with the prevailing lack of social justice.

16. Yahweh saw that there was no one on earth who could intervene. He was appalled, but his own arm brought him victory, and his own righteousness upheld him. The arm of Yahweh may be a veiled reference to his servant, and if so it reminds us that this servant-Messiah would, like Yahweh himself, be overcome with grief and anger at the people of Jerusalem when he journeyed there towards the end of his ministry (Lk 19:41-42, 45-46).

17. The armour and clothing symbolise God's salvation and his just retribution. He has no need for real armour or weaponry; his pure and intense rejection of anything that is evil will suffice him. The image of God's armour was introduced by the first Isaiah (11:5) and would later be taken up by the Apostle Paul (Eph 6:13-17) when he urged believers to put on the armour of God. Here the meanings of the attire used by God as he goes to war are as follows: his garments are his just retribution or *vengeance*, his mantle is his justified wrath or *fury*, his breastplate is his *righteousness*, and his helmet is his wonderful *salvation*.

18. In the judgement to come, Yahweh will judge all people according to what they have *done*. For his impenitent enemies there will be wrath and requital. This verse is characterised by words that imply retribution: *repay* and *requital* (twice).

19. The test is not national but spiritual. Being a Gentile will not disqualify anyone from membership (v 18b, 19), just as being a Jew will not automatically qualify anyone (v 20). Some from the Gentile nations will be requited (v 18b), some will fear the glorious name of Yahweh. He would come in power, intent on victory like a pent-up stream that was driven by his breath or Spirit.

20. He would also come to redeem those who *turned from their transgression* in Zion and in Israel. Without repentance there can be no redemption.

21. The *covenant* here is the new covenant that God would make with his people thanks to the Messiah. Those who entered into it would all know Yahweh (Jer 31:34). They would all speak for him as a nation of prophets (Num 11:28-29, Joel 2:28). The thought in this verse adds the idea of perpetuity. God's Spirit and God's words which Yahweh put in their mouths would never again depart from them, nor from their children and grandchildren.

Meditation: Both Word and Spirit

Verse 15b-16 are not just fine poetry. They express a great truth. There is in the Holy One a heart that throbs on behalf of his people and a will that strikes for their cause. This is a simple truth, and it is a truth that ennobles us. God is out there, always invisible and able to hide even the sense of his presence. He feels passionately for men and women, and he is willing to act speedily in order to save them. There is only one thing that prevents his people from seeing his work in their midst, and that is their sin. He is always aware when a society loses its values because of flagrant selfishness. He does not immediately step in with a wonderful rescue plan. Sometimes he must remain distant so that those who are selfish may taste the bitterness which accompanies the consequences of sin.

Now, however, God decides to turn to his people once again. They have called out to him in deep lamentation in verses 9-15a. When people mourn their past misdeeds, he intervenes. He knows that their situation is beyond human help, so he decides to intervene personally. His own arm will secure victory for him, and his righteousness will enable him to persevere. He puts on his clothing, his mantle, his breastplate and his helmet (v 17). His salvation is good news for those who are crushed and who fear his glorious name. But it is also bad news for anyone who is selfish and impenitent (v 18). People behave selfishly because they do not fear God's glorious name (v 19a). Those who do fear him will turn from their selfishness in repentance, and then they will be redeemed (v 20).

Among the various promises of the new covenant that God would make with his people, we may now savour a new one. His Spirit that he put within them, and his words that he put in their mouths, would never depart from them, nor from their children, nor from their great-grandchildren (v 21). This combination is a very helpful one: word and Spirit, the word of God in the Bible which nourishes us, and the Holy Spirit who lives in our hearts and strengthens us. The promise is about both: all the followers of Yahweh or of his servant-Messiah are promised that the Holy Spirit will come and dwell in them, and that the word of God will always be in their mouths. For this to prove true, those who know and fear God should of course welcome the Spirit into the inner recesses of their personality, and they should also read and meditate on the scriptures regularly.

The promise breaks down if we focus on one part of the promise at the expense of the other. It is possible to be so evangelical that we ignore the promise of the Holy Spirit, and then we may miss out on the beautiful fruit which he forms in our lives (Gal 5:22-23) and the individual gifts he gives to each believer (1 Cor 12:4-11). It is also possible – and indeed this is quite the fashion in ecclesiastical circles today – to be so charismatic that we ignore the scriptures, thereby missing out on the teaching that is so vital for us to attain maturity in our faith (1 Tim 3:14-17). Somebody put it like this: if you have the word but not the Spirit, you *dry up*. If you have the Spirit but not the word, you *blow up*. If you have neither, you *throw up*. But if you have both word and Spirit, you *grow up*. It is worth comparing Ephesians 5:18-20 with Colossians 3:16-17. In both we are exhorted to be filled with something – the Spirit in one case and the word in the other, and then to sing praise to God and give thanks to him. In the Apostle Paul's mind, the Spirit and the word were complementary and believers needed both.

The promise at the end of our passage is that the Spirit of God and the divine word will not depart; they are Yahweh's life and Yahweh's truth. Both of them will continue to characterise the people of God in all subsequent generations.

CVII

60:1-16 The Triumph of the Faith

Chapters 60-62 are radiant with future glory. They tell of blessings that would surpass anything that happened in Old Testament times, although they are written in the language of the post-exilic period when the Jews were rebuilding the city of Jerusalem. They lend themselves to two different interpretations. (i) They may apply to the people of God under the new covenant, after the time of the Messiah. (ii) They may apply to the New Jerusalem whose maker is God, where the godly will live in glory after the present age has been wound up.

1. The prophet addresses a renewed Zion (v1-7). Because the light of her salvation has come and the glory of Yahweh has risen upon her, her people are urged to rise and shine! She is like a city that is glittering in the first rays of the morning sun. What makes her shine is not the sun but the glory of Yahweh.

2. The rest of the world, however, is shrouded in thick darkness (25:7). This will make the radiant divine glory of Zion very attractive to the peoples of the earth.

3. The Gentile nations will be attracted to Zion because she is full of light. Kings will come to her because dawn has broken in on her with great brightness.

4. The people of Zion will look up and see many people coming towards the city from every direction. Her sons and daughters are returning from the faraway nations, carried by their nurses (49:22). This is a promise of the ingathering of many Israelites. They include further exiles from Babylon, and also members of the ten tribes of Israel that were dispersed all over the world.

5. The people of Zion will see the resources of the world, brought on ships and then carried to Jerusalem. These treasures will be placed at the disposal of the citizens, who will be exultant with joy.

6. A vast number of camels will arrive from the deserts of Midian and Ephah in Arabia (Ephah was the oldest son of Midian, Gen 25:4). They will also arrive from Sheba, which is now Yemen. Those who enter Israel are not only the returning Jewish exiles, but also Gentiles of every nationality (Ps 87:3-6). Among the riches they bring are gold and frankincense. These were two of the gifts of the Magi, who were to be the proto-migrants (Mt 2:1-12).

7. Flocks of sheep will come from Kedar, and rams from Nabataea, both regions in northern Arabia. The livestock that is being brought will provide sacrifices for the altar, and the treasures (mentioned in v 5) will be used to glorify the Temple, already built and requiring only to be adorned.

8. From here on Yahweh is the speaker (v 8-16). Ships with white sails converge to the ports west of Jerusalem, like white doves on the wing to their dovecote.

9. The foreign nations have been waiting expectantly for Yahweh. Now they will bring dispersed exiles back to Jerusalem, and also their own treasures to give to Yahweh. They will do this for the sake of the name of Yahweh, who is the Holy One of Israel, who has glorified his people.

10. It is not clear in this verse and elsewhere whether the Gentiles are converts or just foreigners who are subject to Israel. If the latter, their submission is a willing one. They will gladly build the walls of Jerusalem, and their kings will serve God's people. At this stage the walls of Jerusalem are still unbuilt; we have not yet reached the period when Nehemiah was the governor of the city. This also points to Yahweh's renewed favour towards Israel: he has been angry with them and struck them down, but from now on he will favour them with his mercy.

11. There is no risk of invasion, so Zion's gates will be open at all times. Through them a constant stream of treasures will flow in, brought by foreign kings.

12. The nations that do not come to serve Yahweh will perish. Quite simply, if the glory of Yahweh is available, if his radiance is glittering, then those who will not come and take hold of it must face destruction. To reject God's way is suicide. Those countries that will come to Zion to pay homage to her are wise, but those that will not serve her will be laid waste, and their people will perish.

13. Forest trees, including cypresses, planes and pines from Lebanon, will be brought to beautify the sanctuary in the Temple, where Yahweh met with Israel.

14. Because of the radiant glory of the sanctuary, the former oppressors of God's people will come and bend low before Zion, and those who previously despised her will bow down at her feet. They will call Zion the city of Yahweh.

15. Previously Zion had been forsaken and shunned, but now she will be majestic forever. She will become the joy of the whole earth.

16. Thanks to the foreign labourers and the other blessings that come to her from the nations of the world, Zion will flourish. Yahweh promises the triumph of

his kingdom and everlasting blessedness for his people. They will know that Yahweh is their Saviour and their Redeemer.

Meditation: Treasures for the Glory of God

The interpretation and application of this chapter to the people of God down the ages has been controversial. According to George Adam Smith, there are three main lines of homiletical teaching that have been drawn from it:

(i) To describe the ingathering of the Gentiles to the church. (ii) To prove the doctrine that the church should live by the endowment of the nations of this world. (iii) To enforce the duty of costliness and magnificence in the public worship of God. Of these, (i) has been gently disputed by some, who prefer a futuristic eschatological interpretation in which the renewed Zion represents the New Jerusalem in the world to come, but the real heat of profound disagreement has been generated by (ii) and (iii), to which we should pay further attention.

Should the world subsidise the church? Put like this, the answer, in our 21st century pluralistic society, must clearly be No. In some European states there is a popular opt-out clause whereby people need not pay that part of their tax that is used for endowing the state church. In England the state church must look after its own finances, although some help is available in the form of financial grants. These contribute to the upkeep of some of the great church buildings, which form part of the national treasure.

Historically there is some evidence that a close link between church and state has been deleterious for the spiritual growth and maturity of the church. In ancient times the church flourished when it underwent the fire of persecution, but after the Emperor Constantine brought it under the aegis of the Roman Empire, it acquired a tendency to stagnate and become corrupt. In modern times the church seems to be at its purest and best when it is oppressed, or at any rate when times are very difficult for everyone.

The doctrine that the church should live by being endowed by the nations of this world has become an embarrassment to her. The church does her job better when she is under God than when she is obliged to compromise with the world. Some other interpretation of the prophesied involvement of Gentiles in the rebuilding of Jerusalem and the decoration of the Temple must be found. If the coming of the Gentiles in this passage is represented as bringing wealth to the church, then our going out to the Gentiles in order to reach them with the good news would imply for the church the spending of its wealth on things other than the adornment of a cathedral. Besides the heathen, there are also many who are poor and needy for whom God asks for our money, in order that he may be glorified.

Should public worship be costly and magnificent? In verse 12 Yahweh says, ". . . to beautify the place of my sanctuary, and I will glorify where my feet rest".

When these words were written, the sanctuary and the place where the divine feet rested was the Temple in Mount Zion. But when the servant-Messiah came to live with us and tread on this earth, where were his feet resting then? On a few rare occasions it was in the Temple. More often, it was where the sick and paralysed lay, where the demonised were raving, and where the bereaved were weeping. These were the places where his feet most often rested, and which he glorified. Would he not also wish us who are his followers to use our wealth to make these humble places glorious today?

Some godly people are troubled because the godly and reverent no longer build great cathedrals as they did in the Middle Ages. This is true, but on the other hand they build hospitals, refuge-houses, food banks and counselling centres instead. Who would dare to say where God is more greatly glorified? Is it in the great cathedrals or in the humble places of care for the poor and needy?

But the argument is not so simple. To return to the resting place of the Messiah's feet, there was an occasion (Mk 14:3-9, Jn 12:1-8) when he was enjoying a dinner given in his honour, and his wealthy hostess took her costliest treasure, a jar of perfume worth a year's wages. She anointed the Messiah's feet with it and wiped them with her hair. The house was filled with the fragrance of her offering. Some of the Messiah's closest followers objected, saying exactly what we might have said in similar circumstances, namely that the perfume should have been sold and the proceeds given to the poor. To which the Messiah replied, commending the wealthy lady, "Let her alone, why do you trouble her? She has performed a good service for me. She has done what she could".

The worship of God, Father, Son and Holy Spirit, should be more than thoughtful reflections on the great liturgical affirmations or emotional expressions of love. For godly people there should be something sacrificial about worship, because it is the best that they can give. It should be lavish and joyful, the giving of their whole selves, body, heart and mind, to their wonderful God who created them and then redeemed them at such vast cost to himself. If they thought it through, they might conclude that no other response would be sufficient.

CVIII

60:17-22 God is the Glory of his People

This passage is so packed with new glories that, as Derek Kidner wrote, "It can only be portraying the final perfection". God's future community will have none of the faults that we are all accustomed to in this fallen world. There will be a complete and ongoing state of prosperity in all matters material or moral. Instead of the sun and moon, the natural luminaries of heaven, Yahweh himself will be the everlasting light of the new world. Every inhabitant will be righteous and possess the land for ever, as a branch planted by God himself.

17. This verse brings six wonderful and typically divine exchanges, and there are more to come in this passage and later, for example in 61:3, 7. They contrast with our human exchanges, which tend to be devaluations (as, e.g. 1 Ki 14:26-28 and

Lam 4:1-10). Where there is *bronze* now, there will be *gold* then. Where there is *iron* now, there will be *silver* then. Where there is *wood* now, there will be *bronze* then, and where there are *stones* now, there will be *iron* then. For a people who are now perfected, no *overseer* or *taskmaster* will be needed. The guidelines will be *Peace* and *Righteousness*, which are personifications (as in 59:14).

18. There will be no more *violence*; it will be something unheard of. There will be no *devastation* or *destruction*; they too will be in the past. City *walls* will be unnecessary because *Salvation* has arrived. City *gates* will be redundant because of the trust that prevails throughout the city, which leads to glorious *Praise* being sung to God in every corner.

19. People will no longer depend for light on the sun by day and on the moon by night. The immediate presence of Yahweh will provide all the light they need. Their God will radiate a clear and illuminating glory.

20. When the sun goes down and the moon has withdrawn, there will still be light. Indeed, Yahweh will be the everlasting light of his people. Rev 21:23 and 22:5 pick up on this assurance of ongoing light in verses 19-20. Also a promise is made that the days of mourning will be ended; all sadness will be past (57:18, 61:2).

21. The community, composed exclusively of righteous persons, will possess the land for ever. Each one is a shoot of Yahweh's planting, and in every sense his own handiwork. Because of this, he will be glorified in them.

22. The one who is least prominent in the new world will engender a clan, and the smallest and least important will become a nation. At the right moment – once the present age is wound up – Yahweh will accomplish it speedily. This vision not only goes beyond the best ideals of the Old Testament, it also goes beyond the blessings promised for the followers of the Messiah in this life. These verses, like the last two chapters of the Bible, express the coming glory in earthly terms that we shall encounter again in 65:17-25.

Meditation: What will the next Life be like?

In this passage statements about transformation are piled one on top of another to provide a description of abundant richness, superlative quality, and unimaginably favourable conditions. It will be as when the Queen of Sheba saw all of King Solomon's treasures: for a while she was rendered speechless (1 Ki 10:3-9, 21, and 27). Here is a particularly mind-bending challenge. Try to imagine what it will all be like in the next life. You may shut your eyes if you wish.

All the buildings will be strong enough to last for ever. The materials used in their construction will include iron and bronze to provide durability, as well as precious metals like gold and silver for decoration. To our amazement, we shall take part in the building works, but there will be no overseers and taskmasters to boss us around. The work will be enriching and fulfilling, and we shall experience a deep sense of harmony and appropriateness as we give ourselves to it (v 17). Can you imagine this? The beauty of the city, the joy of creativity as we build together with God, and the freedom of working without any discouragements.

There will be no wars between nations and no wars between people. People will forget what the word "war" means. Violence and destruction will be unknown, and our painful memories of them will gradually fade away. The city of God will be without city walls, for it will be utterly secure because of God's salvation. No gates will be needed, and those who go through its entrances will enter entranced with praise (v 18). Can you imagine it? There will be no cowering fear, because there will be nothing to be afraid of. Destructiveness will be gone forever. Every action, word and thought will be constructive and positive.

Everything will be suffused with a pure light that will make the new world seem radiant and beautiful. This light will not be the old physical form of light, but a new spiritual radiance that will make objects gleam with their own God-given beauty (v 19-20). The sun and moon may still be there, but they will not be the luminaries any more. God is light and in him there is no darkness at all (1 Jn 1:5). This is why when God is excluded, as he often is in this life, a dense darkness covers the land (v 2), like a shroud that is cast over all peoples. That is what happened on the terrible day when the Messiah died. But when God is present, his glory is enough to provide just the right amount of light for everyone to see clearly. Can you imagine it? His perpetual divine presence will bring to everyone a delighted and unbroken joy. There will be no darkness and the days of mourning will be past (v 20), for every tear will be wiped away (25:8).

People will "all be righteous". The present author remembers how, over fifty years ago, people in his city could keep their front doors unlocked during the day. There were few petty thefts or burglaries then. In the 1970s the national level of righteousness plummeted, and it became necessary to keep front doors locked. In the renewed Zion everyone will be trustworthy. Homes will not need front doors. God's people will enjoy God's generous and plentiful salvation for ever. They will live in perfect security because evil will no longer exist, and the glory of God will be the focus of everyone's attention (v 21). Can you imagine it? It is difficult for us who live in dark times to picture a place where everyone is perfectly good – the mind boggles! The sense of freedom, security and peace will be blissful beyond words. We shall have the liberty to be truly ourselves at last.

There are some sayings that are hard to understand towards the end of this great chapter. What exactly is meant by "The least of them shall become a clan, and the smallest one a mighty nation"? In some way that we cannot understand yet, we shall be able to influence others for good (Lk 19:15-19). All these changes will not be painful, and they will not take long. We shall be transformed in the twinkling of an eye (1 Cor 15:51-54). God says, "In its time I will accomplish it *quickly*" (v 22). Can you imagine it? We shall live new lives, full of purpose and achieving great good. Our innermost hearts will instantly be transformed from flawed and sinful to flawless and perfect. What will that be like?

CIX

61:1-11 What God's Servant will be like

Verses 1-4 are reminiscent of the "servant songs", and the Messiah would see his mission revealed as clearly in this passage (Lk 4:16-21, 7:21-23) as in them. The author of this passage may have been II Isaiah: the style and content are not unlike his. The speaker, whom most commentators reckon to be the servant of Yahweh, is commissioned to bring comfort and cheer to the distressed people of God by proclaiming a new era of spiritual freedom and blessing.

1. The servant-Messiah would be endued with God's Spirit (11:2, 42:1, 48:16) and anointed as the Davidic King. The Hebrew word for "anointed" is *masach*, from which we get the word *Messiah*, literally "the anointed one". The Messiah would proceed to his ministry of helping the poor and needy in a holistic way that would release them from the bonds that held them captive, and bring them into the kingdom. He would bring good news to the oppressed, and gently heal those who were broken-hearted. He would proclaim freedom to those held captive by sin, and set prisoners free. Was this release of prisoners to be literally fulfilled? John the Baptist, the forerunner of the Messiah, may have thought so (Lk 7:18-19), and it was indeed fulfilled literally in a few cases (Acts 12:1-19). In general, however, the fulfilment would be a spiritual one, the release of people who were imprisoned in the dark and dingy dungeon of their own ego.

2. The Messiah would announce *the year of Yahweh's favour*, and *the day of vengeance of our God* (63:1-6). The Messiah would often (but not always) tacitly omit mentioning *the day of vengeance of our God* in the early stages of his ministry. Towards the end it would be a major theme of his preaching in his parables of judgement, and especially in his vision of the Day of Judgement (Mt 25:31-46). The mourners are singled out in verses 2-3: they would be comforted.

3. Those who mourn would also be provided for. The Messiah would replace their ashes, mourning and faint spirit with a garland, some oil of gladness and a mantle of praise. They would in due course become *oaks of righteousness*, planted by Yahweh in order to display his glory. To become an oak tree is a slow process. In one day an acorn cannot become an oak, but it can sprout a shoot and become something that you could imagine will turn into a sapling.

4. Likewise, ruined cities are not transformed in a day. It is a matter of decades, but it is amazing how much progress can be made in the first year or two. The original setting of this lovely song (in v 1-4) was the ruins of Jerusalem as its people returned and began the work of rebuilding. The more important fulfilment of the passage took place in the life and ministry of the Messiah, when he inaugurated the blessings of the kingdom, destined for the downtrodden.

5. The best explanation of this verse is that the people of God will enjoy a position of privilege in relation to those who do not know him, as priests do in relation to lay people. The latter may wish to help the former in various ways.

6. Israel's calling was to be a kingdom of priests (Ex 19:6), and to be ministers of God. Under the new covenant those who followed the Messiah would have the same calling. As they ministered the things of God to the unchurched, the latter might wish to repay them for their labours, and contribute to their stipend.

7. The prosperity that the people of God will enjoy in the future will be a double recompense for the tribulations they have endured in the past and present. This *double portion* of joy may perhaps be related to the fact that they have received from Yahweh's hands "double for all [their] sins" (40:2).

8. When ungodly people steal from the godly, this is displeasing to Yahweh, who *loves justice* and *hates robbery*, which is taking by force things that belong to someone else. He will *faithfully recompense* his people and will make a new covenant with them that will be *everlasting* (55:3, 59:21).

9. The descendants of God's people will be renowned among the nations. People will say of them that they have been blessed by Yahweh.

10. Who is the speaker now? Some commentators believe it is new believers who are realising the wonder of their salvation. Their outburst of joy is not unlike 12:1-6 and the songs in chapters 24-27. The believers rejoice in God, their whole being delights in their God. They have been clothed with the garments of salvation and given the status of being righteous. Two metaphors are used for righteousness, the first being a robe (as in Lk 15:22). This robe is festive and undeserved, and it is *imputed* or conferred on them from outside (Rom 3:22). Their joy is like that of a bridegroom decked with a garland or a bride adorned with her jewels.

11. The second metaphor used for righteousness is that of shoots springing up in a garden. God sows righteousness in his people. It is *infused* or grown from within (Rom 8:10). It will be seen by the nations, who will praise God for it.

Meditation: The Saviour and the Saved

First it is the Saviour who speaks (v1-4). He is anointed by Yahweh with the Spirit of God. He comes with good news! The groans of the oppressed will be replaced by smiles. The Saviour will slowly bind up those who are crushed and destroyed. He will proclaim liberty to those held captive by sinister forces, and set free the prisoners of sin. Then he will proclaim the year of Yahweh's favour.

Barry Webb explained the phrase *the year of Yahweh's favour* as follows. "This is almost certainly an allusion to the Year of Jubilee as described in the Law of Moses (Lev 25:8-55). Every fiftieth year was to be proclaimed a year of release in which debts were cancelled, slaves were freed, and people who had been forced to sell their family property because of poverty received it back again. It was literally the year *of the Ram's horn*, because of the horn trumpet that was blown to announce its arrival. The expression *proclaim liberty* (in v 1) employs exactly the same Hebrew words as the command in Leviticus 25:10 to *proclaim liberty* in the Year of Jubilee. The preaching of the servant-Messiah is like the blast of the ram's horn which ushered in the Year of Jubilee; it proclaims the arrival of a time of grace, a time of release".

The use of that phrase would have meant a lot to the Jewish exiles on their arrival back in Jerusalem. They had heard the good news of their impending release, and their shattered morale had been gently rebuilt. Now they were back: *the year of Yahweh's favour* had begun, a time of grace and blessing, but also a time of challenge. It would not be easy to rebuild a city. It would take decades.

The year of Yahweh's favour is a phrase that also means a lot to those who are followers of the Messiah. They too have heard good news, and have responded to it. Their inner wounds have likewise been bound up. They also have been set free from their captivity to the world, the flesh and the devil. For them a period of God's favour has begun, in which God will faithfully build them up from a ruin to a city, and enable them to grow from a tiny acorn to an enormous oak of righteousness. This process will take more than a year; they will gradually realise that his grace will continue for ever. They are now saved, and we will hear their reaction to their Saviour in a moment.

In his reading from Isaiah 61:1-2, the Messiah stopped when he had read out "the year of Yahweh's favour". He did not go on to "the day of vengeance of our God" (Lk 4:18-19). By this he made it clear that the first time he visited this world as a man, he did so in great humility. His mission then was not to condemn the world but to save it (Jn 3:17). One day he will return to earth a second time, but then in great glory, and he will execute the judgement which the Father has committed to him (Jn 5:22-29). He came the first time as a suffering servant in order to save. He will come a second time as a conquering warrior in order to judge.

Now it is the turn of the saved to speak. They are filled with wonder and joy (v 10-11). They love to rejoice in their Saviour and to exult in their God. Their salvation is like a garment that they wear at all times with quiet humility, and which they cover with a robe – the robe of righteousness, which they always have on. Dressed in this way, they walk around with their heads held high, like a garlanded bridegroom or a bejewelled bride. Their Saviour loves them and gave himself for them. This gives a huge value to their lives. They remember that they are like a garden planted by God, with shoots of righteousness springing up all around and growing into beautiful plants. They will be seen by those who are as yet unsaved, who will praise God for what he is doing in the lives of the saved. All this will redound to the glory of God.

CX

62:1-12 The Joy and Beauty of Zion

This is another poem depicting Zion as a woman who longs for a happy reunion with her family, but in this case the stress is on her husband's solicitousness on her behalf. Yahweh is described as being anxious that she should be vindicated and seen to be beautiful, and he pours out his love for her in remarkable expressions of affection and declarations of protectiveness.

1. Yahweh declares that he will neither be silent nor rest until his people, here personified as the city of Jerusalem, are vindicated and their salvation is evident. The word aptly translated *vindication* is really *righteousness* as in 61:10-11. Since Yahweh is declaring his intention to restore Zion to a state where the other nations will see her righteousness shine forth, the word *vindication* is appropriate.

2. The nations would then see the vindication and glory of God's people, who would be given a new name, symbolic both of their new character and their new relationship with God. At present this name is a mystery yet to be disclosed (Rev 2:17), and is not necessarily related to the two new names for Zion in verse 4 or the four new names for her in verse 12.

3. The people of God are now compared to a beautiful crown or diadem which Yahweh holds in his hand.

4. The words that foreign people previously applied to Jerusalem were *Forsaken* and *Desolate*. Now it would be different: there would be some new names or characterisations for Zion, for Yahweh says, "My delight is in her" and he would be "married" to her and to her land. The Hebrew words for *My Delight is in Her* and *Married* are *Hephzibah* and *Beulah*, which in the previous two centuries formed part of the English Christian vocabulary. The metaphor of God as the husband of his people is indicative of his fidelity towards them.

5. Just as a young man is very happy when he marries a young woman, so would Yahweh be when he married Zion. He would rejoice over his people in delight.

6. God gives certain people the task to have as great a concern for Zion as his own. He calls the "sentinels" to pray importunately for her. Who were they? The most appealing theory, put forward by Jewish commentators over the ages, is that they were the angelic guardians divinely appointed to look after the city of God. They were to act as remembrancers, as those who reminded Yahweh of his promises made on Zion's behalf (v 8-9). They were to take no rest, reminding God ceaselessly.

7. The sentinels were not to take any rest, nor were they to give Yahweh any rest either, until he had carried out his promises, established the city as his own and given it a universal renown.

8. Yahweh takes a solemn oath that hostile strangers will no longer be permitted to

rob his people of the fruit of their labours. None of the people's grain would go to their enemies, nor would any of their wine be drunk by them.

9. The Israelites who sowed their grain would eat it and give praise to God, and those who had tended their vines would drink their wine in the holy courts of the newly rebuilt Temple. This is a reference to the Temple festivals, where the first fruits were eaten and drunk with rejoicing before Yahweh (Deut 12:17-18, 14:23).

10. The present inhabitants, recently returned from exile, were to prepare the city for the arrival of further exiles. They were to go out of the city and clear stones away from the highway that led to her. They were to lift up an ensign over the foreign nations so that they might bring further displaced exiles to her (49:22).

11. Yahweh himself will make known throughout the earth the great salvation that would come to Zion. The nations of the world would tell the city how very fortunate she was. She would be lavishly rewarded and recompensed.

12. The fourfold name by which the ransomed community would be known provides a triumphant climax to this group of chapters. They now were *The Holy People*, the priesthood of the earth. They would be thought of as *The Redeemed of Yahweh*, bought back from oppressive captivity. They would be called *Sought Out*, for their advice would from then on be courted and valued. Their name would be *A City Not Forsaken*, for Yahweh now delighted in her.

Meditation: The Guardians of God's City

There is a remarkably helpful model for prayer in verses 6-7 of our passage. In this passage certain sentinels or guardians had been posted on the city walls of Jerusalem. They had been given the job of interceding on behalf of the city. Their task was to be remembrancers, who kept reminding God of the promises he had made concerning the city where his people live. They were not to pause for rest. All day and all night, they were not to be silent. They were required to go on praying for the city. They were not to give God any rest but to be importunate in their cries for God's people to be established and blessed before the unbelieving world. This and this alone was God's wish.

The people of God used to dwell in Jerusalem, and their sentinels were either angelic guardians (according to the principal Jewish interpretation) or prophets (according to other commentators, mainly Christian). These sentinels were full of passion, just as Yahweh himself was. They were never to be silent (v6) just as Yahweh declared that for Zion's sake he would not be silent (v1). They were to take no rest (v6) just as Yahweh said that he would not rest (v1). The sentinels were to be bold and unceasing as they kept repeating to God, "You promised! You said that you would do it! You swore that worldly people would not steal the good things you promised for your people!" (v8-9).

Today those involved are different. The people of God, the equivalent of the old Zion, are distributed throughout the different countries of the world. They are the followers of the Messiah who is now known as Christ. They suffer from growing pains. They struggle towards maturity. They need sentinels to keep watch over them by praying for them. Who are the sentinels today? They are the Christian intercessors, themselves also carefully distributed throughout the world. Their task is to intercede for God's people.

They are to watch and pray ceaselessly, not in the sense of praying 24 hours per day, seven days per week, but in the sense that their task will not be finished until the present age is wound up. They will watch and pray in ways that differ, for they are different people. Some will do so in the morning, others in the evening. Some while they commute to and from work, others while they do the housework. Some watch and pray as they read the Bible, others as they prepare their meals.

They pray for their fellow believers throughout the world. They pray for the unfinished task of bringing the good news of the Messiah to the most remote parts of the earth. They watch and pray ceaselessly, because they do so every day. They are God's intercessors, whom he has installed as sentinels or watchmen on the walls of God's renewed city, so as to remind him of his promises to bring his work to a glorious completion (Phil 1:6). They will keep praying until every Christian believer in the world is rightly classed among *The Holy People* and *The Redeemed of Yahweh*, until they are collectively seen as people who are *Sought Out* and *A City Not Forsaken*. This is what God has promised for his people (v12) and the intercessors are to keep reminding God of what he promised.

To be bold in prayer does not mean to be presumptuous. Since intercessory prayer consists of reminding God of his promises, it is bold but it is not presumptuous. The Bible is full of wonderful promises (2 Pet 1:4). They are there, waiting to be claimed by intercessors. "Lord, you promised such-and-such, and I claim this for so-and-so". The great blessings of God await in heaven. It is by intercession, by reminding God of what he has promised, that they are brought down to earth. We have a good example of this in Acts 4:23-31.

Would you like to learn some of God's promises? Here are a dozen encouraging ones from the many that can be found in the book of Isaiah.

1.   A promise of sins forgiven for the willing and obedient. Isaiah 1:18-19.
2.   A promise of a great Messiah, fully God and fully man. Isaiah 9:6-7.
3.   A promise that everywhere there will be those who know God. Isaiah 11:9.
4.   A promise that God will swallow up death for ever. Isaiah 25:7-8.
5.   A promise that God will give peace to those who trust in him. Isaiah 26:3.
6.   A promise that we will be made strong through quiet trust. Isaiah 30:15.
7.   A promise that our human strength will be renewed. Isaiah 40:29-31.
8.   A promise that we need not fear, because God is with us. Isaiah 41:10.
9.   A promise of spiritual refreshment for the thirsty. Isaiah 41:17-20.
10. A promise that the Messiah will deal gently with the broken. Isaiah 42:3.
11. A promise that God's word will accomplish his purpose. Isaiah 55:10-11.
12. A promise that God will dwell with those who are humble. Isaiah 57:15.

CXI

63:1-6 The solitary Avenger

This passage is similar to 59:15b-21 in its treatment of judgement and salvation. Verse 5 has the same message as 59:16. The dramatic dialogue here highlights the *day of vengeance* (v4), which was combined in 61:2 with the year of Yahweh's favour. The great restoration of the latter must be accompanied by the just retribution meted out in the former. The avenging warrior of this passage is the same as the one in Revelation 19:11-16, namely the Messiah himself. Those who face God's judgement do so out of their own choice: there is, of course, an alternative provided by God through the Messiah (53:4-6).

1. The prophet is surprised by his vision of a solitary and majestic figure, dressed in splendid crimson garments, who is approaching Jerusalem from the south-east. We have already encountered Edom and its chief city Bozrah as they represented the impenitent world opposed to God's people in 34:5-6. There is a pun on *Edom* (meaning *red*) and *Bozra* (a word similar to *grape-gatherer*). The prophet asks who this divine figure is. He replies, "It is I, announcing vindication". This means "Speaking in righteousness", for God always speaks the truth and fulfils what he says he will do (45:23, 55:11). Even here, in this sombre passage on judgement, the divine figure declares that he is *mighty to save*.

2. The prophet then addresses the advancing figure, asking for the meaning of his red robes and the crimson stains on his garments, which remind him of the stains on the clothes worn by those who tread the grapes in the wine press.

3. The solitary figure replies that he has trodden the wine press alone, for nobody else was with him. He goes on, "I trod *them* in my anger, and trampled *them* in my wrath". At this stage the reader realises that *them* does not refer to grapes. The divine figure has destroyed *them* in his *anger* and in his *wrath*. His wrath is his settled and holy opposition to those people who persist impenitently in their sin. They must face the righteous judgement of God. It is *their* juice or lifeblood that has stained his robes. The word translated *juice* in this verse is translated *lifeblood* in verse 6 in the New Revised Standard Version. The solitary figure is, of course, the Messiah (the identification is clear from Rev 19:15). John Skinner writes, "It is difficult to say which is the most to be admired, the dramatic vividness of the vision, or the reticence which conceals the work of slaughter and concentrates the attention on the divine Hero as he emerges victorious from the conflict".

4. The terrible *day of vengeance* was in the purposes of the divine figure. It has come and gone. It was something that had to be accomplished, because it was a necessary preliminary to *the year for [the] redeeming work*. The day and the year are both mentioned, in reverse order, in 61:2.

5. The solitary figure was unable to find any worthy human assistant to help him in the execution of God's will. He looked intently, but no one would support him in the fulfilment of God's purpose. He had to do the task himself, and he did it successfully. Difficult though it was, he was kept going by his profound sense of right and wrong. It was his holiness that made the just retribution necessary. This verse is very similar in meaning to 59:16. It suggests that the task of judgement, entrusted by God to the Messiah, was a distasteful one, undertaken by the Messiah as a necessary part of his God-given mission.

6. This verse repeats the message of verse 3b. We can now see that the terrible work of judgement involved trampling people down and crushing them, and then pouring out their lifeblood on the earth. Because these people persisted in their rejection of the means appointed by God to secure his own propitiation, the divine anger and wrath of God could only be appeased by their destruction.

Meditation: A necessary but lonely Mission

Apart from the questions uttered by the prophet, the speaker in this poetic lament is the Messiah. An earlier passage, 61:1-4, and this one, 63:1-6, could have been termed the fifth and sixth "servant songs" if the speaker in each had been referred to as the servant of Yahweh. He was not and that is why we have four "servant songs", not six. The fact remains, however, that the Messiah's mission as the servant of Yahweh involved launching the day of God's vengeance as well as the year of his favour and redemption (v 4, 61:2). Because of this, the keynote of this passage is the loneliness of the solitary and majestic hero who carries out the distasteful task assigned to him. We are left to ponder the pity, the sadness, the agony, and the unshared and unaided effort which the divine Saviour must go through so as to complete the redemption of his people.

The servant had to suffer in order to win a great salvation for us. He had to take away the sin of the world. His sacrifice on their behalf makes it possible for all sinners to be redeemed (52:13-53:12), but the benefits of his passion and death need to be appropriated. If a sinner avails himself of the forgiveness that the Messiah has won for him, he is redeemed; but if he does not do so, he must face the terrible judgement that awaits the impenitent. That judgement is destruction, which will be carried out on the Day of Judgement by the lonely figure of the Messiah. He may shrink from this terrible task, but he will carry it out, for he is both saviour (Jn 3:16-17) and judge (Jn 5:22-29). The judge in this case is also the executioner. He must wholly rid the world of sin in order to redeem it.

The Messiah says something remarkable in our passage (v 5). He "stared", but there was no one to sustain him in his work of destroying impenitent sinners. That is why he had to do this on his own. Some commentators have suggested that the Messiah was not looking for help in the judgement, but instead seeking support in advance of his lonely work on the day of vengeance. All people will be free to decide how they react to his white-hot holiness and fierce hostility towards recalcitrant and impenitent sinners. Some will want to praise him for it, but others may presume to criticise him for it.

The Messiah will in the end destroy people in his righteous wrath. The Holy One who came to put things right will return to destroy what is irremediably wrong. The prophet sees him marching mightily but pensively towards Jerusalem, his garments splashed in blood. He has trampled down and crushed those who themselves had trampled down and crushed the poor and needy. He has poured out the lifeblood of those who poured out the lifeblood of his people (Mt 25:41-46). As people did to others, so he has done to them. That is the definition of just retribution. The great day of vengeance was in his heart, and on it he finally put right every wrong and vindicated his people.

It would take a day for the lonely figure to do his "strange deed" and perform his "alien work" (28:21). It had to be done. To reject God's way of salvation is to choose to be destroyed on the day of vengeance. That dark day would be followed by the year of God's favour, the year of the Messiah's redeeming work. The "year" is certainly figurative, for it would go on for ever (25:8, 26:19, 60:20).

Will the impenitent dead be given a second chance to change their minds and repent? Those who espouse universalism would have us believe this, but the whole trend of scripture, both Old Testament and New, is against this view. John Skinner thoughtfully summed up the position as follows: "While it is true that the judgement is the prelude to the redemption of Israel, the passage that is before us exhibits only the judicial aspect of the divine dealings, and it is not permissible to soften the terrors of the picture by introducing soteriological conceptions which lie beyond its scope".

CXII

63:7-19 Thanksgiving and Penitence

The prophet has been stirred by the glories of chapters 60-62 and the vision of the day of vengeance in 63:1-6. He is prompted to pray, and pours forth his soul in one of the most eloquent intercessory prayers to be found in the Bible. He brings together the goodness of God in the past and the present difficulties of his people.

7. The prophet turns remembrancer (62:6), for his resolve *to recount* means *to bring to remembrance*. He begins his prayer with praise as he remembers the kind deeds of Yahweh in times past. Yahweh showed favour towards Israel, according to his mercy and his steadfast love.

8. In the early days Yahweh thought of the Israelites as his faithful people, free from idolatry. The prophet also picks up the theme of Yahweh being their father, and they his children, from the early prophetic writings of Isaiah (1:2, 4 and 30:9). Yahweh would later be their saviour in all their distresses (Ex 3:7).

9. The prophet remembers further episodes from the book of Exodus. Yahweh did not use either a messenger or an angel in assisting them. It was he himself who accompanied them by means of his presence; it was he who saved them in person (Ex 33:14). In love and pity he redeemed them from their Egyptian slave-owners. In those good old days he would lift them up and carry them through their wanderings in the wilderness, keeping them safe from danger (Ex 19:4).

10. Sadly the Israelites rebelled and grieved God's Spirit. When God who is perfectly holy is grieved and hurt, there are bound to be dire consequences. Those who refuse to walk in God's way become his enemies (1:24) and as an immediate consequence of this, Yahweh becomes theirs. So Yahweh ceased to be their saviour and instead fought against them. The old cliché that [God] hates the sin but loves the sinner needs the corrective of passages such as this, which teach that through our unholy behaviour we become enemies of God. In the final analysis, sinner and sin cannot always be treated separately like this. Notice the prophet's emphasis on the *Holy* Spirit. Because he is the Spirit of the Holy One of Israel, he is called the Holy Spirit here and in verse 11. He is called the Holy Spirit in only one other Old Testament text, Psalm 51:11.

11. In times of distress the people looked back on the ancient wonders of God's grace, and they longed for him to renew his goodness towards them and save them once again. They remembered the days of Moses. Where was the one who had taken them and their leaders through the Red Sea? Where was the one who had endowed their leaders with his Holy Spirit? (Num 11:17, 24-25).

12. Yahweh had transferred the strength of his arm to the right hand of Moses, and had divided the waters of the Red Sea so that all of the Israelites could cross it, and so be delivered from their oppressors (Ex 14:16, 26). In this way God had made an everlasting name for himself.

13. The Israelites had walked on the depths of the Red Sea, and their steps were as firm and secure as the trot of a horse in open country.

14. Cattle may find it difficult to descend into a valley, but once they are in it they find peaceful pasture. The Israelites likewise were frightened when Pharaoh was pursuing them, but once Yahweh had saved them his Spirit gave them peace and security in their resting place. The Exodus had been a glorious time, when God brought great renown to his name.

15. The prophet now turns from remembrance to penitence. He begs Yahweh to look down on his people from his holy habitation, and see their plight. God had withdrawn or at least postponed any intervention on their behalf, and his people feared that he did not fully realise their suffering. They wondered what had become of his zeal and his might. They desperately longed for some fresh demonstration of his yearning heart and some new proof of his compassion.

16. Yahweh alone, and not Abraham or Jacob / Israel, was the father of the nation. The plea "you are our father" is used twice in this verse, giving the prayer a special intensity. Yahweh was not only their father, but also their Redeemer – that was his nature. The people of Israel felt estranged from their God, but when they realised he was their father they felt accepted once again.

17. The prophet remonstrates with Yahweh with increasing intensity of emotion. Yahweh's displeasure with his people had led to his withdrawing his helping hand from them, and this in turn had resulted in their hearts being hardened. Why, then, had Yahweh so arranged things that they ended up straying from his ways in this way? Why had he so overruled the gradual hardening of their hearts that they no longer feared him? The prophet begged Yahweh to turn back to his people both for their sake and for his own, for they were his heritage.

18. By now God's people were back home after their return from exile. They had finished rebuilding their Temple, but they still thought back to the painful lesson Yahweh had taught them. They had possessed the Promised Land for a while, but then their enemies had taken over their land, destroyed their Temple and trampled down their sanctuary. They knew it was their fault.

19. God's people had long ago become like ordinary people, like those who were not ruled by Yahweh. This is what led to their national and religious catastrophe.

The great prayer of intercession is not yet finished. It continues in chapter 64.

Meditation: Answers to difficult Questions

In this passage we may hunt around and find the beginnings of an answer to four difficult questions.

1. **If we have free will, how does God deal with our selfishness?** In the beginning Yahweh said, "Surely they are my people, children who will not deal falsely" (v 8). The word *surely* does not come from divine foreknowledge, but from the hope and confidence of divine love. As the passage makes clear, God's love was disappointed. This is clear evidence that we have free will. Our conduct is an uncertain thing, because we may exercise our free will and go our own way instead of God's way. God's wisdom may well know whether or not his love will emerge triumphant on the final day, but God's love keeps inspiring him to give us yet another chance. God's love will keep trying to redeem the least promising of all his wayward people. This fact alone is very powerful: it can affect people more profoundly than many great theological tomes.

Can it really be true that God's love in some sense overcomes his holiness as he strives for the umpteenth time to woo and to win our recalcitrant hearts? George Adam Smith wrote, "What a religion is this of ours, in the power of which someone may rise every morning, and feel thrilled by the thought that God trusts him or her to work according to his will throughout that day; in the power of which someone may look around, and see the sad and hopeless human lives around him glorified by the truth that, for the salvation of such people, God did adventure himself in a love that laid itself down in death. The attraction and power of such a religion can never die". There is something magnetic about the love of such a great God. God **so** loved the world that he gave his servant-Messiah, so that anyone who puts their trust in him will not perish but have eternal life.

2. When did the idea originate that God was our heavenly Father? The idea of the fatherhood of God appears a few times in the Old Testament (in Isaiah, only in this prayer, 63:16 and 64:8), but always implying that God is the father of the Israelite nation. God's fatherhood is not extended in the Old Testament to the individual believer, although a remarkable anticipation is found in the Apocrypha (Ecclesiasticus / Sirach 23:1, 4-5, written around 180 B.C.): "O Lord, Father and Master of my life, do not abandon me to [the] designs [of my lips], and do not let me fall because of them! O Lord, Father and God of my life, do not give me haughty eyes, and remove evil desire from me".

We have to wait until the teaching of the Messiah for the fullest development of the idea of the fatherhood of God. The Messiah was vividly aware that he was greatly loved by his heavenly Father (Mk 1:11, 9:7), and this assurance sustained him as he fulfilled his mission. He identified himself so closely with sinners in general, and with his humble followers in particular, that he taught them to think of God as their Father just as he did. He gave them a model prayer to pray which begins, "Our Father, you who are in heaven".

3. Can the idea of the Trinity be deduced from the Old Testament alone? It can indeed. We have already encountered it in 6:1-8, and some other examples are cited in the Meditation for section XIII (p.44-45). The Trinity can also be discerned in this passage. God the Father is, of course, Yahweh (v7 and throughout). God the Spirit is, of course, Yahweh's Holy Spirit (v10, 11). He is a person separate from Yahweh because we are told that he can be grieved (v10, Eph 4:30). Where is God the Son? He is recognised in the book of Isaiah as the Branch / the Davidic Messiah, or as the servant of Yahweh, but where does he appear in this prayer? The answer is: in verse 9, in the words translated *his presence*, literally "the Angel of his face", also known in the Old Testament as "the Angel of Yahweh", an undefined figure who is identified as God, but who is distinct from Yahweh. So the truth of the Trinity begins to be revealed in Old Testament days, and is faintly visible here as Yahweh, Yahweh's presence, and Yahweh's Holy Spirit.

4. Do we harden our hearts or does God harden them? There are people who persistently resist God's will, and they can be said to be hardening their own hearts. The heart that is resolutely intent on disobedience hardens itself progressively against the will of God until a moment arrives, known only to God, when God takes the initiative and himself hardens it. One example is the behaviour of the Egyptian Pharaoh prior to the exodus. He first hardened his own heart and persisted in his opposition to Yahweh (Ex 7:13, 7:22, 8:15, 8:19, 8:32, 9:7). At a certain moment God took action. Respecting Pharaoh's free will, he hardened Pharaoh's heart (7:3 which looks to the future, 9:12, 9:34, 10:20, 10:27, 11:10). Another example of God hardening people's hearts may be found in Romans 1:18-32 (See the Meditation for section VII, p.27-28). In the prayer we are studying, the people of God complain that God has hardened their hearts (v 17). The very fact that they are concerned lest they lose out on their salvation suggests that it is they who have hardened their own hearts, and that they have not yet reached the perilous point when God adds his own hardening and makes their hearts as hard as diamond. That would be a point of no return.

CXIII

64:1-12 Prayer for renewed Mercy

The prophet longs that Yahweh might intervene spectacularly and prays that he would save his people through extraordinary acts (v 1-3). Then he thoughtfully seeks for a reconciliation between Yahweh's love for Israel and his righteousness, which has caused him to withdraw his support for Israel.

1. The prophet longs that Yahweh might tear open the heavens and come down. Such a theophany would have terrifying consequences on earth. The mountains would quake, and perhaps the hardened hearts of Yahweh's people might be softened at his presence, opening the way for their salvation.

2. As fire burns brushwood, so Yahweh's appearance might burn away the sin of Israel. As fire causes water to boil, so Yahweh's anger might break through the spiritual inertia and unresponsiveness of his people. Then Yahweh's nature would be revealed to his enemies, and the nations would tremble at his presence.

3. In the past Yahweh had acted in awe-inspiring and unexpected ways in order to rescue Israel from their Egyptian oppressors. When he did so, the mountains did indeed quake at his presence.

4. The prophet enlarges on Yahweh's nature. He is the one and only God, so no ear has heard and no eye has seen any God except him. He intervenes mightily on behalf of those who wait for him (see 1 Cor 2:9, which quotes this verse).

5. Yahweh meets with those who happily do what is right in his eyes and who remember him and his ways. But Yahweh became angry, and it was because his people had sinned. This led Yahweh to hide himself from them, and they sinned all the more, deepening the rift between them and their God. The results of sin, as described in verses 5b, 6 and 7 are very serious. The prophet lucidly describes the power of sin to distance, to deprave and to disintegrate.

6. All of God's people had become unclean in God's sight. Like women during their menstrual period, they were unworthy to enter the Temple precincts. Even their righteous deeds, their best efforts to fulfil God's will, were like a filthy menstrual cloth. Like autumn leaves they were fading away, and their sins would hasten their fall and their destruction.

7. A general listlessness makes the condition of God's people incurable. None of them call upon Yahweh for help, none try to take hold of him. He has hidden his face from them, and delivered them into the hand of their iniquities. God is not to blame for their plight; it stems from their helpless addiction to sin.

8. The prophet approaches the end of his prayer with a humble petition that Yahweh may somehow be able to bring his ongoing righteous anger against his people to an end. He appeals to Yahweh as their Father, who loves those whom he created and formed. They are his handiwork, he has determined the course of their lives. Will the potter allow his choice pots to be destroyed? (Job 10:9).

9. The prophet entreats Yahweh to moderate his anger and forget their past sins (Zech 1:12). Instead, he should remember that the Israelites are his people.

10. The evidence of Yahweh's punishment is everywhere to be seen. Surely the devastation is sufficient: the towns are ruined, Jerusalem is a desolate wilderness.

11. The Temple where Yahweh had been praised over the ages had been burnt with fire, and their pleasant places had become ruins (Ezek 24:21, 25).

12. Surely Yahweh cannot look on these tragedies and maintain his stony silence. Surely he cannot prolong his punishment? The prayer is a model for all who find themselves crying to God out of the depths of their hearts. But it ends with a question, and God's answer to it will make clear how much of the prophet's contrition is shared by the people.

Meditation: The Prophet intercedes for Israel

If little is known for certain about II Isaiah, even less is known about the third author of the book of Isaiah. He was another prophet who wrote much of chapters 56-66, and was probably the editor of the whole book. Writing around 530-520 B.C. after the exiles had begun to return to Jerusalem from Babylon, he had to come to terms with the sense of anti-climax that began to characterise the lives of the Jewish people as they settled down to the task of rebuilding.

In chapters 60-62 the prophet had been caught up in the glorious future that awaited the people of God, but after he wrote those chapters the outlook began to look distinctly gloomy. Perhaps something had gone wrong. At any rate, the people were changing. The prophet was deeply disenchanted by their attitude. So much was this the case, in fact, that he wondered whether his prophetic work had been in vain. The people seemed to be losing all interest in Yahweh.

They had been protected during their journey back from Babylon. They had slowly begun the work of restoring their city. Then, quite suddenly, they realised what a huge task lay in store for them. Once again their spirits were crushed, as they had been during their years in Babylon. Yahweh had promised that glorious things would happen to them in the future, but the reality seemed to be the same as it was back in Babylon: work, lots of it, and very little prosperity.

The prophet felt that all those years of being disciplined by Yahweh in Babylon had done the people of Israel no good whatsoever: "You were angry, and we sinned; because you hid yourself we transgressed" (v5). The people of God had all become thoroughly unclean in God's eyes. Like a rotting leaf they were fading away (v6). The prophet reacted to this by sinking to his knees and praying. This lengthy prayer (from 63:7-64:12) gives us the gist of his intercession on behalf of the people to whom God had asked him to prophesy.

In his prayer the prophet admitted that, together with all the people, he had become like one who was unclean, and that all his righteous deeds were like a filthy cloth (v6). The word used here means a tampon or menstrual cloth. The prophet made use of this offensive noun to inform us how he felt about his best prophetic efforts. It teaches us how God feels about human self-righteousness. Even our best actions, the ones which we feel good about, our times of worship and our contributions to social justice, are like a filthy rag in God's eyes.

One of the striking aspects of this great prayer is how the prophet identifies himself with his people. Throughout the prayer he does not use the third person plural pronoun but the first. As he prays about the sins of the Israelites he says *we*, *us* and *our* instead of *they*, *them* and *their*. He includes himself as one of the hopeless rebels who desperately need God's forgiveness and cleansing.

The prophet takes a dim view of his fellow Jews: "There is no one who calls on your name, or attempts to take hold of you; for you have hidden your face from us, and have delivered us into the hand of our iniquities" (v7). He includes himself among them, even as he attempts to take hold of God in intercession for them. Twice he calls God *our Father* (63:16 and 64:8). The prophet was generous in spirit and his heart was large enough to long that none of his contemporaries should miss out on divine restoration. He pleads with God, saying, "We are all the work of your hand" (v8).

This prayer, which the prophet recorded for posterity, is perhaps the finest part of his prophetic writing. In it his warm heart echoes the heartbeat of God himself. He identifies with God's people in their sins, and he carries them all in his heart as he prays for them to their amazingly patient God.

CXIV

65:1-16 Owned by God or disowned?

What is Yahweh's answer to the prayer of his prophet? Has Yahweh really hidden himself from his people? Have they gone so far with their sinning that he no longer wants anything to do with them? Let us listen, for the Holy One of Israel is about to speak. He will heighten the contrast between light and darkness, and the book of Isaiah will soon come to an end on a searching and disturbing note.

1. The New Testament (Rom 10:20-21) interprets the opening verse as referring to the Gentiles, and the subsequent verses (v2-7) to rebellious Jews. Yahweh was going to be sought out by those who did not ask for him, and he would be found by those who did not seek him – the Gentiles, who did not know about him. He said, "Here I am" to nations who had not been taught to call on his name. The Gentiles were nevertheless going to be brought in and become part of his family.

2. Far from hiding himself from his people who had rebelled against him, Yahweh held out his hands in a gesture of invitation to them. They walked in a way that was not good (Ps 36:4), looking to their own devices and desires.

3. They were returning to some of the old forbidden rites (57:3-10). But while the earlier deviations had mainly been sexually orientated, some of the current ones were provocative and "in Yahweh's face", ignoring the altar set aside for him and instead sacrificing beasts in gardens (1:29), or offering incense on roof-tiles, a practice which some scholars believe they may have learnt from the Babylonians during the exile (v7b, Deut 12:2-7).

4. The people of Yahweh were also dabbling in necromancy, which was rooted in ancestor worship and which provided "oracles from the dead" (Deut 18:11). They defiantly ate forbidden flesh, another unpleasant habit they had picked up from the Babylonians. Sometimes they first sacrificed the unclean animals, and then stewed them, producing a "hell-broth" (66:17, Deut 14:3, 7-8).

5. The rebellious people of God went as far as claiming a magical "holiness" from their perverted practices. They warned other people not to draw too near in case they were harmed by their spell. Yahweh said that these rebels were repellent to him, like smoke in his nostrils coming from a smouldering fire. The trouble with a smouldering fire is that it is alight, but it is not a light.

6. Yahweh therefore proceeded to pronounce his sentence on these rebels. Their misdeeds were recorded in the heavenly books that were open before him, so he could not stay silent. He was forced to pay them back for what they had done.

7. The punishment was for their own sins, inherited from the sins of the ancestors whom they worshipped. It would be for the incense they had offered on the hills and for the way they had spoken contemptuously about Yahweh on the hilltops. Full payment for their misdeeds would be measured onto their laps (Jer 32:18).

8. Verses 8-10 reaffirm the existence of a godly remnant among the Israelites (10:20-23).The simile of the good grapes in a poor cluster relates the theme of the remnant to that of the ruined vineyard (chapter 5). For the sake of the remnant, here called his servants, Yahweh would not totally destroy the whole cluster.

9. Once the separation of the bad grapes from the good ones had taken place, Yahweh would give the land of Israel, together with its mountains and hills, to his servants, descended from Jacob, who would inherit it and settle in it.

10. Theirs would be Sharon towards the west, the northern plain from Carmel to Joppa, where they could pasture their flocks. Theirs too would be the valley of Achor towards the east, with its troubled history and promise of a better future (Josh 7:24-26, Hosea 2:15). All of the Promised Land would be for the people of God who had sought him. It is clear that Yahweh's dividing line is not between Jews and Gentiles, but between those who seek him and those who forsake him.

11. A different fate awaited those who had forsaken Yahweh. Here we see their crowning insult. They ignored the mountain of Yahweh with the new Temple, and instead worshipped *Fortune* (or *Gad*), and *Destiny* (or *Meni*). These gods of luck were worshipped in Syria and in Babylon.

12. Note the pun on the god *Destiny*: "I will destine you". God spells out the fate that awaits the impenitent rebels among the people: they would be destroyed. Why? Because when Yahweh called out to them, they did not answer, and when he spoke, they did not listen. They did what was evil and made wrong choices.

13. Verses 13-16 are a taunt-song. Its sharp contrasts are similar to various contrasts we may find in the gospels (e.g. Mt 25:31-46, Lk 6:20-26, Jn 3:36). The godly remnant who were Yahweh's servants would eat, drink and rejoice, but the rebels would be hungry, thirsty and shamed. There is no mention of a *via media*, an in-between way, but only of the blessed and the accursed.

14. Yahweh's servants would sing out of the gladness of their hearts, but the rebels would cry because of the pain in theirs, and they would wail because of the anguish they experienced in their spirits.

15. The rebels would leave their name, i.e. their essential nature, to be used as a curse. Its words would be "The Lord Yahweh will put you to death". Yahweh's servants, however, would be given a different new name (62:2, Rev 2:17).

16. Whoever invoked a blessing in the land would do so in the name of *the God of faithfulness*. Whoever took an oath would likewise swear by *the God of faithfulness*. By fulfilling both his threats and his promises Yahweh would show forth his faithfulness. The word used for *faithfulness* is *amen*, which describes what is utterly reliable. The Messiah would use the words amen, amen to mean "truly, truly", and he would be given the title *the Amen* in Revelation 3:14. So the former troubles would be forgotten and hidden from sight. This inspired the prophet's imagination to great flights, as we shall see in the next section.

Meditation: God's Answer to the Prayer

At the end of his intercessory prayer the prophet had asked Yahweh whether he would persist in his stony silence, and continue his severe punishment (64:12). Yahweh began his answer to the prayer by insisting that at every moment he had sought to win his rebellious people by his love and to meet them with his salvation (v 2a). But they were descending ever more deeply into evil practices old and new, thereby following the devices and desires of their own hearts (v 2b). So it was not a case of Yahweh not being on speaking terms with them, but rather it was they who were responding to his warm overtures with stony silence.

Yahweh then went on to detail their sins of idolatry, necromancy and concoctions of abominations (v 3-7). This was his answer to his prophet's appeal. In his prayer the prophet had argued that because Yahweh was the potter and the rebels were the clay, it was therefore up to Yahweh to do something to make his evil people good, for they were his handiwork (64:8). And Yahweh said no, this was not the case. This was not how things worked. The prophet's proposal did not conform to reality. There was something the prophet had not considered.

This was the fact that Yahweh had created people with a free will of their own. This being so, Yahweh was not free to intervene in ways that rode roughshod over his people's free will. They were free to disobey him. They were free to persist in evil. They were free to turn a deaf ear to his ongoing pleadings. They were free to choose between Yahweh and the abominable idolatries of the heathen nations. They were free to shut the door of their lives in Yahweh's face, and they were free to resolve to keep him out forever. Faced with this, Yahweh might perhaps let some time go by and then try again, but in the end his hands were tied. If his people persisted in their rejection, Yahweh would have to respect their decision. He would do so with a tear in his eye. He would send his servant, that lonely figure, to tread the winepress alone and return sadly, his garments spattered with blood. It would have to be done. There was no alternative.

This was a sufficient answer to the prophet's prayer. Love is not omnipotent. If people reject and turn away from the persistent appeals of love, no hope remains for them. Nothing else can save them. It is unforgivable to sin against love in this way, because to reject God's love is to reject the fountain of all forgiveness. The sin of these rebellious Israelites was the ultimate blasphemy against the Holy Spirit of God. It is the sin that the Messiah himself would describe as leaving without any hope anyone who was foolish enough to commit it (Mk 3:28-30). Not even almighty God can help those who abuse and despise his grace.

In the remainder of his answer to his prophet's prayer, Yahweh promised that the Israelite nation, the congregation of God's people here on earth, the church – call it what you will – will be saved for the sake of the faithful remnant within it (v 8-10). But the rebellious will not be saved. Those who persistently refuse to respond to God and instead choose to do what is evil in his eyes will perish (v 11-12). They have directed the course of their lives in the opposite direction to the godly remnant, and cannot expect Yahweh to treat them in the same way.

The godly remnant who did not forsake Yahweh but instead sought him will find that he is the God of faithfulness, and will acknowledge him as the God of amen, because the former troubles are forgotten and are hidden from his eyes (v 16). It will be deeply moving to see the fatherly eyes of Yahweh, some of whose children would run away from him and be destroyed. He will wipe away every tear from our eyes (25:8, Rev 21:4), but who will wipe away the tears in his eyes?

CXV

65:17-25 New Heavens and new Earth

The *former troubles* (v16) will be forgotten in the glories of the new creation, in which all things will minister to the welfare of Yahweh's renewed people. The new is portrayed in this-world terms, except that there are no more sorrows. We are in a familiar setting, Jerusalem, but it has been wonderfully renewed. The satisfactions are familiar: the best things in the world are ordinary and simple things like enjoying the work of one's hands.

17. There will be a new universe, for Yahweh will create *new heavens and a new earth*. We have already met the idea of nature being transformed so as to be in harmony with a new humanity (11:6-9, 29:17, 30:23-26, 32:15, 35:1-10, etc.) This more complete new creation may have been suggested to the prophet by 51:6, although here it is taken several steps further, even if the prophet finds it difficult to express it in its fullest New Testament terms involving the absolute absence of any sin whatsoever and the everlasting duration of the new life. With everything being wonderfully renewed, people will be so delighted with the new earth where they are living that they will forget about the old one. The new fields will be so green, the new flowers and trees so beautiful, and the new hills so solid and majestic, that people will forget about the beauty spots of the present earth. And of course, all the old hurts will be forgotten, they simply will not come to mind. For nothing will prey on people's minds: the "former things" will not be remembered or come to mind any more.

18. There will be great joy. Yahweh encourages us to rejoice as we think ahead to what his new creation will be like. He will create the New Jerusalem, his city, as a place of joy, where people will be delighted to live.

19. The joy will be divine. Yahweh himself will rejoice and delight in his renewed city. There will be no more weeping and no more distress there (25:8, 35:10).

20. There will be ongoing life. There will be no infant mortality. There will be no more death among the elderly. If anyone was to die at the age of a hundred it would be tragic, like the death of a youth. If anyone was to die aged less than a hundred it would seem as if he was under a curse. Instead the power of death will be destroyed over the whole course of life, from infancy, past maturity and into old age. Death will not be part of the new life in the new earth.

21. There will be the pleasures of normal life, with the simple delights that God always intended us to have. People will enjoy the reward of their own labour.

They will build their own houses and live in them, they will plant vineyards and eat their own fruit (62:8-9). In this world, life doesn't get any better than enjoying the ordinary things, the smell of fresh air, the refreshment of cool water, and the taste of healthy food. This delight in simple things will continue in the new earth.

22. There will be perfect security and protection. The strong will no longer prey on the weak. The houses that the people of God build will not be taken away from them. The fruits of the trees that they plant will not be stolen from them. They themselves will live on and on, like a great tree (Ps 92:12-13). They will continue to enjoy the work of their hands.

23. There will be purposefulness. The labours of God's people will not be in vain (1 Cor 15:58). Miscarriages will be unknown: instead their children will have a wonderful future ahead of them. The people and their descendants will have God's blessing resting on them.

24. There will be a close and intimate knowledge of God. When any need arises, people will naturally turn to prayer, and they will find that their prayers receive an immediate answer, even as they are being prayed.

25. Finally, there will be peace among the animals (see 11:6-9, which this verse largely quotes). The serpent, who is the ancient tempter, will no longer escape his doom. He once brought sin and death into the world; but his toxic work will be fully undone, and he himself will have to bite the dust (Gen 3:14). History will be perfected and paradise will be regained. Nobody will cause hurt or destruction anywhere on God's holy mountain.

Meditation: How can you describe the next Life?

In the life to come God will entirely transform the conditions of human existence. The prophet describes this transformation as the creation of "new heavens and a new earth". God will take great delight in creating a world that is so wonderfully new that when the people of God are taken to it, they will not remember the previous one (v 17). The prophet then proceeds to paint a very beautiful picture, characterised by serenity and happiness, of this new world where there will be no sorrow or distress (v 18-19). He provides some amazing details.

Premature death will be unknown, and instead there will be patriarchal longevity (v 20). People will enjoy undisturbed possession of their property. Their labour will never be in vain, for God's richest blessing will always accompany them and their families (v 21-23). So deeply will they know and love God, that they will receive prompt answers to all their prayers (v 24). There will be harmony in the animal world, for there will never be any hurt or destruction in Yahweh's holy mountain (v 25). This prospect is worthy of the name given to it by the prophet: new heavens and a new earth. It is a captivating picture.

Imagine you are the prophet, and in the year 520 B.C. you are about to describe to the Jews who are resettled in Jerusalem the new world that God is preparing for those who love him. How would you go about it? You might have thought in terms of a world that was similar to the one you were used to, except that it would be without "the bad bits". There would be no more weeping or distress, no people dying before their time or failing to fulfil their potential, no people criminally deprived of their property or possessions, no work done in vain, no nature "red in tooth and claw", as Tennyson put it, and last but not least, no causes of sin. All of this the prophet included in his message. The new earth will be made wonderful because of what will *not* be there. But it will also be made wonderful because of what *will* be there. What would you want to include?

You might begin by saying that the next life would be characterised by joy and delight at the beauty and the goodness of everything in the new earth. Then you might move on to say that the redeemed would enjoy eternal, unending life. The idea of everlasting life was unknown in those days, although the seed of it had been sown (25:8, 26:19). So the way you might put it would be that life would be unimaginably long. If someone died aged a hundred, that would be an unnatural catastrophe. Life would just go on and on, like that of a giant tree.

After that you might want to describe the purposefulness of life in the new earth. You would talk in earthly terms that people would understand – people would build new homes and live in them, plant vineyards and eat their fruit. The work that people undertook would be secure and it would not be in vain. You might wish to make the point that life will be as good as can be, and so you would mention the simple pleasures of our present lives – creation, procreation, and the fulfilment of one's existence through good creative work. You might mention that the harmful and destructive aspects of nature would no longer be part of life because they would be forever abolished. The different animals, for example, would live together in constant harmony.

Finally you might want to highlight the sheer bliss of having a much deeper friendship with the only true God, who is the creator and saviour of all his people. How could you do this? The thought would come to you: he is a real God, for he is always there and is always ready to hear and answer our prayers. But in the new earth, the answers to our prayers will be immediate, "no sooner said than done", for all our prayers would be according to the will of God. And so you might wish to add that little detail to your description.

If this is how you think of the new life and how you would try and describe it to other people, award yourself multiple extra marks. Your description would match that of the prophet exactly in every detail. Great minds really do think alike. You have described the glories of the future life brilliantly.

Passages like this one are included in the Bible not to satisfy our curiosity but to kindle our hope. If we are followers of the Messiah, we have a great future in this life and an even greater one in the next life. God has said, "I am about to create new heavens and a new earth". Our new lives there will be wonderful beyond description. This does not mean that they will be unimaginably wonderful, for we are certainly allowed and even urged to imagine them, using what is revealed in the Bible as our guide. But the reality will surpass even the inspired descriptions of it, and our most illumined imagining will fall far short of the reality. "From ages past no one has heard, no ear has perceived, no eye has seen any God besides you, who works for those who wait for him" (64:4).

CXVI

66:1-14 Trembling at God's Word

In verses 1-6 Yahweh forthrightly declares what he thinks of a religion that emphasises ecclesiastical form and ritual at the expense of knowing him and trembling at his word. In verses 7-14 he further sharpens the division between the godly and the selfishly rebellious that will take place in the end-time.

1. Yahweh speaks and declares that heaven is his throne and the earth is his footstool. This means that his people should take careful thought as they rebuild and adorn the Temple according to Yahweh's instructions (Hag 1:2-11). What exactly do they mean by saying that the Temple is Yahweh's house and resting place? If their real intention is to build walls around God so as to make him "safe", this is completely unrealistic (2 Sam 7:6-7, Acts 7:48-50, 54).

2. Yahweh is the creator of everything apart from himself, so it makes little sense for people to claim to erect what will supposedly be his dwelling-place. They could not build a house big enough to contain him. They could not constrict the God who made and sustains the world into just the local deity of Israel. Yahweh expects all those who build the Temple and who worship in it to be *humble and contrite* in spirit, and to *tremble at his word* (Ezra 9:4). Men and women are small and sinful, unworthy of God (Lk 18:9-14). But if they humble themselves a miracle will take place: Yahweh will come and dwell with them (57:15).

3. A ritual that is merely correct, carried out according to Yahweh's instructions but with no conscious regard for him, is little more than senseless slaughter and idolatry (1:13, Jer 7:21-26). The verse may be saying more than this, however. The Hebrew reads "The one who slaughters an ox, a killer of a human being; the person who sacrifices a lamb, one who breaks a dog's neck; the one who presents a grain offering, one who offers swine's blood; the person who makes a memorial offering of frankincense, one who blesses an idol". Those who worshipped God in the Temple may have combined holy worship with unacceptable practices. They had chosen their own ways and delighted in their abominations.

4. Yahweh would duly mock these people and visit them with the judgement they dreaded. Yahweh had called to them, but none of them had answered him. He had spoken many times, but they had not listened. They did what was evil and

displeasing to Yahweh. The last part of the verse repeats the last part of 65:12.

5. Those who combined Temple worship with idol worship tended to persecute those who were godly and trembled at Yahweh's word. They rejected them "for the sake of the name" (3 Jn 7). Yahweh promises the godly that their persecutors would be put to shame. Their intolerance would later be inherited by those who persecuted the followers of the Messiah (Jn 9:24, 34).

6. All are bidden to hear Yahweh speaking loudly from the Temple: he announces retribution to his enemies. This will be picked up later in verses 15-16.

7. Verses 7-9 describe the suddenness of the events of the end times. The godly will be renewed instantaneously (60:22), like a woman giving birth before she has labour pains. "We will all be changed, in a moment, in the twinkling of an eye, at the last trumpet" (1 Cor 15:51-52).

8. Such quick procreation is unheard of and has never before been seen. How can a people be born in one day? Will a nation be delivered in a moment? But as soon as mother Zion had pictured her renewed children, she gave birth to them.

9. This verse is Yahweh's triumphant answer to the question which King Hezekiah asked Isaiah (37:3). Will Yahweh open the womb and not deliver his people in childbirth? No, of course not. He does not advance as far as that with his purposes and then abandon them before they are fulfilled. Having opened the womb, will he not deliver? Yes, of course. Yahweh does not begin a task unless he intends to finish it.

10. In verses 10-14 we have the final poem in the series on Zion as the mother of God's children (49:14-23). It is addressed to Zion's children, the godly remnant. The prophet urges them to rejoice with their mother Jerusalem, whom they love and whose destruction they once mourned (61:2-3).

11. Now they will be able to nurse at her breast and be consoled and satisfied. To drink from her glorious bosom will be a great delight for them.

12. Yahweh promises to prosper Zion like a river, and to give her all the treasures of the nations as if in an overflowing stream. The godly would be nursed by her and carried on her arm. They would be fondled on her knees.

13. Now comes a revelation: Zion is not the real source of the wealth and comfort of her children. It is Yahweh, who is described here as their real mother, though he uses the redeemed community to dispense his gifts: "I will comfort you ... in Jerusalem". Yahweh and Zion are related to each other in the same way as our fellowship with God and our fellowship in the church.

14. The prophet tells the godly that they will see their new abode and the one who created it for them, and their heart will rejoice. The Messiah echoed this line as he prophesied his resurrection from the dead (Jn 16:22). The godly will flourish in the New Jerusalem and will be as fresh as grass in springtime. It will be evident to all that Yahweh favours his servants and is angry with his enemies.

Meditation: The Birth of religious Hatred

In verse 14 we read that "It shall be known that the hand of Yahweh is with his servants, and his indignation is with his enemies". One of the sad laws of the spiritual world is that the revelation of God's favour for certain people may lead those who are not favoured to envy and hate those who are.

In our passage there is a remarkable description of those who try to get the best of both worlds (v 3). They do what is lawful and what is unlawful (one slaughters an ox, he also kills a human being). They practice what is ordained and what is weird (one sacrifices a lamb, he also breaks a dog's neck). They present what is pure and what is abominable (one presents a grain offering, he also offers swine's blood). They worship the God of heaven and a false and forbidden god (one makes a memorial offering of frankincense, he also blesses an idol).

Such double loyalties are not only wrong, they are also impossible (Mt 6:24). God will not favour those who attempt to worship him if they also worship idols, for the simple reason that if they are worshipping idols then they are not worshipping him. The worship of God is the natural and reasonable response of a person to the one through whom they were created and saved, and who alone is worthy of worship. The worship of the one true and uncreated God immediately precludes the worship of anyone or anything that has been created (Ex 20:3-6). It is written, "Worship the Lord your God, and serve only him" (Deut 6:13, Mt 3:4, Lk 4:8).

This is why God loves the humble and hates the proud. The humble turn naturally to God and delight to worship him. The proud resent being told how they are to worship, preferring to choose their own way and to delight in abominations (end of v 3). They will not listen when God calls them; instead they will do what is evil in his sight and choose ways that displease him (v 4). Therefore the proud and unrepentant will not be favoured by God. They cannot expect God's favour and, indeed, unless they turn wholeheartedly to him, they are certain to be the recipients of his holy and righteous indignation (v 14).

The text in verse 2b is important and striking: "This is the one to whom I will look, to the humble and contrite in spirit, who trembles at my word". It suggests that our reaction to the word of God is all-important. Barry Webb wrote, "What ultimately divides the true from the false in the church is faithfulness or unfaithfulness to the word of God. Clinging to the promises of God will always seem fanatical and foolish to those who have abandoned them. [The Messiah] warned his disciples that they themselves would experience the same kind of rejection. Religion that loses its anchorage in the word of God either becomes pathetically ineffective or turns into a monster".

Those who try to become righteous in their own way will not only fail in their attempt, but their proud approach is liable to lead them to oppose bitterly those who are humble and contrite. Yahweh here speaks to the latter on those occasions when they are persecuted by the proud. He says, "Hear the word of Yahweh, you who tremble at his word: Your own people who hate you and reject you for my name's sake have said,

'Let Yahweh be glorified, so that we may see your joy'; but it is they who shall be put to shame" (v 5). The true people of God are being persecuted by the nominal people of God, who hate and reject them for the sake of Yahweh's name. What does this mean?

The godly love God and they follow and worship him because of his "name", i.e. because of who he is and what he has done for them. Their persecutors do not know or love God, so they hate the godly "for the sake of Yahweh's name". In our own day, believers who have a simple Biblical faith are despised by some in the church who think of themselves as sophisticated and consider it simplistic to tremble at God's word. The latter may refer to godly believers as "fundamentalists" and create a culture of contempt in the church. This makes it difficult for believers to feed on God through the scriptures. A vicious circle is formed. The church is now very weak. It could become strong again, but only through Bible study. This is frowned upon by some in high positions in the church. The followers of the Messiah do everything except serious Bible study. The church gets weaker.

Derek Kidner comments that in this verse we have "one of the earliest allusions to purely religious persecution and theological hatred, one of the darkest stains of the church". Because of this religious hatred, this venting of the spleen on God's people who take his word seriously, a cry is heard in the city. It comes from the Temple. From there Yahweh speaks, in order to encourage his children. He will deal retribution to his enemies, to those who discourage his people (v 6).

God will fulfil his purpose of having children who take his word seriously and tremble at it. He turns away from those who pretend to worship him but in fact choose what is displeasing to him. He is indignant with those who offer him half of themselves. With God, it is all or nothing. He is everywhere in your life, or else he is nowhere. If he is not Lord of all, he is not Lord at all.

CXVII

66:15-24 The Reign and Judgement of God

15. Verses 15-16 pick up the thread of retribution from verses 1-6. A terrifying fire and whirlwind will accompany the appearance of Yahweh as he comes to rebuke and to pay back his anger in fury.

16. The fire and the sword are the harsh aspect of God's interventions (Mt 10:34, Lk 12:49-51), especially of his final intervention (2 Thess 1:7-10). The judgement will be executed on all flesh, and we are told that those who will be slain will be *many*. From the context the special objects of God's wrath will be those who seek to combine worship of Yahweh with worship of idols (v 1-6, 17). These people have known the light and yet they have despised it.

17. The false followers of Yahweh are described in similar terms to 65:3-5. They take pains to prepare themselves for their heathen rites and then go to the gardens

where their leader, "the one in the centre" (Ezek 8:11), leads their worship of false gods. They eat the flesh of unclean animals and drink their "hell-broth". They participate together, and they will meet their final end together (v24).

18. Verses 18-21 are an epilogue about the coming of Yahweh to the world in the person of the Messiah. This verse informs us about Yahweh's purpose for the world. He knows every person's works and thoughts, and he wishes to gather the nations together so that they may see his glory.

19. The means by which Yahweh will fulfil his purposes is through a sign that he will set before them, possibly looking ahead to the death and resurrection of the Messiah (Mt 12:38-40). The *survivors* are those among them who will be saved. They will be sent to every nation in the world, including those who have never heard of Yahweh, and they will declare his glory. *Tarshish* is Tartessus in Spain, *Put* and *Lud* are places in Africa, near Ethiopia (Jer 46:9, Ezek 30:5), *Tubal* is in the far north (Ezek 39:1-2), and *Javan* is the Hebrew word for Greece.

20. The God-fearing people from all the nations will go to Jerusalem, making their way there by various means of transportation, bringing dispersed Israelites in order to present them before God. Once they arrive there they will gather on Yahweh's holy mountain, like God's people when they bring homage offerings to Yahweh on clean vessels.

21. The Gentiles will be much more than just clean vessels. Yahweh declares that they will be incorporated as full members of God's people together with the godly Jews. They will have all the privileges and responsibilities of God's people.

22. The book of Isaiah ends by describing in Old Testament terms and language the final states of glory and perdition. The new heavens and new earth (65:17), which Yahweh would proceed to make, will remain before him forever. So will the names and the descendants of all who are godly.

23. The new moons and Sabbaths are no longer binding on God's people, but mere shadows of what is to come (Col 2:16-17). Here they stand for all kinds of occasions when worship is given to God. All flesh, all the godly in the new earth, will gather to dedicate their whole lives joyfully to God in worship.

24. The godly will go and look at the dead bodies of the people whom God has destroyed (See Dan 12:2b, Mk 9:43-48). This sombre reminder of the fate of the unrepentant is not an inappropriate ending to the book of Isaiah. Throughout the book there has been a positive note about the importance of fearing God, waiting for God, trusting in God, and being forgiven and loved by God. But there has also been a repeated warning that those who fail to turn to Yahweh in repentance and simple trust will in the end have to face his terrible judgement.

Meditation: The End

In chapters 65 and 66 the two possible final destinations of men and women have been coming into sharper and sharper focus. They are either life or destruction, just as the Messiah said towards the end of his famous Sermon on the Mount (Mt 7:13-14). We have been skipping from one to the other as follows:

65:1-7 is about destruction.

65:8-10 is about life.

65:11-12 is about destruction.

65:13-16 contrasts the two.

65:17-25 is about life.

66:1-6 is about destruction.

66:7-14 is about life.

66:15-17 is about destruction.

66:18-23 is about life.

Finally, 66:24 is about destruction.

It is perhaps surprising to end on a sad and sombre note. We must look closely at the end. Why does the book of Isaiah have a negative conclusion?

As they come to the city to worship, the redeemed go out of their way and walk to the valley outside, in order to visit the cemetery and remind themselves that it is only by the extraordinary grace of God that they have been spared the fate of those who have perished for their impenitent rebelliousness.

There has been a carefully crafted build-up to this grim ending. As Alec Motyer writes, "On the one hand, [the final chapters] have been alight with the glory of the new creation, the new city and its new people. But equally, on the other, they have been solemnised by the note of vengeance (59:17, 61:2, 63:4), the wine-press of the wrath of God (63:3, 6), the fiery sword of judgement (66:16) and the record that *many* will be those slain by Yahweh (66:16)".

But why did the book not end with the new heavens and the new earth, and with the multitude of the redeemed coming to worship God? This could have been achieved easily if verse 24 had been inserted just before verses 22 and 23. Indeed, in Hebrew Bibles, part of verse 23 is repeated after verse 24 so that the readings of Isaiah 66 in the synagogues may "close with words of comfort". There must be good reason why the book has come down to us with the ending as it is.

Could it be something to do with the name or character of God's city, Jerusalem? It means "City of Peace", but throughout its existence it has been anything but that. Many wonderful godly people have been associated with it, but also many who have chosen to go their own way and not God's. In the first 39 chapters of the book of Isaiah it was the home of the prophet who gave his name to the book, but his was a lonely prophetic voice among a crowd of disobedient and rebellious Israelites. Then it was a city in ruins, to which the exiled Jews returned with reluctance and apprehension. Finally it was the resettled city of God which fell far short of the expectations of the resettlers and of the standards that God had set for it. Jerusalem has not only been the city chosen by God *par excellence*, it has also been a city ripe for God's judgement.

The Messiah wept over Jerusalem (Mt 23:37-39). In his final discourse, which he delivered there, he divided the wise from the foolish, the loving from the selfish, and the sheep from the goats. He likewise was sharpening the focus of his teaching, with judgement playing an increasing role in it, as the day of his sacrificial death drew near. It was as if Jerusalem had come to symbolise the ultimate antithesis between life and destruction.

George Adam Smith wrote of verse 24, "It is a terrible ending to a prophecy such as ours. But is any other possible? We ask how this contiguity of heaven and hell can be within the Lord's own city, after all his yearning and jealousy for her, after such a clear revelation of himself, such a long providence, and such a glorious deliverance. Yet it is plain that nothing else can result, if the people on whose ears the great prophecy had fallen, with all its music and all its gospel, and who had been partakers of the Lord's restoration, did yet continue to prefer their idols, their swine's flesh, their mouse, their broth of abominable things, and their sitting in graves, to so evident a God and to such a great grace".

It is indeed a terrible ending, but no more so than one of the grim alternatives open to people according to the Messiah's teaching. He who taught us more sublimely than anyone else about the love of God also taught us most terribly than anyone else about the judgement of God. He wanted the seed of the gospel to be cast wide, but he said that only one of the four types of soil would bear good fruit on the field of judgement. He cried out to all people, "Come to me!" but he also prophesied that on the final day he would sadly have to say to some of them, "Depart from me".

It is a terrible ending because people have free will. God is love, but we are free to turn away from that love and to live as if grace and mercy did not exist. If we do so, we shall face the terrible end in verse 24. But perhaps reading about that terrible end will deepen our resolve to avoid it at all costs, and to give ourselves afresh to the God who loved us so much that he gave his servant-Messiah for us, and who was kind enough to make the possibility of judgement so clear. Like the redeemed who went and had a look at the people in the terrible abyss, where worms and fire cannot be stopped from their destructive work, we may realise what we have been saved from, and at what great cost.

Almighty and most merciful Father, you have caused the book of Isaiah to be written so as to be the revelation of your amazing love for us, and of your power and determination to save us. Grant that our study of it may not have been in vain on account of the hardness of our hearts, but that by it we may be confirmed in our repentance, lifted up in our hope, strengthened in our service and, above all, filled with the true knowledge of yourself and of your Son Jesus the Messiah, in whose name and for whose sake we ask this. **AMEN.**

Appendices

Appendix 1. A most intriguing Text – Isaiah 45:7

"I form light and create darkness, I make weal and create woe; I Yahweh do all these things" (Isa 45:7). We are happy with the first part of each clause. There is no problem in ascribing to God the forming of light and the making of weal, which means the state of well-being. "For everything created by God is good, and nothing is to be rejected, provided it is received with thanksgiving" (1 Tim 4:4). This makes perfect sense. Of course God created everything that is good.

The difficulty many people have has arisen because God goes on to say, "I create darkness, I create woe". God is altogether good, so everything he creates must be good. How then can he declare that he created darkness and woe? Did God create evil as well as good? The text we are puzzling over may be read in a number of different ways. It asserts God's ultimate control over evil (as in 1 Sam 2:6-8). The writers of the psalms struggled to express their feelings as they wrestled with the problem of evil.

At a basic level, in Psalm 17 David is aware of God's searching eye, and is bold enough to invite God to try his heart. He likes to think that his lips are free from deceit (v1), that there is no wickedness in him (v3), and that his steps have not strayed from God's paths (v5). He asks God to guard him "as the apple of the eye" (v8), and is angry because his wicked enemies seek to destroy him (v9-12) and speak arrogantly (v10). He is comforted by the thought of God's just retribution (v13-14), and knows that when he wakes up in the next life he will be satisfied by seeing the face of God in righteousness (v15).

The writer of Psalm 44 thinks at a deeper level. He was probably an exile in Babylon. He loves to think about God's exploits of old in the exodus (v1-3), and of his more recent victories (v4-7). His boast is in God and he delights to thank God for past glories (v8). And yet it is all very different for him now that he is exiled. God has rejected and abased his people (v9). They are humiliated by their captors. They have become a source of derision for their neighbours, and a laughing-stock among the peoples (v10-16).

Psalm 73 is attributed to Asaph, who perhaps had even greater insight. At first he is envious of the arrogant and the wicked, because it seems that they have no pain and are never in trouble (v3-9). Instead they are at ease and increase in wealth (v10-14). Thinking about the unfairness of this becomes a burden to him (v15-16), until he prays about it (v17). Then he perceives that the ultimate end of the arrogant and the wicked will be ruin and destruction (v18-20). This realisation inspires him to write down one of the most magnificent personal prayers of the Old Testament, in which he pours out his soul in a moving expression of love and commitment to God (v21-28).

It is in Amos 3:6 that we have the nearest Old Testament approximation to Isaiah 45:7. The earliest of the writing prophets exclaims, "Is a trumpet blown in a city, and the people are not afraid? Does disaster befall a city, unless Yahweh has done it?" For the prophets of the Old Testament, God himself was the first cause of everything. If a disaster befell a city, it was because God had planned it as part of his mysterious purposes. Perhaps this is the sense in which Isaiah declared that Yahweh created darkness and woe.

We should also go back to one of the most basic questions asked by many thoughtful people. If God is both altogether good and all-powerful, why did he not arrange things differently, so that there would be no sin and no suffering? The answer is, because he wished to create people in his own image, who had free will and were able to choose between loving and obeying God on the one hand, and rebelling against God and disobeying him on the other.

God could have created us without free will. He could have made us a race of robots programmed to please him at all times, never to put a foot wrong. Had he done so, he would have found all of us intensely boring, and perhaps we would in turn have found our existence dull and monotonous. Life is only interesting and exciting when it contains real choices. Of course, it is maddening for us when other people exercise their free will in ways that disadvantage us. It was Jean-Paul Sartre who wrote the famous line "Hell is other people", and it can be said without irreverence that God himself has sometimes been deeply frustrated and grieved by the consequences of human rebellion and sin (see, notably, 63:1-6). On the last day he will tread the winepress alone and destroy those men and women who refused to repent and persevered in their proud disobedience.

The question we may legitimately ask is, was it worth it for God to take such trouble over the human race, when inevitably they would turn away from him and prove to be such a difficult and troublesome part of his creation?

There is only one answer to this question. We may all work it out for ourselves by considering the care God took over his whole creation and providence (40:12-31), the pains he went to in order to secure our redemption (52:13-53:12), and the greatness of the glory he has in store for those who love him (64:4, 65:17-25). To cap it all, we read that the suffering servant will eventually look back at his self-sacrifice on our behalf, and know that it has all been worthwhile. "He shall see the fruit of the travail of his soul and be satisfied" (53:11, Revised Standard Version).

So what exactly does God mean when he says "I create darkness and I create woe"? (45:7). He means that he created us with real free will. By doing so, he made it possible for us to rebel against him and bring darkness and woe to planet earth. It is in this sense that he created evil. He is indeed the first cause of everything, including our rebellion and sin. We might then argue that because God did this, he should therefore take responsibility for what he has done. In the book of Isaiah, as in the rest of scripture, his reply is that he has done just that.

Appendix 2. For Isaiah: the End and the Beginning

The book which is now called *The Martyrdom and Ascension of Isaiah*, part of the Old Testament Pseudepigrapha, may have been written during the persecution of the Jews by Antiochus Epiphanes in 167-164 B.C. so as to encourage the people of God to be faithful unto death as they faced opposition. It may have been based on reliable traditions. It states that, sometime after 686 B.C., the Prophet Isaiah was put to death by the evil King Manasseh, who had him sawn in two. There is a tiny echo of this in the New Testament: in the book of Hebrews there is a reference to some of the Old Testament heroes of faith who suffered persecution, some of whom are said to have been *sawn in two* (Heb 11:37).

The Old Testament Pseudepigrapha are generally considered unreliable sources, so this story may be legendary. We are, however, told that King Manasseh "shed very much innocent blood, until he had filled Jerusalem from one end to another, besides the sin that he caused Judah to sin so that they did what was evil in the sight of Yahweh" (2 Ki 21:16). Assuming that Isaiah was aged 20 in 740 B.C. when he was called to be a prophet (6:1), if he had lived until Manasseh had fully taken over the reins of power from Hezekiah in 686 B.C., he would by then have been nearly 75 years old. It is not impossible that he may have died under these distressing circumstances, for Manasseh was keen to reverse the religious reforms of his father Hezekiah, and would probably have been disinclined to spare the elderly prophet.

In medieval books of hours there are occasional paintings of "the martyrdom of Isaiah". There are two ways in which the prophet is depicted as having been sawn in two, and examples of both can be cited in paintings.

(a) Isaiah could have been placed inside a hollow tree trunk, with his head jutting out at one end and his feet at the other. Then the trunk would have been sawn transversely at the halfway point, dividing Isaiah into two across his waist.

(b) Alternatively, Isaiah could have been hung by his feet from two fixed elevated points a yard apart, so that his legs formed a V with his body hanging upside down. The saw was then aimed for a downwards cut, midsagittally, from the point of intersection of his legs down towards his head.

In either case one or two executioners could have been at work, depending upon whether the saw being used was longer than usual with a handle at one end, or an even longer one with handles at both ends.

Whatever the method and the type of saw being used, death would come speedily due to loss of blood. After a minute or two of intense pain, unconsciousness would set in, and death would follow soon after.

It would have been an inappropriate end for a godly man whose writings have been so greatly valued during the past 27 centuries. But there have been other godly men and women who have been put to death for their faith in the one true God. The Messiah himself was subjected to torture and crucifixion.

We do not ultimately know how the Prophet Isaiah died. He may have passed away peacefully, surrounded by his sons and his followers. Whichever way he died, his end was also a beginning. The end of his life on earth would have been the beginning of a new life in the new heavens and the new earth created by God for those who love him (65:17-25, 64:4). God, who swallows up death forever (25:8) would have spoken the regenerative word. His dead prophet would then live once again, his corpse would rise (26:19). If he had been bisected, the two halves of his body would be reunited. Indeed, his body would be completely renewed. He would then begin to enjoy the glory of his God and to worship him forever.

In medieval times monks compiled martyrologies or books commemorating the godly who had died. Perhaps the most beautiful of them is the priceless Girona Martyrology made around 1410, which has been reproduced in facsimile. Most of the martyrs are commemorated on the anniversary of their "birth" (in Latin, *natalem*) and their place of "birth" is mentioned also (*natale*). It took the present author some time to realise that these were the anniversaries and places of their death or martyrdom. In medieval times Christian Europeans were brought up to think of their own deaths as being their "births" into eternal life.

When Christians die they go home, in order to be with God. All their sins are forgiven, and for them anxieties and tears will be a thing of the past. Their new lives will be purposeful, and all their gifts will find fulfilment. It may be helpful for us to think of their deaths as coinciding with their births to new life. We shall of course miss them in this life, but if we know and love God, we may look forward to a wonderful reunion with them. Perhaps we shall also meet Isaiah, and have the opportunity to thank him for his prophecies.

Appendix 3. For us: the Arrival of the Messiah

It finally happened one day. We do not know the year for certain. It was around 5 B.C. when the Messiah (or in Greek, *Christ*) was born. When the calendar was reviewed over 500 years later, it was intended that the birth-year of the Messiah should be the year zero, but a sixth-century monk from Scythia called Dionysius Exiguus (Dennis the Unimportant) got his calculations wrong, assigning Christ's birth five years too late. His dating was followed by the Venerable Bede in England, and the system caught on. As a result, the calendar is incorrectly dated by Christ's birth, even though our births are correctly dated by the calendar. The Messiah is unique amongst people in that we all indeed date our births by the calendar, whereas he can date the calendar by his birth.

Any reader of the gospels will be struck by the extraordinary humility of the Messiah's birth and subsequent life. He was born in a building normally inhabited by animals, and his cot was a manger for livestock. After he was born, he was visited by lowly shepherds. Later he had more distinguished visitors who gave him gifts. One of these gifts was gold, which enabled his parents to flee from an attempt on his life by the local despotic ruler. The Messiah lived a life of poverty. When he asked God for his daily bread, this was a prayer from the heart for a real need, and not an empty form of words to be repeated every day. On one occasion, he wished to make a point that required the sight of a coin. He was so poor that he did not own a coin, and had to ask for one to be brought to him.

By means of his birth, and in his life, death and resurrection, he fulfilled numerous prophecies that were written in the book of Isaiah. Here are 46 of them:

1. The Messiah would be descended from David (11:1).
2. Someone who was a young unmarried lady, and perhaps a virgin, would bear a son, the Messiah (7:14).
3. The Messiah would be born out of the blue, with no labour pains (66:7).
4. The Messiah would be brought up in Galilee (9:1-7).
5. One of the Messiah's designations would be Immanuel, which means "God is with us" (7:14).
6. The Messiah would be a relatively obscure person, from a modest background, whose development would be hidden away by God. (49:1-2).
7. The Messiah would be like a shoot from the stump of a tree, which would then grow to be a branch (4:2, 6:13, 11:1).
8. Someone else would prepare the way for the Messiah (40:3-5).
9. The Messiah would grow up before God like a young plant, and like a root out of dry ground. This would fill God with delight and pleasure (53:2).
10. The Messiah would not shy away from identifying with his people, for example by being baptised like them (50:5).
11. The Holy Spirit of God would rest upon the Messiah so as to empower him (42:1, 48:16, 59:21, 61:1-3).
12. The Holy Spirit of God would endow the Messiah seven times over (11:2).
13. The Messiah would not have a striking appearance, nor would people find him particularly attractive (53:2).
14. The Messiah would come and enhance the life of anyone who was weak and lowly (40:29-31, 57:15).
15. The Messiah would gently love those who were damaged or hurting (42:3).

16. The Messiah, as Immanuel, would be with his people, accompanying them when they were oppressed (7:14-17, 8:5-8).
17. The Messiah would bring good news for those who were oppressed (61:1).
18. The Messiah would bind up and bring inner healing to those who were broken-hearted (61:1).
19. The Messiah would be the great liberator of those who were captive or held prisoner by evil forces (61:1).
20. The Messiah would comfort those who mourn (61:2-3).
21. The Messiah would heal the blind, the deaf, the mute and the lame (35:5-6).
22. The Messiah would be utterly straightforward, without any deceit (53:9).
23. The Messiah would attract converts from among the Gentiles (11:10, 49:6).
24. The Messiah would set his face like a flint as he faced opposition (50:7).
25. The Messiah would refuse to argue his way out of trouble (53:7).
26. The Messiah would offer his back to those who would smite him, and his cheeks to those who would slap him and spit at him (50:6).
27. The Messiah would be despised and rejected by others; he would be a man of suffering and acquainted with infirmity (53:3).
28. The Messiah would be condemned in a most unjust trial (53:8).
29. The Messiah would have his hands and feet pierced (53:5).
30. The Messiah would be lifted up as a banner (11:12).
31. The Messiah would pray for those who put him to death (53:12).
32. The Messiah would suffer and die for our sins (53:4-6).
33. The Messiah would be disfigured beyond human likeness (52:14).
34. The Messiah would be God-forsaken when he died (49:14, 53:6).
35. The suffering of the Messiah was a key part of God's rescue plan (53:10).
36. The body of the Messiah would be laid in a rich man's tomb (53:9).
37. The Messiah would be brought back from the dead (53:10-12).
38. The Messiah would see the fruit of the travail of his soul, and be satisfied (53:10, Revised Standard Version).
39. The Messiah-king would reign in righteousness; his subjects would also be righteous, for his qualities would take root in them (32:1-8, 53:11).
40. The lowly followers of the Messiah, those who feared and waited for God, would become his temple and dwelling-place (40:29-31, 57:15, 66:1-2).
41. The Messiah's kingdom would embrace all the nations (9:7).
42. One day everyone would contemplate the Messiah-King in his beauty (33:17).
43. Every knee would bow before the Messiah, and every tongue confess that he alone is God; there is no other (45:22-23).
44. The Messiah would not only proclaim the year of God's favour, but also the day of God's vengeance (61:2).
45. The Messiah would one day destroy the impenitent in hell (63:1-6).

46. The Messiah would be worshipped as the Wonderful Counsellor, the Mighty God, the Everlasting Father and the Prince of Peace (9:6).

In his prophetic oracles II Isaiah described a mysterious figure who bore our sufferings, endured our torments, was pierced for our transgressions, and by whose scourging we are healed. The suffering servant of Yahweh would take our sins, which are our minus sign, and somehow turn them into a positive new start, into a plus. The cross on which he died is like a big plus sign for the penitent.

The Messiah whose coming was prophesied in the book of Isaiah would not, however, appeal to everyone. Some people would feel threatened by him as he came among them, just as some people felt threatened by the preaching of the prophet Isaiah (28:9-13). Not everyone is happy with a Messiah who comes to them humbly, riding on a donkey (Lk 19:28:40). Not everyone is happy with a Messiah who longs to save them from their sins, and laments and weeps publicly over them (Lk 19:41-44). Not everyone is happy with a Messiah who gets angry with them and purifies their worship (Lk 19:45-48).

Not everyone accepted the Messiah when he came to live on earth. Not everyone accepts him as their Saviour and Lord today. "But to all who [receive] him, who [believe] in his name, he [gives] power to become children of God" (Jn 1:12).

Appendix 4. The last Word is for Yahweh

The American theologian Richard Niebuhr (1894-1962) summed up a certain type of preaching as follows: "A God without wrath brought men without sin into a kingdom without judgement through the ministrations of a Christ without a cross". Such a statement is prophetic of the state of the church today. The God many Christians hear about in the church today is a small and ineffectual God. It is barely worth our while to strike up a distant acquaintanceship with him, let alone make an effort to get to know him intimately. He is ever benevolent and grandfatherly towards us.

The God that is presented in many churches has no wrath, for he is a purely constitutional monarch whose greatest wish for us is that we should always treat each other with mutual tolerance. He would never dream of displaying such bad taste as to judge people. We in turn should never harbour pathological traits such as fearing him. Even if God did judge people, we ourselves are not all that bad, are we? And even if we do occasionally behave selfishly, he is surely there to forgive us. "C'est son metier" – it is what he is there for. There was surely no need for all this fuss about the Messiah coming to die for our sins on the cross.

This portrayal of God seems to be fashionable in our dwindling contemporary church. But the God so described is most certainly not the same God as Yahweh, who is presented to us throughout the book of Isaiah.

Yahweh is to be feared. For those who know and love him, the fear we have of him is primarily a fear of letting him down, of disappointing him. We love him so much that it is a tragedy when we fail, although there is always forgiveness and grace available provided that we return to him in repentance and trust. Those who do not yet love him nevertheless have some hope of redemption provided that they fear him. If they do not fear him, they have little to look forward to, for they will continue in their disobedience, and the wrath of God will linger on them (Jn 3:36).

Yahweh will judge the world. On that day, he will be especially severe on those who are proud. Pride is the sin he hates the most. In chapter 2, Isaiah gives us one of the two most vivid and powerful visions of the Day of Judgement that have ever been written. The other is in Matthew's Gospel (25:31-46). Nobody can read the book of Isaiah without becoming painfully aware of his or her own sin. This work of judgement is described in the book of Isaiah as Yahweh's "strange" work. It does not come easily to him. His natural work is to forgive and to bless, but where there is persistent disobedience without any repentance, Yahweh must be true to his holiness. There will come a day when he will judge and destroy.

For many readers of Isaiah, the most haunting picture of God in the entire book is that of the unnamed figure who comes from treading the wine press, his garments stained with blood (63:1-6). He had looked, but there was to be no helper. He had to do his strange work alone. We know that the figure is God the Son, the Messiah. The task of judgement and the punishment of everlasting destruction (2 Thess 1:7-10) will not come easily to him, but he is the one entrusted by God with them (Mt 25:31-46, Jn 5:22-29, Acts 17:30-31).

The Bible teaches that God will judge the world through his Son Jesus, the Messiah. Although this is an unpalatable truth and one that should only be mentioned with restraint and sensitivity, it is a truth that may not be omitted in the teaching plan of any church. It is part of the "whole purpose" or complete counsel of God, which the apostle Paul did not shrink from declaring to his churches (Acts 20:27). Nowadays strong pressure is sometimes placed on church leaders not to allow the truth of God's judgement to be broadcast in the church.

The present author has come across this on a number of occasions during his life. He knows someone whom we shall refer to as V. It was made clear to V, by the priest-in-charge of his very small church, that it was wrong even to mention the future judgement in the public teaching and worship. V had submitted some intercessions for a Sunday service, based on the readings for that Sunday. One of the readings featured the text "The harvest is plentiful, but the labourers are few, therefore ask the Lord of the harvest to send out labourers into his harvest". The prayer written by V and linked to this reading was, "Holy Spirit of the Lord, send out ever increasing numbers of your people with your good news to those who have not yet heard it. Convince those who hear about Jesus Christ of their great need for him, of the way of righteousness that is theirs in him, and of the certainty of judgement if they ignore God". By return V was informed by the priest-in-charge that the final phrase was inappropriate because "It is true that Jesus says this, but we feel that only Jesus can say this". V then made the pertinent comment that a few weeks earlier the priest-in-charge had preached against certain unnamed evangelicals who made use of "orthodoxy tests". V pointed out that the priest-in-charge's remarks to him themselves constituted an orthodoxy test, namely that there were certain truths which Jesus said, but which only Jesus was allowed to say (whatever that bizarre statement might mean).

The priest-in-charge replied, writing that "As well as orthodoxy, there is also orthopraxy – right practice. When I read your prayers the phrase I asked you to remove jumped out at me as sounding judgmental against the people of [the church]. I'm sure you didn't intend that but I was worried that that was how it might be heard. To make sure it wasn't just me, I sent them to [the assistant priest] who reacted in the very same way, hence my request to you which arose primarily out of pastoral concern". The word *orthopraxy* was new to V, who is a deeply committed evangelical Christian and who found himself at that time in a vulnerable position, desperately needing affirmation. He felt that on this occasion his only crimes were orthodoxy of belief and a longing to help other Christians to know the full counsel of God.

Having been accused of lack of orthopraxy because of his orthodoxy, and because the matter had been raised by the priest-in-charge with the assistant, and with the final communication involving a perceived difference of churchmanship which might cause offence to other members of the church, V could see no alternative other than to leave that church. He experienced anger and a sense of injustice as he wrestled with the limited range of options open to him after receiving what he considered to be a dose of spiritual abuse, but after a few hours he came to the decision that he would indeed leave that church and not return to it. As soon as he had arrived at this unhappy and inconvenient decision, he immediately felt a proverbial "burden being lifted off his shoulders".

It could be argued that this was just a case of a Christian leader being somewhat manipulative and indulging in a spot of "heavy shepherding". As such this would not have been an uncommon occurrence. What was unusual in this case was that a church leader attempted to stop a church member from sharing his faith and teaching his fellow Christians the full counsel of God. This church leader wanted him to behave as if the book of Isaiah had never been written and as if Jesus Christ, the founder of their religion, had never spoken of a final day of reckoning. Above all, there was the unexpressed longing that this church member should present the worldly and distorted portrait of God that was then fashionable in that church, namely that God is a God of love, full stop. This is, of course, one side of the picture, and arguably love is the most important attribute of God. But it is only one side of the picture. God is a

God of love *and* he is also a holy God. Because he is holy, he commands his followers to be likewise holy. When they fail, they will wish to repent and avail themselves of the forgiveness that was won for them at a great price by the Messiah. But if they choose never to repent, and if they persist in unholy living or in propagating wrong beliefs about God, they will be liable to the judgement. They may try to carry humble believers with them, but they cannot succeeed (Rom 16:17, 2 Tim 4:3-4).

What would God make of this trivial incident in English church life?

The book of Isaiah presents us with the amazing patience and persistent striving of Yahweh with his people. He confronts them with their sins and urges them to repent. Some of them do. Others persist in disobedient beliefs and unrighteous living. So Yahweh tries again, yearning for them, longing that they might turn away from their sins and turn back to him. When they do so, he welcomes them like the Father in the Parable of the Prodigal Son, with open arms and a special celebration for the child who had been lost, but was now found.

But what if they never turn back to God? What if they persist to the bitter end in their unholy beliefs and actions? What will God do then?

There will be a year of Yahweh's favour, but there will also be a day, "the day of vengeance of our God" (61:2). Yahweh has a day against all that is proud and lofty, against all that is lifted up and high (2:12). On that day a solitary figure will tread the wine press alone. He will look, but there will be no helper; he will stare, but there will be no one to sustain him; so his own arm will bring him victory, and his wrath will sustain him. He will trample certain people in his anger, and crush them in his wrath (63:1-6). The end of these people will indeed be bitter. Who is this lonely avenger? He is the servant of Yahweh. He is the Messiah. He is God the Son. He will do this. It will actually happen. It will only take one day. That terrible day will be followed by the year of the Yahweh's favour. There will be a glorious future for God's redeemed people. God is already busy devising it. "From ages past no one has heard, no ear has perceived, no eye has seen any God besides you, who works for those who wait for him" (64:4).

The greatest blessing on this earth is to know Yahweh and Jesus the Messiah whom he has sent (Jn 17:3), and the greatest blessing on the new earth will be to know Yahweh and the Messiah perfectly (1 Cor 13:12-13). The word used for knowing God in the Old Testament is the same word as is used when a man and a woman "know" one another in the intimacy of a marriage relationship. In the book of Isaiah we have the marital language of Israel as the bride of God. This is why unfaithfulness to him is called spiritual adultery. The rich experience of knowing Yahweh which a few of the Old Testament saints enjoyed became a more common experience when the holy remnant of the pre-Christian era became the Spirit-led Church after the resurrection and exaltation of Christ. In the new earth this experience will be universal. Everyone there will know Yahweh. We shall all love him with a perfect love.

For Further Reading

Adam Smith, G., *The Book of Isaiah I-XXXIX* (Hodder & Stoughton, 1889)

Adam Smith, G., *The Book of Isaiah XL-LXVI* (Hodder & Stoughton, 1889)

Adam Smith, G., *The Book of the Twelve Prophets I* (H & S, 1886)

Adam Smith, G., *The Book of the Twelve Prophets II* (H & S, 1887)

Blocher, H., *Songs of the Servant* (IVP, 1975)

Bruce, A. B., *The Training of the Twelve* (T & T Clark, 1877)

Coggan, D., *God of Hope* (Fount Paperbacks, 1991)

Coggan, D., *Psalms 1-72* (Bible Reading Fellowship, 1998)

Coggan, D., *Psalms 73-150* (Bible Reading Fellowship, 1999)

Coggan, D., *The Servant -Son* (Triangle SPCK, 1995)

Edersheim, A., *The Life and Times of Jesus the Messiah* (Eerdmans, 1971)

Ellison, H. L., *The Servant of Jehovah* (Paternoster Press, 1983)

France, R. T., *Matthew* (TNTC, 1985)

France, R. T., *The Gospel of Mark* (NIGTC, Eerdmans, 2002)

Gordon, S. D., *Quiet Talks on Power* (Fleming H. Revell Co., undated)

Gordon, S. D., *Quiet Talks on Service* (Fleming H. Revell Co., undated)

Gordon, S. D., *Quiet Talks about the Tempter* (Fleming H. Revell Co., undated)

Green, E. M. B., *The Message of Matthew* (IVP, 2000)

Griffith Thomas, W. H., *Christianity is Christ* (Longmans, 1916)

Kenber, P. J., *The Life that is truly Life* (Sarsen Press, 2019)

Kidner, D., *Isaiah*, in *The New Bible Commentary Revised* (IVP, 1970)

Kidner, D., *Love to the Loveless* (IVP, 1981)

Kidner, D., *Psalms 1-72* (IVP, 1973)

Kidner, D., *Psalms 73-150* (IVP, 1975)

Kidner, D., *The Message of Jeremiah* (IVP, 1987)

Lane, W. L., *The Gospel of Mark* (Eerdmans, 1974)

Meyer, F. B., *Christ in Isaiah* (Lakeland, 1970)

Meyer, F. B., *Elijah* (Lakeland, 1972)

Moore, P., *Straight to the Heart of Isaiah* (Monarch Books, 2016)

Morris, L., *Luke* (TNTC, 1974)

Morris, L., *The Cross in the New Testament* (Eerdmans, 1965)

Morris, L., *The Gospel according to Matthew* (Eerdmans, 1992)

Morris, L., *The Gospel according to John* (Eerdmans, 1971)

Motyer, A., *The Prophecy of Isaiah* (IVP, 1993)

Packer, J. I., *Knowing God* (Hodder & Stoughton, 1973)

Pawson, D., *Come with me through Isaiah* (Terra Nova Publications, 2010)

Skinner, J., *The Book of Ezekiel* (Hodder & Stoughton, 1895)

Skinner, J., *Isaiah I-XXXIX* (Cambridge University Press, 1896)

Skinner, J., *Isaiah XL-LXVI* (Cambridge University Press, 1898)

Skinner, J., *Prophecy and Religion* (CUP, 1948)

Stalker, J., *Imago Christi* (Hodder & Stoughton, 1901)

Stalker, J., *The Life of Jesus Christ* (T & T Clark, undated)

Stott, J. R. W., *Basic Christianity* (IVP, 1958)

Stott, J. R. W., *The Cross of Christ* (IVP, 1986)

Stott, J. R. W., *The Incomparable Christ* (IVP, 2001)

Taylor, J. B., *Ezekiel* (TOTC, 1969)

Webb, B., *The Message of Isaiah* (IVP, 1996)

Xenophon, *The Education of Cyrus* (Cornell University Press, 2001)

Acknowledgements

I would like to thank Chris B, Robert and Renée K-D, Elizabeth L, John M, John W, and Tim Y for reading the text of my book. They all made comments that resulted in numerous changes for the better, and none of them should be blamed for the flaws that remain on account of my ineptitude or stubbornness.

In my own writing, I have been influenced by several books I have read about the book of Isaiah. There are some which I must acknowledge openly.

First of all I must declare my huge debt to John Skinner and George Adam Smith for their superb two-volume commentaries, written in each case during the final decade of the nineteenth century. From them I gleaned hundreds of small but important insights into the text, many of which I have made my own and included in my verse-by-verse commentary in this book. As I read other commentaries written much later, it was interesting to see how much their authors likewise owed to these two seminal works. I have also made good use of some insights propounded by Derek Kidner, Alec Motyer and Barry Webb in their commentaries, and by F. B. Meyer, Phil Moore and David Pawson in their books of sermons on Isaiah. I also found two monographs on the Servant Songs, by Henri Blocher and H. L. Ellison, very helpful.

Finally, I am once again deeply grateful to Tony Hill at Sarsen Press, who guided me with patience and kindness through the steps of the process of getting this book into print, and to Tim Underwood who did the setting up so beautifully, greatly enlivening the text with his judicious use of two distinct typefaces. Not only did they both do a superlative job; they did it in a way that enhanced the sense of adventure that I felt throughout the project. If the end result is pleasing and attractive, it is (as it was with my previous book) because of the delightful way in which they gilded the lily.